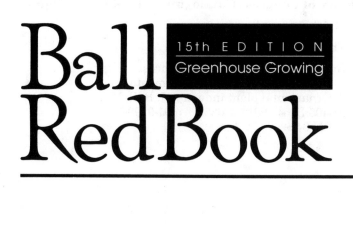

Ball RedBook

15th EDITION
Greenhouse Growing

VIC BALL
Editor

Geo. J. Ball, Inc.

Geo. J. Ball™
PUBLISHING

Library of Congress Cataloging in Publication Data

Main entry under title:

The Ball RedBook

Includes bibliographical references.
1. Floriculture. 2. Plants, Ornamental.
3. Ornamental plant industry. I. Ball, Vic.
SB405.B254 1991   635.9   91-91994
ISBN 0-9626796-2-3

Production supervision/interior design: Janet E. Sandburg

10   9   8   7   6   5   4   3   2   1

Printed in the United States of America

PRINCIPAL CONTRIBUTORS

Todd Bachman	*Bulb Crops*
Vic Ball	*Various chapters and crops*
Warren Banner	*Tissue Culture*
Frank Batson	*Azalea*
Ron Beck	*Lily, Hybrid*
Michael Behnke	*Gerbera*
Henk Berbee	*Iris*
Mark Bridgen	*Alstroemeria*
Charles Conover	*Foliage Plants*
Paul Cummiskey	*Exacum, Gloxinia*
Bob Danielson	*Various crops*
Gus De Hertogh	*Various crops*
Nancy Drushal	*Various crops*
Paul Ecke Jr.	*Poinsettia*
Arnold Fischer	*Saintpaulia*
Ralph Freeman	*Carbon Dioxide*
Ed Harthun	*Various crops*
David Hartley	*Poinsettia*
W.E. Healy	*Alstroemeria*
Debbie Hewlett	*Primula*
R.K. Jones	*Tomato Spotted Wilt Virus*
Michael Klopmeyer	*Disease Indexing*
Roy Larson	*Vernalization*
Marj Laskey	*Herbs*
Richard Lindquist	*Insect Control*
Bob Lyons	*Cyclamen*
Jeff McGrew	*Carnation, Godetia, Iris*
Robert Miller	*Lily, Easter*
Russell Miller	*Several crops*
J.W. Moyer	*Tomato Spotted Wilt Virus*
Jim Nau	*Many crops*
David W. Niklas	*Calceolaria, Cineraria*
Richard C. Oglevee	*Geranium*
James B. Shanks	*Hydrangea*
Andy Stavrou	*Credit*
Jack Sweet	*Exacum, Gloxinia*
Heidi Tietz	*Begonia, Bougainvillea, Foliage*
Anne Whealy	*HID Lighting, Impatiens*
Dick Widmer	*Cyclamen*
Gary J. Wilfret	*Caladium*
Harold Wilkins	*Alstroemeria, Hibiscus*

I also gratefully acknowledge help by the following: Ron Adams, Teresa Aimone, Joe Basgall, David Beattie, Bob Bernacchi, Irene Christiansen, Simon Crawford, Jeff Deal, George Dean Jr., Tom Doak, Bill Hamilton, Ed Higgins, Jay Holcomb, Kenneth Horst, Dan Jacques, Knud Jepsen, Bill Kluth, Dave Koranski, Shawn Laffe, John Landahl, Ian McKay, Ed Mikkelsen, Marvin Miller, Grace Price, Werner Rader, Janet Sandburg, Laurie Scullin, Mark Snyder, Roger Styer, Harry Tayama and Jan Umstead. Cover photo by Kurt Reynolds.

CONTENTS

Section VI   *Culture by Crop, 303*

DEDICATION

This 15th edition of the *Ball RedBook* is dedicated to my father, George J. Ball, a fine grower, founder of the Ball Company, the *Ball RedBook* tradition and *GrowerTalks* magazine.

INTRODUCTION

Flower growing of the early '90s is a whole new ball game. So much change! Much of this 15th edition has been rewritten to cover these important new production technologies, new automation, the remarkable evolution of bedding plants into now 80% plugs and finally new pressures on growers from environmentalists.

Another example is the strident changes occurring in insect control: Our pesticides are accused of contaminating the environment and bugs have already gained much resistance to sprays. New ways are available—and must be mastered. Computers appear more each year in greenhouses controlling environment, crop planning, accounting, etc. Truly, growers of the '90s must strive to master all of these new ways. And students training for crop production and marketing must also be knowledgeable of it all. The threat of lower priced pot plants, especially from Europe, is real, but if U.S. growers will automate and produce quality, they can be fully competitive!

Another facet of all this (and a key part of the 15th edition) is crop automation. Moving crops in and out of greenhouses is the key labor cost—and you'll find several approaches to this task in this volume. Handwatering crops is still widely practiced in the United States and Canada. The job can be mechanized—a few growers are doing it—and still producing quality. You'll find a review of equipment for the job in the book.

A key goal of the *Ball RedBook* is to bring to growers (and to students in horticulture) the latest in all these new technologies and growing systems.

The *Ball RedBook* also provides practical commercially-oriented crop culture—in fact, 120 crops, large and small. You'll find chapters on the majors, such as bedding plants, poinsettias, foliage, etc.—all done by experienced authorities. Most are updated with new varieties in commerce. These chapters are aimed to help the new grower, to provide a reference for an old hand trying a new crop or to help in troubleshooting.

Last (but not least!) warm thanks to many specialists who have contributed so generously to this 15th edition of the *Ball RedBook*. And to brother Carl Ball whose encouragement and interest in our various publications is much appreciated. And to the dedicated Ball staff people, many of whom have helped editorially—especially Jim Nau—and others who have pitched in on the job of producing this book: John Martens, our able publisher, Peg Biagioni, my secretary, who organized the flow of chapters from authors to editors to printer and who put the whole book onto word processing equipment, to Charles Spanbauer, printer of the book, and to Debbie Hamrick for her help. My thanks also goes to Julie Martens and John Saxtan, who edited the whole book. Without all of them, it just wouldn't have happened!

Most of all, we all hope our readers will find this new edition helpful and useful in the tough and exciting challenge of growing at a profit in the 1990s.

Now, we'll all start thinking of the XVI edition!

Vic Ball

SECTION I

The Physical Plant

Chapter 1

GREENHOUSES FOR THE 1990s

by Vic Ball*

So much change in greenhouse structures since the *Ball RedBook's* 14th edition (only six years ago). Polyethylene is still king (it's a different poly), but the rigid structured sheets have improved greatly—and are successfully challenging both glass and fiberglass and poly, too! And there's a whole new approach to heating.

FIRST, DEFINITIONS

For those new to growing, here are some of the buzzwords.

Fan jet. A unit that combines hot air with outside air and blows it down the greenhouse—end to end—through a large poly tube. (See photo in Chapter 2.)

*Thanks to Laurie Scullin of PanAmerican Seed Company, West Chicago, Illinois for help in all of this.

3

Fiberglass. A milky sheet, rigid, nearly always corrugated, widely used as a greenhouse roof. Always used as a single layer.

Hoop greenhouse. From 15' to 25' wide structures supported by wood or metal hoops, arc shaped (see photo).

Polyethylene (poly). Flexible, soft, milky plastic sheets widely used as a greenhouse roof. Poly sheets are available in local hardware stores—but often they are not the ultraviolet-treated material used for a greenhouse roof.

Roof bar. Wood or metal strip that supports glass or other roofing materials.

Structured sheets. Clear rigid sheets 6 to 16 millimeters thick, transparent. Some single layer, some two layers ribbed together with ¼" to ½" dead air space between for insulation. Used for the greenhouse roof and sides.

Thermal sheets. Normally a plastic sheet extended gutter to gutter on winter nights to conserve heat.

Traditional greenhouse. Old style greenhouses were built with purlin pipe supports (see sketch) and purlin pipes that support the roof bars. Not built today, but many are still in use.

Truss greenhouse. Usually 25' to 40' wide. The truss supports the roof so it is a clear span greenhouse (no interior posts except gutter posts).

Unit heater. Usually installed overhead, a small burner/blower heater used to heat greenhouses. Also used in industrial buildings.

Venlo greenhouse. The narrow greenhouse, normally a 10½' wide roof, but built in multiples of two or three greenhouses clearspan gutter to gutter. On glass houses, a single pane of clear glass extends from gutter to ridge. Also done with poly roof.

NOW GREENHOUSE COVERINGS

Ask half a dozen greenhouse builders, "What roof and sides are being used on new greenhouses today?" Here's the consensus:

Poly Still Clear #1

Poly is used on the majority of new greenhouses built today. It's nearly always a double sheet blown 3" to 9" apart by a "squirrel cage," a small blower fan. That air space provides great insulation, but the two milky sheets do cut down some on precious winter light. Most greenhouse roofs use 6-mil thick plastic on the outside; 4 mil is sometimes used on the inner sheet. A good, tight, inflated poly greenhouse will burn 1/3 less fuel than a single glass roof.

4

Poly greenhouses are very low cost to build. In acre volume in a single sheet, good 6-mil poly costs about 6¢/sq. ft., 12¢ for a double sheet (it is available in double sheet rolls up to 24' wide. You roll out the two layers on the roof and fasten them both down at one time). A gutter-connected hoop house covered with double poly (the skin only) costs around $1.50 for material only—no ends, no heat, no benches.

A "budget" hoop house—free-standing single house, no heat, no fan jet, 16' to 20' wide—can be had for around 50¢/sq. ft., material only. Source: Agra Tech [phone (415) 432-3399].

Al Reilly, Rough Bros.: "A complete, first-class inflated double poly greenhouse with pad and fan cooling, benches, overhead unit heaters and fan jets will cost around $8 to $9/sq. ft. covered, all labor and material. Very roughly that's $3.50 for structure with sides and ends, $2.50 to $3 for benches (rolling) and $2 for unit heaters with fan jets."

The good news: The new polys of the 1990s will last three summers, sometimes even four. The greenhouse must then be recovered. It is finally destroyed by ultraviolet light, of which there's a lot more in Southern areas than in the North. By the way, growers in subtropical areas such as Florida often use one layer of poly—fuel expense is less here, so there's less reason for a double layer roof. FVG is a major producer of poly for greenhouse roofs. Armin Tufflite is also widely used.

Poly hoop houses will easily accommodate overhead unit heaters (not so with venlo houses). Again, it's a low initial cost approach to growing. Poly houses plus unit heaters plus fan jets for heat distribution are widely used worldwide.

Crop uses (Skip Smith, X.S. Smith Inc.): "Inflated poly is widely used for spring bedding production, often combined with fall poinsettias in the North or South. Light limitations are not a problem for either crop. Many growers use poly for other pot plants and cut flowers even in Northern areas, although this is more challenging to the grower, especially in low light areas, such as Cleveland and Seattle. HID light is used some to offset this." Poly generally does not allow enough winter light to do quality roses in the North.

Huge areas of winter vegetables are grown across the Mediterranean nearly always under single sheets of poly. I hear there are about 40,000 acres there versus 10,000 acres total of all greenhouses in the United States.

Inflated double poly hoop houses (or any greenhouse) can be built as single greenhouses or gutter-connected. Initial cost is higher per square foot covered, and fuel cost is much lower for gutter-connected houses—there's much less exposed roof area to radiate heat. Also, managing a gutter-connected range is better—you can see what your help is doing, and it's easier to move materials back and forth. Gutter-connected double poly hoop houses are now built up to 42' wide clear-span—21' roofs supported by a truss (X.S. Smith).

Most of all though, the $818 million American bedding plant crops—from the single 100' greenhouse "start-up grower" to a 20-acre range—is done mostly under inflated double poly that's hoop supported.

There is a four-year poly, recently put on the market. There just hasn't been enough experience with it to rate it at this time. It's promising.

There are several innovative new polyethylene sheets just coming onto the market. Examples: infrared reflective poly, such as Sunsaver and Cloud Nine, which offer an important added fuel saving but with some less light penetration than regular poly. Also there are anti-drip polys, such as Fog Bloc and Armin Drip Less. And still other new materials are in the pipeline—many from Israel.

A new trend in greenhouses— high gutters. The 14' gutter pictured here, at Norm White's, Chesapeake, Virginia, raises the black cloth sheet high enough so that the heat conducting poly tube can be installed below it— and still keep good head room. Another advantage: With high gutters it's cooler at bench level in summer. The automated black cloth was installed by Cravo, about $1.10/sq. ft.

#2 Spot—Glass or Structured Sheets

Glass is probably #2 today—and probably structured sheets will beat glass in the early 1990s. So let's talk glass first. It's still the Cadillac. Glass is used:

- **Where winter light is critical,** like with Northern cut roses and often by quality-oriented Northern holiday pot growers. Glass provides substantially better winter light versus double poly.

On the right is Dallas Johnson, owner of Red Oak Greenhouses, Red Oak, Iowa, with Vince Nierste, Ball Seed Company. Dallas says, "A glass greenhouse does far better quality versus poly." He grows mainly pot plants in 4 to 5 acres of mostly glass (some double poly). His comment: "Much better quality on winter crops under glass versus poly. There's no comparison certainly on our lilies. Geraniums bud up earlier under glass."

Gene Young, a major pot and bedding plant grower in Auburn, Alabama, reports clearly better quality poinsettias under glass versus poly.

- **Where the grower is well-capitalized.** On the 20-year haul, glass costs less per square foot per year, but initial cost is much higher. And, you don't have to replace it unless it breaks!

- **Where fuel cost is less critical.** Fuel cost per square foot of glass is higher versus double poly. If thermal sheets are used under both, poly still costs less to heat.

Glass tends to grow the best crop. It allows maximum light; it "breathes" (glass laps between panes allow air to enter). Poly and structured sheets tend to be air tight and can result in excessive humidity if not carefully managed.

Which will stand hail better? Poly, by far (unless tempered glass is used). High winds? Probably a draw if both are well-designed. Snow load? Probably glass is better, again depending on snow/wind load design. A 20 lb./sq. ft. roof will hold better than a 15 lb./sq. ft. roof, of course. Most U.S. greenhouses today (of any roof material) are built to a 15 lb./sq. ft. design load. Normally a safety factor of two is built in so a 15 lb./sq. ft. roof will carry a 30 lb./sq. ft. load safely. The ultimate design load is 30 lbs. Some overseas houses in low-snow areas are designed with only a 1.25 safety factor—now the 15 lb. roof will carry 19 lbs. safely. (For a copy of the Greenhouse Design Load Standards put out by the National Greenhouse Manufacturers Association, write NGMA, P.O. Box 567, Pana, IL 62557.)

A brand new venlo roof in Holland. Note the single sheet of glass extending from gutter to ridge, and the very narrow bar spaced 2' apart. All of which allows more of precious mid-winter Dutch light to the crop.

Wood bars, used until recently to support glass, require costly painting. Most new glass bars today are aluminum—zero maintenance. Trusses are galvanized; again, no maintenance.

Several firms are building new Dutch-style glass in the United States and Canada, predominantly venlo types. They permit a very high percent of winter light to reach the crop (narrow bars, wide glass panels). Combined with a heat sheet, they are reasonably fuel efficient.

These venlo structures are very widely used in Holland today—including new construction. They provide an answer to Holland's very low winter light, since they allow a very high percent of available light to reach the crop.

They are, however, less fuel efficient versus inflated double poly, but Holland doesn't have the extreme cold of the northern United States and Canada.

I hear that Dutch tomato growers are seriously probing the idea of not using thermal sheets on their glass venlo greenhouses. Reason? Even when rolled back during the day, these sheets tend to reduce amount of daylight available to the crop by about 4%. But, new curtains that extend and retract just inches from the inside of the roof or sidewall—rather than gutter to gutter—are helping to solve the light problem.

In several ways, the double poly house is best suited for the northern U.S. grower and glass/venlo for the Dutch grower.

By the way, most glass used today is DSB (double strength B, 3 millimeter/⅛″) grade glass. This glass alone costs around 60¢/sq. ft. There is a stronger and more expensive type called "triple strength." It is 4 millimeter, about 5/32″ thick. Also there is a tempered "triple strength" glass. There's also a low iron glass that permits more and better light transmission. The question here is the amount of PAR (photo-

A typical venlo installation—the new Egon Molbak range in Woodinville, Washington. Low winter light makes glass a considerable advantage on winter crops in this part of the world.

synthetically active radiation) that passes through the glass—part of the light spectrum that makes plants grow.

Lastly on glass, in the fast changing world of flower production today, is it wise to invest in a 20-year glass structure? The grower can recover his investments from a poly greenhouse in several good years. The banker would like that!

Doug McCrimmon of Nexus, greenhouse builders, says that substantial new glass is being built these days for research—both university and commercial firms. Optimum light penetration is critical here!

Structured Sheets

Sharing the #2 spot with glass, structured sheets are clearly on the way up. They're not cheap, but they offer compelling advantages.

Probably the most widely used structured sheet today is polycarbonate. Until recently it was short-lived and discolored rapidly, but new technology puts an ultraviolet inhibitor coating onto—or in some cases it's blended into—the sheets. The result: Much of today's polycarbonate is sold with a 10 year guarantee. Some suppliers even guarantee against hail loss—within prescribed limits—and labor to recover is not that bad. Sheets can be "point fastened"—nails or screws can be

An example of a structured sheet. It's two layers of rigid plastic, perhaps ¼" apart. Structured sheets show a lot of promise as North American greenhouse roof coverings. Note the "roof bar" designed to hold the sheets together.

driven into the material (single or double) to secure it to a roof bar. Not possible with acrylics, which tend to shatter if this is done. Also, newer polycarbonates are drip-less, helping to control condensation problems that often arise in such tight houses.

Polycarbonate is used two ways:

- **As a "sandwich"**—two very thin, rigid, flat sheets of polycarbonate held together by polycarbonate ribs. Total thickness of the two sheets is 8 millimeters (5/16"). These sheets are great for insulation. Cost for sheets alone, about $1.25/sq. ft.

- **A single sheet, now corrugated,** costs about 90¢/sq. ft. It's a good glazing material for retail greenhouse gables and ends, because it allows a good view of what's in the greenhouse.

- **A flat single sheet**—not commercially available for greenhouses.

Both offer good light penetration, although the single one is better. Acrylic allows about 86% of sunlight to reach crops, polycarbonate about 80% and glass about 88% to 89%. Figures based on new material. On all the above subtract light loss from interior structures, pipes, shade cloth, etc.

A key selling point for polycarbonate: It resists hail well. It's widely used in the Colorado-Texas hail belt for this reason. Also it's used on sides and ends of glass and poly ranges everywhere—to minimize vandalism damage. Polycarbonate is very fire-resistant.

Polycarbonate, even double sheets, can be bent around the shape of a hoop greenhouse. That's a real advantage. Acrylic bends only slightly. Polycarbonate is easily installed, is "builder-friendly."

Polycarbonate is appearing on more and more new pot plant/bedding plant and cut flower ranges these days, both new and retrofit. John Pound of Agra Tech Inc., Pittsburg, California: "We've built several new polycarbonate ranges out here recently for roses, carnations, etc. Also a 750,000-sq.-ft. polycarbonate range in Boise, Idaho, to grow fish in huge tanks!"

Trade names for polycarbonates are confusing! Several of the common trade names of the early 1990s for polycarbonates are Dynaglass (corrugated), Twex, Cyroflex and Lexan Thermoclear.

Acrylics

Acrylics give some more light penetration versus polycarbonates; some growers say growth is definitely better. It is long lasting—some manufacturers guarantee it up to 8 to 10 years for light transmission, not guaranteed against breakage. World War II fighter plane windshields were made of acrylics and they're still okay.

Acrylics make a fine house for such winter-light sensitive crops as cut roses, although it costs a bit more than polycarbonate. It's normally used twin wall—two flats sheets ¼" to ½" or so apart. The air space between the two sheets provides insulation, so it's very fuel efficient. Acrylic may not be point-fastened—no screws or nails can be driven through the sheet—so it costs more to secure it to a roof (it needs gaskets). Also, it is simply less impact-resistant than polycarbonate; it will shatter. Severe hail can cause crazing or even holes. And, it's more prone to burning—about like fiberglass.

I see it a lot more on Northern rose ranges and generally in New England. Research greenhouses also use it, probably mostly for better light penetration. Of the two, ultraviolet inhibited polycarbonate seems to be more widely used—both for retrofit and new ranges.

One trade name under which acrylics are sold is Exolite and also Exolite No-Drip, which causes condensation to run down to gutters rather than dripping onto crops.

#3—Fiberglass

Widely used in the 1960s and 1970s, fiberglass is dropping in popularity today. Corrugated fiberglass is a fairly low-cost sheet, varying from 50¢/sq. ft. to $1 for top quality, Tedlar-coated fiberglass. Light penetration on new sheets is good. A case is made for a more diffused light reaching the crop—better than with most other roofs. Hail is less of a problem than with glass, but some hail will penetrate or craze it.

The problem: It burns easier than other covers (some severe fires have occurred). It does discolor after 7 to 10 years, depending on ultraviolet radiation levels; faster darkening occurs in Southern areas. It is not an especially fuel-efficient roof—a reason it has been widely used in the Deep South and California, where fuel is less of an expense.

An interesting point: Anyone considering building or retrofitting a greenhouse would get a lot of good background on roofing materials and structures by attending one of the major trade show/seminars in the United States. I think of GrowerExpo held near Chicago in January, the International Floriculture Industry Short Course held in Ohio in July, Professional Plant Growers Association conference held in October or the Canadian Greenhouse Conference, Guelph, Ontario, Canada, in October. There are exhibits by principal manufacturers with samples of all these materials available for inspection and qualified people there to talk about them. Watch the trade press for announcements of these meetings.

COST ESTIMATES
FOR SEVERAL COMMON GREENHOUSES TODAY

The following cost analysis figures are from several greenhouse manufacturers:

- **Inflated double poly hoop house** with unit heaters, pad fan cooling, 20 lb. snow load roof, no benches: $6 to $6.50/sq. ft. of ground covered, labor and material.

- **A very low cost small hoop house** with single poly, no heat, no fans or benches: to 60¢/sq. ft., material only.

- **A good 2- to 3-acre Dutch venlo range,** 11½' wide, gutter-connected greenhouse: all labor and material, $6 to $7/sq. ft. of ground covered, labor and material, including hot water heating system, but not the boiler, no benches. For pad and fan cooling, add 50¢/sq. ft. (figures from V&V Noordland).

- **Nexus Teton house,** double poly, gutter-connected truss house, material only, delivered, about $1.94/sq. ft. covered. This does not include benches, heat, water, fans, pads, etc. and is for a group of four greenhouses. For a single greenhouse, 29' x 96', figure about $2.50/sq. ft. It is a widely-used design across the United States and Canada.

SUPPORTING STRUCTURES

Here are several commonly used ways to support the greenhouse roof.

- **Hoop.** Most inflated double poly is supported by hoops, bent over from ground to ground. Low cost. Some polycarbonate is done on hoops.
- **Trusses** provide clear span support; there are no purlin posts. They're used for glass, acrylic, polycarbonate and fiberglass roofs and also a good bit for polyethylene houses.
- **Venlo** is a special structure design to support a single 5- to 6-foot pane of glass from gutter to ridge. Commonly two or three 10½' roof units will be supported by one truss. The venlo is a special-purpose design from Holland—it adapts well to their mild winter temperatures and very low winter light levels. It's a low-cost structure and relatively inexpensive to erect. I hear that in Northern winters, the space between glass and the thermal sheet becomes quite cold and tends to put heavy frost on the inside of the glass.

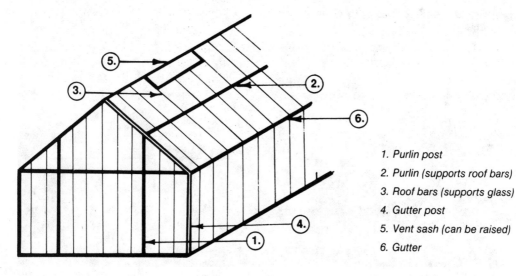

1. Purlin post
2. Purlin (supports roof bars)
3. Roof bars (supports glass)
4. Gutter post
5. Vent sash (can be raised)
6. Gutter

The typical purlin-type glass structure was widely built across the world until a few years ago. Lots of them are still around. An important point: modern houses leave clear, open space free of posts—it's easier to operate.

13

BUDGET BUILDING

An interesting way to ease the problem of raising money for new greenhouses is budget building. John Pound, Agra Tech, and a major California greenhouse builder, counsels his grower customers to "take it a step at a time." In other words, build a good, sound, basic structure, as much as you can handle financially at the time. Then, as your cash flow position gets stronger, you can go back and add some of the fringes. Examples:

- **Environmental controls:** You start out with a lower cost, solid state control. Later on, add a mainframe computer, which really controls your whole business—accounting figures, dollars per square foot, yield data, crop planning, etc.
- **Thermal and short day sheets** can save a lot of fuel, but they're expensive. Again, start off without them, add them later as you can.
- **All sorts of interior automation.**

COLD FRAMES 1990s STYLE

Here's the widely used "cold frame"—a very low cost poly hoop house. Material is only about 50¢/sq. ft. The grower is Bob Miller, a lily bulb specialist in Smith River, California.

A generation ago, cold frames were sort of outdoor beds covered with a sash of glass or poly. Today, the term is applied to a very low cost, budget, poly-covered hoop house (see photo). They are great for spring bedding plants even in the North—if a bit of heat and a vent fan is provided. As of the early 1990s, they are very, very widely used! Agra Tech alone does 2 million sq. ft. per year.

A good example would be Agra Tech's 20′ wide house. It's free-standing—a separate house, roof supported by a metal hoop extending from ground to ground. It was originally designed for a single layer of poly only for spring use, but in fact many growers are putting double poly on them, adding a little heat and a fan, and using them for spring bedding plants.

Cold frames are low-cost. For example, for a 20′ x 100′ house, about 2,000 sq. ft., the pipe hoops alone are under 50¢/sq. ft.—about $100. If you add a double poly roof to this, a Modine heater and one 36″ fan, it now goes to $1.25/sq. ft. material only, or about $2,500 for a 20′ x 100′ greenhouse. And again growers are using these now for year-round growing, even in the North. Great for early crops of pansies, carnations, snaps and other semi-hardy annuals.

For the record, such a house has limitations. First, the framework is light-weight; second, more complete greenhouses are better-ventilated—and spring plants don't like high temperatures. Of course, it is a free-standing separate house—not as efficient as a gutter-connected range—and of course unit heaters are very definitely less fuel-efficient than hot water heat, which costs a lot more initially.

There's another adaptation of this being promoted early 1990s as the "Ball Plant Factory." It's the same low cost hoop house, but now a purlin pipe is built in at about head height on either side of the house. On this, a trolley is installed, which permits moving product from anywhere in the greenhouse out to the end of the house. This structure, by the way, can be gutter-connected later, is a bit stronger than the real budget hoop house described above and costs in the neighborhood of $3,000 for 20′ x 100′ or 2,000 sq. ft. That's now $1.50/sq. ft.

START FRESH!

So often I see growers struggling to adapt old ranges to modern mechanization, heating, etc. In many cases, it just won't work. I do see quite a few growers who simply move a few miles out of the city, find some fresh open land, spend some money leveling it—and then they are ready to really start building a modern greenhouse range. Examples: Alexander Masson, Kansas City, or really any one of the Van Wingerden ranges anywhere. Mechanization demands, first of all, flat, well-drained land to build on; second, wide, hard-surfaced aisles. And, of course, any new project of this kind should have ample land available for expansion.

There is something psychological about doing all this—it says that you and your staff are committed to the future. Bankers like that. (Note the section "To Remodel or Rebuild," later in this chapter.)

One possible exception to all this: I do often see growers with a smaller, old greenhouse range that the city has grown around. Such growers often convert their

A fascinating glass-roofed garden center in Sydney, Australia. The design is based on the famous 1850 Crystal Palace in England. Right is the late Alan Newport and on the left is Neryl McDonald, who built the structure with her husband, Larrie.

places into retail outlets. The public likes to buy from the grower—and when they see a glass roof they think everything was grown there by the proprietor. Besides, the public just loves to wander around a glass greenhouse. Often such growers build attractive "store front" structures upfront. And, of course, such places always have good signs and parking. It's expensive—but I've seen a lot of growers buy expensive next door lots for just parking (Kramers, Neenah, Wisconsin).

One more thought on all this: If you're going to pull up stakes from the old family range and build a modern producing unit, are you sure you're in the right part of the country? I see a light scattering of Northern growers moving into the Southeast, Texas and California. This does mean moving from the population center (the market), but there are major advantages in winter light and fuel costs. Many larger growers operate both Northern ranges and new operations in the South or the Far West.

Speaking of all this, there is a point that has puzzled me for a long time: Why are bedding plants grown in the North and shipped to the South? There would be a lot of reasons for doing it just the other way around. Again, winter/spring light is better in the South, fuel need is lower, and labor might tend even to be less expensive. A few growers are moving this way.

16

This is another tough and very important question facing many growers today. A brand new range can save a lot of labor, on fuel costs—and many times will produce better quality versus old glass. Yet, it costs a lot of money to rebuild, and, in balance, it may not be good business for you today. Often there are tax and interest rate considerations. Also available capital.

Tom Doak, Yoder Brothers, brings much experience to this question from his long involvement in Yoder operations. A few comments from Tom:

"If you do go to the expense of building a new range, be certain that when you are through you will have important savings in both energy costs and labor costs to show for your investment. Example: Double poly, we find, does save an honest 25% to 30% against a single glass roof. Also, heat sheets (gutter-to-gutter applied at night) yield between 25% to 40% savings in our experience. We just did 3 acres of heat sheets at Leamington, Ontario, cost about $1/sq. ft. of ground covered. We figure it will pay off in about 1½ years in fuel savings.

"You do have to watch snow load here, though. When snow accumulates to dangerous weight loads, you want the outside of the roof warm—to melt that snow off. That means no heat sheet. Automated heat sheets also mean automated shade for mums, etc.

"We figure fuel cost alone is about $1/sq. ft. per year for 60°F in the North today [about 1985]. So, if you can save 1/3 of your fuel bill, you are saving $15,000 a year. How many years will it take to pay for your new heat sheets or Lapseal?

"Certainly crop turnover has to be watched, too. It is simply that more crops, more dollars per bench per year—increase your ability to carry overhead costs such as fuel and labor.

"Moving benches, however you do it, eliminate most of that walk space. You not only cut the fuel bill 15% to 20%, but really you can build 20% less greenhouse area and turn out the same amount of crops.

"We think a lot about material handling devices. Unfortunately, most old greenhouses were built in an era of cheap labor and often don't lend themselves well to this.

"Decisions on rebuilding or remodeling also have to be looked at from a tax point of view. Talk to your tax accountant.

"Another point: It takes a lot of money to rebuild—and even for extensive modifications. In some cases it may be a question of whether capital is available for this purpose. Greenhouses are not the best collateral—to many bankers."

Tom talked about industrial revenue bonds tax-free, which, in effect, make capital available for improvements or rebuilding at "tax-free bond" rates. In some cases, you can get 100% financing. The usual range is seven to 10 years. They are done in cooperation with the local municipality. One requirement is they must create new jobs or save existing ones. But the low interest rate is very helpful.

Finally, the question of rebuilding or remodeling boils down to this: Which route will enable you to recover your investment sooner? To make an intelligent decision you really have to put down all the factors involved.

A promising new American design—Rough Bros.'s White House. Note the thermal sheet extending lengthwise of the house and horizontal air fans.

Chapter 2

GREENHOUSE HEATING—
AGAIN CHANGES!

by Vic Ball*

In greenhouse heating there are again important new trends versus the 1985 14th *Ball RedBook*. First, the major new root zone heating development—heat the plant not the air—which gives much better growth with much less fuel input. In boilers, there's a whole new family of "minis." The huge old 20' to 30' steam generators are being replaced by these very efficient small hot water boilers. They do the job well—and with only 2' x 3' or 6' x 8' of floor space. It's the end of the boiler shed—and of big brick chimneys (how will seed salesmen find their customers?!).

Greenhouse heating for the 1990s is mainly hot water systems, some root zone heating, plus a good bit of overhead unit heaters. I see almost no new steam systems. There are also much fewer overhead heating pipes. Some pipes are on walls and ends, but more heat each year is with hot water—with pipes below the bench or in a porous cement or gravel floor. Heat the roots and plants, not the air above the plants!

*Thanks to Laurie Scullin, PanAmerican Seed Company, for background on this chapter.

19

First, why is hot water taking over for steam?

- **Steam traps** are an endless maintenance problem. (I still remember hammering sticky traps on a zero degree midnight with George J. Ball.)

- **Hot water systems** deliver heat more evenly and with less fluctuation. Modern hot water systems gradually modulate water temperature up and down to control greenhouse temperature. If you turn steam into a steam pipe, it roars down and heats one end first. Most of all, there are only two steam pipe temperatures—hot or cold. Steam does sterilize benches of soil, so it's especially important for cut flower crops. A wagon load of soil can also be steam pasteurized for pot and bedding plants, but chemicals do most of soil sterilizing now—and most pot and bedding plants are grown in commercial mixes that growers usually don't sterilize anyway.

Types of Boiler-Firing Systems*

1. **On/off** means that when a call for heat is made, the boiler will fire at the input on the rating plate. This is the least expensive, but has a tendency to over and under shoot setpoint. Less efficient operation is the result if it cycles too rapidly. It's best used only on single or dual zone systems. (A zone is a greenhouse area kept at the same temperature with perhaps 5,000 sq. ft. or maybe an acre or more.)

2. **Two stage** has the ability to fire at 50% or 100% of the input on the rating plate. This system is less expensive than full modulation and provides somewhat greater flexibility in matching the actual heat load. It's best used on any system up to three zones.

3. **Full modulation** has the ability to fire down to 20% (10% at inputs over 1.7 million BTUs) of rating plate input. Boiler water temperatures will be maintained within 2 degrees of setpoint continuously, and very little cycling of the burner occurs. There is generally a slight loss in efficiency that is more than offset by no cycling losses.

How Greenhouse Temperatures Are Maintained

The simplest of systems is a boiler, generally gas-fired, that's set to maintain a given water temperature. This boiler is allowed to fire only when there is a call for heat in the greenhouse zone(s). Temperatures are maintained within 2° to 4°F of setpoint throughout the zone(s), depending on the firing system used. Zone temperature is monitored by either a single thermostat per zone or an inexpensive multiple zone electronic controller.

*Much of this data on hot-water boilers is from Jeff Deal, Hamilton Engineering, Livonia, Michigan.

Next is the more advanced generation of temperature controls. Temperature of the water pumped through the crops is controlled by mixing more or less cooler water (coming back from the greenhouse pipes) with hot water from the boiler. As the crop calls for more heat, the pipes get warmer water—and pipe surfaces warm. All this is constantly adjusted by typically solid state computerized controls. Properly controlled, this system delivers even temperatures—only a maximum 1° to 2°F difference end to end with a minimum fluctuation. Systems like this with mixing valves are typically used only for large systems—an acre or more—and are generally required on any steel or cast iron boiler systems operating a low temperature (140°F) hot water heating system. Other applications would be combination systems (high and low temperatures).

How is the Warm Water Distributed?

There are several ways:

- **Under bench pipes.** For larger areas with acres of greenhouse crops, the most common system is aluminum, copper or steel pipes from ¾" to 2" diameter installed below the benches. Soil and crops are heated; air above the crop gets less. Some of

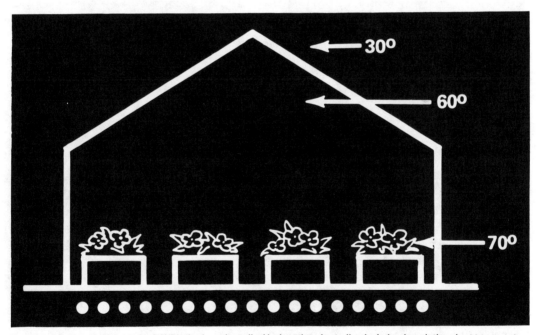

Another way to save big on fuel: With the heat installed below the plants (buried pipe here), the plant temperature will be warm (70°F), the attic temperature cooler—maybe 60° or 65°F. Given a 30°F outside temperature, there's 30°F difference (60° minus 30°), and fuel requirement is in direct proportion to the difference between inside and outside temperature. The same house with overhead unit heaters might well have 75° to 80°F attic temperature, now 50° difference inside versus outside. If you cut the inside versus outside difference in half, you cut your fuel bill in half.

21

these pipes are fitted with fins to deliver more intensive heat in a given area. Pipes are also installed along end and side walls of the greenhouse to prevent cold spots and often under the gutter to melt snow.

An interesting fact: One foot of 1″ bare pipe delivers 90 BTUs/hour. A foot of fin type pipe delivers 893 BTUs/hour.

But the big point of under-bench pipes is that soil and plants are heated first and foremost, while air above the plants and in the greenhouse "attic" gets less heat and is much cooler.

- **Very small root zone* tubes** on the floor of the bench. For example, on a 5′ x 20′ bench used for seed germination or rooting cuttings, small ⅛″ plastic tubes are extended over the (empty) bench surface with lines 2″ apart down the bench end to end (see photo). Warm water is piped through these tubes. Soil or flats above them are kept at the desired soil temperature.

  The same principle is used to heat large areas—even acres. Again, it's with small tubes laid lengthwise down the bench bottom.

- **Root zone tubes on the bench floor.** Small 5/16″ EPDM tubes are extended over the (empty) bench surface with lines generally about 2″ apart and down the bench end to end (see photo). Water is piped through these tubes. Soil or flats (and plant

The Rutgers University floor heating plan (Bill Rogers). Plants grow so much faster with warm feet and fuel bills are so much lower with the heat down at the plants, not up near the roof. Tubes here will be buried in a 4″ layer of concrete.

*Root zone is a registered trademark of Vary Industries Ltd. 1982.

canopy) above them are kept at the desired temperature. Again, the roots and plants are warm, air above is cooler.

- **Root zone tubes now on the ground.** Here's a different application. Now the EPDM tubes are spread out on the ground, again about 2″ apart from end to end of the bench. It's low cost (no bench cost), and again roots and plant canopy are kept warm, air above is cool.

- **Buried root zone tubes.** Other growers bury smaller PVC or ⅜″ EPDM pipes in a porous concrete floor 2″ to 6″ below the surface with pipes spaced about 4″ to 6″ apart. EPDM, by the way, is a synthetic rubber material that is much longer-lived than PVC. It stands ultraviolet exposure better than polybutelene. Large areas—acres of pot and bedding crops, even plugs—are grown on these porous, self-draining, heated cement floors. It's the same result: warm soil/roots and plants, cooler air above.

  A lower cost option is to bury the heat pipe in pea gravel instead of concrete—which is being done some by bedding plant growers. I understand, though, that burying these small pipes in pea gravel is very inefficient in terms of heat getting to the crop. It's much better to put the little ¼″ tubes on top of the pea gravel.

ROOT ZONE HEATING PRO AND CON

Many growers and researchers have strong opinions on the pros and cons of root zone heating for large-scale production of both pot plants and bedding plants. Root zone is generally accepted as best for seed/plug germination and rooting cuttings. I've talked to perhaps a dozen growers in preparation for this book. Here's a fair summary of what I hear and see:

- **First, pot plants.** It's probably a fair consensus to say that most growers who have had experience find pot plant production on tubes either on the floor or a raised bench or on the open ground surface or even buried in concrete produces good quality plants. You keep the roots and the plant canopy warm, *and* you save major fuel—simply because the overhead air (up under the roof) is cool.

  This reminds me of a comment by Don Fleischman of Vary Industries in Grimsby, Ontario, of a case where outside air temperature was 0°F, root zone heating maintained 70°F at the plant canopy level and temperature just under the thermal curtain at night was 40°F. Just above the curtain but below the glass the temperature was 25°F. The result: a difference between 25°F and 0°F of heat loss. In the same situation with overhead unit heaters, the overhead air temperature could quite likely be 70°F, so the difference between inside and outside would now be 70°F. With root zone the difference was 25°F, so the result was a staggering ⅓ as much heat loss in the root zone house.

- **Jim Dickerson,** a grower in Gobles (Kalamazoo), Michigan, has recently installed 2 acres of root zone tubes on the ground (actually a hard plastic mesh is spread out first, then tubes are put above that). He has been growing poinsettias, pot mums and other pot plants for about two years. The quality that I've seen several times

Root zone heating is small, plastic tubes laid down the bench. They put heat just under the crop—just where it's needed. It's great, especially for germinating seeds, rooting cuttings, etc.

has been excellent. Jim is very happy with the system. He reports ⅓ less fuel cost— dollars/sq. ft./year— versus his other range that's heated with overhead unit heaters. And with the root zone beds there is no bench cost! All this is the subject of a story in *GrowerTalks* "Viewpoint" column, April 1990.

Another example is Bill Swanekamp of Kube Pak Corp., Allentown, New Jersey, who has about 500,000 sq. ft. of pot plants. Most of the range is equipped with root zone tubes buried in porous concrete. Bill reports that quality of pot plants on the root zone porous concrete is fully as good as any other system. He does report problems with bedding plants. It's simply that when flats are set flat to flat on this surface the heat is trapped below the flats, roots become very warm, and especially with cold weather, it's hard to keep air temperature at any reasonable level. It's this kind of problem that prompts most growers with root zone heating to have some form of overhead heating available.

- **Propagating.** Germinating seed, rooting cuttings and growing plugs is a sure winner for root zone heating. In fact, most of the root zone installations so far have been relatively small areas installed to support the various forms of propagation. Germinating seed, rooting cuttings and growing plugs need warm soil temperature—and more and more require the ability to maintain a set temperature for different plant species. In other words, you need the ability to keep the soil warm and to keep it at a desired level of warmth.

- **Conclusion** as of the early 1990s: The great majority of propagating—seed germination, rooting cuttings and plug growing—is done on some form of root zone heat. A substantial scattering of innovative growers are finding that root zone is

An important point on fuel: An acre of separate hoop houses (top row) will almost double the fuel cost versus the same acre of gutter-connected houses (bottom row). It's simply that you eliminate all those sidewalls, which means about half as much exposed surface. The downside: gutter-connected houses cost a lot more per sq. ft., mostly due to the expensive metal gutters needed.

a practical, cost-efficient way to grow acres of pot plants, especially when you can reduce fuel costs by ¹/₃ versus unit heaters and eliminate bench costs by putting the tubes on the open ground. This is Jim Dickerson's case—he saves ¹/₃ of his fuel costs, saves $1 to $2/sq. ft. cost for benches, and the whole heating system (including the boiler) costs $1 to $1.10/sq. ft. versus $1.50 for hot water with pipes. Unit heaters are less expensive initially (50¢/sq. ft.) but not as fuel efficient.

For one last example, let's look again at Kube Pak in Allentown, New Jersey. They grew one 60,000-sq.-ft. block of poinsettias, about 35,000 6″ pots, on unheated floors without thermal sheets. This poinsettia crop required 28,000 gallons of oil. The next year, in the same area with floor heating and thermal sheets overhead, the same crop was grown with about 5,000 gallons of oil. Striking!

The following table underscores the effectiveness of root zone heating in keeping the heat down with the plants and not heating the overhead air:

	Root Zone Heat— Cool Air Overhead	Unit Heaters— Warm Air Overhead
Outside air	30°F	30°F
Inside air under the roof	60°F	80°F
Difference outside versus inside the roof	30°F	50°F (66% more fuel needed)

Again, fuel consumption is in direct proportion to the difference between temperature inside the greenhouse roof and outside.

There's a helpful University of Georgia extension service bulletin published by the College of Agriculture, Athens, GA 30602, with valuable, practical background data on root zone heating—especially as it applies to producing pot plants and other crops. Good engineering background has been included. Ask for "Commercial Flower Grower Notes," January-February 1990, by James T. Midcap.

EXAMPLES OF HOT WATER BOILERS USED TODAY

Again, there's a whole new family of efficient hot water boilers that need perhaps ⅛ or ¹/₁₀ the floor space of old steam boilers (and no coal bin or stoker). Here are examples from small to large. Areas heated are very rough approximations!

- **A 45,000 BTU copper tube** hot water boiler, 84% efficiency, will heat roughly 500 sq. ft. of Northern greenhouse. Cost including piping to the bench and controls is about $1,700. It uses a gas burner. Floor space requirement is less than 2' x 2'.

- **A 270,000 BTU** hot water boiler will heat roughly 3,000 sq. ft. of Northern greenhouse and costs about $4,200. Again, there's a very small floor space requirement, about 2' x 3'.

- **One million BTUs:** Occupies only 2' x 3' of floor space and can even be installed outdoors! Fuel efficiency 88%. Costs around $10,000. Such a boiler will heat roughly ¼ to ⅓ acre of Northern greenhouse, and, of course, growers can use multiple units. It's a good example of high efficiency, very small floor space and modern hot water boilers. This one's made by Hamilton.

- **For boilers up to 4 million BTUs** of capacity (up to one acre of Northern greenhouse), we have many options: in copper tube, Raypak and Hamilton; in steel tube, Kewanee, Cleaver Brooks, Johnston, York Shipley; and in cast iron, Weil Mclain and Burnham.

- **Dutch boilers.** The Dutch also build very advanced, large, hot water boilers for greenhouses. Virtually all their new ranges today are hot water heated. For information I suggest a call to Jan Van Heyst, president of V&V Noordland Inc., Medford, New York. Peter Van de Wetering has an excellent installation of such a boiler in Calverton, Long Island.

Other Points on Hot Water

- **Copper tubes versus steel versus cast iron.** The point behind all this: Heating a greenhouse has situations that don't typically occur in other heating installations. After a full day of sun in which no heat from your boiler has been required, the sun goes down, and wham—all of a sudden your boiler is called on for full heat. And now all of the water in the system is at a cool 70°F. As this water begins to circulate and the boiler is firing away, shock can occur (cold water hitting a hot boiler). If your boiler is copper tube, it's okay; it was designed to operate under these conditions. But if it's steel or cast iron, you have a problem.

Steel or cast iron cannot handle these wide variations in water temperature. Two things can happen: It will condense and it may even pull a tube or crack a section. If it only condenses, you will loose efficiency rapidly and the boiler life will be drastically shortened. What's the answer? If you are using steel or cast iron, especially on a low temperature system that is designed to keep the boiler hot, make sure the return water temperature never drops below those shown in the accompanying table. With a properly designed system you can expect 20 years or more out of any boiler. Otherwise, look for five years at best.

Materials used in Construction	Fuel Type	Input Ranges	Efficiency Ranges	Minimum Return Water Temp.*
Copper tube	Natural or LP gas	45,000-4 million BTUs	75-88%	70°F
Steel tube/ tubeless	Natural, LP gas & oil	45,000-6.5 million BTUs	70-85%	140°F
Cast iron	Natural, LP gas & oil	50,000-6 million BTUs	70-82%	170°F

*Minimum allowable return water temperature—to prevent damage.

Local heating contractors tend to install steel tube and cast iron boilers in greenhouses (there is a very big residential market for these mini boilers, by the way)—they just don't appreciate the special problem of greenhouse heating loads. Beware! Greenhouse heating engineers understand all this better.

- **Ten mini boilers at 100,000 BTUs versus one at 1 million.** Another option available to the grower. And there are things to be said on both sides of this one!

First, big boilers are not necessarily more efficient than small ones. Second, there typically is not a major difference in floor space using one big one or several small ones.

The case for the 10 small boilers is that, especially with computer control, as the load increases, more boilers will fire up automatically, so this means that each boiler will only operate when it can operate at full capacity. These boilers are not efficient cycling on and off every few minutes. Using one big boiler may well mean it will be operating at 10% or 20% of capacity some of the time, which again is not efficient. Modulating burners, however, can go down to as little as 25% of capacity with fair efficiency.

Remember that hooking up electricity, gas lines, water and computerized controls is 10 times more work for 10 boilers than it is for one. Another point: If you do go the one boiler route, it's almost surely better to split the load between two boilers—so you have backup. Boilers, too, will fail.

Maintenance: With 10 boilers you have 10 times the amount of breakdown that you'll have with one.

An interesting example of 10 mini boilers designed to heat a half acre or so of greenhouse. They're installed away from the crop area in a separate passage house. The grower is Tom Smith, Detroit, Michigan area.

A modern mini boiler requires perhaps 2' x 5' of floor space and is installed right out in the greenhouse. It heats an area about 80' x 250' at Jim Dickerson's Gobles, Michigan, range. No boiler shed here!

An example of a horizontal air flow blower, designed to circulate the air more efficiently in a greenhouse. It's widely used.

Costs: 10 minis at 100,000 BTUs will cost roughly $12,700. Two boilers at 500,000 BTUs cost around $9,800. The two bigger boilers are cheaper—plus you have the added installation cost of 10 boilers versus two.

- **What's the case for installing one 100,000 BTU boiler in each of 10 greenhouses** versus buying one 1 million BTU boiler and piping the hot water out to the greenhouses? Again, it's done both ways. Obviously, putting 10 hot water boilers in 10 houses means delivering electricity, water, gas and computer controlled wiring to 10 boilers in 10 greenhouses, which is quite a lot of work. On the other hand, with one central boiler (or probably, in fact, two), you now pipe hot water through 10 greenhouses. Also, if the houses are separate and one burner fails, you're in trouble. With a central system with two boilers you have a backup.

- **Boiler location:** Jeff Deal of Hamilton makes a strong point that putting these hot water boilers in an open greenhouse is bad. Pesticides and other chemicals used tend to get onto metal surfaces of the boiler and cut length of life drastically. A far better plan is to put the boiler in a separate structure, which can be in a greenhouse if the area is sealed off from crops. In either case the boiler will need a fresh air supply from outdoors and an exhaust outlet somewhere (but no chimney). I often see sidewall exhaust vents.

- **From Jan van Heyst of V&V Noordland:** "Unit heaters have rather small combustion chambers, and as a result, more heat goes out the chimney. Hot water boilers can be modulated versus on/off operation—that's more efficient. And hot water provides more even temperature to the crop."

- **An interesting point about modulating boilers:** A 1 million BTU boiler without modulation, 88% efficient, costs around $10,000. The same 1 million boiler now with a modulating burner costs about $7,400 and has an 80% efficiency. Both are copper tube boilers. The modulating boiler requires 3' x 6½' of floor space; the boiler without modulation requires 2' x 3'.

- **A strategy for start-up growers:** For the grower starting a small new operation—always limited on capital—here's an interesting plan. At the start, install a unit heater per greenhouse or two or as many as are needed—accepting the relatively lower fuel efficiency—and inability to deliver heat below the crop. Then, after two to three years, install gas fired hot water boilers. Now you can install one boiler, and you can rely on the old unit heaters for backup. Once you are using hot water boilers, you gain that important fuel efficiency. It's clever!

OVERHEAD UNIT HEATERS—ALSO IMPORTANT

There are a lot of overhead unit heaters (hot air heaters) being installed these days—Modine, Reznor, etc. The pros and cons of unit heaters versus the new mini hot water boilers are important—especially for the half acre to 1-acre grower where both are widely used. What is a unit heater? Answer: an open flame burner combined with a blower in a 3' to 4' metal cabinet. The blower fan forces the heat out through the greenhouse.

The case for unit heaters that I see:

- **Lower initial cost** versus hot water. There is a substantial saving using unit heaters. This is especially important to the smaller and new start-up grower. A hot water system (boiler, pipes, pump) costs around $1.50/sq. ft. covered (for small ranges) versus 50¢ or less for unit heaters. That's a huge difference!

- **Flexibility.** If you add a house or two, you can add unit heaters to accommodate the new area. Not so with a central hot water boiler. There are smaller boilers, one per greenhouse, but there are disadvantages to going this way.

- **Combined with fan jets,** heat from unit heaters can be efficiently and evenly distributed down the length of a greenhouse.

- **As backup.** Many growers using bench-top root zone heat feel more secure with some overhead unit heaters as backup. It's mainly for an occasional, extremely cold, windy night; it's rarely used.

These same growers often report that with only small tube bench-top heat the crops are warm and fine, but the air above them is uncomfortably cool for the workers. So they install a few unit heaters to keep the staff happy.

Typical Comments From Suppliers

a. Jeff Deal of Hamilton: "Many quarter-acre bedding plant/pot plant growers use mini hot water boilers."

b. Skip Smith of X.S. Smith: "Most often quarter-acre growers put in unit heaters."

c. Doug McCrimmon of Nexus: "A new 5-acre poly range (pot plants, bedding plants) may go either unit heaters or hot water with under bench pipes. Probably the trend is toward more hot water."

d. Al Reilly of Rough Bros. "A new quarter-acre pot plant/bedding plant grower would probably use the new high-efficiency Modine unit heaters. A one-acre range used for propagation or plugs probably would use hot water and under bench heat or root zone tubes on the bench floor. For pot plants/bedding plants probably unit heaters. A 5-acre pot plant/bedding plant range would likely go hot water with below bench heating pipe—more fuel-efficient."

e. John Pound of Agra Tech Inc. (California) felt the same way: "Energy is not a big deal in California today, but gas prices will probably rise again."

Here are additional comments on typical installations being done today:

- **For a 10,000 sq. ft. range** maintaining 60°F nights in the Northern states, two very roughly 550,000 BTU copper tube hot water boilers (exact size depends on outside minimum temperatures, wind, etc.)

- **For one acre,** 60°F crops, Northern area, about two 1,750,000 BTU boilers—again subject to calculations on assumed inside/outside temperature, wind, etc.

- **Tom Smith,** Detroit, uses 10 of these tiny mini boilers to heat a half-acre area.

Down Side of Unit Heaters

Overhead unit heaters cost a lot less initially than hot water. But on an annual basis, fuel cost tends to be a good bit higher versus hot water boilers. Two reasons:

- **With unit heaters,** you're heating the air above the crop and losing much more heat through the roof and sidewalls. Root zone with hot water heats the soil and the crop more.

- **Some hot water boilers** modulate with the load. The unit heater is on/off, which is inherently less efficient.

- **Crop quality:** Some growers will tell you that hot water heat will grow better crops than overhead heaters. They say, "More uniform heat, less on/off cycling, less cold soil." It's a judgment call. Probably tropical plants would be more at home with hot water, while cool crops such as many bedding plants do better with overhead heat.

I have seen growers install unit heaters in ways that still permit delivering under-bench heat. It can be done, but it's awkward spacewise. See Ivey's greenhouse, Lubbock, Texas, *GrowerTalks*, December 1989.

By the way, unit heaters don't work well in venlo greenhouses—there's not enough space overhead for the heaters unless quite high gutters are used.

Unit heaters mainly burn gas. In remote areas propane may be used. It is expensive. There are also oil burning unit heaters available and unit heaters built to use hot water from a central hot water boiler.

Lots of small growers and many start-ups have gotten off the ground with double poly hoop houses and low cost unit heaters.

Heat Distribution—From Unit Heaters

Now, let's talk about distributing heat from overhead unit heaters. This is where the fan jet shines! It's an ingenious combination using an overhead unit heater plus a blower that forces heat from the heater down the length of the house through an 18″ poly tube. There are holes on the side of the tube that permit heat distribution down the house (see photo). It works! I've seen two to three degrees or

A typical fan jet installation. The unit heater (the 2′ metal box, above right) blows hot air to the left. It is drawn into the poly tube by a fan at the end of the tube, then it's blown on down the house and distributed by holes in the poly tube. The heat is also pushed from the heater by the fan (on the right of the unit heater) towards the poly tube. The louver (on the left in the photo, in the open position) is closed in cold weather but can be opened to draw in a bit of fresh air on early spring days. Note the critically-important exhaust tube, the "chimney" for the unit heater.

less temperature difference end to end of houses with overhead unit heat distributed this way.

The fan jets have another strong advantage. On sunny days in winter, greenhouses often require some ventilation—to control humidity and avoid excessive temperatures, even though it's cold outside. The fan jets have the ability to draw in a limited amount of outside fresh cold air, mix it with the air from inside the greenhouse and deliver it down the overhead tube throughout the house. This avoids a blast of cold air (bad for crops) that would result from the use of normal ventilators. For much more detail on fan jets see Chapter 4.

TWO TYPES OF UNIT HEATERS

- **PA-style unit heaters** (propeller-driven) cost about a third less than BA-style heaters (blower-driven). It is not possible to use an overhead poly tube to carry the heat down the length of the greenhouse with a PA heater—you must use a fan jet to conduct the heat from the heater into the overhead poly tube. Alternately, however, you may use HAF (horizontal air flow) blowers instead of fan jets. Now, the heater just blows heat toward the fan, and the fans pick up the heat and conduct it down the length of the house and back up the other side—in a circular trip around the greenhouse. This is a lot less expensive and simpler—and is being done quite a bit these days by growers.

- **BA heaters** are blower-driven. They involve more moving parts—but now the grower can use an overhead poly tube hooked directly to the heater without a fan jet unit. It's one less piece of equipment, but you lose the ventilating capability of fan jets, which is important.

Here's an alternative ventilating plan. What growers are doing in lieu of fan jets in some cases is to first open a small shutter at the end of the greenhouse, then at the opposite end of the house turn on one large 36″ cooling fan. At the same time the grower turns on his HAF blowers. The result is a small volume of cold air from outside drawn into the house and mixed and distributed throughout the growing area. The 36″ cooling fan is also exhausting humid air from the greenhouse. Typically a grower will dehumidify this way in short, 1-minute "bursts"—to let the cold, dry air warm up. Usually this dehumidification cycle is done late in the afternoon partly to aid in drip elimination.

Part of what has brought on this new system of distributing air from heaters is the problem of the overhead tubes from fan jets interfering with thermal and short day curtains. See Chapter 4.

HORIZONTAL AIR FLOW (HAF)

Skip Smith of X.S. Smith reported very wide use of HAF fans with both hot water and unit heaters. They move air around the perimeter of the greenhouse— avoids stratifying warm air up high, cool air below. Other greenhouse builders I talked with reported wide use of these HAF fans. Typically HAF fans are 16" to 20" diameter and move 2,000 cu. ft./minute per fan.

INFRARED HEAT

Infrared heat systems are available and have certain points in their favor, and, like all systems, have problems and limitations, too. Since they are not widely used except in the Northwest I won't go into a lot of detail. It is very fuel-efficient. In moderate winter areas and especially with high humidity (the Northwest), it does tend to keep foliage dry—a real help in disease control. For more details I suggest a call to Jim Youngsman, Skagit Gardens, Mt. Vernon, Washington [phone (206) 424-6144].

BASIS FOR CALCULATING BTU REQUIREMENTS

Not that every grower should be a heating engineer—but it will help growers appreciate the factors that influence heat loss in a greenhouse if they understand how the BTU requirement for a heating system is calculated.

In principle, it's rather simple. The heat loss (in British thermal units per hour) of a given greenhouse equals the exposed area (roof, sides and ends of the greenhouse) times the difference between inside and outside temperature, divided by the "R" factor (rate of heat loss through the roof). (One British thermal unit (BTU) is the heat needed to raise one pound (AVD) of water one degree F at 39°F.)

Let's assume that the total exposed area of the roof, sides and ends of a greenhouse is 10,000 sq. ft. Let's also assume that we want the capability of maintaining 60°F with 0°F outside—a 60°F difference. 10,000 sq. ft. x 60 (degrees difference) x 1.13 (U factor of glass) results in heat loss of 678,000 BTU/hour. This loss can be satisfied by two 400,000 BTU/hour heaters or four 200,000 BTU/hour heaters, assuming an 85% heater efficiency.

There are other considerations! Condition of the roof is important. Glass slippage or even the glass lap cracks can affect this. Frequent high winds obviously increase the demand for heat. A glass roof with lap cracks will freeze over on a very cold night, greatly reducing heat demand. Snow does insulate. And, of course, different roof materials each have their own "U" factor or heat loss factor.

Another factor: Where heat distribution systems (pipes or bench top tubes) are positioned below or on the bench and below the crop—or better yet in the soil—the temperature up just under the roof tends to be a good bit lower which influences heat load importantly.

Lastly, I again urge talking with greenhouse heating engineers or suppliers of this equipment. Trade shows and seminars are also a gold mine of information (see Chapter 1).

OTHER HELPFUL DATA

U Factors

First, here are the U factors for various greenhouse roofing materials. The lower the factor, the more fuel efficient the roof:

Material	U Factors
Glass, single layer	1.13
Glass, double layer	.65
Polyethylene, single film	1.15
Polyethylene, double-film inflated	.70
Fiberglass	1.00
Acrylic, double sheet	.56
Polycarbonate, double sheet	.62
Concrete block 8″	.51
Asbestos board ¼″	1.10
Polyurethane foam applied at site, 1″ thick	.14
Black sateen	.65
Polyester fabric, spun bound, reemy 2016	1.20

Which Month Uses the Fuel?

Heating Requirements by Month at State College, Pennsylvania, Expressed in Degree Days and Percentage of Total

	Average Degree Days per Heating Season	Percent of Total Heating Season
July	0	0
August	12	0
September	83	1
October	439	7
November	766	13
December	1,130	19
January	1,401	24
February	933	16
March	608	10
April	379	7
May	139	2
June	44	1
Total	5,934	

Credit: Pennsylvania State University, Dept. of Horticulture, University Park, Pennsylvania

How Much Saved When You Lower Temperatures?

Percent Reduction in Fuel Use
When Greenhouse Temperatures Are Lowered

Average Outside Temperature (°F)		Inside Greenhouse Temperature Percent Reduction From A to B					
	A	65° to	65° to	60° to	60° to	55° to	55° to
	B	60°F	55°F	55°F	50°F	50°F	45°F
	—	%	%	%	%	%	%
20		11	22	12	24	14	28
24		12	24	14	28	16	32
28		13	26	16	32	19	38
32		15	30	18	36	22	44
36		17	34	21	42	26	52
40		20	40	25	50	33	66
44		24	48				
48		29	58				

Credit: *Pennsylvania State University, Dept. of Horticulture, University Park, Pennsylvania*

Chapter 3

CONTROLLING THE GREENHOUSE ATMOSPHERE

by Vic Ball*

Again, much improvement here versus the 14th edition—in performance and efficiency. Like most computerized things, each year you get more for less money. Also there are more suppliers competing for this expanding market.

THREE LEVELS OF ENVIRONMENTAL CONTROLS

There are three basic categories of controls:
1) Thermostat ($50 to $250). Available from your local heating contractor.
2) Analog ($800 to $1,600). Examples:
   Wadsworth STEP 50A, STEP 500
   Acme Grotron II
   Barber-Coleman CP-8161, CP-8102
   Pacific Controls Stage 12
3) Computer ($3,000 to $50,000+). Examples:
   Wadsworth MicroSTEP/SA
   Priva CV 750
   Q-COM GEM

*I acknowledge major input to this chapter by George J. Dean Jr. of Wadsworth Control Systems Inc., Arvada, Colorado. It was really a joint project.

- **Thermostats** come in two varieties: On/off and proportioning. On/off thermostats simply switch (heat or vent) with a change in temperature. Proportioning thermostats provide a continuously variable resistance that changes with temperature. On/off thermostats can control fans, heaters and other equipment directly. Proportional thermostats work as sensors for electronic controllers that operate equipment.

- **Analog controls** use proportioning thermostats or electric sensors to gather temperature information. This information drives amplifiers and electronic logic (i.e. decision making) circuitry. These controls cost more than thermostats, but are more versatile and offer better performance.

- **Computer controls** replace the amplifiers and logic circuits of an analog control with a microprocessor—a "computer on a chip." This computer can combine information from a variety of sensors (temperature, relative humidity, sun, etc.) to make complex judgments about how to control the environment.

A thermostat controls one piece of equipment. An analog temperature controller controls one environment. A computer typically controls multiple environments (several different ranges of a greenhouse) and considers multiple sensors in each environment when it makes a control action.

Interesting point here: I hear often of growers building greenhouses (or adding to them) usually short of capital. Suggestion: Build a good solid greenhouse structure, often with simple thermostat or analog type environmental controls, and do the rest of controlling by hand. Then as your cash position improves, go into computerized controls—and gain importantly both in efficiency (fuel costs/better crops) plus turning a lot of busywork chores over to computers. The grower lives much better!

Now let's take the whole list of the greenhouse environmental control functions—and comment on different ways each might be done. Here we go!

- **Greenhouse temperature controls.** Analog controls will do it. Says George Dean, "Our Wadsworth Step 50 will do it—it's very widely used today. Step 500 handles more equipment."

    But computers will do it more accurately! First, the computerized system can bring in readings from many sensing points (versus one for the analog system) and average them out. Computers can anticipate heat load—at winter sunset, for example, they can start the boiler earlier and gradually feed heat into the houses. That means more boiler efficiency and more even temperature in the houses. Dutch research proves that a greenhouse averaging 1% above set temperature over a one-year period can add 5% to your fuel bill. Three degrees means 15% more fuel cost.

    Analogs turn heat on and off. Temperature rises, heat goes off; greenhouse cools, heat goes on. Computers modulate—they can maintain very close to your set temperature. A computer will convert from day to night temperature at the correct time for each day of the year. Remember that sunset (increased heat load) varies from 4 p.m. in winter to 9 p.m. in summer (in Northern latitudes). Analogs can be set manually each day—but will you? Ranges with several boilers (five or

10 of the new mini hot water boilers) need only one boiler for light loads. The computer will fire up additional boilers as they are needed. A larger boiler working at only 10% of its capacity means very low efficiency. There's a case for many small boilers.

So—let's put all these facts together. Now we see how computerized heating controls save money. That's why commercial control firms will go to large office buildings and guarantee 15% to 20% fuel saving with these more advanced controls—and they usually deliver. And why greenhouse growers, too, can save a lot of fuel with such controls. This can amount to big savings, and again, computers save the grower a lot of busywork.

Priva, the major Dutch environmental control supplier, also offers these advanced fuel saving computers. Often I see them in larger ranges over the United States and Canada. These larger, more advanced controllers are available also from American manufacturers: Wadsworth, Q-Com and Denmark's DGT-Volmatic.

Priva greenhouse atmosphere control equipment is widely used worldwide, especially on larger ranges. Shown right is Jan Prins, president of Priva, and on the left is Andy Olsthoorn, owner of Lakeshore Produce Ltd., Jordan Station, Ontario. The white "can" is an aspirated sensor—to pick up temperature and humidity readings. Above left is a CO_2 generator.

George Dean Jr., Wadsworth Control Systems, with an example of one of his control panels. For many years George has been a leader in control equipment for small- to medium-size ranges across the United States and Canada.

- **Vent controls.** Analog controls do raise/lower vents to maintain a set temperature. Typical equipment will raise and lower vents in three stages, from fully closed to fully open. Again, computerized controls modulate—they provide an infinite number of adjustments as called for by appearance of sun or lack of sun, outside air temperature changes, wind, etc. I've stood in such greenhouses and listened to the constant tiny adjustments in vent position to maintain a set temperature.

    So again, the computer does a much more accurate job. It saves fuel and grows better crops, but it costs more!

    Speaking of automated vent controls, many growers will remember the days of manual ventilators, the problem of forgetting to open vents on a sunny morning. You walk into the house, it's up to 90°F and very humid. Bad news!

- **Cooling pads/fan controls.** Analog controls will do this. As temperature rises, it turns on a few fans and then more as needed. Then, at a still higher setpoint, it turns the water flow over the cooling pad. Finally, as greenhouse temperatures exceed the setpoint, all fans run and all pads deliver maximum water circulation.

40

- **Humidity control.** Humidity control is a common problem for growers. On a typical late winter afternoon the sun dives, and greenhouse temperatures drop rapidly. It soon goes down to the dewpoint, and moisture appears on leaves—making a fertile breeding ground for disease spores.

  Maintaining desired levels of relative humidity (RH) is obviously critical. More advanced growers consider precise RH levels as a key way to control crop diseases. Mildew, for example, occurs and spreads with high RH. Rose black spot and poinsettia botrytis are also humidity-related. In fact, if RH is controlled accurately (mainly to keep foliage dry) and if crop temperatures are unfriendly to key disease problems, the need for extensive fungicides should be minimal—and losses from disease the same. All pathogens have a rather narrow range of temperature and humidity through which they can and do spread seriously. Avoiding these ranges with precise computerized RH and temperature controls is the way sophisticated growers control diseases.

  Analog controls will do this job. As RH exceeds the setpoint, the control will introduce a bit of heat, also a bit of ventilation. It's the classic "heat and air" used by old-time growers. Says George Dean: "The grower can do this job with analog controls. But again, computerized control will do all this with much more precision. Computers have more accurate controls, faster response."

- **Thermal and daylength sheet controls.** Installed overhead, gutter-to-gutter in most modern greenhouses today, thermal sheets are applied sunset to sunrise in winter. Again George Dean says, "Dozens of growers do this job with analog controls. The typical result: 25% to 35% reduction in fuel cost. Other sheets reduce daylength to force short-day plants into bloom. The short-day sheets are applied from about 5 p.m. until 8 a.m.—to provide a 15-hour night (short day). Still other sheets are applied during summer when natural sunlight is too strong for certain crops."

  All of these applications can be controlled by computers. Thermal sheets are applied at sunset (sunset varies each day of the year) and stay in place until sunrise. The short day sheets are on a rigid schedule to always provide a pre-set daylength. And the light reduction sheets—to reduce excessive summer sun—are applied when a setpoint of footcandles is reached.

- **About weather records.** Computers can receive, record and display weather data—received from sensors in your greenhouses. This includes temperature indoors and out, outdoor sunlight (it measures sun energy), wind direction/velocity and RH indoors and out. Especially such things as sunlight and temperature can be presented in graph form which is very useful in managing crops.

  The point here: Computers don't grow crops, growers do. Computers (and analogs) help growers greatly by:

- Giving them weather information on which to base growing decisions.

- Making it vastly easier to implement growing decisions. You just set the computer to extend the thermal sheet at sunset each day—and it will get done!

  But like all mechanical things, someone must be there to monitor all of this.

- **CO_2 application.** Analogs will trigger injection of CO_2 during pre-set hours each day. If vents are opened or a fan goes on, analogs will stop the CO_2 flow. Analog controls are used a lot for this. Computers will do all this, and they have the capability to measure CO_2 levels in your greenhouses—and add enough to maintain a setpoint level.

- **Adding heat or cooling during winter afternoons.** Given a row of unit heaters/fan jets in a gutter-connected range, analogs can turn on unit heaters as needed. At first, perhaps every fourth heater fires, then every second, then finally all of them. On a sunny winter day, analog controls will turn on fan jets and bring in fresh air as needed. Again, just a few jets go at first, then more as needed.

- **HID lights.** High intensity discharge lights are becoming ever more common in northern greenhouse areas in the United States, Canada and Europe. They are a rather obvious and simple application of any electronic controls, analog or otherwise.

- **Applying black cloth shade.** More and more of the application of black cloth or black plastic for daylength control is being automated and handled with analog controls or computers. A simple application relieves the grower of a pesky burden.

- **Water temperature control in hot water boiler systems.** Modern hot water boilers, teamed up with computers, can deliver desired temperature in the greenhouse— above or below the crop (or soil). As heat is needed, temperature of the water circulating in the greenhouse pipes is raised. Temperature in the greenhouse pipe is controlled by mixing varying levels of cooler return water (from the greenhouse) with hot water from the boiler. And finally, as load increases, the boiler is fired up more. The computer makes all this happen—a key reason most modern ranges today are hot-water heated.

- **Alarms.** Computers can detect such alarm points as too low or too high a greenhouse temperature, pressure of hot water systems below or above setpoints, or a greenhouse temperature falling below a set point. In such cases, the computer will phone you at home. If no one answers, then it will ring your foreman, etc.

MORE ADVANCED COMPUTER APPLICATIONS

Beyond all the above, there are other very important tasks that computers can do for more efficient growing. Many are tied to new, more sophisticated growing technology.

It's the way of the future! Examples:

- **Managing cool day/warm night height control.** *GrowerTalks* through 1988 and 1989 carried many reports on the new Michigan State University technology for controlling crop heights by temperature. In a word, cooler days versus night temperatures greatly slow down plant stretch. See the chapter on this elsewhere in this 15th *Ball RedBook* edition.

The big problem: Especially in the South, growers just don't have cool days when they need them. Example: Much of Easter lily growth occurs during March, a month that sees many warm days in the South. So how can you have a warmer night temperature when the day is 80° or 85°F?

Research tells us that the plant "senses" its day temperature mainly during the first two hours after sunrise, so if you can open vents and turn on cooling pads and fans at sunrise you'll be able to, in effect, apply cool days more or less for the whole day. The same is true for poinsettias. By the way, there's a videotape on cool day height control for Southern lily growers available from *GrowerTalks*.

But who wants to get up at 5 a.m. each day and do all these chores? Answer: The computer. It's just the kind of thing computers will do well.

First, the computer knows when the sun rises on each day of the year. You "tell" it to do these things at precisely sun up:

Turn off the heat.

Turn on fans/pads.

Open vents if appropriate.

Then, two hours later, tell it to go back to normal daytime temperature/RH control.

- **Ramping.** This is another temperature control trick that can do important things for growers. Example: (Again using cool day/warm night technology) we want to raise temperatures 4 degrees at sunset (60° to 64°F)—to achieve the warm night part of it. With simple analog controls, the system immediately strives to reach 64°F. The boiler suddenly goes on full force, all greenhouse controls call for more heat. It's a crash program.

  But with computerized controls, the changeover is done in steps—over maybe 30 minutes. Temperature goes up one or two degrees per 15 minutes. Result: No sudden load on the boilers—and sudden loads are hard on them! No sudden temperature changes on crops, sudden increases/decreases are not good growing. You "ramp" from day to night temperatures or vice versa.

  Hank Mast, Grand Rapids, Michigan, grower, does cool day lilies and poinsettias very well and does ramp. Hank reports it is almost a necessity to ramp cool day treatments.

- **Sunny day/warmer night.** Research tells us that a plant can "grow" more if there's more sunlight. A key part of this "growth" is the respiration that occurs at night. Here, sugar built up by the day's photosynthesis is "used" at night, which means the sugar is converted to new plant tissues, leaves, stems, flowers, etc. So, if there is more sunlight today, more sugars (carbohydrates) are built up in the plant, then more respiration can occur at night. The next important fact is that respiration occurs more rapidly at higher temperatures. You can use up more of those sugars to build more plants if the night temperature is a bit higher.

  So, if we have a full-sun day, and if we do raise temperatures that night by maybe 3 to 5 degrees for four or five hours, then more new growth will occur—and now we're able to use that added sugar.

Again, enter the computer. It measures sunlight each day, can sense an increase of sun versus a norm—and can respond by increasing night temperatures by a set amount. This is being done commercially today.

- **Vent controls.** This is a more applied application of computers, but again it's important to the grower. The computer can measure light rain, a storm (high winds), and a severe storm (very high winds). It can also measure wind direction.

  And modern computers can respond: to light rain, by setting all vents to a shed position—that means no rain on crop; to storm/high wind, by closing the vent on the windward side, leaving some air on the leeward side (shed position); to severe storm (very high wind), by closing all vents to shed position. After the storm, normal temperature controls resume.

FOR VERY LARGE OPERATIONS

For the 10- to 20-acre or more ranges, there are several possibilities.

- **Several separate computers** can be installed, one for each major section of the operation. One such a separate computer might serve four or five separate temperature control zones.

- **Use a larger microcomputer with hard disk.** It can record weather and graph temperatures both indoors and outdoors, received from the smaller computers. It will tell the grower at a given moment what happens over his entire range—temperatures, RH, light, etc.—and also record outside conditions.

- **A large mainframe computer can do accounting/general ledger records.** It can send out statements, maintain accounts receivable and accounts payable records. Crop planning, especially for pot growers, can be computerized. See the separate chapter on this elsewhere in the book. Even this job is usually done by microcomputers today—at least for businesses up to $10 to $20 million per year.

Chapter 4

OTHER POINTS ON THE PHYSICAL PLANT

by Vic Ball

WHICH FUEL TO BURN?

Annual fuel costs for 60°F nights for the Northern states, year-round grower as of the early 1990s is around $1-$1.25 per square foot of ground covered. That's 10% to 15% of total production costs. (Figure 60¢ to 70¢ for growers who carry some houses much cooler in January-February.)

All too often, there are ways growers could reduce this cost. The big three fuel cost cutting opportunities that I see:

- A fuel-efficient roof.
- A high-efficiency boiler with well-insulated mains.
- Selecting fuel with the least cost per 100,000 BTUs—in your situation.

How to Select the Lowest Cost Fuel

To appraise actual BTU cost for various fuels you must first reduce the available alternatives to a common language. You've got to compare apples with apples!

The most practical language: Appraise each fuel according to cost per BTU. That's a British Thermal Unit—a basic way to measure heat. Don't worry about details. Just know, for example, that if your grade of oil at your cost delivers 100,000 BTUs for 90¢—and gas per 100,000 BTUs is 60¢—well, let's switch to gas! This comparison is so easy to do—the accompanying charts are self-explanatory. Remember, you're not buying coal or oil or gas—you're buying heat. And buy it as cheaply as you can.

Compare Fuel Costs

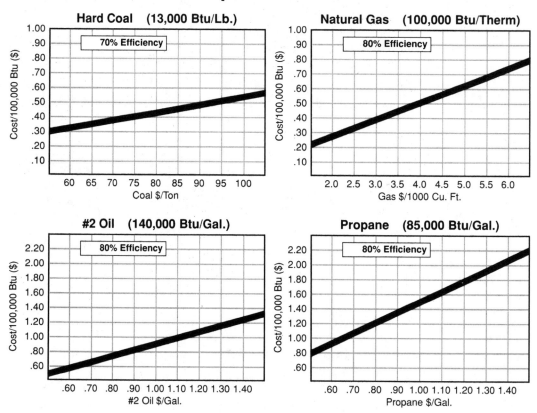

A very handy way to convert the dollar cost of a fuel to BTUs. An example: Assume $70/ton for coal. You go up from the $70 to the black line and go left to the margin—at about 42¢/100,000 BTU cost.

The Main Four Contenders

- **Gas—most used today.** By far the most used fuel for greenhouse production in the United States (and most of Europe) is gas. Why? It is clean, very convenient and is generally competitive cost-wise. Equipment for burning gas is far less than for coal and even less than for oil. There are no storage tanks, as with oil, and no coal or ash handling.

Speaking of gas, it is very widely used where overhead unit heaters are installed in greenhouses. Other fuels are difficult to handle in these small burners (except propane, which is expensive).

Before committing to gas, just be sure you couldn't heat your range for 25% less if you burned oil—or even coal—even allowing for the added cost of burners and handling the fuel.

- **Oil.** It's a close #2 to gas—many growers do use light oil especially for smaller ranges. A few large growers, 3 to 5 acres or more, burn No. 6 heavy oil, which must be preheated before burning. But BTU cost is lower than for light oil! Again it's a question of cost per 100,000 BTU versus gas or coal.

  Oil burners are costly and require maintenance. Oil storage tanks are also expensive, and today's government agencies are very tough on possible leaching of oil, etc. from leaky tanks into the ground water, especially from underground storage tanks. Some large growers invest in large above ground storage tanks and fill them in the summer—thus hedging oil prices going into winter.

  There are practical oil-burning overhead unit heaters available.

- **Coal.** There was a strong trend toward coal, especially on larger ranges, in the early 1980s. It was triggered, of course, by skyrocketing oil prices. There are still a lot of big ranges (5 to 10 acres or more) burning coal, especially Northern roses. On large modern Northern ranges of this type, growers often install highly automated coal handling and burning equipment. With modern handling and burning, the labor cost and labor problem become minimal. As the *Ball Red Book* goes to press in early 1990, the country is experiencing a 30% to 40% increase in cost of fuel oil and propane—which will certainly send especially larger growers back to shopping for coal and stokers. Many large growers maintain the flexibility to use both coal and oil to fire their boilers.

  There's another problem with coal: Environmental contamination. More each year, various government agencies are tightening down the amount of sulfur dioxide that can be emitted into the atmosphere by coal boilers. Of course, hard coal is less of a problem here, but doesn't get off free. Regulations and their interpretation seem to vary even from city to city. If you can make your peace with the EPA and other agencies on a reasonable basis, then this barrier is out of the way. Often, it's a politicking job.

  But on a BTU basis in some cases, coal can save big bucks. When doing your calculation on fuel cost, include depreciation of the stoker and labor and facilities for unloading the coal, storing it, moving it to the burner. For the record, coal deteriorates in heat value over long-term storage.

  One coal burner supplier reported rough cost for a 145 hp Scotch Marine boiler with burners (or stokers) of roughly $30,000 for the gas/oil burner versus $90,000 for coal. The 580 hp level was about $80,000 for a gas/oil burner versus $150,000 for coal. Those are figures from the early 1980s.

- **Propane.** It's clean, very convenient and can be used by growers out in rural areas where gas lines are not available and where other fuels are hard to bring in. Another advantage: It can be used with overhead unit heaters—by small rural bedding plant growers. Many do just that. They heat their houses only in late February/March.

The big problem, of course, is that it is very expensive. On bedding plant crops, especially in Southern areas where there is only a short-term fuel need and no severe cold, it is rather widely used in spite of its cost. Incidentally, there does seem to be a lot of price dealing in propane—especially for larger users. The cost for storage tanks, piping and burners is modest.

Here's an interesting and very neat approach to the traditional greenhouse coal pile—a metal silo. Note the loading crane. The grower is Jack Van de Wetering, Ivy Acres, Calverton, Long Island.

- **Sawdust and logs.** Occasionally I come across growers who heat sometimes large ranges with sawdust, chips or rough logs. The Houweling Brothers in Vancouver, British Columbia, located in the midst of major timber cutting, still get sawdust practically free. They've been heating 27 acres of bedding plants and pot plants for some years with sawdust—with no problems. Their equipment comes from Kara Engineering Co., Almelo, Holland. Their comment: "Sawdust is practical for ranges of 3 acres or more. Not for the small grower."

There are a few growers in the Southeast who heat ranges with low cost rough logs. Again, the fuel cost is very low, handling is some labor, but on balance it is a major economy for these growers.

A Good Example of Picking the Best Fuel

Hans Pein, Urbana, Illinois, grower, operates 3 acres of double poly bedding plants, geraniums and pot plants. He's been struggling with the available fuel alternatives for six or eight years. His conclusion (as of early 1990):

- **Gas:** Not available. "It would cost me $40,000 to pipe it in from the main 5 miles away." (In some cases I hear of a gas company paying for the pipeline given a long-term contract from the grower.)
- **Coal:** Illinois soft coal is by far the lowest cost per 100,000 BTUs. But after five years Hans gave up. His problems? "First, I can't get clearance from the Illinois EPA—and if anything, they're getting tougher," he says. "Next, was a major cost for a modern coal stoker—I just can't afford it. Finally, I had hostile neighbors concerned about fly ash."
- **No. 2 oil:** "I'm using it today (early 1990)," Hans says, "but the cost of No. 2 oil and propane is fluctuating widely just now. I use the one that delivers the lowest cost per 100,000 BTUs—and I check them weekly."
- **Propane:** A viable alternative—again depends on the cost per 100,000 BTUs.

Here are fuel options with cost comparisons available to Hans Pein 1990:

	Cost January 1990	Cost per 100,000 BTUs	Annual fuel cost (estimate)
No. 2 oil	94¢/gal.	83¢	$125,000
Propane	85¢/gal.	$1.25	$188,250
Illinois soft coal	$42/ton	42¢ approx.	$ 63,250

ROLLING BENCHES—BIG SPACE SAVERS

With rolling benches, the benches may be rolled several feet sideways either right or left. A typical house with four benches and normally four walks will now have only one walk (plus a gutter walk), and that one walk can be positioned anywhere the grower wishes, simply by rolling the benches sideways. Normally the rolling is accomplished by turning a crank that's at the head of the bench or simply pushing the bench to the side. It's not hard to do. As of the early 1990s, hundreds of greenhouses have converted to these rolling benches across the United States, Canada and Europe. They are becoming rather standard equipment on modern new ranges. If you're converting to rolling benches, realize that if purlin posts are installed in the greenhouse, it complicates the use of rolling benches.

The obvious advantage is that with rolling benches you now use perhaps 86% to 88% of the available space for crops versus 62% to 66% with the old-style fixed walks. Stated a different way, that means perhaps 35% less fuel cost and 35% less of all overhead cost (depreciation, salary, taxes, insurance, etc.) per square foot per year. That is a major cost reduction, and the grower still has access to his crop. You produce one-third more crop per year on your range!

Inevitably we find ourselves comparing rolling benches with the tray mechanization concept (covered elsewhere in the *Ball RedBook*). With tray mechanization, the benches (or trays) can be moved back and forth to the headhouse. Both plans offer a much higher percentage of space utilization. In fact, the trays do use more greenhouse space better than rolling benches. Both provide access to the crop—trays can be spread a foot or so apart anywhere for this purpose. Of course, the major feature of the tray approach is very fast and very low cost movement of the crop from headhouse to bench and back to headhouse. And that's most of the labor cost to grow a crop today. Again, these tray conversions are more costly. It's a whole different way of managing a greenhouse!

Another interesting point: I'm hearing of a few cut-flower growers doing cut-flower crops on raised benches—with sliders. This provides the same one-third increase in production per acre that the pot plant and bedding plant grower gets.

One American manufacturer of rolling benches, Rough Brothers Inc. [phone (513) 242-0310], offers a commercial version of the rolling bench. Figure about $2 per square foot of bench cost (including the bench).

ALL-IMPORTANT HEADHOUSES

An adequate headhouse (workroom) is absolutely basic to any efficient growing operation. Also, it's essential for much of modern mechanization—potting for pot plant growers, flat fillers and seeders for bedding growers. They all need a good, dry, well-lighted area—with reasonable temperature control and certainly with cement floors. Most pot plant specialists are designing loading ramps so that trucks can be backed up to the headhouse doors—with the truck bed the same level as the headhouse floor. One of the basics of tray mechanization is that potting, spacing, etc. can be done in the headhouse, the crop moved to the growing area, then back to the headhouse for packing—all of which demands adequate work area.

Probably most headhouses I see are metal roof or sometimes fiberglass roof structures. But several quality growers with good physical plants I know of do this job under an inflated double-poly roof, like the Van de Weterings on Calverton, Long Island, New York.

Depending on the operation, the headhouse is normally the storage place for major supplies. For bedding growers, that's soil mix, packing boxes, trays and packs. For pot growers, it's storage for flower pots and shipping boxes and space for pot bulb coolers (refrigerators). For cut flower growers, it's a space for grading, bunching, refrigeration and tray storage.

And don't forget parking space! Headhouses are often used for parking large trucks. Do you want them indoors in winter? On the next page are some examples of good operations, comparing the amount of headhouse space provided to total growing area.

Here's a very practical answer to building a headhouse. The two right "hoops" with a very high gutter are the headhouse for this range. This is located at Ivy Acres, Calverton, Long Island. See the adjoining photo for an inside look.

The interior of the headhouse at Ivy Acres. With cement floor, heat and lights, it's a fine place to work.

Grower	Greenhouse Area (sq. ft.)	Headhouse Area (sq. ft.)	Work Area is What % of Total Range	Crop	Remarks
G&E Greenhouse Batavia, Illinois	136,000	12,560	9.2	pot plants	not including cooler
G&E Greenhouses Elburn, Illinois	69,000	5,805	8.4	pot plants	
Masson's Kansas City, Kansas	240,000	40,000	16.5	bedding plants pot plants	Note 1
Frank Clesen South Elgin, Illinois	137,000	11,760	8.5	pot plants	
Mid-American Growers Granville, Illinois	880,000	66,000	8	bedding plants pot plants	Note 2
Ivy Acres Calverton, Long Island, New York	860,000	73,000	8.5	bedding plants pot plants	Note 3

1 *Alexander Masson: "Our ratio is 1:6. Keep in mind, however, that we garage most delivery trucks inside. Secondly, we produce and market a diversified line of product, and this activity needs more space than, say, the producer of just potted mums."*

2 *Mid-American Growers: "Our support buildings, by the way, include soil mixing, peat storage, transplanting, sowing area, offices, cafeteria, bathrooms, shipping pick up area, storage, cooler, shop, chemical room."*

3 *Ivy Acres: Their new range consists of a 10-acre block (430,000 sq. ft.) plus an additional 10 acres created by their unique outdoor bench system (see mechanization section). Interestingly, if you add the two 10-acre areas together, you again come up with a headhouse area about 9% of the total area of greenhouse.*

An interesting conclusion: There is a remarkable consistency of work area to total roof area—very close to 9%—except for Alexander Masson, who keeps trucks inside and who does substantial assembly and packing of other related products in his work area. The percent of headhouse area needed seems to stay fairly constant regardless of the size of the operation. Hearty thanks to these growers for providing this enlightening picture.

CURTAINS, NOT JUST FOR ENERGY SAVING AND SHORT DAYS ANYMORE!

Here's more new technology and new and important products since the 14th *Ball RedBook* edition. They are: thermal sheets, light reduction/cooling screens, daylength control for short-day crops and frost protection sheets.

Many of these newer products serve both as thermal sheets (reduce fuel loss on winter nights) and to reduce summer sun/heat. One new product is effective for frost protection on outdoor areas and also for reducing summer sunlight.

In total, these various sheets are very widely used by bedding plant, pot plant and foliage growers all over the United States and Canada. They are important! The trend on use of such sheets is up sharply.

Thermal/Light Reduction Sheets

These are sheets installed gutter to gutter or lengthwise in the greenhouse perhaps 8' to 12' above the ground. They serve two basic functions and both are important.

- **Reduce excessive sunlight.** Many crops just can't tolerate full summer sun. Put a different way, the capability of restricting sunlight to a set level (often done with computers) is a major assist to growers striving for quality crops. Also reducing summer sun especially in Southern areas substantially reduces water requirement. Pete Peterson, major San Antonio, Texas, bedding and pot plant grower, reports 8° to 10°F cooler temperature with light reduction sheets. Also water demand by plants down a surprising 50%, which means a lot less fertilizer and less of scarce good water. Southern growers are achieving these results using LS16 (65% light reduction, and 60% night time energy reduction).

- **Fuel saving.** Equally important: By extending these sheets daily sunset to sunrise (in winter), major fuel economies can be realized. Typically 25% to 35%.

Much higher gutters—often 10' to 12' high or more—are being built in the early 1990s. Reason? Better air circulation, more even temperatures. Also important: Higher gutters mean cooler summer temperatures at the bench levels, and also with high gutters, fan jet tubes can be placed below the thermal sheets.

A complete automated installation, all labor and material, of these new, improved energy sheets will cost $1 to $1.50 per square foot of ground covered. Growers can compute the number of years needed to pay back their investment in such equipment. Example: Given a $1/sq. ft. fuel cost and 35% fuel savings, that's 35¢/sq. ft. per year saved. Divide this 35¢ into the $1.50 cost for the thermal sheet. That gives you 4.3 years to recover your investment—in fuel savings alone.

Sources. An important supplier of these sheets is Ludvig Svensson (U.S.) Inc., a Swedish manufacturer, with U.S. offices in Charlotte, North Carolina [phone (704) 357-0457]. Here are some of the Svensson thermal sheets, all of which are combinations of aluminum and various plastic materials.

- **LS13.** Extended at gutter height sunset to sunrise in winter, it will reduce fuel costs about 30%. Total summer sunlight reduction: 30%. Cost for the sheet alone is about 50¢/sq. ft. Ludvig Svensson reports typical costs for mechanized installation in a greenhouse are around $1.50/sq. ft., all labor and material. LS13 sheets are widely used by Northern greenhouse growers and many vegetable growers across the United States.

- **LS15.** 50% to 55% fuel saving (manufacturer's figures) and 50% summer sunlight reduction. Cost for the sheet alone: 38¢ to 45¢ per square foot. Used very widely by bedding and pot plant growers in the Northern states and Canada—for example, Nick Van Wingerden, Mid-American Growers, Granville, Illinois.

- **LS16.** Roughly 60% fuel saving, 60% summer light reduction. Used primarily in sub-tropical areas such as Florida and Southern California where excess summer sun and heat are a problem. In fact, this material is a real help in cooling greenhouses.

Note: All the above sheets are lightweight enough to be adaptable to flat surface mechanical applications, typically gutter to gutter. Mechanical installations of these sheets are available from Van Wingerden Inc., Fletcher, North Carolina; Van Rijn, Toronto; Wadsworth Controls, Arvada, Colorado; and Cravo Equipment Ltd., Brantford, Ontario.

Short-Day Sheets

Here the purpose for the sheet is to reduce daylength. It's the same as the black cloth idea—giving near zero light for at least 12½ to 13 hours per night to trigger flowering in such crops as mums, kalanchoes and poinsettias. (Actually it's the long night that does it.) Materials used today:

- **Black sateen cloth.** Skip Smith of X.S. Smith reports black sateen as the most used shading cover by growers generally. It can be done over one bench at a time or from gutter to gutter mechanically. It will last five to seven years depending on use. Cost is 65¢ to 70¢/sq. ft. Black sateen can be used with automatic installations.

- **Black polypropylene** can be taped and grommeted for installation. It's low cost—about 6¢ to 7¢/sq. ft. Short-lived, especially if abused.

- **LS100.** It's a black polyester, woven material. Some growers report longer life than sateen. It can be used to shade single benches of plants ground to ground. It's less energy-saving than LS11+1. Cost is around 70¢/sq. ft.

- **LS11+1.** This is 99% blackout cover. Durable. Costs about 60¢/sq. ft. Adaptable to automated installations.

- **LS11+7.** Here's the plastic "black cloth" that will provide short day shade yet allow enough light so that crews can work with the crops under the cover. It blocks out the near red part of the light. Both LS11+1 and LS11+7 can be used with automated installations gutter to gutter and cost about 60¢/sq. ft. LS11+1 and LS11+7 reflect more sun than LS100 so there will be less heat build-up. Sateen tends to absorb more heat.

Shade House/Cloth House/Saran Mesh

A different application of light reduction, these are plastic mesh materials normally around 15-20 threads per inch. In general, these are materials formally referred to as "saran mesh." They are available in several different shades—some reduce light 50%, some less, some more. They are used mainly in Southern and Western mild climates—widely used by Florida foliage growers, mum cutting producers and outdoor pompon growers in Florida. They are also used for a weed control mulch. The cloth house installations are normally semi-permanently installed overhead, often to last several years. These materials are too heavy to be used in greenhouse light reduction/thermal sheet applications.

Two examples:

- Polypropylene is a woven plastic. Two brand names: Chicopee, Pak.
- Knitted mesh. Some more tear-resistant. Used as a semi-permanent "roof" for cloth houses. One material is produced by V-J Growers Supply in Florida [phone (800) 327-5422].

Automated Outdoor Frost Protection Sheets

A new LS product (PLS-50) can be applied overhead to large areas and be mechanically extended or retracted. Growers are using it mainly for frost protection. It will also provide 50% light reduction. Examples of users:

- **Billy Powell,** Troup, Texas has 6 acres of this material (slightly modified)—used importantly for pansy plants outdoors in March subject to late freezes. Billy installed polyethylene sides and maintains 50°F with some portable heat.
- **Tom Van Wingerden,** Charlotte, North Carolina, covers 4 acres of roll-out bedding plants with PLS-50.
- **DoRight's,** Camarillo, California, has an acre or two. They use it for frost protection on late winter bedding plants.

A Specialized Shade-Thermal Sheet Installer

Cravo Equipment Ltd. (Richard Vollebregt) is a specialist in installing these various shade and thermal sheet mechanical installations [phone (519) 759-8226].

For a helpful compilation on all these automatic curtains see the April 1990 *GrowerTalks* (there are over 50 different sheets available).

Chapter 5

GREENHOUSE COOLING/VENT SYSTEMS

by Vic Ball

FAN/PAD COOLING

Nearly all serious U.S. and Canadian production of year-round pot plants and major cut crops such as roses are equipped with fan/pad cooling. The only exception would be cool summer areas such as Washington State and Vancouver. A pot mum crop without cooling even in the Midwest or the East is a good bet for major losses from heat stalling in summer. Further south or in the Southwest, cooling is an absolute must. Surprisingly, there are major greenhouse ranges even in Florida with fan/pad cooling. In spite of the relatively high humidity, there is enough cooling to make it economical. For the record, there is substantial use of high-pressure fog/mist for cooling, especially in propagating areas and for cut roses. See later in this chapter for details.

The rapid rise of electricity costs has caused growers in some areas to reconsider rows of giant fans and pads as a cooling system. A big example: Aldershot Greenhouses near Toronto, with many acres of year-round pot mums, are taking a serious try at relying on 50″ roof ventilators to do the cooling job. Their climate (almost between two of the Great Lakes) takes a lot of the hot weather pressure away.

But still, nearly all serious production of pot plants and cut flowers in North America is fan/pad cooled.

How It Works

Evaporative cooling of greenhouses is accomplished by drawing air through a wet pad and in the process evaporating water, cooling the air by absorbing 8,100 BTUs of heat energy for each gallon evaporated. Cool air comes out of the pad and into the greenhouse.

A wet wall, consisting of pads, water distribution system to wet the pads, water pump and sump, is erected continuously along one side or end wall of the greenhouse. The pads must be kept wet to facilitate the evaporation process. On the opposite wall, exhaust fans properly sized for the greenhouse size and location are installed and placed to provide smooth airflow across the greenhouse. Pads should be sized to provide the most economical and efficient system possible. Cellulose pads 4″ thick operate best at an air speed of 250′/minute through the pad, and 2″ aspen pads work best at 150′/minute. For 6″ cellulose pads, use 400′/minute.

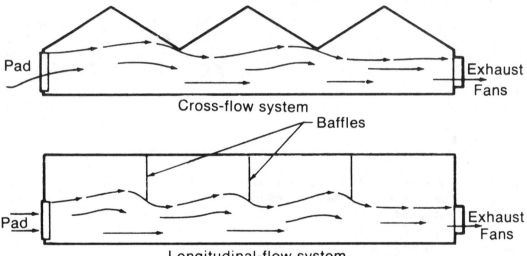

Cross-flow system

Longitudinal-flow system

A good schematic drawing of cooling. The top range: ridge and furrow. Note how the gutter keeps the cool air down near the crop. The lower sketch is a separate house, the cool air now drawn lengthways from pad (left) to fans. In this case, baffles are needed to keep cool air down at crop level. Drawing credit: Acme Engineering.

How Cool?

The amount of cooling achievable by evaporative cooling varies with the dryness of the air—the differential between the wet bulb and dry bulb temperatures. This differential varies not only with location and season, but also during each day.

Although the dry bulb could vary as much as 25°F in one day, the wet bulb varies approximately ⅓ as much. Therefore, cooling can be accomplished even in normally high humidity areas in the middle of the day when it is really needed.

A well-designed evaporative cooling system should be able to reduce the dry bulb temperature inside the wet wall to approximately 85% of the difference between the outside dry bulb and wet bulb temperature. A temperature rise of about 7°F from the pad to the exhaust fans should be expected.

Please do not "cheat" on the size of the intake air openings—the larger the better. A smaller size than called for creates static resistance, which greatly reduces the efficiency of fans and causes increased electricity usage. I prefer continuous vents whenever possible.

How Many Fans—How Big a Pad?

The calculations are simple—the problem is that the need varies by localities. Some areas have consistently high 90% humidity summer days (Dallas, Texas, for example). Others, like Chicago, will be typically low 90s many days. Generally, fan and pad systems work best in dry climates. Systems must be "oversize" in high humidity areas like Houston, Texas and Florida.

To give a rough idea of equipment needed for cooling an acre of conventional gutter-connected greenhouses, here's the way it's figured: Length of houses x width x distance from ground to gutter height tells CFM (cubic feet per minute) required for air movement. To figure pad area required, divide that total CFM by 250 for 4" thick pads and by 400 if using 6" thick pads, and that total by the number of linear feet of wall the pad vent will cover. This last number will tell you how tall the system will have to be. In humid climates, I recommend oversizing fans and pads by 20%. For growers interested in calculating pad and fan requirements, I suggest writing to Acme Engineering & Mfg. Corp., P.O. Box 978, Muskogee, OK 74402, for a copy of a manual entitled "Controlled Environment Equipment for Greenhouses." Also ask for their excellent "The Greenhouse Climate Control Handbook." Both are available at no charge.

Cautions on pad installations: Pads cause resistance to airflow, so be sure that all air passes through the pads and that all other openings are closed. Even an open fan-jet shutter will greatly reduce pad efficiency.

Sample Calculations

Example: 14 bays each 21' wide by 144' long have a total area of 42,336 sq. ft. With an 8' gutter height, this greenhouse section requires moving 338,688 cu. ft. of air per minute for proper fan/pad cooling. Assuming use of a pad that will move 250 cu. ft. of air per minute per sq. ft. of pad area, we divide the 338,688 by 250 and will need 1,355 sq. ft. of pad area. Again, 4" paper pad moves air at 250 cu. ft. per minute, 6" thick pad at 400 cu. ft. per minute. Assuming pads are mounted to gables, we have 294' available to mount the system (14 bays x 21'). The square feet required divided by the available linear feet of mounting space means pads will have to be at least 4.61' tall to do the job. Always figure pads up to the next even foot, not down. In this example, then, 5' tall pads should be used.

To select fans, we again must move 338,688 cu. ft. of air per minute. A fan drawing air through a 4″ pad will move air at 250' per minute and can move 21,090 cu. ft. of air per minute per fan (see Acme's bulletins for fan capacity specifications). So we divide 338,688 by 21,090 cu. ft. of air per minute capacity of each fan. Answer: We need 17 fans.

When the house temperature becomes too high and cooling is needed, the equipment controller or cooling thermostat simultaneously opens the motorized shutter (covering the fans) and energizes exhaust fans. When the desired temperature has been reached, the equipment controller or thermostat closes the inlet shutter and turns off the exhaust fan, thereby shutting off the outside air supply.

When the relative humidity in the house exceeds the desired level it can be reduced by bringing in cooler, outside air that has a lower water vapor content. The humid house air is expelled by the exhaust fan while the drier, incoming air is heated and mixed with the house air.

A good example of a "wet pad" installed across the end of a pot plant range. Air is drawn from the outside, through the wet pad and then to the crop. The evaporation occurring as air rushes through the pad does the cooling.

Which Pad?

In recent years, new types of pads have come on the market that offer important advantages. Here they are—pro and con—versus the traditional aspen pad. Each has its own pluses and minuses to consider when choosing a pad system.

- **Paper pads** are a patented design of paper coated with a special glue formed into a honeycomb shape. It is presently available from Munters Corp., 1205 6th St. S.E., Ft. Meyers, FL 33907. Paper pads are also available from Glacier Cor, Div. International Honeycomb of IL, 1149 Central Ave., University Park, IL 60466. They market the pad under the name of Glacier-Cor. The paper pad has a much greater surface area than aspen per sq. ft. of pad, thus providing more cooling per sq. ft. of pad. Its life varies from two to seven years depending on how many months a year they are used and water pH. High alkaline water seems to deteriorate or dissolve the glue that holds the pads together. Water should be pH adjusted to provide the longest life. Algae buildup on pads can be controlled chemically with an algaecide such as Agribrom. These paper pads are very widely used—in fact, aspen pads are almost off the market at present. Additional paper pad manufacturers are expected as the patents for paper pad systems expire.

- **Aluminum pads,** now on the market, are made of a number of layers of expanded metal with a special surface texture to help hold moisture. They are too new for much testing to have been done at this printing. Because the pads are made completely of aluminum they should last a long time. Cost is approximately $1/sq. ft. more than paper pads. It's worth looking into; just remember that some of the engineering and testing under various climates is yet to be done.

As of this edition, 90% plus of pads in North America are paper. The aluminum pad is promising, but as yet unproven.

Fan Maintenance

For fans to work at peak efficiency with the minimum amount of electrical usage, certain maintenance steps and general guidelines should be followed. Keep all the belts very tight to eliminate slipping, which reduces not only the air output of the fans but can also increase electrical use on the motor. Be sure that all air leaks in the greenhouse are kept plugged in order to get top efficiency from your pads. Pads create air resistance, and air leaks in the house can increase temperatures in the greenhouse 4° to 10°F because air intake is going through air leaks and not the pads themselves. Be sure the pad area is kept completely wet without any dry spots. Control algae by using chemical algaecides or even common bleach. During winter months, check for air intrusion through fan shutters or inlet shutters to reduce heat loss. These simple steps will help to keep your greenhouse cooler in summer and warmer in winter.

There is substantial interest and activity in the use of high-pressure fog for cooling and humidifying greenhouses for ornamentals, vegetables and nursery stock. Fog offers some important advantages, especially in certain applications—both in the dry Southwest and in the northern United States and Canada. I talked with Gene Parsons of Baumac International, Mentone (San Bernardino), California [phone (714) 794-7631]. Baumac's is a 35-year company that deals about half in fogging greenhouses (flowers and vegetables) and half in livestock applications. It is one of several firms, including Mee Industries [phone (818) 350-4180], that are prominent in supplying fog to ornamental growers.

Several of the key fog advantages that developed in the talk with Gene:

- **Humidity for roses!** It's a given that roses need humidity—some are in the 60% to 70% RH level. Providing this humidity plus moderating high summer temperatures apparently has produced substantial benefits for rose growers. Rose growers report better production and fewer problems with mildew under fog. Several major producers in the Toronto area (Jake and Otto Bulk, for example) have acres of roses under fog cooling for these reasons. The chronology: Growers intall sophisticated Priva-type environmental controls, are then about to monitor their humidity levels and realize the humidity deficiency. This has led them, in some cases, to fog.

  A recent paper presented by Alan Darlington of the University of Guelph offers the results of testing controlled humidity levels with certain types of roses. Alan compared the performance of rose cultivars Samantha and Royalty in a humidity-controlled environment (by using a high pressure, high efficiency fog system) versus a non-controlled environment. The net result of this testing demonstrated a 5% increase in length with the Royalty and a 10% increase with the Samantha cultivar grown in the humidified greenhouses. In addition, according to this research, the quality of the rose harvest increased dramatically (as much as 25% in the Royalty variety), and there was a 15% to 20% higher yield per growing cycle.

- **Another important application for bedding plants** is in plug production and seed germination. The point here has to do with preventing transpiration of moisture from the plant into the surrounding atmosphere. By increasing the RH of the environment, the air no longer acts as a sponge to draw moisture from the plant. The net result is reduced irrigation and therefore fewer occurrences of disease problems commonly experienced by overwatering. Furthermore, there is less stress on the plant so the yield is substantially greater.

- **Pot plants.** Again, I heard of the benefits, especially on certain crops, of maintaining relatively high humidity—along with moderating very high summer temperatures.

- **Pesticide application.** Due to the unique nature of these systems, fog offers an excellent vehicle for the distribution of pesticide/fungicide agents due to the billions of aerosol particles generated. Not only do growers experience a more uniform coverage with a high efficiency fog system (which offers increased effectiveness with a reduction in the utilization of material), but they find that these treatments can be performed in a fraction of the time of conventional spraying practices.

As with any chemical agent it is absolutely essential to verify that the material a grower chooses to use in a fog system meets with state and local approval.

- **Greenhouse peppers.** A 5-acre greenhouse pepper grower in the Toronto area recently converted to fog in his venlo glass greenhouses. The reason was to gain both higher relative humidity and moderation of high summer temperatures. The results: earlier set and heavier, better yield.

Pro and Con

In fact, fog systems and pad systems work on the same evaporative principle (evaporation). Therefore, it is not possible to say one system can cool more efficiently than another. The only real difference between the two systems is how they

Alex Gerace, Welby Gardens, a major Denver bedding plant producer, operates this plug finishing area with high-pressure fog cooling.

suspend the moisture into the incoming air stream. A pad system uses a celluous material to suspend moisture, whereby a fog system generates literally billions of aerosol size droplets, which are then suspended in the air where they quickly evaporate and thus cool and/or humidify as required to meet growing demands.

The advantages of fog systems include more efficient utilization of the water supply (a concern that is growing ever more popular each year), the ability to adapt the fog system to almost any ventilation design and a more uniform cooling effect. The fog system can be utilized in conjunction with adequately designed naturally ventilated structures, offering excellent cooling efficiencies without the initial purchase or ongoing electrical consumption of exhaust fan assemblies. It is important to remember that the cooling performance achieved with any evaporative cooling system is in direct relation to the ventilation supplied. If a naturally ventilated house cannot provide this necessary ventilation, then exhaust fans are required.

Care must be taken to prevent nozzle blockage when designing and installing high efficiency fog systems. Fortunately, all impurities in a given water supply can be treated to prevent nozzle blockage within a fog system. Provided these impurities are addressed and counter measures adopted, the nozzle blockage occurrences typically are less than 3% per month.

Fog systems from several firms are used by dozens of growers in the Southwest and West and in the eastern United States and Canada. It's often used for propagating, germinating seed and plugs, for rooting vegetative material and also importantly for cut rose production.

FAN-JET SYSTEMS

Here's an ingenious and widely used system of fans/inlet louvers/polyethylene tubes used both to distribute heat and to ventilate greenhouses.

Stage 1—Ventilation

Fan-jet systems provide for necessary ventilation, especially on warm early spring days, without a rush of cold air hitting the crop. This is done by drawing air in through the louver by means of a fan and then forcing it through a large 12" to 30" diameter polyethylene tube that runs overhead the length of the greenhouse. A series of small holes down the length of the tube permits small amounts of outside air to enter the greenhouse atmosphere—without damage to crops.

The same fan and polyethylene tube system is used to distribute heat from overhead unit heaters. Now the heat is simply drawn from the outlet of the unit heater into the fan jet—and again it's distributed down the length of the house through the perforated polyethylene tube. The system provides a quite uniform temperature from one end of the greenhouse to the other during heating operations.

I thought the following paragraphs from "The Greenhouse Climate Control Handbook" published by Acme Engineering and Mfg. Corp., Muskogee, Oklahoma, were helpful in understanding this equipment.

A typical fan jet installation. The unit heater (right) blows hot air to the left. Heat is drawn into the fan jet assembly on the left by a fan in the end of the poly tube, then is blown on down the house and distributed through holes in the tube. The louver (open in this photo) is closed in cold weather but can be opened to draw in fresh air on early spring days. Note the exhaust tube above right—it's very important.

Fan-Jet Minimum Ventilation Systems

During cool spring, summer and fall nights and on most sunny winter days, minimum ventilation is needed to control house temperature. This type of ventilation, using cool or cold outside air, is quite different from summer ventilation and evaporative cooling. The flow must be turbulent with small to moderate quantities of air required, while in the summer the flow should be smooth using large quantities of air.

The minimum ventilation system is an important part of climate control and requires several distinct characteristics. First, it must have ample air flow capacity to maintain a proper heat balance by removing the excess solar heat on mild sunlit days.

Second, the minimum ventilating system must be able to introduce very cold winter air into the greenhouse without producing cold drafts on plants. This requires a very thorough mixing of cold outside air with warm inside air before the plant level is reached. Since powered ventilating has the energy available to produce the turbulence necessary for thorough mixing, it supplies properly tempered fresh air.

Third, it is important that all parts of the greenhouse be at the same temperature. To achieve this, the ventilating system must distribute air very uniformly throughout the house and maintain positive air movement and continuous circulation. A powered ventilating system has a real advantage over gravity systems that rely on thermal air mixing.

Continuous circulation also produces a gentle air movement that maintains a better leaf surface microclimate and prevents pockets of disease-producing high humidity.

For average conditions an airflow of 1½ to 2 cu. ft. per minute/sq. ft. of floor space holds the house temperature within 15°F of outside temperature.

Using exhaust fans for mechanical ventilation of greenhouses combined with perforated transparent plastic tubes makes an ideal method of introducing cold air into a greenhouse in winter without cold drafts. The development of these principles has produced the Acme Fan-Jet Climate Control System. This is a multi-purpose system that can alternately heat, dehumidify, ventilate or recirculate air in a greenhouse for proper climate control in fall, winter and spring. This system is not designed to provide temperature control in warm seasons, although this system's exhaust fans can also serve as fans for the summer fan and pad cooling system.

The Fan-Jet system consists of a specially constructed pressuring fan attached to a custom-designed perforated plastic tube. The tube is located in the upper section of the house and extends along the length of the greenhouse with its far end closed.

The pressurizing fan runs continuously, inflating the tube and blowing air through the holes in the form of jets into the greenhouse space. This distributes air uniformly for the full length of the tube, creating turbulence, thorough mixing and active air motion throughout the entire greenhouse. It maintains a more uniform temperature and humidity and prevents cold spots.

The fan is mounted inside the greenhouse at a specified distance from the gable end wall in front of a special-sized motorized shutter that functions as the fresh air inlet. Several sizes of Fan-Jets with matching air inlet shutters and perforated tubes are offered for different requirements. Often two or more units are needed for a greenhouse depending on its size.

Supplying Heat

Quoting from the Acme bulletin on the role of this Fan-Jet system and distributing heat:

While the Fan-Jet ventilating system provides excellent distribution and circulation of air, it can also serve as a highly efficient heat distribution system. When equipped with an accessory "heat kit" package it becomes part of a heating system without affecting its other functions of minimum ventilation and recirculation. The heat kit comprises a baffle arrangement that permits using conventional horizontal-discharge-type unit heaters in combination with Fan-Jet units to make an efficient and economical heating system.

Since the Fan-Jet Climate Control System works directly with the air, it reacts quickly to changes in requirements. By using high velocities and the rapid mixing turbulence of the jets, it achieves the maximum capability of the equipment in a matter of seconds and provides quick response necessary for maintaining a uniform climate.

The Fan-Jet system is designed to both heat and ventilate in fall, winter and spring. When high summer temperatures arrive, however, larger fans and usually a fan/pad cooling system are needed.

Rough costs for the Fan-Jet system—for the fan, the shutter, the poly tube, tube hangers, tube support systems and heat accessories, not including the heater—on a 150' gutter-connected greenhouse, is about $525 FOB factory.

SECTION II

Labor Saving/Mechanization

Chapter 6

BACKGROUND ON MECHANIZATION

by Vic Ball

First off, mechanize we must—if U.S. and Canadian bedding plant and pot plant growers will survive world competition on the long term. Sooner or later, it will be a free trade world flower industry, and the country that produces each crop most efficiently will win leadership in that part of the market.

Europe, especially the Dutch and Danes, have automated a lot. Certainly not all, but maybe one-third to one-half of their pot plant production is under Dutch tray systems in the early 1990s. Almost no one there hand waters pot plants and bedding plants. Their internal competition forces them to automate irrigation—and as much else as possible.

A key factor in this strong move to automation in Europe is their very high labor cost. Including social cost, Holland in the early 1990s often pays $12 to $15 per hour. Compare this against $6 to $7, especially in metropolitan areas of the United States—plus $3 to $4 retirement/medical/vacation cost here—and we are not too far behind. Certainly labor costs in the United States and Canada are going up rapidly, and in some areas, help just can't be had for any price. An inevitable result of all this European automation is that their prices (to growers) for pot plants and bedding plants are generally one-third or more below current U.S. price levels. Again these prices are forced down by internal competition over there.

The alarming point about all this for U.S. growers: If and when free trade actually occurs between the United States and Canada and Europe, there will obviously be some very tough low price competition for American growers—coming from across the Atlantic. Yes, there is shipping cost, but modern jet freight is so fast and so cheap. And with a 30% to 40% lower price to the grower, Europeans can afford to fly plants across the Atlantic. There is a $100 million cut flower trade from Holland to the United States alone today. If cut flowers can be flown over in that volume, pot plants are surely a possibility. Interesting point: I hear already of major shipments of potted foliage plants from Holland to Taiwan.

As of publishing this book, Quarantine 37 (designed to keep foreign insects and diseases out of the United States) is under heavy attack. If it is substantially withdrawn, certainly major and very tough competition will face American growers. The irony here is that European growers in fact have no inherent advantage over U.S. producers. The Dutch and Danes have less winter light, higher labor costs, the same fuel costs, and they are 3,000 to 4,000 miles from the U.S. market.

So, in balance, there would seem a compelling case for American growers to automate—now. In fact, a dozen or two larger producers have moved into acres of Dutch trays, automated irrigation, and other labor saving approaches. A clear

Speaking of specialization, here's a Danish grower who grows a major area of pot vinca for summer sales—an acre or more. He follows this with pot asters and poinsettias in the fall, azaleas in spring—in other words, a series of crops. During each of these crops they are a "specialist" in that one crop. In this way they are able to achieve most of the benefits of mechanization.

majority of U.S. pot plants and bedding plants, however, are still more or less done the old way. Lots of handwatering, lots of wheelbarrows and even hand-carrying plants around the greenhouses.

But automation for American growers is not that simple! There is a particularly major problem:

- **Specialization—a basic to automation.** All too often even larger American growers will have three or four different crops in a single greenhouse. Modern automation simply doesn't work unless the grower does a substantial area of one crop at one time. Maybe several acres—but even better if it's 5 or 10 acres. I think of Knud Jepsen in Denmark who operates a single range, 13 acres of glass, year-round 4″ kalanchoe production, totaling about six million 4″ plants per year. Other Europeans achieve fair specialization with a *succession* of crops through the year, devoting major areas to one crop in the fall, a second crop in the winter, etc. Many European growers operate this way. Also, of course, if an American grower is very large, even up to 20 to 30 acres, he can operate a section, for example, of pot mums, which will be perhaps 3 to 5 acres by itself year-round, and that will accommodate specialization.

But, by and large, most U.S. pot production is done the old way—with a variety of crops at a given time in a several-acre range. Automation just doesn't work unless there is a major area of one crop at one time.

The real heart of the specialization problem is the frankly archaic marketing system in most of the United States and Canada today. So often the typical several-acre U.S. pot grower says, "I have to grow a wide variety of plants to sell my product." Given today's system, that's true. So, really, the American grower can't specialize until our marketing system is in some way changed to better support the specialist grower. Today a grower produces what crops he thinks his market wants, and sells them himself the best he can.

- **How to do it?** Again, we look to Europe. For 50 years, the Dutch and Danes have been developing their very sophisticated co-op markets. Much of it is done under auction clocks, some not. But the majority of Dutch and Danish production goes to markets through these co-op marketing systems. Probably one-third of pot plants are sold directly by growers or through private wholesalers and even a higher percentage of bedding plants. The co-ops are grower-owned and provide an efficient market for dozens of small specialist producers, most of whose production goes through the co-op market. Another key advantage of this system: The major chains in Europe can now go to the Dutch or the Danish auction and buy major quantities of a variety of quality plants—and all from one source. Buyers like that!

There are private wholesalers across Europe who do sell pot plants/bedding plants for growers—but clearly the very large grower-owned co-ops market the majority of the production—and in most cases set the prices.

Why not such auctions in the United States and Canada? There have been several attempts. There are today (in 1990) auctions operating in Vancouver, Toronto, Montreal, Los Angeles and San Diego. The one real success story so far is

Vancouver—doing about $25 million to $30 million in sales per year. Most others are down in the $5 million to $8 million per year volume and, in fact, are not handling the majority of production in their areas. The Vancouver auction has created a climate where a smaller grower may specialize and market through the auction. Why this success? First, a major concentration of growers with 5 to 6 million sq. ft. of greenhouse in the greater Vancouver area. Also, growers give the auction major support—the majority of Vancouver production goes through the auction today. Another factor is that so many growers in this area are themselves Europeans, often Dutch and Danes, and they are used to this sort of marketing. Americans generally are firmly entrenched in free enterprise and are hesitant to commit marketing their product to a cooperative system—which is often seen as socialistic. Perhaps another factor: The major market for their products is the Northwest states and California.

Here's the auction clock at work at the Vancouver, British Columbia, auction.

72

There are areas in the United States and Canada with enough grower concentration to support what is happening in Vancouver. As an example, I think of the San Francisco Bay area, Los Angeles, Florida, the New Jersey/Long Island area and Toronto. As I mentioned before, there are two auctions operating in the Los Angeles-San Diego area today. One is rather new, in downtown Los Angeles, and the other is at the new Ecke Floral Center in Encinitas.

One rather encouraging thing I see here is the emergence of giant food/discount/home improvement chains as a market for plants and flowers. In a certain way, a giant like Kroger is today a market for a one-crop specialist. One case of violets a week to each of 800 stores would surely provide a market for one or several specialist violet producers. Automated! It's probably already beginning to happen.

Another approach to this I'd like to call a "free enterprise answer" to the problem. Here, commercial firms, either growers or wholesalers (or often firms doing both), function in the role of the European auctions. They receive products from a variety of growers and, in many cases, combine this with their own production. They are now able to supply major chains with a wide variety of quality plants year-round.

That's a little overstated, but it's a goal that I see starting to emerge in several cases. An example is Van's Inc. in Alsip (Chicago area wholesaler), Illinois, who receives plants—especially from several central Michigan growers—and markets to Midwest chains. Gary Miller of Milgro at Oxnard, California, is a major producer (close to 1 million sq. ft.) and also is today marketing products from other smaller nearby growers. Bill Vermeer, Westbrook Greenhouse Systems in Grimsby, Ontario, Canada is again a major grower and markets products from other growers. His stated goal is to use his new marketing facility mainly for moving production from other growers.

Interesting note: There is a sort of cooperative project emerging in England to market bedding plants. Four or five major bedding growers are booking orders for their crops through a marketing pool arrangement called "NOMAD." The group can deliver major quantities of plants to large chains.

So, there it is: The United States and Canada must automate to survive in the long haul, but growers can't really do major automation with the marketing system we have in place today. Granted, several very large pot plant and bedding plant producers are specializing—simply because of their size (Green Circle Growers, Oberlin, Ohio, for example; Powell's Plant Farm, Troup, Texas; Nurserymen's Exchange, Bay City Growers, Sunnyside Nurseries in the Salinas area, Milgro in Oxnard, California, and others).

But still, today the substantial majority of U.S. and Canadian pot plants and bedding plants are done by traditional, rather high labor cost methods and are marketed again by our traditional system with each grower selling what he grows the best he can. We must do better!

The remainder of Section II on mechanization will describe several key ways it can be—and in some cases, is being—done today.

Chapter 7

TRAY MECHANIZATION

by Vic Ball

Tray mechanization (in Europe, they say "container") is a way to reduce hand labor dramatically, especially on pot/bedding/foliage plant crops. The same is true for rooting cuttings/young plants, 2¼" and plug production. Combined with specialization and properly done, trays have repeatedly reduced staff on pot ranges from seven to eight people per acre to two or three.

They're found mainly with crops that require moving plants in and out of the greenhouse often—a minimum of three to four times per year.

WHAT IS TRAY AUTOMATION?

Briefly, it's a system where crops are grown on aluminum trays from roughly 4' x 5' up to perhaps 5' x 20' (length and width) and normally with a 4"- to 5"-sidewall. The tray is the bench and is also used to move crops in and out of the greenhouse. The key to trays: Crops on trays can be moved in or out of the greenhouse very easily—with near zero labor costs.

Some trays have solid aluminum sheet bottoms, others have expanded metal, a mesh that permits air flow upward and water drainage downward. Trays are normally placed crossways of the house, filling the greenhouse area from gutter to gutter except for normally one aisle. A 22'-wide house might have trays set crosswise in the house with two feet allowed for an aisle. They are set at waist height, and they roll freely from end to end of the greenhouse on normally 1½" pipes (see photo for all of this). One man can easily push a dozen of these trays up to the center or end walk of the greenhouse and onto some sort of conveyance to get them into the headhouse—and, of course, do the same thing in reverse.

This is a typical Dutch tray layout—maybe 20'-long trays set crosswise of the house and moving back and forth on ingenious rollers (under the trays), which ride on the pipe (foreground). This photo is of Aart Van Wingerden's Dover, Delaware, range.

Again, the key to the system is the ability to move these trays (filled with plants) from the greenhouse area to the work area, back and forth, with near zero labor. This, in turn, means that all hand operations—potting, spacing, pinching, sleeving, boxing—can be done in the headhouse under very favorable, efficient conditions, and potting machines, flat fillers, assembly line transplanters and all supplies (soil, pots, flats) are centralized, again in the headhouse. The point is that the greenhouse aisles are a very inefficient place for all of this work.

With a tray system a pot crop is potted on potting machines in the headhouse and pots are fed mechanically onto these aluminum trays. Then they are moved, tray and all, out to the growing area until the crop is completed, after which they can be rolled back to the headhouse to be sleeved and packed. Crops are also rolled back to the headhouse for other activities, such as spacing or disbudding. The tray is both the growing bench and the vehicle for moving plants back and forth from work area to growing area.

Why Are Trays So Great?

The key case for trays is simply that all the work with the crop can be done with machines in the headhouse, and the crop can be moved from headhouse to greenhouse and back almost labor-free. Potting mums, for example, is done in the headhouse. This means that potting machines that are large and awkward to move into a greenhouse can stay in the headhouse. Also, other machines move plants from the potting machines and place them mechanically into the trays at any spacing desired. Potting lily bulbs, planting poinsettias—it can all be done in the headhouse the same way. All work crews stay in the headhouse, which means much more efficient working conditions, a short trip to the toilet, dry, comfortable working temperatures and a cement floor. It gives better control of staff by management. Other advantages to trays:

- **Similar important economies of labor are realized at shipping time.** Poinsettias, for example can be rolled into the headhouse where crews are ready to pick the pots off the tray and drop them into a sleeve (even this can be done mechanically now). Plants are then dropped into corrugated boxes for shipping and moved on pallets to nearby truck loading docks. If 10% of plants on a tray aren't ready for market, they can be consolidated into several trays and rolled back to the greenhouse. The result: important space efficiency.

- **Crops can be spaced mechanically.** The tray is first moved into the headhouse. Full trays and empty trays are placed side by side. For mechanical spacing, equipment picks pots off the trays onto a belt and back onto another tray at the new spacing. Or the spacing can be done by hand. Then the crop goes back to the growing area filled with pots at the new spacing.

- **All watering and feeding can be done mechanically**—by ebb and flow irrigation in the trays. They are waterproof. Water level is raised an inch or so and then dropped back again mechanically. It is a closed recirculating system with no runoff to create environmental problems. Or, plants can be irrigated mechanically using overhead nozzles. For more details on watering system possibilities, see the chapter on automated irrigation.

Knud Jepsen (right) does 4 million plus, mostly 4" kalanchoes, in Denmark. Like many European pot growers, he does the rooting and young-plant stage of the crop on trays, the rest on stationary benches. You'll first see a half-acre headhouse almost wall to wall with trays filled with pots and a dozen or so women sticking kalanchoe cuttings into the pots. The pots are then moved on the roller wheels (shown) out to the rooting area, an acre or two, still on Dutch trays. From there, they go by flats on very fast, ingenious, self-powered carts to the growing bench. On the left is Henning Rasmussen.

- **Bedding plant plugs can be planted** into packs or 4″ pots, flats set into trays in the headhouse (soon this will be done mechanically), and then trays are moved back to the growing area.

The net effect is to eliminate the majority of the hand labor—depending on the crop. All of this really works—it's being done on hundreds of acres of pot crops both in Europe and the United States and Canada today. The concept was first developed by Toen Boekestijn of de Lier, Holland, with the first tray equipment built by HAWE, a Dutch builder. The other major supplier is Intransit, located in Holland. Rough Bros., U.S. greenhouse builder, also offers this equipment.

The second effect of using trays is a more efficient use of space: Normal greenhouse aisles mean that about 65% of the ground covered by a greenhouse is used for a crop. The rest is taken up with aisles. Under trays, normally one aisle is left in the greenhouse to provide access to the crop. This means 85% to 90% utilization of space—about a one-third improvement. This is critically important! Of course the same benefit can be gained by sidewise rolling of benches, which are described elsewhere in this book. But the grower does not gain in the major labor saving he would realize with trays.

Now, About Tray Movers

There is a wide variety of automated equipment available to move the trays from headhouse down the end walk of the greenhouse and to the "bench area." A simple four-wheel d cart designed to receive the trays as they roll off the "bench," carrying perhaps one or maybe two or three trays, is often used. The cart is pushed by hand into the headhouse or can be electrically powered. Normally they are guided from growing house to headhouse by a rail buried in the concrete end walk.

More sophisticated versions of these wagons or carts are electrically powered and computer-controlled. Equipment in commercial use in Holland and Denmark today actually takes trays of newly-potted plants out to the designated area where they are to be grown, depositing them in the designated growing area. Then it picks up plants from some other house along the way back, delivering them to the work crews in the headhouse. It's all totally automatic and unattended.

It's eerie to see these "robots" moving back and forth down the end walk of a greenhouse doing their job. They can be programmed in the morning to bring a certain flow of material from greenhouse to work area or vice versa—all hands-off. One potted palm specialist in Holland does his potting, growing, spacing and packing/shipping with well under one person per acre. It is a four- to five-month rotation in a one-crop specialized range.

Another approach to moving trays from greenhouse to headhouse is using a system of self-powered rails. Trays dropped from the bench onto the rails move automatically down the end or center walk to the headhouse or vice versa. Be sure to see photos of all this equipment elsewhere in this chapter. Other rail systems provide for hand-pushing the trays back and forth on the rails.

Tray Systems Must Be Used—A Lot

All this automated tray equipment is expensive. And obviously it pays off best where there is frequent moving of crops back and forth from headhouse to greenhouse. A rotation that provides for moving crops in and out of the greenhouse only two or three times a year would be marginally profitable. One of the most advantageous applications of trays and one of the first growers to use it extensively are mum propagators. Here the crop rotation is two to three weeks and there will be eight or 10 crops grown a year in each house. Lots of crop moving back and forth is involved (at a very minimal cost) and lots of hand work is done in sticking and removing cuttings from the trays—which again can be done very much more efficiently in a headhouse.

Some remarkably advanced automation is being used in Holland today for mum cuttings where flats of rooted cuttings are moved to the growing area, set in a pre-determined position to be rooted, then picked up by the robot weeks later and brought into a shipping area. About the only hand labor involved here is sticking the cuttings—and the Dutch are looking carefully at that. It's incredible to see thousands of these flats of newly-stuck cuttings moving out to the rooting area and then later called back to fill orders.

It's a matter of saying, "We want 10,000 Bright Golden Anne today." And the computer will deliver them.

Cost

When you consider that good metal benches (expanded metal floor) cost $2 to $2.50/sq. ft., the cost of tray automation is not really excessive. The trays themselves with rails and supporting posts for a 1-acre installation are on the order of $3.50/sq. ft. of bench. The equipment to move them back and forth, greenhouse to headhouse, can be either simple and inexpensive or, in case of intensive use, may be automated or robotized at more expense.

Here are some approximate cost figures supplied by Intransit (1989), one of the two leading Dutch suppliers of this equipment, for a 1-acre tray installation. More on trays and pictures of several of these tray movers can be seen on a video available from *GrowerTalks*.

Cost, Material Only, For an Acre Greenhouse	Cost Per Sq. Ft.	
$113,000	$2.63	For 520 trays, 63″ x 103″ expanded metal bottoms.
10,800	.25	Pipe supports and pipe "rails."
$123,800	$2.88	
$ 22,900	.53	For one 33′ transport car, electric powered, manually operated—can carry three trays end to end, headhouse to greenhouse.

All the above is FOB Holland, plus tax, and for material only. Fully automatic, computer-controlled transport cars are available at about $68,000.

Several growers (early 1990s) report labor and material costs, for complete tray installations at about $5.50 to $6/sq. ft. of growing area. This does not include sophisticated transport carts. The costly Dutch guilder is a factor here!

Several Approaches to Moving Dutch Trays

The Strijbis brothers in Holland do three or four million, mostly 3" pot mums, a year. There's much moving from rooting area to long day to short day to packing shed. It's all on Dutch trays, but the tray moving is strictly budget style. This cart carries one tray, is drawn by a small garden tractor and guided by a small groove in the walk (shown in the lower left corner of the picture).

Here's the latest (early 1990s) in computerized equipment to move trays from potting area to the growing bench and back for shipping. It's all done by the small cart on the right. Trays are fed automatically from potting area to the cart (two per load) and down to the preselected house number where the tray is inserted into the growing area. This set-up is at a large adiantum fern operation in Holland.

Another way to move trays. The tray is rolled out of the growing area (left) and onto the roller wheels (center). They are pushed on the roller wheels down to the packing area. Some systems include powered wheels so you just drop the tray on the wheels and off it goes. This system is at Burnaby Lake Greenhouses, Vancouver.

Another approach to moving trays: Jim Leider, a major U.S. pot grower, faced with the problem of an existing range (many subranges), opted for trays moved around on rails by hand. He reports major labor saving.

Dutch Trays for the 1- to 3-Acre Grower

Somehow Dutch tray installations across Europe and America so far have been almost entirely on quite large ranges—10 to 20 acres and more. However, just as the *Ball RedBook* is going to press, I came across the John Van Bourgondien range at Peconic, New York, where there are 2 or 3 acres of top quality seed geraniums, among other crops. The interesting thing was that while they have installed belts throughout the range, they have, in the past year (1990), installed 25,000 sq. ft. of full-scale Dutch trays. This includes automated pot moving from the potting machine into the tray. Trays are moved from the headhouse to the greenhouse manually, but says John, "I can move five or six of the trays myself at one time."

The Van Bourgondiens are very pleased with the system. They see:

- **Major labor saving**—in getting crops in and out of the greenhouse and in filling orders, especially for their pot geraniums.

Dutch trays are economical and practical for the 1- to 3-acre grower, provided the grower is at least semi-specialized. The Van Bourgondiens (shown), Peconic, New York, installed 25,000 sq. ft. of trays for geraniums (spring), 6" pot annuals (summer) and poinsettias (fall).

- **Watering is fully automated**—the trays are used for an ebb and flow irrigation system. Again, it's major labor savings.

- **They have complete freedom to space** and re-space pots as they wish—without having to move either spaghetti tubes or, even worse, to hand water.

- **They like the quality** of geraniums they can grow in the trays.

- **Last, but certainly not least,** the trays provide a 100% recirculating system—no drainage from the crop enters the ground water. And this was the key reason for the Van Bourgondiens going into the system in the first place.

As of the early 1990s, the Van Bourgondiens are committed to moving into more trays. That's quite an exciting prospect considering, of smaller growers, they are one of the very few in the world who are using trays—and finding a reasonable payback on their investment.

THE ROUND ROBIN TRAY CONCEPT

Still in final testing stage as this book is published, this is a different application of trays—and a very interesting one. It was designed and built by Aart Van Wingerden, a major pot and bedding plant grower headquartered at Fletcher, North Carolina.

Two houses are again filled with trays, set crossways in the house. They fill the area really wall to wall and end to end with growing crop. The trays move down the length of one house to the end, are transferred over to the other house and then move up the length of the second house. They are transferred across the other end and then moved back down to the original position. In other words, the trays go around a circular pattern. Normally, the trays would not leave this closed circuit.

The point of this system is that crops can be fed onto the trays or taken from the trays at one point along the end walk of the greenhouse. For example: The potting machine can be brought into the greenhouse, pots are filled, planted and mechanically moved onto these trays. In the same way at shipping time, plants can be taken from the trays—either mechanically or by hand—and moved on a belt to a packing area, or packing can be done in the greenhouse. One of the great advantages of this Round Robin system is that a single pair of houses, perhaps 25' x 150', can be built and used by a smaller grower—reaping much of the benefits of automation available now only to the larger specialist with normal tray automation. Also, crops can be watered and sprayed as they pass by a certain point on their trip around the greenhouses.

The transfer of trays (when they reach the end of the house) over to the adjacent house is accomplished with little steel carts that move on rails—again it's all automated. The trays can move around the circle 24 hours a day unattended.

Another plus: With Round Robin, 90%+ of the area in the greenhouse is used for crops. There's near zero walk space.

Time to get a tray to the shipping point at the end walk from the furthest distant point would be about 60 minutes.

The Round Robin concept is still in development and will probably be on the market by the time this book is in print. For details call Aart Van Wingerden [phone (704) 891-4116]. See *GrowerTalks* December 1988, for more details.

ROLL-OUT BEDDING PLANTS

Here's a fascinating application of these Dutch trays to the bedding plant world! A greenhouse is equipped with normal Dutch trays as described above. But, on a roll-out range, the tracks that move the trays up and down the greenhouse extend right out through the end wall of the greenhouse and outdoors. The result: A 250'-long greenhouse full of trays can be rolled right outdoors in perhaps 20 minutes of work by several men.

Roll-out requires those "tracks" (in fact they are pipes) on which trays roll. They must be installed to carry the trays out to the 250' (or whatever size) outdoor growing area. Most growers provide concrete walks—to accommodate order filling carts, etc. Orie Van Wingerden, a Pompton Plains, New Jersey, grower, just completed an acre of new roll-out. Cost for the set-up (outdoor pipes, rails, cement walks):

Cost for One Acre	Cost/Sq. Ft.	
$108,000	$2.51	Includes 20' trays, pipe supports and rails.
30,000	.70	Cement—6' aisle between each of eight rows of trays.

All costs are material only. The Van Wingerdens did the installation. Note that the combined cost of all of the above is still far below, probably half, the cost of a new poly greenhouse with heat, benches, etc.

Orie Van Wingerden has about 2 acres of roll-out, and it's all automated. Here's the machine that moves the plants in and out in minutes at the touch of a button. The result: major improvement in quality of annuals plus two crops per year from the greenhouse.

Why is this so exciting?

- **With this arrangement, one crop** of spring plants can be grown on the trays and rolled out during the day. A second crop can be grown on the ground under the trays. Since the upper crop is outdoors all day, the lower crop gets full light. The result is two crops from each greenhouse instead of one. There is added cost for the pipe rails to roll the crop outdoors—but in balance the system is being used more each year. Already there are dozens of applications across the United States and Canada. Jack Van de Wetering, bedding plant grower on Calverton, Long Island, pioneered the concept and uses it extensively today.

- **"The far superior quality is the key advantage,"** says Orie Van Wingerden of roll-out. It's simply a matter that the plants are outdoors all day long. Unfortunately, most bedding plants are growing in inflated double polyethylene greenhouses, which are often poorly ventilated. This means high temperatures during warm sunny spring days. Heat always deteriorates the quality of bedding plants—most of them are cool-temperature-loving plants.

  Most of all, though, we have learned from research at Michigan State University that all plants will be much shorter and more compact if the day temperature is cooler than the night temperature. Even the same day and night temperature is better—but the worst of all worlds is a very warm day and a cool night. That, unfortunately, is what happens to most bedding plants in polyethylene greenhouses today. The poor ventilation means very warm days, and expensive fuel keeps many growers from heating at night.

  On the other hand, plants in a roll-out situation (outdoors all day, indoors in a warm greenhouse at night) do have a cooler day and a warmer night. The result: a major improvement in quality! And this, perhaps, is the biggest payoff of all from roll-out bedding plants.

  Listen to Orie Van Wingerden [phone (201) 694-7222], who has 100,000 sq. ft. of roll-out: "Buyers coming to my place always go for the outdoor plants first. They are just a lot better." I asked Orie what neighboring growers' responses would be to his experience. Said Orie, "These plants are so much better that other growers are going to have to go this way to have competitive quality. The main reason we have gone to roll-out is for the far superior quality. We are running greenhouse temperatures 65°F nights. Days (outdoors) have been 40° to 50°F. The result is a strong negative DIF—much cooler days versus nights. Plant quality is really remarkable. Plants are very compact and sturdy. We are giving our greenhouse crops the coolest day possible and again 65°F nights—but they're not as good as the outdoor-grown roll-out plants."

  Another facet of roll-out: The outdoor area created by the rolled out trays can do summer and fall crops with much better quality (versus greenhouse). I've heard of growers filling these trays with 4″ annuals planted in late May and sold through June and July. Other growers use them for garden mums. Usually some sort of watering facility is available, either overhead or, in the case of Orie Van Wingerden, the trays can be watered as they pass in and out of the greenhouse. Using a row of nozzles that can be turned on as the plants are moving back and forth.

Last point on roll-out: Moving plants in and out of the greenhouse can be automated. Orie Van Wingerden has an automated system. He can move his 100,000-sq.-ft. of trays in and out in minutes—with the push of a button. Cost per acre (for the automation only) is roughly $15,000 for a one-acre block, eight bays, eight machines at $1,500 each. That's about 28¢/sq. ft. of ground covered.

By the way, there is a *GrowerTalks* videotape showing Orie Van Wingerden's automated system.

Here's roll-out used on Catapano's retail growing range, Southold, Long Island, New York. Neal Catapano is in the photo.

Roll-Out for Retail Growers

Just starting to appear is the application of this roll-out idea for a retail grower. An example is Neal Catapano, Southold, Long Island, who grows several acres of bedding plants, both retail and wholesale. They are located on a busy highway, but as you drive by you see only plastic greenhouses. Several years ago they installed a quarter-acre of roll-out that enabled them to move a quarter acre of plants out right next to the highway. The expanse of color did the trick! They reported their retail business up a full 50% the first year they had plants outdoors. Again, there's a major improvement in quality—and the ease with which plants can be moved back into the greenhouse if frost threatens. Again, there is a video available from *GrowerTalks*.

Chapter 8

BELTS/CARTS— MAJOR LABOR SAVERS

by Vic Ball

Here are ways both smaller and mid-size growers can reduce labor costs to move plants in and out of the greenhouse.

Trays and belts won't reduce staff from eight per acre to one, but especially for the small to mid-size grower they can eliminate a great deal of heavy hand labor— and the original investment is a small fraction compared to Dutch trays. Both are widely used among pot and bedding plant growers today, especially carts, which are almost standard for most growers. Either belts or carts are almost the standard way of moving plants from the transplanting area to the growing greenhouse and for the laborious task of gathering orders of flats.

FIRST, CARTS

There are a variety of carts available to the grower today. Cannon carts (Cannon Equipment Co., Cannon Falls, Minneapolis [phone (800) 533-2071] are widely used and a good example. Here are their models currently available:

- **Plant transport cart** model 83-0157 is probably the most widely used and can be hooked together into a sort of "train" drawn by a small garden tractor around the greenhouse and out to the shipping area. It can be collapsed at the garden center

The much-used 4-wheel cart for moving flats, pot plants and baskets in and out of the greenhouse.

Many, especially larger, growers tie half a dozen of various carts into a "train" towed by, most often, a small garden tractor.

after unloading and many more can be accommodated per truckload on the return trip to the grower. The carts can be and often are forklifted to the truck floor—and back down to the ground at the retail outlet. This transport cart is 58¾″ long, 21⅜″ wide and 80″ high. It costs about $285. Each shelf is about $28 (early 1990 prices). This is the model so widely used by growers to move plants from the transplanting area to the growing area, for order assembly, from greenhouse to the truck and then to the garden center.

- **Display cart** model 83-0083 is designed especially for retail display. Shelves slope outward facing the buyer! It may not be pulled in a train. Dimensions: 81″ long, 22¼″ wide and 58″ high. It costs $197; shelves run about $47 each. The weight capacity for this model is 750 lbs. It knocks down for shipping and storage.

All this applies to a variety of potted and foliage plants. It's the same opportunity for easier moving of plants about the greenhouse and to the shipping area.

There are other reliable cart suppliers for greenhouse use. Some good examples: Andpro, Ltd., RR 4, Waterford, Ontario, Canada N0E 1Y0; and Hodge Manufacturing Co., Inc., Springfield, Massachusetts 01107.

A bit more expensive cart, self-powered but fast, maneuverable and carries a lot of flats or pots!

An ingenious cart that can double both for moving plants and as retail displays. Think how many more plants per sq. ft. of precious floor space can be displayed on such a cart!

An obvious point: These carts are far more useful on a range equipped throughout with good cement walks. Rough walks just don't make for satisfactory moving of heavy flats with carts.

Automated Order Assembly

I'm seeing several of the larger bedding growers who have installed automated systems of assembling orders of bedding plant flats—based on the use of Dutch trays and belts. The flats are moved to the assembly area on the Dutch trays and, in some cases, are moved automatically from the 10'- or 15'-long tray onto a belt. From here flats are moved by belt to a series of long belts installed side by side. Each of these several dozen belts is kept filled with flats of one color or one variety of bedding plants. Also they are sloped so that as you remove one flat from the low end of the belt, the other flats move into the front position. Then, of course, the order assembly people can go down the low end of the belts and pick as many flats of each color or variety as are needed for the order—and off they go to order assembly. Several photos with this chapter will help explain this. These systems are expensive but do move a lot of flats through order filling in a hurry.

European Carts

Several widely used cart systems in Europe:

- **The Dutch cart** is very widely used by growers sending plants to their auction—in fact the auction is built around the carts. They are used to get plants from the greenhouse to the auction and are used to move plants within the auction, through the auction hall and then to the buyer's truck. It's a pool system: The grower buys so many carts, sends carts to the auction every morning and gets back the same number of carts he sent in. These carts are a very basic part of the whole Dutch auction system.

- **The Danish CC cart** has different dimensions and is used for shipping plants to the auction. It carries more flats per cart—and more carts per cu. ft. of truck.

NOW, BELTS/CONVEYOR TRACKS

Belts are less widely used than trays but important to many bedding and pot plant growers. I see more of them each year. They offer a practical way to move plants from headhouse to greenhouse and back for order filling. There are several big advantages of belts:

- **Belts mean a steady flow of material** from Point A to Point B—inherently a lot more efficient than carts that must go back and forth, half the time empty.

- **Complete flexibility**—you can put belts wherever you wish—uphill, around corners, through the greenhouse wall, etc. With belt equipment, there's less need for cement walks.

- **Belts can be used to assemble** flats and pot plants for orders—and bring them into the headhouse.

There are a variety of belts and tracks at a variety of prices. Examples:

- **The basic conveyor track.** Normally made of aluminum, 10' sections can be joined together and laid down the length of a bench or down the end walk. There are 90 degree turns available. These are commonly available from greenhouse suppliers. Generally plants and pots moved on these tracks are in flats.

- **Power belts** are rubber belts normally 6", sometimes 8" wide or more. They are electric-powered and normally in 10' sections. Sections can, of course, be joined together, they will turn corners, go through walls and go up and down hill. They give maximum flexibility. These are much used by bedding and pot growers everywhere and are widely available.

A Danish hibiscus specialist developed this system of belts to carry plants from potting room to the farthest greenhouse. It's strange to see these little pots moving up and down the houses.

Here's Jim Dickerson, Gobles, Michigan, with his ingenious belt system at work. A belt goes down the center walk to the end of each greenhouse then plants go on a separate belt down the individual houses. Most of all, the belt can be rolled from left to right to pick up or deliver plants to any bench in the house.

92

Belts can carry flats almost anywhere. There's no limit on belt length since each section is self-powered. But they are expensive! Figure roughly $100 per linear foot of self-powered belt. A 10' section is roughly $1,000.

- **Combination power and coaster belt** is a system devised in Holland. Here, a 10' self-powered section of rubber belt is laid down, then the grower sets in 30' or 40' of conveyor track—not self-powered. The flats are pushed by the one 10' powered section across the conveyor track. At the end of the 40' track they are picked up by another powered section and moved along. In this way only a fraction of the track need be powered—and that's a lot less expensive. This combination track is available, to my knowledge, only from Holland. Contact HETO, Postbus 49, 2370 AA, Roelofarendsveen, Holland [phone 01713-19111, FAX 01713-15103].

- **Aldershot's belt range.** There is a major range located in Ontario run by the Vanderlugt family. It produces mainly year-round pot mums and covers 3 to 5 acres. The entire operation is done with belts—moving plants from potting area to growing bench, then back to shipping area when plants are ready. Full details are available in *GrowerTalks*, September 1982, or by phoning the Vanderlugt's [phone (416) 632-9272].

- **The Dickerson system** is an innovative plan developed by Jim Dickerson, major pot plant grower in Gobles (Kalamazoo), Michigan. Jim recently built a new 2-acre range with the houses each 40' x 200'. Growing benches run from the center

Another belt application, now for order assembly of bedding plants. On the right are perhaps 3' x 10' blocks of different annuals slanted toward the belt in the center. The order filler goes down the line with the order in hand, picks off what's needed for the order, sets them onto the belt and off they go to the truck.

walk either way 100′ to the end wall. Jim has developed a belt that will bring plants from the far end of the bench to the center walk. The exciting thing is that this belt can be rolled across the house—from bench #1 to bench #3 or #4. Now it can pick up plants from any one of the six benches in the house, set them onto the belt and move them to the center walk. In shipping poinsettias, for example, you roll the belt over to the bench from which you are shipping, move plants from bench to belt and up they go to the center walk. Here they are picked up by another belt that goes down the center walk to the headhouse/shipping area. See photo. Pot plants are normally moved in flats; hanging baskets move right on the belt. Jim figures the rough cost for the whole system, both the individual bench belts, the rollers that carry the belt crossways across the house and the center walk belt, for the whole range, roughly $1.25/sq. ft. of ground covered by the range. Growers interested might contact Jim Dickerson [phone (616) 521-3838]. The belts used here come in longer sections and cost much less per sq. ft.

Here's an exciting, new approach to moving plants in, out and around the greenhouse. It uses conventional 4' wheeled carts as shown here, except that they are self-propelled. For example, you load poinsettias onto a cart in the greenhouse, instruct the computer gadget (lower right corner of the cart) where you want it to go and five minutes later the cart shows up at the shipping dock. In the same way, newly potted pot and bedding plants can be moved from transplanting room to growing area. For much more detail, see GrowerTalks, February 1991. The innovative grower (in the photo) is Gene Young, Young's Plant Farm, Auburn, Alabama.

Another point: That belt that goes on the center walk also serves as an assembly line belt. Workers pick plants off the belt, sleeve them, put them on and put them back. At the end of the belt crews pick up the sleeved plants and box them—very fast! *GrowerTalks* has a videotape available that shows all of this.

Again, much more information and background on carts and belts is available from major trade shows such as International Floriculture Industry Short Course, GrowerExpo and Professional Plant Growers Association. You can see actual equipment on the trade fair floor and talk to people at these meetings who produce it. And often there are seminars about them.

Chapter 9

NEW IRRIGATION CONCEPTS

by Vic Ball

Almost since commercial growing started, ornamental crops have been watered with the hose. In recent years, much of this tedious hand work has been taken over by "spaghetti tubes" (with pot plants), various nozzles (with bedding plants, cut flowers), ebb and flow or mats.

In the past several years, other very major changes in watering practices have also occurred:

- Thanks to new, much improved automatics, most watering today can be done mechanically—without penalizing quality. And growers are starting to move this way. Competition will soon make handwatering a too-expensive luxury. It's already happened in Denmark and Holland.

- Recent research has also established clearly that the old philosophy of watering crops "thoroughly"—so that ample runoff occurs—is wasteful and unnecessary.

- Close on the heels of all this, environmental protectionists are realizing that the runoff water from that overly generous old-style watering and feeding is dumping nitrates and pesticides into our streams, lakes and ground water (wells). It's also wasting ever more of our scarce water. Restrictive legislation is already on the horizon.

So again, I see much change from the ways of the 14th *Ball RedBook*. These changes are what this chapter is all about.

Poinsettias ebb and flow irrigated on Dutch trays. The grower is Henry Schneider, G&E Greenhouses, Elburn, Illinois. G&E operates several acres of ebb and flow pot plants. To his left is visitor Richard Anderson, a major Napier, New Zealand, grower.

AUTOMATIC WATERING CAN GROW QUALITY!

Many growers keep telling me that you just can't grow quality bedding plants or poinsettias without more or less of handwatering. Yet I see many growers across the United States and Canada who are in fact growing excellent quality—without hose watering—including bedding plants, poinsettias and plugs, too. The Dutch and Danes are almost entirely weaned from the hose, saying, "We can't afford it."

I am quite aware that probably the majority of bedding plants today are more or less handwatered, especially earlier in the crop. Common wisdom says that you just can't grow quality poinsettias (without botrytis) without handwatering, especially in the later stages of the crop. Yet again, it's being done. See *GrowerTalks*, February 1989, page 28, for details on this. Here are three successful poinsettia crops grown without handwatering: Carl Blasig, Hightstown, New Jersey; Green Circle, Oberlin, Ohio; and Henry Schneider, G & E Greenhouses, Elburn, Illinois. For a good example of quality bedding plants grown with almost zero hose watering see Orie Van Wingerden, Pompton Plains, New Jersey [phone (201) 694-7222]—including both indoor and outdoor roll-out plants, by the way. Orie also mechanically waters plugs. Carl Blasig, Hightstown, New Jersey, does the same on 2 to 3 acres of both bedding plants, poinsettias and plugs. For a 10-acre range of quality bedding plants almost entirely mechanically overhead irrigated, I suggest Carl Loeb, Summersun Greenhouse, Mt. Vernon, Washington.

Almost always, growers today will, if feeding is needed, inject fertilizer into their irrigation water. See Chapter 20 for details.

You can grow quality with automatic watering!

MOST USED AUTOMATICS

The first big change: better automatics. Question: What are the best automated ways to irrigate bedding and pot plants as of the early 1990s? Here's my list, including the important new ways. First, here's a summary ranging from the most precise, quality-oriented and costly to the least. All this for pot plants, bedding plants and foliage:

1) Ebb and flow
2) Trough irrigation systems
3) Drip irrigation
4) Spaghetti tubes (Chapin)
5) Boom irrigation
6) Mat irrigation
7) Stationary overhead sprinklers

1) Ebb and Flow

Yes, it's the most expensive, but what is it worth to eliminate handwatering yet grow top quality? And do this on any size pot at any spacing (4″, even 3″ and 2″ pot plants are booming these days). Hundreds of growers across America and Europe have gone to ebb and flow—and more are moving that way each year. Besides, ebb and flow done in aluminum trays ties in with tray automation, which eliminates 90 percent of hand moving crops in and out of the greenhouse. It's a winning combination.

In principle, ebb and flow is certainly not new—it's simply subirrigation of plants. Plants are placed in watertight containers and water (usually with fertilizer) is piped in an inch or so deep and then immediately drained away. Water soaks up from below and the job is done. Probably the most common application is in connection with tray (container) growing—the 15′ or 20′ long aluminum trays that serve both as growing bench and as a way to move crops in and out of the headhouse efficiently. Most container growers do take advantage of the waterproof aluminum container and practice ebb and flow irrigation. See Chapter 7 on tray automation.

A real help in ebb and flow watering of trays is a Danish device that enables growers to pre-set the water depth during an irrigation cycle. When water reaches the desired level, the tray automatically starts to drain.

Ebb and flow in Dutch trays. The large tube in the foreground feeds the water in; the 4" black tube is the Danish device that starts draining the water at whatever level you set. An important point on ebb and flow: Regularly monitor EC soil levels at both the top and bottom inch of the pot. Salts accumulating at the top could be a problem when the final customer waters the plant and washes the salt down.

As of the early 1990s we're beginning to see some ebb and flow cement floors. The grower simply cements the entire floor from gutter to gutter, pitches it slightly toward a center drain—and pumps in water, wets the plants and drains it away. It's seen a good bit in Holland. Also, Norwin Heimos, a major St. Louis pot grower, has a large installation of cement ebb and flow pot culture. He reports good quality and effective irrigation with this system.

What are the points for and against ebb and flow?

Pro:

- Easy spacing. An ebb and flow system permits any spacing or re-spacing of any size pots or flats or whatever. It provides complete flexibility. Most importantly, ebb and flow irrigates smaller pot sizes—4", 3" and even 2", which are clearly becoming an increasing part of pot production. Example: There are many millions of 2" poinsettias grown in Europe today. Obviously spaghetti tubes in such tiny pot sizes would be impractical—but ebb and flow works fine with them.

    In fact, if these small pots become the majority of the pot business, growers will be under real pressure to go to either ebb and flow or to use modern boom irrigation—or a combination.

100

Ebb and flow irrigated geraniums. The peat particles are filtered out each time the water is recirculated.

- Growers report actually superior growth of such things as poinsettias in ebb and flow—as compared to other irrigating systems. I hear this rather consistently.

- Keeps leaves dry. Ebb and flow does not wet plant surfaces. That's obviously important in disease control. Bacterial spores, for example, don't germinate on a dry leaf surface.

- Ebb and flow adapts well to recirculating systems. Here the water drains from plants, can be piped first to a filter to remove soil and peat particles, next to equipment that adjusts pH and EC (soluble salts) to desired levels and then back to the crop. Again the grower has flexibility of nutrient levels and pH. With such recirculating systems, both water and fertilizer costs are greatly reduced—versus plans where surplus runoff from watering is simply dumped into the land drain, which is fast becoming a forbidden practice (see Chapter 31 on environmental problems). Water and fertilizer are both becoming expensive and in some cases extremely scarce.

- As with most systems, ebb and flow can be, and often is, computer-controlled.

- Humidity. It may be an advantage or otherwise—but whichever, ebb and flow does provide more humidity in the greenhouse.

The downside:
- First, ebb and flow is expensive. A complete ebb and flow system from the ground up, including aluminum tray "benches," costs around $5.50/sq. ft. of bench space,

all labor and material. Around $4.25 is material for trays, plumbing, tanks, etc. Add $1 to $1.50/sq. ft. for labor (trays must be precisely leveled).

But this must be put into perspective—against the alternatives available to the grower—especially for pot crops:

1) Good all-metal rolling benches (slide sideways to eliminate aisles), with spaghetti irrigation installed, costs around $4/sq. ft. of bench space—$3.50 labor and material for the bench, 50¢ for spaghetti tubes, installed. For $1.50 more (now the total is $5.50), you have a Dutch tray automation with ebb and flow. You get a super irrigation system (can handle 3″ and 4″ pots, not practical with Chapin), and re-spacing is simple (can be automated). You also gain major economies of labor in moving crops in and out of the growing area. In a broad sweep you cut total staff per acre from seven or eight down to two or less.

Now it's easy to see why many growers over the world have opted for Dutch tray/ebb and flow irrigation systems. Growers also say Dutch trays with ebb and flow grow better quality than Chapin tubes.

Put against $12 to $13/sq. ft./year of sale (for a pot plant rotation with overhead baskets), $5.50 doesn't sound out of order, especially for a well-capitalized operation. And that's point #2.

2) The low investment route. Pot plants can be, and again, many hundreds of acres of them are, grown on inexpensive wood benches, often with cement block legs—and Chapin irrigation. The cost of such benches varies widely, but most growers say around $1.50 to $2/sq. ft. labor and material. Quality can be and is grown on such benches (Norm White's of Chesapeake, Virginia, a top-quality mum grower, for example). If you add the 50¢/sq. ft. of bench area for spaghetti tubes, you're still at or below $2.50/sq. ft.—less than half versus the Dutch tray/ebb and flow route.

The main things you gain by going the Dutch tray/ebb and flow route are: first, major economies in the labor of moving crop in and out of the greenhouse; second, the Dutch tray system is all metal and permanent, not so for a wood bench; and third, you have a recirculating system, end of concern about ground water contamination. Add a rather indefinite plus for better quality with ebb and flow—growers do say this.

Henry Schneider, G & E Greenhouses Inc., Elburn, Illinois, a top-quality 100,000-sq.-ft. pot grower, has installed about 2 acres of ebb and flow in aluminum trays and reports a cost of around $5.50 for both trays and the ebb and flow irrigation system—as of the late 1980s. He likes ebb and flow, feels it grows some better quality than handwatering or Chapin tubes—including poinsettias. He does an excellent crop of them.

- Disease spread. It would seem that with water flowing from plants to a central tank, then back to plants, that disease spread would be a major problem. It just doesn't seem to happen. Hundreds of growers, especially in Europe, use this system—without problems. They do take care to use only disease-free cuttings, bulbs, etc. There is a system available in Holland that pasteurizes water during the circulating cycle.

A Dutch cement floor subirrigation installation. It's done quite a bit in Europe and the United States. The flooded floor system requires some getting used to to produce consistent quality.

2) Trough Irrigation of Pot Plants

Here the pots are placed in metal troughs, typically 4″ to 5″ wide, 1″ or less deep, set across the bench. The troughs are pitched slightly to one side of the bench. Water is fed in at the high end, often through a spaghetti tube, flows to the lower end, is collected in a gutter and piped back to the high end. The pots placed in the trough are subirrigated in the process (see photo).

Pro and con

First, in favor, such a system is substantially less costly than ebb and flow with aluminum trays. And the troughs become the bench—again major saving. As with ebb and flow, growers who get used to this system report crop quality very good—fully as good as any other way. Says Jim Leider, major pot producer: "It does take some getting used to, but once you get the hang of it, it does good quality." Another plus for troughs: excellent air flow through the crop canopy.

The main downside: There is less flexibility and spacing of pots. You may slide the troughs closer together or further apart, but unless you have a different set of

Saintpaulia in trough irrigation at Aart Van Winderden's, Fletcher, North Carolina. One key advantage: air circulates up from below through the plant canopy.

Trough irrigation at Paul Ecke Poinsettias, Encinitas, California, for pot poinsettia production.

narrower troughs it would be hard to accommodate, for example, a 4" or 3" pot plant, or a 7" or 8" pot.

Trough systems can recirculate water—an important economy in water and fertilizer, and an increasingly necessary accommodation to environmental contamination problems. Examples of successful trough systems I've seen recently: Ecke's at Encinitas, California, on major areas of pot poinsettias; Jim Leider at his Houston, Texas, range, mainly 6" pot mums; and Yoder's Leamington, Ontario, range with major production of 4½" pot mums.

3) Drip Irrigation

In a way this is an adaptation of the spaghetti tube system—except that now instead of an open line of water flowing through the tube onto the individual pot soil surface, there is instead a slow, steady drip. The drip application occurs intermittently and can be turned on or off by computer.

Several advantages: First, drip irrigation tends to mean a lot less of both water and fertilizer used. With careful management, you just don't have water and fertilizer running out the bottom of the pot! The drip process applies only the amount of water needed, and it's soaked up by the soil as it is applied. There's very little runoff, and that fits in with today's environmental pressure on runoff.

Drip is relatively inexpensive. Cost is roughly 50¢/sq. ft. versus 40¢ for spaghetti tubes. The added cost, of course, is for the individual emitters—which drip from the line into the pot soil. Again, plant leaf and stem surfaces are not wet—so there are fewer disease problems. The system can be turned on perhaps for 10 or 15 minutes out of every 2 hours or whatever is needed, which can be done by computer.

Again, pro and con: An advantage is that less water volume is needed to water a bench or a house of pot plants with drip irrigation versus spaghetti tubes. While a given water main might be adequate for two or three benches of spaghetti tubes, the same main would do perhaps 10 benches of drip. Drip systems tend to deliver a half gallon per hour per nozzle, more or less.

An obvious use and, in a way, advantage of drip irrigation is for use on hanging baskets. I see drip irrigation installed very widely on overhead baskets. It does the watering job—and the drip irrigation system means a lot less runoff coming out of the baskets onto the crop below. And handwatering overhead hanging baskets is a tough job.

One limitation of the drip system—in the case of smaller pot plants (4″, 3″ and less)—a great many outlets must be installed. This is expensive and it just isn't practical.

Drip irrigation is used some amount commercially (not nearly as much as spaghetti tubes). Several success stories include: Westbrook in Grimsby, Ontario, and Welby Gardens in Denver, Colorado.

The main case for drip irrigation today is that it greatly minimizes runoff—which is fast becoming a forbidden procedure for pot plant growers. Since the system applies only enough water to soak the soil ball, there's very little runoff. Spaghetti tubes tend to apply a larger volume of water rather suddenly, so some of it inevitably runs out through the drain. Expect to see a lot more of drip irrigated pot plants in the early 1990s.

4) Spaghetti Tubes for Pot Plants

Spaghetti tubes are ⅛″ or so plastic tube installed so that one tube irrigates each pot on a bench of pot plants (see photo). Chapin was the originator, but since then there have been many other suppliers. They are commonly available and very commonly used by most pot plant growers today. See photo on how water is piped into these tubes on a typical bench. Also note the several different devices installed at the end of each tube. Some use a small weight that holds the tube end onto the top surface of the flower pot; others use a little wire that's driven an inch or two into the soil.

Norm White, top-quality pot mum grower, Chesapeake, Virginia, installs a Coke bottle at the head of each bench. A tiny tube, just like those that go into each pot in the bench, goes into the Coke bottle. When they water the bench they turn the water on until the Coke bottle is filled (to a mark). That means that each plant has a fair watering.

Does the last pot in a 150' bench get as much water as the first pot? Generally it seems that if the pots furthest from the inlet get a good watering, then it's not a problem. Sometimes growers pipe the water into a 150' bench from the center rather than from one end, for this very reason.

Spaghetti tubes are very widely used by pot plant growers across the world today. About the only downside is the cost. For rough figures: Cost per pot (labor

Spaghetti tube irrigation—now pot geraniums. A small, lead weight holds the tip of the tube inside the pot. Other growers use a 2" or 3" wire inserted into the soil to hold the tube in place. Spaghetti tubes are very widely used, probably ¾ or more of all U.S. 6" and larger pot plants are watered this way.

Here are some of the headers available to feed water to spaghetti tubes. Note the 1" main on the right, the ¾" tube leading from there to the center and feeding the small header, which feeds the line to each pot. There are many variations of this equipment available.

and material) to install spaghetti tubes will be around 35¢ to 50¢ per pot. Figure 20¢ for the tubes, 5¢ for fittings and headers, 10¢ for labor.

Spaghetti tubes work best on 5", 6" and larger pots. Four-inch or smaller pots tend to be a lot of work and expense to set up the tubes—an awful lot of tubes for a bench of 4" pot plants! Some growers set pot crops out pot-tight, handwater during this brief phase and then install tubes after pots are at final spacing.

Spaghetti tubes are clearly the most-used system for watering 6" and larger pots as of the early 1990s.

5) Modern Boom Irrigation Technology

Overhead moving booms have been with us for a long time. In the late 1980s, however, a new batch of them arrived on the scene—including quite helpful computerized controls. There are several excellent suppliers. I can't describe them all but I finds ITS Inc. one of the leaders (P.O. Box 1406, Hightstown, NJ 08520, [phone (609) 448-6533]). Here's what ITS can do for the grower:

1) First, thanks to an ingenious bit of technology, the grower can quickly set the system to water the first 10' of the bench, skip the next 10', then water the rest of

107

An ITS irrigation system at work. The boom with the hose reel travels suspended from overhead. I get good reports on uniformity of irrigation/feeding with this equipment. In the photo is Gary Lucas, president of ITS, at Carl Blasig Greenhouse, Hightstown, New Jersey.

the bench—whatever areas you want watered. Most importantly, the machine can change speed at each area of the bench so that different crops or different container sizes are each watered correctly. A simple barcode label on the track identifies each crop location.

2) The boom rides on an overhead pipe. As the nozzles move down the bench they may strike an impediment—a wheelbarrow or anything. If this happens the computer turns the water off, stops the boom from traveling and says in a loud, recorded voice, "Help, we have a problem here." The idea is that the machine should never do crop damage because of a mechanical problem.

ITS boom irrigation does a very thorough job of watering. For example, there are 25 nozzles on a boom across a 25' span of plants (more if you wish). Nozzles are generally on 14" centers plus extras at the ends. Lots of nozzles mean uniform application. Growers say that "it does a more even job of watering and feeding than I can do by hand."

There are several models available:
• Grower Jr. is a boom that rides on two overhead rails. The basic model rides up and down one greenhouse on command (computerized). It has a split boom—so you can still walk down the center aisle and irrigate one side or the other—or both. It's used for both plugs and flats of bedding and pot plants.

Here's ITS equipment—the unit that will water one house and can be moved in several minutes to the adjoining house. In the photo is Bruce Gibson, Summersun Greenhouse, Mt. Vernon, Washington.

There is a side shift option that permits rolling the Grower Jr. manually from one greenhouse to the next. Now one machine can do four or five gutter-connected greenhouses—bedding plants, pot plants, etc.—and it's often done that way. The shift from one greenhouse to the next requires one person for two or three minutes. Gary Lucas, president of ITS, recommends one such unit for each four or five greenhouses—less if the houses are short. Plan covering up to 20,000-sq.-ft. per machine.

Costs:

$5,855 boom, rail system, hose, trolleys for one greenhouse 30' x 210'. 93¢/sq. ft.

$10,246 same unit, with side shift option—one boom irrigates four greenhouses 30' x 210'. Boom is shifted greenhouse to greenhouse manually. 41¢/sq. ft.

- Mini grower. A single overhead rail machine is used mainly for bedding and pot plants. Since the whole boom and machine are moved about on one overhead monorail, this is really a monorail conveyor system—and growers do use it for moving plants back and forth. Now the boom can be moved wherever the overhead rail goes. Some growers run the monorail out the end of a hoop house and into the next house. This makes one machine do four or five greenhouses.

The mini is simple to install—it's often done by the grower. It provides only one boom; you do the whole greenhouse width, gutter-to-gutter. It still waters different crops correctly using the same barcode system as the Grower Jr. model.

109

Costs:

$4,808 boom with overhead monorail, hoses, controls for one greenhouse 30′ x 210′. 76¢/sq. ft.

$6,857 with side shift option—the one boom now covers four greenhouses, 30′ x 210′. It is shifted manually from greenhouse to greenhouse. 27¢/sq. ft.

All the above costs are material only; installation is by the grower.

Notes on costs: Plainly a longer and wider greenhouse means much lower costs per square foot for ITS equipment. Also plainly it is much cheaper to do four or five greenhouses with one machine—and time to shift the boom from one house to the next is only several minutes. It works. Gary Lucas, president of ITS, suggests that one boom or one machine in most cases is best utilized when it covers about 20,000-sq.-ft.

I have talked with several growers who have used ITS boom irrigation on plugs—with generally very good results. They say, "It does the watering and feeding more evenly than I can do myself." And it is automated! It can, of course, be set to water every hour or once a day.

Summersun Greenhouses, Mt. Vernon, Washington, is a good example of what ITS equipment can do. Carl Loeb, owner, reports that virtually all watering of his 10 acres of bedding plants, potted annuals and pot plants is done with automated ITS booms. Quality at Summersun that I have seen on several visits has been very good. An interesting example: One summer Sunday, the several watering crew men failed to show up. The manager on duty watered the entire then 6-acre range of mainly bedding plants himself during that one day—using ITS equipment. Yes, he hustled, but he got it done.

There are several other competing automated boom irrigation units that are also proven performers:

- Boomerang is produced by Art Thorsby of Thorsby Industries, Milton, Florida, and is a less sophisticated, less expensive and quite widely used new system. It operates on a 12-volt battery that can be recharged at night. Costs run about 40¢/sq. ft. on larger areas. It can be shifted manually from greenhouse to greenhouse.

- Dana Cable's Growing Systems, Milwaukee, Wisconsin, is an established supplier of greenhouse automation equipment. He offers an automated boom irrigation system perhaps a bit less sophisticated than ITS, but less costly. It's widely used by pot plant and bedding plant growers.

- Andpro, Waterford, Ontario, Canada, is another established, reliable supplier of this sort of automated boom irrigation equipment. Peter Van de Wetering, a several acre plug grower on Long Island, uses both ITS and Andpro equipment.

- Bouldin & Lawson, McMinnville, Tennessee, at press time is getting into boom irrigation. The boom is supported by a mobile electric cart from the base. This makes retrofit an easier task. The electric cart reads magnetic cards that you place on the walk. The cards signal it to start, stop or alter the volume of water. It's

A new contender in the boom irrigation field is from Bouldin & Lawson. It's a cart that makes its way down the aisle carrying overhead boom irrigation. Interesting!

an interesting approach to this new boom technology. One drawback is that the cart needs a wide walk, about 3', to operate. In most ranges this should not be a problem.

6) Mat Irrigation

Here, porous mats, perhaps ⅛" thick or so, are spread across the bench. Plants are set onto the mat, and irrigation is done by simply wetting the mat—I've seen spaghetti tubes or an overhead nozzle used sometimes. Moisture soaks up into the soil in the pots or flats. The system has been with us for many years, and although it is not that widely used, it somehow seems to still be commercial practice on some ranges. It has some strong pros and cons!

First, in favor:

- Mats are relatively low-cost—and an easy installation. Waterproofing benches or containers is not required.

- Complete flexibility on spacing and size of pots. Great for a bench of 2″ poinsettias!

- Mats keep foliage dry—which minimizes disease problems.

- Easy, low-cost installation.

- There's minimal, almost zero, runoff from a mat irrigation system.

I've seen much mat irrigation in Europe in recent years, especially for very small plant production, 2″ and up, of which many millions are grown these days. There are acres of mats—including a variety of pot plant crops grown on them—and often with very good quality. It seems to be a system that certain growers get used to and like. There's a good case for mats. A special application, by the way, is in retail display areas, especially where thousands of especially smaller pot plants are on retail display, and the task of keeping them watered is almost impossible. Mats permit easy watering—without spraying water all over a retail display area. Egon Molbak operates a major acre or two retail garden center near Seattle and uses mats extensively to water pot plants that are on display. The public moves things around—but they still land back on a mat—and get watered.

Cons:

- Some extra care is required to establish capillary flow from the mat to the soil in the pot or flat. Perhaps try wetting agents in the soil mix.

- Mats tend to develop algae and become green and scummy. A system has been devised where a thin sheet of plastic is spread over the fiber mat. The plastic sheet has tiny holes across its surface that permit moisture movement from the mat up to the plant—but the total effect is a lot less algae growth on the mat surface. Also there are chemicals, such as Agribrom, which will effectively inhibit algae development. Shig Otani, Greenwood Greenhouse, Seattle, Washington, a top quality, 2-acre bedding plant grower, does his plugs all on mat irrigation. He solved the algae problem by incorporating 15 parts per million Agribrom in the irrigation water for the plugs. I also noticed during a recent visit that the walks in this area were free of algae.

7) Stationary Overhead Sprinklers

Here, a variety of fixed nozzles are installed above the crop—at spacings that will ensure reasonably even watering of the plants. A wide variety of nozzles are available that cover different shapes and sizes of crop area, break water up into different particle sizes and vary greatly in cost. They are widely used on cut flower and foliage crops, some on pot plants and even on plugs. One major 10- to 15-acre poinsettia crop is watered entirely with such overhead nozzles—and without disease problems. That's done by carefully adapting the system to the threat of botrytis—watering only in the morning, ventilation and heat after watering to dry plants off, use of fungicide to minimize botrytis, etc. Also with this system, saucers are often installed below each pot to gather the water that falls between the pots and feed it by a sort of subirrigation system back up into the pot itself (see photo). Results: much less frequent irrigation. Overhead nozzles are often used in bedding plants where wetting foliage is less of a problem.

The main advantage of overhead nozzles is simply low initial cost. They will water plants adequately and can be computer-controlled. Obviously there is also complete flexibility of spacing plants—the system works fine for small 2″ and 3″ pots and also for bedding plants. Disadvantages: wetting foliage, which aggravates disease problems in some crops. Also, such systems tend to waste water and fertilizer. Probably the main disadvantage of these overhead nozzles is that unless

A success story for overhead boom irrigation. Green Circle Growers, Oberlin, Ohio, do 10 or 15 acres of poinsettias all on the ground and all overhead irrigated from start to finish. I've seen their crop at flowering date. There's no botrytis. They irrigate early in the day, use heat and air to dry the plants, and use fungicides for botrytis control. The "saucers" above gather the water falling from the canopy, which flows to the center of the saucer and is soaked up by the pot. The result: much fewer irrigations and almost no ground water runoff problems.

Another overhead nozzle success is plug production at Ivey's, Lubbock, Texas. Monitored with appropriate control equipment (10 seconds every hour or whatever you wish), it produces plugs for Ivey's one acre of bedding plants.

carefully engineered, they tend to apply water unevenly. By nature they deliver water over a circular area. Even if these areas overlap, there is not perfect uniformity. In many crops, the crop is overwatered a bit—to ensure that all plants in the area are adequately watered. This obviously demands a well-aerated, open, loose soil mix. Also it obviously means increased runoff, which is presenting more and more problems in terms of environmental contamination. Using plastic reusable water collector trays (one under each pot), you can eliminate a good portion of the water that falls between the plants or drips from the canopy. It is held by the cup-shaped tray until it is soaked up by the plant.

Often I see bedding plant growers who tend to handwater during late winter, but as they get into the warm days of late April, they're glad to have overhead nozzles to keep plants from drying out.

Overhead nozzles are obviously very important in many cut flower crops. Also they are very widely used in nursery stock production.

114

It's not strictly a watering system, but mist is used for maintaining humidity and applying moisture, especially to plugs, germinating seedlings and rooting cuttings. Mist systems apply water in very small particle sizes—generally from 10 to 20 microns (versus 100 microns for a raindrop). Overhead propagating nozzles (normal water pressure) generally apply water in larger particle sizes—from 50 to 70 microns. The great advantage of mist, especially in the case of plugs and rooting cuttings, is that moisture can be applied to surfaces of seed or seedlings or to newly stuck cuttings to minimize drying—yet the grower applies much less volume of water. And it is so easy to overwater both cuttings and germinating seedlings, especially in plugs. Plugs tend to fill with water and drain poorly (too shallow a container), minimizing oxygen in the soil mix, all of which causes big problems. Mist systems are expensive, but they are appearing more and more as growers strive for quality plugs or quality rooting operations.

Mist systems also reduce greenhouse temperature during hot weather. For this they are much more effective in dry desert areas.

There are several manufacturers of mist systems. Examples are Mee Industries, Baumac International, Mentone, California, and Agritech, Broadway, North Carolina, offering an innovative approach to mist—each with its own pros and cons.

SECOND BIG CHANGE: WATER/FEED MUCH MUCH LESS

As this 15th edition is being prepared, there is another very basic and important change developing that will affect watering and fertilizing of crops very much. It should be studied and understood by growers and be part of any decision on new equipment to water and fertilize crops.

- **We've been watering/fertilizing entirely too much!** Recent work at Michigan State University makes it clear that existing feeding and watering practices have been seriously overdoing the job in both cases. Clearly most greenhouse crops can be done just as well with a fraction of the amount of water and fertilizer—and fertilizer concentrations—than we have been using. This has major implications on both crop profitability and pollution problems. It's a whole new concept—a basic change in watering and feeding practices—and it's just coming onto the scene in the early 1990s. Large scale commercial growers, though, are already starting to adopt these low feed, low water practices. And they are still growing very good quality crops.

  John Biernbaum at Michigan State University has been doing these studies—pioneering this very important new approach to watering and feeding crops. In the following report (from *Grower Talks*, September 1989), John presents his ideas on this. Read it twice!

IRRIGATION AND FERTILIZATION GO HAND IN HAND TO REDUCE RUNOFF

by John Biernbaum, Mark Yelanich, William Carlson and Royal Heins
Michigan State University
East Lansing, Michigan

Subirrigation with recirculated solutions has been getting a lot of attention as a method to reduce fertilizer and water runoff from greenhouses. Even though it's a great system for many reasons, not many growers are willing or able to make the investment in the necessary hardware and plumbing. The good news is that our research with subirrigation has helped point out some important lessons that every grower can use to reduce runoff.

Subirrigating Cuts Fertilizer Use

One of the must important differences with subirrigation is that less fertilizer is required than with traditional top watering systems. In our experiments comparing top watering and subirrigation of poinsettias, Easter lilies, mums and bedding plants, we subirrigated plants with half the fertilizer concentration used for the top watered treatments—and they grew just as well.

Soil test values of media taken from subirrigated plants' root zones almost always have a lower than recommended level, even though the plants look well fertilized. Some growers using subirrigation confirm that media levels test low but plant tissue analysis indicates adequate fertility.

At first we thought reduced fertilization and media analysis levels were something unique to subirrigation. The effects are probably partly due to the fact that there's no leaching, but perhaps plants take up nutrients more efficiently with subirrigation.

After several subirrigation experiments, we're taking a closer look at traditional watering methods. Even with traditional top watering, you can grow good crops with much less fertilizer. The important thing to recognize is that irrigation method determines how much fertilizer you need.

Fertilizer Concentration Versus Rate

Since the industry has moved to using fertilizer injectors and water soluble fertilizers, most recommendations suggest a concentration of fertilizer applied at a certain time frequency, such as 400 parts per million weekly or 200 ppm constant liquid feed. While this system has worked for many years, it doesn't adequately account for differences between root media, irrigation systems and solution volume applied by different growers.

Few growers recognize that fertilizing pots doesn't just depend on applied fertilizer concentration. The amount or rate of fertilizer in the container after several feedings is determined by concentration and volume of applied solution. The greater the volume of solution applied, the more fertilizer salts are leached from the pot; the lower the volume of solution applied, the more fertilizer is left in the pot.

In one experiment at Michigan State University using 6″ poinsettias, we maintained a similar media nutrient level with 200 ppm applied with 12% leaching as with 400 ppm applied with 50% leaching (half the solution applied is leached out). In each case, root media electrical conductivity (EC) or soluble salt level was comparable and provided adequate nutrition for the poinsettia crop.

In growing these poinsettias, total nitrogen applied—from the lowest to highest rate—varied almost tenfold, from 620 milligrams to 6,500 milligrams. The estimated amount of nitrogen runoff from 100 ppm with 12% leaching to 400 ppm with 50% leaching is 40 times different. This is an indictment of our current fertilization techniques.

Leaching: How Much is Really Needed?

A standard recommendation passed down from the days of soil-based media is that 10% to 15% of the volume of fertilizer and water applied to container plants should be leached to prevent salts accumulation. As growers moved from poorly drained, soil-based mixes to well drained, peat-based soilless mixes, leaching amounts have increased. Since current soilless media drain so well, it's easier to apply excess solution to make sure the media is well saturated and leached, whether or not it's needed. It's likely that many growers have never measured how much leaching occurs when they irrigate and have no idea of how little water it actually takes to get 10% to 15% leaching.

Drip irrigation has also led to higher leaching rates. With automated drip irrigation it's easy to water and leach a crop heavily; leaching rates of 40% to 50% are not uncommon. This may be due to the fact that water from drip tubes doesn't rapidly and uniformly saturate some peat-based media. This problem can be addressed by changing media components or adding wetting agents. Adding water slowly, in short pulses rather than one long irrigation, will also allow uniform wetting with less runoff.

Sometimes heavy leaching may be due to the fact that the drip system on a large bench isn't properly engineered. If the drip system on a large bench is pressurized from one end, water may begin flowing from one end of the bench 20 to 30 seconds before the other end of the bench. This can lead to significant waste of water and fertilizer. If 20 to 30 seconds of drip time can significantly contribute to runoff, what happens when drip systems are manually controlled and allowed to run for 10 minutes or more?

Irrigation water quality plays a critical role in determining the amount of leaching required in a given production situation. In many cases, little or no leaching is required; with saline water or water containing high levels of certain nutrients, heavy leaching may be required. One reference recommends water with an EC below 0.75 mS (before fertilizer is added) shouldn't cause problems that require heavy leaching.

Levels between 0.75 and 1.5 mS will probably require some leaching, and an EC higher than 1.5 mS will require regular leaching. If root media EC levels are too high, be sure to find out if it is due to water quality or over-fertilization.

Tracking Nutrient Levels

How do you know if you're applying enough fertilizer? Traditionally it's been easier to apply high concentrations with heavy leaching than to take regular media samples. Many growers only take media samples when there's a problem. If fertilizer runoff is to be controlled, growers must test media frequently to determine when nutrients are required.

With this new emphasis on testing media, we must evaluate accepted media test values. These test values evolved over the years from soluble salt levels acceptable for soil-based media and from observations of what worked most of the time. This has been good enough in the past but must be refined for the future. We cannot afford to provide luxury levels of nutrients with frequent leaching to prevent imbalances. Neither can we afford to give all growers one concentration that—when applied in excess—will work under a wide range of conditions.

Just as we have learned to use graphical tracking to know what height our plants should be throughout the crop, we must learn what our media nutrient level must be throughout the crop. Monitoring nutrients and graphing levels over time has been proposed for some time by media test labs. Perhaps we can call it graphical tracking for the root zone. With additional information about how to change root zone EC and what factors influence EC, many growers will be able to use EC more effectively as a nutrient management tool.

Relating Fertilization to Irrigation

The industry must develop fertilization programs that are suitable for subirrigation or drip watering without contaminating the environment with excess fertilizers. To do this will require knowing how much fertilizer our crops need and at what stages it should be applied. Do we need to start crops at a high nutrient level? What EC level is best to finish a crop and for the consumer?

There are many questions that need to be answered. We need to use media analysis to guide our fertilization programs, which may include refining our guidelines for acceptable root media nutrient levels. The first step is for growers to recognize that the method and quantity of irrigation will play an important role in determining how much fertilizer is applied—and how much wasted.

118

Pressures are building on growers to stop contaminating ground water, wells, streams, lakes, etc. See details on this in Chapter 31 but for now, a key part of the pressure on growers as regards environmental contamination concerns runoff water from greenhouses into ground water. Pressures are mounting mostly from local government agencies—on growers to stop dumping both nutrients and pesticides into the environment—and very likely federal legislation will be with us before long to require growers everywhere to severely restrict or discontinue dumping fertilizers and pesticides. Certainly anyone planning new crop production facilities and new irrigation/fertilizing systems should have this in mind—surely built around a system that will not dump these materials as most growers are now doing.

A classic answer to this whole problem is the case of El Modeno Gardens, Irvine, California. Operated by the Groot family, their Irvine ranch alone includes about 100 acres of various pot plants, mostly flowering, including 6", gallon can annuals, poinsettias, geraniums, etc. In the late 1980s, the Groots were served notice by the local water conservation board that the runoff from their growing operation was seriously contaminating the nearby very prestigious Newport Yacht Harbor—and an equally important wildlife preserve. Such actions, by the way, are nearly always triggered by a disgruntled citizen complaint. In any case, the Groots, and several large gallon-can neighbors, were given several years to either clean up the dumping of especially nitrates into the Newport Bay or get out. Up to this point they had been doing normal spaghetti tube and overhead nozzle irrigation on their crops, following normal fertilizer practices.

Their response was prompt, enlightened and effective. In the process they developed, to me, a whole new, important and innovative way to solve the problem. The basis of it all is what Peter Groot calls "pulse irrigation." This means that instead of pouring water on a pot plant until surplus runs out the bottom, a limited amount of water/nutrient solution is applied to the pot four or five times a day (with spaghetti tubes). In this way, the water and fertilizer slowly soak into the soil, maintaining appropriate soil moisture/nutrient levels—and reducing leaching or runoff to near zero. The four or five irrigations of each of those 100 acres of pot plants is done by computer; Q-Com engineered the computerized control part of the job.

The net effect is that—still using the existing spaghetti tube and overhead nozzle irrigation systems but greatly minimizing the amount of water/nutrients supplied—they have been able to drastically reduce the amount of runoff and also greatly reduce fertilizer use. Most of all they've made peace with the government agency involved.

Cost-wise, Peter Groot reports the whole conversion as roughly a three- to five-year payoff. For more details on this I suggest reading the report on Peter Groot in *GrowerTalks,* September 1989, page 24.

Polyethylene tubes used for watering cut flower crops. Photo courtesy of Chapin Watermatics Inc., Watertown, New York.

SYSTEMS FOR CUT FLOWERS

by Roy Larson
North Carolina State University
Raleigh, North Carolina

Cut flowers have been watered automatically for many years in most greenhouse ranges. Here are several systems used today.

- **Perimeter watering systems.** Perimeter watering of cut flower crops has been used by growers for many years, but some recent improvements have made the system even more acceptable. Plumbing is so much easier now with the improved plastic or PVC pipe and fittings. White PVC pipe doesn't expand and move out of the bed or bench as black plastic pipe does. Nozzles with different distribution patterns (45°, 90° or 180°) can be easily installed.

The system can be operated semi-automatically or automatically, with time clocks turning water on and off. There are some precautions that must be observed if watering is to be done successfully. Long benches require that water mains come to the middle of benches so the distance water must travel will not be excessive. There must be sufficient water pressure so plants in the center of the bench will get watered.

Some growers remove bottom foliage on chrysanthemums, as they believe the larger leaves block water dispersal. This perhaps is true on wide benches and with low water pressure, but I do not remove leaves on chrysanthemums growing on benches 42″ wide. Removing bottom foliage is labor- and time-consuming, and those larger leaves are very beneficial to plants, particularly in early growth stages.

A grower must be able to disconnect the system from the water main and raise the pipe during soil pasteurization or fittings will be damaged by the high temperatures. It is also a good practice for the pipe and fittings to be surface-sterilized with a disinfectant prior to re-installation on the soil surface.

Perimeter watering is often used on carnations and roses. Some rose growers have quit putting corn cobs, straw and similar mulches on the soil surface, as perimeter watering has made the important task of watering so much simpler than watering with the hose. An interesting statistic is that one carnation flower reportedly can use one gallon of water by the time it is harvested, indicating the volume of water utilized by a carnation crop.

Advantages of perimeter watering are the savings in labor and time, and it is relatively easy to install and maintain. Water quantity and pressure must be adequate to provide uniform irrigation. A newly planted crop of snapdragon seedlings might be blown over with excessive force, while a mature mum or carnation might have dry plants in the center with inadequate pressure.

- **Polyethylene tubing.** There are different types within this system (see photo). One of the earliest types consisted of flat black plastic tubing, placed lengthwise on the bench, with at least two tubes per bench. Water would move down the tubing, which would swell, and water would then be dispersed through regularly spaced holes in the tubing. A newer system consists of a perforated plastic pipe within a flat polyethylene tube, and the water slowly seeps through the stitching in the tube. Such tubes should not be further apart than 8″, as the lateral movement of water will only be about 4″ from each side of the tube.

Tubes are attached to ¾″ plastic pipe at one end of the bench, and that pipe is connected to the water main. Tubes are plugged at the other end of the bench. The length of tubes on the bench should not exceed 60′, and water pressure should be within the range of 4 to 9 lbs./sq. in. (psi).

There is no splashing of water with this latest system, installation is quite easy, and the tubing lasts longer than material used in earlier systems. As with perimeter watering systems, the tubing must be removed between crops and should be surface-sterilized if the soil is pasteurized.

A similar system can be installed across the bench rather than down the length of the bench. A polyethylene pipe is installed on one side of the bench, and a thin polyethylene tube is connected to the pipe at 8″ intervals. Water is slowly applied to the crop.

Installation perhaps takes longer for this system than when fewer tubes are run the length of the bench, but the advantages and disadvantages are similar.

- **The nutrient film technique (NFT) system** has also been used on cut flower crops in Europe. It perhaps is more popular among tomato and cucumber growers, but it is a system to watch with interest.

Tremendous advances have been made in automatic watering of floricultural crops. It is difficult to predict what innovations in watering practices will be in the future, but only the most foresighted of growers of 25 years ago might have guessed at some of the systems available now. There is no reason to believe that ingenuity among manufacturers and growers will cease suddenly and no further advances will be made.

Chapter 10

AUTOMATED BEDDING PLANT TRANSPLANTING

by Vic Ball

For years, transplanting bedding plant seedlings has been done by the neighborhood ladies, high school people, etc. on most U.S. and Canadian ranges. It was part-time work that provided them with some added income—and got a big job done for the grower.

Again, there's been change—to automation. The basis for this automation is the conversion of U.S. bedding *plants* to plugs. As of the early 1990s, probably 70% of the estimated 4 billion bedding plants grown per year in the United States were plug-grown. And soon it will be 90%. See the plug chapter for more details on plug growing.

Plugs have already made one big change in bedding plant production: the conversion on many ranges to assembly-line transplanting. The basis for this is a mechanical belt, perhaps 12' to 15' long, that carries flats filled, dibbled and ready for transplanting to the half-dozen or so people doing the transplanting. The transplanting crew stands on either side of the belt. Typically each person is assigned one pack in each flat or some part of the pack, and that person places plants in that pack as each flat goes by. The rate of movement of the flats is adjusted to provide reasonable time for each of the people to do their share of the flat. See the photo. It's a system also widely used to plant hanging baskets, 4" and 6" pot annuals, etc. The

Here's assembly line transplanting of bedding plants. The belt moves flats by the transplanters.

results in flats per person, per hour, has been quite remarkable—especially when the grower converted to plugs. With plugs, a person simply pulls up a handful of plugs from a nearby plug sheet with the left hand, picks out one plug with the right hand and places it in a pre-dibbled hole. It is a simple job, and it really needs no training. And most of all, even with a moderate pace on the belt movement, transplanting cost per flat has gone down substantially. I've seen hand-transplanting of bareroot seedlings (minimum labor rate) costing growers up to 50¢ per flat of 72 plants. With a normal assembly line system, this cost goes down to 15¢ to 20¢ and sometimes 10¢ to 15¢. That's an important economy. Equally important: The transplanting job now gets done on time. The crews, and often the grower/owner, don't spend their Saturdays and Sundays transplanting during busy spring weeks. It has been a real step forward—and is widely used among bedding plant growers today. The total assembly line—belt and other parts—costs around $4,000.

NEXT STEP: AUTOMATIC TRANSPLANTING

As this 15th edition goes to press, several automatic transplanting machines are just coming onto the market. All are designed to remove plugs from the plug sheet and plant them into a pot or flat. Today's machines are still more or less on a shakedown basis—working out problems. But it is quite clear that soon enough the job will be fully automated. This will mean the end of the "neighborhood ladies" tradition. It's sad in a way. Here, very briefly, are several of the candidates as of the early 1990s:

- **The Harrison Transplanter**, designed by Richie Harrison in cooperation with grower Jack Van de Wetering of Ivy Acres, Calverton, Long Island. The system has a design capacity of 450 to 500 flats per hour, with a crew of 4 workers (5¢ per flat). Two of these people fill in skips since the machine also transplants plugs in which germination did not occur. It costs in the range of $30,000 to $40,000. The machine extracts the plugs from the plug sheet by inserting long needles into the soil ball. Details in *GrowerTalks*, May 1989, page 24. Availability is planned for 1991. For details write Ivy Acres, 128C Edwards Avenue, Calverton, Long Island, New York 11933.

- **The Visser Transplanter** is Dutch-designed and manufactured and also just entering the market. As of publication of this edition, the Visser transplanter is expensive—but shows important signs of being able to do the job. One Dutch

Baskets can be done on the assembly line, too.

grower, John Ammerlaan, as of June 1990, had successfully transplanted 4½ million plants with the Visser machine. Comments:

First, growers using the Visser transplanter must convert to a special plug tray (by Visser). The individual plug containers are sort of star-shaped. The little "points of the star" are a key part of the way the machine grabs a plug.

Skips (non-germinated plugs) must be replaced by hand, at an average of 3 to 4 plants per tray of 32 plants.

The machine transplants 6,000 to 8,000 plants per hour, doing 2,500 flats a day with about 82,000 plants in 32 trays.

Ammerlaan's still manually transplants crops with low germination.

John Ammerlaan reports being impressed with the lack of transplant shock—or rather the speed with which plugs grown in the star trays take off in the pack. "You can already see the roots growing after transplanting in just one day."

The machine has been working perfectly for three months.

Cost of transplanter alone: 150,000 guilders (about $82,400 U.S.). The entire work line with flat filler, dibbler, etc. is 400,000 guilders ($219,780 U.S.).

Ammerlaan's reports saving 4 to 5 people in their operation (about 6 million plants a year). Their only major problem with this system now is replacing non-germinated plugs.

For details, write Visser, Beneden Havendijk 115a, Postbus 5103, 's-Gravendeel (Holland).

- **Coverplant,** a French company, has developed a transplanter that eliminates inferior plants and transplants about 7,500 plugs/hour. No other details are available.

- **The Gerplant Transplanter,** also French, operates at about 15,000 plugs/hour. No other details are available.

- **In early 1990, Lannen,** a Finnish company, introduced a prototype transplanter that attaches to potting machines.

- **The Timmer Industries Plug Transplanter** (Jenison, Michigan), [phone (800) 828-9238] plants 12,000 to 20,000 plants/hour and also ejects bad plugs. Price is about $40,000.

An interesting point on automated transplanting and irrigation and other bedding plant jobs: They do eliminate a lot of jobs. But, on the positive side, automated bedding plant production means that U.S. growers can be competitive cost-wise with low-labor areas. The point is that labor, with this automation, will be such a small percent of cost of production that south-of-the-border producers will have no real labor advantage over U.S. or Canadian growers. And, of course, it is always a real step ahead when production is located in the area where the product is marketed.

Chapter 11

SIX LABOR SAVERS

by Ron Adams
Ball Seed Company

LOW VOLUME APPLICATORS FOR GREENHOUSE SPRAYING

Chemical application without exposing the grower reduces the hazard to the applicator. Treating greenhouses during the night without an operator seems too good to be true, but low volume application equipment makes this possible. Low volume applicators reduce the particle size to less than 10 microns, allowing the insecticide or fungicide to mix with the air current for distribution. Deposition studies show that both the upper and lower leaf surface is covered with more than the 45 particles per sq. mm. needed to achieve effective control with normal air flow. The benefits?

- **The amount of chemical required** is less than with high volume equipment.

- **Treatment can be made during the night** by setting the timer, allowing the machine to shut itself off in a closed greenhouse. After treatment, houses should be ventilated for 3 to 6 hours before entering.

- **The small particle size eliminates any residue** problems unless the mist combines with large water drops when the relative humidity is 90% or higher. It is not recommended to treat when the air temperature is above 86°F and relative humidity is 90% or higher.

Here's the ultra low volume spray pesticide applicator—it works while you sleep!

Low volume applicators come in different sizes depending on the area to be covered. Small applicators cover 15,000 to 20,000 sq. ft. of pot crops and 5,000 to 10,000 sq. ft. of cut flowers. Medium size applicators cover 30,000 sq. ft. of pot crops and 15,000 sq. ft. of cut flowers. Large applicators will treat 60,000 sq. ft. of pot crops and 30,000 sq. ft. of cut flowers.

This exciting new development in pesticide application equipment reduces the exposure to pesticides in closed greenhouses while effectively controlling insects and diseases. This new ultra low volume equipment is available from most grower supply firms.

Ultra-Low Volume Application Versus Standard Manual Sprayer

	Standard Hydraulic Sprayer	Ultra-Low Volume Sprayer
Cost	$1,500	$4,500
Applications/year	52	52
Application time (employee hours/ 30,000 sq. ft.)	5 hours	zero hours
Employee hours/ 5-year period	1,300 hours	zero hours
Labor rate	$7.50	N/A
Labor costs/5 years	$9,750	N/A
Total costs	$11,250	$4,500
Chemical exposure	yes	no

FERTILIZER INJECTORS

Fertilizing virtually all commercial flower crops today is done along with irrigation. Fertilizer is automatically injected into the irrigation water just ahead of application to the crop. Modern injectors permit varying the concentration of the fertilizer being injected. Also, these injectors handle other chemicals in some cases. See the fertilizer chapter for details on injectors.

AUTOMATED CLOTH APPLICATION

Automated cloth is used for shortening daylength to control flowering of mums or kalanchoes, reducing summer light on crops that can't stand full sun, and providing thermal insulation. All three operations are very much a part of many growing ranges; all are energy-related and certainly offer mechanization possibilities. Let's pull it all together in this chapter.

Short-day shading cloth on mums—automated. The black poly sheet is drawn across the house mechanically from gutter to gutter.

Short-Day Control

The classic way to create short days is just to pull a big piece of black sateen over the bench supported by a metal and wire framework. It's applied at 5 p.m. and removed at 7 a.m.—manually, of course. In some cases it's done with black poly sheets, but they don't stand much of this kind of wear.

Years ago growers found that they could stretch a sheet of black poly from gutter to gutter supported by wires drawn across the house. They'd just fasten the sheet to one gutter and draw it across the house, often securing it to a wire at the other gutter with clothespins. It's still a manual operation—but it takes a great deal less man hours than pulling shade over individual benches. The obvious disadvantage: You've got to shade the whole house as one. There's no more option of individual bench shading.

The next step—and actually a by-product of energy conservation—was to mechanize that sheet of material that was drawn across the house gutter to gutter. Ideas to mechanize this were spawned as a result of the roughly ⅓ fuel savings affected by stretching such a sheet from sunset to sunrise during winter. And the same sheet, if it's opaque, will do the short-day job in spring and summer. Just set it up on a time clock and it's fully mechanized. The whole installation, for both energy saving and short-day control, is not that terribly expensive: $1.25 to $1.50 per sq. ft., for starters.

That's the way a great many of the pot and cut mum ranges are being operated today. With all the competitive pressures of the 1990s, pulling cloth by hand is going out fast.

Light Reduction

Many crops just can't stand the full 10,000 to 12,000 fc. of mid-summer sunlight—especially under a glass roof, which aggravates the problem. Also, by the way, in many cases *people* have the same problem standing this intensive heat and sunlight. The result of all this is that almost a majority of crops are put under some sort of light reduction in hot summer weather.

The old shade plan was just to make up whitewash in buckets and use a tin can to throw it up over the roof. It did the job, but with a lot of hand labor, and, maybe worst of all, it was hard to get off in the fall. Often that shade is still there in November when the crop desperately wants every bit of light it can get.

By the way, such shade can be—and really should be—removed in late September. Simply make up a solution of Lightening Crystals, available from Florist Products Inc. [phone (800) 828-2242], spray it on the roof and hose it off with water. It should leave the glass clear.

Now, the light reduction job can be mechanized, and it's easily done with the same mechanical equipment that applies both black cloth for daylength control and the white polyester fabric for energy conservation. It is, again, just mechanically spreading a basic sheet of fabric across the house from one gutter to the other.

Fortunately the white polyester fabric that is so widely used for energy conservation also provides about a 45% reduction in summer sunlight. So it's widely used, especially for foliage crops and for other crops that just don't want that intensive light and heat. Many acres of greenhouses use this white polyester fabric to provide light and heat reduction.

See elsewhere in this book for details on the wide variety of fabrics available from Ludvig Svensson in Sweden [U.S. phone (704) 357-0457] for light reduction, short-day purposes and fuel conservation.

AUTOMATED CUT FLOWER HARVESTING

There is a whole array of equipment available both in the United States and Holland that does a variety of things related to harvesting cut flowers. All of the following examples are offered by Olimex in Holland. U.S. address: Olimex USA, 110 San Juan Rd., Watsonville, CA 95076 [phone (408) 722-0831].

- **Rose graders:** electronically sorts roses according to stem length.
- **Carnation counters:** counts carnation stems into bunches of 25 or whatever.
- **Mum stem strippers:** removes leaves from the lower several inches of stem.
- **Stem cutters:** cuts entire bunches off at a designated length from the flower head.
- **Bunch tiers:** ties a bunch of pompons or 25 carnations or roses or whatever.
- **The Dutch pompon harvester** is another little interesting combination of labor-saving equipment and ingenuity. I recently visited a grower named Middelburg in the Westland area of Holland. He and his three sons grow and harvest a remarkable 6 acres of year-round pompons with no outside help. The point of my story is the harvesting system. They have built a 3' x 5' tray that is suspended by two overhead rails. On this tray from left to right you see a stem cutter, a leaf stripper, a bunch tier and, suspended from in front of the shelf, a pack of sleeves.

   The grower quickly pulls up five stems of pompons and lays them on a belt going to the center walk. There, the ends set into the stem cutter, the stem stripper and the tier. The bunch is put stems down into the pack of sleeves and quickly picked up with one sleeve around the bunch of pompons. To finish it off, there is a proper corrugated box on the shelf into which the bunch is placed by hand—and it's all ready to go to the auction the next morning. No, they're not put in water overnight.

OTHER WAYS TO MOVE THINGS

- **Roller tracks.** These are aluminum tracks in typically 10' sections with rollers. You just lay them down the length of the bench or down a walk hooked end to end, and you can push all sorts of stuff back and forth on the roller track. They are most often used for filling a bench with pot plants. You just put the pots in flats on the track and push them down the bench.

- **Overhead monorails.** Hundreds of greenhouses use them to move things back and forth. They are often adaptations of the manure rack used by farmers.
- **Greenhouse carts**—much detail on available carts elsewhere in this book.
- **Dutch trays**—see the separate chapter on this.
- **Jim Dickerson's** remarkable belt system—elsewhere in this book.

POT AND FLAT FILLERS

Use of potting machines and flat fillers have shown significant labor savings once properly installed. There are several types of machines available for greenhouses that can work in a variety of growing operations. Pot and flat fillers can be more efficient by organizing support systems, such as the bulk bin for growing mix. The bulk bin system fills the machinery directly, without having extra conveyors or emptying several bags to keep a constant soil supply. Pot or flat fillers can be adapted to fill either pots or flats, increasing the utilization of specific equipment.

The decision on what to purchase depends on the primary product of the operation. If you handle more pots than flats, then a pot filler would be the best

A modern potting machine is almost standard on 1-acre or more ranges. Pots are filled by the machine, plants can be dropped in, and filled pots move off on the belt to the right. This machine is by Javo.

Meet the bulk bin—a great way to cut the labor of handling mix. The media comes from the supplier in the bag, is picked up by a forklift, suspended over the potting machine or flat filler (build your own rack), and you just release the media from the bag as desired. There's no labor of emptying bags and no bag disposal. It's great!

choice. But, if there are more flats with pot filling secondary, then a flat filler would be the best choice. In some operations there is enough filling for both types of equipment.

Source locations on equipment:

1. Javo USA Inc., 1900 Albritton Drive, Suite G & H, Kennesaw, GA 30144 [phone (404) 428-4491; FAX (404) 424-6635].

2. Bouldin & Lawson Inc., Route 10, Box 208, McMinnville, TN 37110 [phone (615) 668-4090; FAX (615) 668-3209].

3. Ball Seed Company, 622 Town Rd., West Chicago, IL 60185 [phone (708) 231-3500; FAX (708) 231-2774].

4. Gleason Industries Inc., 13670 S.E. 132nd, Clackamas, OR 97015 [phone (503) 698-5504; FAX (503) 698-2048].

SECTION III

Plugs

Chapter 12

PLUGS—THE WAY OF THE 1990s

by Vic Ball

My best estimate says that ¾ or more of all U.S. and Canadian bedding plants are grown from plugs—as of the early 1990s. And the prospect for plugs is steadily upward. Again, at best guess, the United States grows about 4 billion bedding plants per year—and probably 3 billion or more of them are from plugs—plus a lot of other ornamentals (cut flowers, etc.) and vegetables. Greiling's at Apopka, Florida, operate about 35-plus acres of greenhouses in plug production in season—Spark Plugs. And commercial vegetable growers' plug use is surely several times that of ornamentals, as plugs lend themselves to automatic field transplanting. One 5-acre range in Gilroy, California, is all plugs (in season), mainly market vegetables, some cut flowers. By the way, perennials are also moving into plugs.

Ernst Walz, a major German seedsman, has just completed a 5-acre range (1990) to produce plugs and seedling flats. The trend here: more plugs. There's also a very large "plug factory" just north of Venice—heavily producing vegetables for European market growers.

Shig Otani of Greenwood Greenhouses, Seattle, Washington, says, "Plugs have given our bedding plant production here (2 acres) a major boost. First, we can hold plugs for several weeks and transplant according to demand, which is not possible with bareroot seedlings. Second, the time from planting plugs to sale of plants is 1/3 less than with bareroot, and third, seed sowing was a big job here and is now automated. By the way, we use Agribrom at 15 parts per million on all our plug

For 10,000 Flats 72 plants/flat		
Type:	Square Ft.	% of finished area
Mass	1330	6 ½
648	2240	11
400	3640	18
273	5330	26

An interesting point about growing your own plugs: Using 273 per tray plugs, 26% of your finished area will be used to grow plugs—5,330-sq. ft. for 10,000 flats.

plants. They are mat irrigated and Agribrom keeps the algae down and also controls fungus gnats."

Plugs are important!

Why this rather sudden and major move to plugs?

- **Plugs take 30% less time overall, plant to sell,** and that means 25% to 30% more flats per house per spring. Also, plugs give more second crops and the opportunity to sandwich other crops in, especially before bedding plants. You don't need the space until about three weeks later than you would with bareroot seedlings. Even allowing space for self-grown plugs, there is still a major gain.

- **Transplanting is much faster**—especially where assembly line transplanting is done (see Chapter 10) and the flats move down a belt past the transplanting people. Each person does perhaps one pack out of each flat. Labor costs per flat for 72 plants have gone from 35¢ to 50¢ down to 15¢ or less. The traditional weekend and evening overtime at spring transplanting time is no more, and the job is getting done on time. That's very important.

- **Plugs adapt to automatic transplanters.** As the 15th *Ball RedBook* edition goes to press, the first automatic plug transplanters for bedding plant growers are at last being used commercially. Automatically transplanting plugs into bedding containers is coming soon. And these transplanters are all tied to the use of plugs.

- **Almost no skips.** A well-established plug set into a dibbled hole in a pack is almost a sure bet to grow. The result is that almost no skips need to be replanted.

138

- **Flexibility.** Plugs can be held at least several weeks without losing final plant quality. The same is not true with bareroot seedlings, which will quickly crowd and stretch.

- **Shorter crop time.** Time from sowing seed to sale of bedding plants is shortened by 7 to 10 days—you don't lose that recovery time from transplanting shock if plugs are used.

- **Seed sowing itself is now automated.**

- **Each seedling now has its own space.** The result: definitely higher percentages of transplantable and usable seedlings.

SCHEDULES AND TEMPERATURES

There is much specific detail on this in the bedding plant chapter elsewhere in this book. You'll find weeks from plug sowing to transplanting for several crops in several areas. Also, these schedules are all tied to a growing temperature during the plug stage.

THE PROBLEM SPECIES FOR AUTOMATED SEED SOWERS

There are several common bedding plant species that, for different reasons, cause problems in automatic seeders. Here they are, with the status of each as of the early 1990s.

- **Begonia** seeds are very small (300,000 seeds/oz.). Several seeders will handle them bare, but most growers seem to be opting for pelleted begonia seeds. Several reported sowing two pellets per plug; many use only one. One limitation of pelleting is that seed must be sown within 4 to 6 months of the pelleting process. But, of course, the great advantage is that most automatic seeders will handle the pellets very nicely.

- **Marigolds**—the fuzzy little tail on each seed is the problem. The answer: Seed producers are "de-tailing" marigold seeds of most important varieties, which permits, of course, handling in most automatic seeders. In addition to de-tailing, various coatings are used on some marigolds.

- **Tomatoes**—a very big and important bedding plant (often listed as #1 in total flats). Tomato seeds are naturally fuzzy so seeds stick together in a mechanical seeder. It's a big problem. The answer is to defuzz the seed. Defuzzed seed of all major commercial varieties is available and generally used in automatic seeders.

- **Ageratum** seed—there's some pelleting here. The seed is rather odd shaped so automatic seeders don't handle it well.

- **Zinnia** is a "sticky" seed type. The best answer, to my knowledge, is that the Old Mill seeder will handle them—not rapidly, but reliably. The same is true for scabiosa.

Meet "Mr. Plug," Dave Koranski, of Iowa State University. The flat on the left was fed with a weak nutrient solution the same day as sowing. The flat on the right received no nutrients on the sowing day. The moral: Feed plugs from the very beginning. Also, Dave has done so much for plug growers.

WATERING AND FEEDING PLUGS—IMPORTANT!

Originally plug sheets were almost always hand watered. Even today many good growers do this job mostly by hand. This means at least three or four trips over the bench on a sunny spring day. You've got to really live with them.

The past several years I've seen more growers doing quantities of plugs with automatic irrigation—and doing them very well. Partly this is the result of the improved boom irrigation systems now on the market. Examples are ITS, Hightstown, New Jersey [phone (609) 448-6533], and Growing Systems, Milwaukee, Wisconsin [phone (414) 263-3131]. I've seen excellent plug sheets done with either system. ITS is more sophisticated, offers more flexibility and more automation, and costs more. Ray Banko, Banko's Greenhouse, Dayton, New Jersey, does several bedding plant acres, mostly self-grown plugs, and does the job very well with the Growing Systems equipment. Orie van Wingerden, Pompton Plains, New Jersey,

Specialist producers typically use Dutch trays to move plug sheets back and forth. Here is Peter Van de Wetering's Jamesport, New York, operation where irrigating and feeding of plugs is done with booms, mostly ITS. Left to right are Jerry Mahoney, Ball Seed Company, Joyce Van de Wetering and Peter Van de Wetering.

reports that with ITS equipment he turns the watering job over entirely to automatics—except that he carefully monitors the setting on irrigation frequency. But says Orie, "The machine can do a more even watering job and plug sheet feeding than I can do by hand." I've heard other growers make the same statement.

Another option: ordinary overhead mist nozzles. There are nozzles available that will do this job satisfactorily. Again I've seen many growers doing it this way. A good example is Ivey Gardens in Lubbock, Texas. It's a relatively low cost system. When combined with a good automatic mist controller and monitored carefully by the grower, it will grow good plug sheets. There's a video available describing the Ivey system; write *GrowerTalks*.

Fog nozzles (much smaller particle size versus mist) are used by some plug growers. They are great for keeping plugs moist without pouring gallons of water onto trays. But true mist is expensive. Examples are Mee Industries, El Monte, California [phone (818) 350-4180] and Baumac International, Mentone, California [phone (714) 794-7631]. You'll find fog system details in Chapter 5.

Part of the problem is that plugs grow in a very shallow container—usually under an inch deep. This means poor downward movement of water and a tendency to waterlogging. It is critically important that plug sheets not be overwatered, and, by the same token, not be allowed to dry.

More and more growers are starting a low feeding concentration almost at the same time seed is sown. I often see 50 ppm and then a little later 100 ppm of nitrogen. It helps get the plugs started off better and sooner.

Growth chambers were originally an idea used by research people—they offered the capability of carefully controlling growing conditions for research projects. Commercial growers tended to open benches using sophisticated misting systems and several ways of maintaining soil temperature precisely as desired. Probably the majority of plugs are grown that way today—and certainly many excellent quality plug sheets are produced on open benches.

More and more though, as of the early 1990s, I see growers using growth chambers as a supplement, mostly as a way to provide special temperature and humidity conditions during sprouting of certain seeds. Why?

Pansy plugs are needed by Southern growers in midsummer—a time of very high temperatures in the South. Here's the 90% plus germination sheet produced by Ron Wagner, a Minneapolis specialist in a cooler climate!

- **First, pansies/perennials.** Especially pansies used heavily by Southern growers are very difficult to germinate and to grow on in the high temperatures of the Deep South in mid-summer. With a growth chamber it's possible, using mechanical refrigeration, to control the temperature as desired—especially during sprouting. Ronald Wagner, a Minneapolis plug specialist, does summer pansies in a refrigerated growth chamber—and reaches above 90% germination on most of his plug sheets.

In the same way, perennials are difficult to germinate in the summer and often need lower temperatures to get good germination. Again, it's a case for refrigerated growth chambers.

Bill Swanekamp of Kube Pak in Allentown, New Jersey, acquired a retired 40' truck body, installed specialized misting equipment (see the bedding plant chapter for details) and is able to handle species with special temperature and other requirements. He only uses it for a few special things, but it's important as a specialist plug producer to win with everything.

Gene Young, Auburn, Alabama, again a major bedding grower, has opted for growth chamber starting of all his plug flats. As soon as seeds are sprouted they are moved out to an open bench.

One penalty of this procedure is the peril of allowing plugs to stretch and over-grow in the growth chamber. They must be moved out promptly as soon as they are sprouted. And in some cases only ¾ of the seed has sprouted—and still you've got to get them out into the light or they'll stretch ruinously. This means that temperature and humidity must be maintained on the open bench to germinate the rest of the seeds.

More and more I see Dutch-style trays 12' or 15' long being used as a bench for germinating plugs—and permitting mechanical moving of thousands of plug trays from one position to another. Again it's a product of specialization.

CONTROLLING PLUG STRETCH

There are several means available to growers to do this:

- **Chemical retardants.** Use the ones as indicated for each species in the bedding plant chapter. An important point: It's easy to over-do retardants on plugs. One result: Plants may fail to grow out of the retardant after reaching the home gardener's flower bed! In other words, don't over-do, but a light B-Nine spray on petunias, for example, will make a shorter, stockier and better plant. There are excellent details on chemical retardants used on plugs in *Grower Talks*, February 1989, page 52.

- **Cool day/warm night.** The cool day/warm night (DIF) system from Michigan State works very nicely on plugs. Five degrees cooler day than night will very definitely retard stretch on plugs and improve quality. Especially with more than 5°F difference, there's a tendency for plugs to turn yellow, or chlorotic, which they will easily grow out of as night and day temperatures are put closer together.

Producing a good, even sheet of plugs with 85% or 90% germination is one of the toughest challenges facing any grower. I see many marginal plug sheets, 50% to 60% germination or less. All this is a key reason that more and more plug production seems to be moving into the hands of specialists.

Here are some of the common problems I see:

- **The hard water/climbing pH** syndrome may be the most common breakdown. In many parts of the United States, growers have quite hard water and this in a plug situation results in climbing pH. The result: Such critical things as iron are no longer available to the plant. Chlorosis occurs, and the plug dies. Begonias are especially susceptible. See Chapter 9 about irrigation and Chapter 25 about soil and water testing. Salt (EC) and pH levels must be monitored carefully. A good overall goal is to maintain pH about 5.8 to 6.

- **Excess salt level.** Many crops are very sensitive to excess salt, especially in the plug stage. It is a tiny, very tender plant! Monitor salt levels with a solubridge and aim for EC levels of 1.0. A coarse, well-drained medium plus an occasional leaching will help.

Plugs are often grown on a heated cement floor. Here's Carl Blasig, a Hightstown, New Jersey, grower. Note the inverted plastic liner used to keep flats off the floor and discourage root-through.

After holding petunia plugs for three weeks in the greenhouse, there is a noticeable size difference between 200 and 800 cell seedlings. Plugs grown in smaller cells don't hold as well.

- **Temperature control.** Actually the temperature spread within which many species will germinate satisfactorily is rather narrow. Dave Koranski at Iowa State University has prepared a tabulation of these temperatures (elsewhere in this chapter). It is critically important that growers stay reasonably close to these optimum temperatures. That requires some sort of root zone heating system that permits fairly precise temperature control of the media. Also growers should have and use a glass rod thermometer with which they can check media temperatures frequently.

- **Plugs not fed.** Again, given the intense culture—a plant growing in such a tiny volume of soil—it is imperative that some fertilizer be applied almost from the sowing of seed. I've seen crops where nitrogen has simply been leached away and the crop is starving.

- **Minor element deficiencies** occur in plug growing, especially calcium, magnesium and boron. Occasionally minor element deficiencies or excesses can upset a plug crop. Beware. See Chapter 25 for more details about minor elements.

- **Excess light—leaf burn.** With such sensitive things as begonias, plugs can and often do simply sunburn, especially on the late spring crops. I see many growers either applying shade to their greenhouse roof or using light reduction curtains to control the light level.

    There are other problems. When all else fails, Iowa's Dave Koranski is a knowledgeable and helpful problem-solver [phone (515) 294-1916].

- **Holding plugs too long.** Holding most bedding annuals too long in plugs will result in delayed flowering and impaired growth. Impatiens particularly, if held 4 weeks (sow to transplant), will grow on normally; if held 8 weeks, there is a definite delay in flowering and growth. More or less the same thing occurs for petunias, salvia and seed geraniums. Fibrous begonias showed little difference—they are slower-growing anyway. As you would expect, the impaired growth and flowering of

An example of the kind of sheets that are used worldwide for growing plugs. The "648" on the left provides 648 plugs per 21" flat.

these annuals was worse in smaller plugs and less a problem with larger plug sizes, all this based on research at Michigan State University and at Iowa State. See the details in *Grower Talks,* January 1985, page 48, December 1989, page 72 and December 1990, page 76.

PLUG SIZES

There are many different sizes available. Most plugs are done in a 10½″ x 21″ plastic tray or flat. The widely used "392" plug sheet offers 392 cavities per 21″ flat; each cavity is square, ⅝″ across x ⅞″ deep.

Here are the most common sizes used:

Cell Size	Depth	Cells Per Flat	Shape	Remarks
¹³/₁₆″ x 1¼″	⅞″	288	square	Used where larger size plugs are wanted. Many geraniums are started in 288s. The 288 square holds 28% more soil versus the 288 round.
¹³/₁₆″ x 1″	⅞″	288	round or square	Easier to remove round plug versus square plug.
⅝″ x ⅝″	⅞″	392	square	A size widely used (#1 for most bedding plant crops, but trend is toward 512).
⁹/₁₆″ x ¾″	⅞″	512	square	Used where a smaller plug, more per flat is wanted. Increasingly popular due to lower cost per plug and less freight.
⁷/₁₆″ x ¾″	¾″	800	square	See note below.

Note: The 800 cells per flat tray is being used substantially as of the early 1990s. It is a very small cell size and makes it difficult to produce a good, even stand of plugs! But it is very economical—the cost per plug is very low. Some specialist plug growers are producing up to 25% of their plugs in 800s. It's controversial. Obviously, any plants received in 800 plug sheets must be planted within a day or so of arrival. They just don't keep very well and overgrow rapidly.

146

Important! If you scrub plug sheets with bleach after use (or use any other disinfectant) be sure to rinse thoroughly to remove all the chemical. The flat on the right was treated with bleach and not rinsed thoroughly.

Plug sheets are often mechanically fed into seeding machines. Be sure the flat you select fits your machine.

The last point on plug flats: Some growers reuse them and sterilize them with an LS10 wash. It's okay but I have seen problems where the LS10 or bleach was not completely washed from the tray and there was an adverse affect on the next crop. Beware!

THE ROLE OF THE SPECIALIST PLUG PRODUCER

More each year I see a clear trend in plug production toward specialists. It's the old story—the specialist puts his total resources and effort and time into this one crop and does it better. There were several of these type of growers reported in much detail in the December 1989 issue of *GrowerTalks*. The point in general is that they bring in computerized and more sophisticated and more accurate control of such things as temperature, humidity and light levels and because they do a larger

One of the efficiencies seen at plug producer operations. Here, Ron Wagner, a Minneapolis plug specialist, moves flats of plugs from seeding room to sprouting chamber in Dutch trays loaded on a wagon. There's much less cost versus small carts.

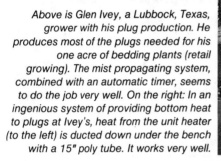

Above is Glen Ivey, a Lubbock, Texas, grower with his plug production. He produces most of the plugs needed for his one acre of bedding plants (retail growing). The mist propagating system, combined with an automatic timer, seems to do the job very well. On the right: In an ingenious system of providing bottom heat to plugs at Ivey's, heat from the unit heater (to the left) is ducted down under the bench with a 15" poly tube. It works very well.

volume they are able to provide the special environmental conditions that at least the major species require. Begonias early in the season are a case in point. They want to be warm and humid. Pansies in mid-summer are another example. It's all this sort of thing that I see causing a steady trend toward more growers buying from the specialist—especially the harder-to-do things like begonias and impatiens.

SOME BASICS ON PANSY PLUG CULTURE

An important refinement frequently adopted by growers is "stage culture." You break the plug culture into four stages. I think the following plan for producing pansy plugs is a good example of this approach. It's by Roger C. Styer and Shawn R. Laffe of Ball Seed Company.

Pansy plugs for fall sales (most are plug-grown today) must be grown during the hot summer months of July, August and September. Warm temperatures (85°F and higher) inhibit germination, cause pansies to stretch quickly, promote soft growth, and blast flowers. Even the most extensive cooling systems for greenhouses have difficulty maintaining 75°F or lower in August, therefore, many growers use refrigerated growth chambers to sprout pansies in hot weather. To help alleviate some of these stress problems, or at least to help the grower be aware of what's ahead, the following pansy plug culture guidelines are recommended:

Stage 1: Time of radicle (root) emergence (3 to 7 days after sowing)
- Cover trays to maintain moisture around the seed during germination. A thin layer of coarse vermiculite or growing medium can be used.
- Temperature 65° to 75°F soil, no warmer!
- Relative humidity: soil moist but not saturated.
- Light is not necessary for germination until radicle emergence.
- Medium pH 5.5 to 5.8 and EC less than .75.

Stage 2: Stem and cotyledon emergence (the next 7 days)
- Temperature 62° to 76°F soil.
- Moisture level: Allow the soil to dry out very slightly between watering to encourage root development. Pansies should not be kept saturated.
- Nutrition: Maintain pH 5.5 to 5.8 and EC .75; begin supplementing with balanced fertilizer at low rate, such as 50 to 75 ppm.

Stage 3: Growth and development of true leaves (the next 14 days)
- Temperature 60° to 76°F soil. The cooler the temperature, the slower and more toned the plant growth.
- Allow the soil to dry slightly.
- Nutrition: Maintain pH 5.5 to 5.8 and EC less than 1.0; fertilize with balanced feed at 100 ppm.
- Growth regulation may begin at this time, chemical or cultural. B-Nine is not registered for pansies, but has been applied experimentally at 2,500 to 5,000 ppm starting at the first-true-leaf stage with effective control.

Time To Produce Plugs—Weeks From Sowing To Mature Plug

| | Plugs per 22" flat | | |
	800	406	112
North, spring	5 to 6	6 to 7	8 to 9
North, fall	4½ to 5	5½ to 6	7½ to 8
South, spring	4 to 5	5 to 6	7 to 8
South, fall	4 to 4½	4½ to 5	7 to 7½
	Time from transplant to sale (weeks)		
	800/72	406/48	112/4"
55°F nights	7 to 8	6 to 7	6 to 7
70°F nights	5 to 6	4½ to 5	4½ to 5

GrowerTalks on Plugs, a collection of *GrowerTalks* feature stories on plugs, is available from *GrowerTalks.*

GrowerTalks special plug issues: January 1987, January 1988, December 1989 and December 1990. Each contains a lot of basics on plug growing updates on research.

Automatic Plug Seeders

Company and Address	Seeder Type	Begonia, Raw	Marigold, De-tailed	Tomato, Defuzzed	Alyssum, Raw	Pepper, Raw	Petunia, Raw	Impatiens, Raw
Berry Seeder Company Elizabeth City, NC (800) 327-3239	Berry Precision Seeder	no	yes	yes	yes	yes	yes	yes
BFG Supply Co. Burton, OH (800) 321-0608	Hamilton Tray Indexing	yes	yes	yes	yes	yes	yes	yes
	Hamilton Electric Conveyor	yes	yes	yes	yes	yes	yes	yes
	Hamilton Drum Seeder	no	yes	yes	yes	no	yes	yes
Blackmore Co. Inc. Belleville, MI (800) 874-8660	Blackmore	yes	yes	yes	yes	yes	yes	yes
Bouldin & Lawson Inc. McMinnville, TN (800) 443-6398	Precision Drum Seeder	no	fairly well	yes	yes	yes	yes	yes
Gleason Industries Inc. Clackamas, OR (503) 698-5504	Gleason	no	no	yes	no	yes	no	no
Growing Systems Inc. Milwaukee, WI (800) 792-3504 ext. 325	Vandana Direct Seeder	yes	no	yes	yes	yes	yes	yes
	Vandana TLXL Tubeless Seeder	yes	yes	yes	yes	yes	yes	yes
Jack Van Klaveren Ltd. St. Catharines, Ontario Canada (416) 684-1103	Niagara	yes	yes	yes	yes	yes	yes	yes
H.J. Kern & Son Perrysburg, OH (419) 874-2844	Note[3]	—	—	—	—	—	—	—
Lannen Inc. Camarillo, CA (800) 426-8124	Note[4]	—	—	—	—	—	—	—
Little's Machinery Inc. Concord, NC (704) 786-1774	Little's Seeder	no	yes	yes	yes	yes	yes	yes
Seed E-Z Seeder Co. Inc. Prairie du Sac, WI (608) 643-4122	E-Z Seeder	pelleted	yes	yes	yes	yes	yes	yes
Speedy Seeder Inc. Lodi, WI (608) 592-3873	SS-I	pelleted	yes	yes	yes	yes	yes	yes
Klaas Visser International Aalsmeer, Holland 02977-27274	Visser Tuinbouw Technick	(handles cyclamen seed only)			—	—	—	—

Note[1]: Pelleted seeds are larger, round, generally uniform in size in all species. Following are currently available as pellets: marigolds, begonias, alyssum, lisianthus, lobelia, petunias, dusty miller. More species being added each year. Pellets work well with drum seeders.
Note[2]: Besides de-tailing, coating seed is done currently only on marigolds. It is a thin coating, does not change the shape or size of seed, but facilitates handling seeders.

Pelleted Seed Note[1]	Coated Seed Note[2]	Flats Seeded Per Hour; 390 Seeds Per Tray	Approx. Cost for Basic Seeder	Largest Tray It Will Handle	Feeds Trays Mechanically	Can Sow Single or Double	How Operated
yes	yes	250	$ 495	Todd (Speedling)	can seed trays directly on a moving conveyor	yes	vacuum
yes	yes	90	$ 7,200	17"x17"	yes	yes	air compressor
yes	yes	120	$ 9,400	17"x17"	yes	yes	air compressor/electric
yes	yes	600	$16,000	17"x17"	yes	yes	air compressor/electric
yes	yes	240	$ 9,000	128 plug tray; direct sows flats also	yes	yes	mechanical drive vacuum seed pickup
yes	no	900+	$16,500	18"x6" without modification	yes	yes	vacuum seed pickup; water seed delivery
yes	yes	900	$ 2,935	14"x26"	yes	yes	vacuum
yes	yes	240 to 500	$ 3,500	13"x26"	yes	yes	vacuum
yes	yes	120 to 240	$ 1,110	13"x26"	no	yes	vacuum
yes	yes	120	$ 8,000	all commonly used	fed by conveyor	yes	vacuum
—	—	—	—	—	—	—	—
—	—	—	—	—	—	—	—
yes	yes	100	$ 4,500	14" wide	yes	yes	electric with built-in vacuum
yes	yes	120 to 240, depending on varieties	$ 599 with one plate	512 holes	no	yes	vacuum
yes	yes	300	$ 495	any (can custom design)	no	yes	vacuum
—	—	100 trays	N/A	+ or - 40 cm x 60 cm	yes	double	vacuum

Note[3]: *H.J. Kern makes a variety of seeders tailored to the job and the crop. Contact Harold Kern for more information.*
Note[4]: *Lannen offers a drum seeder mounted on a belt conveyor.*

151

How to Grow 18 Plug Crops*

		Stage 1		Stage 2			Stage 3	
Crop	Covering	Germination Temp. (°F)	Time (Days)	Temp. (°F)	Fertilizer (ppm)	Time (Days)	Temp. (°F)	Fertilizer (ppm)
Ageratum		78 to 82	2 to 3	72 to 75	50 1 to 2/week	7	65 to 68	150 1/week
Begonia		78 to 80	6 to 7	72 to 78	50 to 100 1 to 2/week	21	70 to 75	150 2/week
Celosia		75	4 to 5	72 to 75	50 1 to 2/week	7	65 to 70	100 to 150 2/week
Coleus		72 to 75	4 to 5	72 to 75	50 to 75 1 to 2/week	10	68 to 72	150 2/week
Dahlia	yes	78 to 80	3 to 4	68 to 70	50 1/week	7	65 to 70	100 1 to 2/week
Dianthus		70 to 75	3 to 5	70 to 75	50 1/week	7	65 to 70	150 1/week
Dusty Miller		72 to 75	4 to 6	70 to 75	50 1/week	14	65 to 70	150 1 to 2/week
Geranium	yes	70 to 75	3 to 5	70 to 75	50 to 100 1/week	10	65 to 70	150 2/week
Impatiens		75 to 80	3 to 5	72 to 75	50 to 100 1/week	10	68 to 72	100 to 150 1/week
Marigold— African	yes	75 to 80	2 to 3	68 to 70	50 to 75 1/week	5	62 to 65	100 to 150 1/week
Marigold— French	yes	75 to 80	2 to 3	68 to 70	50 to 75 1/week	7	62 to 65	100 to 150 1/week
Pansy**	yes	62 to 68	4 to 7	62 to 68	50 1/week	7	60 to 62	100 1/week
Petunia		75 to 78	3 to 5	72 to 78	50 to 75 1 to 2/week	14	62 to 68	150 1 to 2/week
Salvia		75 to 78	5 to 7	70	25 1/week	7	62 to 65	100 1/week
Snapdragon		70 to 75	5 to 8	65 to 70	none	14	62 to 65	100 1/week
Tomato	yes	70 to 72	2	68 to 72	none	7	60 to 65	100 1/week
Verbena	yes	75 to 80	4 to 6	72 to 75	25 1/week	14	68 to 72	100 1/week
Vinca	yes	75 to 80	4 to 6	72 to 78	25 1/week	14	68 to 72	100 1/week

*by Dave Koranski, professor of floriculture, Iowa State University. Adapted from GrowerTalks magazine, December 1989.
Special comments:
   Covering: Certain seeds need to be covered to exclude light. In these seeds light causes desiccation, so they do not maintain adequate moisture levels to germinate. Germination percentages decrease significantly under lighted conditions.
   Fertilizer: Fertilizer is shown in parts per million (ppm) of nitrogen. The source is a commercial 20-10-20 fertilizer with calcium added. You can also fertilize by adding separate components NH_4NO_3, $Ca(NO_3)_2$ and KNO_3. The components need separate injector heads to prevent precipitation.
   If ammonium is used in Stage 2, be careful to keep temperatures above 68°F.
   Stages 3 and 4 fertilizer may be 20-10-20 as long as temperatures are above 68°F. Because most 20-10-20 fertilizers lack calcium,

Stage 4		Time (Days)	Total Plug Crop Time (Weeks)	Comments
Time (Days)	Temp. (°F)			
14	60 to 62	14	5 to 6	
21	62 to 68	14	8 to 9	When seedlings are in Stage 2, they tend to lose vigor. Check soil for low and high fertility. Ammonium should be less than 20 ppm in soil.
14	60 to 62	7 to 14	5 to 6	Salt levels and moisture levels should be maintained to avoid premature flowering. Use preventive fungicides. Stage 1 temperature is critical for uniform germination.
14	60 to 62	7	5 to 6	Growth regulators and lower finishing salt levels help to keep plant compact.
7	60 to 62	7	3 to 4	Difficult to sow mechanically. Low salt levels may be beneficial for growth and development.
14	60 to 62	7 to 14	5 to 6	Lower salt levels to prevent burn. Night interruption with 50 fc. light can be used to promote flowering. Watch for stem elongation.
21	60 to 62	7 to 10	6 to 7	Low germination percentage; use multiple seed. Moisture levels on dry side after Stage 1 may be helpful. Preventive fungicide for alternaria is suggested.
14	60 to 62	14 to 21	6 to 7	pH must be maintained at 5.8 or greater to prevent iron manganese, sodium and zinc toxicity. Germination temperatures highter than 75°F may be detrimental.
14	60 to 62	7 to 14	5 to 6	Keep Stage 1 wet for first two to three days, then decrease moisture. Use growth regulators to maintain compact growth if fertilizer is used. HID lights for two to three weeks will provide vigorous plant with thicker stem.
14	60 to 62	7 to 10	4 to 5	Need two to three weeks to flower. pH levels below 5.8 result in toxic levels of iron, zinc, manganese and sodium; appears as necrotic spots and burned edges on lower level.
14	60 to 62	7 to 14	5 to 6	Phytoxicity can appear from iron and manganese deficiency.
14	55 to 60	14 to 21	6 to 7	Stage 1 65°F and high moisture for three days, then reduce moisture. Medium with low nutrient charge and low phosphorus helps to prevent stem elongation.
14	62 to 65	7 to 10	5 to 6	Near saturation moisture level critical for first two days of germination, then decrease moisture thereafter. Medium pH should be less than 6.8 to prevent iron deficiency.
21	60 to 62	7	5 to 6	Refined seed may improve germination. Low fertilizer levels during Stage 1 and 2, increase in Stage 4. Do not hold plugs.
14	60 to 62	7 to 10	6 to 7	Alternating 70°F day and 80°F night temperatures may be beneficial for germination. Use low salt levels.
7	60 to 62	7	3 to 4	May stretch when germinated without lights. Moisture stress is effective to control height.
14	65 to 68	7	5 to 6	Dry conditions during germination may be beneficial. A preventive fungicide program may improve germination.
21	65 to 68	7	6 to 7	Cover seed, but sparingly. Maintain temperature, high moisture for three days, then reduce.

it may be necessary to use a CaNO$_3$ fertilizer in addition but separately.
When a toned plant is desired, CaNO$_3$ and KNO$_3$ may be used.

Definition of Stages:
Stage 1—time of radicle emergence.
Stage 2—stem and cotyledon emergence.
Stage 3—growth and development of true leaves.
Stage 4—plants ready for transplanting, shipping or bedding.

**See above cultural information.*

153

SECTION IV

Insect Control

Chapter 13

INSECT CONTROL—TOUGH!

by Vic Ball

Ask 20 growers to identify their most pressing problem. The majority will start talking bugs. And as the years go by the problem gets steadily worse. Why?

- **Insects have developed resistance** to many or most of our most effective pesticides. The result: Sprays of these materials give poor or zero control.

- **Some of our most effective** (and most poisonous) pesticides have been withdrawn from the market. A classic example: Temik, which has raised such havoc in Long Island, Florida and Wisconsin. And few really good new pesticides are taking the place of the ones we're losing.

- **Pressure from various environmental groups** and new, very restrictive laws make pesticide use by growers ever more difficult and expensive. Growers must be licensed to apply pesticides and must pass examinations to get that license. Furthermore, pesticides that inevitably appear in greenhouse runoff or ground water are fast becoming a serious offense and will probably be subject to legislative control soon. The public just doesn't want pesticide poisons in their drinking water—can you blame them?

- **Along with all this I hear** many examples of growers themselves rebelling at constant exposure to these powerful chemicals. They just don't want themselves, their families or their employees to risk buildup of these chemicals in their bloodstreams. I hear, "Tell me how I can go about using those parasites to control whiteflies on my poinsettias this year."

- **Especially mass outlet buyers insist on zero tolerance**—no bugs allowed! Somehow U.S. and Canadian chain buyers must realize what the Europeans learned years ago: Zero tolerance is just too expensive and not worth it in terms of the price of product versus customer satisfaction. European buyers do not accept poinsettias, for example, which yield a cloud of whiteflies when disturbed—but they do live with an occasional insect.

- **Another facet** of the evermounting insect control problem is new re-entry laws. These are very specific laws that require a certain number of hours between the spray application and re-entry into the greenhouse by the grower. In other words, if you apply a given spray you are required to stay out of the greenhouse for a certain number of hours. That can be very tough when you need to water and ventilate your crops.

So, clearly insects are a far more difficult challenge to the grower than was the case only a decade ago. All this has been aggravated by recent "epidemics" of several insects—a phenomenon that didn't occur a generation ago. Example: In the mid-1980s leafminer simply decimated many chrysanthemum growers, especially in cut mum crops in California and England. And then came whitefly on poinsettias and thrips on nearly everything.

WHAT CAN GROWERS DO ABOUT ALL THIS?

Fortunately there are answers—some short term to ease the problem today, plus longer term measures. It's not at all a hopeless outlook!

But, to live with this new dimension of insect problems, growers must change and adapt to new and different control measures. Unfortunately the *Ball RedBook* just doesn't have space for all insects/all crops—especially on these new measures. I do, however, offer:

- In broader terms, the several new approaches with which growers can keep their crops reasonably clean.

- The current Ohio State tabulation—recommendations for control of most pests by crops and by insects (in the following chapter).

- Many references, particularly recent stories from *GrowerTalks*, often from top entomologists, which offer very specific plans for control of most common pests, using both chemicals and biologicals—including parasites that are steadily coming into use by growers.

First, the New Approaches

Specialize we must. Pressures build steadily each year on growers to specialize—grow fewer of more crops. First, most crops have a particularly troublesome insect—whitefly on poinsettias, leafminer on mums, etc. A single greenhouse with half a dozen crops tends to have four or five major insect problems versus one for the specialist. Furthermore, the plant toxicity (crop injury) problem is also multiplied by five or six—there are six crops to be concerned about rather than one. Clearly these multi-crop houses present a much more difficult challenge for insect control in light of the world of the 1990s. It's tough enough to control one insect in a house, but far tougher to manage half a dozen. Biologicals—parasites and predators—are also all specific to one crop and one insect—again, it's just not practical for use in a multi-crop house.

Interesting to note: The biggest and most practical use of parasites/predators in U.S. and Canadian ornamental ranges is in response to the poinsettia whitefly. A major factor: Many growers virtually fill their entire range with this one crop for three or four or five months a year. Now, at least for that period, they can focus their attention on this one insect and one plant toxicity concern. I'm seeing dozens of growers across the country who are actually winning the whitefly battle on poinsettias with the parasite *Encarsia formosa*.

Of course, insect control is not the only pressure growers feel to specialize. The whole world of automation works far better in a one-crop situation versus multi crops in one house. The Dutch particularly do specialize—whole 5- to 10-acre ranges of cut pompons, the same for tomatoes, cucumbers, etc. Of course their marketing system supports this specialist grower—that's one of our problems. See elsewhere in this book on that.

But many growers today can and are starting to reduce the number of crops—and buy in from other specialists some of their lesser crops.

Bedding plants are a particular problem here because by nature they include dozens of species and many different insects. Fortunately it's a very short-term crop, and there's not normally a major insect problem. Some growers have had trouble with aphids recently, but so far it's been controllable.

Expect the gradual disappearance of many spray chemicals. Reality today says use them, but sparingly. Consider them a slowly vanishing resource. The more you use them, the faster they will vanish. Hoard them—get as many years of help as you can. Heavy continuous use of pesticides (weekly preventive sprays, for example) accelerate the buildup of resistance and make your problem in your range more difficult. Each grower does develop his own strains of resistant bugs. The more you spray, the more resistant the insects will be in your houses.

Michael Parrella, one of our leading entomologists, suggests using substantially lower dilutions in a spray than are recommended. Quoting from a *GrowerTalks* article by Mike, March 1987, page 140: "A good example of low-dose strategy can be given for the leafminer. We have found that the material Citation gives approximately 80% leafminer control at $\frac{1}{5}$ the recommended rate. This is good control at a lowered rate but more importantly excellent compatibility with parasites is achieved with this rate. At the recommended rate, Citation's compatibility with parasites is considerably reduced. Similarly, a lower rate of Avid has been shown to give leafminer control equivalent to the labeled rate."

A key point: If the grower monitors his crops regularly (more later on this), he can often detect a "hot spot"—a new outbreak of an insect on a few plants. A

Spraying, like everything else, is done so efficiently in Holland. The grower draws the hose down the walk, then sends a radio signal back to the center walk. Now the hose automatically retracts. Note, though, that this grower is not using protective gear.

handsprayer application several times to these few plants will often avoid a major, costly application to the whole crop. It's a great way to minimize the use of sprays and resistance buildup.

Start moving toward alternate control methods—a variety of generally nonpoisonous yet effective methods. See more later in the chapter.

Mostly, adopt a new approach to pesticides. Use them, but sparingly. And only after you have exhausted all alternative control methods.

You'll see the acronym IPM a lot these days. It means integrated pest management, which in turn simply means integrating all the different means available to you to control insects on your crops—including chemical pesticides—but surely emphasizing other control measures a lot more.

Lastly, use pesticides "smart"—get to know life stages and which stage is vulnerable to which spray. Again, more on this later.

All this can easily cut your frequency (and annual cost) of pesticides in half or less. Now. It's there. It needs only the grower's conviction that doing these things is vital, that alternate controls do work and that they are good business.

Jim Kussow, Madison, South Dakota, does a serious job of monitoring yellow sticky tapes. In fact, the job is done by Ray Vantelz who goes through the entire operation weekly, checks all tapes and records what he sees. He's shown here with his portable equipment.

Cornell's IPM Scouting/Record Keeping

Cornell has a great way to achieve most of what I've been saying so far in this chapter. As of the early 1990s, Rod Ferrentino, Cornell extension coordinator and champion of this scouting/record keeping idea, reports that in just one year, 30 New York state growers reduced their pesticide applications by half or more. I've talked to growers who are part of this plan, and they readily support this claim!

To do this, the grower needs only a 10 power hand lens, a good notebook, a supply of yellow sticky tapes and a real conviction and dedication to the concept. Important also is a large scale floor plan of your range showing each bench.

The heart of this plan is twofold:

1. Regular scouting—looking carefully down each walk of each house for any signs of insects. It's done at least weekly and by someone who knows what to look for.

2. Use yellow sticky tapes positioned one/1,000 sq. ft. all through your crops.

Of course, the key part of this weekly scouting is careful reading of these sticky tapes—which insect, precise location and the number of insects that appear on the tape. All are carefully recorded by location and date.

The other key to Rod's plan is the grower's ability to identify life stages of key insects. The point again is that certain sprays at certain life stages are very effective, but at other life stages, all sprays are a waste of time and money. Again, spray smart.

Records are a must! Certainly recording all infestations with location, date and severity (on that map) is basic. Also, do record all pesticide applications. At first you have a lot of uncoordinated notes. But after a while the records develop a pattern—a small infestation on bench 9, several spray applications on that hot spot, and hopefully this ends the problem. And that's critical—clean up that hot spot early, before the whole range requires frequent, heavy spraying.

That's what Rod Ferrentino's plan is all about. Again, it's hoarding pesticides.

Rod works closely with especially poinsettia growers on the whitefly problem. He stresses the careful inspection of newly-received plants from propagators on arrival. Says Rod, "In my observation, most plants received by growers do carry at least a little of some pests. Clear them up in a quarantine house before they get out into your range."

Before new poinsettia stock plants arrive, give the stock plant house a thorough cleaning—eliminating certainly all weeds, all old plants of other crops, any trash or debris. Use disinfectant on walks and benches.

Start all this inspection/record keeping the day the stock plants arrive. A key point: Never let a whitefly buildup occur. Once they are well-established and a canopy of foliage develops, it's very tough to get at the insects, especially those down deep in the plant.

The whole idea is the preventive approach. Never let insects build up. I've talked to growers who have followed this system. They say it does keep whitefly infestations on poinsettias down and greatly minimizes spraying.

I'm talking only poinsettias here—but surely the approach is just as applicable and as effective on other crops, especially for the grower who is able to at least semi-specialize.

Parasites/Predators

In the natural ecology, insects (and all species) are kept in balance by natural predators. Yes, all insects do have natural enemies. The ladybug feeds on aphids, etc. In my observation, a real part of our insect problems these days is simply that the saturation of our growing areas with sprays kills these natural predators. Is this not the reason we have such devastating epidemics of leafminers, whitefly, etc.? The

John Vandermey, Fraser Nurseries, Surrey, British Columbia, does an especially thorough job of whitefly control (see text). Shown is the screening of the poinsettia stock plant area to ensure that no outside infestation gets at the stock plants. In the photo is James Robertson, Ball Superior.

natural predators intended by nature to keep the leafminer population in balance have been exterminated by our heavy, continued pesticide use. We're killing the good guys and shooting ourselves in the foot!

So now, a whole new science has built up. It first selects a predator that will feed on our problem insect—let's say whitefly. A usable predator here is *Encarsia formosa*. Large populations of them are released in poinsettia houses, build up (feeding on whitefly) and, in fact, can very effectively reduce and control the whitefly population if managed properly.

Listen to John Vandermey, who operates Fraser Nurseries in Surrey, British Columbia, [phone (604) 531-6225], with several acres of quality pot plants, "We have used Encarsia for three years now and are getting reasonable control. It's not perfect, but there's an acceptable level of whitefly—and without chemical pesticides.

"The key consideration that's moving us away from chemicals and toward these parasites is concern about all of us on our staff, including myself, being exposed to pesticide poisons. I just don't like to have them around. So, we're going to a lot of trouble to find other ways to do the job.

"Also, we are becoming increasingly aware of the problem of runoff water carrying dangerous pesticides to the ground waters in our area.

"A key to success with Encarsia in our experience has been to start early in the game. Before stock plants come in (March), we empty the houses, then cook the stock plant house (100°F for 4 days), then we spray the walks and benches with a 5% bleach solution. Of course all weeds, trash and any leftover plants from other crops are carefully removed. Also we cut back outdoor weeds, etc. near the greenhouses to minimize reinfection. We do lime under our benches.

"As stock plants are received, we first carefully check them for possible whitefly. They are then set into the stock plant area (about 10% of our 1-acre poinsettia crop). Immediately as stock plants arrive we introduce Encarsia. We start at 2,000 per week and continue weekly introductions of fresh Encarsia until late November.

"One of the key problems is reinfestation—whitefly are everywhere, especially in warm weather. We do screen our stock plant area for this reason. We use a fuzzy material that seems to allow enough air through the cooling pads to keep reasonable temperatures. It's called 'Insect Barrier' from Hydro-Gardens Inc., Colorado Springs, Colorado, [phone (719) 495-2266]. We have not found it necessary to screen our entire acre of poinsettias so far.

"From here on we watch the crop carefully weekly. As the crop spreads out to the full acre area we increase the weekly Encarsia introduction to 5,000 or even 10,000 per week. We would even double that if the infestation appeared to be serious. Our sticky tape tells us that, for example, in one 2-week period our Encarsia population increased twice as much as the whitefly. So, if managed carefully, Encarsia will control the problem.

"I've heard the rule of four wasps per plant that are needed to get whitefly control. If the fly population builds up, you may have to go to five per plant.

"You do have to sort of 'grow the Encarsia crop.' Be very careful about sprays that will kill them. They seem comfortable in normal poinsettia temperatures and light levels.

"We obtain our Encarsia population from Koppert, the Dutch firm specializing in predator/parasite populations—through a local outlet, Green Valley Fertilizer Company, Surrey, British Columbia, [phone (604) 591-8461]. There are many other sources for Encarsia (see later in this chapter).

"Several other area growers have been using Encarsia—with generally encouraging results. An example is Wes-Can Greenhouses, Eric Voogt, [phone (604) 530-9298]. As far as cost is concerned, we don't have accurate figures but, to us, the expense of the Encarsia is well worth what we're getting.

"Our market is accepting a small percentage of whiteflies on poinsettias. It must be very limited, though.

"An interesting sidelight: We've been fairly successful in controlling aphids in our cineraria crops (important here) with Safer soap. It seems to work!"

Another interesting comment I hear from growers in the Vancouver area: Growers who really depend on DIF (cool day/warm night technology) for plant height control are finding that cool days (mid-60s or lower) are too cool for Encarsia. They go dormant. These growers can and do rely on Encarsia from the arrival of poinsettia stock plants until mid-August—the start of cool days. From then on they use sprays heavily, I hear.

The following are, at least in most cases, prime producers of parasites and predators for growers.

American Insectaries
Escondido, California
(619) 432-0485

Applied Bionomics Ltd.
Sidney, British Columbia, Canada
(604) 656-2123

Better Yield Insects
Windsor, Ontario, Canada
(519) 727-6108

Gerhart Inc.
North Ridgeville, Ohio
(216) 327-8056

Hydro-Gardens Inc.
Colorado Springs, Colorado
(719) 495-2266

IPM Laboratories Inc.
Locke, New York
(315) 497-3129

Necessary Trading Co.
New Castle, Virginia
(703) 864-5103

Praxis
Allegan, Michigan
(616) 673-2793

Brinkman B.V.
The Netherlands
31-174811333

Richters
Goodwood, Ontario, Canada
(416) 640-6677

Rincon-Vitova Insectaries Inc.
Oak View, California
(805) 643-5407

Biotactics Inc.
Riverside, California
(714) 685-7681

Abbott Laboratories
North Chicago, Illinois
(800) 323-9597

Koppert B.V.
The Netherlands
31-189140444

Mycogen Corporation
San Diego, California
(619) 453-8030

Brinkman Horticultural Inc.
Stoney Creek, Ontario, Canada
(416) 643-6630

Whitmire Laboratories
St. Louis, Missouri
(800) 325-3668

Pathogens

There's a group—fungi, bacterium, virus and the nematode group—all of which cause a fatal disease in the host pest. In most cases, toxicity to humans is very low or nil. And in many cases they are very effective for control of specific insects. There are four groups:

- **Bacterium** is the most important group economically today. Several of these materials have been on the market and are used commercially. Most are from the genus Bacillus:

  1. *Bacillus thuringiensis* (Dipel commercially available), especially for control of caterpillars and other worms. There are many, many strains of *B. thuringiensis*.

  2. *Bacillus israelium* (commercially available as Gnatrol). Controls fungus gnat.

  3. *Bacillus thuringiensis San Diego* from Mycogen Corporation, [phone (619) 453-8030], for control of beetles. The commercial form is called M-1. Used for Colorado potato beetle control.

  Another form, *Bacillus pompilli*, is used commercially for grub control in turf.

- **Virus**—several being developed experimentally for use on Lepidoptera (worms), especially beet army worm. One material is *Beauveria bassiana,* which shows promise for worm control (beet army worm). It is not yet on the market. Lance Osborne, University of Florida, who knows this pathogen group well and is working actively on them, considers this an important potential group.

- **Nematodes** as carriers of bacteria. Here "friendly" nematodes are sprayed on crops. They carry a bacteria and when the target insect feeds on the nematodes it becomes ill from the bacteria and dies. This offers much promise for the control of leafminer, beet army worm (pupae), black vine weevil and also fungus gnat. In general, the nematode carriers are used on soil-inhabiting insects.

- **Fungi.** One material is used commercially in England for whitefly and aphid control. It is not licensed in the United States as yet. Another, *Bacilli paecilomyces,* is promising but not yet commercially available (patent applied for by Lance Osborne, University of Florida).

This whole group of pathogens offers important promise for the future. Mostly they are not toxic to either crops or people.

Several Other General Points on Insect Problems

- **Blood tests.** There are tests available that monitor the level of serum cholinesterase in the bloodstream. It will provide an early warning of too much exposure to organophosphate pesticide. Testing is recommended at a minimum of several times yearly (some doctors recommend monthly testing). If the level rises excessively (the doctor's opinion), stop applying organophosphates. For more details, see *GrowerTalks*, March 1987, page 106.

- **Low volume sprayers.** As of the early 1990s, there is a new group of sprayers available that permit pesticide application without the grower being in the greenhouse. At the end of the day, the grower sets the machine up, fills the tank, turns it on and leaves promptly. The machine fills the area (maximum half an acre) with a very penetrating fog. The machine turns itself off after 4 or 5 hours of operation. All this is after hours and after employees have all left. It is reported to be effective in control of many insects, no labor is required for application of the sprays, and best of all, there's almost no exposure of staff to pesticides. They are available from greenhouse supply firms across the United States.

Some Helpful References

These are mainly stories from the past several years in *GrowerTalks* magazine. These articles will be part of a book, published by *GrowerTalks*, on pest control, available in 1991. Here are a few of the most practical and helpful:

"IPM Scouting and Record Keeping Tips You Can Use," by Russell Miller, May 1990, page 25.

One of several excellent, new, low-volume spraying units. They operate at night after staff leaves and effectively clean up many insects at minimal cost.

"New York Poinsettia Growers Slash Pesticide Use and Achieve Better Whitefly Control," by Russell Miller, January 1990, page 56.

"Identifying the Most Serious Problem We Face Today—TSWV," by Russell Miller, July 1989, page 100. A good rundown on tomato spotted wilt virus.

"An Integrated Approach to Preventing Western Flower Thrips and TSWV in the Greenhouse," by Karen Robb and Michael Parrella, March 1989, page 26. An authoritative and very complete report on the wilt virus problem, including some comments on screening houses for thrip exclusion.

"Can We Beat the Bugs?," by Vic Ball. January 1988, page 40. A penetrating report by Robert Metcalfe, one of America's top entomologists, points up the perils we face and some answers he sees shaping up.

"Making Biological Controls Work for You," by Russell Miller, May 1988, page 52. An excellent and thorough review of predators/parasites available for control of principal insect problems.

"Resistance to Insecticides: What a Grower Can Do," by Michael Parrella, J.R. Baker, John Sanderson, R.K. Lindquist and A.D. Ali, March 1987, page 136. An excellent and very complete report on the general problem of insect resistance and what growers can do about it.

"Five Pests That Really Bug You," by five leading authorities, June 1987, page 34. An excellent, detailed report on the latest available control measures, both pesticide and biological for whitefly, thrips, spider mite, mealybug and leafminer. Each is written by a top entomologist and covers detailed, current, best methods to control the insect. There's practical help for the grower here.

"Sweet Potato Whitefly—This Pest Intends to Stay," by Russell Miller, November 1987, page 56. A complete report on the sweet potato whitefly problem—with current best controls.

GrowerTalks, August 1990, is a special insect control issue including several very helpful, practical articles.

Chapter 14

INSECT CONTROL—
A TABULATION

Table 1. Shelf Life of Selected Pesticides*

Pesticide	Shelf Life	Comments
Insecticides		
Carbaryl, WP (Sevin)	several years	WP formulations have been stored up to 5 years without loss of effectiveness. Settling will occur in flowable formulations.
Diazinon (Spectracide)	5 to 7 years	Diazinon formulations will last 5 to 7 years provided concentrate containers are tightly sealed (granular and dusts are kept dry).
Disulfoton (DiSyston)	2 years	Under normal conditions.
Azinphosmethyl, WP (Guthion)	2 years	Under normal conditions.
Malathion, WP	indefinite	Very stable when stored under proper conditions (decomposes when exposed to high temperature).
Oxydemeton-methyl (Meta-Systox-R)	2 years	Under normal conditions.
Methoxychlor, WP Resmethrin (SBP-1382)	indefinite 6 mos. to 2+ years	Stable under normal conditions; stable at 70°F for at least two years; and at 80°F for 6 months.
Aldicarb (Temik 10G)	indefinite if kept dry	Moisture causes active ingredient to be released from granules.
Acephate (Orthene 75SP)	2+ years	Under normal conditions.
Bacillus thuringiensis Dipel	6 mos. to 3+ years	WP formulations in closed containers, stored at 30% RH, should be stable for at least 3 years; use liquid formulations within 6 months.
Fungicides		
Benomyl, WP (Benlate)	2 years	If kept tightly sealed, shelf life should be at least 2 years. Keep dry (will decompose if exposed to moisture).
Captan, WP	3 years	Under normal conditions.
Herbicides		
Ammonium sulfamate, soluble salt (Ammate)	at least 2 years	Keep dry and under 100°F—no low temperature limit.
DCPA, WP (Dacthal)	at least 2 years	Under normal conditions.
Glyphosate, liquid (Roundup)	at least 2 years	Quite stable when stored under 140°F (do not allow to freeze).
Pronamide, WP (Kerb)	at least 2 years	Under normal conditions.
Paraquat, liquid	indefinite	Extremely stable, but do not allow to freeze.
Simazine, G, WP (Princep)	indefinite	Stored as long as 9 years under good conditions.
Oryzalin, WP (Surflan)	3 years	If stored at high temperatures, it should be mixed well before using.
Trifluralin, G (Treflan)	3 years	Loses 15 to 20% activity when stored at 100°F. Stable for 3 years when stored under dry conditions and temperatures no higher than 80°F.

Prepared by Richard K. Lindquist and edited by Harry K. Tayama, The Ohio State University, Columbus, Ohio.

Table 2. Insect and Mite Control*

Insect or Mite Pest	Chemical Control			Registered Crops	Comments
	Common Name	Brand Name	Formulation		
Aphids	Acephate	Orthene	75SP	anthurium, cactus, carnation, chrysanthemum, foliage plants, orchid, poinsettia, rose	Apply as foliar spray. Injures some chrysanthemum cultivars and foliage plants.
		Pt 1300	aerosol	airplane, aloe, begonia, bird of paradise, bloodleaf, Boston fern, cactus, calendula, carnation, chicken-gizzard, Christmas cactus, chrysanthemum, coleus, columbine, croton, dusty miller, euonymus, gardenia, geranium, German ivy, grapeleaf ivy, impatiens, jade plant, Moses-in-the-cradle, night-blooming cereus, ornamental pepper, orchid, pansy, peperomia, peperomia (variegated), philodendron, poinsettia, polka-dot plant, sansevieria, santolina, schefflera, shrimp plant, snapdragon, spider plant, sprengeri asparagus, velvetleaf, wandering Jew, white-edged Swedish ivy, zinnia	
	Bifenthrin	Talstar	10WP	all greenhouse ornamentals	Not effective against green peach aphid.
	Chlorpyrifos	Dursban	50WP	all greenhouse ornamentals	Be careful, might injure plants.
	Cyfluthrin	Tempo Decathlon	2EC 20WP	all greenhouse ornamentals	
	Diazinon	Diazinon	fog	carnation, chrysanthemum, rose	
		Pt 265 Knox Out	2 FM (micro-encapsulated)	African violet, agapanthus, ageratum, aluminum plant, alyssum, arrowhead, azalea, begonia, bird's nest fern, Boston fern, bottlebrush, cactus, calendula, camellia, celosia jewel box, chrysanthemum, cockscomb, coleus, cotoneaster, crepe myrtle, croton, daisy, dianthus, dogwood, escalonia, euonymus, flat-topped sedum, floss flower, friendship plant, gardenia, gazania, geranium, gold-dust, honeysuckle, hydrangea, ilex, impatiens, ivy, jade plant (crassula), Japanese aralia, juniper, leucothoe, lilac, malus, maranta, marigold, nandia, oleander, orchid, osmanthus, pachysandra, periwinkle, petunia, photinia, pineapple guava, pittosporum, podocarpus, primrose, privet, pyracantha, raphiolepsis,	

171

(continued from previous page)

Insect or Mite Pest	Chemical Control		Formulation	Registered Crops	Comments
	Common Name	Brand Name			
Aphids *(cont.)*	Diazinon *(cont.)*	Pt 265 Knox Out *(cont.)*		rhododendron, rose, salvia, sansevieria, scarlet sage, snake plant, snapdragon, spider plant, star jasmine, strawflower, Tahitian bridal veil, velvet plant (gynura), verbena, virvia, wandering Jew, wax plant, zinnia	
	Dichlorvos	Vapona	fog, smoke	all greenhouse ornamentals	Effective at lower greenhouse temperatures.
	Endosulfan	Thiodan	50WP, EC	all greenhouse ornamentals	Effective at higher greenhouse temperatures.
	Fenpropathrin	Tame	2.4EC	anthurium, bedding plants, chamomile, chrysanthemum, columbine, foliage plants, geranium, gladiolus, impatiens, liriope, lily, marigold, poinsettia, snapdragon	
	Fluvalinate	Mavrik	2F	all greenhouse ornamentals	
	Horticultural oil	Sunspray		azalea, begonia, camellia, chrysanthemum, crown-of-thorns, dieffenbachia, ferns spp., gardenia, geranium, jade plant, palm spp., philodendron, poinsettia, portulaca, zinnia	
	Insecticidal soap	Safers Conc.		all greenhouse ornamentals	Wet foliage thoroughly by spraying or wiping.
	Kinoprene	Enstar	5E	all greenhouse ornamentals	See label for precautions about plant injury.
	Lindane	Lindane	foliar spray, smoke, fog	all greenhouse ornamentals	
	Malathion		fog	carnation, chrysanthemum, geranium, rose, snapdragon	
	Naled	Dibrom	fog, smoke, vapors	all greenhouse ornamentals	
	Nicotine		emulsion, smoke	all greenhouse ornamentals	
	Oxamyl	Oxamyl	10G	allspice, aluminum plant, ardisia, artillery plant, asparagus fern, azalea, bird's nest fern, Boston fern, caladium, carnation, chrysanthemum, croton, dieffenbachia, dracaena, gardenia, gladiolus, gypsophila, hoya, iris, ivy, jade plant, leatherleaf fern, maranta, palm (chamaedorea [elegans] and Madagascar), peperomia, philodendron, rose, sansevieria, snapdragon	

Insect or Mite Pest	Chemical Control			Registered Crops	Comments
	Common Name	Brand Name	Formulation		
Aphids (cont.)	Oxamyl (cont.)	Vydate	2L	aloe spp., alyssum, ardisia, areca palm, asparagus fern, bird's nest fern, Boston fern, bromeliad, caladium, calathea, calendula, camellia, cactus (Christmas), carnation, chamaedorea (elegans) palm, chrysanthemum, citrus, coleus, crassula, dieffenbachia, dracaena, ficus, fuchsia, gardenia, gazania, geranium, gerbera, gladiolus, gynura, gypsophila, hedera, hibiscus, hoya, hypoestes, impatiens, iris, kalanchoe, lantana, leatherleaf fern, Madagascar palm, maranta, marigold, nephthytis, Norfolk Island pine, oleander, orchid, pachysandra, pansy, peperomia, periwinkle, petunia, philodendron, pilea, pittosporum, podocarpus, portulaca, pothos, pyrancantha, rhododendron, Rieger begonia, rose, royal palm, saintpaulia, salvia, sansevieria, spiraea, Ti plant, verbena, wandering Jew	
	Sulfotepp	Dithio Dithione	fog, smoke	all greenhouse ornamentals	May be formulated with tetradifon. With non-systemic insecticides, repeat application at 7-day intervals, as needed.
Caterpillars (e.g. loopers, cutworms, leafrollers, plume moths, beet armyworms)	Acephate	Pt 1300	aerosol	same as for aphids	
	Bacillus thuringiensis	Dipel	WP	all greenhouse ornamentals	Apply as foliar spray. Thorough coverage necessary.
	Bifenthrin	Talstar	10WP	all greenhouse ornamentals	
	Cyfluthrin	Tempo Decathlon	2E 20WP	all greenhouse ornamentals	
	Fenpropathrin	Tame	2.4EC	anthurium, bedding plants, chamomile, chrysanthemum, columbine, foliage plants, geranium, gladiolus, impatiens, liriope, lily, marigold, poinsettia, snapdragon	
	Fluvalinate	Mavrik	2F	all greenhouse ornamentals	
	Lindane		WP	all greenhouse ornamentals	Apply as foliar spray.
Fungus gnats (larvae)	Bacillus thuringiensis H14	Gnatrol	AS 12AS	all greenhouse ornamentals	Apply as drench.
	Diazinon	Pt 265 Knox Out	2FM	same as for aphids	

| Insect or Mite Pest | Chemical Control | | | Registered Crops | Comments |
	Common Name	Brand Name	Formulation		
Fungus gnats (larvae) (cont.)	Kinoprene	Enstar	5E	all greenhouse ornamentals	See label for precautions about plant injury.
	Oxamyl	Oxamyl	10G	same as for aphids	Apply as described for aphids. Repeat in 4 to 6 weeks.
		Vydate	2L	same as for aphids	
(adults)	Resmethrin	Pt 1200	aerosol	all greenhouse ornamentals	Repeat applications at 4- to 5-day intervals (adults).
Leafminers	Abamectin	Avid	0.15EC	all greenhouse ornamentals	Apply as foliar spray.
	Chlorpyrifos	Dursban	50WP	all greenhouse ornamentals	See label for precautions about plant injury.
	Cyromazine	Citation	75WP	container-grown chrysanthemums	
	Dichlorvos	Vapona	fog	all greenhouse ornamentals	Effective at lower greenhouse temperatures.
	Naled	Dibrom	fog	all greenhouse ornamentals	Might injure plants.
	Nicotine	several	emulsion	all greenhouse ornamentals	
	Oxamyl	Oxamyl	10G	same as for aphids	
Mealybugs	Acephate	Orthene	75SP	anthurium, cactus, foliage plants, orchid, poinsettia	Apply as foliar spray. Repeat at 2- to 3-week intervals. May injure some foliage plants.
		Pt 1300	aerosol	same as for aphids	
	Bendiocarb	Dycarb Ficam Turcam	76WP	African violet, ageratum, aglaonema, antirrhinum, ascarina, asplenium, azalea, baby's breath, begonia, calathea, calendula, celosia, chrysanthemum, cineraria, cissus, coleus, cyrtomium, daffodil, dahlia, dianthus, dieffenbachia, dracaena, dryopteris, epipremnum, fern spp., ficus, four-o-clock, fuchsia, gardenia, gazania, geranium, gladiolus, guava, hydrangea, hypoestes, impatiens, iris, ivy, lily-of-the-valley, maranta, marigold, mondograss, nasturtium, nephrolepis, nicotiana, ochrosia, pachysandra, pansy, petunia, philodendron, plumella, poinsettia, polypodium, portulaca, rose, sago palm, salvia, sansevieria, schefflera, shasta daisy, spathiphyllum, sprengeri asparagus, vandaonomea, verbena, vinca, wandering Jew, zinnia	Apply as foliar spray. Avoid use of alkaline water for best results.

Insect or Mite Pest	Chemical Control		Formulation	Registered Crops	Comments
	Common Name	Brand Name			
Mealybugs (cont.)	Bifenthrin	Talstar	10WP	all greenhouse ornamentals	
	Chlorpyrifos	Dursban	50WP	all greenhouse ornamentals	See label for precautions about plant injury.
	Cyfluthrin	Tempo Decathlon	2E 20WP	all greenhouse ornamentals	
	Diazinon	Pt 265 Knox Out	2FM	same as for aphids	
	Dichlorvos	Vapona	fog, smoke	all greenhouse ornamentals	Effective at lower greenhouse temperatures.
	d-Phenothrin	Sumithrin	2EC	same as for aphids	Foliar spray. Repeat at 10- to 14-day intervals.
	Fenpropathrin	Tame	2.4EC	same as for aphids	
	Horticultural oil	Sunspray		same as for aphids	
	Insecticidal soap	Safers Conc.		all greenhouse ornamentals	Repeat at 1- to 2-week intervals.
	Kinoprene	Enstar	5E	same as for aphids	
	Naled	Dibrom	vapor, fog	all greenhouse ornamentals	
	Oxamyl	Oxamyl	10G	same as for aphids	Repeat at 3- to 5-week intervals.
		Vydate	2L	same as for aphids	
	Sulfotepp	Dithio Plantfume 103	smoke, fog	all greenhouse ornamentals	
Millipedes	Malathion	Malathion	50WP	none	Greenhouse bench spray.
Mites (cyclamen mite)	Dicofol	Kelthane	WP, EC	all greenhouse ornamentals	Apply as foliar spray.
	Endosulfan	Thiodan	WP, EC	all greenhouse ornamentals	Apply as foliar spray.
(Two-spotted spider mite)	Abamectin	Avid	0.15EC	all greenhouse ornamentals	Apply as foliar spray.
	Bifenthrin	Talstar	10WP	all greenhouse ornamentals	
	Dichlorvos	Vapona	fog, smoke	all greenhouse ornamentals	Effective at lower greenhouse temperatures.
	Dicofol	Kelthane	WP fog	all greenhouse ornamentals	Apply as foliar spray on carnation, chrysanthemum and rose; apply as fog on other greenhouse ornamentals.
	Dienochlor	Pentac	WP, F	all greenhouse ornamentals	Apply as foliar spray.
		Pentac	fog	carnation, chrysanthemum, rose	

175

(continued from previous page)

Insect or Mite Pest	Chemical Control			Registered Crops	Comments
	Common Name	Brand Name	Formulation		
Mites (Two-spotted spider-mite) (cont.)	Fenbutatin-oxide	Vendex	WP, F	all greenhouse ornamentals	Apply as foliar spray.
	Fenpropathrin	Tame	2.4EC	same as for aphids	
	Fluvalinate	Mavrik	2F	all greenhouse ornamentals	Use higher rate for mite control.
	Horticultural oil	Sunspray		same as for aphids	
	Insecticidal soap	Safers Conc.		all greenhouse ornamentals	Repeat applications at 7- to 10-day intervals.
	Naled	Dibrom	EC	all greenhouse ornamentals	Apply as vapors.
	Oxamyl	Oxamyl	10G	same as for aphids	
	Sulfotepp	Dithio Dithione	fog, smoke	all greenhouse ornamentals	
Scale insects	Acephate	Orthene	75SP	anthurium, cactus, foliage plants, orchid, poinsettia	Apply as foliar spray. Repeat at 2- to 3-week intervals. May injure some foliage plants.
		Pt 1300		same as for aphids	
	Bendiocarb	Dycarb Ficam Turcam	76WP	same as for mealybugs	
	Chlorpyrifos	Dursban	50WP	all greenhouse ornamentals	See label for precautions about plant injury.
	Diazinon	Pt 265 Knox Out	2FM	same as for aphids	
	Horticultural oil	Sunspray		same as for aphids	
	Kinoprene	Enstar	5E	same as for aphids	
	Malathion		fog	all greenhouse ornamentals	
	Oxamyl	Oxamyl	10G	same as for aphids	
		Vydate	L	same as for aphids	
	Sulfotepp	Dithio Dithione	fog, smoke	all greenhouse ornamentals	
Slugs	Metaldehyde	Snarol Slugit Bug-Geta	bait, dust, emulsion	all greenhouse ornamentals	
	Methiocarb	Slug-Geta Mesurol	bait	all greenhouse ornamentals	

Insect or Mite Pest	Chemical Control			Registered Crops	Comments
	Common Name	Brand Name	Formulation		
Sowbugs	Cyfluthrin	Decathlon	20WP	all greenhouse ornamentals	
	Malathion		WP	none	Spray or dust growing medium surface.
Springtails	Malathion		WP	none	Spray or dust growing medium surface.
Thrips	Acephate	Orthene	75SP	anthurium, carnation, cactus, chrysanthemum, foliage plants, orchid, poinsettia	Apply as foliar spray. May injure some cultivars.
		Pt 1300	aerosol	same as for aphids	
	Bendiocarb	Dycarb Ficam Turcam	76WP	same as for mealybugs	
	Chlorpyrifos	Dursban	50WP	all greenhouse ornamentals	See label for precautions about plant injury.
	Cyfluthrin	Tempo Decathlon	2E 20WP	all greenhouse ornamentals	
	Diazinon		fog	aster, carnation, chrysanthemum, snapdragon	
	Dichlorvos	Vapona	fog	all greenhouse ornamentals	
	Fluvalinate	Mavrik	2F	all greenhouse ornamentals	
	Lindane		several	all greenhouse ornamentals	Apply as foliar spray, dust, fog.
	Malathion		fog	carnation, chrysanthemum, geranium, rose, snapdragon	
	Naled	Dibrom	EC	all greenhouse ornamentals	Apply as vapors.
	Nicotine		several	all greenhouse ornamentals	Apply as spray, dust, emulsion, smoke.
	Resmethrin	Pt 1200	aerosol	chrysanthemum	
	Sulfotepp	Dithio Plantfume 103	fog, smoke	all greenhouse ornamentals	Repeat applications of all materials (except granular formulations) at 4- to 5-day intervals to protect flowers.
Whiteflies	Acephate	Pt 1300	aerosol	same as for aphids	
	Bifenthrin	Talstar	10WP	all greenhouse ornamentals	
	Cyfluthrin	Tempo Decathlon	2E 20WP	all greenhouse ornamentals	
	Dichlorvos	Vapona	several	all greenhouse ornamentals	Apply as fog, smoke.

177

(continued from previous page)

Insect or Mite Pest	Chemical Control			Registered Crops	Comments
	Common Name	Brand Name	Formulation		
Whiteflies (cont.)	d-Phenothrin	Sumithrin	2EC	same as for aphids	Apply as foliar spray. Apply late afternoon or night. Repeat weekly.
	Endosulfan	Thiodan	several	all greenhouse ornamentals	Apply as foliar spray, dust, smoke.
	Fenpropathrin	Tame	2.4EC	same as for aphids	
	Fluvalinate	Mavrik	2F	all greenhouse ornamentals	
	Horticultural oil	Sunspray		same as for aphids	
	Insecticidal soap	Safers Conc.		same as for aphids	
	Kinoprene	Enstar	5E	all greenhouse ornamentals	See label for precautions about plant injury.
	Lindane		several	all greenhouse ornamentals	Apply as foliar spray, fog, smoke.
	Malathion		fog	carnation, chrysanthemum, geranium, rose, snapdragon	
	Naled	Dibrom	vapor, smoke	all greenhouse ornamentals	
	Oxamyl	Oxamyl	10G	same as for aphids	
		Vydate	L	same as for aphids	
	Pyrethrum	Pyrenone	EC	African violet, aster, azalea, begonia, camellia, carnation, chrysanthemum, dahlia, geranium, gladiolus, marigold, rose, rubber plant, wandering Jew	
	Resmethrin	SBP-1382	EC	ageratum, azalea, aster, begonia, calendula, chrysanthemum, coleus, geranium, ivy, petunia, poinsettia, rose, salvia	Apply as foliar spray. Apply during late afternoon or night. Repeat weekly.
		Pt 1200	aerosol	all greenhouse ornamentals	
			fog	arum lily, azalea, begonia, bird-of-paradise, Chinese fan palm, coleus, crane lily, dieffenbachia, English ivy, foundation palm, gardenia, geranium, India rubber tree, Norfolk Island pine, poinsettia, palm spp., snapdragon, wandering Jew, zephyr lily	
	Sulfotepp	Dithio Plantfume 103	fog, smoke	all greenhouse ornamentals	

Note: This chart is current as of October 1990. Note that much change has occurred in this field!
Prepared by Richard K. Lindquist, extension entomologist, The Ohio State University, for Ohio Florists' Association Bulletin.
Before purchasing and using any pesticide, check all labels for registered use, rates and application frequency. Generic names have been used for all pesticides. This list is presented for information only. No endorsement is intended for products mentioned, nor is criticism meant for products not mentioned.

SECTION V

Other Basics for Profitable Crops

Chapter 15

COMPUTERS

by Vic Ball

SUGGESTIONS ON GETTING STARTED

Already today (early 1990s), at least some computers are a part of most substantial commercial growing operations. And their role in efficient production is expanding rapidly.

Typically in such a situation, many growers are debating over whether to move on computers. Since computers can do three basic jobs for the growers, the other question is, which one first? Let's take a try at that one.

- **Accounting**—printing invoices, statements, doing payroll (including checks) and creating monthly and annual operating statements and balance sheets. Computers can also do cash flow projection and regular surveying and aging of accounts receivable and accounts payable. Computerized tax calculations and financial planning can also be done by growers. These applications are clearly the most widely used by growers today.

- **Crop planning**—does such tasks as crop planning, space planning, keeping inventory of plants available for sale, providing cost data and much more. They also provide much of the data helpful to the grower in planning his workload, his buying, etc.

- **Environmental control computers**—a newer, more specialized application used worldwide today. These "EC" computers do the basic temperature control job, but

George Lucht, a major geranium propagator in Minneapolis, relies heavily on computers for controlling the production of geranium cuttings. George is at home with his computer.

they also can do much more—on hundreds of ranges. Some key examples: controlling humidity, affecting major fuel savings (often 15% to 25%) by more efficient operation of the heating system. And equally important, they can make life so much easier for the grower. You'll find information about environmental control equipment, including computers, in Chapter 3.

WHICH ONE FIRST?

Clearly, controlling the greenhouse environment is the #1 job for computers in most ranges. Good, practical equipment is freely available. It does control temperature, humidity, light levels, etc. very well and at reasonable costs.

My vote for #2: accounting computers. To me, they affect the most direct help in labor and in cash management, the fastest payback for equipment cost and are the easiest to learn.

And for #3, especially for pot plant growers, the new pot plant production software. It can be a big help, especially in crop planning and costs, also in planning for cuttings, pots and labor for weeks out ahead.

The following paragraphs provide more details on both accounting and crop planning computers. Again, see Chapter 3 for more on environmental control computers.

COMPUTERIZED ACCOUNTING

The challenge here is to computerize (automate) the following activities in your business:
1. Entering the original sale into your system—order entry.
2. From this, prepare the invoice to the customer.
3. Prepare customer shipping documents, both for your shipping crew and the customer (to go with the product).
4. Update accounts receivable as a result of each sale.
5. Update general ledger.
6. Update balance sheet/operating statement.

Here's equipment needed to do these things, let's say on an acre or so of greenhouse, wholesale or retail:
1. Computer
2. Printer
3. Hard disk drive. Floppy disks are slower and, most important in greenhouse applications, are subject to corruption from moisture and dust in the air.
4. Appropriate software—readily available

Software needed for accounting-only application would be as follows:
1. Order entry/inventory control. This is the program used to enter all customer orders and sales tickets into your system. It is the basis for keeping inventory control records.
2. Accounts receivable
3. Accounts payable
4. General ledger
5. Payroll (the ability to write checks and keep tax records)

Each of these will come to the grower on a floppy disk, which the grower can immediately transfer to his hard disk (built in).

Larger users: The owner of a half acre or perhaps an acre of wholesale pot plant range with a limited number of sales tickets can probably handle his entire work-load of accounting and crop planning activities with one computer and one printer. However, the same acre of greenhouse with an active retail department with thousands of sales tickets, especially a lot of credit sales, would probably need several terminals (a computer with typewriter console).

A busy or larger retail operation might need half a dozen or even several dozen of these terminals depending on the volume, especially of invoices, to be written.

An important point here: A single terminal might handle the job if you are willing to delay writing invoices in order to create payroll or to do financial statements, for example. But if a business is to be operated efficiently, there should be enough terminal capacity to keep both the flow of invoice writing and the other accounting activities up to date. It's the old story—how can you manage your business efficiently if you don't have up-to-date information?

Training

Another important point in selecting equipment is to select the supplier who offers good training for you or your staff person who will do the computer work. This should mean both initial training upon receiving the equipment and also ongoing support, answers to questions and problems, updating of software as better programs become available. Software is constantly improving, of course.

Security of Information

A point in favor of computerizing: It permits real security. It's standard practice and, by the way, highly recommended that all computerized data be copied off the hard disk daily or at least weekly and stored out of the building. What this means is that in case of a fire, no matter how severe, you will still have such vital records as your accounts receivable, accounts payable, etc. We've all heard the story that 80% of businesses who lose their accounts receivable in a fire never reopen their doors! With manual records, you just can't keep the copies elsewhere—it isn't practical.

How About Nursery Production?

Growers producing both flowers or bedding plants and hardwood nursery stock can certainly include their nursery production in all this computerized equipment. Of course, nursery production can also be handled with almost the same equipment.

Sources of Equipment

Some sources of equipment are IBM computer stores, Inacomp computer stores and Computer Land.

COMPUTERIZED POT PRODUCTION

There is presently available very practical and helpful software for pot plant production. The Gartplan system (PKM in Denmark) described here was created in Denmark by Per Kaerlof Moller. It's available in the United States from Midwest GROmaster [phone (708) 888-3558]. I saw it in use at Knud Jepsen's range in

You'll find production control computers on the desks of major growers worldwide and, most often, they know how to use them! Here's Adrian Moerman, a major northern England pot grower, who uses the Gartplan system from Denmark.

Denmark and had a good discussion with Knud, who is a major kalanchoe and mini pot rose grower. These notes are based on Knud's experience.

He reports that about 50 Danish, 10 Dutch and several English growers are using the equipment now (early 1990s). "Most Danish pot growers are using this equipment today," he says. Knud is a 250,000-sq.-ft. grower, very much a leader in efficient production and twice a speaker at GrowerExpo, by the way.

The Gartplan system includes three modules:
- Production planning. This can be tied to their Danish marketing co-op, by the way.
- Sales/P & L—sales by units, by dollars and profitability.
- Labor cost analysis.

I asked Knud about his goal—what he wanted to get from this software. His response:
- First, maximize space use. In fact, he reported 98.4% space utilization in a recent year.

- Maximize sales versus production—to sell as high a percentage of available production as possible.
- Maximize the use of labor—have the amount of labor needed on a given day and no more.
- To have available all supplies needed each day: cuttings, pots, mix, etc.
- To be able to plan labor availability to have the number of man hours each day that are needed for that day's work.

Knud was quite pleased with the system and is continuing to use it as the basis for his pot plant and direct stick pot rose production.

Space Planning

A key benefit of the system is that the grower can see (visual presentation) six months or a year ahead what percent of each house will be filled with plants, according to present production plans. He shows you a bar graph on the computer—one bar for each greenhouse. If the bar reaches the 100% line, the house is full. If it's a little over, there's excess product for the space available. Again, it's a visual presentation. It's all done in square meters of bench space per week; the U.S. system is done in feet and yards. Knud plans all kalanchoe crops a full year ahead.

Given this accurate preplanning of space, Knud is now able to forecast supplies and manpower needed each week for up to 52 weeks ahead. He gets the number of unrooted cuttings to be stuck in pots, the schedule of pots, soil needed and man hours of labor needed for each week. This goes to his production foreman. Of course, as the week arrives, he and his production people know exactly how many cuttings they will be sticking in pots and how many plants will be moved to the production area, etc.

"The Computer Helps Us Sell Plants"

The software provides for each week ahead how many kalanchoe plants will be available for sale, how many were sold for that same week a year ago, and, for a given week, let's say several weeks ahead, he can always tell how many plants by variety are unsold for that week. The result: You sell what you have and don't sell what you don't have.

The system also gives Knud records of past sales by week, by customer and by pot sizes (10½ cm., 9 cm., 6 cm.). On a given Monday morning he can bring up from his computer the number of plants that were sold last week, along with who bought them, the number of plants booked for this week and number available. Knud says, "We used to do a lot of this on a big wall chart, but it's a whole lot less work with a computer and much easier to change."

On Costs and Profitability

The system gives Knud accurate costs per plant, per variety and per pot size. Given the number of units forecast a year ahead and the price per unit, it's now possible to budget sales and also costs for labor and other components of the plants.

The system creates a profit and loss statement for each crop on a monthly or even more often basis. Knud says, "The computerized profit and loss for the crop for the year will match our accounting figures normally within 1%."

Other Comments

For one thing, who manages the computer process? Knud reports one half-time person enters the data, and he says, "I do some of the planning myself. I spend time with the computer studying sales past and future and constantly adjusting production plans."

Costs for the system: The software in the early 1990s is $4,000 to $5,000 and the IBM hardware is $2,000 to $5,000 (including the printer).

Knud says, "Per Moller has made a new version of his software. I have tested this new version and it seems to be very user-friendly."

An interesting comment: Recently Knud was working toward tying the system in with their Priva environmental control computer so that night temperatures could be bumped a bit following a sunny day—to better utilize the sunny weather that occurs.

The problem with books about computers for growers is that the equipment and software available changes so fast! Lastly, I understand that there are a number of other database systems that growers can set up themselves to achieve at least some of these objectives. Also, software is available providing computerized links to on-line locations within your range.

OTHER USEFUL SOFTWARE

There are several spreadsheet softwares on the market today that are extremely useful for certain applications. Examples are Lotus 123, Symphony and Excel. You get, say, Lotus 123 on a floppy disk, and you can sketch out ideas and plans right on the terminal. It enables you to make an electronic spreadsheet. A good example: You've got 20 greenhouses. You put numbers from 1 to 20 across the top of the screen, then you list your 10 major crops down the left margin. This information is all "typed" onto the screen. Then you can start filling in the crops. Fill greenhouses 1 to 10 with Easter pot mums. If it doesn't quite fit, you quickly "rub it out" and start over. As you get to know it, Lotus 123 and systems like it can multiply, divide, etc. It can divide a whole row of figures by a constant. Lastly, when you get your "plan" all done, it can be fed directly to your hard disk—and, of course, be printed.

An example of word processing software is WordPerfect. It's very helpful in preparing letters, writing papers and articles. (This 15th *Ball RedBook* edition is all being done on a word processor.) Now you can create a form letter to go to 500 customers. They will all be typed originals, and the computer can automatically type in each customer's name and address and change a word or two at the bottom of the letter if you wish.

An example of an electronic filing system program is dBase. You can put 1,000 names and addresses into your "file" (that hard disk again) in any order. You can call up all the Bs or Cs or all those who live in various nearby towns. It's great for keeping your customer list sorted out by groups as you wish. For instance, you can write a spring promotion letter to all of your homeowner accounts.

Chapter 16

COLLECTING YOUR BILLS

by Andrew C. Stavrou
Ball Seed Company

Granting credit involves taking on risk. The control you administer regarding who you give credit to and the techniques you employ to collect past-due amounts owed your business will have a real impact on the profitability of your business.

The following points have to do with two basic areas of effective credit and collection management:

1. Control—who you give credit to and why.
2. Collection tips—how to get your past-due monies paid to you as quickly as possible.

Before proceeding, let me emphasize one very basic, often overlooked, point. That is, no matter how good a collection technique you employ, you will only be paid when the other party has the money to pay you. Today's greenhouse grower who wholesales material is being called upon more and more to grant credit. That doesn't necessarily mean that it is in his best interest to do so. Being prepared when entering into a business relationship with information as the basis for making your credit decision will make your accounts receivable portfolio a better quality portfolio for now and in the future. Before you jump into an open credit situation, remember:

Control your receivable by knowing your customer. I am not of the school that mandates signed credit applications from everybody. If you know that the account that you have called on is solid (national chain store, long-time local merchant with a great reputation), that should be good enough. But, there are always going to be those

189

situations coming up where you really don't know too much about the other party. Being prepared to ask for specific information is just plain, good business sense. I recommend that you employ the use of a short form credit application in these situations to get this information.

XYZ Greenhouse

Confidential
Credit Application

Firm Name		Phone	Date	
Mailing Address	City	State	Zip Code	
Street Address	City	State	Zip Code	
Shipping Address	City	State	Zip Code	

Company Owners or Officers

Name	Title	Social Security No.	
Home Address	City	State	Zip Code
Name	Title	Social Security No.	
Home Address	City	State	Zip Code

Corporation	Partnership	Sole Proprietorship	Date Established	Sales Tax No.

Mortgage Holder/Landowner	Are you operating under the jurisdiction of any court?		Yes ☐ No ☐
Name	Present Balance	Monthly Payment	
Address	City	State	Zip Code

Bank Reference

Bank Name	Name of Banker		
Address	City	State	Zip Code
Checking	Account No.	Savings	Account No.	Borrowing	Non-Borrowing

Trade References

Name	Amount Owed	
Address	City	State	Zip Code
Name	Amount Owed	
Address	City	State	Zip Code
Name	Amount Owed	
Address	City	State	Zip Code

Credit Line Desired

I certify that the above information is correct.

Signature _____ Title _____ Date _____

As you can see, the short form credit application is asking for the names of the principals, how the business is set up (corporation, partnership, proprietorship), when it started, a bank reference and three trade references. Also on the short form is a line specifically related to the credit line the customer desires.

This single piece of paper will give you a good deal of background information and should be enough to take care of the credit relationship question. Assigning the credit reference checking to an office person would be a good idea. If you know of any other companies that the customer in question is doing business with, have that person check with them as well. Run a check for uniformity in the way that they pay their bills; all references should show payment as being prompt, with banking relations being satisfactory and no NSF checks whatsoever showing up. If you see a disparity between the references that the customer supplied and the references that you supplied yourself, you can figure that trouble is brewing and what they have probably done is cherry-picked the references that they wanted you to contact, neglecting those that they have not been taking care of.

I believe what you will find is that most credit worthy accounts will be glad to share their trade and bank reference information with you on this short form. As a group, these customers are proud of the relationships that they have built up through the years and are eager to show off. By seeking out that information along with the credit line desired, you are starting your business relationship in a very healthy manner. Both sides know exactly what is expected.

Properly invoice the transaction. Delays in payment are often brought about for reasons other than lack of ready cash. Your invoices should always contain complete information. That would include, but not be limited to, the following:

- Full name and address of the customer along with the telephone number and name of your contact.
- The invoice number and date of invoice.
- The date of shipment.
- The full product description.
- Customer purchase order number (if applicable).
- Specify the terms of sale. If net 30 days, say so.
- Specific amount owed.
- If allowing a prompt pay discount, spell out the latest day the prompt pay will be considered as a full payment.
- The specific due date.

There have been many instances, especially with larger chain stores, where if a piece of information is missing, not only are you not contacted about the missing information until you request payment from the customer, but you are also put on the bottom of their payments list once you supply the correct information to them. Needless to say, this will negatively impact your cash flow. Be your own best friend. Be sure your invoices have all the necessary information, and if you have specific customers who are requesting additional specified items, be sure to include it on the original invoice. So much of what you control rests on documentation. Follow through on the front end; dividends will come in the form of prompt payments.

Be timely. Invoices should be generated immediately after the ship date; do not delay. It will only delay your payment. Remember, inventory equates to accounts receivable once it is out the door. There should be absolutely no lag time between your taking that inventory internally and equating it with an accounts receivable entry. Generally speaking, the payment terms begin not on the date of the shipment, but on the date the invoice is generated. Again, this is a question of your being your own best friend. Get the invoice out as soon as the material ships.

COLLECTION TIPS

Assign one person to collection. If possible, give it to somebody who is not in the sales function. You will also want to give this person a title (collection supervisor, account representative, credit manager). Any of these titles would be appropriate, depending on just how important the collection function is to your operation. The larger, more diverse your customer base is, the more I would lean to making the title that of credit manager.

Track your past-dues at least twice per month. A letter should go out requesting any past-due money when the account has invoices that are 15 days or more beyond the due terms. On an initial letter request, especially with any institution (school, hospital) account, it is a good idea to include a copy of the invoice with the letter. This should and will cut down on some of the collection time necessary to get paid.

Keep track of all letters you are sending. This should include the name of the contact and the date the letter was sent. Copies aren't really necessary as long as you know the tone of the letter, thus making a follow-up easier.

Telephone accounts that have not responded to your letters. I would say within 10 to 15 days after the letter is sent out, a follow-up phone call is the thing to do. Again, keep a log by account of exactly what activity has taken place. You should indicate who was spoken to and what was said. This will allow you to build a historical file with which you will be able to match promises with results. Therefore, you will be able to track those accounts that were able to keep their word versus those who were stalling for more time.

Make every call count. If you can't get to your contact, leave a complete message and get the name of the person you are leaving the message with. Always inquire and be sure to listen. You will find that many times you can spin off to another party and get the answer you need. For those situations where that simply isn't the case, be sure to leave yourself in a position where your next phone call won't be a surprise to anybody. Also insist on a return phone call, and ask when you can expect it. If you contact the correct person, you should always attempt to work out a complete payment arrangement on the entire account. It is very easy to get on the phone and work up a partial payment situation, necessitating an additional phone call down the road. Pushing for a comprehensive payment plan is a great idea. You will also be able to figure out whether the slow payment that you are calling about is a one-time deal, or whether you can expect the same sort of thing to happen in the future.

Follow up any commitment such that if the commitment does not come through, you are contacting that party by phone within three business days after the account failed to live up to its promise. Again, here it is important to be as specific as possible. If someone tells you a check will be in the mail within a few days, see if you can get them to indicate a specific date. This will allow for easier tracking of what money you are expecting.

Use new shipments or orders as leverage to collect old balances. It is important that the person who is in charge of your collection area interface closely with the sales area. It is meaningless to try to collect an open account receivable balance that you are concerned about when you keep shipping material to the account. You are sending a very clear signal to the customer that they can get away with pretty much anything they want.

Keep a running tab of your aged trial balance and build up a historical file. This should be done with each account as well as your total A/R portfolio. This will enable you to see how much of your total receivables are current, past due by one to 30 days, etc. It is a great tool to use in order for you to weigh out your short-term borrowing requirements, should you have any, in that you can have a better handle on what you can expect your receivable portfolio to be doing. These reports should also be used for purposes of reviewing open accounts. Regular meetings between your collection person and ownership is always time well spent. Monthly meetings of this nature are advised. It might take 10 minutes or three hours. Either way, it is good to review what is there.

Don't state something you don't mean. This is where sales and credit areas interfacing becomes very important. Before you allow your collection person to use an order as leverage, make sure you are prepared to cancel. It is important not to bluff, as credibility will quickly slip away.

If the collection looks hopeless, plan ahead and talk to a collection agency or attorney before the next critical phone call takes place. By getting your ducks in a row, you will know exactly what is in the offing should something not take place. Collection agencies are extremely competitive; most of them base their fees on strictly a contingency basis. (They get a percentage of what is collected. If nothing is collected, they get nothing.) If you do plan on sending something to a collection agency or attorney, do not ship anything further until the old collection situation has been resolved. This is also a great opportunity for the boss or owner to take the account over from the collection person. This move adds a sense of urgency to the situation that may just get some cash rolling in.

Not to be overlooked is the importance of setting credit lines and revising them as needed. As a basis for revision, use historical data (how the account has paid and kept commitments, as well as information on the short form credit application). Everyone in your account portfolio should have a credit line (a credit limit) assigned to them. This doesn't mean that it is an out-and-out maximum limit. It also doesn't necessarily mean that it has to be exceeded before you do anything on the collection end. The invoice due date should trigger a collection response. If you see that an account is not able to take care of its obligations in a timely manner and it looks like their credibility is slipping, you might want to lower the credit line to the existing accounts receivable balance that you have open and start holding orders.

On the contrary, if you have a customer who has been paying his bills on the button, and you now have a situation where your sales volume can grow appreciably, ask yourself the questions that you would be asking the customer on the short form credit application. Is there enough there, in your mind, that would enable you to lift up the credit line to a point where you could please them on the sales end of things and also make you feel good about your specific situation? If the answer to that question is no, then I would recommend that you contact your customer and have him fill out the credit application, explaining to him that your credit exposure is going up and you need this additional confidential information.

I have spoken in this article about the need for being timely for charting out the trial balances of your accounts individually and in their entirety, about the importance of getting invoicing out promptly and so forth. Needless to say, the use of a computer would make a lot of these functions easier. I personally recommend using a computer for at least aged trial balance purposes, as well as invoicing purposes, for any operation of 20,000-sq.-ft. or more. The price of a computer with a printer and off-the-shelf software has gotten low enough where it is affordable for an operation of this size. The nice thing about off-the-shelf software packages that are now available is that they do not demand programming expertise by anyone in your company, but rather only data inputting onto a disc in formats that, by and large, are easily understood and flexible enough to meet your business needs. The only recommendation I would make when choosing your hardware is that you purchase something that is compatible with more sophisticated software. You never know—down the road, you may want to upgrade, and why start all over again?

Credit and collections is a game of persistence. Doing your homework on the front end, knowing who your customers are, having background information on them and keeping background information to use when you need it makes the collection effort much easier. It also allows you to set a realistic credit line based on the risk involved. If a collection effort is necessary, making each call count, documenting what you are doing and keeping track of the success ratio that your collection person is having will make credit and collection decisions easier to make down the road. It also makes the credit and collection function easier to take over from someone who may have left your company; you will already have housed information that speaks for itself.

It is also important to remember that chronic collection problems may best be dealt with by simply not doing any additional credit business with them. This, of course, assumes that you have a home for the material that otherwise would have gone to this company. You should always strive to pool your orders toward companies that can pay within your terms. Chances are you have some good customers, and you have some customers who could get better. Being your own best friend in this scenario will make life easier for you and will allow for a healthier A/R portfolio that will serve as the foundation for your business growth.

Chapter 17

XERISCAPING

by Vic Ball

Especially in certain areas (Santa Barbara, for example), drought in the early 1990s is importantly limiting bedding plants sales. Local authorities are imposing severe restrictions on water use for ornamentals. It's an especially serious problem on lawns, but certainly a real limitation on bedding plant use. Also, to some extent, on the use of woody ornamentals, especially evergreens, which do require water. The following points on this are from a circular published by Shemin Nurseries [phone (708) 773-8090]. I think it brings some constructive thinking to the problem.

XERISCAPE CAN HELP YOU:

- To respond to water use restrictions resulting from drought conditions.
- To plan ahead *before* municipal water conservation regulations.
- To save on maintenance labor and material costs.
- To ensure basic continuation in times of drought or severe water restrictions.
- To expand landscape contractor/interiorscaper business.

195

Basic Steps

1. **Good design and planning.** Group plants according to their water needs. There is no need to completely eliminate high water use plants. Simply group them together so that they can be watered properly, yet efficiently.

2. **Improve the soil.** Prepare the soil properly, ensuring that there is an adequate amount of organic matter available. Equip it to conserve moisture.

3. **Use hydro-gel.** Apply additives to the soil that aid in water retention and better availability of water to the planted material. Hydro-gel can realize up to a 50% savings in water use.

4. **Use ground cover.** The lawn is the biggest water user in the landscape. Try to limit it by using alternative ground covers. Besides retaining soil moisture, ground covers offer a wide variety of textures.

5. **Low-water-use plant selections.** Select plants that have minimum water requirements. This need not limit selection as there is a wide range of plants that survive well with minimal watering. The variety includes natives as well as exotics, ranging from ground covers to trees to flowering plants and shrubs.

6. **Use mulches.** Mulching reduces evaporation and keeps the soil moist. Seventy-five percent of water that falls is lost through evaporation or runoff. Mulching can save 90% of lost water.

7. **Incorporate low volume irrigation.** Irrigate efficiently. Use water systems that are designed specifically for economy of usage. State-of-the-art sprinklers offer spray patterns that can be adjusted to cover sharply defined or variably shaped areas. Whenever possible, use drip irrigation systems or soaker hoses because they pinpoint the water exactly where it is needed.

8. **Proper landscape maintenance.** After the first year's establishment, xeriscaped gardens almost always require less watering and weeding.

Chapter 18

SOIL MIXES

by Vic Ball*

Using the correct soil mix is just as important as choosing the right variety or proper temperature control. The soil mix serves several important functions.

- **Provides for air and water exchange.** If a mix is too tight with too little porosity, then it will hold too much water in its pore spaces, not allowing sufficient air for developing a healthy, well-branched root system. This will slow down growth, often missing scheduled flower dates. On the other hand, if the mix is too open, it will require too much water too often, increasing production labor costs, not to mention the quantity of water and nutrients needed to produce the crop.

- **Serves as a reservoir for nutrients.** While the mix serves as a reservoir for nutrient exchange, it also is critical for buffering pH and fertilizer salts. Soil pH is extremely critical for optimum nutrient uptake. With such a soil mixture as one part soil, one part peat and one part perlite, the optimum soil pH should be approximately 6.2; whereas with an organic mixture of bark, peat, perlite and vermiculite, the optimum pH is 5.2 to 5.5, a whole unit lower. Also, the ability of the soil to hold and release nutrients will help maximize the efficiency of the fertilizer, whether it's a slow release or water soluble.

*Ron Adams, Ball Seed Company, contributed much of this chapter.

- **Should adequately support the plant.** Keep in mind, though, a plant in a bedding plant container requires a different support than does a tall pot plant such as a 4″ geranium. If a plant is not properly supported, then extra care will have to be taken to stake or tie up the plant. This means extra labor, increasing production costs. An inadequately supported plant with poor soil structure or too lightweight soil can also reduce plant shelf life. For instance, many times when plants are being shipped, they are jostled during shipping. In a lightweight mix, plants will not be adequately supported and will be floppy and loose when they reach their destination—not being of excellent quality.

- **Should be reproducible.** You should be able to consistently reproduce that mix time after time, season after season. Just imagine growing on a year-round pot mum schedule and changing your mix every week. This would definitely increase your frustrations in handling that crop, trying to adapt to each drainage or fertilizer requirement.

- **Should be readily available.** Historically, this item has not been a traditional function of the soil mix, but today as we're dealing with larger production areas, any soil mix or the materials for the soil mix should be readily available when you need it—be it a commercial mix from a factory or local components. For instance, if you are making your own mix and peat moss is an ingredient, I have seen seasonable outages of peat moss due to poor harvest conditions at the peat bogs.

  Another aspect of it is where you store your mix. Is it properly stored where the mix is available? For instance, if you store it outside and you encounter an extremely wet and rainy period, can you get out and bring your mix into the greenhouse? Another example is in the middle of winter—is your soil mix pile frozen to the point that it is unavailable? These are things that you want to consider—whether it's your own mix or whether it's a commercial mix—the availability of the material when you need it.

  Commercially prepared soil mixes are currently receiving much attention. These mixes contain ingredients from straight peat moss to blends using bark, perlite, vermiculite and peat. It is important to understand that you can grow in almost any medium. But if you compare the media functions to your own conditions, there will be one best medium that fits your needs.

The Case for Specialist Mixes

There are several factors that have created this shift away from growers making their own soil mixes. Let's take a look at some of these:

- **Consistency.** A large firm making soil mixes on a year-round basis can specialize and consistently make the same mix to the same standards. Therefore, you have peace of mind when you place an order that the mix is the same as in the previous batch that you have been using.

- **Scarcity of materials.** As communities have developed around greenhouses and major metropolitan areas, good top soil has either become unavailable or very expensive to prepare and store on site. Weed killer contamination is a very real problem in field soils today. One clear trend of the early 1990s is that outdoor field soil use as a component of growing mixes is rapidly vanishing. Grower after grower I talked with in preparing the 15th edition reported, "We included 10% of field soil last year but that's the last of outdoor soils for us. Too hard to get and too many weed killer problems."

Other ingredients can also become scarce, such as Canadian peat moss during a year of poor harvest or a local supplier of bark not having his normal quantity of supplies because the housing industry has not created the demand for lumber, slowing down bark production.

Large specialist firms making mixes are able to overcome these commodity shortages and are able to maintain larger supplies because of economy of scale. Therefore, they can ensure a consistent supply to the marketplace.

- **Cost.** More growers have recognized that considerable man hours have gone into soil preparation, competing with the time that could be spent in production. It not only takes time to put the mixes together, but it also requires management time and organizing, planning and resource commitment, such as inventory dollars, for raw materials. As with any production materials, you want to tie up as few dollars as necessary in materials or labor. Buying mixes has freed up this time and resource dollars so you only have to inventory finished, ready-to-use mix, and you can schedule it to arrive when you need it.

- **Convenience.** Using a commercially prepared mix allows you to concentrate your efforts on other areas of the growing operation. Let's face it, there are several things to consider in making your own mix, such as particle size, pH adjustments, soluble salt levels and sterility. It is much more convenient to depend on an outside supplier who specializes in mixes and manufacturing than to dilute your own time and resources.

Cost Estimates

Next, just to give you an idea of what it costs to make mixes, Paul Nelson at North Carolina State University sat down and figured it out using a fixed-cost determination method of preparing mixes, depending on management size and how much it would cost when he figured in all the components, as well as the physical equipment required. This just goes to show that if you take the same factors into consideration that most commercial manufacturers use, the mix cost range per cubic yard that he showed was anywhere from $48 to $75, depending on your operation size. Commercial mixes are available in the marketplace from approximately $40/cu. yd., depending on where you are located, up to $70/cu. yd. depending on the type and quality of the mix.

The fact is, growing in the 1990s is done mostly in artificial mixes. All but the very large growers use a specialist-produced mix.

Chapter 19

STERILIZING SOIL

by Vic Ball

In the days of field soil growing, sterilizing soil, often with steam, was the rule. Today, many pot plants and bedding crops are growing in commercial mixes, and growers generally do not feel sterilizing these mixes is necessary. Why?

- Pine bark, a component of many of these mixes, is known (from scientific research) to have a depressant effect on many soil pathogens. Plants grown in mixes with pine bark seem to resist most diseases. Peat moss comes from "below ground" and therefore tends to be generally free of pathogens and weed seed.

- Vermiculite, perlite and polyurethane particles are all manufactured products that are generally considered disease-free.

For whatever reason, most crops today are grown in commercial mixes, and rarely do I see growers sterilizing them for most of today's commercial crops.

Some growers do use some soil, however, and, especially in some disease-prone crops, do sterilize either with steam or by chemicals. Here briefly is the way sterilizing is generally done.

STEAMING BULK SOIL

Two systems generally used:

- **Commercially produced soil-steaming wagons.** Bouldin & Lawson [phone (615)

Here's the late Len Shoesmith with an example of a steam sterilizing cart. It's simply a box mounted on wheels with steam pipes across the bottom of the box. Soil is piled onto the box, covered and steamed, and then potting can be done right on the cart bed.

Used cement mixers are often used to mix and steam soil mix.

668-4090], a Tennessee firm, offers a rubber-tired, four-wheel wagon designed to steam sterilize soil. It has pipes across the bottom with holes that allow steam to escape. The wagon is filled with soil, the steam is turned on, and the job gets done. Bouldin & Lawson makes these on a custom basis.

- **Concrete mixers.** I still occasionally see growers steaming soil mixes with salvaged concrete mixers. The mix is dumped into the mixer, live steam is injected until the soil reaches the desired temperature, and then it's dumped out.

For a guide on temperatures needed for sterilizing, see the following thermometer graph.

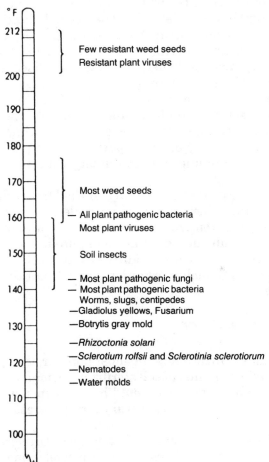

This graph shows temperatures necessary to kill pathogens and other organisms harmful to plants. Most of the temperatures indicated here are for 30-minute exposures under moist conditions. (From Baker, K. F., ed., "The U.C. System for Producing Healthy Container-Grown Plants," California Agriculture Experiment Station and Extension Service Manual 23, 1957.)

203

by Kenneth Horst
Cornell University
Ithaca, New York

A number of chemicals have been formulated as liquids to be applied to soil for killing nematodes, certain insects, weeds and more recently, fungi. Most of these chemicals become gases and diffuse in soil to bring about kill. Soil temperature must be 50°F or above at the 6″ level to permit good gas dispersion. Soil must be tilled to reduce or bury crop debris and be in good planting condition when treated.

One of the problems arising from sterilization or near sterilization of soil with materials such as chloropicrin, methyl bromide or steam is that such treatment removes most organisms—beneficial as well as disease-producing—from the soil. Under such conditions, the first organisms to be introduced have very little competition and can develop very rapidly. If a disease-producing organism is introduced first, serious problems may result. For this reason, when using soil treated this way, it is imperative to use clean planting containers, tools and other equipment, and especially clean or pathogen-free planting stock. Because of the difficulty of doing this under most nursery conditions, other approaches to the problem need to be found.

Of course, nearly all soil steaming in the United States is done to the 180°F, 30-minute standard. Where less than a complete kill of soil life is wanted, however, one approach is to pasteurize the soil at temperatures of 160°F for 30 minutes—the so-called aerated-steam method. Another approach is through the use of fungicides applied either as drenches or as additives to the soil. These may either prevent the re-entry of disease-producing organisms or prevent their development in the soil, should they become introduced.

Chemicals—Pro and Con

While steam sterilization is the most popular, the most reliable and generally the most economical method of soil sterilization, many occasions arise where steam is not available and chemicals would be less expensive than setting up a steam system. Certainly, over the last several years, progress has been made in the field of chemicals.

Donald E. Munnecke, plant pathologist, University of California at Los Angeles, says, "An ideal chemical for treating soil is one that kills a variety of fungi, bacteria, insects and weeds; is inexpensive and harmless to the operator and equipment; is quick-acting and effective deep in the soil as well as on the surface; is harmless to nearby plants; and is not toxic to subsequent plantings in the soil."

As yet, the above-described chemical has not been developed. Therefore, there are three general types of material available: those that will control diseases, those that will control insects and nematodes, and herbicides that will control weeds. Of the classes of organisms to be controlled, the diseases are the most difficult. If a chemical will control the soil-borne fungi, chances are it will control the other organisms as well.

One major drawback of chemicals for treatment of greenhouse soils is the time required for complete aeration of the chemicals after treatment. Planting too soon will result in loss of roots—or even the crop. Waiting two weeks for soil aeration is an expensive process. This period for aeration is much less critical in terms of outdoor areas that are cropped only once a year. Also, great care must be used in working with chemicals under glass to ensure that gas escaping from a bed doesn't get to other plants in the house.

There are several materials available now that can be used safely in the greenhouse with no damage to crops. These will be discussed separately.

Which Chemical?

There are dozens of materials sold for treating greenhouse soil. Before discussing individual materials, it should be pointed out that results of chemical treatment may vary widely according to soil texture, moisture and temperature. Dosage should vary accordingly. Heavy, dry, cold soils generally require more chemical to get the same results.

- **Aliette,** a systemic fungicide, has given good control of pythium root and stem rot with drench applications to azalea, rhododendron and schefflera and foliar applications to aglaonema, azalea, bougainvillea, hibiscus, pothos, leatherleaf fern and rhododendron. Allow foliage to dry before overhead irrigation. Follow label directions for application rate and frequency.

- **Banol** can be used as a seeding or transplant application on bedding plants or bareroot dips at potting to control pythium root and stem rot. Follow label directions for application rate and frequency.

- **Banrot** is a broad spectrum fungicide made up of 15% wettable powder Ethazol plus 25% Thiophanate-m. Use as a soil drench and follow label directions for control of root rots caused by pythium, rhizoctonia, sclerotinia, sclerotium, fusarium and thielaviopsis. Be sure to check label before using.

- **Benlate,** a systemic fungicide, has given excellent control of a number of soil pathogens including rhizoctonia, sclerotinia, sclerotium, fusarium, thielaviopsis, verticillium and cylindrocladium. The 50% wettable powder is available as Benlate for ornamentals and Tersan 1991 for turf. Follow label directions for application rate and frequency. Most plants are not injured, but try it on a few plants first to make sure injury does not occur. Plant roots must be confined to the treated area as "container plantings." Results of field tests have been erratic, but not inconsistent, with the postulation that a large percentage of the root system is required to take up the fungicide.

- **Chloropicrin and methyl bromide.** Combinations of chloropicrin methyl bromide and chloropicrin, 98% and 2% mixtures, respectively, are more effective against fungi than the materials used alone. The combination must, of course, be covered with polyethylene sheeting. Some authorities state that, when using chloropicrin sealed in with plastic, the control of verticillium approaches the results obtained with steam. Chloropicrin applied under glass, however, is apt to cause injury to other crops in the same house. Methyl bromide is less dangerous, but has been known (along with other chemicals containing bromide) to be toxic to some crops, especially carnations. Therefore, it is not wise to use methyl bromide on carnation soil. A good precaution, where chemicals are considered, is to try them on a small scale first to see how they affect specific plants grown under your conditions.

- **Subdue.** The water molds pythium and phytophthora are found occurring naturally in most soils, and, in addition, they are rapid invaders of sterilized soil. Subdue is a fungicide that has been found to give excellent control against water mold root rots of many plants including gloxinias, African violets, chrysanthemums, poinsettias, azaleas, snapdragons and geraniums. Follow label directions for application rate and frequency. Application frequency depends partly on the crop and the disease severity.

- **Terraclor (PCNB).** This material, though commonly grouped with fungicides, is not really a fungicide, but a fungistat. This means that it does not kill most of the organisms against which it is effective but prevents their development. It is extremely good for controlling certain soil-borne, disease-producing organisms such as rhizoctonia and various sclerotinia species. In addition to this, it has the advantage that it has a relatively long residual action and is practically insoluble in water. Thus, once it has been added to soil, it will remain effective for periods as long as six months to a year.

  Terraclor is best applied to soil prior to planting. Follow label directions. Terraclor is not effective against pythium. Do not make repeated applications of Terraclor.

- **Truban (Ethazol).** Specifically for water mold control, Truban is often combined with other materials in a soil drench program. Follow label directions for application rate and frequency. Follow the application with an additional watering to improve the penetrability of the material into soil. Foliage must be rinsed with water immediately after application to avoid phytotoxicity. Drench application is preferable to soil mix incorporation.

Cost

Ease and cost of doing the job vary greatly, depending upon which type of chemical is being used. For instance, applying such chemicals as methyl bromide is far from an agreeable task—and it is dangerous if not handled properly. Vapam is much easier to handle, but probably less effective.

We may conclude from the above discussion that chemicals might be most profitably and effectively used under the following conditions:

1. **Where overhead costs are low,** so that time for aeration is not expensive. In general, this means outdoor areas that are cropped only once or twice a year.

2. **Where weeds and perhaps soil-borne insects** are the main reasons for sterilizing. Chemicals are generally not dependable for control of certain hard-to-kill disease organisms.

3. **On less valuable crops**—outdoor flower and vegetable crops—where the cost and potential return are lower than for more intensive forms of culture.

4. **Where steam boilers are not available.** Boilers cost money! Rental of a portable boiler may be the best solution for some growers.

Safety Precautions

1. **Always read the label** before using pesticides. Note warnings and cautions each time before opening a container. Read and follow directions for use.

2. **Keep pesticides away** from children, pets and irresponsible people. Store pesticides in a secure place away from food and feed.

3. **Do not smoke** while using pesticides, and avoid inhalation.

4. **Do not spill pesticides** on skin or clothing. If they are spilled, remove contaminated clothing and wash exposed skin areas thoroughly.

5. **Dispose of empty containers** so that they pose no hazard to humans, animals or valuable plants.

6. **If symptoms of illness** occur during or shortly after using pesticides, call a physician or get the patient to a hospital immediately. Physicians now have available information for quick and effective treatment of accidental overexposure to pesticides. If possible, take along a label from the pesticide container.

7. **You may obtain prompt,** up-to-date information on symptoms and treatment of cases resulting from exposure to toxic agricultural chemicals by calling your Poison Control Center.

Sterilizing Open-Field Soil

There may be occasional situations where growers have need for weed or disease control of either flower bed areas or large open crop areas. For example, the Ball Seed 8 acres of trial grounds are treated each fall with a combination of 1/3 methyl bromide and 2/3 chloropicrin applied at the rate of 350 lbs./acre. The soil temperature must be a minimum of 60°F at least 4″ deep. Cover soil with a sheet of plastic for 24 hours after application. Wait one week after application before planting. The soil is rototilled for aeration before planting is done. This procedure gives excellent weed control (chloropicrin) and considerable help on fungus and diseases (methyl bromide).

Chapter 20

MODERN FERTILIZING METHODS

by Ron Adams
Ball Seed Company

Plant nutrition has become more exact as we are gaining more control over our growing environment. A fertilizer program should balance soil and water chemistry to provide an optimum level of plant nutrition for the type of growth or methods of application. There are two primary methods of fertilizing greenhouse soils: 1) feeding a water soluble fertilizer along with irrigation water through an injector; 2) incorporating a slow-release fertilizer into the soil prior to planting or top dressing on the soil after plants are established. Optimum growth often occurs when growers use both a slow-release and constant water soluble feed.

HOW TO FIGURE PARTS PER MILLION

Parts per million can be determined by many methods. A simple way is to figure 1 oz. of fertilizer per 100 gals. of water equals 75 ppm. If we want to use a 20-10-20 at 200 ppm N and K, then we would need 13.3 oz. of fertilizer (75 x .20=15 ppm, 200/15=13.3 oz.). When reading a fertilizer formula, the numbers are percentage values so we have to place a decimal in front of the formula number before multiplying by 75 which equals 15 ppm N and K and 7.5 ppm P for each ounce of fertilizer from the 20-10-20 formula.

209

Because there are so many formulated products available, charts are easy to use to look up a particular formula and determine how much fertilizer is required depending on injector ratio. Many labels give specific dilution rates so the label is an important source of information in determining what type of fertilizer it is, what it consists of and how the fertilizer can be used correctly. See Table 3.

FERTILIZER INJECTORS

Constant feeding of greenhouse crops has made fertilizer injectors standard equipment for greenhouses. There are several types of injectors available to fit a wide variety of growing situations. The wide range of available equipment increases the difficulty of matching injectors to the operation. Some greenhouses use small injectors in each house, and others install a central injector system to conveniently feed all houses from one location.

Here's a typical fertilizer injector (Smith) and the concentrate container on the right.

210

Hozon siphon proportioners have been used for feeding and drenching for years but are not preferred because they make feeding a chore. One limitation of the Hozon siphon is the requirement of having a high flow rate, which results in a forceful spray from the hose that often knocks pots over. A central injector with a high flow rate can be augmented with portable injectors that provide specialized treatment in specific areas.

There are many types of injectors available from many suppliers. The key things to keep in mind when purchasing an injector are:

- **Water flow ranges** in which a particular model works. For example, a Smith R-3 has a rated range of 3 to 12 gals./minute; an Anderson 200 series is rated 1 to 20 gals./minute.

- **Proportioning** is another consideration. How many gallons of water is the concentrate blended into? How is the concentrate blended? Is it surged into the water line giving a dose of fertilizer followed by just water or is there a blending of the fertilizer and water before entering the water line? Does the system require a blending tank? Is the proportion adjustable or fixed?

- **Portability** often determines what type of injector is required.

- **Is acid injection needed?**

- **Will pesticide applications** be harmful to the equipment?

- **Service**—Can the injector be easily repaired or does it have to be replaced after its useful life? Can the old unit be traded in for a credit on a replacement model?

As you can see, choosing an injector is complicated and requires careful planning to ensure that the unit is a benefit to getting fertilizer applied and not a limitation to production. See Table 4 for details on available injectors.

Proportion Is Not PPM

An injector is not set for parts per million. Most have a variable proportion, which means that, with a given volume of water going through the metering device, a certain amount of concentrate will be drawn or injected into the water system. The rate at which you mix the concentrate determines ppm. If you look at tables for determining the amount of fertilizer per gallon of concentrate, the table shows common proportions available from standard equipment.

Checking Fertilizer Injectors

There are two primary methods of checking an injector for accuracy: 1) check the blended fertilizer/water solution as it is applied to the crop using a solubridge to measure electrical conductivity; 2) measure uptake of the fertilizer concentrate by using a known amount of water.

Method #1 is the easiest because it does not require collecting large amounts of water and can be sampled anywhere water can be collected. To perform a conductivity check you need a reliable conductivity meter that has been calibrated with a standard solution before testing. First check the untreated water and obtain a salt reading. Then test a sample of the fertilized water and subtract the raw water reading from the combined reading. Look up on a fertilizer chart how the measured reading compares with the standards. Constantly checking your conductivity levels alerts you to improper fertilizer mixing or a malfunctioning injector.

Method #2 is a physical measure on the amount of fertilized water collected from the injected solution. To do a physical check you need to collect a known volume of water such as 50 gals. of solution at the hose just before plant application. The concentrate solution has to be measured before and after the collection to measure the exact amount siphoned into the injector and blended with the water. A 1 to 100 ratio injector would draw ½ gal. of concentrate for every 50 gals. of dilute solution. This test can be done in larger or smaller samples, but the sample should be large enough to even out sample variation and assure that the equipment is fully functioning and working at a normal rate when feeding.

Table 1. Fertilizer Salts and Their Chemical Formulas, Analyses, Percentages N, P and K and Effects on pH*

Compound	Formula	Analysis	Nitrogen	Percentage Phosphorus	Potassium	Effect on pH
Ammonium chloride	NH_4Cl	25-0-0	25	0	0	acid
Ammonium nitrate	NH_4NO_3	33.5-0-0	33.5	0	0	acid
Monoammonium phosphate (Ammophos A)	$NH_4H_2PO_4$	11-48-0	11	21	0	acid
Diammonium phosphate	$(NH_4)_2HPO_4$	21-33-0	21	23	0	acid
Ammonium sulfate	$(NH_4)_2SO_4$	20-0-0	20	0	0	very acid
Calcium nitrate	$Ca(NO_3)_2$	15-0-0	15	0	0	basic
Sodium nitrate	$NaNO_3$	16-0-0	16.5	0	0	basic
Urea	$CO(NH_2)_2$	45-0-0	45	0	0	acid
Superphosphate	$Ca(H_2PO_4)_2 + CaSO_4$	0-20-0	0	8.7	0	neutral
Treble superphosphate	$Ca(H_2PO_4)_2$	0-42-0	0	18.3	0	neutral
Phosphoric acid	H_3PO_4	0-52-0	0	22.7	0	very acid
Potassium chloride (muriate of potash)	KC_1	0-0-62	0	0	51	neutral
Potassium nitrate (saltpeter)	KNO_3	13-0-44	13	0	36.5	basic
Potassium sulfate	K_2SO_4	0-0-53	0	0	44	neutral
Magnesium nitrate	$Mg(NO_3)_2.6H_2O$	11-0-0	11	0	0	neutral
Monopotassium phosphorus	KH_2PO_4	0-53-34	0	23.1	28.2	basic
Dipotassium phosphate	K_2HPO_4	0-41-54	0	17.9	44.8	basic

*Source: *Ohio Florists' Association Bulletin* No. 631, May 1982.

The analysis values used in this table were obtained from commercially available products. The analysis of compounds may vary slightly from listed values as a result of differences in processing among various chemical companies.

Table 2. Amount of Various Fertilizer Materials Needed to Supply 200 PPM Each of Nitrogen and Potassium*

Fertilizer Combination	Fertilizer Analysis	Ounces to Add to 100 Gals. of Water
1. Ammonium sulfate	20-0-0	13.3
Muriate of potash	0-0-62	5.6
2. Ammonium nitrate	33.5-0-0	8
Muriate of potash	0-0-62	5.6
3. Urea	45-0-0	6
Muriate of potash	0-0-62	5.6
4. Calcium nitrate	15-0-0	10.6
Potassium nitrate	13-0-44	7.5
5. Calcium nitrate	15-0-0	16.7
Muriate of potash	0-0-62	5.6
6. Sodium nitrate	16-0-0	10.6
Potassium nitrate	13-0-44	7.5
7. Ammonium sulfate	20-0-0	8.5
Potassium nitrate	13-0-44	7.5
8. Ammonium nitrate	33.5-0-0	5.1
Potassium nitrate	13-0-44	7.5
9. Urea	45-0-0	3.8
Potassium nitrate	13-0-44	7.5
10. Ammonium nitrate	33.5-0-0	6.1
Calcium nitrate	15-0-0	4
Muriate of potash	0-0-62	7.8

Example: 13.3 oz. of ammonium sulfate added to 100 gals. of water, applied directly to the crop, will supply 200 ppm of nitrogen.

*Source: *Ohio Florists' Association Bulletin* No. 631, May 1982.

The following table gives the amount of fertilizer (in ounces) for making a 100-150-200 ppm nitrogen solution. Example: To apply 200 ppm of nitrogen through an injector, first make up a concentrate of 9 oz./gal. of 30-10-10 (line five in the table immediately below). Apply this concentrate to the crop with an injector set to 1:100 (left column).

Table 3. Injection Ratios and Concentrations for Constant Feeding with Commonly Used Formulas

30% Nitrogen Formulas (30-10-10, etc.)

Injector Ratio	Per Gallon of Concentrate		
	100 ppm N	150 ppm N	200 ppm N
1:300	13.5 oz.	20.25 oz.	27 oz.
1:200	9 oz.	13.5 oz.	18 oz.
1:150	6.75 oz.	10.125 oz.	13.5 oz.
1:128	5.76 oz.	8.64 oz.	11.52 oz.
1:100	4.5 oz.	6.75 oz.	9 oz.
1:50	2.25 oz.	3.375 oz.	4.5 oz.
1:30	1.35 oz.	2.025 oz.	2.7 oz.
1:24	1.08 oz.	1.62 oz.	2.16 oz.
1:15	.675 oz.	1.012 oz.	1.35 oz.

25% Nitrogen Formulas (25-5-20, 25-10-10, 25-0-25, etc.)

Injector Ratio	Per Gallon of Concentrate		
	100 ppm N	150 ppm N	200 ppm N
1:300	16.5 oz.	24.75 oz.	33 oz.
1:200	11 oz.	16.5 oz.	22 oz.
1:150	8.25 oz.	12.375 oz.	16.5 oz.
1:128	7.04 oz.	10.56 oz.	14.08 oz.
1:100	5.5 oz.	8.25 oz.	11 oz.
1:50	2.75 oz.	4.125 oz.	5.5 oz.
1:30	1.65 oz.	2.475 oz.	3.3 oz.
1:24	1.32 oz.	1.98 oz.	2.64 oz.
1:15	.825 oz.	1.237 oz.	1.65 oz.

20% Nitrogen Formulas (20-20-20, 20-5-30, 21-7-7, etc.)

Injector Ratio	Per Gallon of Concentrate		
	100 ppm N	150 ppm N	200 ppm N
1:300	20.25 oz.	30.375 oz.	40.5 oz.
1:200	13.5 oz.	20.25 oz.	27 oz.
1:150	10.125 oz.	15.187 oz.	20.25 oz.
1:128	8.64 oz.	12.96 oz.	17.28 oz.
1:100	6.75 oz.	10.125 oz.	13.5 oz.
1:50	3.375 oz.	5.0675 oz.	6.75 oz.
1:30	2.025 oz.	3.037 oz.	4.05 oz.
1:24	1.62 oz.	2.43 oz.	3.24 oz.
1:15	1.012 oz.	1.518 oz.	2.025 oz.

15% Nitrogen Formulas (15-15-15, 15-30-15, 16-4-12, etc.)

Injector Ratio	Per Gallon of Concentrate		
	100 ppm N	150 ppm N	200 ppm N
1:300	27 oz.	40.5 oz.	54 oz.
1:200	18 oz.	27 oz.	36 oz.
1:150	13.5 oz.	20.25 oz.	27 oz.
1:128	11.52 oz.	17.28 oz.	23.04 oz.
1:100	9 oz.	13.5 oz.	18 oz.
1:50	4.5 oz.	6.75 oz.	9 oz.
1:30	2.7 oz.	4.05 oz.	5.4 oz.
1:24	2.15 oz.	3.21 oz.	4.32 oz.
1:15	1.35 oz.	2.025 oz.	2.7 oz.

Use of slow-release fertilizers to produce quality bedding and pot plants is not as popular as it has been. The decline of usage is attributed to growers' increased use of soluble fertilizers through injectors. The water solubles are better understood and allow growers better control, although several growers have reliably supplied all the nutrients necessary to produce an excellent crop with slow-release fertilizers. The advantages of using a slow-release are:

1) providing a constant fertilizer source that can be safely incorporated into the soil mix prior to planting;

2) reducing the constant need to mix and proportion water solubles or apply dry soluble fertilizers;

3) maintaining a more constant supply of nutrients between waterings than water solubles when waterings are not as frequent;

4) using capillary watering systems to minimize algae buildup on mats;

5) increasing plant shelf life by providing nutrients after plants leave the greenhouse. Hanging baskets, foliage plants and pot plants such as African violets can use the additional fertilizer, which sustains the plants for a longer period of time.

Slow-release fertilizers have proven themselves over a number of years, but there are some disadvantages when using them:

1) cannot easily change the salt level, especially to lower it, when plants are growing at a slower rate;

2) should be incorporated throughout the soil mix prior to planting for the most uniform distribution of nutrients;

3) can provide too high a fertility at the crop finish making growth at sales difficult to control, particularly in the South, as in the case of foliage plants fed at too high a level for reduced growing conditions during and after acclimatization for indoor plantings;

4) some top-dressed slow-release materials will float out of the container under flooding conditions, reducing the effective rate;

5) some slow-release fertilizers are temperature- or bacterial-dependent, so the release rate varies depending on conditions.

We can use either slow-release or soluble feed to produce plants. Though the trend is to more soluble, the best growth is with a combination of slow-release and water soluble. If you plan to use the combination, it is best to reduce the effective rates by as much as 50% to provide an optimum level. For example, if you use a slow-release at 10 lbs./cu. yd. and feed at 250 ppm N, then you should try 5 lbs./cu. yd. of slow-release and feed at 125 ppm N.

COATED FERTILIZERS

There are two basic types of complete slow-release fertilizers: coated and granulated. Coated fertilizers consist of water soluble fertilizers coated with a plastic resin or sulfur that allow the fertilizers to become available over time. Osmocote and Nutricote use a microporous plastic resin to lock up the fertilizer until osmotic pressure initiates release. Then the fertilizer diffuses through the coating until the fertilizer is depleted. Release times can be controlled by the coating thickness. Formulas can be timed to release anywhere from 40 days to a year. Osmocote or Nutricote can be either top-dressed or incorporated into the soil. They should not be mixed ahead of time by more than two to three weeks and cannot be steam sterilized. There are several formulas of these products available, and the newer formulas are adding trace elements and changing the nitrogen type in order to make a more complete fertilizer for soilless mixes.

Another type of coated slow-release fertilizer is sulfur-coated urea. It was first developed by Tennessee Valley Authority Research Lab. Sulfur coats use a waxed sulfur to coat urea nitrogen, and through bacterial action the coating degrades to make the nitrogen available over time. Other nutrients can be co-blended with this fertilizer. Since sulfur coats depend on bacterial break-down, release is variable and cannot be totally predicted. Sulfur coats cannot be steam sterilized.

GRANULATED FERTILIZERS

The most commonly used granulated slow-release is MagAmp. MagAmp is a co-granulated blend of nitrogen, phosphorus, potassium and magnesium with a formula of 7-40-6 plus 12% magnesium. MagAmp or magnesium ammonium phosphate is what we consider a true slow-release fertilizer where only 1% of the fertilizer is available in a 24-hour period under saturated conditions. The MagAmp formula is high in phosphorous and could be considered as a phosphorous source for mixes with the additional benefit of nitrogen, potassium and magnesium. MagAmp is not temperature sensitive, and soils including MagAmp can be steam sterilized prior to planting, without any harmful effects. MagAmp release rates can be changed by varying the particle size.

There are two grades available: 1) medium grade—the most desirable for greenhouse production—lasts four to six months in the soil; and 2) coarse grade—typically suited for outdoor nursery stock and outdoor plantings—can last up to 24 months in the soil. MagAmp has to be incorporated in the soil to be effective and should not be top dressed, but it can be mixed and stored for several months ahead of using.

216

Table 4. List of Equipment Available

Injector	Manufacturer	Models	Proportion	Cost
HOZON	Distributed through many local suppliers		1-15	$10 to $15
Comments: Requires high flow rate; accuracy variable.				
DOSATRON	Dosatron International	7GPM, 40GPM, 100GPM	1-50 to 1-1,500	
Comments: Two to three year life.				
DOSMATIC	J F Equipment	Dosmatic Plus	1-5 to 1-1,000	$250 and up
Comments: Two to three year life.				
GEWA	MFG in Germany, distributed by Brush King, Naples, Florida	GE04, GE06, GE15, GE26, GE04	1-100	Others variable
Comments: Portable fertilizer in rubber bladder that can leak, losing accuracy.				
SMITH	Smith Precision	R-3, R-4, R-6, R-8	1-100 standard 1-200 standard	$847 and up
Comments: Several options available; has exchange program; works in set flow range.				
ANDERSON	H.E. Anderson Co.	201, 301, 501, 1001, 1601	1-200 other options 1-200 can be 1-100 1-200 with 2 pump heads	$865 and up
Comments: Works over wide flow range; requires blending tank.				
VOLMATIC	MFG in Denmark, distributed by Midwest Trading, St. Charles, Illinois	AMI series Computer controlled		
Comments: Can be integrated to conditions and acid inject, as well as several stocks.				
POLY FLO	Florist Products	Poly Flo	1-12 to 1-200	$1,200 and up
Comments: Compatible with pesticide solution and acid injection.				
BAHM	Bahm, Inc.	Bahm 10-370	Variable	$50,000

There are several other proportioners available such as Merit Commanders, M-P Mixer, Fert O Jet and HPA that can fit a variety of growing needs depending on how an individual unit can be serviced.

Chapter 21

SEED GERMINATION

by Vic Ball

Probably two thirds or more of most seed-grown crops today are started as plugs. You'll find much detail on temperatures, mixes and other special conditions needed to get good germination in plugs in Chapter 12.

There are still a lot of growers out there, however, who sow seed in open flats for bedding plants and other crops. I am including the following notes on seed germination for these growers.

Germinating seed is one of the more difficult parts of the growing job—so often seed is sown and germinated by the proprietor. Here are some suggestions:

1. **Sow good seed.** Remember, seeds are living things! No one can guarantee a perfect stand. Reputable seedsmen, through dry storage and regular germination tests, generally supply good seed. There are low-priced flower seeds, but the occasional problems that result more than wipe out the savings.

2. **Soil medium—use the right kind.** A wide variety of soil (or no soil) mixes will germinate seed. To do the job it must be:

   • Loose, porous, well-drained.

   • Low in salts. High salts damage tender roots.

   • Disease-free. You can't win if the soil is full of damp-off organisms. The mix must either be naturally sterile (for example, Ball Growing Mix) or else be steamed 180°F for 30 minutes. Include flats, labels, etc.

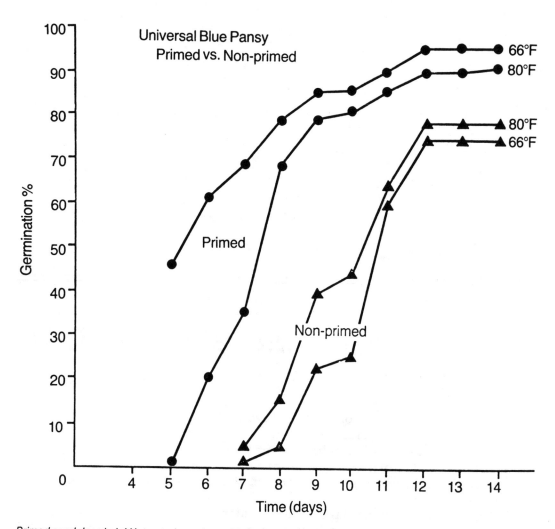

Universal Blue Pansy
Primed vs. Non-primed

Primed seed does help! Untreated pansies at 80°F germinate in the upper 70% range; primed seed at the same temperature germinate in the lower 90% range. This is from Dave Koranski's work at Iowa State (shown in GrowerTalks, *January 1988).*

• Reasonably fine-textured. You don't sow petunia seeds in big lumps of soil.

In fact, the majority of growers I see simply use a commercial growing mix. It's sterile, has enough nutrients to make seedlings grow, has okay texture and does drain. Some growers add some sand. The reason: Seedling separation during transplanting goes faster (be sure to sterilize the sand).

Such mixes have enough nitrate so that further fertilization is normally not needed. In mixes without fertilizer, use 1 oz. of 20-20-20/3 gals. of water.

3. **Keep soil warm.** Here must be the #1 stumbling block—especially with the more "difficult" things like impatiens and geraniums. They really aren't difficult!

The majority of bedding annuals should have a soil temperature (day and night) of 75°F to achieve prompt germination. This is not a house temperature, but actual temperature in the soil. This applies to petunias, geraniums, impatiens, begonias, salvias, lobelias, marigolds and vincas. 70°F honest soil temperature will sprout most of these annuals most of the time, but 75°F does it more promptly and generally gives a better percentage. Why not! You must have a suitable thermometer to know where you stand.

Moisture evaporation from the soil surface will cool the soil 5° to 10°F. Ken Reeves, Toronto bedding plant specialist, says, "Soil temperatures in my flats are frequently 10°F or more below the house temperature. I check it!"

Water applied to seed flats (mist, etc.), often at 50° or 45°F, will cool soil down sharply. Tests at Michigan State show that 70°F soil took 8 hours to get back up to 70°F after an application of cold water.

Growers who consistently win with the tough ones (geraniums and impatiens) insist on "mid-70s in the soil."

A good way to really control soil temperature is by use of hot-bed cables. Depending on length, these cost around 50¢ to 70¢/sq. ft. Now you set the thermostat (in the soil) where you want it. Growers often use steam pipe below the bench to warm soil.

CHECK LIST FOR GERMINATION TROUBLES

SUFFICIENT MOISTURE? ABSOLUTE NECESSITY — UNIFORM - NOT EXCESSIVE.

CORRECT TEMPERATURE? — USUALLY 65-70° — SOME PLANTS COOLER.

SEEDS COVERED TOO DEEP? AIR IS AS ESSENTIAL AS HEAT AND MOISTURE!!! FINE SEEDS REQUIRE LITTLE OR NO COVER — WILL "WASH" INTO SOIL.

ANTS-MICE — MORE OFTEN RESPONSIBLE THAN PEOPLE GENERALLY REALIZE — EVEN FLORISTS!

CLEAN, DISEASE - FREE STERILIZED MEDIUM?

YOUR SEEDSMAN IS ONLY HUMAN -- DOES HIS BEST. IF YOU THINK HE IS AT FAULT, WRITE AND GIVE HIM A CHANCE TO HELP!

ABOVE ALL, REMOVE SEEDLINGS TO COOL AIR AND PLENTY OF LIGHT AS SOON AS SPROUTED -- BEST DAMP-OFF PREVENTATIVE!

More recently I'm seeing Biotherm and similar tiny hot water tubes running lengthwise down the bench 2″ to 4″ apart. They provide ample bottom heat at a lot less energy cost than electricity. In fact, Bill Swanekamp, a major bedding grower in New Jersey, does much of his seed germination right on the ground— but with hot water tubes buried right in the floor to maintain the necessary 70° to 75°F soil temperature in flats.

There is a group of bedding annuals that need a lower temperature for sprouting. Soil temperature of 65°F is recommended for pansies, phlox and snapdragons.

4. **Keep the soil surface moist until sprouting.** George J. Ball used to say that if a seed started to soak up moisture, then was allowed to dry, it would die. Once you start, the soil surface must be kept moist. Ways to do it:

- Mist 6 seconds per 10 minutes during sunny daylight only. Actually, the best growers seem to prefer misting by hand. They live with their flats that carefully. Says one good Virginia grower, "Automatic mist tends to get my seed flats too moist. I'd rather watch them myself."

- Another way: Wrap flats in poly or cover the bed with a sheet of poly, or better yet, use one of the new porous materials, such as Remay or Vispore—both are white, so they reflect the light, and porous for air circulation. If flats are well-watered before sowing, there is normally ample moisture to sprout seeds. Be sure to remove the poly as soon as seedlings are through. Beware of full sun on flats covered with poly. It's easy to burn plants! Leonard Osborne, Piney Flats, Tennessee, says, "It gets too hot here under poly. I prefer to cover the seed flats with newspaper and keep a close eye on them." Leonard always wins!

5. **Cover the seed?** The winners all leave the fine seed uncovered—petunias, begonias, etc. The tiny seeds soon wash down into the mix. Nearly all growers do cover the larger seeds, such as tomatoes, salvia and zinnia. Marc Cathey, U.S. National Arboretum, says that many seeds need three days of darkness to germinate. Examples are verbena, larkspur, dusty miller, pansy, phlox and portulaca.

After-Sprouting Care

Under the 75°F, high-moisture regime, good seed should be well up in five days or less for most annuals. Very soon now these flats should be moved into a 50°F house. Don't let them dry to wilting, but gradually withhold moisture. "Cool and dry" from here on produces well-rooted, sturdy seedlings—and a minimum of damp-off problems. As seedlings mature, they're best with full sun and lots of fresh air.

Grower Comments

Jim Crouch, Jonesboro, Tennessee: "We had some damp off after transplanting annuals and hit the flats with a drench of Dexon and Terraclor. It seemed to stop the problem."

Phil Couch, Rogersville, Tennessee: "It's important not to sow seed too thickly. You crowd seedlings, encourage damp off. I use $1/256$ oz. of petunia seeds to a 24″ flat. At 75° to 80°F soil temperature, they jump through in no time. Sowing in rows helps, too—if damp off starts, it will just go down the row and stop."

From Val Maxwell of Green Thumb, a large Apopka, Florida, producer: "All flats here are watered in with Dexon after transplanting. Everything."

Begonias—And Other Tiny Seeds

A special problem. How often have you seen a flat of fibrous begonias that sprout well, then most of them just fail to grow?

The usual case: The seed (and seedlings) are both very small and shallow-rooted. Especially under mist, all nutrients are promptly leached out of the surface of the mix soon after sowing, so the tiny seedling simply starves! The answer: 1 oz./3 gals. of 20-20-20 applied as soon as seeds sprout.

Chapter 22

TISSUE CULTURE—AN OVERVIEW

by Warren Banner
Ball Seed Company

Tissue culture (micropropagation) of ornamental crops in the 1980s became an important source for providing select crops to the grower. There are several crops today that are produced almost exclusively by micropropagation, such as syngonium and spathiphyllum. The 1990s will see an expansion of tissue culture methods in commercial applications and an increase in the crops produced by tissue culture. Although this production technology has greatly improved the quality and performance of several crops, it has yet to replace many crops produced by traditional methods of propagation. The next decade will probably pass with many more crops commercially produced through some form of tissue culture production.

The exciting opportunities related to tissue culture in the 1990s center around new production methods that will include many other crops being produced in vitro (growing in an artificial and sterile environment in culture). There are two to three promising methods being pursued in labs around the world.

- **Somatic embryogenesis** produces many viable somatic (seed) embryos from plant tissue. Here an embryo (a seed less the protein and the coat) is "grown" by tissue culture. It is then "germinated," much as a normal seed is done. This technology could be used to cost effectively reproduce crops that are normally vegetatively propagated. Scientists envision seeding plugs with these embryos and providing a germinated plug seedling.

- **Micropropagation** (commercial propagation of crops using tissue culture) has been very labor intensive and scientists are seeking methods of automation to reduce this cost. The automation may include the possible use of robots and other forms of mechanization.

- **Liquid batch culture** is being used to increase bulb crops such as lilies. Each liquid culture produces hundreds of thousands of disease-free bulblets. The bulblets are then grown for one to two more years in the field before going to the commercial greenhouse grower.

These technologies and others are certain to make this decade very dynamic with regards to supplying our industry with superior young plants.

Tissue culture has also become a valuable tool in several other important fields of horticulture. Many crops produced by traditional vegetative propagation now depend on obtaining base stock free of viruses, fungi and bacteria and to certify clean plant production. For many years, this practice has been used in carnations, mums and geraniums; it is now being expanded to include crops like New Guinea impatiens and Rieger begonias.

Breeders are integrating aspects of tissue culture to speed up new product introductions and expand their product lines. Some of these applications include increasing variability in horticultural traits to create potential new varieties, rescu-

A tiny (1 mm.) bit of tissue is placed in a special medium and soon develops plant parts—roots and stems. It's called "multiplying in vitro."

226

ing embryos from seeds of select crosses to obtain new hybrids that normally could not be obtained, selecting varieties under specified selection pressures and preserving varieties or selections in vitro for long periods. This storage method is called "in vitro germplasm preservation."

Breeders also rapidly scale-up new varieties for faster introduction using micropropagation. These and other applications for the pathologist and breeder will continue to expand.

There are five major horticultural crop segments that have benefited from micropropagation: foliage, cut flowers, landscape ornamentals, pot plants and agricultural crops. The first four of these segments are discussed below. The discussion also includes a partial list of commercially produced crops.

FOLIAGE

Foliage plants benefit greatly from micropropagation. The foliage industry is very dependent on micropropagation as a source of microcuttings. Micropropagation provides a disease-free cutting that is vigorous and in most cases exhibits good basal branching. The elimination of soft rot bacterial diseases and the formation of superior basal habits in tissue culture produces superior crops relative to the plantlets produced by traditional propagation. This is especially true for syngonium and spathiphyllum. The basal branching is thought to be a carry over effect due to the growth regulators (cytokinins) used in the culture media. In addition, new varieties can be rapidly scaled up for rapid and broad distribution throughout the world. There are several varieties commercially produced by tissue culture listed below.

Syngonium	Philodendron	Ferns
Spathiphyllum	Calathea	Cordyline
Dieffenbachia	Anthurium	Banana
Ficus	Alocasia	Dracaena

POT PLANTS

The use of tissue culture is less prevalent for pot plants than for foliage. There is no clear reason for this trend, other than the lack of cost efficient technology. Many pot plants could benefit from disease-free micropropagation and the subsequent uniformity possible from microcuttings. The 1990s may be the decade for tissue cultured pot plants if some of the emerging technologies come on line. One crop particularly helped by micropropagation is gerbera. A key selling feature is the ability to produce plants with an identical flower color. Since the plants are clones, uniformity is also apparent within a selection. Pot plants commonly produced from tissue culture include:

Gerbera daisy	African violets	Lilies
Pot roses	(limited)	Rex begonia
Anthurium	Aloe vera	Orchids

227

CUT FLOWERS

Several significant cut flower crops benefit from micropropagation. Gypsophila can now be produced free of crown gall, and cut-type lilies are produced free of viruses that previously decreased quality. Disease-free micropropagation of lily bulblets produces flowers with true colors, larger petals and increased plant vigor. Cut type gerbera benefit from being reproduced with genetic purity, which ensures the unique color pattern for each variety. Several commercial cut flower success stories include:

Gypsophila	Cut roses
Gerbera	Perennial asters
Lilies	Delphinium (some of the new hybrids)
Orchids	Anthurium andreanum
Statice	Alstroemeria

LANDSCAPE ORNAMENTALS

This classification of plants includes woody ornamentals and perennials. Many of the woody ornamentals are very difficult to propagate by traditional means. Tissue culture has made this task much easier. Due to the slow growth of woody plants relative to many pot plants or annuals, tissue culture allows for a quicker build-up of new varieties. This speeds new products to market and cuts years out of the product development cycle. Perennials such as daylilies have benefited from tissue culture because many rare and beautiful varieties—previously very difficult to reproduce and seen only by a select few—can now be mass produced. Landscape ornamentals propagated through tissue culture include:

Hemerocallis	Rhododendron
Landscape gerbera	Kalmia (Mt. Laurel)
Hosta	Lilac
Liriope	Birch
Amelanchier	

Chapter 23

THE IMPORTANCE OF CARBON DIOXIDE

by Ralph Freeman
Cornell Cooperative Extension
Riverhead, New York

During the 1960s the subject of carbon dioxide (CO_2) was one of the hottest topics in the greenhouse industry. Everyone, it seemed, was asking, "What is it?," "Is it really worth using?," "How much does it cost?" or "Will I obtain results?" All of these were valid questions. This presentation will attempt to answer each of these questions and provide you with some realistic guidelines on how to use carbon dioxide as a production management tool for producing quality plants. Yet the question remains: "Does CO_2 benefit bedding plant growers?" In this chapter I'll attempt to answer that one also.

As the late 1960s and early 1970s passed, many cut flower growers invested in CO_2. The results were quicker cropping, stronger stems, stockier stems, improved quality and higher yields. Growers rapidly discovered that with CO_2 they needed to step up fertility programs, increase growing temperatures and water more frequently. In the period 1968 to 1973 there were crop changes from cuts to pots, as well as more bedding plants grown. With all this activity, interest in CO_2 lessened. Then, in 1973 to 1974, the energy crisis hit hard! Fuel prices quadrupled, resulting in only a small percentage of growers continuing to invest in CO_2. These were primarily the rose growers. The attention previously focused on CO_2 was quickly drawn to conservation strategies.

Carbon dioxide (CO_2) is one of the basic compounds found in the atmosphere. The approximate concentration is about 300 parts per million by volume. Generally, we refer to the concentration as being 300 ppm. CO_2 is one of the raw products required for photosynthesis.

The compound CO_2 is a colorless, noninflammable gas that is heavier than air. The gas solidifies under atmospheric pressure at -109.3°F. Solid CO_2 possesses the interesting property of passing directly into the gaseous state (sublimation) without going through the liquid state at atmospheric pressure.

Photosynthesis and CO₂

Photosynthesis is a biochemical process using the sun's energy to chemically combine CO_2 and water (in the presence of the catalysts chlorophyll and solar radiation) to yield chemical energy in a usable form. The actual products of photosynthesis are carbohydrates (sugars and starches), complex chemical compounds, water and oxygen. A simplified explanation of the process of photosynthesis is seen in the following formula:

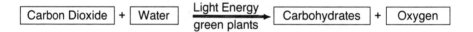

$$\boxed{\text{Carbon Dioxide}} + \boxed{\text{Water}} \xrightarrow[\text{green plants}]{\text{Light Energy}} \boxed{\text{Carbohydrates}} + \boxed{\text{Oxygen}}$$

Dramatic evidence of the effect of maintaining correct levels of CO_2. The top two plants were treated, the bottom two were not.

230

Carbon dioxide has been shown to be a limiting factor for proper plant growth and development in greenhouses during the fall, winter and spring. This occurs because greenhouse vents are normally closed to conserve heat for extended time periods. Without adequate ventilation, the CO_2 level drops below the normal 300 ppm atmospheric level. Plants have a tremendous need for CO_2. With vents closed, the CO_2 is quickly used up, thus becoming a limiting factor for plant growth. Plant growth with inadequate CO_2 is put under stress, resulting in poorer growth than might be realized. Figure 1 shows approximate CO_2 levels measured in greenhouses and outdoors during the course of daylight hours.

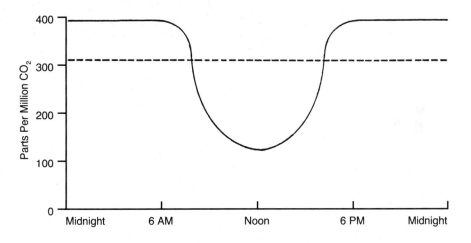

Figure 1. Carbon dioxide levels as measured in a greenhouse (solid line) and outdoors (dotted line) in a typical 24-hour period.

Over the years research has shown that adding CO_2 during the daylight hours to the greenhouse atmosphere in concentrations of three, four or five times greater than that found in the natural atmosphere will give increased yields, higher quality and often shorter cropping times.

When to Use CO_2

The results in Figure 1 demonstrate a very low level of CO_2 occurs in green-houses for a significant portion of daylight hours. Research has clearly shown that deficient CO_2 levels occur in greenhouses generally between 9 a.m. through 3 p.m. during the fall, winter and spring months. Therefore, if CO_2 is limited at any time during daylight hours, photosynthesis and, ultimately, plant growth will be limited. It is during these hours that CO_2 should be added to the greenhouse environment to help overcome this limiting factor.

Chrysanthemums, for example, have been found to respond more favorably in the young plant stage (up to the time of visible flower buds) than they will when mature. Other plants may respond similarly. In plants showing this response pattern a grower could stop using CO_2 in the finishing-off period.

How Much to Add?

Research results have been inconsistent from university to university as to the exact amount of CO_2 to add to the greenhouse air for maximum plant growth and development. There are many reasons for all this variability, but there are some common threads. Based on both research findings and commercial CO_2 usage, we can suggest that growers try to maintain levels between 600 and 1,500 ppm.

Do not permit the CO_2 level to exceed 5,000 ppm. First, it is wasteful (costly), and second, somewhere beyond that point headaches and listlessness may become troublesome.

Sources of CO_2

There are many different sources of CO_2. Some are ventilation (exchanging greenhouse air with fresh outside air), decomposition of mulches, compressed CO_2 gas, dry ice, liquid CO_2 and combustion of various fuels (propane, natural gas or kerosene). Many growers remove the CO_2 from flue gases after boiler fuels have been burned. In order to do this, special stack scrubbers must be used that separate the CO_2 from the noxious gases. The CO_2 is then collected and injected into the greenhouses. Table 1 provides some basic information on each of the more commonly used fuels.

It is important that sufficient oxygen supplies be provided to all fossil fuel burners so that noxious gases such as ethylene and sulfur dioxide do not cause deleterious effects to plants.

Table 1. A Listing of Some of the More Common Sources of CO_2 and General Comments Regarding Each.

Source of CO_2	Comments
Organic matter	As organic matter breaks down, CO_2 is generated. In this aerobic process there is little control over the levels maintained in the greenhouse environment.
Solid CO_2	Dry ice is placed in special cylinders and CO_2 is released as the dry ice sublimes. The amount of CO_2 going in the greenhouse is regulated with gas flow meters or pressure regulator valves.
Burning of fossil fuels*	Burning of kerosene, propane or natural gas results in the CO_2 generation. The regulation of CO_2 concentrations is controlled by the firing rate and/or the number of units being used.
Liquid CO_2	Stored in special vessels. The CO_2 is released to controlled rates via gas flow meters or pressure regulator valves.

*When purchasing fuel be sure the fuel supplier is aware that you'll be using fossil fuels for CO_2 generation. If by chance he has a lot with a sulfur content higher than normal, it would be undesirable for your purposes and he'll choose not to deliver it.

Light, Temperature, Fertility

As carbon dioxide can become a limiting factor reducing growth of plants, likewise light, temperature and fertility can become limiting factors in plant growth. If, for example, the ideal CO_2 levels for a particular crop were between 800 and 1,000 ppm and either one or more of the light, temperature or fertilizer levels were not up to par, growth would be restricted and the full potential of adding CO_2 would be lost. Therefore, each grower must discover proper light levels, temperature and fertilizer rates that would be optimal in his specific situation, as well as the levels and rates for different seasons of the year. This sounds difficult but experience has shown the following to be a starting guide:

- **Light.** Know your crop needs. Provide as much light as possible, yet not so much as to scorch leaves or blooms.

- **Temperature.** Higher levels may be needed, 62° to 65°F nights and up to 80°F days. Start ventilating at 80° to 82°F and turn CO_2 generators off automatically or manually when top vents are open 4″.

- **Fertility.** Fertilizer programs will have to be stepped up—with increased growth more fertilizer and water will have to be applied. Keep fertilizer levels up at all times. Use soil tests and foliar analysis. Some growers have had to nearly double the amount formerly used when they start a CO_2 program.

Most important—for maximum growth, don't allow any growth factor to become a limiting factor.

Caution

- **Upper limits.** As growers may have a tendency to keep adding CO_2 to reach the "upper limits," a note of caution is in order here. The Mine Safety Appliance Company reported that a concentration of 8% to 10% CO_2 can be fatal. CO_2 concentrations of 1% (10,000 ppm) may cause headaches and listlessness. Concentrations too high make it impossible for the lungs to accomplish their function of eliminating CO_2 from the blood, and suffocation can result from prolonged breathing of such a high percentage of the gas. A small amount of CO_2 in the blood is necessary, however, to stimulate the brain centers controlling respiration. Our basic guideline may be taken from the research. Most results indicate plants respond favorably to levels up to 2,000 ppm. Let's not exceed this level.

- **Safety controls.** Each CO_2 generator should have approved safety controls. Some of these include a flame failure safety valve, solenoid valve that automatically switches the fuel on and off, gas filter, fine reading gauge showing true jet pressure, and a thermocouple that will shut off the gas flow if the pilot light is not functioning.

- **Use low sulfur fuels.** When purchasing fuels for CO_2 generation, be sure your fuel supplier is aware that it will be used for CO_2. This will aid him in avoiding delivery of batches with abnormally high sulfur content.

- **Fuel leaks.** Unburned fuels escaping into the greenhouse air can cause serious plant damage. Leakage from the piping system or from a burner operating incorrectly has resulted in flower and fruit abortion, abnormal growth and numerous other problems.

Avoid Air Pollution Problems

Self-induced air pollution problems are those caused by burners and furnaces in greenhouses that are not burning properly. Failures are usually due to inadequate amounts of oxygen supplied to the combustion process. Other causes may be dirty nozzles, off-center fires, delayed ignition, oil or gas leaks, pulsating fuel pressure, etc. Any of these factors and more can cause difficulties such as incomplete combustion, resulting in noxious gases contaminating the greenhouse atmosphere. When these gases are present in excessive concentration for sufficient time, damage such as glazing of leaves, parallel veins, necrotic flecks, spots and areas between veins or twisted and distorted growth may occur.

Does CO_2 Benefit Bedding Plant Growers?

Certainly! The literature reveals bedding plants such as geraniums, petunias, marigolds, tomatoes, lettuce and numerous other crops benefit from the use of CO_2. If used, expectations should be faster seedling growth, faster crops and improved plant quality.

The greatest responses and most benefit would take place in the young plant stages, not near maturity of the crop. One place where CO_2 could be particularly beneficial would be immediately following germination until bud set. Propagators could make real use of CO_2, especially during rooting of geranium cuttings, but also in growing seedlings and plugs to the point of transplanting.

Beware—if bedding plant growers use CO_2, expect all your scheduling to change. Plants do grow faster in CO_2-enriched environments. Watch your scheduling carefully.

Costs

Even though growers today are "energy conscious," the costs of installing and operating CO_2 generators are not that high. Investments in CO_2 generators amount to approximately 10¢ to 12¢/sq. ft. to install. Now that's a one-time investment! Equipment maintenance is generally minimal.

The cost of generating CO_2 from either liquid CO_2 or fuels such as kerosene, propane or natural gas amounts to approximately 10¢ to 15¢/sq. ft./year. Keep in mind CO_2 will only be used from October through April with operational hours of 9 a.m. to 3 to 4 p.m. or a total of around 1,000 hours annually in the North.

When one considers the increase in production and improved quality as a result of using CO_2, there is no question about the economics. If used properly and the

This is the CO_2 sensing equipment produced by Priva that activates an additional flow of CO_2 into the atmosphere when levels fall below the set point.

grower keeps all factors affecting plant growth managed well, the investments in equipment, maintenance and costs of generating CO_2 are soon paid with a good return on the investment.

MEASURING CO_2 LEVELS

Over the years a number of different "CO_2 test kits" have been made available to the greenhouse industry. Their purpose was to provide an indispensable aid to help the grower measure the amount of CO_2 in the greenhouse at any time.

Grower reaction to many of these CO_2 test kits has varied. Some comments were positive, others negative. Costs of the kits and supplies were often another problem area. It seemed most of these kits soon found their way to dusty corners and were forgotten either due to costs, time to take the test, inaccuracies or whatever.

There are, however, very accurate instruments available for measuring CO_2 concentration in air. Unfortunately, these are very expensive.

Well, then, what is a grower to do? How can he know how much CO_2 is in the greenhouse air? First, he can calculate the volume of the greenhouse(s) in which CO_2 will be injected or generated. For example:

Volume of Greenhouse = (width) x (length) x (average height of 12′)
Volume = (25′) x (100′) x (12′)
Volume = 30,000 cu. ft.

Second, calculate the hourly CO_2 requirements. To do this, keep in mind that plants on the average need at least 400 ppm (0.04%). Then,

$$\frac{(30,000 \text{ cu. ft.}) \text{ x } (400 \text{ ppm/hr.})}{1,000,000 \text{ ppm}} = 12 \text{ cu. ft. } CO_2/\text{hr.}$$

Knowing that 12 cu. ft. of CO_2/hr. are required for 400 ppm, the grower can set the pressure regulator flow control valve on the liquid dry ice converter or set the gauge pressure (on gas-fired units) on the setting to deliver an adequate amount of CO_2/hour. All reliable gas equipment should have charts to relate gauge pressure, propane or natural gas used/hr. and the number of pounds of CO_2 generated/hr. Although the exact concentration may not be known, good judgment, experience and continued use should be combined to make necessary adjustments for daily weather changes so excessive concentrations can be avoided.

Chapter 24

UNVENTED HEATER PROBLEMS

by Vic Ball

Every so often I come across a crop of bedding annuals or mums or something that is just plain unhappy and in obvious trouble. The grower doesn't really know why. But, there is a problem. The name is epinasty! All too often, the culprit is a defective, open-flame heater.

Each winter I come upon clear examples of gas damage from poorly vented unit heaters or heaters with no provision for air inlet to the burner. In some cases, the damage is minor, located just close to the heater. In others, it is devastating: maybe one whole crop of bedding plants—40,000 sq. ft. or so of poly greenhouses—perhaps a total loss; in another case, 35,000 sq. ft. of cut mums—a total loss.

Most of these problems occur in polyethylene greenhouses—probably because the poly houses are so airtight. But, one of the serious losses described above was in a glass greenhouse. So, it can happen under glass, too!

When you see these major losses, you wonder how many other crops are just not quite what they should be—again because of poorly vented heaters. And the grower never knows the difference. So, I'm taking a little space to describe the problem in some detail—and the remedy.

THE TYPICAL PROBLEM

Most cases of injury from heaters look about like this. First, it is usually a polyethylene structure and usually almost airtight, which is easy to do with poly.

237

The problem, of course, occurs only with open-flame unit heaters installed right in the greenhouse. Steam-unit heaters are never a problem, simply because there is no open flame.

The problem can occur where such open-flame gas or oil-fired heaters are either vented poorly or not at all. By venting, I mean that there is simply no provision for the "smoke" from the fire to get out of the greenhouse. What would happen if you tried to operate a regular coal boiler in your greenhouse without a chimney? There would be no place for the smoke and gases from the fire to escape—so they just all pour into the greenhouse. Some growers who had severe damage have reported gases from the fire were so dense that they would make your eyes burn on cold nights. Obviously, there should be no noticeable smoke and gases from the fire in a greenhouse where heaters are properly vented, even on a cold night.

The problem can also occur where there is no provision for an air inlet from the burner. When carbon-containing fuels are burned completely, the final end products are carbon dioxide and water vapor, but if incomplete combustion occurs because of oxygen deficiency, reduced substances such as ethylene, carbon monoxide and formaldehyde may be formed instead. Because large quantities of oxygen are needed for combustion during severely cold weather, and because the tight construction of plastic houses (particularly the popular, double-layer, air-inflated houses) prevents normal air infiltration or exchange with the outside atmosphere, inside oxygen levels can be reduced too low for complete fuel combustion, with subsequent production of harmful air pollutants.

In regular glass greenhouse structures, there are usually two or more complete air changes per hour (depending upon outside conditions) by infiltration between laps of the glass, which maintains an adequate oxygen supply inside the structure for fuel combustion, except during extremely cold periods when cracks might be filled with frozen condensate. For these reasons, it is essential that you provide a supply of fresh outside air to each burner unit by installing a duct through the plastic wall, having a minimum cross-sectional area of 1 sq. in. for each 2,000 BTU heat output rating of the heating device being used. For example, if you have a burner rated to put out 100,000 BTUs of heat for your greenhouse, you need an air inlet pipe of a minimum of 8″ in diameter.

What are some of the indications that you might be having self-induced air pollution problems? If you find that your heating units have gone out during the night during severely cold weather, you should consider the possibility of insufficient oxygen to support combustion of the fuel necessary to provide the large amounts of heat needed. If you detect unusual odors or smells emanating from your heater when you enter the house from the outside, you should also be suspicious. Both carbon monoxide and ethylene gases are basically odorless, but under combustion conditions where either or both of these might be produced, other substances such as aldehydes are also often produced that do smell and might be detected by your nose. If you find that your heating unit is suddenly producing great quantities of soot, you should also have it checked, because this is another indication of poor combustion.

In addition to ethylene, burners can produce other harmful gases that can cause difficulty. I have often been consulted about cases in early spring in which bedding plants or other young seedling plants were showing severe marginal leaf burns, stunting and failure to grow—even in cases when tomato plants in the same greenhouse were not showing epinasty typical of ethylene injury. When we followed up on these cases, we generally found out that when outdoor temperatures moderated so that less heating and more ventilation was being used, the problem seemed to disappear and was no longer troublesome. Judd (1973) reported on such a case in which sulfur dioxide was eventually determined to be the problem.

Symptoms

- **Bedding annuals.** Serious injury from heaters will actually curl the leaves of such plants as tomatoes, petunias, salvias and marigolds. Soon, the top growth is deformed, stunted and obviously unhappy. Impatiens seem to be very susceptible. Tomatoes are especially unhappy in these fumes—again, leaves curl badly and plants just stop growing. Actually, all plants seem to be more or less affected by it—perhaps tomatoes are particularly sensitive.

Tomato test plants showing typical ethylene-injury symptoms. Left, untreated control plant; center, plant exposed to 1 to 2 ppm ethylene for 24 hours; right, plant exposed to 1 to 2 ppm ethylene for one week. A few tomato test plants in active growth should be maintained at all times by a grower who suspects that he might be experiencing ethylene problems. Then, if the plants begin to show these epinastic symptoms, he will be aware of his problem and may be able to correct it before it causes trouble to his other, less-sensitive plants.

239

Typical ethylene-injury symptoms on chrysanthemums. Left, control plant given 5 weeks of short-day treatment in an ethylene-free atmosphere. Right, plant of same age given same amount of short-day treatment in an atmosphere containing 1 to 2 ppm ethylene. Note the closely-spaced leaves, failure to initiate a flower bud and loss of apical dominance as indicated by the breaking into growth of the axillary sideshoots. Similar symptoms developed on plants grown in tightly constructed plastic houses heated by gas-fired unit heaters lacking a chimney or other provision for air intake to supply the needs of the combustion.

- **Mums.** Response of mums to fumes from heaters is very typical, really very easy to spot, once you get to know what to look for. As each stem comes up and starts to form its bud, the gas injury seems first to simply delay bud development. The bud will grow to perhaps a ⅛″ to ³⁄₁₆″ size, then it will stop developing. Soon vigorous side buds will start to grow out past the center bud. They will be typically half-hearted, semi-vegetative shoots. There is a bud in the tip of each of them, but something is holding the buds back from normal flowering date—and we still have only these half-hearted little ¼″ or less buds. It's a little like heat delay in midsummer. If the problem is caught in its early stages, the side buds are quickly removed and the problem of the heater corrected, the buds might go on and develop. Once it gets out of hand and once side buds have passed the original center bud by an inch or two, probably the best thing is to discard the crop and start over.

240

Typically on the mum problem, by the time the crop should be in full flower and ready for market, we have only the aborted center bud and several 2″ or 3″ half-vegetative side shoots to show for our efforts.

Remedy

When making a new installation or trying to troubleshoot the problems of an old one, call upon engineers and service personnel of the firm supplying the heaters for consultation and assistance. They are anxious to help you use their equipment so that it performs properly and successfully for you, so you will come back year after year with additional business.

It would be almost certain that any unit heaters installed by a reputable firm would have built into them an adequate-sized vent to allow for escape of smoke and gases from the fire. Be sure that the vent is carried out through the roof so that the gas can escape. To ensure a proper draft, the outside exhaust stack must be tall enough to be well above the roof peaks of nearby structures. It is also a good idea to have a proper cap on its top to prevent downdrafts, to prevent exhaust gases being carried back downward into your greenhouses by gusting winds. If exhaust fans for ventilation in the greenhouse go on while the burner is still operating or just after it has shut off, this may also pull exhaust gases back into the greenhouse. Many growers have interconnected controls to prevent such occurrences. Birds' nests built in your flues during summer when heating units were not in use have also been found, in a few cases, to be preventing escape of exhaust gases.

Still one other point needs to be watched. Each unit heater needs to be disassembled regularly—at least once a year before the major heating season begins—so that the heat exchanger panel inside can be inspected for possible cracks or holes caused by rust. The flames and heated exhaust gases pass through the inside of the heat exchanger panel on their way up the exhaust stack. Heat is in fact "exchanged" through this panel. Air on the other side of the panel is blown out into the growing area. Obviously, if this panel develops cracks, then flue gases will get into the growing area, and again, this causes major problems. Since nearly all unit heaters are completely enclosed in an outer sheet metal cover, it means that you have to dismantle them to make your inspection possible, but it is an essential type of preventive maintenance that needs to be carried out each fall without fail. It is possible to purchase unit heaters in which the heat exchanger panel is constructed of stainless steel, but these are considerably more expensive than the stock models. However, if you lose a greenhouse full of salable plants from self-induced air pollution, that might have been an inexpensive form of insurance.

Finally, be sure to have properly sized air intakes for each gas- or oil-fired heater unit. On the coldest nights, there is a great temptation to stuff an oil sack in them to keep all that cold air from coming into the greenhouse unit, but that is the time when air is needed most for combustion. If you try to save a few pennies during the night by doing this, you may have plant injuries worth dollars or hundreds of dollars the next morning!

AIR POLLUTION EFFECTS ON ORNAMENTAL CROPS

The 14th edition of the *Ball RedBook* and several editions before that included an excellent, quite detailed chapter on air pollution effects on ornamental crops—by Marlin Rogers, University of Missouri. It covers a wide range of air pollutants detailing their effects on crops. I regret that space does not allow including this chapter in this 15th edition, but I refer anyone interested in the subject to the 14th edition, page 213. Copies are available from many local libraries.

Chapter 25

SOIL AND WATER TESTING—AND NUTRITION GUIDELINES

by Vic Ball

Greenhouse crops do vary importantly in their nutritional and pH needs. Most of especially the major crop chapters in this book deal with the specific needs of that crop. But we felt that the whole subject of testing soils and water—and in general terms, defining reasonable limits for nutrient levels for most crops—needed attention in this new edition.

Another preface: This chapter assumes that growing media will be all or mostly artificial. Most growers today are using mainly artificial mixes; a very few still use a small percent of organic soil, occasionally half or more.

Important point: Note that artificial soilless mixes generally want a lower pH (from 5.2 to 5.5) versus a higher level for field soils (from pH 6.5 to 6.8). Sometimes you'll read about "organic soils" that are natural or field soils—for example, the topsoil from a farm field.

And lastly how much (and how often) should growers test media and water supplies? It's done many different ways. I'd suggest:

- **Thorough testing of soil, water and tissue** when important problems appear. It's the first step in finding the answer!

- **Some sort of routine testing**, especially of soil and water systems, on a regular schedule (at least several times a year). The point here is that you may well pick up a problem before it shows up as a poor or chlorotic crop—not after. I know growers who test each lot of commercial mix as it arrives—as a precaution. Most good growers test their water supply at least annually.

WHO WILL DO THE TESTING?

- **Soil, water, and tissue tests** are done by many state extension services, usually for a fee. If testing is not available in your state, contact one of the following:
  1) Ohio Agricultural Research and Development Center-Research Extension Analytical Laboratory (OARDC-REAL), Wooster, Ohio, [phone (216) 263-3760]
  2) Soil and Plant Laboratory Inc., Santa Clara, California, [phone (408) 727-0330]
  3) Grace-Sierra Horticultural Products Co., Fogelsville, Pennsylvania, [phone (215) 395-7104].

- **Self-testing.** Any serious grower should be equipped to do two tests himself: pH and soluble salts. For pH tests, try a battery-operated pH pen, available for about $40 from E.C. Geiger Inc., Harleysville, Pennsylvania, [phone (800) 443-4437]. It provides quick and accurate pH testing. Litmus paper also works for pH testing, but it's less accurate.

  For soluble salts testing, use some sort of solubridge, equipment to test total salts (EC) in growing media. One possibility is a soluble salts pen available from most greenhouse supply firms for about $45; it is also available from Geiger. Again, it provides a quick reading of total soluble salts in your soils. A step up (more accurate) is the Kelway salinity tester from Florist Products Inc., [phone (708) 885-2242]. These units cost about $140 and provide a simple way to test total soluble salts (EC) in the media and avoid either excess soluble salt problems or a serious overall nutritional deficiency.

  A solubridge also tests your fertilizer injector—is it delivering the correct concentration? It can also define salt content in your water supply.

  Many growers we know manage their crops with frequent checks on pH and soluble salts—which they do themselves. A full range of NPK tests can also be done by the grower—but very few do it themselves.

THE BIG FOUR NUTRITIONAL PROBLEMS

Here they are at a glance along with the underlying cause:
- **Too high pH.** Most frequent cause: highly alkaline water. Fertilizer selection and concentration and excess lime can also affect this.
- **Low pH.** Probably the most common cause: using acid forming fertilizers. It's also aggravated by water with very low alkalinity. Peat is acid!

244

- **Excess soluble salts.** Cause: usually a combination of high salt water and excess fertilizing. It's often associated with subirrigation systems that force salts up to the surface. Occasionally high fertilizer levels in commercial mixes can aggravate the problem.

- **Low soluble salts.** Causes: excess leaching, inadequate and infrequent feeding, malfunctioning fertilizer injector.

NUTRITIONAL LEVELS—AN EXCELLENT OVERVIEW

Following is an excellent paper on media testing and nutrition. It's a Michigan State University Cooperative Extension Service Bulletin that gives an exceptionally clear presentation on desirable levels of nutrition, pH and soluble salts plus practical considerations on many related problems. You'll find it an excellent starting point in managing nutrient, pH and salt levels (EC) of your commercial flowering and foliage crops.

Two prefaces:

- **Total soluble salts** in a media or water sample are expressed in one of several ways. For clarity:

  Millisiemens (mS) used in the following text are a way of expressing the reading of total salts in a soil or water sample from a solubridge. It represents the same value as millimho and also is the same value as EC. The term "EC" is used by commercial growers today the world over to express salt levels. Roughly, EC 0.25 is a too-low nutrient level; 3.0 is too high and may cause soluble salt injury. These values are based on a solubridge test using one part medium to two parts water—volume to volume. In today's publications, seminars and in this book, you will hear mainly EC to express salt levels.

  PPM is parts per million—of any soluble material in a solution. To convert millisiemens to parts per million, multiply by 700.

- **Again, for those unfamiliar** with industry jargon: You'll see on a fertilizer bag, for example, 20-10-20. It simply means that this fertilizer mix contains 20% nitrogen, 10% phosphate, 20% potash.

- **pH** is the way of expressing degree of acidity. From pH 0 to 7 is acid, from pH 7 to 14 is alkaline. pH 7 is neutral.

GREENHOUSE GROWTH MEDIA: TESTING & NUTRITION GUIDELINES

by Darryl D. Warncke and Dean M. Krauskopf
Michigan State University
East Lansing, Michigan

Greenhouse growth media have chemical and physical properties that are distinctly different from field soils. Over the past 20 years, greenhouse operators have changed from using mixes containing soils to peat or bark-based mixes containing other manufactured materials such as perlite, vermiculite and expanded polystyrene beads. The "soilless" growth media have good moisture holding and aeration properties, but limited nutrient holding capacities. As a result, fertility management in the greenhouse is more important than ever before.

Being knowledgeable about physical and chemical properties is a prerequisite for good management. An analysis of a growth medium (growth medium or media refer to any material in which plants are grown) provides basic information on which to build a fertility program. Prior to using any new lot of growth medium, test for pH, soluble salt content and available nutrient levels. Even though most companies maintain quality control programs, variations in growth media properties do occur. Knowing the initial chemical properties is essential to avoiding costly plant growth problems later.

The Michigan State University Soil Testing Lab offers a testing program specifically designed for analyzing "soilless" growth media used in producing greenhouse crops. Technicians analyze greenhouse growth media using a saturated media extract (SME) procedure. Approximately 400 cubic centimeters of a growth medium are mixed with sufficient distilled water to just saturate the medium sample. pH is determined on a saturated mix. After one hour, the saturation solution is removed with a vacuum filter. All subsequent analyses are then performed on the extracted solution.

In soilless greenhouse growth media, the concentration of essential nutrients around the root is critical to plant growth and depends upon the medium's moisture holding capacity. With a given amount of nutrient in a container of growth medium, the nutrient concentration around the root decreases as the moisture content increases. Since growth media vary widely in bulk density (weight per unit volume), it has been difficult to develop a single set of fertilization guidelines. With the saturated media extract procedure, it's possible to use a single set of fertilization guidelines (Table 1) since the amount of water held at saturation is directly related to the moisture holding characteristics of each medium.

Table 1. General Information Guidelines for Greenhouse Growth Media Analyzed by the Saturated Media Extract Method

Analysis	Category				
	Low	Acceptable	Optimum	High	Very High
Soluble Salt, mS/cm	0-.75	.75-2	2-3.5	3.5-5	5+
Nitrate-N ppm	0-39	40-99	100-199	200-299	300+
Phosphorus, ppm	0-2	3-5	6-9	11-18	19+
Potassium, ppm	0-59	60-149	150-249	250-349	350+
Calcium, ppm	0-79	80-199	200+	—	—
Magnesium, ppm	0-29	30-69	70+	—	—

Desirable pH, soluble salt and nutrient levels vary with the greenhouse crop being grown and management practices. General guidelines for the most important fertility parameters are given in Table 1. Acceptable sodium and chloride levels depend upon the total soluble salt content.

To obtain maximum crop growth, adjust growth media to optimum nutrient levels before planting. Consider the following when adjusting growth media nutrient levels.

246

Media pH

Growth medium pH influences the availability and plant uptake of all essential plant nutrients. In peat-based medium, the most desirable pH is 5.6 to 5.8 for most plants. Most irrigation waters in Michigan are alkaline, containing excess calcium carbonate. Watering plants with alkaline water gradually raises growth medium pH; over a three-month period, the pH may increase 0.5 to 1 pH unit. Thus, it is extremely important for growth medium pH to be properly adjusted prior to planting. Too high a pH, greater than 6.5, increases the chances of micronutrient deficiencies. Too low a pH, less than 5.3, may result in calcium and/or magnesium deficiency or manganese toxicity.

The amount of lime to add for pH adjustment depends on the buffering (ability to resist change) capacity of the growth medium. To bring about a one pH unit change (4.5 to 5.5) in weakly buffered growth media may require only 2 lbs. of finely ground lime per cubic yard, whereas 5 lbs. or more per cubic yard may be required in a more highly buffered growth medium. Amendments such as perlite, expanded polystyrene beads and expanded vermiculite have little or no buffering capacity. Fibrous peat and shredded bark or wood also have limited buffering ability. Somewhat decomposed peat, muck, well-composted bark and field soil provide a higher degree of buffering.

When adding lime to a greenhouse growth media, remember that it is better to under-lime initially than to over-lime. Mix up a small batch (0.1 cubic yard) of growth medium using the lime rate judged to be correct. Moisten the medium as you would before planting, place it in a large plastic bag for two weeks and then sample and check the pH. If the pH is between 5.5 and 6, the lime rate is acceptable. If the pH is outside this range adjust the rate accordingly. Always use finely ground lime passing through a 100-mesh sieve. Coarser liming materials, such as agricultural lime, may take up to six months to fully react and bring about the desired pH change. Lime will not react in dry, stockpiled growth medium; when the growth medium is moist, however, fine lime will fully react within two weeks. Calcitic lime supplies only calcium, whereas dolomitic lime contains both calcium and magnesium.

Avoid growth medium with too high a pH—lowering the pH is more difficult than raising it. Acidify high pH growth medium by mixing in iron sulfate. Approximately a one pH unit decrease (pH 7.5 to 6.5) can be brought about with 3 lbs. iron sulfate per cubic yard. The exact change depends on the buffering nature of the mix components.

Adjusting the pH in pots, benches or flats with growing plants present is more difficult and may cause plant injury. Use limewater to neutralize acid growth medium (raise the pH). Adjustment is not suggested if the pH is 5.4 or above. Stir 1 pound of finely ground lime or ½ lb. of calcium oxide into 100 gals. of water, let settle overnight and apply the clear solution, avoiding or filtering out any settlings. The growth medium should be quite moist at the time of application to minimize root shock and injury. Avoid getting the solution on the foliage or wash off the foliage immediately after application. *Do not apply ammonium containing fertilizer immediately before or after a limewater application. Ammonium reacts with lime to release volatile ammonia, which may burn plant foliage.*

Gradually lower the pH of alkaline growth medium by watering with an iron sulfate solution. Dissolve 2 lbs. of iron sulfate in 1 gal. of water and inject through the watering system at 1:100.

Acidify alkaline irrigation water using phosphoric, sulfuric or some other acid. The amount of acid to use depends on the alkalinity of the water. As a starting point, 1.5 oz.

of 85% phosphoric acid or 0.6 oz. of concentrated sulfuric acid added to 100 gals. of water will bring the alkalinity closer to the acceptable alkalinity of 100 ppm and lower the pH to about 6. Precise adjustment requires some trial additions and monitoring the resulting water pH. Injecting acid into the irrigation system also cleans out the irrigation lines and sprayer on drip nozzles. Exercise extreme caution and care when using acid. Be sure to keep sodium bicarbonate on hand to neutralize any acid spills.

Soluble Salts

All soluble ions or nutrients, such as nitrate, ammonium, potassium, calcium, magnesium, chloride and sulfate, contribute to the soluble salt content of a growth medium or water. Total soluble salt content in water or a growth medium extract is determined with a solubridge (conductivity meter) and expressed in millisiemens (mS). To convert mS to ppm multiply by 700.

Greenhouse operators commonly use a one part growth medium to two parts distilled water (volume:volume basis) to determine soluble salt content. A 1:5 ratio may be used if more solution is needed. The MSU Soil Testing Lab determines soluble salt content on the saturation extract. Guidelines for interpreting soluble salt levels for each procedure are given in Table 2. Mixing fertilizer into a growth medium increases the soluble salt content. In general, each pound of soluble fertilizer mixed in per cu. yd. of medium increases soluble salt content in the saturation extract 1.0 mS per cm. The exact increase depends on the fertilizer used.

Minimize soluble salt buildup by watering to cause some leaching. Reduce excessively high soluble salt levels by leaching the soluble salt content down to an acceptable level. Watering the container or bed so a good amount of water drains out and then repeating this procedure one to two hours later reduces the soluble salt level sufficiently. Extremely high soluble salt levels may require repeating the procedure two or three days after the first.

Table 2. Soluble Salt Guidelines for Greenhouse Growth Media Using Various Media to Water Ratios

| | Solubridge Reading | | |
Saturation Extract*	1 part media to 2 parts water	1 part media to 5 parts water	Comments
—————Millisiemens (or EC)—————			
0-0.74	0-0.25	0-0.12	Very low salt levels. Indicates very low nutrient status.
0.75-1.99	0.25-0.75	0.12-0.35	Suitable range for seedlings and salt-sensitive plants.
2-3.49	0.75-1.25	0.35-0.65	Desirable range for most established plants. Upper range may reduce growth of some sensitive plants.
3.5-5	1.25-1.75	0.65-0.90	Slightly higher than desirable. Loss of vigor in upper range. Okay for high nutrient-requiring plants.
5-6	1.75-2.25	0.90-1.10	Reduced growth and vigor. Wilting and marginal leaf burn.
6.00+	2.25+	1.10+	Severe salt injury symptoms with crop failure likely.

*Used by the Soil Testing Lab at Michigan State University.

248

Nitrate Nitrogen

Plants deficient in nitrogen become light green in color beginning with the older leaves. Some nitrogen-deficient plants may also show a reddish color. Nitrogen is an important component of the chlorophyll molecule. The nitrate form of nitrogen is soluble and mobile in the growth medium, so with watering, some of the nitrate may leach out.

Optimum nitrate-N levels vary with plant age and type. Some guidelines are given in Table 3. Young plants and seedlings do best with low to medium nitrate levels. Most pot and bedding plants in a "growing on" stage require moderately high levels. Crops grown in ground or raised beds do well with high nitrate levels. Adjust the initial level of nitrate-N in a stock growth medium using the guidelines given in Table 4.

Maintain a fairly constant level of available nitrogen by injecting additional nitrogen into the watering system. When injecting fertilizer into the irrigation water, be sure to water adequately to cause some leaching and prevent excess nitrate and soluble salt buildup.

Table 3. Desirable Nitrate-Nitrogen (NO_3-N) Concentrations in a Greenhouse Growth Medium Saturation Extract

	ppm NO_3-N in extract
Seedlings	40-70
Young pot and foliage plants	50-90
Pot and bedding plants—growing on	80-160
Roses, mums, snapdragons in ground or raised beds	120-200
Lettuce and tomatoes in ground beds	125-225
Celery transplants	75-125

Table 4. Nitrogen Fertilizer Needed to Increase the Nitrate Level in the Saturation Extract 10 ppm N

Nitrogen Carrier	N Content %	To increase test level 10 ppm, use: oz./bu.	oz./cu. yd.	oz./100 sq. ft.
Potassium nitrate	13	0.12	2.3	4.6
Calcium nitrate	15	0.10	2.0	4.0
Ammonium nitrate	33	0.045	0.9	1.8
Urea	45	0.035	0.7	1.4

Phosphorus (P)

An adequate phosphorus supply is important for root system development, rapid growth and flower quality in floral plants. Phosphorus-deficient plants exhibit slow root and top growth. In severe cases, foliage turns purple. Phosphorus plays an important role in the photosynthetic process. Phosphorus compounds (being only slowly soluble) are generally subject to limited leaching loss, but leaching may be significant (up to 30%) in fibrous, peat-lite mixes. Sufficient super-phosphate can be mixed initially into a growth medium to supply phosphorus throughout the growth period without concern for undue leaching loss or soluble salt buildup.

Crops grown in ground or raised beds require higher phosphorus levels than pot or bedding plants (Table 5). Plants grown at cool temperatures sometimes develop phosphorus deficiencies, even with adequate phosphorus present, due to limited root growth and activity.

Table 5. Desirable Phosphorus (P) Concentrations in Greenhouse Growth Media Saturation Extracts

	ppm P in Extract
Seedlings	5-9
Bedding and pot plants	6-10
Lettuce and tomatoes in ground beds	10-15
Roses, mums, snapdragons in ground or raised beds	10-15
Azaleas	7-12
Celery transplants	10-15

Table 6. Fertilizer Needed to Increase the Phosphorus Level in the Saturation Extract 2 ppm P

Phosphorus Carrier	P_2O_5 Content %	To increase test level 2 ppm, use:		
		oz./bu.	lb./cu. yd.	lb./100 sq. ft.
Normal superphosphate	20	0.75	0.90	1.8
Concentrated superphosphate	46	0.33	0.40	0.8
Bone meal	25	0.60	0.75	1.5

Raising the temperature 5°F enables plants to grow out of this condition more easily than does adding more phosphorus.

Concentrated superphosphate (0-46-0) is the phosphorus source most available to greenhouse operators, but normal superphosphate (0-20-0) is better for use in greenhouses because it contains extra calcium and sulfur. Table 6 provides guidelines for increasing available phosphorus levels in most greenhouse growth media. Mixes containing greater than 25% calcined clay or muck require about 2.5 times more phosphate fertilizer to achieve the same increase in extractable phosphorus. Do not use superphosphate for lilies because of potential fluoride toxicity. Fluoride is contained in rock phosphate—the base material used for production of superphosphate. Bone meal is a better phosphorus source for lilies.

Take care not to over-fertilize with phosphate. Excessively high phosphate levels may reduce the ability of plants to take up and utilize several micronutrients. If the irrigation water pH is being adjusted with phosphoric acid, additional phosphorus probably is not necessary. Each ounce of 85% phosphoric acid added per 100 gals. of water supplies 83 ppm P_2O_5 (36 ppmP). The percent phosphate listed on the fertilizer label is as percent P_2O_5, and P_2O_5 contains only 43% actual P.

Potassium (K)

The nutrient most often limiting in greenhouse fertility programs is potassium. The lower or oldest leaves of potassium-deficient plants show marginal yellowing or chlorosis. Spotting over the entire leaf is sometimes also associated with potassium deficiency. Many greenhouse plants have a potassium requirement equal to or greater than their nitrogen requirement. As a result, potassium levels are depleted more readily than nitrogen levels. Potassium salts are water soluble and leachable in soilless growth media with low nutrient holding capacities. Soluble fertilizers are commonly injected into the watering system to supply 200 ppm nitrogen, and many of these fertilizers (such as 20-20-20 or 25-0-25) contain equal amounts of N and K_2O. K_2O, however, is only 83% K, so plants are receiving only 166 ppm K in the fertilizer solution.

Table 7. Desirable Potassium (K) Concentrations in Greenhouse Growth Media Saturation Extracts

	ppm K in Extract
Seedlings	100-175
Bedding plants	150-225
Pot plants	175-250
Lettuce and tomatoes in ground beds	200-300
Roses, mums, snapdragons in ground or raised beds	200-275
Azaleas	125-200
Celery	250-300

Table 8. Potassium Fertilizer Needed to Increase the Potassium Level in the Saturation Extract 25 ppm

Potassium Carrier	K_2O Content	To increase test level 25 ppm, use:		
		oz./bu.	oz./cu. yd.	lbs./100 sq. ft.
Potassium nitrate	44	0.19	3.75	0.46
Potassium sulfate	50	0.16	3.25	0.40
20-20-20	20	0.41	8.25	1.03

The demand for potassium is greatest in rapidly growing plants in the vegetative stage. Seedlings and young plants usually do better with a low to medium potassium level. Optimum potassium levels are given in Table 7 for various plant categories.

Potassium nitrate has a K:N ratio of about 3:1 and is ideal for building up potassium content of a growth medium. Since plants use both the potassium and nitrate portions of the salt, concern over soluble salt buildup is less than with other potassium sources. Potassium sulfate is a suitable potassium source but is not very soluble. Potassium chloride is not recommended for greenhouse use because of its high salt index.

Establishing a near optimum potassium level in the growth medium before planting is desirable to ensure a more consistent potassium supply throughout the growth period. The quantities of potassium fertilizer to obtain the necessary buildup are given in Table 8.

Calcium (Ca)

Calcium availability for plant uptake depends on growth media pH and levels of other cations present, especially potassium and magnesium. Calcium deficiency in

251

plants results in abnormal growth or death of the growing tip. As a growth medium becomes more acid (lower pH), especially below pH 5, calcium becomes less available.

Available calcium levels may be marginal in soilless greenhouse media, especially those having an acid peat as the base material, unless amended with lime. To effectively change the pH and available calcium level, lime must be thoroughly mixed in and the growth medium must be adequately moist.

Many of the calcium carriers are slowly soluble so that equilibrium won't be reached if the stockpiled growth medium is maintained dry. As a result, the calcium content in a saturation extract may not accurately reflect the available calcium content of the growth medium.

Increase calcium levels by adding lime to acid growth medium. Calcium sulfate (gypsum) and calcium nitrate can be used to add calcium to growth medium not needing pH adjustment. Appropriate quantities to add are given in Table 9. Calcium sulfate is insoluble and does not water in well, but calcium nitrate is soluble and can be watered in.

Magnesium (Mg)

Reactions of magnesium in growth media are similar to calcium. Lower leaves of magnesium-deficient plants exhibit an interveinal chlorosis. This chlorosis may sometimes also appear on the upper leaves as well. Some soilless mixes are low in available magnesium unless the pH has been adjusted with dolomitic lime. Growth media containing vermiculite usually have magnesium levels since vermiculite naturally contains magnesium. Correct low magnesium levels in acid mixes by adding finely ground dolomitic lime.

Magnesium sulfate (Epsom salts) at 4 to 8 oz./cu. yd. or per 100 gals. (for drenching) is the best material to use in growth medium not requiring lime. *When injecting magnesium sulfate into the watering system, do not mix it with any other material unless you are sure it does not contain calcium or phosphorus. Several injectors have been plugged by precipitates formed when magnesium sulfate was injected with a calcium and/or phosphorus containing fertilizer.*

Nutrient Balance

Potassium, calcium and magnesium compete for similar uptake sites at plant root surfaces. Increasing concentration of one relative to the others changes their relative availabilities. Similarly, a high sodium (Na) level may depress potassium, calcium or magnesium uptake. Hence, the balance among the essential plant nutrients, especially potassium, calcium and magnesium is important.

When expressed as a percent of total soluble salts, the nutrient balance given in Table 10 has been found to give the best plant growth. Although the situation given in Table 10 is the most desirable, having the nutrients present at other levels, but in the same proportions as in Table 10, may also represent a nutritionally balanced growth medium. Plant growth is better with balanced nutrient levels even at low fertility. High soluble salt levels are better tolerated by plants in a balanced nutrient situation.

252

Micronutrients

Micronutrients are essential nutrients required in small quantities. Many artificial mixes, especially peat-based ones, may be deficient in micronutrients unless appropriate amendments are added. For these mixes, it is essential to add a complete micronutrient mix, 3 to 4 oz./cu. yd. (Table 11). This can be done either by a commercial manufacturer or the grower.

All essential micronutrients, except molybdenum, become less available as the pH increases. Hence, to prevent micronutrient deficiencies, it is important to maintain the pH below 6, as well as to add micronutrients.

Iron (Fe) and manganese (Mn) are the two micronutrients most likely to be deficient, especially at pH above 6.5. Total yellowing of the youngest immature leaves is a good indicator of iron deficiency, whereas mottling or striping of the youngest fully-developed leaves may indicate manganese deficiency. For correction of an iron deficiency use 4 oz. of an iron chelate per 100 gals. water. Iron sulfate can be used but is less soluble and less effective in correcting an existing deficiency. Especially with alkaline conditions (pH above 7), iron from iron sulfate becomes tied up, whereas iron in the chelate form remains available.

Table 9. Calcium (Ca) Carriers to Increase the Calcium Level in the Saturation Extract 25 ppm

Calcium Carrier	Ca Content	To increase test level 25 ppm, use:		
	%	oz./bu.	oz./cu.yd.	lb./100 sq. ft.
Calcitic lime	30-34	0.21	4.2	0.53
Dolomitic lime	20-24	0.30	6	0.75
Calcium sulfate	23	0.29	5.8	0.73
Calcium nitrate	19	0.35	7	0.88
Normal superphosphate	20	0.33	6.7	0.84
Concentrated superphosphate	13	0.51	10.2	1.28

Table 10. Desirable Nutrient Balance in Saturation Extract

Nutrient	% of Total Soluble Salt
Nitrate-N	8-10
Ammonium-N	less than 3
Potassium	11-13
Calcium	14-16
Magnesium	4-6
Sodium	less than 10
Chloride	less than 10

Table 11. Suggested General Micronutrient Formulation to Mix into Growth Stock Media

Compound	Quantity to Use Per Cu. Yd.
Iron chelate (6%)	1 oz.
Manganous sulfate	1 oz.
Copper sulfate	0.3 oz.
Zinc sulfate	0.2 oz.
Sodium borate (borax)	0.1 oz.
Sodium molybdate	0.03 oz.

For correcting a manganese deficiency, use either manganese sulfate at 1 to 2 oz./100 gals. or a manganese chelate at 4 to 8 oz./100 gals. *Never use a manganese chelate in conjunction with iron sulfate.* The other combinations of iron and manganese carriers are compatible.

Copper (Cu) and zinc (Zn) deficiencies occur infrequently. Both sulfate and chelate forms of these nutrients are effective. Use 1 oz./100 gals. for the sulfate form and ¼ oz./100 gals. for the chelate form.

Exercise extreme care when applying boron (B)—the difference between deficiency and toxicity is very small. Uniform application is very important and is best done as a liquid solution. Use no more than ¼ oz. borax (11% B) per cu. yd. or per 100 gals. water on a one-time basis. Boron in the irrigation water is a potential source of B toxicity. Levels greater than 0.5 ppm may result in injury to sensitive crops. Know the quality of your irrigation water.

Molybdenum (Mo) deficiency is seldom seen, but may occur when the growth medium is quite acid, near pH 5 or below. Poinsettias are more likely to develop molybdenum deficiency than other ornamental crops. The quantity required is so small that uniform application can only be attained with a liquid solution.

The presence of fluoride (F) may adversely affect the quality of lilies and some foliage plants. More than 5 ppm fluoride in the saturation extract of a growth medium is likely to result in some type of fluoride injury for sensitive plants. Excess fluoride may cause some tip burn and marginal chlorosis. Adding calcium as lime or calcium sulfate (5 lbs./cu. yd.) will "fix" the fluoride in an unavailable form and usually eliminate the adverse fluoride effect.

WATER TESTING AND PARAMETERS

Lack of quality water often causes severe problems for growers. Also, in establishing a new growing operation, an adequate supply of "grower quality" water must be a #1 consideration. You can't grow quality without it! Bad water also seriously inhibits the results from pesticides, growth retardants and floral preservatives. So—what is "grower quality" water? There are two ways to evaluate water supplies:

● **pH and alkalinity levels**—by far the majority of water problems occur here.

● **Excess or deficiency of other elements**—an occasional problem.

254

The following paper by John Peterson and Laura S. Kramer identifies the pH/alkalinity problem in very clear practical terms—it's strongly recommended reading for anyone growing or planning to grow crops. It's adapted from *Grower-Talks*, December 1984, p. 30.

THE RELATIONSHIP BETWEEN WATER pH AND ALKALINITY

by John C. Peterson and Laura S. Kramer
Ohio State University
Columbus, Ohio

Findings of a water quality survey conducted at Ohio State have revealed some very important perspectives relating to water quality, of which all floral industry firms should be very aware. While this comprehensive report reviews numerous aspects investigated as part of the water quality project, it seems there is one issue that needs a high level of awareness: the relationship between water pH and alkalinity.

Nearly 700 samples, submitted by U.S. floriculture industry firms, were analyzed as part of the Ohio State Water Assessment Program. Among the samples tested, more than 80% were found to have a pH exceeding 7. For purposes of evaluating submitted samples, a pH range of 5 to 7 was judged to be desirable. Only a few of the samples analyzed had pH values below 5. Overall, high pH was found to be the water quality parameter that most concerns monitoring and controlling in the floriculture industry.

The Concern for Water pH

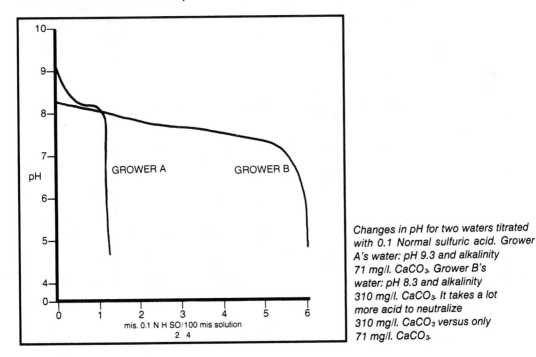

Changes in pH for two waters titrated with 0.1 Normal sulfuric acid. Grower A's water: pH 9.3 and alkalinity 71 mg/l. CaCO₃. Grower B's water: pH 8.3 and alkalinity 310 mg/l. CaCO₃. It takes a lot more acid to neutralize 310 mg/l. CaCO₃ versus only 71 mg/l. CaCO₃.

Adverse water pH can directly and indirectly affect all segments of the floriculture industry, including propagators, growers, shippers, wholesalers, retailers and plant-scapers. Water pH is known to affect the quality and postharvest life of cut flowers; the stability and efficiency of pesticides, growth regulators and floral preservatives; the solubility of fertilizers in solutions; and the availability of nutrients in growing media. These specific situations, plus other possible influences of water pH on cut flower and pot plant quality and longevity, are ample reasons why all floriculture industry firms should be concerned about the pH of their water.

Naturally, the first step in assessing your water pH is to test it. A single test is helpful, but not always dependable. Whereas the pH of a municipal water source is generally maintained at a relatively constant level, the pH of well and surface water (pond, river, etc.) can be highly variable depending on rainfall and other environmental factors. The rule of thumb for testing well and surface water sources is to do so as often as is practical and most certainly when environmental occurrences (such as rainfall) suggest a change might have occurred in the pH level.

Measure pH at commercial and university laboratories or on site at your firm. Test procedures are relatively simple. Purchase either a good quality pH meter or pH papers for this purpose. A good pH meter will generally cost $150 or more; besides testing water, the meter can also be used for other purposes, such as monitoring growing media pH. Using pH paper test strips is also a fairly good procedure for monitoring water pH. Test strips rely on color-sensitive chemical systems and can be quick and easy to use. Both pH meters and papers are available from many industry supply firms and scientific supply companies.

If the pH of your water is within a range of 5 to 7, under most circumstances you have a desirable situation, although it is most desirable to be within a range of 5 to 6. The entire issue does not end here, though, and you should clearly recognize that measuring pH is only half the story. It is especially important to understand and measure alkalinity, particularly if you are interested in reducing the pH of your irrigation water.

Water Alkalinity Relates to pH

Alkalinity is a chemical factor that is, in a manner, related to pH, but in itself is a different parameter. The term "alkalinity" should not be confused with the term "alkaline," which describes situations where pH levels exceed 7. Perhaps "basic" is a better and more accurate term to describe high pH conditions; low pH situations should be described as "acidic."

Water alkalinity is a measure of a water's capacity to neutralize acids. Alkalinity is expressed chemically as milligrams per liter of calcium carbonate equivalents (mg/l $CaCO_3$). Dissolved bicarbonates, carbonates and hydroxides comprise the major chemicals that contribute to the alkalinity of water.

The alkalinity of water is important and related to pH because alkalinity establishes the buffering capacity of a water source. Simply stated, alkalinity affects the ability to change or modify water pH by adding acids.

An important example of the manner in which alkalinity relates to pH modification is as follows: Grower A has water with a pH of 9.3 with an alkalinity of 71 mg/l $CaCO_3$. To reduce the pH of this water to 5, it takes 1.2 ml of 0.1 N sulfuric acid/100 ml of water. In contrast, Grower B has water with a pH of 8.3 and an alkalinity of 310 mg/l $CaCO_3$. To reduce this water to a pH of 5, it takes 6 ml of 0.1 N sulfuric acid/100 ml of water. Despite the fact that Grower B's water is a full pH unit lower than Grower A's, it takes five times more acid to lower the pH to 5. The important perspective to retain from this is that efforts to reduce water pH cannot and should not be based on pH measurement alone! Alkalinity is important and must be considered.

This perspective is especially important whenever and wherever efforts are undertaken to reduce water pH levels. This includes injecting acid to lower the pH of irrigation water, adding acid to water to assure the stability and efficacy of pesticides and growth regulator chemicals, and also using floral preservatives to extend cut flower quality and longevity.

In order to be optimally effective, most floral preservatives reduce the pH of water to about 3.3 to 3.5. This pH reduction is important because it suppresses the growth of microorganisms that "clog up" the water conducting cells in cut flower stems. Often, floral preservatives contain acidifying agents, such as citric acid, to reduce the pH of water to which they are added. If the alkalinity of water is extremely high, a situation exists where the pH of the water may not be sufficiently reduced, and the floral preservative might not be optimally effective. This circumstance might account for the fact that floral preservatives might not seem to work well for you or some of your customers. The alternative is not necessarily to add more preservative to the solution, since other chemicals are contained in these products and might be added in excess amounts. Some floral preservative companies will provide you with a special formulation containing extra acidifier, if you know for certain that the alkalinity of your water is excessively high.

The relationship between pH and alkalinity is also important for growers interested in reducing the pH of their irrigation water. High pH irrigation water applied to a growing medium can cause the pH to rise further.

Generally, the higher the alkalinity of an irrigation water, the more rapidly the medium pH will rise. As might be expected, this pH increase within a growing medium can lead to nutritional imbalances and, consequently, reduced growth and crop quality. Therefore, a program of acid injection for modifying the water might need to be employed. Both alkalinity and pH must be taken into consideration when a program is developed.

Further Considerations

High pH and high alkalinity may cause the breakdown of pesticides and growth regulators. In some cases, the effectiveness can be dramatically reduced or completely eliminated. For example, the growth regulator ethephon (Florel) is optimally effective when the pH of the spray solution drops to about 4 after the ethephon concentrate is added to water. If the pH reduction does not occur, then this material may not have the desired effect when applied to plants. Water having a high alkalinity may resist adequate acidification by the ethephon concentrate. The resolution to this situation might be to reduce the alkalinity level (by adding acid) prior to adding ethephon.

As is the case for pH measurements, alkalinity can be measured by submitting a water sample to a lab. But as with pH, on-site alkalinity measurements can also be performed easily, quickly and inexpensively by all floriculture industry firms.

A suitable alkalinity test kit is manufactured by Bausch and Lomb. I have utilized this test kit and found it to be an inexpensive, simple procedure.

The Bausch and Lomb Portable Spectro Alkalinity Kit is available through Fisher Scientific Company. Fisher Scientific is headquartered in Pittsburgh, Pennsylvania, and has branch offices in other major cities throughout the world. The alkalinity test kit costs approximately $36 and tests about 100 samples. Samples can be tested in three minutes or less. The system is similar to test kits used for monitoring swimming pool water. An indicator dye is added to a small measured volume of water, then drops of a test solution (dilute sulfuric acid) are added to the sample until it changes from a blue to a pink color. Each drop of test solution equates to 20 mg/l of $CaCO_3$.

When interpreting results of an alkalinity test, we have found water with an alkalinity of 100 mg/l $CaCO_3$ or less to be most desirable. Within this range, if pH modification is performed, small additions of acid will generally bring about rapid reductions in pH levels. As alkalinity levels increase above 100 mg/l $CaCO_3$, the amount of acid required to bring about a pH reduction increases. We have noticed a need for a very acute awareness about potential pH/alkalinity problems as they relate to floral preservative, pesticide and growth regulator effectiveness; also problems of rapid, undesirable rises in growing media pH when the alkalinity level of water exceeds 200 to 250 mg/l $CaCO_3$. Among the water samples we tested from floriculture industry firms, levels as high as 500 mg/l $CaCO_3$ were found. Levels this high may present very serious problems.

In summary, water pH is an extremely important issue that the entire floriculture industry should be aware of and concerned about. But in addition to pH, alkalinity is an important part of the overall perspective. Alkalinity should be understood and considered when evaluating pH problems and methodology for modifying water pH.

Other Deficiency-Excess Problems

Occasionally other elements appear in either excess or deficiency in grower water supplies and can cause severe problems. Here are the main elements involved and approximate parameters of upper and lower levels desirable for most crops.

Desirable Ranges for Specific Elements in Irrigation Water

Sulfate (SO$_4$)	24-240 mg/l	Soluble Salts	0-1.5 mmhos
Phosphorus (P)	0.005-5 mg/l	Zinc (Zn)	1-5 mg/l
Potassium (K)	0.5-10 mg/l	Sodium (Na)	0-50 mg/l
Calcium (Ca)	40-120 mg/l	Aluminum (Al)	0-5.0 mg/l
Magnesium (Mg)	6-24 mg/l	Molybdenum (Mo)	0-0.02 mg/l
Manganese (Mn)	0.5-2 mg/l	Chloride (Cl)	0-140 mg/l
Iron (Fe)	2-5 mg/l	Fluoride (F)	0-1.0 mg/l
Boron (B)	0.2-0.8 mg/l	Nitrate (NO$_3$)	0-5.0 mg/l
Copper (Cu)	0-0.2 mg/l	Ammonia (NH$_4$)	Undetermined
SAR	0-4	Alkalinity	0-100 mg/l $CaCO_3$

Chapter 26

HIGH INTENSITY DISCHARGE LIGHTS

by C. Anne Whealy
Ball Seed Company

The application of greenhouse supplementary lighting, specifically high intensity discharge (HID) lamps, continues to increase in low light regions of North America and Europe. With proper cultural and environmental control, supplemental lighting enables greenhouse growers to increase productivity, reduce crop time and produce consistently high quality plants year-round, regardless of the weather or season.

Plants produced under insufficient light levels have reduced vigor, stretched narrow stems, poor breaking, small leaves and grow slowly. Adequate light levels produce high quality plants that are more compact with good breaking, have thick stems and dark large leaves, grow faster and flower earlier.

Low light is due to natural shortening of daylength, lower angle of the sun or an increase in number of cloudy days. In the northern United States, the light intensity during November, December and January is less than one-third of July's. Natural light levels are adequate April through August, and supplemental lighting is not economically justifiable.

The greenhouse structure, type and condition of the glazing material, and overhead equipment and hanging baskets can further reduce light levels inside the greenhouse to one-half that of outside the greenhouse. During low light periods, light becomes the limiting factor to plant growth.

Increased profit from increased yield of high quality crops when the market price is most favorable is the driving force behind supplemental lighting installation. When considering supplemental light installation, consider the following: location, crop(s) to be produced, available markets, electric energy rates (present and future) and cost-benefit.

ECONOMIC CONSIDERATIONS

It is estimated that supplemental lighting costs about $2/sq. ft. for installation or about $250 per lamp/fixture; the lamp is about 30% of this cost. Operating costs (including ballast energy) are 0.47 KW and 1.1 KW per 400- and 1,000-watt lamp, respectively. Payback on supplemental lighting system investments, given substantial crop improvement, is estimated to be from 2½ to 3 years.

Some power companies offer greenhouse growers reduced rates for off-peak use of electricity for lighting. Rebate incentives on lighting system purchases are also available from some utility companies.

Supplemental lighting provides supplemental heat, which reduces operating costs by decreasing heating fuel usage. Four hundred- and 1,000-watt HPS (high pressure sodium) lamps/ballasts produce about 1,600 and 3,750 BTUs per hour of operation, respectively. Or, 28 1,000-watt HPS lamps operating for 1 hour will produce the same amount of heat as one gallon of fuel oil or 140 cu. ft. of natural gas. It is estimated that HPS lighting can reduce heating costs by as much as 25% to 30%. The higher the light levels and longer of duration of use, the more heat produced and greater reduction of heating costs. Lighting can also reduce greenhouse humidity levels. It is obvious that the heat given off by supplemental lighting reduces the payback period.

Light and Plant Responses

Sunlight contains visible light of all colors in the rainbow and invisible radiation in the form of infrared and ultraviolet radiation. The wavelength of the radiation, measured in nanometers (nm), determines the color of the light: violet, 400 nm; blue/green, 500 nm; yellow, 600 nm; and red, 700 nm. The visible spectrum is the radiation emitted between 380 and 780 nm. Light is composed of particles called "photons" that have a distinct energy level with respect to wavelength. The amount of energy increases as wavelengths become shorter. For example, blue light photons have a higher energy level than red light photons. Both visible and invisible light becomes heat when absorbed by an object, except for the energy utilized by the plant as chemical energy in the process of photosynthesis.

Plants respond differently to different wavelengths of light. Maximum plant sensitivity for photosynthesis occurs at 675 nm. Plant leaves contain chlorophyll, a yellow-green pigment that reflects or transmits yellow-green light and absorbs blue and red light. Red light is necessary for photosynthesis and chlorophyll synthesis and promotes seed germination, seedling growth, stem elongation, flowering and anthocyanin formation. Blue light is also necessary for photosynthesis and chlorophyll synthesis and reduces stem length and dry weight, but increases branching and stem strength. Blue light has also been shown to improve leaf and flower color. There may be possibilities to decrease growth retardant use by manipulating spectral distribution.

Supplemental Light and Plant Responses

Maximum plant densities result in the most economical use of HID lighting. Therefore, during early developmental stages lights are the most beneficial. Give light to bedding plants when the first true leaves are green and continue for 4 to 6 weeks. Lighting beyond 6 weeks is not economically worthwhile. On vegetatively produced crops, cuttings benefit from supplemental lighting during propagation and continued until flowering.

Irradiation level and duration depend on crop, daylength, latitude and cultural conditions. A lower irradiance level for a longer period of time is preferable to a higher irradiance level for a shorter period of time. For example, it is better to give 300 fc. for 24 hours than 600 fc. for 12 hours. For most cut flowers and potted plants, light levels of 400 to 500 fc. for 18 hours per day will increase plant growth, quality and profits. For plugs, 300 fc. is the minimum for economic return. Light levels of 600 to 700 fc. will increase growth, but are not economically justifiable. Levels of HID higher than 700 fc. may cause plant damage.

Supplemental light is becoming a major aid to growers in both North America and Europe.

In growth chambers or growth rooms, 2,000 to 6,000 fc. are used. Typically metal halide (MH) or a combination of HPS and MH are used to balance the spectral distribution. In interiorscapes, MH lamps providing 100 to 350 fc. should be used.

For most cut flowers and potted plants, provide lights for four to six hours on sunny days and 12 to 16 hours on cloudy days. Most bedding plants should be lighted for 18 hours. Extending to 24 hours does not result in appreciably more plant growth. Given very low power costs, lighting may be done more economically at night.

Types of Supplemental Light

There is no one light source that can simulate growth effects caused by the sun. Most light sources emit radiation from 300 nm to 2,500 nm, but not all wavelengths are emitted by all light sources. In theory, the most effective assimilation lamp would be the one that emitted most strongly in the red range, at 675 nm, but without blue light, plants would be elongated.

Besides spectral energy distribution, other factors such as efficiency, output, uniform light distribution and the crop are critical considerations. Efficiency—the best return on the electricity used—depends upon light source, type of reflector and amount of benefit to the crop. Uniform light distribution translates into uniform production. Uniformity depends upon lamp wattage, amount of area lighted, reflector design, lamp spacing and height of lights above the crop. Light distribution uniformity should be at least 85%.

- **Incandescent lights** emit light primarily in the far red range and are considered rather inefficient. Incandescent lamps convert only 6.5% of the energy consumed into light energy; the remainder is emitted as heat. Incandescent lamps have a relatively short lifespan (1/10 of fluorescent lamps), but initial investment costs are low. Because of these factors, incandescent lamps are used primarily for photoperiod control and not recommended for supplemental lighting.

- **Fluorescent** are cooler, more efficient, have a better spectral balance and a longer lamp life than incandescent. Fluorescent are expensive, however, and cause shading problems due to their large fixture size. Because of the lamps' bulk, they are generally only used in special situations such as growth chambers, where they are installed in combination with incandescent lamps to balance the blue to red light ratio for plant growth. Fluorescent lamps are half as efficient as HPS lamps in converting electricity into light energy. Lower efficiencies mean that more fixtures are required, adding to shading problems. Also, lamp degradation is more than three times greater for fluorescent lamps than for HPS lamps.

- **HID lights*** are preferable to incandescent and/or fluorescent lamps because of high efficiency, uniform light distribution and lower amount of shading.

*High intensity discharge (HID) is a generic term. It includes MH, LPS and HPS lamps. Incandescent and fluorescent lamps are not technically considered to be HID lights.

Metal halide (MH) lamps emit white light, which is similar to daylight as perceived by the human eye. This white light is very effective in retail areas or interiorscapes where color and plant appearance are important. HPS lamps are not desirable in these areas as they cast a yellowish light. MH lamps provide the best spectral distribution of all lamps for plant growth, providing more reds, far reds and blues than HPS lamps. They are less efficient, however, less cost effective and shorter lived than HPS or LPS lamps. MH lamps have an energy conversion efficiency of 120 to 125 lumens per watt compared to an efficiency of 135 to 140 lumens per watt for HPS lamps.

Low pressure sodium (LPS) lamps are the most efficient light source since they have the highest rating for lumens per watt, generating less heat than other lamps. The disadvantages of LPS lamps are undesirable spectral distribution, high cost and large fixture size that causes shading problems.

High pressure sodium (HPS) or sodium vapor lamps emit mostly in the yellow-orange-red range, 550 to 700 nm. HPS lamps are considered to be the best supplemental light source because they provide more photosynthetically useful light per unit of electricity than other light sources, and their efficiency is almost as high as LPS lamps: 25% versus 27% conversion efficiency. HPS lamps degrade slowly and have longer useful lives than other lamps. For example, 400- or 1,000-watt sodium lamps are rated to last 24,000 hours; MH, 20,000; LPS, 18,000; and fluorescent, 15,000. HPS fixtures are more compact with less bulky reflectors and cause less shading problems than fluorescent or LPS lamps.

HPS lamps are available as either 400- or 1,000-watt units that provide an output of 50,000 and 140,000 lumens, respectively. The trend is going toward the 400-watt units, which are more compact and less expensive to install and maintain. One-thousand-watt lamps require a high mounting height that may not be possible in many greenhouses.

A lamp reflector is a mirror that directs the light from the fixture to the crop. The objective in reflector/fixture design is to maximize light output, light distribution uniformity and power consumption efficiency. Reflectors allow increased distances between lamps and decreased mounting height. Therefore, better reflectors reduce the number of fixtures required. Well-designed reflectors direct 90% of the light to the plants; poorly designed reflectors may direct less than 50% of the light.

Increasingly HID units are being developed that use less electricity, operate more efficiently and coolly, are more compact to reduce shading problems and cost less to install and maintain. To benefit from supplemental lighting, it is imperative to provide optimum temperatures and levels of carbon dioxide, water and fertilizer to maximize plant growth. Supplemental lights will eliminate light level as a limiting factor in plant growth, but if other factors become limiting, the use of supplemental lights will not be advantageous.

Chapter 27

ATTENTION YOUNG PEOPLE! EXCELLENT CAREER OPPORTUNITIES HERE FOR YOU

by Vic Ball

Flower growing, including bedding, pot plants, foliage and cuts, is a strong, expanding industry. U.S. Department of Agriculture numbers (dollars sold) in 1989 for these crops were about $2.7 billion. Many growers are automating, expanding and tooling up for the expanded floriculture markets of the 1990s.

A key problem I hear so often is the critical shortage and need for well-trained young people. Men and women. Ask a grower, "What is well trained?" Most will want first, people with solid classroom training in the basic plant disciplines: pathology, entomology, agronomy, physiology, chemistry, etc. Two years will do it, and there are some excellent two-year schools. Four years is better—now time for some broadening, liberal education. The United States and Canada have many excellent four- and two-year universities.

Back to that grower: He also very much wants people with some hands-on growing experience and people management. Much of the world has well-established programs that include both classroom and recognized apprenticeship plans. You spend several years with a proven "master," growing crops under his watchful

265

eye. It's a good system, especially strong in countries such as Holland, Germany, Scandinavia, England and New Zealand. In fact, in my opinion, their ample supply of such thoroughly trained young people will be a major advantage to those countries as flower production becomes ever more openly competitive worldwide. Soon enough that will be the way. The United States is committed to free trade. The United States and Canada can ill afford to enter this world competition with the penalties of an incomplete system for training young people.

Well, back to the ranch! What can today's U.S. and Canadian young people do about all this? My thoughts:

- **If possible, do get at least two years** at one of our excellent four-year universities. Again, basics. Examples of schools with good four- and two-year programs: Michigan State University, East Lansing, Michigan; North Carolina State University, Raleigh, North Carolina. Better yet, do four years if you can.

  Another option: Try one of the many fine local community colleges where these basic plant subjects are taught. Many of these schools welcome students who live at home. Many are part-time in the classroom and are working in local flower production commercially during the rest of their days. Some do evening classes. A good combination! Good examples are Sand Hills Community College, Pinehurst, North Carolina; and New York State, Cobleskill, New York.

  Another option: There are good correspondence courses available. An example is the University of Guelph, Horticultural Correspondence Program, Guelph, Ontario, Canada N1G 2W1 [phone (519) 767-5050].

- **Hands-on experience.** We don't have a recognized apprenticeship system (nearly all other U.S. professions/trades do—for bricklayers, airline captains, doctors, etc.!), but you can seek out a top grower in your crop preference, apply for two to three years of employment with him, tell him frankly that you want hands-on experience growing crops, that you have had basic classroom training and that your goal is to be a grower of top quality plants. Most importantly say, "I'm willing to work." Many growers (not all) will welcome such an approach.

- **As circumstances permit, do try to visit other nearby growers.** Talk to them, watch their crops. The major seminars/trade shows held yearly are another great place to learn. Examples: GrowerExpo, Chicago, Illinois area, early January; International Floriculture Industry Short Course (formerly the Ohio Short Course), Cincinnati, Ohio, in July; and Professional Plant Growers Association (formerly BPI), early October. All are great learning opportunities.

About Compensation

Flower production in years past has had a reputation for hard work and low pay. Happily, though, in recent years this is changing. The hard work is fast giving way to a wide variety of automation and computers. And compensation, especially for people with good training and some on-the-job experience, is quite good. People who can grow several acres of quality crops and can manage a dozen or two people are much in demand—at salaries (with some experience) at $30,000 to $40,000 per year and higher. If you can produce!

Flower Growing in the 1990s

Flower growing in the 1990s will be ever-increasingly dominated by new technologies, new automation, new precision scheduling of crops. There'll be more computers. Crops are being tailored very precisely to achieve a set height, number and size of flowers, etc.—all done in a carefully controlled number of days. Mass outlets are publishing "specifications" and holding growers to them. Competitive pressures are pushing growers to very tight rotations. Our open market system is pressing our whole industry to produce "smaller bites (smaller pot sizes) of top quality"—at lower prices. All of which can be and must be done profitably, but only with carefully thought out schedules, spacing and temperatures using all available modern technology. It's a whole new world into which growers are being led mainly by mass outlets. As we learn to accommodate these new markets, clearly there is ever increasing demand for our products. Europe, with basically much of our lifestyle, already uses several times more flowers per capita than here in the United States and Canada. We are moving that way.

Back to automatics: The Dutch and Danes are already down to as little as two and three people per acre on at least semi-specialized ranges—partly made possible by their very efficient marketing systems. Somehow we must adapt our own marketing capabilities to achieve such efficiency.

So, the old days of hard physical work have gone and, to me, a fascinating new era of technology/automation/computers is coming in. Fast.

Floriculture needs good young people who can manage these precisely scheduled crops and the machines and computers that will do the "work."

A key goal of the 15th edition of the *Ball RedBook* is to help bring these new technologies to the grower—and to students. Better heating and cooling systems, better plug culture, such things as cool day/warm night growing.

We need you!

Ball Institute Seminars

With a different approach to training, Ball Institute conducts a series of 1- and 2-day seminars on a variety of crops and other grower subjects. Examples: plugs, modern structures, control of the greenhouse atmosphere, and media/water management. Some are held at the Ball Institute headquartered in West Chicago, Illinois, most are held out across the United States and Canada in key growing areas. For more details write Ball Institute, P.O. Box 335, West Chicago, IL 60185 [phone (708) 231-3600].

Chapter 28

THOUGHTS ON LAUNCHING A NEW BUSINESS

by Vic Ball

Every year many young people (and some not so young) start up a new flower growing business. Partly that's because growing flowers is one of the few businesses in which a new entrepreneur with limited capital has a fair chance. It's not dominated by franchises, chains, etc. Many people do start—and many (not all) of them succeed.

I like to point out that my father, George J. Ball, founder of the Ball company, started up many years ago as a modest 2- or 3-acre outdoor cut flower grower—raising asters for the Chicago wholesale market.

I'd like to offer suggestions on all this.

TRAINING

You've got to know basic growing—and if you will retail, some basics of retailing. How to get this?

- **Schools help.** There are dozens of four-year universities offering horticulture, plus many community colleges and technical schools (some one year, some two year). They also offer evening classes or perhaps part-time day classes. Often they are close by—no living costs involved.

Jim and Judy Gordy, J & J Greenhouse, Claxton, Georgia [phone (912) 739-4567]. In 1980, Judy started growing a few bedding plants in a 50' greenhouse as mostly a hobby. It went so well that Jim joined the business in 1984. Today they operate a very successful 100,000-sq.-ft. pot and bedding plant business. According to Judy (swamped with poinsettia orders in mid-December), "We enjoy it!" Note: Any of these start-up success stories welcome phone calls from anyone thinking of going the same way.

Schools are a good way to get basics, but I suggest that the classroom alone doesn't qualify you for running a business.

- **Hands-on experience** is important. Some classroom is great, but if you must pick between the two, I'd consider several years actual experience with a successful grower as more apt to breed a successful entrepreneur. Pick someone who does your crops—bedding, pot plants or perhaps foliage, and if you plan to be a retail grower, find someone who also does a good retail garden center and maybe a retail flower shop.

Somehow the whole world has well-developed apprentice systems in flower production—always coordinated with ¼ to ⅓ time in the classroom. Formal training gives you much more depth and understanding of growing and business. But again, the odds for surviving the first several years (if you must choose) are probably better with in-depth apprenticeship experience. The odds for a successful, satisfying, lifelong career are better with formal training. Try hard for some of both. See Chapter 27 about training in floriculture.

Mike Behnke, Highwoods Nursery, Winter Haven, Florida [phone (813) 324-3151] started in business with his wife Joy in 1982 with about 15,000-sq.-ft. After quite a struggle, they are well established, growing pot and bedding plants in 3 acres of greenhouses plus 3 acres of Saran. Says Mike, "We had a super spring 1990, heavily into chain business. Things are going very well now but it is nerve wracking."

- **How big, what to grow, how to sell.** Basic decisions that must come first:

First, size. I see many couples where the man has an outside job (income), the woman likes growing, and somehow they find the land and money to put up perhaps 10,000 sq. ft. of plastic, typically for growing bedding plants. They are clearly most profitable. Often they sell both retail and wholesale to local garden centers, hardware stores, etc. They say, "We sell 'em wherever we can." The man takes his vacation in May to help out at peak season. Often he builds the greenhouse and is the "repair guy."

In a successful case, they go on for several years, build up a customer list and a lot of know-how. Things learned the hard way are not soon forgotten! All this begins to develop a financial structure, some assets (net worth), several years of reasonably profitable operation and perhaps money borrowed and paid back, which is important in borrowing bigger money later on. See *GrowerTalks,* September 1986, page 82, for Mike Behnke's start-up story.

Then, in several years, comes the point of decision. "Shall I quit my job, go for some financial help and expand enough so the enterprise will support our whole family without my job?" Let's say the decision is yes.

How big to build? It depends on what you grow and how you sell. A retail/garden center operation (bedding plants, poinsettias) with even a half acre might do it. Wholesale would probably struggle to support a family with less than an acre.

I've seen people with good on-the-job experience and lots of ambition launch a 1-acre wholesale bedding and pot plant operation with heavy borrowing and make it go. It needs a lot of hard work and cash hoarding, especially at first and you've got to grow quality plants.

What to grow? Most new flower growing operations I see do spring plants, pot plants and often some perennials. Cut flowers are promising, especially in California and Florida, but tend to be larger operations and not commonly done in the North (except outdoor summer cut flowers). Foliage in Florida also favors the not-too-small size operation.

Retail or wholesale? It depends a lot on you. See the bedding plant chapter for some ideas on what makes a good retailer.

Do a Thorough Plan/Budget/Cash Flow

Of the three, cash flow is by far the most important, but do start with a detailed plan. First, a detailed floor plan for the whole show—driveway, parking area, some kind of headhouse (can be a poly greenhouse), and will it be raised benches or on the ground. Overhead unit heaters mean lower initial costs by far. Do see Jim Dickerson's (Gobles, Michigan) unique on-the-ground root zone hot water heating with mini boilers right out in the greenhouses (*GrowerTalks*, "Viewpoint," April 1990). There is also a *GrowerTalks* videotape available describing Jim's system.

Your plan must include heat, water piped out through the houses, electricity the same, probably a well and gravel for a driveway, etc. Include a fertilizer injector of some sort, a sprayer and some sort of vehicle. Then put a fair price tag on all this and add it all up.

The next suggestion: at least a rough plan for what you're going to grow and sell year #1—10,000 4" geraniums in May, 2,000 flats of annuals in April, etc. Again, extend prices. There's your total income for year #1, by month. Be sure to deduct a 10% shrink.

Now the last, somewhat difficult but most important planning step of all: a cash flow. It's a bit of trouble but strongly recommended. Start with the day Jones Greenhouse opens its doors. List how much cash is on hand (checking account, savings account, securities, etc.)—liquid assets only. Then, for each month, you add the cash income (mostly sales) and subtract all you spend—wages, supplies, electric bills, mortgage payments, etc. You'll soon begin to see a projection of the lifeblood of

Steve Barlow, Barlow Flower Farm, Sea Girt, New Jersey [phone (201) 449-9189]. Steve and his wife Leslie bought a 13,000-sq.-ft., run-down range in 1983. Today it's up to 48,000-sq.-ft. and still growing. Says Steve, "Pot and bedding plant business is fantastic. We built 4 new houses last spring, and planted all in 4½" (4 plugs each). They sold out in 4 weeks at $2 retail." Steve's comment to others considering starting up: "It's a wonderful opportunity today!"

your entire project. Profit is important. That's where cash comes from! Many businesses (large and small) make good money but go bankrupt. They just run out of money (spend too much on new equipment, accounts receivable too high, too much salary), and the bank says no.

You'll soon see, too, how critical cash flow accounting is to the decision on spending—how much greenhouse area you can afford to build and still keep up the loan payments. You may well be able to borrow money from that banker, but it's a great deal easier for him to help you if you have a reasonably accurate cash flow.

Many growers say, "I'm going to need $25,000 about February 1. Everything's going out then, but no sales. I'll have a surplus (to invest) July 1." It's called seasonal borrowing and most businesses do it. Farmers, too.

Two other basic financial records every business needs:

- **An operating statement** (profit and loss) lists all expenses and income, shows your profit or loss by month.

- **Balance sheet**—do a good one at least twice a year. It will show you what you own and what you owe. A good goal is to own over half of your enterprise all the way. Too often banks own over half and they become uneasy—and they should, too.

273

Jack Knox (right) of Lubbock, Texas [phone (806) 745-7820], shown here with his son Jerry, had a different start-up approach. In 1982, with one 50' house, he turned to growing for a retirement income and "something to do." Today it's 6,000-sq.-ft. generating sales of $30,000 per year. He grows poinsettias, baskets and 6" geraniums ($3.50 wholesale). Top quality (I saw them). Combined with his wife's teaching salary, they are financially independent and he enjoys growing! In 1985, Jerry started nearby with 3,000-sq.-ft. and today is at 6,000-sq.-ft. He's doing well, too.

A good accountant can do these things in simple form, and it shouldn't cost you a fortune. He can also be a helpful financial adviser.

You are going into business, and businesses must know how they are doing so they can make intelligent decisions. The most critical and common business problem: an impending cash shortage. If you know it's coming you have a lot better chance of weathering the storm. Bankers are a lot more comfortable and more willing to help if you have good records. And you sleep better.

Be a Cash Hoarder

Steve and Leslie Barlow, Sea Girt, New Jersey, went through these start-up perils recently and succeeded (see *GrowerTalks,* August, 1987, page 70). Steve spoke at a GrowerExpo seminar about it all. His message: Don't spend money for anything you can possibly do without at first. Make do, borrow it, do it by hand, do as much as you and your family can do without hiring help. Yes, you've got to have quality right from the start, but there are lots of ways to do quality without spending a lot of money. Use low-cost poly greenhouses (put them up yourself) and unit heaters that are less fuel efficient but cost 50¢/sq. ft. initially versus $1.25/sq. ft. for hot water systems.

Aim to time the launching of your operation for the first sales just ahead of Valentine's Day and the spring months. Not just *after them!* Spring is when you make money, summer and fall you try to carry the overhead. Plan your buildings to be completed by August 1. You'll probably be a month or two late, but you'll still be on time for spring crops.

Some smaller growers don't start heating their greenhouses until late February or early March (earlier in the South). They start up bedding plants with bought-in plugs. This costs money, but fuel in January and February is expensive.

Start-up growers so often sell cheap. They feel they must sell below the market in order to break in to sell their products. It's a critical point. Comments:

- **Strive for quality.** If you have it, I urge holding price with your good, established, quality competitor. If you don't have it, I can only urge striving for it. Get things done on time—spacing, transplanting plugs, watch temperatures, don't let houses overheat—it's all tough on quality. Keep things watered, but not too wet.

- **Get out among prospective customers yourself.** Go see them, take samples, try the individual garden centers or the smaller variety store chains.

    If you retail, do hit your local newspapers regularly with ads. Sometimes the local radio station will welcome a Saturday morning talk show—call in with your gardening questions. Are you brave?

- **Lastly, fight very hard to hold the price.** Remember the cash flow business? The only place cash comes from is profit, and it doesn't take much price cutting to squeeze out most of your profit. And somehow even though buyers try hard to get your price down, they do finally respect quality and a firm price.

Last Thoughts

As of the early 1990s, demand for spring plants is "best ever," except occasionally in some areas with especially heavy spring rain. Prices are firm and volume is up. Who knows what's ahead, but for now it's a great business!

P.S. Have some fun along the way.

Chapter 29

THE IMPORTANCE OF DISEASE INDEXING AND PATHOGEN-FREE PRODUCTION

by Michael Klopmeyer
Geo. J. Ball, Inc.

As we head into the 21st century, what future is in store for us concerning disease-free plant production? History has shown that it is difficult to produce top quality vegetatively propagated crops without the use of pathogen-free plant material due to severe losses caused by plant pathogenic fungi, bacteria and viruses. It's a problem that has bankrupt important propagators. Why are many growers today producing top quality vegetative crops? The number one reason, I believe, is that they are using cuttings and/or young plants that index free of known plant pathogens. Unfortunately, too few of our growers today know this.

As many new growers come into the industry, whether they are new to the business or have taken over their family businesses, they may never have experienced a complete crop failure due to disease. For example, the success of a geranium crop may be affected by the vascular pathogen *Xanthomonas,* while a good mum crop may be destroyed by pathogens, including *Verticillium* Wilt or Chrysanthemum Stunt viroid. Thus, it is difficult to understand the need for disease-indexed stock. So now they ask, "Do I really need it?" In order to help answer this question, I have outlined what disease indexing is all about, including how it is done, who is doing it and what crops are indexed. Finally, I will discuss advantages of producing disease-indexed plants in your operation.

WHAT IS DISEASE INDEXING

Disease indexing, simply stated, is testing various plant parts (i.e. cuttings) for the presence of any plant pathogen. If plant pathogenic fungi, bacteria, viruses or viroids are present in the plant part tested, that plant is either destroyed or subjected to various procedures designed to eliminate the pathogen. Only plant samples that test negative for any given plant pathogen are considered to be disease free, and these are increased in large numbers under strict sanitary conditions.

It is important to understand that although these plants index free of all known plant pathogens, they are still susceptible to them and can be infected if they are exposed to them. Thus, pathogen-free production procedures, such as growing mother stock in isolated greenhouses using raised benches and pasteurized soil and replacing the stock on an annual basis, are essential to successful production.

Production of disease-free geranium stock plants to be used to plant production areas at the Ball Certified Plant greenhouse, West Chicago. Critical sanitation here includes growing plants on raised benches, using pasteurized soil and maintaining good pot spacing to prevent disease spread. In the photo is Mike Klopmeyer, plant pathologist.

278

The first step in disease indexing is to test tissue from a clone/variety for the presence of bacterial and fungal plant pathogens. This process is called "culture indexing." Surface sterilized stem sections are placed in a nutrient solution optimal for bacterial and/or fungal growth. If bacteria and/or fungi grow out of these stem sections, that cutting from which the sample came is destroyed. Only cuttings that culture index negative on three separate occasions over the period of one year are used to establish mother plants that are considered certified free of bacterial and fungal pathogens. The advantage of this culture indexing process is that all systemic bacteria and fungi (both pathogenic and non-pathogenic) can be eliminated. (A systemic disease organism is one that exists in the water and food conducting tissues of a plant.)

Once plants are certified free of all systemic fungi and bacteria, they are ready for virus indexing. Plant pathogenic viruses cannot be cultured in an artificial nutrient solution like fungi and bacteria are. There are, however, two alternate methods of virus detection available in the industry today.

The first is the use of antibody tests similar in format to home pregnancy test kits or AIDS testing. These tests utilize antibodies prepared against the target virus and are conducted in a laboratory setting. Test results are obtained in as little as a few hours to one to two days (a commercial plant virus testing service is available through Agdia, Inc., Elkhart, Indiana). The antibody tests are extremely useful since they are easy to use, rapid, specific and very sensitive. Recent developments in biotechnology have introduced the use of extremely sensitive genetic probes to detect the nucleic acids of the target virus. Yoder Brothers is utilizing this technique to detect some virus pathogens of chrysanthemum.

If antibody tests aren't available for certain viruses or for confirmation tests, an additional method is the use of virus indicator plants. Most plant pathogenic viruses are capable of infecting more than one plant host. Research over the years has determined that a few key plant species (tobacco, lambsquarters, pinto bean and cucumber, to name a few) are susceptible to many different plant pathogenic viruses and can exhibit symptoms characteristic of each when inoculated. If these indicator plants are inoculated with sap from a virus-infected plant, they will show virus symptoms in two to four weeks. Another indicator plant technique is to graft healthy indicator plant parts onto a virus-infected test plant or vice versa. If the indicator plant shows virus symptoms, virus was present in the test plant and migrated into the indicator plant. The advantage of biological indicator plants is their ability to detect many different unknown plant viruses.

If plant pathogenic viruses are detected in all plants tested of a desirable cultivar, there are techniques available to free these plants of these viruses. This is typically accomplished by subjecting them to temperatures of 95° to 98°F for anywhere from two to 24 weeks. High temperature therapy inhibits replication of the virus and lowers the virus concentration in the plant tissue. These heat-treated plants are brought into the laboratory, and under sterile conditions, young terminal growing tips (meristem tips) 1 to 2 mm in length or less are excised and placed onto an artificial tissue culture medium. After two to three months, these young shoot tips grow into tiny plants. The young plants are then transferred back into the greenhouse and virus tested again using the methods described earlier. The combination of thermotherapy and meristem tipping is usually effective in obtaining young plants that index free of viruses. Once virus-free plants are established, an effective sanitation program including insect control must be taken to preclude the re-introduction of virus pathogens. Insects, such as aphids, thrips and whiteflies, can transfer a virus from an occasional infected plant to a clean plant.

Finally, after mother plants that index free of known plant pathogens have been obtained, it is of critical importance to determine if they are still of top horticultural quality. In certain instances and with certain cultivars, the heat treatment and, in particular, the meristem-tip culture can result in undesirable horticultural characteristics. At that point, production and flowering trials should be conducted and superior clones selected using horticultural characteristics, such as earliness to flower, number of flowers and overall performance, including basal branching and cutting production. What crops are indexed and who is doing it?

The principal floricultural crops that are disease indexed are those crops that are vegetatively propagated. The reason for this is obvious: Vegetative crops are propagated from mother plants by cuttings, and systemic, fungal, bacterial and viral pathogens can be propagated and spread along with these cuttings. In this way, many plants become infected and losses can be great. Thus, it is of utmost importance to have pathogen-free stock for vegetatively propagated plants.

Disease indexing on a commercial scale was introduced almost 50 years ago, when Yoder Brothers began producing disease-indexed chrysanthemums.*

Two major U.S. suppliers, Yoder Brothers and California Plant Co., now produce culture indexed and virus indexed chrysanthemums and carnations, using many of the techniques described earlier in this article. Yoder Brothers are currently certifying over 400 mum and over 25 carnation cultivars. The major systemic fungal and bacterial pathogens being eliminated are *Verticillium* (wilt), *Fusarium* (wilt) and *Erwinia* (bacterial blight) from mums, and *Pseudomonas* (bacterial wilt), *Fusarium* (wilt) *Phialophora* (wilt) and *Erwinia* (slow wilt) from carnations. The major viruses and viroids eliminated by thermotherapy and meristem tipping for chrysanthemum are Chrysanthemum Stunt Viroid, Chrysanthemum Aspermy Virus, Chrysanthemum Chlorotic Mottle Virus and Tomato Spotted Wilt Virus (TSWV). Major carnation viruses being tested for include Carnation Mottle Virus, Carnation Etch Virus and TSWV.

---

*This was in response to a major invasion of the mum crop by *Verticillium* wilt, and after culture indexed stock free of *Verticillium* was produced, the crop was then affected by chrysanthemum stunt viroid. This pathogen threatened the success of the mum as a commercial crop. Virus indexing produced stunt-free cuttings and the crop was saved. The mum is, to this day, a major worldwide crop, thanks to the actions of Cloy Miller and Conrad Olson of Yoder's and several Cornell University pathologists, especially Wat Dimrock.

Beginning in the late 1950s, Oglevee's of Connellsville, Pennsylvania, provided culture-indexed geranium stock to the industry in response to the decline of commercial geranium production due to bacterial blight, caused by *Xanthomonas*. Their process, termed CVI® (culture virus indexing), now provides both culture- and virus-indexed geranium stock using techniques similar to those described earlier. Since then, other U.S. geranium propagators, mainly Fischer Geraniums USA Inc. and now Ball Seed Company, employ similar techniques to supply culture- and virus-indexed geranium varieties.

Culture indexing of geranium varieties targets the eradication of *Xanthomonas* and *Verticillium,* while virus indexing targets Tomato and Tobacco Ringspot Viruses and Pelargonium Flower Break Virus (PFBV), to name a few. The recent spread of PFBV throughout many of the commercial geranium varieties is now considered a threat to overall plant vigor. This virus causes breaking (streaking) and spotting in both geranium petals and leaves and is easily sap transmissable. The eradication of this virus from some cultivars will significantly improve flower number, quality and color.

Recently disease indexing has been initiated for other vegetatively propagated crops. With the increase in popularity of New Guinea impatiens, coupled with the increase in prevalence of TSWV, the need for disease indexing of this crop is of critical importance. Mikkelsen's, Inc. (Ashtabula, Ohio) provides certified stock of the Sunshine Series of New Guinea impatiens, and Paul Ecke Ranch (Encinitas, California) provides certified Kientzler cultivars of New Guinea impatiens. Other certified vegetatively propagated crops available in the United States today include kalanchoes (Ball Seed Co. and The Plant Co.), hiemalis begonias (Mikkelsen's, Inc. and Oglevee, Ltd.) and streptocarpus (Oglevee, Ltd.). Of course, the foliage plant industry has provided tissue culture explants (which index free of bacteria and certain viruses) for many years.

WHAT'S IN IT FOR ME?

If you have never experienced a severe disease outbreak in your operation due to using non-certified stock, then you may ask, "Why do I need it?" That is a difficult question to answer, because you probably think, "If it ain't broke, why fix it?" First, the very threat of one of the "killer diseases" (mum stunt or *Xanthomonas* in geraniums) is eliminated—a major worry taken from the hard-pressed grower! But there are other factors to consider before making a decision. History has proven that disease-free stock performs better than non-certified stock. In addition to being disease-free, the plants are more vigorous, flower more freely and earlier, and can potentially give you better turnaround and ultimately increase your profits. You will also have increased confidence in your crop knowing that the threat of disease and total crop failure is minimal since you purchased disease-free stock. Likewise, if you replace your stock on an annual basis with certified cuttings (following standard certified production rules), you free up additional greenhouse space originally reserved for holdover stock plants.

Finally, special mention needs to made of the fact that with the increased prevalence of TSWV in many greenhouses throughout the United States, the potential of introducing TSWV into your operation is very high. Purchasing stock plants that are certified free of TSWV prevents entry of this virus— which has a wide host range that could threaten your other crops—into your greenhouses. The use of certified stock, along with an active pesticide program to control the primary vector of TSWV, the western flower thrips, gives you a head start toward a successful and profitable crop.

Chapter 30

COOL DAY/ WARM NIGHT TECHNOLOGY

by Vic Ball

It's a major new technology for controlling stretch of most ornamentals. It came from research of the late 1980s at Michigan State University. The principal researchers were John Erwin and Royal Heins. Its creators call it DIF (difference between night and day temperature). It could well be the most significant research in ornamentals of the 1980s. We need much more of this kind of work!

It's simple. Plants exposed to a *cooler day* than night temperature will stretch (elongate) less. The more difference between night and day temperature, the less stretch. There will be much less stretch if night and day temperature are the same as compared to a *warm day* and a cool night environment. For the record, negative DIF is a *cooler* day versus night. Positive DIF is a *warmer* day versus night temperature.

The one major weakness in cool day retarding of crops is a climate and a time of year with many very warm days. If it's 90°F today, it's obviously tough to create a night warmer than the natural day temperature. Two answers to this problem:

- The same researchers at Michigan found that if a grower is able to cool a crop on a hot day, let's say to 70° or 75°F, the first two hours after sunrise, the crop will "accept" that 75°F early morning temperature as the all-day temperature—for purposes of cool day retarding. This can be done by venting, by fan/pad cooling or mist cooling. Reducing sunlight helps, too.

So, if temperatures the first 2 hours average 75°F and the night temperature is 80°F, the grower will get cool day retarding even though the day temperature may go to 90°F. It really seems to work that way. If the grower is able to maintain the "sunrise plus 2 hours" temperature at the same level as the night temperature, he will have a lot less stretch effect as compared to 90°F day and 70°F night. Actually 3° to 5° cooler day versus night is a fair amount of difference and will very much affect most crops. Ten degrees difference is rather extreme and will really stop stretch dead. Or, with a much warmer day versus night, elongation will be accelerated. Rapidly!

A striking demonstration of the effect of cool days/warm nights on lilies. The plant on the left was kept at 14°C (57°F) days and 30°C (86°F) nights. The plant on the right was grown with 30°C (86°F) day temperatures and 14°C (57°F) night temperatures. It really does work! Photo from Michigan State University.

- The other answer to very warm day temperatures is the use of chemical retardants. Plus, of course, partially withholding soil moisture and fertilizer. Avoiding crowding of plants also minimizes stretch. Excess shading (light reduction) tends to stretch crops.

Graphical Tracking

A helpful extension of this technology is "graphical tracking." Here the grower creates a graph with plant height on the vertical side and weeks from start to maturity on the horizontal scale (bottom). He then enters a desired final height at the top right corner and a beginning height at the lower left corner. He joins the starting height with the final height (not always a straight line). Then each week (or twice a week) he measures actual heights of plants and enters this on the graph. In fact, growers usually enter two target lines—a low and a high side—and height within this "window" is acceptable deviation.

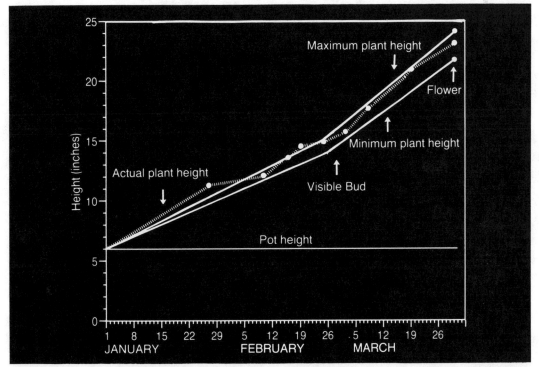

Graph showing the important components of an Easter lily graphical tracking plot. The horizontal axis represents time from emergence to flower. The vertical axis represents total height of the pot and the shoot. Two lines connect the height at emergence with the visible bud height and the final desired minimum and maximum height at flower. The dotted line between the "minimum/maximum window" shows actual heights taken during the growth of a crop that ended up about half way between the minimum and maximum lines. Based on work done at Michigan State University published in American Floral Endowment "Research Report" March 1990.

And, of course, if, on a given week, the actual height line falls above or below this window, the grower responds immediately with more or less DIF, or, if temperature won't do it, then he uses retardants or other means. It's quite surprising to see a crop height exceeding the desired window limits—then with 5° or 6° cooler day versus night, the graph line goes back within the window, often in a week or less.

See crop chapters in the *Ball RedBook* such as lilies for examples of these graphs. Such graphs are widely used by commercial growers—especially on poinsettias, lilies and pot mums. Pressure to hit final height targets within a narrow tolerance has mounted, especially on pot plant crops. Again, many mass outlets have written specifications, including minimum and maximum heights, that they will accept. Plants out of these limits may be, and often are, rejected. Poinsettias exceeding target heights, for example, may not fit the planned packing boxes. A taller box means one less layer of boxes per truck, which is a major increase in trucking cost per plant. Obviously the ability to finish the crop at a predetermined height on such crops as lilies, poinsettias and pot mums with quite good accuracy is a great help in such situations.

As of spring 1990 I found cool day treatment being widely used especially among poinsettia, lily and pot mum growers. Many bedding/spring plant growers are also aware of and are using this plan. Says Abe DenHoed, DenHoed Greenhouses, Boyden, Iowa, a major bedding plant grower, "Thank God for cool days/warm nights."

Several Side Effects

Especially where larger differences between night and day temperatures are used, you may see these effects:

- **Chlorosis.** With 5° to 10° cooler days, some crops suddenly become chlorotic. Plugs are a good example. It will disappear in a few days once the day and night temperature are brought together.

- **Leaves point downward.** Especially on lilies, a pronounced droop or downturning of leaves will occur—especially under an extreme temperature differential (8° or 10° or more difference). Unless the difference is maintained over an extended period, it will disappear as soon as night and day temperature are brought together. There have been cases where lilies were given extremely cooler days for longer periods and did not fully recover.

- **Otherwise there are no other known side effects**—no delay in flowering, no impairment of quality. Bulbs generally seem to be too rapid a crop to respond to cool day treatment.

Specific Crop Comments

Most crop chapters in this book deal with the cool day treatment plan. Here are brief comments on several of the majors.

Poinsettias cool day and warm night effects. The plant on the left was kept at 74°F days and 64°F nights; on the right, 64°F (cool) days and 74°F nights. Cool days will really retard poinsettias.

- **Plugs very definitely respond.** Cool day is a great way to control stretch on plugs. Some annual species display chlorosis, especially under an extreme difference of temperature, but always recover as the DIF is discontinued.

- **Bedding plants.** To my knowledge, all bedding annual species respond well to cool days/warm nights. It is a very effective way to control often troublesome stretch, especially when demand slackens during a wet spring.

    There's a point here: Bedding plants are grown mainly in low-cost poly roof greenhouses, typically not well-ventilated. So as warm days of spring arrive, day temperatures tend to the 80s and higher—warm. At the same time, many growers, reluctant to spend a lot on fuel, allow night temperatures to go quite low. The result is a very warm day (80°F or even 90°F) and quite cool nights (50°F or less), which is exactly the opposite of the desired cool day/warm night. The inevitable result is serious stretch. I see it a lot!

    So I do urge growers to do all possible to cool those spring days, open sides, use fans if available and shade the roof. And do keep night temperature well up. If you can achieve the same, or even nearly the same, night and day temperature, you'll get a whole lot less stretch than you will with 15° or 20° warmer days.

    In a way, that's the key point about roll-out bedding (see the tray mechanization chapter). Growers roll houses of annuals outdoors on Dutch trays during cool spring days, then they roll them indoors for the warm nights. They get short, freely-branching, superb quality.

    Cool day/warm night technology is here to stay!

287

Chapter 31

ARE WE GROWERS CONTAMINATING OUR ENVIRONMENT?

by Vic Ball

Answer: Probably yes. Although even an answer to that question would bring confusing contradictory responses from different sources today. In any case, many growers today are concerned and anxious, partly because of the lack of any well-defined rules. Legislation is brewing. Storm clouds are gathering:

- As of the early 1990s, dozens of growers across the United States are being cited, charged with specific abuses of our environment. These charges come from a wide variety of authorities—from local water management districts, state and federal authorities, especially the EPA. Some of these cases are costing growers hundreds of thousands of dollars, much time and anguish. Some growers are being forced to clean up the problem or close up shop. See *GrowerTalks,* September 1989, for the El Modeno Gardens story where a grower did clean up—and did it promptly and well. There is also a videotape covering the El Modeno story. Call *GrowerTalks.*

- Again in the early 1990s, major federal legislation is in the works that may well impose severe restrictions on flower growers dumping their runoff drainage (including pesticides and fertilizers) into ground water—streams, lakes, etc. The same is true for hundreds of regional authorities that are rapidly developing restrictions on pesticides, fungicides and fertilizers being dumped into ground water. California already has severe state restrictions on pesticide use by flower growers—which is a major nuisance and expense to the grower with forms to fill out, reports to make, etc.

- One alarming facet of all this is that, as of today, growers do not face a clear, reasonable mandate from a single national authority on environmental pollution. Instead, growers can be cited by dozens of authorities from local municipal governments, local water management districts (hundreds of them), many widely different state mandates plus a whole array of federal laws and restrictions and the EPA. One major New York state grower has been under criminal and civil charges for several years, has spent hundreds of thousands of dollars and still is being heavily harassed. A major part of the charges: ground water pollution created by an owner of 50 years ago. How can you win that?

A related problem: U.S. farmers today are applying many tons of pesticides, fungicides and herbicides to millions of acres of farmland and are gradually coming under federal and state restrictions. Question: Will flower growers be swept in with them as laws are passed limiting their use of these chemicals? And will these laws be unreasonable, perhaps impossible for flower growers to live under?

The grower's one hope here: Our national association, Society of American Florists. SAF monitors all new laws, sounds the alarm when needed and fights for the grower.

Put it all together and it's a very bleak picture. At best, there is lots of uncertainty (which all business people dislike), and at worst, severely damaging restrictions ahead. Question: What can and should U.S. and Canadian growers be doing about this now? Suggestions:

1. Plan to recirculate all your runoff water within three to five years.

This problem deeply involves the system of crop watering you use. Runoff from crops grown on (and subirrigated in) Dutch trays is recirculated—100%. There are other major advantages to these trays, including a big labor saving. It's expensive, but a few pioneers have already gone that way—and not only huge growers. John Van Bourgondien, a 3-acre geranium grower in Peconic, New York, has done 25,000 sq. ft. of Dutch trays (early 1990) and will do more in 1991. G & E Greenhouse (Henry Schneider), Elburn, Illinois, has installed several acres of trays in his pot plant range.

A few other growers are moving on cement floor subirrigation, which is again 100% recirculation. Norman Heimos, a large St. Louis, Missouri, pot grower, has made a major commitment to cement floor subirrigation. And it's all recirculated.

For details on watering systems available, see Chapter 9.

However you do it, one good way to improve your odds in the coming environmental contamination battle is to recirculate all your runoff water—the sooner the better.

2. **Cut back on pesticides and fungicides.** It's called IPM (integrated pest management). It means simply that to comply with ever-increasing pressure on your use of chemicals, it's just smart to gradually but surely rely less on chemicals and more on other means of control. There are some very promising other methods.

   For a starter, no more routine preventive spraying. Also, use yellow sticky tapes to monitor outbreaks from the beginning and limited spraying to control these infestations when they first occur.

   Take a hard look at parasites/predators—nature's way of controlling insects. See Chapter 13 about insects.

3. **Support your national trade associations.** The Society of American Florists (SAF) is the grower's only voice in Washington, D.C., our only pressure to keep Congress from imposing unreasonable, unworkable laws on the grower. Join by writing SAF, 1601 Duke St., Alexandria, VA 22314.

4. **Beware of the disgruntled employee or neighbor.** So often growers report that complaints that cost them big money and lots of time and anguish all started because some employee or perhaps a neighbor filed a complaint with some local authority.

   What can you do except help to keep good communication and relations with both neighbors and employees? Hope that they will complain first to you. Most of these cases do not involve substantive abuse of the environment. Many are frankly frivolous attempts to make problems for the grower who has been a "bad guy" in their perspective.

5. **Cultivate members of local boards/authorities.** I know one major grower who is, in fact, a member of the local water management district! What a great way to at least have your voice heard at this all-important table.

Conclusion: Evermore restrictions on contamination of both ground water and atmosphere are ahead. A suggestion: Plan for it.

Chapter 32

TOMATO SPOTTED WILT VIRUS

by J.W. Moyer and R.K. Jones
North Carolina State University
Raleigh, North Carolina

Tomato spotted wilt virus (TSWV) has recently become one of the most important pest problems of floral crops. Reports of significant losses to TSWV began emerging in the mid-1980s. National and international attention was focused on the problem in the floral industry by a 1987 symposium on TSWV and thrips sponsored by the American Floral Endowment and Yoder Bros. This virus has caused hundreds of thousands of dollars of losses in the floral crop industry over the past four years and has been identified in over 20 states. TSWV has also been positively identified by reliable confirmatory tests in floral crops from production facilities throughout Central and South America, Canada, Europe and Israel, in addition to the United States. TSWV is also known to cause diseases in other crops in Asia.

The disease occurs in greenhouse-grown crops as well as in field-grown floral crops. It has also caused significant losses in crops such as peanuts, peppers, tomatoes and tobacco. The wide host range of this virus is one of its most dangerous characteristics in that it is difficult to eliminate from all floral hosts or weed hosts, which may be near by. The other dangerous characteristic is that TSWV is transmitted by several species of thrips. Thrips are doubly harmful insect pests of many floral crops as they cause serious damage from feeding and colonizing on floral crops as well as spreading TSWV. Certain species, such as western flower thrips, are also among the most difficult insect pests to control in floral crops.

SYMPTOMS

Plants infected with TSWV range from complete destruction of the plant to symptomless carriers of the virus. The classical symptoms caused by this virus include chlorotic ring patterns on leaves. The chlorotic tissue may turn necrotic and result in death of the leaves in some plant species. In highly sensitive species, the leaves may develop necrotic spots or lesions along the veins without first becoming chlorotic. These symptoms have been mistakenly attributed to chemical injury and result in leaves and plants that are often severely stunted and deformed. Lesions on the stems, petioles and veins are also common in many species. The lesions may be brown to black streaks, as in chrysanthemum, or shiny black sunken lesions, as in exacum. This is often accompanied by a wilting or "flagging" of the tip of the plant.

Symptoms caused by the same isolate may vary in intensity or type between different crops or between varieties of the same crop. Many symptoms resemble those caused by other viruses, fungi, bacteria or even chemical injury. Further, it should not be assumed that "symptomless" plants are free of TSWV. Mild or intermittent symptom expression, as in dahlia or stephanotis, can indirectly result in significant losses. While these plants do not appear to be affected, they are

Tomato spotted wilt virus injury on a gloxinia leaf.

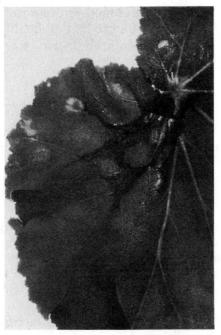

TSWV on begonias.

important sources of TSWV for the insect vector, which moves the virus from plant to plant. Thus, growers should not rely on symptoms alone for diagnosis. Detection procedures are described below.

SPREAD OF TSWV

There are two important avenues by which TSWV can be introduced into a floral crop production greenhouse. Vegetatively propagated crops can become infected by propagating from TSWV-infected stock plants. TSWV is also spread from plant to plant by certain thrips species. The western flower thrips *(Frankliniella occidentalis)* is considered to be the primary thrips species that spreads TSWV in floral crops. The importance of the western flower thrips is due to the difficulty encountered in controlling this species relative to other species. Other species of thrips known to transmit TSWV include *F. schultzei, F. fusca,* and *Thrips tabaci.*

The relationship of TSWV with its vector, the thrips, is somewhat unusual for plant virus-vector interactions. Only the thrips larvae are capable of acquiring TSWV for transmission. Once the larvae mature into adults they remain as potential transmitters of TSWV for the remainder of their lives. At the present time there is no evidence that the virus is maintained into the next generation through transovarial passage. Thus, TSWV can be spread by plants carrying virus-infected adult thrips even though the plants themselves may not be infected or are immune to TSWV infection.

Spread of TSWV by thrips and in propagation material together provides a very efficient system for the movement of TSWV throughout a production facility and then throughout the industry. The only currently available controls are directed at interrupting these two avenues of spread.

CONTROL

Prevention is the only effective strategy for controlling TSWV. Unlike other stresses, such as nutrition or some other fungal and bacterial pathogens, TSWV-infected plants cannot be cured. Plants infected by some fungal pathogens can be cured with the application of a fungicide, whereas TSWV-infected plants—as is the situation with most virus-infected plants—once infected, cannot be returned to a healthy state suitable for sale.

TSWV can be introduced into production areas by infected plant material, by thrips spreading TSWV from naturally infected plants outside the cropping area and by the distribution of thrips-infested propagation material. Once introduced into the cropping area in the presence of thrips, the virus is efficiently spread to other plants. Two simultaneous approaches are necessary to obtain effective control of TSWV.

The first approach is to eliminate sources of TSWV from outside the production area. This can be accomplished by obtaining propagation material that has been shown to be free of TSWV. Nuclear stock should be tested on a routine basis and maintained in a limited access greenhouse that has been screened with a fine mesh material suitable for excluding thrips. In production areas where TSWV has become established it may be necessary to use screened houses for production or else abandon production of highly sensitive crops. Visual inspection is not sufficient to certify plants free of TSWV. Source plants should be assayed using a sensitive indicator host such as *Nicotiana benthamiana* and/or by serologically

TSWV on exacum plants.

specific tests for TSWV. The reagents for the serological tests are available in kit form from commercial sources.

The other is the elimination of spread within the production area. Here the focus is on the elimination of resident populations of thrips and the removal of all TSWV-infected plant material from the production area. Ideally, infected plants should be placed in sealed containers before removal from the infected area so as to reduce the probability of further spread. Thrips populations should be monitored on sticky cards and approved thrips control practices followed. It should be noted that damage thresholds for insects as virus vectors are generally lower than for the same insect as a pest.

Given the present level of understanding and available control practices, it is nearly impossible to eradicate thrips and TSWV once they become established in a production greenhouse. Thus, the goal of control strategies is to prevent its introduction into production areas.

Chapter 33

LOW TEMPERATURES FOR THE CONTROL OF FLOWERING—VERNALIZATION

by Roy A. Larson
North Carolina State University
Raleigh, North Carolina

Some floricultural crops absolutely require an exposure to cool temperatures for extended periods, either to initiate flower buds or to promote further flower development. This need can be viewed either as an asset or liability in crop production. Sometimes it is viewed as a liability when cool temperatures can only be provided by artificial means, such as with cold storage facilities. These facilities do reduce time in the greenhouse but can be a limitation as to how many plants can be grown. The low temperature requirement can be advantageous because it provides growers with the ability to control and accurately schedule flowering of these crops.

In nature, this cool temperature requirement is generally in the range of 32° to 50°F, and it is a survival mechanism. Seedlings that emerge as soon as seed drops to the ground, flower buds that burst into bloom as soon as they are quite well developed, or bulbous plants that sprout in early autumn would not withstand the first killing frost or survive the extremely cold winter temperatures. Instead, the seed or plant apexes become dormant, and nothing visibly seems to happen until the seed or plants have been exposed to an adequate duration of chilling tempera-tures. Warmth, provided either by greenhouse temperatures or naturally warm air outdoors, allows plants to reach the flowering stage.

As mentioned before, nothing appears to be happening during this dormant phase, but it would be a major mistake to consider the crop as inactive at this time. Major biochemical and physiological processes are occurring.

Not all of the floriculture crops that require chilling will be mentioned. Most are covered in the section on specific crops. Only a few representative crops will be discussed now to illustrate the impact of chilling and how diverse its effects can be.

It would be appropriate to begin the discussion with seedlings, since it was with wheat seedlings that the concept of a use for chilling originated. If winter wheat cultivars are sown in spring, they will not flower in summer. In contrast, spring wheat cultivars will flower. It was known over 100 years ago that exposure to chilling temperatures was needed before the fall wheat cultivars would flower. This was defined as "vernalization," which literally means "making ready for spring." Many biennials grown by flower growers have the same requirement as winter wheat, and flowering can be regulated with a low temperature treatment.

Vernalization also has been defined as a process by which floral induction is promoted by exposure of appropriate plants to cool temperatures for a given dura-tion, or, more broadly, as any temperature treatment that initiates or promotes flowering.

Spring-flowering bulb crops also require exposure to low temperatures before flowering will occur. Cool temperatures are not needed to initiate flowers on narcis-sus, hyacinths, crocus or tulips. Flower primordia are formed on the narcissus before bulb harvest, while flower initiation in crocus, hyacinths and tulips takes place during the warm storage period after bulbs are harvested. Low temperatures, however, are required for root development, shoot elongation and continued flower development before greenhouse forcing. Easter lily plants are very different. Flower initiation does not occur until after plants or bulbs have been removed from low temperatures and shoots have emerged at higher temperatures. Easter lily plants that have not had a chilling treatment grow slowly, have many leaves and possibly flower starting about 200 days after planting. There are other plant species that will eventually flower without a cold treatment, but exposure to cool air hastens flower-ing. This gives the grower a mechanism to time a crop for a specific period.

Some perennials, such as foxglove and astilbes, have a cold requirement that must be satisfied or they will not flower.

Hydrangeas and azaleas are prominent floral crops that also require chilling temperatures before uniform flowering will occur. In both instances flower buds are quite well developed before the apexes become dormant, and only cool air or a chemical such as gibberellic acid will release them from dormancy and permit proper flowering. One major difference between these two crops is that hydrangea growers make every effort to retain foliage on their plants in cold storage. It once was believed that removal of hydrangea foliage removed an inhibitor that inter-fered with eventual flowering, but the primary reason for leaf removal is disease control. Approximately six weeks of cold storage are needed for both crops. Then the plants are forced at higher temperatures. Again, temperature regulation enables growers to have precise control of crop scheduling and to produce uniform flowering plants, providing proper cultural practices were followed before and after cooling.

Natural growth substances (inhibitors) have been implicated in the onset of dormancy or whatever process prevents flower development from progressing further without exposure to chilling treatments. Other substances (promoters) have been suspected as the agents responsible for the resumed activity of the reproductive apex, and the substitution of gibberellic acid for low temperatures would support that belief.

Dormancy and vernalization are complex subjects, and some researchers have devoted their professional careers to them. The authors of the chapters in this book do know the temperature requirements of the crops they have covered. Successful flowering can be achieved by following their schedules and cultural recommendations.

SECTION VI

Culture by Crop

INTRODUCTION TO CULTURE BY CROP

For convenience, the material on specific crops is arranged alphabetically. Crops are listed under their common names. Note that several major chapters are included in alphabetical order in the list:

- Bedding plants
- Chrysanthemum
- Foliage
- Geranium
- Lily
- Poinsettia
- Rose

Germination information listed under each crop heading is largely based on the work done by Henry M. Cathey, director of the National Arboretum. "Light" simply refers to the fact that maximum germination is obtained when the seeds are exposed to light. Conversely, "dark" indicates that for top germination the seed should not be exposed to light. If neither "light" nor "dark" appears it indicates that seed will germinate well under either condition, or a combination of the two. "Alt. 70° to 85°F" indicates that a crop should be grown at an alternating temperature of 70°F nights and 85°F days.

About Light Intensity

What is optimum light intensity for crops? The accompanying graph shows the effect of light intensity on the rate of photosynthesis of a single leaf at the top of a

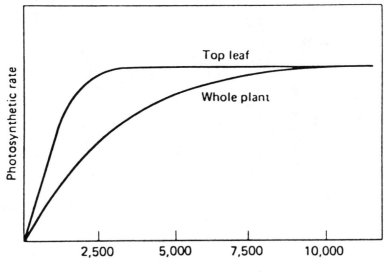

plant and of the whole plant. While the single leaf reaches its maximum rate of photosynthesis at 3,000 fc., an intensity of 10,000 fc. might be required for the whole plant in order to raise the light intensity within the leaf canopy to 3,000 fc. The message here in practical terms: Plants don't need more than 2,500 to 3,000 fc. for optimum growth! Credit Paul Nelson, *Greenhouse Operation and Management*, Reston Publishing Company, 1981.

About Hardiness Zones

Here is the standard U.S. National Arboretum plant hardiness map. It defines 10 zones which are often referred to in this edition of the *Ball RedBook*.

There is a revised plant hardiness zone map now available based on much more data, plus a frost-free Zone 11 has been added. It gives a hardiness zone for each county nationwide! To order a copy, phone the U.S. Government Printing Office, ask for Miscellaneous publication no. 1475 [phone (202) 783-3238].

Zones of Plant Hardiness

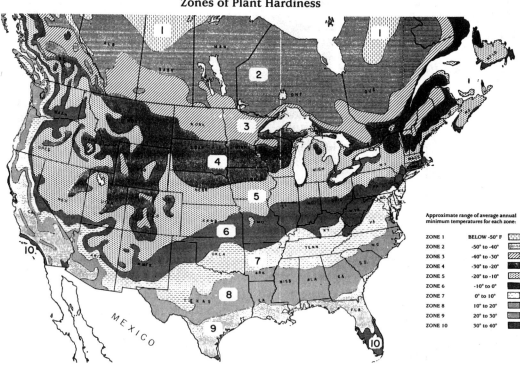

Approximate range of average annual minimum temperatures for each zone:

ZONE 1	BELOW -50° F
ZONE 2	-50° to -40°
ZONE 3	-40° to -30°
ZONE 4	-30° to -20°
ZONE 5	-20° to -10°
ZONE 6	-10° to 0°
ZONE 7	0° to 10°
ZONE 8	10° to 20°
ZONE 9	20° to 30°
ZONE 10	30° to 40°

Map courtesy of the U.S. National Arboretum

Basic to anyone planning or already producing ornamentals: Which crops are healthy and expanding, which are not? What is the outlook for export competition in each?

The *Ball RedBook* certainly doesn't have final answers on these important questions, but several of the major chapters include graphs of recent production trends based on USDA data. The accompanying USDA graph gives an interesting overall view of U.S. ornamental production.

USDA FLORICULTURE CROPS
1984 - 1989 TOTALS

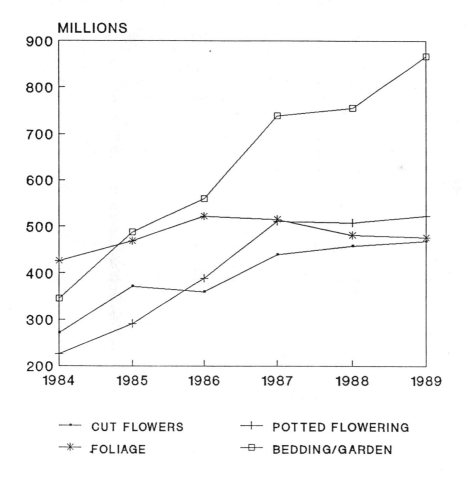

For the record, there are two basic sources of crop statistics in the United States:*

- The U. S. Department of Agriculture National Agricultural Statistics Service (NASS) has been published yearly since 1956. It currently covers only 28 states, only major crops and growers with $10,000 or more in annual sales. There was no survey done for 1982 or 1983, but it has been published yearly since then. While this is only a partial report, its value is that it shows trends. All the crop graphs in this edition are based on these USDA figures.

- The mandatory U.S. Bureau of Census Census of Agriculture covers all growers with over $1,000 of agricultural sales in all states every five years (most recently 1987). It reports cut flowers and cut greens, pot plants, bedding plants, foliage and nursery crops. The Census of Horticultural Specialties is done every 10 years, most recently 1988, as a separate survey in conjunction with the Census of Agriculture. It reports separate totals for cuts, pots, foliage, bedding, bulbs, flower seed, vegetable seed, greenhouse vegetables, sod, mushrooms and nursery products, and includes all growers with over $2,000 per year of horticultural specialty sales. It's historically reasonably accurate and complete.

The 1987 Census of Agriculture total value of the four major floriculture crops at wholesale was $2.66 billion. Lastly, here are totals from the last three censuses taken by the Department of Commerce Census (not the USDA) on ornamentals. These figures cover all states and are considered a penetrating survey. Unfortunately, pot plants and foliage crops in this report are combined in 1982 and 1978. Department of Commerce, Census of Agriculture (in thousands of dollars):

Department of Commerce Ornamental Census (in thousands of dollars)

	1987	1982	1978
Bedding	$817,960	$477,188	$284,939
Pots	648,240		
Foliage	603,174		
Pots/foliage		983,011	804,432
Cuts	594,478	417,695	351,965
Total floriculture	$2,663,852	$1,877,894	$1,441,336

*Thanks to Marvin Miller, Geo. J. Ball Inc. marketing, for help with this data.

ACHILLEA

by Jim Nau
Ball Seed Company

Perennial (species and seed count see below). Germinates in 10 to 15 days at 65° to 70°F. Seed should be left exposed to light during germination.

Commonly called yarrow, there are a number of achillea species and varieties on the market today, several of which are described below.

Achillea filipendulina (Fernleaf Yarrow) (200,000 seeds/oz.) is a rank growing variety reaching 4' or 5' in the garden when grown from seed. Sown in February and transplanted within 24 days after sowing, plants can be sold green in May when grown at 55° to 60°F. This group of yarrows will flower only marginally at best during the summer of the first year after sowing. Flowers are golden yellow in color, blooming plate-like (flat top) in July and August. Plants flower better when sown the year before and overwintered in quart or gallon containers. Seed varieties include Parkers Variety, Gold Plate and Cloth of Gold. In all cases, the varieties perform equally well and are often sold under the same name.

For vegetative material, consider Coronation Gold which is a related variety, though a hybrid. The flowers are golden yellow on plants no more than 3' tall. Coronation Gold is a variety that can be used for landscaping or in the perennial or cut flower garden.

The seed types are excellent for background plantings and especially where long stems are needed for the cut flower trade. Both classes are excellent as dried or fresh cut flowers and will last indefinitely. The flower color holds well during and after drying.

Achillea millefolium (Common Yarrow, Milfoil) (140,000 seeds/oz.) is the most common of the yarrows on the market today and comes in a wide range of pastel colors. Seed sown in February, transplanted within three weeks, and grown on between 65° to 70°F will be salable green in the cell pack in May. Plants will flower more dependably (70% or better) than *Achillea filipendulina* during the first summer after sowing. In general, the flowers of this class are known to shade or fade readily in the sun when temperatures are above 80°F. They make excellent fresh cut flowers, though the flower color fades as they dry. The best blooms are taken when the buds first open. Plants can get 3' tall, though most of the vegetatively propagated varieties are 2½' at best.

As for varieties, those propagated from seed include Cerise Queen which has rose-pink flowers that shade to pink and eventually off white. It performs equal in habit and flower color to Rosy Red. In one opinion, the best varieties from seed in this group are those that flower white since they have the least tendency to shade or fade. However, there is one mixture that deserves special merit for its overall performance, especially in uniformity of both habit and height as well as for flower colors. Summer Pastels is the best overall variety for this class from seed. It is a well-blended color mix on plants to 2½' tall that flower profusely in July and August from a mid- to late-February sowing.

In vegetative varieties, be sure to try some of the new Galaxy varieties on the market. These are the result of a cross of two achillea species and are related to *A. millefolium*. Varieties are sold under individual names like Hoffnang, Sawa Sawa, and Nakuru, to name just a few. Though the flower colors will shade as in the seeded types, the varieties come in colors of gold, rose, lavender, white and several other pastel colors.

Both *A. filipendulina* and *A. millefolium* are hardy to USDA zones 3 to 8, and flower from June to August in the garden.

AGERATUM

by Jim Nau
Ball Seed Company

Annual (Ageratum houstonianum), 200,000 seeds/oz. Germinates in 8 to 10 days at 80° to 82°F. Seed should be left exposed to light during germination.

Ageratum is best used in containers, as a border or edging, and especially in mass plantings in landscape situations. Once sown, seedlings can be transplanted in 15 to 20 days and grown on at 60° to 65°F. When grown in cell packs, plants are salable green in 8 to 9 weeks, or in flower 11 weeks after sowing. If growing for 4″ pot sales, plants are salable in bloom 12 to 13 weeks after seeding (60°F for one to two weeks, then 50°F).

In the southern U.S. allow 9 to 10 weeks for flowering pack sales, and 11 to 12 weeks for flowering 4″ pot sales of dwarf varieties. Sales should begin once all danger of frost has passed, and continue until April for flowering through mid-August.

For varieties, Blue Puffs (also called Blue Danube) is the leading mid-blue flowered, F₁ hybrid variety on the market today—and for good reason: There are few varieties that can compete with Blue Puffs' clarity of flower color, uniformity in height, and dependable performance when grown year after year. At 9″ tall it is a truly reliable variety. For a taller plant in the mid-blue color, consider growing either Adriatic or Blue Blazer. Both of these are F₁ hybrids like Blue Puffs and are dependable varieties in any garden setting, though they are not as uniform in overall appearance.

In the purple flowering varieties, Royal Delft is the best in overall performance and uniformity, though North Sea is a strong contender. Both varieties grow to about 8″ tall in the garden and make excellent 4″ pot plants (one plant per pot).

White flowering varieties are also available in limited supply.

For something a little unusual in the market, there is also a cut-flower variety called Blue Horizon that grows to 3½' and makes an excellent cut-flower or background planting. Planted 12″ apart the variety fills in readily and flowers from June until frost. The flowers can be used fresh or dried in arrangements.

Ageratum, offered in the very widely-used cell packs, is a fine bedding plant!

ALSTROEMERIA

THE CUT FLOWER CROP

by W.E. Healy, University of Maryland, College Park, Maryland, and
H.F. Wilkins, Nurserymen's Exchange, Half Moon Bay, California

The modern alstroemeria cultivars that are available from Europe (see table) are the result of years of interspecific breeding and irradiation to induce mutations of various cultivars. The majority of the new hybrid cultivars have originated from the van Staavern Company (The Netherlands) and Parigo Seed Company (England). Recently, the Wulfinghoff Company (The Netherlands) has introduced several new and interesting alstroemeria cultivars. Plants are normally leased from the breeder; also, a yearly royalty is assessed on the square footage in production. The Fred Gloeckner Company is the United States representative for the van Staavern Company, whereas the other firms, as far as we know, have no U.S. representative.

Alstroemeria species and hybrids come in many different shades of reds and yellows. The native species are found from the snowline of the high mountain plateaus of the Andes in South America down through the highland forests to the coastal deserts. The requirements for floral induction in the hybrids can be separated into two groups: the white/yellow, and the red/orange, which originated from several different interspecific crosses. The white/yellows require a shorter cold period, have a higher "devernalization" temperature and a shorter photoperiod for flowering than the red/orange group.

Some Alstroemeria Cultivars by Color

Bronze	Red
Harmony (S)	Carmen (P)
	Fanfare (W)
	King Cardinal (S)
Orange	Red Sunset (S)
	Red Surprise (S)
Campfire (S)	Result (W)
Harlequin (W)	Valiant (W)
Orange Beauty (S)	
Orchid Florin (P)	
	Red-Purple
Pink	
	Marina (P)
Capitol (S)	
Mona Lisa (S)	**Yellow**
Pink Perfection (P)	
Regina (S)	Canaria (S)
Rosali Staliro (S)	Orchid (S)
Rosita (S)	White Wings (S)
Trident (W)	Yellow Tiger (S)
	Zebra (S)

P = Parigo; Spalding, England
S = M.C. van Staavern; Aalsmeer, The Netherlands
W = A. Wulfinghoff; Rijsuiyk, The Netherlands

Plant Characteristics

As the leaves on an alstroemeria shoot unfold, they rotate 180° so that the adaxial (upper) surface becomes the abaxial (under) surface. The inflorescence consists of a whorl of flowering cymes, with each individual cyme bearing one to five sympodially arranged flower buds.

The alstroemeria plant consists of a white fleshy rhizome from which arises aerial shoots and a root system that is moderately fibrous and can become thickened like a dahlia. The growing point of the rhizome gives rise to aerial shoots. Each new aerial shoot arises from the first node of the rhizome, and a lateral rhizome develops in the second node of the aerial shoot.

The aerial shoots can be either vegetative or reproductive. Normally, shoots that have unfolded more than 30 leaves will not flower and are vegetative. Once rhizomes are induced to flower by low temperatures, all shoots that form will flower until plants become "devernalized" by high temperatures.

Flower Induction

The flowering control mechanism for alstroemeria hybrids appears to be of a biphasic nature, with a primary cold temperature requirement and a secondary photoperiod requirement. As stated earlier, the temperature effect shows a group specificity, with the white/yellow group requiring a shorter cold treatment (two to four weeks of 40°F) for floral induction than the red/orange group, which needs four to six weeks of 40°F for floral induction.

Once flowering begins, the plants will continue to produce flowering shoots indefinitely until the soil temperature goes above 60°F for extended periods of time. Ten plants were grown at continuous 55°F soil temperature; the plants continued to

Alstroemeria does very well outdoors in the Watsonville, California, coastal area. Here's a large acreage of them at the Brothers Brothers location near Watsonville (two of the Brothers in the foreground).

flower indefinitely regardless of air temperature and regardless of photoperiod. Since the below-ground part of the plant must be kept cool (55°F) for continued flowering, deep soil mulches or misting the mulch to encourage evaporative cooling will help maintain a cool soil temperature, along with evaporative air cooling during periods of warm temperature.

The other component that controls flower induction is photoperiod. Once plants have perceived an adequate cold treatment, a 13-hour photoperiod as obtained by using standard chrysanthemum lighting as a night interruption hastens floral initiation. Lighting nonvernalized plants will not induce flowering. Photoperiods longer than 13 hours will not promote any earlier flowering, but may decrease flower production. We have found a 4-hour night interruption (incandescent source, 10 p.m. to 2 a.m.) adequate. Another method we have used is to add the length of normal existing daylength plus x hours of night interruption in order to equal 13 hours. These night interruptions are effective in promoting earlier flowering without decreasing flower production. Lighting should occur from about September 1 to April 15 at 45°N latitude (St. Paul, Minnesota). Check with your local weather bureau to determine the exact dates when the daylength is less than 13 hours at your latitude.

Light intensity has been shown to affect flower development. In northern Europe where light intensity in the winter is significantly reduced, bud blasting is a problem. In Minnesota we have only occasionally observed bud blasting, and this may have been related to soil temperatures that were too cool. Since the number of cymes per stem is positively correlated with the stem diameter, alstroemeria should be grown with the maximum available light so that a maximum number of cymes per stem can be attained.

Propagation

Alstroemeria plants should be divided every second or third year, depending on the cultivar and growth characteristics. About one to two weeks prior to dividing, plants should be severely pruned, leaving only the youngest 6″ to 8″ plants after flowering decreases in late summer or early fall. Care should be taken to dig deep enough to get the growing point, as the rhizome can grow 12″ to 14″ deep. Each new division should consist of a single rhizome with an undamaged, blunt growing point, some new aerial shoots and, most important, some large fleshy storage roots.

The presence of these thickened storage roots is critical for the re-establishment of the plants, since the first new roots will arise from these enlarged storage roots. Normally only the youngest 1″ to 3″ of rhizome is kept, with the older portion of the rhizome being discarded. These older rhizomes are of no value, as the lateral rhizomes that may arise from them are weak and do not appear to regain vigor.

Immediately after the rhizomes are divided or new rhizomes are received, they should be planted. It is essential that pots, soil or ground beds be ready before plants are divided or received. Normally, extra plants are potted up to replace plants that die or are not as vigorous as others. It is expected that 5% to 25% of the plants will not

A short course in physiology of alstroemeria: First, you see a 1" or so rhizome extending horizontally. It's a fleshy "stem" storing starches—the plant's reserve. Extending upward from the rhizome are 5 or 6 shoots, each ¼" or so. Some of these will flower, others will be only leafy shoots (see text). At the tip of the pencil is a tiny node. It is a small bud that will grow out horizontally to form a new rhizome. Around the rhizome you will also see normal roots.

survive transplanting. To increase the survival rate, a fungicidal drench (8 oz./100 gals. of water each of Lesan and Benlate) is recommended at the time of planting and again a month later if vigorous root growth is not observed. Excess watering will quickly rot the rhizomes. After the initial watering with the fungicidal drench, spot water plants as they become dry. Grow the plants at 65°F until they become well extablished (four to eight weeks), before lowering the temperatures to 40°F.

When new growth commences, numerous shoots will form. Removing some of the weak vegetative shoots was shown to increase flower production. Shoot removal acts as a "pinch" and encourages growth or lateral branching of the lateral rhizomes. Shoots should be pulled, since cutting the stem and not pulling it off the rhizome will decrease flower production. A quick upward pull will cleanly remove the shoot from the rhizome. Stems are harvested when the first group of flowers begins to open. Care should be exercised with young or poorly rooted plants because the rhizome may be uprooted or torn loose from the soil if careless stem removal occurs.

Alstroemeria are heavy feeders. We have fed up to 600 ppm N in the form of KNO_3 twice a week to vigorous plants without any adverse effects. Ammoniacal forms of nitrogen fertilizer should be avoided, as at 55°F growing temperatures ammonia is not readily converted to nitrate. Application of minor nutrients may be required to maintain optimum levels within the plant.

Insects and diseases are essentially not a problem on alstroemeria. Whiteflies and aphids may appear during warm weather. We have observed leaf mottling and verified this as a virus infection.

ALSTROEMERIA— A PROMISING POT PLANT

by Mark P. Bridgen
University of Connecticut
Storrs, Connecticut

Alstroemeria, the Inca Lily, has been traditionally grown for cut flowers. However, in 1985, the first commercial cultivar of a "dwarf" alstroemeria arrived in the United States. It has pink and white flowers and is called Rosy Wings. Holland Park Products introduced this plant for Cor Van Duyn (now known as Phytonova) of the Netherlands. At that time, interest by Americans for a dwarf alstroemeria was minimal, propagation of Rosy Wings was difficult and postharvest shipping of rhizomes had tremendous losses. However, since that time, interest in dwarf alstroemeria as a potted crop and as a bedding plant has increased dramatically.

Alstroemeria do make an
attractive pot plant.

Traits such as its ability to be used as a longlasting cut flower, its everblooming characteristic once its been induced to flower, its preference for cool temperatures, and the potential for new flower colors including white, pink, red, purple, lavender, yellow-orange and bicolors have made it a plant in demand. There are now at least four major breeding programs for dwarf alstroemeria in the United States, and prefinished liners are becoming more available. At this time, Erwin Mojonnier Enterprises of Encinitas, California is the largest supplier of liners.

Propagation

Full details on vegetative propagation of alstroemeria and requirements for flowering will be found earlier in this chapter.

Greenhouse Culture

Dwarf alstroemeria can be grown in pots as small as 6″ and still produce a nice, full plant. Due to the extensive root system that develops, standard pots are recommended over azalea pots. Two to three small liners can be planted per 6″ pot. Plant the liners to the outside of the pot, with the growing points leading to the inside. If plants are initially grown in 4″ pots, transplant one full pot into each 6″ pot. The rhizomes should be planted shallow, but should not be exposed on the surface. The large storage roots that sometimes accompany the rhizomes may be planted at any depth.

Proper growth in the greenhouse will help to keep the height under control. If grown properly, the plants generally will not exceed a height of two times the size of the pot. Plants should be adequately spaced to maximize light. If plants are started in 4″ pots, spacing should be 9″ x 9″; when they are moved to 6″ pots they should be spaced 15″ to 15″. These plants respond to pinching and pruning for height control; the more they are cut, the shorter they grow. Every two to three weeks, plants should be "shaped up" by pulling out dead stems and pinching back the top of vegetative stems. This process will encourage new shoots to be shorter. Pulling out dead or unsightly stems, instead of cutting them, will encourage more lateral breaks of the rhizome. Be careful though, if roots are not well established, the whole plant could be pulled from the pot. Also, be aware that these plants are monocotyledons, and once a shoot is pinched back it will eventually turn yellow and die, and these stems will need to be removed before retail sale. No axillary shoots will be produced from that pinched shoot; instead, new shoots will arise from the rhizome. Education of the consumer that these plants are rhizomes that will continue to produce new shoots will also help prevent complications.

Research on height control of alstroemeria with growth regulators is still in the early stages, and no chemical is registered for these plants. The triazoles, Bonzi and Sumagic, and A-Rest create a "cauliflower effect" and prevent flowering; drenches have especially pronounced effects. Cycocel and Florel have little or no effect. B-Nine SP has had the best effect of all the growth regulators. The best height control is obtained when multiple applications are made at lower concentrations

(2,500 ppm); some yellowing of the leaves may occur. Research in this area is ongoing and the possibility of using slow release growth regulators in the growing mix is being examined. Good cultural practices are still the best way to control height: choose genetically dwarf cultivars, grow the plants at full light, space the plants adequately, grow at proper temperatures and do not keep the plants wet.

Alstroemeria grow best in a loose, well-drained growing mix at a pH of approximately 6.5. The plants require large amounts of water, but should never be kept wet, due to potential root rot problems. Water stress, however, can cause flower bud abortion and blindness. Plants respond to heavy feeding, and constant liquid feed of 250 to 300 ppm N or weekly applications of 400 ppm N are recommended.

Inca lilies should always be grown "cool." After planting, good roots form if night temperatures are kept 60° to 62°F. With alstroemeria it is the rhizomes which monitor the temperatures and consequently determine if vegetative or floral shoots are produced. An occasional thermometer placed in pots around the greenhouse helps to determine when to heat and when to cool. Rhizome temperatures should be kept 55° to 60°F for flower initiation; if not rhizomes will become vegetative. The higher temperatures (60° to 65°F) are preferred for the first two to three weeks after planting, and the lower temperatures (55° to 60°F) are preferred during flower production. Temperatures can drop as low as freezing and still have plants survive; however, growth slows as the temperatures drop. Some growers will place plants in cold frames or refrigerators to make space in the greenhouse. Then, as space is available, the plants are removed and induced to flower.

Lighting will hasten flower production with Inca lilies. A night interruption using 100 watt incandescent lights 35″ apart and 33″ above the plants can be used. High intensity discharge (HID) lights will induce flowering faster and produce shorter plants, but they are costly.

ALYSSUM

by Jim Nau
Ball Seed Company

Annual (Lobularia maritima), 90,000 seeds/oz. Germinates in 8 to 10 days at 80° to 82°F. Seed should be left exposed to light during germination.

Commonly called sweet alyssum, the softly scented blooms flower most profusely under cool (60° to 68°F) night temperatures. Recommended for use as either edging or border plants or in hanging baskets mixed with other annuals.

Sow direct to the final container using 8 to 15 seeds in each of the individual cells of a cell-pack. Try for between 5 to 10 seedlings per one cell. For transplanting, seedlings are large enough to handle 20 to 25 days after sowing. Grow on at 50° to

55°F night temperatures until ready to sell. Salable green packs are ready in seven weeks, with flowering packs ready in eight to nine weeks after sowing. For either 4″ pots or 10″ hanging baskets, allow 10 to 11 or 12 to 14 weeks, respectively.

In the southern United States allow seven weeks for packs with color, and nine weeks for flowering 4″ pots. Plant in late summer to mid-winter for plants that will flower as late as June. Plant in full sun to partial shade and space 8″ apart to fill in.

As either a garden or landscape plant, sweet alyssum performs better in spring, early summer, or late summer plantings than it does during the heat of summer. Quite often it is only the white flowering variety which has the vigor to perform during the hottest part of the year in the northern United States. Though they may heat stall (go out of bloom) temporarily in August, the plants will flower again once the night temperatures cool off.

The standard white flowering variety on the market today is New Carpet of Snow. It is a pure white variety up to 6″ tall, and has a reliable performance from year to year. Snow Crystal is a recent introduction which has the largest individual plant size of any white variety in the marketplace. It too is no taller than 6″. For uniform habit and excellent outdoor performance, the Wonderland series is ideal. The three separate colors are well matched in crop time and habit, with the aptly-named Wonderland Deep Rose among the best rose flower colors on the market. Finally, Easter Bonnet is the newest alyssum on the market at the time of this writing. It combines three different colors, white and two shades of purple (one with a hint of rose), and brings to the marketplace the best pastel-shaded mixture available. Others currently available tend to have light yellow in their mixes, which often looks washed out and faded and generally makes the variety look poor.

AMARYLLIS *(HIPPEASTRUM)*

by A. A. De Hertogh
North Carolina State University
Raleigh, North Carolina

Amaryllis *(Hippeastrum)* originate in South America. Flowering is regulated by bulb size, temperature and moisture. The commercial cultivars are the product of extensive breeding efforts. The primary sources of amaryllis bulbs forced in the United States and Canada are Swaziland and The Netherlands. Some bulbs are also produced in Israel. The major use is for pot plant forcings, but they can also be used as cut flowers. The general marketing season is from September to May. Normally, the Swaziland-grown cultivars are forced early and the Dutch-grown cultivars medium to late. With special growing and handling, some Dutch cultivars are suitable for December forcings. The objective is to market a plant that has simultaneously produced a floral stalk and growing leaves.

The amaryllis is a colorful winter pot plant for the home.

The number of floral stalks produced is influenced by bulb size and cultivar. Examples of commercial-sized bulbs are (in circumference): 20/22, 24/26, 28/30 and 32/up cm. The number of flowers per stalk is primarily a cultivar response, and most cultivars produce four flowers per stalk. However, the range is two to six. Larger bulbs tend to produce two floral stalks.

After harvest, the bulbs are quickly dried and cured. During this and all subsequent processes, it is critical that the old root system be kept viable. Normally, the bulbs are cured for two weeks at 73° to 77°F with high ventilation rates. They are subsequently stored at 55°F at 80% relative humidity for at least 8 to 10 weeks. Bulbs stored for longer periods are held at 41° to 48°F. Bulbs should be transported at 41° to 60°F. In addition, they should be protected against freezing and drying out.

Forcers should be prepared to plant bulbs as soon as they arrive. If they must be stored, place them at 41° to 60°F. The precise temperature for preplant storage will depend on the sprouting condition of the bulbs on arrival. If they have begun to sprout, store them at 41°F. If no sprouting is observed, store at 55°F. Keep bulbs from drying out during preplanting storage.

Amaryllis must be planted in a well-drained, fine, pH 6 to 6.5, sterilized planting medium. Never use fresh manure or bark as part of the medium. The medium must be capable of being firmed-in tightly around the roots.

Normally, one bulb is planted per 5½" or 6" standard pot. Plant the bulb with the nose above the rim of the pot, one-third of the bulb should be out of the planting medium. Force bulbs pot to pot on the bench.

Assortment of Amaryllis (Hippeastrum) Cultivars Used for Forcing[1]

Source of Bulbs	Color	Cultivar	Approximate Days to	
			Market Stage[2]	Flowering
Swaziland	red	Barotse	27	34
		Bold Leader	25	35
		Miracle	32	42
		Noel	36	40
		Safari	25	32
		Sundance	20	28
	pink	Blushing Bride	20	28
		Candy Floss	21	29
		Milady	21	28
		Springtime	24	30
		Summertime	20	28
	salmon-orange	Desert Dawn	20	28
	white	Intokazi	20	27
		Masai	27	37
		Wedding Dance	21	28
	orange	Zanzibar	21	31
	bi-color	Carnival		
		(white/deep red flush)	21	29
		Cocktail		
		(red/white striped center)	24	32
The Netherlands	red	Belinda	34	41
		Cicero	27	41
		Red Lion	36	46
		Rilona	26	41
		Telstar	32	40
	pink	Hercules	28	40
		Susan	25	33
	white	Ludwig Dazzler	25	38
		White Christmas	31	49
	orange	Kokarde	21	33
		Orange Souvereign	26	39
	bi-color	Apple Blossom		
		(white/pink flush)	30	40
		Cinderella (light orange		
		with white edge)	24	37
		Orion (red/white flush)	30	38
		Minerva (light red on white)	35	44
		Piquant (red, white striped)	23	33

[1]This is a selected list of available cultivars. There are many other cultivars available.

[2]Marketing stage is when first floral stalk has reached 12" in length. This and the flowering stage usually take a few days longer than average with early plantings and is reached quicker with later plantings. Also, lots are somewhat variable and the information given should be used only as guide.

Amaryllis are tropical plants and they can be forced over a wide range of temperatures, but 70° to 80°F is preferred. Bottom heat should be used. Average forcing time to market stage of development is three to five weeks. It will vary with each cultivar and forcing period (see table). It is also important to note that most lots are somewhat variable. The forcing information in the table should be used as a guide to average dates of marketing and flowering.

Plants should be forced in a low- to medium-light intensity (1,000 to 5,000 fc.) greenhouse. It is possible to start bulbs in a dark, temperature-controlled area before the bulbs are placed under lighted conditions. Force plants in a well-ventilated greenhouse. Do not allow the relative humidity to build up.

After planting, water the medium thoroughly. Subsequently, the medium should be kept only slightly moist. It is important not to overwater the plant in order to stimulate regrowth of the basal root system. Normally, watering once per week is satisfactory. Use tepid water and do not water over the bulb noses.

Initially, the bulbs do not need fertilization. After they are marketed, however, consumers should be advised to fertilize the plants. Care tags should be used when the plants are marketed.

The primary disease of amaryllis is Fire or Red Spot (Stagnospora). Overwatering can sometimes promote development of Fusarium. In addition, it is possible to have mites, thrips and mealybugs.

The plants should be marketed when the floral stalk is 12″ tall. Also, it is desirable to have leaf growth of 6″ to 12″ and a second stalk beginning to grow. Do not cold store the plants. If they need to be held, place them at 48°F. Wholesalers and retailers should use tepid water after they receive the plants.

Whenever possible, plants should be marketed with care tags. The consumer should be informed that amaryllis should be fertilized at least one to two times per month when they are growing. The plants should be kept in the coolest area of the home and out of direct sunlight in order to obtain maximum life of the flowers. Also, they can be placed outside in the pot when the danger of frost has passed. To reforce the plants, they should be taken in the home in the fall, allowed to dry and be stored for at least eight weeks at 50° to 60°F. Then the dried leaves should be cut off, the planting medium watered and the plants placed in a warm area to start the forcing process. If one does not want to store the bulbs, the plants can be grown at 50° to 60°F for 8 to 10 weeks and then forced into flower.

Amaryllis can also be used as cut flowers. They should be cut when the floral buds are colored, but not yet open. To prevent the splitting and outrolling of the cut stems, the flowers can be held in 0.125M sucrose for 24 hours at 72 °F before shipping.

ANEMONE

by Simon Crawford, Dan Jacques and Grace Price
Pan American Seed Company

56,700 seeds/oz. (clean seed). Germinates in 7 to 14 days at 60°F.

Anemone coronaria is the most widely grown species of the *Anemone* genus. It originates in southern Europe around the Mediterranean and is referred to in this section simply as anemone. Anemones are widely grown in Europe as greenhouse cut flowers or as garden plants, but are not well-known in the United States.

Until recently all cultivars were grown from corms produced by specialist growers. Examples of these are the de Caen and St. Brigid (double and semi-double) selections. Although they are still widely grown as cut flowers, they suffer from having a poor color range, small flowers and short stems. Another corm-raised cultivar, St. Piran, has larger flowers and longer stems, but still has a limited color range. More recently F_1 hybrid anemones have been introduced which can be grown from seed and have marked improvements in plant quality. Perhaps the most outstanding of these introductions is the Mona Lisa® series, the result of 40 years extensive breeding work.

Mona Lisa is grown predominantly for cut-flower production. The colors include wine, pink, white, blue, orchid, red and a bi-color red and white. The benefits of Mona Lisa are strong 17" stems, 4" to 5" blooms, high productivity, a vase life of 10 to 14 days, and less disease problems than corms. With a good growing regime and using a planting density of 12 to 15 plants/sq. yard, at least 125 stems/sq. yard can be harvested. Anemones are energy efficient, being grown in cool houses. Compared with many other cool cut flower crops such as carnations, they are less labor intensive as they do not require staking, stringing, or disbudding.

Sowing Seed

Sow seed of Mona Lisa in mid-March to mid-April in a well-drained peat-based medium. If seed flats are used, seeds should be sown ½" apart. Seeds of Mona Lisa are "defluffed," which makes them much easier to sow than other anemones. Cover the seed lightly (0.10") with a soilless medium and use a Lesan/Benlate drench to water the seeds in (1 lb. each/100 gals.). Mona Lisa should be germinated at 60°F. After sowing, flats can be stored at 50°F until seedling emergence (around two weeks), then moved to a cool greenhouse bench. Higher temperatures will definitely reduce germination percentage. Transplant eight to nine weeks after sowing, when the seedlings are about 1" long. Transplant into cells which are 1" in diameter. When seeds are sown in plugs, use 288 size plug trays. Keep plug trays in a cool chamber (60°F) until emergence, then move to a greenhouse bench. It is important to maintain cool temperatures (70°F) and high humidity to obtain high germination. Plugs should be kept constantly moist. A coarse vermiculite cover should help prevent water stress and algae build up. Agribrom or Physan 20 used at the recommended rate should be applied to keep algae under control. Plugs should be kept within a pH range of 5.8 to 6.5. With higher pH, chlorosis can develop. Young plants benefit greatly from a constant or alternate feeding using 20-10-20 peat lite special at 75 to 100 ppm. Seedlings can be transplanted to size 72 plugs four to five weeks after sowing (after the second true leaf appears).

Many cut-flower growers have raised young anemone plants from seed, but the worldwide trend is to buy-in plugs of Mona Lisa, thereby streamlining production.

Preparing For Your Transplants

The kind of growing medium employed will influence the type of spacing and bed set-up that will be used. A raised bed will be of most benefit with a heavy soil while flat beds will be more adequate for a well-drained soil.

Planting schemes may vary and are described below. The aim is to obtain 12 to 15 plants/sq. yard. If a soil-based medium is used, it should be sterilized. Mulch to keep soil temperature down.

Before transplanting, make a soil test to determine specific fertilization needs. It is necessary that the pH of a soil-based medium remain neutral (pH 6.8 to 7) throughout the growing season. The pH of soilless media should be approximately 6.2 to 6.5. Add 2 to 2½ lbs. of superphosphate per cubic yard of medium.

Spacing

Here are several bench spacing plans used in Europe. Most European crops are grown on ground beds. Often the walk is dug out and the bench raised 4″ or 5″ above the walk level. The goal is to ensure good drainage.
1. **Two-row bed.** Two rows spaced 10″ to 12″ apart with plants spaced 6″ to 7″ apart. There is a 28″ to 30″ walk between the double row beds. It's a widely-used plan, especially in Holland, and is easier for flower harvesting.
2. **Four-row bed.** Four rows spaced 10″ apart with plants spaced 6″ to 7″ apart. A rather narrow 16″ to 18″ walk separates the beds. This plan is used on ground beds with, again, soil mounded above the walk level. This spacing is also used on raised benches.
3. **Two-row beds widely spaced.** Two rows 12″ apart, a 30″ space and two more rows 12″ apart. Plants are spaced 3″ apart in the rows. Harvesting is easy and there is good air circulation around the plants.

Transplanting

When transplanting, care should be taken to prevent injury to the delicate root system. Initial root growth can be stimulated by addition of 150 ppm N of a starter

*Mona Lisa anemone is
a colorful, lovely and
exciting cut flower.*

solution (9-45-15), or 150 ppm N of calcium nitrate if superphosphate has been added to the growing medium. After about two weeks drench with Benlate/Subdue (1 lb. Benlate and 1 oz. Subdue per 100 gals. of water).

To grow Mona Lisa in a pot, we have found that the best performance comes from using a 6″ to 8″ pot, one plant per pot. On the bench, place pot to pot or space pots 2″ apart at the rim to provide better air circulation. Pot-grown Mona Lisa may take longer to flower than bed-grown anemones due to the higher soil temperature in the pots.

Water before noon to allow foliage to dry completely before sundown. Every precaution should be taken to keep water off the foliage. If possible, it is better to employ a ground-level watering system.

Fertilizer

It is best to base fertilizer use on media and water tests. We recommend a fertilizer that is low in ammonium or urea N, as acid-forming fertilizers may decrease medium pH when irrigation water has a low buffering capacity. Try 20-10-20 Peat-Lite Special at 150-200 ppm N. If no superphosphate has been added to the medium, it may be best to use 15-16-17 or 15-17-17 (no sodium) Peat-Lite at 150-200 ppm N. It may be advisable to leach with clear water occasionally, in order to decrease media soluble salts. Do not shock Mona Lisa with high fertilizer rates or irregular water schedules as this can cause cracking of the flower stems. For stronger stems fertilize occasionally with calcium nitrate at 200 ppm.

Greenhouse Environment

Anemones grow most successfully in cool, shady conditions. In areas of extremely high temperatures or high light intensity, heavy shading may be required. Shading should be removed in areas where cooler temperatures and cloudy weather persist throughout the growing season. During warm weather when cooler night temperatures are not possible, plants do better when grown in houses equipped with fan and pad cooling.

Diseases and Insects

The control of diseases and insects is outlined in the table below.

Controlling Diseases and Insects on Mona Lisa Anemone*

Disease/Pest Problem	Symptoms	Treatment
Botrytis cinerea	Yellowing of older leaves, soft rot at base of plant, gray mold.	Botran (½ lb./100 gals.), Ornalin (1 lb./100 gals.), Daconil (1½ lbs./100 gals.). Every 2 weeks (alternate products). Exotherm (weekly basis); ventilate greenhouse; keep a clean environment; remove diseased plant material.
Rhizoctonia	Yellowing foliage, softening and blackening of crown at soil level. Associated with wilting.	Terraclor drench (once only). Avoid poor drainage and overwatering.
Pythium	Bluish color on foliage/wilting with a definite blackening in the crown.	Subdue
Downy mildew	White, powdery fungus growing on leaves.	Aliette
Colletotrichum (leaf curl/ anthracnose)	Stunted and gnarled leaves; irregular margins. Flower deformity or discoloration (in severe cases). High temperature and high humidity promote the disease.	Benlate/Ferbam every 7 to 10 days (1 lb. Benlate and ½ lb. Ferbam in 100 gals. water) or Difolatan/ Benlate (1¾ lbs. Difolatan and ½ lb. Benlate in 100 gals. water).
Aphids		Temik, Oxamyl, or Malathion (allow plants to establish before using Temik or Oxamyl)
Whitefly		Resmethrin aerosol spray
Thrips	Mottled tracks on leaves; distortion on flower.	Dursban or Thiodan (harvest and destroy before spraying).

*Disclaimer: To simplify information, trade names of products have been used. No endorsement of named products is intended, nor is criticism implied of similar products not mentioned. Mention of chemicals does not imply guarantee of effectiveness or safety, nor that the chemicals or uses discussed have been registered by appropriate agencies.

Flower Harvesting and Storage

Mona Lisa flowers will close up naturally at night. Flowers are best cut as early as possible before greenhouse temperatures rise and flowers begin to open. Cut the flower close to the crown, but use a clean, sharp knife as this can become a site of disease infection. Sterilize the knife frequently.

Flowers can be cut at the closed bud stage, and stored for several days in water containing an antibacterial agent such as Floralife. This will produce a medium-sized flower. For maximum flower size, allow the flower to open and close once before cutting, bearing in mind that this will reduce the vase life.

Flowers can be kept in cold storage prior to shipping, but we recommend that they be held at 34 °F for no longer than 14 days. Otherwise, stored blooms can be cooled to 40°F when they are in the flower shop.

Stems need not be shipped in water if markets are close by. DO NOT ship stems lying down in a box since "crooking" of the necks can occur. Always demand boxes be shipped with flowers standing upright.

A fine house of Mona Lisa anemone.

ANTHURIUM

by Nancy L. Drushal
GrowerTalks magazine

Anthurium andraeanum **and** *Anthurium scherzeranum;* **family Araceae; common name Flamingo Lily.**

Anthuriums have long been known as a cut flower in the floral industry, but now are also marketed as a blooming foliage plant for interiorscapes. These plants do well under interior lighting conditions, preferring a well-drained organic soil mix and high humidity. *A. andraeanum* sports attractive foliage with large red, pink, white

All important crops
need a specialist
propagator/breeder.
Fortunately, anthuriums have
a good one: on the left is
Nick Van der Knaap in Holland
who does this job very well. He
has an acute awareness of
pathology. On the right, Henk van
Staalduinen, affable Dutch
horticulturist.

or salmon waxy spathe-like flowers. *A. scherzeranum* is a more compact plant with crimson or red and white polka-dot flowers and is more floriferous than *A. andraeanum.*

Due to a widespread, long-term blight problem the only way to safely produce anthuriums now is from tissue culture propagation. *A. scherzeranum* should be potted one plug (three to five seedlings) per 4″ to 5″ pot, while the larger *A. andraeanum* should be started one plug (three to five seedlings) per 6″ to 10″ pot. Spacing on the 4″ pot starts at roughly three pots/sq. ft. and 1½ pots/sq. ft. on the 6″ pot. Crop time for both is six to eight months.

The soil mix is very light, as excellent drainage is required. A 50:50 peat/perlite or similar mix is recommended. Plants should be kept moist but not wet, as they are slow growers and prone to rot.

A. scherzeranum requires 1,500 fc. of daylight while *A. andraeanum* requires 2,500 fc. Even in the interiorscape *A. scherzeranum* requires less light to bloom and prosper.

Growing temperatures should be kept between 70° and 80°F daytime and 55° to 65°F nighttime; above 90°F will be detrimental. *A. andraeanum* is not as affected by higher temperatures as *A. scherzeranum* and can be grown outdoors under saran.

A 200 ppm nutrient solution of 6-2-4 or 20-10-20 fertilizer can be applied on a drip irrigation system, or by overhead if plants are rinsed with clear water afterward.

Anthuriums are affected by several bacterial and fungus diseases, so good drainage, watering practices and air circulation are important. They can also be affected by aphids or mites. Several common fungicides and pesticides are labeled for anthuriums.

It is best to discontinue fertilizer at least seven days before shipping. Blooms on anthuriums will last up to three months.

AQUILEGIA *(Columbine)*

by Jim Nau
Ball Seed Company

Perennial (Aquilegia caerulea or A. hybrida), **15,000 to 22,000 seeds/oz. Germinates in 21 to 28 days at 70° to 75°F. Seed should be left exposed to light during germination.**

One of the most requested of the spring perennials due to its unusual flower form, columbine is an excellent plant for the perennial border, as a pot plant, and as a cut flower. The predominant flower colors in the trade in this species are usually bicolors (blue, white, yellow) though solid colors of white or yellow also are available. Flowers are of an unusual form, having appendages at the base of the

Aquilegia Songbird is an interesting new pot plant.

bloom, called spurs, that can be short or long. These spurs give the flower its unusual character. Plants flower in May and June and are hardy to USDA zones 3 to 8.

Sowings are most often made the summer prior to the spring selling season for flowering pot sales. Germination can be irregular. To improve uniformity, the seed should be chilled two to three weeks at 40°F before sowing, especially if holding seed over from year to year. Sown in July, transplanted 30 to 40 days later to packs, and transplanted to quart or gallon containers when ready, plants can be over-wintered in cold greenhouses or coldframes for sales next spring. Flowering will occur naturally in April in Chicago within the coldframe. Plants can become quite tall in the gallon containers (2' plus) if not treated with any growth regulator. For green pack sales in the spring, allow 15 to 20 weeks, though plants will not flower the same season from seed.

Late season sowings (September/October) over-wintered at 40° to 45°F will flower in March and April. Use one plant per 6" pot.

In varieties the most common one is McKanas Giants, which is a mixture of a number of colors which are often the earliest to flower.

Songbird (F₁ hybrid) is the newest variety on the trade and includes a number of separate colors that are sold under such names as Bunting, Robin, Cardinal, and Dove, to name a few. Check catalog descriptions carefully on this series, since some colors perform better as pot plants while others are taller (which makes them excellent cut flower candidates).

Music Mixture is also an F_1 hybrid and available in a number of colors. It compares in habit and performance to Songbird, though it isn't as early or offer as broad a color range.

In dwarf flowering varieties try Biedermeier, which is a mixture of several different colors on plants to 16″ tall in the 6″ pots. Flowers are held upright and measure no more than 2″ across.

ARABIS

by Jim Nau
Ball Seed Company

Perennial (Arabis causasica), **70,000 seeds/oz. Germinates in six to 12 days at 65° to 70°F. Seed should be left exposed to light during germination.**

Arabis is commonly called Rock Cress or Wall Cress due to its low growing habit and excellent footing for planting into rock gardens or rock walls. Arabis has mostly white flowers, though sometimes they are rose pink in cultivated varieties. Plants are compact and rosetting, and grow to no more than 8″. Flowers are small (to ½″) and fragrant. Double and single flowering varieties are available as well as variegated leaf types. Hardy in USDA zones 3 to 7, arabis will flower in April and May.

Seed is the most common method of propagation, though division and cuttings are popular, too. Many cultivated varieties have to be vegetatively propagated. Division can be easily done in the spring or fall, and cuttings should be taken in the late spring after flowering. Seed sown in winter or early spring will flower sporadically at best during the same year as sown. In fact, usually 10% or less will flower the same year from seed. For green pack sales in the spring, allow 12 to 15 weeks. For flowering pot sales in the spring, sow in July of the previous year and overwinter in quart containers. Grow on at 50°F.

Snow Cap is the most popular variety of arabis on the market, and is sold both as seed and vegetative material. Flowers are white, single, and held on stems to no taller than 6″. Compinkie is a rose-pink flowering variety that is available from seed or can be vegetatively propagated as well. Plants grow to 4″ tall.

A related variety, *A. blepharophylla* Spring Charm is a single flowering rose colored variety that is treated as an annual in the Midwest. Plants do best in mild wintered areas and usually need winter protection in the home garden to survive even in this type of environment. However, sowings made in early October flowered profusely in 4″ pots by Valentine's Day when grown at 55°F nights. Allow approximately 20 to 22 weeks for winter flowering.

ASPARAGUS

by Ed Harthun
Ball Seed Company

Annual *(A. species)*, **500 to 900 seeds/oz. Germinates in three to six weeks at 75° to 85°F.**

Plumosus nanus and *Sprengeri* are the most widely used species. Both of them are used as cut greens in flower arrangements, but *Sprengeri* is more widely used in hanging baskets, urns, and other patio containers, very frequently combined with flowering annuals such as petunias and geraniums. *Asparagus meyeri, falcatus* and *pyramidalis* are other species sometimes used as potted house plants.

New crop seed is usually harvested in January or February, and best results can be obtained by using fresh seed. Since germination is strung out over several weeks, the seed flats must be watched closely. A night temperature of 60° to 65°F promotes good growth. They prefer light shade and regular fertilization after becoming established. A 2¼" size requires 14 to 16 weeks of growing time from seed sowing. A finished 4" takes about 24 weeks. Many growers today start with liners that are 10 to 12 weeks old. These are produced by experienced specialists.

ASTER

Cut Flowers

This versatile flower was one of the favorites of the late George J. Ball, who, over 75 years ago, developed the forebears of some of today's finest varieties. Probably no one series in history was as well known or has been grown by as many florists as the Ball Florist strain, available as a mix. Despite the inroads of diseases like fusarium wilt and the "yellows," they are still grown profitably in some areas, chiefly by specialists.

For outdoor summer culture (cloth houses), the usual handling by retail growers calls for sowing April 15, transplanting to Jiffy-7s or Jiffy Pots two to three weeks later, and planting out to the cloth house May 20 to 25, depending on the weather. Space 12" x 12". It's very important that the plants not be allowed to "draw up," either in the seed flats or in the pots.

About diseases: There are two principal offenders; both can be definitely controlled.

332

- **Stem rot** (fusarium wilt) is a rotting of the plant at the surface of the soil, usually with dark lesions extending up the stem. Steaming soil to 180°F for ½ hour, 8″ deep, should reduce loss to almost nothing. Next to that, planting asters to soil not used for that crop before usually prevents any serious loss.

- **Yellows.** Part or all of the plant just turns a sickly yellow and stops growing. Flowers on affected plants are also more or less yellowed and do not open properly. Plants are normally a foot or more high before the injury appears. Often, one side of a plant is affected first. Infected plants should be destroyed at first signs of infection.

  Yellows is a virus that affects many weeds and common garden annuals. The only way an aster can get yellows is via the aster leafhopper. This little fellow (¼″) looks like a small grasshopper. He picks up the yellow virus from weeds, etc. outside the house, then as he feeds on the aster foliage he infects the clean plant. Aster yellows can be eliminated if plants are grown in a cloth enclosure kept tight enough to exclude the hopper. This calls for cloth that runs 22 threads per inch.

Greenhouse Asters—Year Round

The only important requirements are a 50°F night temperature and additional light that must be supplied continuously from the seedling stage until plants are 20″ to 24″ tall. The only exception is the period from May 15 to August 1, during which daylength is long enough, 60-watt bulbs with reflectors, spaced 5′ apart, or the lighting setup you use for mums is satisfactory. Lights must be turned on from sundown to 10 p.m. daily, or for two hours in the middle of the night. Spacing is usually 8″ x 8″.

A mid-July sowing flowers in January, October 20 sowing flowers in April and a May 20 sowing flowers in September. For varieties, consult the Ball Seed Company catalog.

Perennial Aster—Exciting Pot Plant

[**Editor's Note:** *Although they are not grown in the United States now (early 1990s), pot asters are a major crop, especially in Denmark (9 million per year) and do seem to have potential for the U.S. market. I hear endless pressure always for "something new" in pot plants in this country. Here is a colorful, long-lasting plant with good shelf life—and a proven seller in Europe, especially in Germany.*]

(The following notes are by Irene Christiansen and David Beattie of Pennsylvania State University and are adapted from *GrowerTalks,* November 1990.)

Europeans, especially Germans, have found out that they really like perennial asters as a pot plant. This colorful new plant has become a major crop for the Danes—a new and rapidly expanding segment of their floriculture export sales.

About eight years ago a Danish grower, Flemming Kragh Sorensen, began to produce perennial asters as a greenhouse pot crop. He began by experimenting with long days, short days, and growth regulators. In a short time Flemming has developed a pot plant of reasonably good quality. He has found that asters are a fast and inexpensive crop that take only eight to 10 weeks from sticking to sale. They can be produced and sold during the summer, just when it can be difficult to find a crop to replace traditional bedding plants.

Flemming's success with the crop spread fast to other Danish growers, and production increased. In 1989, 20 Danish growers produced and sold 8 million perennial pot asters, and in 1990 expected to sell 9 million.

As export competition increases, particularly for new markets, crop quality has increased. As a result, production time has increased as growers try to produce fuller plants. Today, asters take 10 to 11 weeks to produce. Production begins in early spring and continues through to autumn. For a few Danish growers who produce asters as their main crop, the production cycle begins in March and continues into October. However, most growers start selling after the bedding plant season in June and sell the last plants in September/October when poinsettias or other Christmas crops need more space.

Varieties

Most perennial pot asters grown in greenhouses are *Aster novi-belgii* and the main cultivar is Royal Blue. Other important cultivars are the red Freda Ballard and the blue Royal Ruby. The most popular white varieties are *Aster ericoides* Monte Casino and White Butterfly. Although cultivars of *Aster noviangliae* have been tried, flowering is difficult to control.

Culture

Most perennial asters are short-day plants, so stock plants must be kept under long-day conditions to produce vegetative cuttings. High light and high temperatures (above 68°F) keep plants vegetative. Some growers who take cuttings weekly run high temperatures and high light levels during fall months to keep stock plants vegetative. The relationship between temperature, light and vegetative growth changes during the year. For example, during the early production season a grower can run cooler temperatures and still maintain vegetative growth. In addition, cutting quality is influenced by stock plant light levels, temperatures more than 68°F and by the age of the cuttings. Aster growers now realize that cutting quality is probably the most important element for developing high-quality, well-budded plants. Some growers want a very vegetative cutting, while others prefer to work with cuttings that are physiologically closer to flower initiation. One is not better than the other, but the choice determines the length of the long-day photoperiod as well as the amount of growth regulator.

The production cycle begins in January or February when stock plants, which are overwintered outdoors, are lifted and moved into the greenhouse for the production of new stock plants. They are potted in sphagnum moss peat mixed with limestone to raise pH to about 6. In addition, low levels of nitrogen, phosphorous and potassium are added to the growing mix. The stock plants are kept under long days at 68°F, and 3″ to 4″ long cuttings are taken every week. No rooting hormone is used. Three cuttings are stuck directly in each pot and are rooted under poly covers or under fog. It takes 10 to 12 days for most cultivars to root.

Culture of the Pot Plant

In Denmark, all pot asters are produced in 4″ pots. The same peat mix used for stock plants is used for growing. Fertilizing starts immediately after propagation; a 20-13-17 is a good fertilizer for pot asters.

After rooting, the plants are kept under long days for one to three weeks, depending on the variety, cutting quality and the time of year. For instance, *A. novi-belgii* cultivars require more time under long days than *Aster ericoides*. Since the plants develop vegetatively during long days, this photoperiod must be maintained long enough for plants to size up. In the initial growing phase, plants are pinched back once or twice, depending on variety. During the vegetative phase plants may become too tall, so they are sprayed several times with B-Nine. Higher growth regulator rates are used in early summer than late summer. After the plants have developed sufficient size they are given short days until sale.

A first-class Danish pot aster must be 8½″ to 9½″ high, 8½″ to 9½″ wide, be well branched and have more than 50 flower buds. They are sold with three to four open flowers and the grower will receive 85¢ to $1.20 for each plant.

[*Editor's Note: Cuttings of these perennial pot asters are currently available from Yoder Bros., P.O. Box 68, Alva, Florida 33920 and from Jens Kristensen Stenbaek, Stenbaekvej, 8220 Braband, Denmark. Unrooted cuttings can be imported to the United States and Stenbaek has them available in season.]*

Pot Asters From Seed

There are several groups of varieties that make very attractive, colorful spring pot plants, normally one per 4″. Most commonly used: Pixie Princess, Pot 'N' Patio, Milady and Dwarf Queen. Normally they are sown around February 1, receive several weeks of long days to develop the plant, then short day to flower. Normally 60°F night temperature. If sown earlier, let's say in December in the North, they would normally flower without short day treatment.

ASTILBE

by Jim Nau
Ball Seed Company

Perennial (Astilbe x arendsii), 384,000 seeds/oz. Germinates in 14 to 21 days at 70°F. Seed should be left exposed to light during germination.

Astilbe is a premier perennial plant with excellent value for either the pot plant market or for perennial plant sales in the spring. Astilbes flower in late spring and early summer and do best in areas where they get light shade in the afternoon. Plants get 24" to 36" tall, and come in colors of red, pink, white, or lavender. Flowers are borne in plumes that measure from 4" to 10" long. Hardy in USDA zones four to eight.

Though astilbes can be propagated from seed, the boldest colors and all the hybrids come from divisions that are done in early spring or fall. Upon receipt of roots, separate the crowns, or pot as is, using one plant per quart or gallon container. February and March planted divisions will be salable by late May, though flowering will not be profuse from these divisions; more flower color will be on next year's plants.

For potted plant sales in flower during late winter and spring, bring the crowns (try to have three to four "eyes") in around September. Pot up into 6" pots and let the plants become established in the container. Chill the plants for 10 to 12 weeks at 35° to 40°F. They can be overwintered with other perennials and brought in when needed. Once the pots have been brought back into the greenhouse, place the pots out of direct light and allow them to warm up gradually over a period of several days, then increase temperatures to no less than 58°F nights and allow 12 to 16 weeks to flower, depending on the cultivar. In general, the early and mid-season varieties will flower about the same time. The late season varieties tend to take longer, though they would work for sales two to four weeks after the start of the sales of the earlier flowering material. It is suggested to stay away from taller varieties to avoid too vigorous a growth. A growth regulator is suggested for keeping the plants dwarf.

For those who would like to grow from seed, pretreat by placing the seed on moist peat moss for two weeks at 70°F. If the seed does not germinate, then give 40°F for three to four weeks. This will help to break dormancy within particularly hard to germinate seed. However, when the seed is fresh, 70°F has been all that is needed to get 70+% germination rates. If following the procedure above, once removed from the 40°F cooler the seed will germinate in 14 to 21 days at 70°F. January seed sowings will not flower the same season.

All seeded varieties are mixtures of the species. While the plants perform well, the flower color is muted at best and dull in its overall appearance. As for astilbe varieties from division, the following cultivars are suggested; Fanal—a deep red to

336

22″, Rheinland—a pink to 24″, and Deutschland—a pure white to 24″. These as well as other varieties on the market are classified by being from early- to late-season performers; check with your favorite supplier in regard to the seasonality of the cultivars in which you are interested.

In related material, *A. chinensis* var. pumila is an excellent variety, with lavender pink flowers, that prefers a well-drained though moist soil in the garden. This dwarf variety (10″) is recommended for use in rock gardens and as a border or edging plant in the perennial garden. It also makes a sharp 4″ pot. However, pumila is an August flowering astilbe in the Midwest garden, which makes it one of the latest to flower.

AUBRIETIA

by Jim Nau
Ball Seed Company

Perennial (Aubrietia deltoidea), 85,000 seeds/oz. Germinates in 14 to 21 days at 65° to 70°F. Seed should be left exposed to light during germination.

A low growing perennial sometimes confused with arabis. Aubrietia flower colors are lavender, blue and purple. Deep rose flowers are also available, but often appear to have blue or lavender overtones. Flowers measure ¾″ across and are held on upright stems over the rosetting foliage. It grows to 8″ tall. Plants flower in April and May and are hardy in USDA zones 4 to 7.

Aubrietia is primarily propagated by seed, though cuttings taken after flowering in late spring, or crown division done as soon as the plants can be dug out of the ground in the spring, are other noted methods. Seed sown in January for May sales will not flower until the following spring. Sow in summer for sales the following year. Sowings made in early October, grown at 50 °F during the winter and transplanted to a 4″ pot, flower in May. For green pack sales, allow 10 to 12 weeks. Growing on temperatures are 50° to 55°F nights.

In varieties, the primary seeded selection is one called Large Flowered Hybrids which is a catch-all name for seed collected from the species. It is a mixture of lavender, lilac, purple, and dark rose. Plants grow to 8″ tall. Purple Gem has ¾″ purple flowers on plants to 6″ tall and is vegetatively propagated. The seeded form is similar and it is sold under the name Whitewell Gem.

AZALEA

by Frank Batson
Angelwood Nursery
Woodburn, Oregon

In today's market there is such a limited number of growers who have the time, space, knowledge, or desire to produce their own azaleas that this chapter will deal only with the how, why, when and where of how to handle budded azaleas once they are delivered to you from the specialist azalea growers. Those wishing for more detailed information on growing azaleas from start to finish or from the liner stage, or even on a year-round schedule, should refer to the 13th or 14th edition of the *Ball RedBook*. If interested in even more complete details, obtain a copy of the University of California's publication #4058, "Growing Azaleas Commercially," by Kofranek and Larson (out of print but probably available from a horticultural library).

The Main Classes

One of the more confusing aspects of azaleas is the nomenclature of types and varieties. Greenhouse-forcing azaleas generally fall into four main groups.

1. **The Indica** varieties are usually large flowered and come in sometimes single, but mostly double-flowered types in a wide range of colors. Our present Indica varieties are thought to have originated from species native to India. These were brought to Europe during the past century where considerable hybridizing produced many varieties in use today. The Belgians did a lot of this earlier breeding and, for this reason, the Indica varieties are sometimes known as Belgian azaleas. Such excellent varieties as Albert and Elizabeth, Jean Haerens, Mme. Petrick, Triomphe and Paul Schame come under this Indica group.
2. **Kurume** azaleas originally were found in and about the city of Kurume in Japan. This type includes most of the small-flowered single varieties that have small, numerous leaves and dense, shapely plants. Such varieties as Coral Bells, Hexe, Snow, Hinodegiri and Salmon Beauty are of the Kurume group. Incidentally, the Kurume class is probably the hardiest for outdoor garden purposes of any of the forcing azaleas. They live over winter, with protection, along the coast lines from Long Island, down the southern coast, and throughout the West Coast to Seattle.
3. **The Pericat** group originated in this country in the late 1920s. It is midway between the large-flowered Indicas and the small-flowered Kurumes in flower size and general habit. The Pericats are generally late-flowering and find their best use for Easter forcing. Such varieties as Marjory Ann, Rival, Sweetheart Supreme (an excellent early-forcing Pericat), Pericat, Rose Pericat and Pink Pericat belong in this group.
4. **The Rutherfordianas** were introduced in this country about 1935 and are the most recent group. They resulted from crosses between Indica and Kurume varieties.

Here's Frank Batson, the author of this chapter, with budded azaleas in Oregon.

Rutherfordiana flowers are midway between the two parents in size, and are known for their keeping quality. Such varieties as Dorothy Gish, Rose Queen, Constance, Alaska, and Snow Queen belong in this group.

Many of the above-named varieties are no longer generally available, but have been included here as a matter of historic reference.

Growing Areas

The production of budded greenhouse forcing azaleas has definitely become a specialty of a few large growers centered in three major areas of the country: on the East Coast there are a few growers located in Virginia or the Chesapeake Bay area; in the Deep South, the Semmes, Alabama area; and on the West Coast, the Portland, Oregon area. The latter is by far the place where the vast majority of budded, pre-cooled plants are being produced today.

Dormant Plants

Dormant budded azaleas were once 100% bed grown, then dug and shipped to the forcer to repot prior to forcing. Now, however, most of the azaleas being produced today are pot grown in 4", 5" or 6" pots.

Azaleas are normally shipped "out of pot" since this increases the number of plants that will fit in a shipping box because they can be laid flat and stacked on top

A different approach to azalea growing: larger Northern pot growers buy "liners," roughly 2½" to 3" pot size plants, in May, grow them outdoors all summer, pot them in the fall and then precool them for forcing in the winter and spring. The grower here is Dick Holmberg of Nelson & Holmberg, Plainfield, Illinois.

of one another. If grown in a standard azalea pot, the azaleas can usually be slipped into a new pot and set out on a bench at once. West-Coast produced plants are another matter, as they are usually grown in a more straight-sided nursery "can," which means they are too large to slip into a standard azalea pot without removing part of the root ball. This in no way harms the plant, and some of the leftover root-ball material may be used in the re-potting operation. Otherwise, use either straight peat or a soil mix high in peat content if it is necessary to add soil to make the root ball fit firmly into a different size pot.

Receiving Plants

Most dormant azaleas are sold by the growers to a brokerage house, who in turn sells them to the individual forcers. There are a few dormant-azalea growers who sell direct, but they are in the minority.

One of the advantages of buying through a broker is that if any trouble arises, either in transit or in forcing, or if there is any misunderstanding about size, color, count, etc., the local salesman can be contacted immediately and arrangements made for him/her to come out and inspect the shipment. It would be impossible for the dormant grower to do this himself. Also, the broker can arrange for drop points and coordinate shipments from different dormant growers as part of their service.

Actual shipment time from the West Coast to East Coast or Midwest forcers should take only a week's time; anything over this should be reported to the salesman in case a problem develops. However, remember that once the shipment is accepted by the trucking company, it, and not the producer, is responsible for any transit or delay problems that may occur.

Plants obtained from non-West Coast growers may need to be placed in refrigerated cold storage to ensure adequate pre-cooling if they are to be used for December forcing. Northern forcers may be able to supply enough cold treatment by holding plants in a cold house or cold frame for three to six weeks prior to being forced.

Whether you buy pre-cooled plants or not, their care upon arrival at your establishment is most important. They will most likely have been shipped by refrigerated pool trucks direct from the area in which they were produced. They should be immediately unpacked, unless frost damage en route is suspected. Azaleas that have arrived in a partially-frozen condition stand an excellent chance of recovery by placing the unopened cases in a cooler or cool greenhouse and letting them thaw out gradually over a two- to four-day period. Do NOT place them in a boiler room, etc., in an attempt to warm them up fast. Be sure to notify the trucking company immediately if frost damage is suspected, so you have a basis for a claim if any of the plants do not recover.

Plants should be unpacked and either potted up at once or set out on a bench for potting later. Some leaf drop and yellowing of leaves on some varieties may have

Here's Ken Fessler, Fessler's Nursery, Woodburn, Oregon, a large producer of liners and budded azaleas for shipping to Eastern growers for forcing.

341

occurred while in transit and, unless it is excessive, it is nothing to worry about. However, if you deem it excessive, let both the trucking company and your salesman know in case a future claim must be made. If leaf drop or yellowing occurs at all, it is most likely to happen during the October shipping season. Due to weather conditions on the West Coast, the plants may have had to be packed with wet foliage, as a lot of the Christmas crop is grown outside in lath houses.

Watering the root balls and syringing the foliage helps restore the plants to their natural condition, as they will be somewhat flattened-out after having spent several days, usually on their sides, in a dark shipping box. Forcing temperature of 60° to 65°F can begin at once.

Budded, pre-cooled plants will be shipped from the growers to the forcers according to when they are wanted in flower. Plants received in mid- to late October are for Christmas forcing. Those shipped in late December are for Valentine's Day, and those sent in January to February are for Easter. If a continuous supply of flowering plants is desired, other shipments may be scheduled. However, these will usually not go by the pool trucks, therefore freight cost may be higher. Another way to do this is to have excess holiday plants shipped and spread out the forcing dates, but this does mean one must have a cool storage area.

Some growers are able to artificially cool plants and supply forcers with budded pre-cooled plants for forcing from September through May or even on a year-round schedule. Those plants shipped in early August or September are usually referred to as "early birds."

Pre-Cooling

Azaleas need a ripening or conditioning period at low temperatures (35°F to 40°F) before they can be forced evenly; this is known as "pre-cooling." Pre-cooling seems to be an accumulative process, with azaleas needing approximately 1,000 hours of such cooling. This can be accomplished either by storing in a cooler at a constant temperature for five to six weeks (34°F without lights, or 45° to 50°F with lights, maintaining at least 10 fc. intensity for 12 hours each day), or by natural means, which may extend over a three- to four-month period. This can occur only in those areas of the country that have very cool nighttime temperatures, even during the summer months.

It's obviously important at these low temperatures to be sure that the buds are not allowed to freeze.

Oregon and Washington comprise one such area. October shipment of some varieties from these states will be pre-cooled and bloom for Christmas—the hardest holiday to force azaleas for and be absolutely certain that they will be in bloom at the appropriate time because of the pre-cooling factor. Some Northern forcers may elect to do their own pre-cooling, receiving budded plants in September to October and placing them in their own coolers or into heavily shaded greenhouses or cold-frames that can be held at a cool temperature. During this self pre-cooling treatment, uniform temperatures are very necessary. For instance, if plants are

342

stored in a cool greenhouse and temperatures get up into the 60s during warm, bright days, the plants may not force uniformly. Plants should be kept only moderately wet during this cold-storage treatment. Excessive watering or excessive dryness of the roots may cause leaf drop.

Good air circulation within the cool greenhouse, cold frame, or the cooler is a must to prevent botrytis from developing. The use of small horizontal-air-movement fans aids greatly in this respect. All watering should be done in the morning so the foliage may dry off completely before nightfall.

Any flower buds that show color prematurely should be removed as these are an ideal place for botrytis spores to grow.

Spacing

During the forcing period it is best if the plants are spaced out so the foliage is just touching—this permits fairly good air circulation around the plants. If unable to provide this much space, try to provide extra air movement over the top. During the forcing some leaf drop may occur, especially if any yellow leaves have developed during the pre-cooling or storage period. This is normal. Excessive leaf drop, on the other hand, may indicate overwatering while in storage, letting the root ball dry out too much, or even botrytis problems that might have started while in storage due to overcrowding and lack of good air movement.

Fertilizing

The pre-cooled plants that you receive as a forcer have, in all likelihood, not had any fertilizer applied to them since early September. This is done to help harden-off the plants, and some dormant growers believe it also helps in obtaining a good, well-developed bud set. If you are going to keep some of these plants back for a later forcing period in a cool house, do not fertilize them, as in some cases severe leaf drop may result. For those plants going directly to a forcing house, hold off feeding for at least the first two weeks so that some root regrowth may take place. The first feeding should be no more than half-strength of a complete fertilizer, plus iron chelate or S.T.E.M. (soluble trace element mix). A once-a-week application or constant feeding program can then be followed right up to sales time.

Forcing—and Varieties

Azaleas are classified by their natural blooming dates as Early, Mid-season, or Late. Only Early types will force in time to ensure making Christmas, and even some of the Early types will force better than others for Christmas. Some of the newer and better varieties from Europe to consider for Christmas are: Helmut Vogal (red), Pink Vogal, Coral Vogal, Inga (pink-and-white variegated), Nordlicht (red) and Poloma (white). Some of the older varieties still very much in use are: Erie (salmon-and-white variegated), Dogwood (white), Variegated Dogwood, Alaska (white), Red-Wing (red) and Mission Bells (red). Chimes (red), the old Christmas standby for many, many years is almost out of the picture today due to its poorer keeping quality when compared to any of the newer varieties. Most forcers use West Coast pre-cooled plants as being the most dependable for Christmas flowering.

Forcing temperature can be anywhere between 60° to 70°F. Day temperature should not exceed 80° to 85°F. The higher the night temperature is, the faster azaleas will flower. However, a better keeping quality of blooming plant is achieved by maintaining as low a forcing temperature as possible, but still hitting a scheduled holiday period.

In the North no shade of any kind should be used over the plants. Southern forcers may need a light shade such as a single layer of tobacco cloth. Overhead syringing to maintain atmospheric moisture usually hastens flowering, but only up to when color begins to show. Be sure the foliage is dry before nightfall, and also watch out for aphids, red spider, and whitefly during this period.

As forcing proceeds, shoot-bypassing of the flower bud may be noticed. These should be removed before they are ½" long, or "blasting" of the bud may occur. Do not pinch them off, but remove the entire shoot using a quick sideways movement right down to the base of the bud. On some varieties, it is best to hold onto the bud with one hand as you strip off the bypassing shoots with the other. This is especially true if there are several shoots and they have grown out 1" to 2" or more and have hardened up at the base; otherwise, the bud may be ripped off along with the shoots.

As forcing continues, the temperature may be raised or lowered to time the flowering. A plant that is in the "candle" stage, or is just showing color the full length of the bud, may be stored in a 40° to 48°F cooler, using 12 hours of light, for a period of two weeks, without detrimental effects.

Plants that are going out to a shop or to a customer should be slightly beyond the "candle" stage (petals not opened out) if they are to open up properly. A plant that is still in tight bud, but showing some color, if placed in a low-light-intensity area, may "stick" and never open as it should. An exception to this may be when dealing with some of the new super-early German varieties such as Inga and any of the Vogal varieties. These come on so fast that they can be sent out to the shops when some of the buds are in "candle" and the rest are not yet at that stage, providing they will receive ample light while in the shop.

Again, we stress that to make Christmas, order only early-forcing varieties that have been adequately cooled. To try and force later types, such as Lentengroot, will often mean missing the holiday completely. Such varieties, it seems, must go through a longer cold pre-cooling and ripening period, or "gestation period," as one broker calls it, and no matter how hard they are forced, they will not flower until this ripening requirement is satisfied.

Any of the previous named varieties, as well as Dorothy Gish (salmon), Gloria (salmon-and-white variegated), White Gish, Flamenco (red), Friedhelm Scherrer (red), Kingfisher (pink-red) and Roadrunner (pink-red) may be used for Valentine's Day. At that time of the year, usually four to six weeks at 60 °F will force most varieties quite easily.

344

Lowell Hall and son, Steve, Lowell Hall Nurseries Inc., Hubbard, Oregon, are also major forcers of budded, dormant azaleas.

Easter is a difficult holiday to force for, due to the variability of the date, but material obtained anywhere in the country will force readily for it. In fact, if Easter is late the biggest problem is to hold plants back from flowering prematurely. If one has a cooler, the plants may be held back much better than if only a cool, shaded greenhouse or storage shed is used. For an early Easter, two to three weeks at 60 °F is all that is required. If it is late, one to two weeks will be sufficient.

Some of the better late-blooming cultivars are Dewales Favorite (pink-and-white variegated), Knut Erwen (red), Heidi (white), Mistral (pink), Whitewater and Madame deWales (white).

The only way to hold plants for Mother's Day is by storing them in a cooler. They should flower one to two weeks after being removed from cold storage. The extra work and effort of storing is usually well worth it at that time of the year.

Trends and Predictions

Azaleas have historically been produced in large size containers, i.e., 6″ to 8″ or more. One of the trends that has been developing during the last ten years is the production of smaller and smaller sizes to meet the needs of chain stores and even full-service florist shops located in areas that cannot command the high price that a large-size azalea could and should bring. As a result, we are now seeing a lot of 5″ or 4″, and some even smaller, blooming azaleas on the market.

345

To meet this trend, many of the large West Coast dormant producers have shifted a large part of their production away from the standard 6″ pot size to the smaller sizes. This accommodates the demands of the Midwest and Eastern forcers in two ways. It provides them with a smaller plant ready to drop into a 4″ or 5″ pot, and it also saves them on freight costs because 40 to 50 four-inch size plants will fit into the same size shipping carton that will hold only 24 of the standard size dormant plants.

This shift toward more and more smaller sizes will probably continue. The azalea is, and always will be, "The Aristocrat of Pot Plants," but the price that a retailer has to charge for a large well-budded azalea really puts it out of the reach of many of today's consumers.

Some of the dormant growers who also force plants for their own local markets have been experimenting with a "mini-azalea" in a 3″ or even a 2″ pot. They do this by using a rooted cutting that has been pinched only once or twice and then treated with a growth retardant to set up a flower bud. This will work only by using very early varieties such as Inga or one of the Vogals that require very little, if any, pre-cooling. These minis are proving quite popular and should be showing up in other areas of the country. Then there is another grower that is marketing azaleas in hanging baskets, like the poinsettia growers have started to do.

For those forcers that want to be able to provide their customers with the ultimate in floricultural classic creations, there are the "standard" or tree azaleas which are being produced in limited numbers by a few specialty growers. These are grafted and require anywhere from three to five years to grow. They range in height from 3′ to 6′. Needless to say, these are high ticket items, but for those forcers or retail growers lucky enough to service a high income clientele, a tree azalea in candle stage or even in full bloom is a sight few people can resist.

There is also another very clear trend developing: forcers are no longer aiming most of their flowering azaleas for the Christmas market as was the practice in the

Smaller "mini" pot azaleas are becoming important, especially for the major chains. Plants such as these (3″ pots) provide a lot of color at a price that fits in the chain store world. Look for much more of mini azaleas!

346

past. Today's forcers want a large portion of their dormant azaleas to arrive from the West Coast just a few days before Christmas or right after, just so they have enough time to force for Valentine's Day and later. This has come about partly because of the greatly improved keeping quality of the Christmas poinsettia.

This need to hold an ever-increasing portion of the dormant crop until mid-December instead of shipping it the first part of October for Christmas forcing, has stimulated a large expansion of greenhouse facilities on the part of the dormant azalea growers. When they could ship most of their product in October, there was no need to provide as much freeze protection for the crop which could be grown outdoors under lath or saran cloth. But now this is no longer the case.

I hope this chapter has been of some help to those of you now engaged in, or contemplating, the forcing of azaleas for the wholesale market or the retail shop, and I leave you with this thought: To grow them is heavenly...but to force them is divine!

Azalea Vocabulary

Dormant, budded azaleas. Words used by growers. An azalea starts as a cutting and is grown on for perhaps a year or so to flowering. In late summer it's ready to set bud and is exposed to cool temperatures (35° or 40°F or so). This vernalization process ensures prompt, even bud set and development. The plants are then ready to ship to the local greenhouse grower who will "force" them into flower—just warm them up and open the buds. The fall plant isn't really dormant—the leaves stay on, the buds stay there. It's "budded" in the sense that buds are present.

Forcer. Budded, dormant plants are produced in the Northwest and the Southeast or Florida. Typically they are shipped in the fall in bud to greenhouse growers all over the United States who cool-store them until they are ready to "force" them into flower, which simply means exposing them to a warmer temperature (60°F) for a few weeks to open the buds. So, a forcer is the guy who warms the plant up, opens the buds and sells the plant.

Pre-cooling/vernalization. This is the cool temperature period following 8 to 9 months of growth, normally done in early fall, which is necessary for proper bud formation and development. Many plants require this vernalization process—most perennials, Easter lilies, tulips, etc.

Dormant azalea grower. These are the specialists in the Northwest or Southeast who grow azalea plants for 8 to 10 months, usually precool them (vernalize) and ship them to greenhouse growers across the country to be forced. By the way, some producers of budded plants do not do the cooling; they leave it to be done by the local greenhouse grower, which of course requires refrigeration.

BEDDING PLANTS FOR THE 1990s

by Vic Ball

Bedding plants—all spring, summer and fall garden plants—are very much alive and well! There are major changes in the *kind* of bedding plants people buy, but overall the demand is steadily up. The accompanying graph of U.S. sales is very clear on this. Total bedding plant sales for 1989 were up substantially versus 1988.

And again there *are* major changes since the 14th *Ball RedBook* edition, in the way bedding plants are grown and sold. The great majority of all bedding plants are grown from plugs—a giant step forward (see separate chapter on plugs). Equally important: Consumer demand is steadily moving from the traditional pack of small plants to pot annuals and various patio planters—instant color. And, automation is moving in rapidly. Marketing channels are changing—ever more bedding plants are being sold to various mass outlets. And landscape contractors responding to public demand for color in the landscape are becoming major users of bedding plants. And last but not least, breeders are bringing us a steady stream of really exciting new varieties—even new species.

People love the color of bedding plant flowers around their homes, work place, etc. Overall it's an exciting prospect. Lots of potential here for the grower willing to dig in and adapt to the new ways.

One more bit of good news: In a world dominated by giant chains and franchises there is still much opportunity in bedding plants for new start-ups. It's not easy—but it is being done (see Chapter 28).

BEDDING PLANT TRENDS

Some real surprises here!

This graph reflects four years of all bedding plants: flatted flowers and vegetables, pot annuals (flowers and vegetables), pot geraniums, garden mums and hanging baskets (flowers only). All of this is in units (flats of annuals, pots of geraniums, etc.). No inflation here! My conclusion: bedding plants are booming! Here's a 57% steady increase in units spread over four years, or about 15% per year!

Where is it happening? *Clearly the real excitement is in pot annuals, hanging baskets and a variety of preplanted patio containers.* All are forms of bedding plants where the bedding grower does more of the

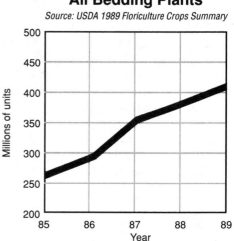

All Bedding Plants

Source: USDA 1989 Floriculture Crops Summary

348

work for the consumer. The public wants an instant garden (larger potted annuals), instant color and they love hanging baskets—just hang them up and enjoy! Look at the numbers:

Pot Annuals Flower and Vegetables

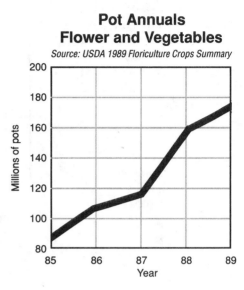

Source: USDA 1989 Floriculture Crops Summary

Pot annuals have doubled in four years: 25% per year and still zooming. Surely landscape contractors' heavy demand for pot annuals is a part of this.

Floral Hanging Baskets

Source: USDA 1989 Floriculture Crops Summary

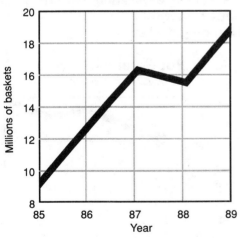

Flowering hanging baskets. More than double in four years! A 108% increase, or 27% per year, and still up 27% between 1988 and 1989. And remember, the millions of preplanted color bowls, whiskey barrels, etc. are not even included. Again, the public wants us to make color for them—now!

Here's a 14-year look at flats of **flowers and vegetables,** again in units. They're still the backbone (a full half) of the bedding plant business, but clearly plateauing the past three years. Are they giving way perhaps to those new forms of instant

349

color—pot annuals, hanging baskets, preplanted patio urns, and color bowls—that are already well over ¼ of total bedding plant sales and climbing fast?

Flats of Flower and Vegetable Bedding Plants

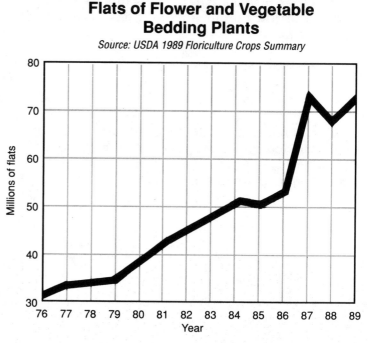

Source: USDA 1989 Floriculture Crops Summary

Now geraniums: seed below left and cuttings below right. Again, the last three years show a clear plateauing of both seed and cuttings. Question: Isn't the rampant expansion of New Guinea impatiens taking a share of the traditional geranium market—windowboxes, flower beds and hanging baskets?

Pot Geraniums (seed)

Source: USDA 1989 Floriculture Crops Summary

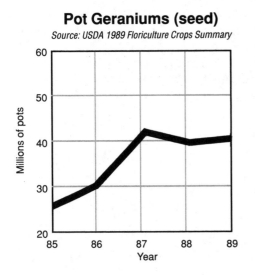

Pot Geraniums (cuttings)

Source: USDA 1989 Floriculture Crops Summary

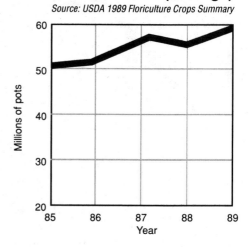

350

The geranium is still a heavyweight—almost $120 million per year at wholesale in 1989 and still gaining ground. But, again, changes!

Garden mums are clearly in strong demand and continue to increase. Up nearly 15% 1988 to 1989. They require low labor, have attractive fall colors, and offer diversion from poinsettias.

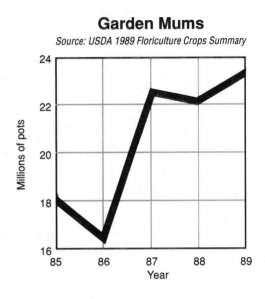

Garden Mums
Source: USDA 1989 Floriculture Crops Summary

All This in Dollars

Again, the preceding figures are all in units. Here is a look at some of the highlights in dollars—affected, of course, by inflation.

First, the tabulation:

	1984	1989	Change
Flats of flowers (excluding geraniums)	$196 million*	$383 million	Up 70%
Flats of geraniums	$ 25 million*	$ 28 million	Up 12%
Flats of vegetables	$ 62 million	$ 60 million	Even
Potted annual flowers	$ 59 million	$131 million	Up 120%
Potted vegetables	$ 4 million	$ 10 million	Up 150%
Pot geraniums from cuttings	$ 57 million*	$ 82 million	Up 43%
Pot geraniums from seed	$ 21 million*	$ 37 million	Up 79%
Garden mums	$ 26 million	$ 36 million	Up 39%
Hanging baskets—flowers	$ 45 million	$100 million	Up 122%
Total bedding plants	$495 million	$867 million	Up 79%

*No 1984 totals available, 1985 figures were used.

Comments:
- Total dollars for all bedding plants are up 79% in the past four years versus a 53% increase in units. It's inflation at work.

- Are those pot annual and hanging basket increases really an important part of the bedding plant business? Answer (1989 figures):

Hanging baskets $100 million, potted flowers/vegetables $141 million, totaling $241 million. For comparison, flats (flowers and vegetables) were $443 million.

The bedding plant business is indeed changing! A suggestion: Start moving into these new forms of bedding plants in your business!

Landscape contractors, in a certain way, are moving in the same direction. They are under contract to keep color in often very large flower beds around shopping centers, hotels and offices. They prefer 3" to 4" plants in color. Which again means instant color for flower beds, which are often replanted three to four times a year, especially in the South and West.

So what about the rest of the United States—and Canada? Florida has already gone the same way. One large Marriott resort hotel on Marco Island, Naples, Florida spends around $10,000 per month mainly on potted annuals. It's quite a show. Patio planters are definitely coming in—and 4" annuals are clearly king—today. The small pack plant is fast disappearing. On Eureka Road at Homestead, Florida (south of Miami) two major growers are (early 1990s) doing 100+ acres of mostly pot annuals. And there are many other such growers across the state—including a 15- to 20-acre operation in Naples. Florida has gone "California style" already!

Across most of the rest of the United States and Canada you'll still find mainly pack annuals—now 42 or 36 per flat cell packs. They are still very impor-

Gary Baucom, a major Charlotte, North Carolina bedding plant grower with color bowls!

352

tant, although clearly plateauing. But, especially in metropolitan areas, you'll find 4″, even 6″, potted annuals clearly moving in. Four- or three-inch pot bedding sells mainly in June and July, 6″ seems to sell in July or even August. Millions of them. They're used by both homeowners and landscape contractors. And here and there across the Eastern United States you'll find major success stories with patio planters, especially among larger growers. One major Midwest grower is producing 250,000 1-gal. containers, each with four plugs of colorful annuals. And they sell! Several other major bedding plant growers are doing four to five acres of assorted patio planters, whiskey barrels, color bowls, etc.

All of this would seem to indicate that the California style of bedding plants is in fact steadily moving across the United States. So often growers tell me, "We've tried 4″ annuals here—they just don't sell." But others who stuck with it for several years find that they soon do develop a market for them. It's like anything else new, you have to push it. But as Gene Campbell, a Wichita, Kansas, grower says, "These 4″ pots are a lot more profitable than packs, they stand up much better on the display counter. And people like them. We're moving that way." As is so often the case, the new product earns the extra buck—during the innovative years.

Why the Big Change?

All this change really is the result of changes in the lifestyle of the people who buy our plants. And changes there are! Examples:

- **The working woman.** Today over half of American women work outside the home. And when they come back from a long day on the job they're a lot less apt to want to go out and find tools and hoses and plants and make a garden. They'd much rather spend a few extra bucks, buy some nice patio planters to set on their front porch or patio—and get some color that way. Now.

- **The impatient American.** Back to the shift from small pack annuals to 2¾″ to 4″ potted plants. Again, changing lifestyles and attitudes of people at work! Today's consumer wants everything now. We swarm to McDonald's and Wendy's Hamburgers, not because it's especially good food, but because in three or four minutes you can be sitting, eating your lunch—instead of waiting 20 minutes for service. The same mentality, I feel, is affecting plant sales. The 4″ potted annual has a nice display of color today, you plant the bed and you have color now. The pack annual, on the other hand, requires three or four weeks of patient care, watering, etc. People just don't want to wait that long.

- **The shrinking American yard.** Mainly because of skyrocketing land prices, America's yard and garden areas are shrinking fast. Especially lovely 3,500 sq. ft. to 5,000 sq. ft. homes that would get a half acre or an acre a decade ago, today are being built shockingly close on small 100′ or less frontage lots. And that means less space for gardens. And that means more of patio color and less of flower beds.

353

Here's Jack Van de Wetering,
Ivy Acres, with preplanted
patio containers at
Ivy Acres, Calverton,
Long Island, New York.

- **Water shortages.** Somewhat, the chronic and ever-troublesome shortages of water in some areas of the country are tending to drive people way from flower beds. And those patio urns and planters take a lot less water than a flower bed. Yes, there are ways that flower beds can be irrigated with a lot less water than an overhead sprinkler—but it just doesn't seem to happen.

MARKETING—PLAN BEFORE YOU PLANT

So few bedding growers I know of really do give marketing their product serious thought. They like and they think growing—then they sell the product "best they can." The following pages are meant to provide a sort of road map—how to study your own marketing opportunities. Steps. Suggestions. Try them.

Basic Decision—To Be Pure Wholesale or To Retail

You will get $12 a flat at retail (12 packs at $1), maybe $6 to $7 wholesale. But it's a different world. Not all easy. And for the record, either retailing or wholesaling can certainly be profitable.

Do you enjoy dealing with the public? If so, odds for success at retailing go up. Are you a friendly type? Is your present location on a high traffic street—critical to

354

success in retailing? Lots of room for parking? Are you in an affluent neighborhood? These folks want quality and will pay for it. I think of Herman Wallitsch in Louisville, Kentucky, a classic "affluent supplier." Are you well known in your community? Can you breathe life into a newspaper ad—or maybe do a radio or TV talk show? Great for retailing.

Now let's talk the attributes of a good wholesale grower. First, are you a reasonably good businessperson (really basic to either wholesale or retail)? Are you a good money manager? Can you collect old bills, buy hard? Can you manage people? Do you really enjoy growing, managing production and help? Are you a quality grower (important in the tough competitive world of wholesale growing)? Are you good with mechanical things? Bedding production is moving steadily toward mechanization and so often successful wholesale growers I see are good builders and fixers of greenhouses, etc.

Study the competition. Go see their facilities during the spring rush, talk to them. See what parts of your local or regional markets are well serviced today, which are less covered. What areas are flooded with very cheap competition. Marketing people call it "seeking a niche in the market." Sometimes you'll find a smaller corner, some part of the market that no one else is doing. Reminds me of Curtis Pickens, Orlando, Florida, who came into the growing business several years ago. Small, new, he took a one-year try at pack annuals, found the competition of

Here's a way to stir up business. Send a truck with samples of your bedding plants out among garden centers and other outlets with a good sales person. Ivy Acres, Calverton, Long Island, New York.

Here's the classic parking lot bedding plant greenhouse display very widely used across the upper Midwest, especially in areas with severe late frosts, which can damage retail displays. There are probably 1,000 to 1,500 erected annually for the spring season only.

All garden centers need an "information booth." Here's a special one at Egon Molbak's super garden center in Woodinville, Washington. Note the folks waiting to get at it!

very large mechanized producers tough. So, on the advice of his friendly Ball Seed salesman, he dove into the 4″ annuals. He's doing great, expanding. A classic niche. By the way, the niche probably won't be there forever, but it's been a great thing for Curtis Pickens.

All of this bears on what marketing people call "market segmentation." What they're saying is that the market for a typical product will have many different "segments." In bedding plants there will be the price-conscious discount outlet, and at the other end of the spectrum the garden center appealing to the super affluent buyer—at top quality and top price. And a wide variety of other special markets. Like the wholesale landscape contractors who want to buy 500 flats for planting at a large shopping center. Or a truck load of 4″ plants for some big contract job.

The point of all this: Pick the segment where you see opportunity and where you can serve most efficiently and most profitably.

The very large wholesale growers, highly mechanized, make tough competition for the wholesale market. With their advanced mechanization, they can produce at a lower price and make a fair profit. The smaller grower quite often gets started in retailing. It's a world where being big and mechanized doesn't count much.

By the way, speaking of retailing and competitors—do check out some of the garden center chains in your local area. They are almost everywhere across the United States today, and they typically do an excellent job of laying out retail displays, price marking, and other little details of retailing. It's all there for you to see and copy where it fits your world. Learn from your successful competitor! Study him. Talk to him, shop his prices and quality and pack sizes.

Containers—a Critical Choice

A key way you implement your marketing strategy is by your choice of growing containers. Back to our friend Herman Wallitsch and his affluent customers. A key item here is a tray of twelve 2¼" Jiffy-Strips (two strips of six each). The 12 plants in a plastic tray retail at $5.75.

Perhaps the other extreme would be the very large wholesale grower producing for discounters who tend to insist on 18 packs per 21" flat. This gives the discounter the cheapest pack in town (which they seem to cherish). Growers don't like this very much, but giant chains are insisting—as of the early 1990s.

The great majority of petunias, marigolds, etc. are grown either in AC 4-12, 48 cells per 21" flat (12 packs of four plants) or some in an AC 3-12—12 packs of three plants (impatiens and begonias).

Again, Curtis Pickens (Orlando, Florida) grows the same petunias and impatiens now in a 4" square plastic pot. And again, the container is one of the ways you make your marketing strategy work.

An interesting thing happened in the world of flat and pack annuals several years ago: a major Southern grower decided to try a flat 20% smaller than the

The point here: Far better to have retail displays up off the ground and convenient to the shopper. This photo at Thomson's Garden Center, Danvers, Massachusetts.

standard 21" Handi-Flat®. It really didn't seem to make that much difference to his market so he went over all the way to the smaller flat—now grows 20% more flats per house. Same overhead cost. Also he has less cost per unit for flats and packs. Oddly enough, one top quality Eastern bedding grower adapted the smaller flat and it didn't seem to make much difference in his market either. But the great majority of the eastern United States pack bedding business is done in the 21" flat today. By the way, there is a Connecticut flat somewhat smaller, different dimension. Also a West Coast flat which is different. This lack of standardization means higher costs per unit for the grower.

An important point on selecting the right container: So often I see good quality retail grower operators offering a very large pack size at a somewhat higher price. Typically there will be six of these packs to a 21" flat—with maybe six or eight plants in a pack. The grower probably tells you that he gets $1.49 at retail versus the 59¢ pack at the discounter. But look at what happens to the return *per flat*:

Pack	Retail price per pack	Pack price times packs per flat
6 packs per 21" flat	$1.49	$ 8.94 retail grower
18 packs per 21" flat	.59	10.62 discounter

So now our quality-oriented retail grower friend is getting about 15% less for a flat of his plants than the super-cheap discount store! In fact, he should be getting 50% more. His quality is often a lot better (better care of display). Also, he can offer the customer a wide variety of annuals and other plant material, typically real help on laying out a garden, solving other problems. Also, he typically offers a variety of gardening supplies: peat moss, fertilizer, etc. He has so much to offer compared to the low price chain—but in fact he ends up getting fewer dollars per flat. The rationale is always the same: "I want to have a bigger pack than the chain." He too is striving for a niche, but ends up losing the battle.

I am seeing a clear trend among many growers both retail and wholesale, moving from six or eight packs per flat to 10 or 12. All 22" flats. Reason: lower cost per pack to the retail outlet whether it be the grower's own garden center or the retailer he is supplying. $6.50 per flat divided by six is $1.08 per pack. Same flat divided by 12 cost the retailer only 54¢. And annuals today are sold by the pack, not per dozen.

Other Marketing Comments

Speaking of marketing—and niches—the food chains (large and small) seem to be emerging as a potentially important market for bedding plants. The big Southern chains, such as TG&Y, typically display pack annuals in front of their stores in early spring. But less so in the North—where food chains are so very strong in pot plants and cut flowers. Somehow the major Northern and Western chains have simply not gotten into bedding plants yet. One grower (Ivy Acres, Long Island) reported last spring designing and offering a display cart to supermarkets that

I see more tents each year set up in parking lots to market bedding plants. Here's one in Ontario—colorful red and white stripes.

handle his plants. The cart is perhaps 5' x 2' (three or four shelves), on wheels, and is made available at no charge to the super. Since there are four or five layers of plants on the car, this minimizes the floor space tied up in plants. If only there could be some way of mechanically irrigating displays of annuals at supermarkets and discount chains, it would do so much for our whole industry! Dry plants are a chronic and continuous problem.

Watch out, by the way, for high cost of delivering plants to retail outlets. Bob Bernacchi, major LaPorte, Indiana grower, reports that 10% to 12% of his total bedding cost is delivery cost. "We bought some new steel racks. Each holds 64 flats, 10 racks to a 40' truck. Now we can load a Hertz truck in 20 minutes. That helps."

Beware of Dump

In making your marketing plan for the spring ahead, one important clue can come from records of the years past. Particularly plants dumped, also what you ran out of and which week items were short. All of which demands good records—more on this later. But it's obviously critical to cover this spring's shortage with a little more production of the same item next spring.

Price—Key Part of Your Marketing Strategy

In a way, price is the very essence of your marketing plan. So many growers I see just stay with their competition—or often a bit below—which is a poor basis for setting price.

- **What's the market?** Clearly the major consideration in setting price should be what the market will pay for what you have to offer. Here again the niche—the new product, the new idea—can often command an extra 10% or 20%. Sometimes a new variety will do it. The first Happipot gerbera brought surprising prices, for example. The very essence of good business is sensing when you have something in demand, not offered freely on the market, and which will support a little higher price.

- **Cost.** Again, not many growers really know their cost—but they should! In any case, it's obviously courting disaster to sell at cost or below. If you can't mark up an item substantially above cost, better get out of it. But most of all, know your cost.

- **Your competitor.** No, you can't ignore him, but again certainly don't be tied to his price.

- **About bundling**—it's a buzzword of the marketing profession. What you do is first separate out the components of your price. For example, a pot mum at retail (don't be concerned about the prices, they are only for example):

$10 for the mum
$ 2 for the wrap/bow
$ 2 for delivery
$ 2 for credit

Total $16

The point of all this: If you separate and identify the things you are charging people for, you can price the product at different levels for different parts of the "bundle." For example: The pot mum above at $10 is a cash and carry price. The retailer might offer each of the other three components at the customer's option. Or various combinations.

Part of the point of all this is to be sure that your competitor is not offering a $10 mum and not including the wrapping, delivery and credit—which you may include in your price.

A Last Thought on Pricing

If you're consistently selling out every spring, a good case can be made that your prices are too low. Bring them up 5% to 10%. If you still sell 95% of your production, you gained a lot.

How do the really successful growers build ever-increasing retail sales of bedding annuals? Important clues:

1. Often such successes bear the clear stamp of the owner's personality. Fred Pence, Lawrence, Kansas, gets on the local radio station on Saturday morning and talks gardening. Everyone knows Fred, and a lot of the listeners buy from him. Or take big, affable Andy Hauge of Fairmont, West Virginia, who, like hundreds of others, knows and is known personally by most of his customers. People just love to be greeted by name. Don't you?

2. They just do a lot of the right things at the right time and do them reasonably well. Let's call it good management.

- **Use the newspaper!** Newspaper ads are clearly the number one way the winners go. The great majority use newspaper advertising heavily—generally more so than TV/radio. The number one mission of your advertising program is to get people into your shop—and the local press seems to do it best.

    One problem in using newspapers effectively is just getting the job done—and on time. You really must lay out a plan months ahead. Start hitting readers several weeks before the season. Hit them hard during the peak weeks—and keep after them until it's over. You just can't do such a program on a week-at-a-time

Dan Milaeger is a great promoter and here's one of his many ads that appear in the Racine, Wisconsin press this time promoting a free flat of flowers if you buy your lawn fertilizer today.

basis. Good newspaper ads are a lot less a matter of inspiring copy and a lot more just getting them in regularly and at the right time. Tell people what you've got to sell. Use pictures.

Push your money-makers! You know the things that earn for you—and what you have in supply. Push good, new items. Push your good service—"Let us help you plan your garden"—things that low-price chain outlets tend not to offer. Important! Most papers have a garden editor. It's a fact of life that good steady advertisers get helpful plugs in these garden columns ("Madness™ petunia is great, you can get it at Jones' Garden Center"). Cultivate your local garden writers. They can help you.

What should your newspaper advertising budget be against your total sales? Andy Hauge, Fairmont, West Virginia, a successful retail grower, says, "We have both a flower shop and a garden center. Total advertising budget is 6% to 8% of sales. Besides newspapers, we are promoting on radio and TV, especially at the height of the spring selling season."

Sam Perino, successful garden center/bedding plant outlet, New Orleans, says "We use newspaper ads for our publicity. It works. Radio just doesn't seem to get the same results."

- **Radio/TV.** Again, newspaper ads generally are number one among retail growers—but in some situations radio and TV do a bang-up job. My own observation: if the proprietor takes a personal interest in radio and TV, it can really do a job for him. Classic example: the proprietor who knows gardening (growers all really do) and who has a knack for talking about it on radio or TV. Local stations generally are pleased to have someone talk gardening for 10 or 15 minutes weekly in the spring—"What you should be doing in your garden this week," or "Here are the new rose and petunia varieties for the season—as I see them for our locality." Or just a troubleshooting program—one fellow keeps a phone hotline open. Folks phone in questions, he fields them as they come. (An interesting challenge!)

There are "garden writers" in radio/TV, too—important, well worth cultivating.

- **Price list/direct mail.** Great sales builders. Most successful retail-grower garden centers I know do publish a price list. Some represent a major effort (20 to 30 pages or more), lots of 4-color, helpful ideas on gardening, etc. Typically, they go out by mail to the full list of retail customers and prospects—well in advance of the season. The substantial investment made here by successful growers says these lists must be effective sales builders.

Home gardeners love to read, plan, on those cold nights in February! Your message should be there. Some good examples I've seen: Bruce Bordine, Rochester, Michigan (very colorful), also Weall and Cullen Garden Center/Nursery catalog (in the Toronto area).

Great opportunity here for helpful ideas for your home gardener customer. Help on the terribly important question of matching shade-loving plants with shady borders. Which plant can stand how much shade? Did you know the browalia will provide great blue in shady spots? Also, which of the new varieties this season are really great for your particular climate?

- **Have an open house.** So often a part of the marketing program of successful retail growers, garden centers. They're done in different ways. Gerhard and Guenther Siegert, Crystal Springs Florist, Benton Harbor, Michigan, operate an acre of greenhouse, grow pot plants, some cuts—and bedding plants. Early December there are thousands of well-done poinsettias ablaze with color, so they invite the town in for a day. Not to sell, mainly to get new faces into their shop. Builds business.

I like this "welcome" sign at Bryfogle's in Pennsylvania.

A good sign is an important part of retailing.

The Zoerbs, LaCrosse, Wisconsin, grow a lot of fine geraniums each spring. An open house in early May, just before the bedding season begins, brings a lot of new prospective customers into their houses. Again, not much in direct sales that day—but surely good for business.

- **Have a good sign.** Good signs cost money, but they are very much a part of success in retailing bedding plants. For an example of a good sign see the photo of Carl Padgett's Dogwood Nursery, Gulfport, Mississippi. The sign cost $2,500 plus the maintenance contract.

You often see such signs with provisions for a weekly special below the name of the nursery. "Special this week—pack petunias 89¢."

The emphasis by such retail giants as Holiday Inn and McDonald's must tell us that a good sign is one key weapon in bringing people into your shop. One of the major national motel chain's signs cost around $285 per month per motel—and more than pay their way!

• **Use point-of-sale aids!** When Mrs. Home Gardener walks up to your display of impatiens plants, for example, it's critically important that several things be instantly apparent to her.

    1. That impatiens will flower well in shade—but not dense shade.

    2. What actual color she can expect from Elfin® Red, for example.

    3. What spacing to allow—and how tall she can expect them to grow.

    4. Price per pack or pot.

    5. An 8″ x 10″ color poster along with the plant is a great sales aid.

Give her a picture in color of what a great show those plants will make in her garden a month or so from now. PPGA (Professional Plant Growers Association) offers such material to members.

A good retail display provides height, spacing, shade preference, price, etc.—all part of a well-organized, self-service display.

A classic, well-done retail operation—Great Swamp Greenhouse, Gillette, New Jersey. Left and right are Michael and Joseph Beneduce, the co-owners; Dennis O'Keefe, Ball Seed Company, in the center. Note the sign: no smoking and "please keep children in hand."

How to do all this? Again, here's what some winners do:

Color labels are very widely used. I see more of them each season. They give color presentations of the variety—and a label can go out with each pack!

Color labels also relieve much of the pressure to have such annuals as petunias sold in flower. In my travels among growers, more than half of all petunias I saw went out green. Comment: "Gardeners are coming to realize that short, bushy, soft green plants will do a far better job in their gardens. And now with colored plastic labels, they can plan their color combinations."

Hascal Collins, Collins, Mississippi: "If we use a color label on each pack, we can sell petunias to our local PGY chain before they flower. It's a better plant, takes less time for us to produce. They don't demand petunias in flower here—but they do want color labels."

Chatty little signs. Here and there I find a grower who makes cardboard signs and puts them up among displays. Just inexpensive white cardboard lettered by hand with a felt-tip pen. The messages: practical pointers about the plants you offer; (Impatiens) "Great in that shady spot—but not for dense shade;" (Portulaca) "They're happy right in the hottest, driest place you've got;" (Vinca) "No good in the shade—need full sun. They like it hot."

Here's a chance for you to use your expertise to help your customers—and serve them better. They'll remember.

Garden books are a sales builder, too! I see people thumbing through these colorful booklets and books. You know they're getting ideas on how they can use annuals around their homes. The Kmart store manager, Oxnard, California, says: "These books sell big here. We make money on them—and they help fire people up about gardening." Three sources for books: Sunset Books, Lane Publishing Co.,

Menlo Park, CA 94025; Countryside Books, Countryside Publishing, A.B. Morse Co., 2280 U.S. Highway 19 N., Suite 22, Clearwater, FL 33575; Ortho Books, 575 Market Street, Room 3188, San Francisco, CA 94105.

Well-organized self-service builds sales. Virtually all garden centers operate on a "serve yourself" basis. The point is if it's organized well so that shopping here is easy and convenient, people buy more. Some points:

1. Display plants at convenient waist height—not down on the ground.
2. Aisles—wide, surfaced (never muddy).
3. Carts—I see all sorts of things, even children's wagons. Just have plenty of them and be sure they're big enough.
4. Ample parking. Eric Schaefer, Montgomery, Illinois, has 60 spaces for roughly a $2,000 turnover of bedding plants per parking space per year.
5. Ample checkout facilities.
6. Have someone around who can answer questions, talk gardening. Good point-of-sale aids (Master Tags, posters) go a long way, but often gardeners like help, especially on "what will grow in that bed just in front of my house?"
7. Someone to help the customer load heavy plants into the car.

Self-service carts are a critically important part of well-organized self service. In the photo is Ben Miller, Stutzman's, Hutchinson, Kansas.

Grow quality. There's no sales builder quite like good plants. Stocky, well-grown cool-finished annuals. Not too crowded—better 48 or 36 to a 21″ flat. Good varieties—include the new things that gardeners do call for these days. When plants become overgrown, second class, throw 'em out!

Just like a good restaurant, the word spreads about good annuals, and most of all, plants that perform well this year will bring that customer back next spring.

GROWING THE CROP

Keeping Plants Short—A New Way

Some very helpful new technology here!

I'm talking about the new cool day/warm night system (DIF)—a remarkably effective way to control stretch of nearly all ornamental plants. Certainly all bedding plants. It's a result of research at Michigan State University by John Erwin and Royal Heins.

It's simple. If plants are exposed to, let's say 6° to 8°F cooler day versus night temperature, plant elongation nearly stops. You'll notice it within several days—if you are measuring your plants daily. For the record, it applies certainly to poinsettias, lilies, pot mums, practically all ornamental crops (see Chapter 30). What a great way to control ruinous stretch on petunias, impatiens, etc. during a late, wet spring! If temperatures are even held the same day and night, stretch will be noticeably less. Conversely, if the day temperature is perhaps 3° to 5° or more warmer versus the night temperature, plant elongation will be notably accelerated.

The researchers call it "DIF"—the difference between day and night temperature. Cool days/warm nights is positive DIF and retards growth.

The only important limitation of cool day culture of bedding plants (or any crop) simply is that, especially in Southern areas, it's difficult to keep the day temperature cool enough. Remember, the night must be warmer than the day so if the day is, let's say 80° or 85°F, then the night temperature must be perhaps 90°F. The other limitation is that many bedding plant growers simply carry very low night temperatures both to improve quality and to save fuel. If you're going to keep the night warmer than the day, it tends to mean more of 60° or 70°F night temperatures, which does add to fuel costs.

There is an answer to this problem. Again, Michigan researchers say that if you maintain the day temperature cool *for the first hour or two after sunrise* the plant tends to accept that as the all-day temperature. In other words, if you can keep 50°F for the first hour or two in the morning, the plant thinks that it has a 50°F temperature all day. So if the night temperature is kept at 55°F, then we have achieved a cooler day than night. This also seems to really work.

Another point about cool days: Especially if there is a strong difference, perhaps 10°F cooler day for an extended period, many plants tend to become chlorotic. Normally a few days with warmer day temperatures will correct the problem.

Here's Michael Vukelich Jr., Color Spot, a major West Coast bedding plant grower, with a typical outdoor supermarket display of bedding plants in northern California. It's mainly 4".

Now let's talk cool days and conventional poly greenhouses—so much used for growing bedding plants. The fact is that most bedding plants are grown in poly hoop houses, typically not well-ventilated, and typically growers tend to not heat much at night due to fuel cost and quality of plants. Result: For all these years our bedding plant crops have so often been getting a warm day and a very cool night, which, as we saw in the preceding paragraph very strongly aggravates stretch—plant elongation. In other words, the structures we have been living with all these years couldn't have been designed worse in terms of producing quality compact bedding plants. The system strongly encourages warm days and cool nights instead of cooler days and warm nights.

What to do about it?

- **Ventilate more.** There are ways to ventilate poly greenhouses. There's an interesting new system of inflatable tubes that run lengthwise on the side of the greenhouse. When deflated they open the side to provide ample cross ventilation. Another obvious answer is the use of cooling fans.

    Stuppy offers a poly greenhouse with conventional ventilating sash that can be opened and closed as needed. A last help is simply reducing light either with whitewash shade on the roof or with one of the new light reduction sheets that can be extended gutter to gutter as needed. Especially in hot Southern areas, 50% light reduction does a lot to keep temperatures down and sharply reduces water need, especially in warm areas.

- **Warmer nights.** The other obvious answer is to maintain higher night versus day temperatures. Again it's costly, but it's one of the two keys to making cool days work, and producing quality plants.

Within limitations it's possible to reduce the effective average temperature on a crop and still use the cool day system. Example: If you're growing bedding plants at 55°F days and 60°F nights, the temperatures can be reduced to 50°F days and 55°F nights—which reduces the average effective temperature on the crop by 5°F. And you still have a cooler day.

Cool days really work!

Chemical Retardants—Another Valuable Tool

In the bedding world of today it's mainly B-Nine used as a retardant. Almost all growers I know of do use it, at typically the standard 0.25% dilution. Petunias respond beautifully to B-Nine—it keeps the plants short and stocky and doesn't seem to delay flowering appreciably. Many other annuals also respond. A dilution

Retardants do work on impatiens! Here they are with and without. The growers are Dave and Martha Wright, Plantersville, Alabama.

369

rate of 0.25% (2,500 ppm) is made up with 0.4 oz. of 85% wettable powder per gallon of water. A 5,000 ppm solution requires 0.8 oz./gal.

See the accompanying table on response of various annuals to retardants. This table, prepared by John Holden, Ball Seed Company, gives the response of most bedding plants to several key retardants.

Many growers use growth retardants such as B-Nine (Alar), Cycocel or A-Rest to reduce stretching and maintain good compact habit in the pack. This permits them to stay on schedule without having to allow extra time as in the case of using lower temperature.

Warning: Chemical retardants are no longer legal on any vegetable plants in the United States.

Response of Bedding Plants to Retardants

Class	Cycocel	Responds To: A-Rest	B-Nine
Ageratum		x	x
Aster		x	x
Begonia, tuberous rooted	x		
Browallia		x	x
Calendula			x
Carnation	x		
Celosia		x	
Centaurea		x	x
Cleome		x	
Coleus		x	
Dahlia, dwarf	x	x	x
Dianthus	x	x	
Geranium	x	x	x
Impatiens		x	x
Marigold, dwarf		x	x
Marigold, tall	x	x	x
Petunia			x
Salvia Splendens	x	x	x
Snapdragon		x	
Verbena		x	x
Vinca Rosea		x	
Zinnia		x	x

Note: Gay Heibert, a topnotch Sioux Falls bedding grower, gets excellent height control on petunias using Bonzi at a very low concentration and a very light application. Says Gay, "We applied Bonzi at 10 ppm early in the crop, only a light application—definitely not to runoff. Repeat once later if needed. We get good height control and no delay in flowering on petunias. It is also helpful with impatiens. We can water crops four hours after application. Caution: 25 ppm will stop petunia growth cold."

Another caution about retardants: If they are overdone, plants will be permanently retarded in the consumer's garden. Unfortunately, I see too many examples of this. Go easy on all retardants. Use cool day/warm night technology as much as possible and cut back on watering and feeding.

How to Hasten Flowering

Since most markets want color on annuals, petunias, impatiens, etc., it's worth taking note that flowering on most annuals can be advanced by adjusting growing conditions. And that's the story of the famous John Seeley trials done at Penn State and described briefly below. The conclusions:

- **Higher temperatures.** Petunias, and really most annuals, flower earlier at warmer temperatures. Example: Pink Magic petunias sown March 9 were 96% in flower grown at 60°F, 4% in flower grown at 50°F. Here's the reason some growers grow annuals at 68°F rather than 60°F. Warmer temperatures do tend to stretch the plant, discourage bottom breaks, but they do flower earlier.
the plant stays in flower when it's planted out. It's practical, it's real, and it's done by many growers. Note that the earlier sowings made in January and February water more, get earlier flowering—and still not have too tall a plant—with careful use of retardants. Says Ken Reeves of Toronto, "I'd rather control height with retardants than with cool temperature which will delay flowering. And B-Nine does not delay color."

- **Soil moisture.** On most annuals, more frequent watering means earlier flowering. Again, John Seeley's classic trials at Penn State: Comanche petunias sown March 2 flowered 70% May 21 if watered daily, 7% if run dry. John adds, "The real wet ones (plunged in soil and watered daily) did flower first of all—but they were too tall."

- **Feeding:** Same story. More feed on most annuals means earlier flowering. Certainly on petunias. Allegro petunias sown March 2, not fed, are 33% in flower May 21, fed weekly, 90% in flower.
What do growers do about this feeding question? I see a lot of people using fertilizer injectors, but often going back to clear water as the plants become established. Frankly to harden the crop and sometimes to hold it back. A few other growers do use slow-release (MagAmp and Osmocote) only, often at half or less the recommended rate. In general, a pot mum crop will probably get liquid fertilizer injection from start to finish. Bedding plants generally are fed a lot less than that, some crops not at all. It's a judgment call that you get good at only with experience.

- **Daylength control.** The giant flowered African marigolds clearly respond to short days. Just spreading a sheet of 1 mil. black poly over a bed of Moon Shot 7 a.m. to 5 p.m. will flower the crop several weeks earlier—and perhaps half the height. And the plant stays in flower when it's planted out. It's practical, it's real, and it's done by many growers. Note that the earlier sowings made in January and February often flower just as fast without short day treatment, because of natural short days at that time of year. Note also that the French marigolds don't respond appreciably to daylength control.

371

Carol Troendle, Ball Seed Company,
and 4" marigold production at
George Caple's, Homestead, Florida.

Interesting point about petunias: On a short 9-hour day, petunias will be bushy, free breaking, great quality, but delayed flowering. On the other hand, grown warm and under a 12-hour or longer day they will flower earlier, but tend to be tall and spindly. So Ohio State's Harry Tayama says, "Start them on long days at 60°F, apply B-Nine; then as flower buds are visible, stop the lights and cool them down."

Salvias have a complex day length response. The tall late types are naturally short-day plants, flowering only in late summer as the day length shortens. The very short early flowering kinds like St. John's Fire will flower short and compact in mid-summer, obviously they are long day plants.

How Most Growers Do This

Here comes the delicate compromise between high temperature, frequent watering and feeding that cuts crop time and gives earlier flowers and a more lush plant, versus cool/dry/low feed culture that produces a sturdy, a bit harder plant and a better shelf life.

Growers I see can be divided into perhaps four groups.

- **Cool-dry growers.** These fellows sow very early, and as soon as seed germinates drop the crop back to 50°F or even 45°F. It can be a 20-week crop from sow to sell. The plants at sale time will be tough, rather hard, good shelf life, and they will perform for the customer.

- **Start at 60°F drop to 50°F.** A great many growers across the United States do it this way. The crop is kept at 60°F nights for a week or 10 days after transplanting, then dropped to 50°F or even cooler to harden the plant and improve quality. More bottom breaks. Probably now about a 14-week crop sow to sell. This plan is widely followed.

- **Straight 60°F.** Again, a large group of growers follows this plan—60°F from transplant to sell. Now down to about 12 weeks sow to sell. Not quite the quality of the fellow who cools down to 50°F the later part of the crop. Maybe two more weeks total time sow to sell versus straight 60°F.

- **Straight 68° to 70°F.** This will probably cut two weeks off the straight 60° to 50°F growers' time sow to sell—important, especially when you're working for a second crop, which many growers do, and for early color on petunias.

Southern growers aim for a peak sales period of April 1 (versus May 1 in the North). All my records point to perhaps a week or so less time sow to sell on their April 1 crop versus the Northern May 1 crop (see J & J Greenhouses, Claxton, Georgia, schedules later in this chapter). The reports on straight 60°F crops I hear average about 11 weeks sow to sell. Probably the warmer more favorable spring, especially in the Deep South, is responsible for this.

The following table puts it all together.

Weeks Sow to Sell for the Northern States

Sow Date	Crop Salable	Weeks Sow to Sell	Early Temperature	Finishing Temperature	Remarks
About Dec. 1 (Nov. 21 to Dec. 10)	March 1	13 to 14	68° to 70°F	70°F	Warm grown—early crop
Jan. 25	April 15	11½	68° to 70°F	70°F	Warm grown, peak week
Jan. 23	May 1	14	60°F	50°F	Peak week
Jan. 7	May 1	16	60°F (only 1 to 2 weeks)	45°F	The slow, dry, cool, Northern grower
Feb. 6	May 5	12 to 13	60°F	60°F	Many Northern growers

Petunia Schedule for Typical Southern States

Sow Plugs	Transplant Plugs	Crop Salable	Early Temperature	Finishing Temperature
Jan. 15	Feb. 25	April 1	60°F	60°F

An interesting adaptation of all this: Bobby Bearden, a major Plantersville, Alabama bedding specialist, grows a crop of about 20,000 flats of petunias, sown December 5, transplanted about January 5. Kept at 60°F in the greenhouse for a week or 10 days then moved right outdoors. No protection! Result, superb quality, heavy bottom breaks—and lots of ulcers worrying about a hard freeze. It happened once, he just stacked the flats five high and hauled them into the shipping shed with a forklift. It worked! Total time sow to sell (a green plant), by the way, is now 14 weeks—but most of that time is spent right outdoors in the field. Color appeared on these petunias about April 1.

- **HID to hasten bloom.** Several growers' experiences clearly confirm that exposing plug annuals, especially petunias, to HID light for even several weeks will hasten flowering. It's Marc Cathey's "head start" at work. It does work!

Bill Craigie and his son-in-law, Frank, are super quality bedding growers in Sydney, Australia.

SPECIFIC CULTURE—SIX MAJOR GROWERS

I'm trying a different way to communicate bedding plant growing in this edition. On the following pages you'll find specific temperatures and schedules from six growers—from cool/dry up to warm/faster-grown crops. Also a California grower and a Deep South operator.

"How we do it"—six different approaches to growing bedding plants. Not good guy/bad buy, rather growers in very different climates and growing for different markets.

Here we go!

The Bernacchis—Midwest/Quality-Oriented

The Bernacchis are a classic family operation (like the Ball company). Location: LaPorte, Indiana. They operate about four to five acres of holiday pot plants (top quality/price) plus a rather new two- or three-acre bedding plant range. They're nearly all done from plugs.

I talked here with Jerry Bernacchi, also with his uncle, veteran grower, Bob Bernacchi.

374

- **Schedules/temperatures.** Here are dates—all based on plug growing.

Sow Plugs	Transplant Plugs	Crop Salable	
Jan. 15	March 1	Apr. 20	Begonias (slowest crop) first sowing
Feb. 5	March 5	May 1	Last lot of begonias
Feb. 5	March 10	Apr. 15	Impatiens—first lot
Apr. 1	May 1	May 20	Impatiens—last lot
Feb. 1	March 5	Apr. 15	Petunias—first lot
Apr. 1	May 1	June 1	Petunias—last lot

For bare-root seedlings add one week sow to sell.

The black plastic support on which these flats rest keeps the flats clean, off the floor and well-drained. In the photo: Tony Bernacchi, A. Bernacchi Greenhouse, LaPorte, Indiana.

Plug Growing

Temperature for plugs here is 75°F night and day.

Plugs are grown on raised benches with steam pipes below the bench and poly skirts on the side of each bench. By the way, water for most of the plugs is heated to 65°F—"does help a lot."

Plug sheets: 200 plugs per 21″ tray for geraniums, 392 for begonias and most bedding plants, 512 for petunias, celosias, snaps, etc.

Plug media: A commercial peat/vermiculite material (Sunshine No. 5).

Begonias: All pelleted and double-seeded. Vinca same.

375

Watering of plug sheets: "A good bit by hand early in the game, later in the spring we use overhead mist. On a sunny day we will often handwater the area three to four times. The nozzles are three gallons per minute."

Cover seed? "Most larger seeds are covered with vermiculite, not so with small seeds. We use all defuzzed tomato seed and de-tailed marigolds."

Seeder: "There's a Blackmore and a Hamilton here. We use Hamilton on the bigger seeds. We produce about 14,000 trays of plug sheets a year."

"We use Genesis® seed on pansies and dusty miller. High Energy on all petunias and impatiens."

On feeding: We start feeding plug sheets with a weak solution (50 ppm) at time of sowing, and a bit stronger later on (75 ppm)."

"We watch water acidity carefully. Goal: pH 6 to 6.3. We use phosphoric acid, 2 fl. oz./100 gals. as needed. If pH climbs, begonias get yellow."

"We test our water supply twice a year."

"Plug trays rest on an expanded metal mesh bottom, rolling benches."

"A few things need shade in late spring, especially begonias."

"We use no retardants on our plugs, it's not needed."

"We do re-use our trays, it would be costly to dump them. We use Agribrom in irrigation water on all plugs. We dip used plug sheets in Greenseal (an algaecide). We have problems dipping used sheets in chlorine—unless they are washed thoroughly."

Culture of Bedding Plant Flats

First, temperature: Flats are grown at 65° to 68°F night and day. Ventilation in the day is done at 65°F. Next, media: It's a commercial mix (Sunshine No. 1) plus 15% of soil. But, "No more soil after spring 1990. We just can't find good, clean soil, and besides it requires sterilizing. We don't have to sterilize a commercial mix. We used to have three men working all summer to mix and steam soil. No more!"

- **Growing containers.** "Most bedding plants here are grown in 48 cells (plants) per 22″ flat (12 packs of four plants). We do use 36 per flat (2 x 18) on African marigolds and dahlias. No more 72 plants per flat.

  "We do a few 4″ here—mostly seed geraniums. Four-inch annuals haven't sold too well up to now."

- **Transplanting.** "We do use assembly line transplanting—a belt which moves the flats past the transplanting crew, each one does part of one pack. We operate three lines at peak season, six to eight women per line. Plus one person at the end of each line who inserts color tags in each pack."

- **Other comments:** "Bedding plants are grown on the ground, but we use a plastic riser which holds flats about 3″ off the ground" (see photo).

  "Our market here does want color on pack annuals."

  "We deliver to about 50 stores of one of the major supermarket chains—once a week, minimum 200 flats, normally 400 to 600 per trip."

Next: Kube Pak in Allentown, New Jersey

It's a rather large operation, 13 acres of greenhouse. I saw mostly Bill Swanekamp. Besides bedding plants and a major poinsettia crop they do produce 40 million plugs a year primarily for resale (early 1990s). The other distinction: All bedding plants here are grown in preformed cubes of mainly peat: "Kube Paks." They do about 350,000 flats of bedding plants a year.

- **Media.** Media here is their own: 80% peat, 13% vermiculite (for cubes), plus lime as needed. They do use about 7% soil as a buffer—again not sure they will continue this; too hard to get good soil.

- **Plug culture.** Plugs are grown on a heated porous cement floor 3″ thick, pipes 3″ deep, 11″ apart. Soil temperature on most crops is about 78°F nights, 85°F days (impatiens a little cooler). Begonias get an even higher soil temperature, around 80°F. Pansies and some perennials not over 68°F. By the way, they have equipped a 40′ truck body with refrigeration, which is used as a growth chamber for

Meet Bill Swanekamp with the unique Kube Pak bedding plant (pressed peat blocks), done at Kube Pak's, Allentown, New Jersey.

sprouting summer pansies and perennials. Pansies like cool temperatures. Also vinca and salvia are done in the truck body—to accommodate temperature requirements. Good reports on Genesis pansies here. Much faster sprouting with many things in the growth chamber—and more uniformity. Kube Pak is moving toward more of the growth chamber idea, for better control during sprouting. By the way, there is an interesting air/water mixing valve installed in the truck body to provide humidity. It provides 40 psi air mixed with three psi of water, and it does make a fog at a lot less cost than mist equipment.

"You must provide a drip sheet under a plastic roof for plugs otherwise the drip will do damage."

Some plugs are covered—especially the smaller seeds.

"We do have our water tested once a year."

"We use ITS boom irrigation on all our plug areas."

Plug sheets. They use a 13¼" x 19½" plug sheet containing 600 cells. This is roughly equal to the 512. Cells are ⅝" in diameter. Says Bill, "The square plug is harder to extract from the plug sheet, but it does hold a larger soil volume." Their plug sheet, by the way, includes no drain hole—"roots grow through and make the plug hard to extract." Why no drain? Answer: It speeds removal of plugs and allows for growing plugs on a heated greenhouse floor. Also, eliminating drain holes is one of the keys to a good, even sheet of plugs.

"We're not using the 800 sheet—we'll try it next year."

Interesting point: In a way the plug was born on this range—in the early 1970s by Fred and Bernie Swanekamp (father of Bill). You can see the first automatic seed sower ever built—dated 1971. It's a drum model, all stainless steel and still very much in use. It does 1,200 flats per hour. They also use an Old Mill seeder.

Now, Growing On of Flat Annuals

First, schedules/temperatures. Immediately after transplanting, begonias and impatiens go to 65°F nights, 75°F days. Petunias and many other annuals 60°F at first. All flats start out for several weeks on bottom heat—"root zone." After two or three weeks the bottom heat goes off, then overhead heat is used. Says Bill, "Bottom heat all the way will grow plants very fast, but they will be soft and not quality. Also with bedding plants, sealing the heat below the flats, soil temperature will be 65°F, air temperature 45° to 50°F. Result: continuous 'rain' all over the crop (only with a polyethylene greenhouse. Under glass we don't see these problems)."

On temperature: Kube Pak does use cool day (DIF). It was done very much on poinsettias, they got clear control of stretch with a night temperature of 62° to 64°F and a pulsed DIF—an early morning cool temperature. The first several hours after sunrise will be around 47° to 52°F. All the rest of the day at 75°F. This early morning cool period does give plants a "cool day" response. Even Hegg poinsettia leaves stood up.

A widely used system for assembling orders on large, flat-annual ranges. There's a 5' or 10' block of each color of each plant arranged down the house and a track in the center. Employees go down the line of annuals and set flats onto the track as needed to fill the order.

To spread out availability of things like petunias, Kube Pak will grow part of a sowing at 45°F nights, 55°F days immediately after transplanting. The rest of the sowing will be at normal temperatures and will, of course, mature earlier.

For spring 1989, Kube Pak reported 4″ and 6″ pot annuals at 7% of their production, perennials 7%, pot and patio urns very little but promising, "because they are more profitable." The rest was all flat annuals.

On transplanting: "We do use an assembly line. Our people average 45 flats per hour; our cost is 26¢ flat for mostly 48 plants per flat."

On watering flat annuals: Says Bill, "We do it by hand, six people for our spring peak weeks, balance of the year fewer than that. We figure the cost of installing automation on our whole area would not be justified in view of our annual cost of handwatering.

"All our bedding plants are in peat moss cubes, mostly 1½″ x 1½″ x 3″ deep in a flat 13″ x 18″. We are doing some 3″ cubes, finding a good market for them and will probably move more that way." A different form of pot annuals!

"We do constant liquid feeding, but with judgment. Some crops less. Example: ageratum no feed until we see color; same for marigolds.

"Our market wants color on annuals—unless the demand is too tight. Peak shipping weeks here May 1 to 15. We shipped out 90,000 flats one week recently."

- **Kube Pak schedule.** Remember, all flat annuals here are grown in cubes of peat moss. Somewhat, growing in peat might shorten the weeks from sow to sell.

Sow Plugs	Transplant Plugs	Crop Salable	Weeks		
			Sow to Transplant	Transplant to Sell	
Jan. 1	Feb. 19	Apr. 23	7	9	Begonias—our slowest crop—lot #1
March 13	Apr. 24	June 15	6	6	Last lot
Feb. 11	March 11	Apr. 15	4	5	Impatiens—lot #1
Apr. 17	May 15	June 15	4	3	Last lot
Feb. 11	March 11	Apr. 15	4	5	Marigolds—lot #1
Apr. 14	May 12	June 5	4	3½	Last lot
Jan. 14	Feb. 18	Apr. 15	5	8	Petunias—lot #1
Apr. 3	May 1	June 5	4	5	Last lot
Jan. 28	Feb. 18	Apr. 15	3	8	Dahlia—lot #1
Feb. 5	March 26	Apr. 30	7	5	Dusty miller—lot #1
Jan. 14	Feb. 18	Apr. 15	5	8	Salvia—lot #1
Apr. 3	May 1	June 5	4	5	Last lot
Feb. 12	March 19	Apr. 23	5	5	Verbena—lot #1
Feb. 16	March 30	May 4	6	5	Vinca—lot #1
March 27	May 1	June 5	5	5	Last lot
Feb. 26	March 26	Apr. 30	4	5	Pepper—lot #1
Apr. 17	May 15	June 5	4	3	Last lot
Feb. 26	March 26	Apr. 30	4	5	Tomato—lot #1
Feb. 18	March 18	Apr. 15	4	4	Alyssum—lot #1
Feb. 19	March 26	Apr. 30	5	5	Lobelia—lot #1
Jan. 21	March 4	Apr. 15	6	6	Pansy—lot #1
Jan. 8	Feb. 5	Apr. 23	4	11	Geranium—lot #1
Jan. 21	Feb. 18	Apr. 15	4	8	Ageratum—lot #1
Apr. 3	May 1	June 15	4	5	Last lot
Feb. 19	March 26	Apr. 23	5	4	Celosia—lot #1
Apr. 17	May 15	June 5	4	3	Last lot

DoRight's—The Davises

DoRight's (Dudley and Dianne Davis) operates about three acres of greenhouses plus a new 1-acre "frostproof" area located in Camarillo (Ventura) and Oxnard, California. Bedding plants are the backbone of the business. And like so many others they do a poinsettia crop plus some follow-ups. It's the nature of their bedding crop that I especially would like to talk about. Partly because they are typical of most California bedding growers.

First and up front, you will see very few cell pack 72 plants/flat or 48 plants/flat bedding plants here at all. The traditional "flat bedding plant" has pretty well left California. Even American Plant Company, where the "Pony Pack" was originated by the late Carl Tasche, now does only about 7% of their production in packs. Instead you see the following at Davis' (and more or less the same across California):

380

This heavy-duty forklift can move plants on these carts from growing area to the truck and right up on the endgate. And off they go! The grower, Bo Pinter, Ypsilanti, Michigan, says, "It costs the price of a Cadillac, but it's worth it!"

- **Some 4″ annuals—petunias, impatiens, etc.** They made up about 20% of the DoRight's crop in 1989, will be less than that in 1990. They grow them 16 in a 17″ x 17″ flat. Four-inch annuals were the backbone of California bedding plants, but they, too, are backing away now.

- **The famous 6-pack** is really taking over in California. Dudley Davis reports that they were about 70% 6-pack in 1989, will be 80% in 1990. The 6-pack really is a sort of compromise 4″ annual. The consumer gets 2¾″ "pot annuals" in a pack of six plants. They're always sold in flower, giving the consumer the benefit of instant color, larger soil volume, more apt to survive transplanting. Plus, the retail outlet has less of a problem keeping them watered versus smaller pack plants. Another point in favor of the 6-pack: It gives the consumer a longer flowering season versus the pack annual. You don't have to wait three or four weeks for it to flower! Still, this 2¾″ (sometimes 3″) form of bedding gives the consumer much of what he got from the 4″—which dominated California several years ago. Question: Will this 2¾″ 6-pack form, like all other things from California, move East?

- **Now patio annuals.** They take several different forms but they are already an important part of California bedding plants—and most important, there are more being grown each year. Dudley reports 15% of their 1989 sales were in gallon cans, typically planted from plugs, using petunias, impatiens, bellis, nemesia, dwarf snaps, etc. "Demand is increasing rapidly." Elsewhere across California you see acres of such patio planters as color bowls, whiskey barrels, cedar boxes, etc. A wide variety and lots of them.

- **Hanging baskets.** The Davises do a lot of baskets, too—mostly 10″ and heavily in petunias, impatiens, etc. The sales trend on baskets generally is up across California. People like things they can set out on their patio or on their front porch which will give them color now. Now they don't have to dig up a garden, plant small plants, water and wait. It's all done for them—for a price. And people are buying it.

And there you have it: The California evolution from packs and flats to 4″ annuals (very big five years ago) and now to the 6-pack—2¾″ plants in a pack of six taking over. And a good bit lower price per plant versus 4″. But still profitable to the grower.

Bedding plants are more or less a year round crop in California, with some buildup in mid-April. At this time, sow to sell (with plugs) takes about eight weeks for impatiens, seven weeks for petunias. In central California (Davises) many annuals are kept in a 60°F greenhouse for seven days after planting from plugs, then moved right outdoors. Days will be 40° to 50°F in early spring. Impatiens and begonias are more tender and aren't moved out until into April. Same for African marigolds.

- **Temperatures for plug germination:** It's all done in a growth chamber here. Night and day 75°F for most crops.

- **Media:** All annuals here are done "in our own peat perlite vermiculite mix, no soil."

- **Cool day/warm night** retarding is very much a part of things at DoRight's. Fans go on at daylight for 1½ hours. Says Dudley, "It does help a lot to retard such things as petunias. Actually all of our greenhouse area is operated on this daylight cool temperature plan."

- **A growth chamber** is used for germinating all plugs here.

- **Media for plugs:** W.R. Grace—a typical commercial plug media.

- **Plug sheet size:** All 392 plugs per 21″ flat, all square.

- **Genesis seed** is used, "Works okay."

- **The "frost proof" area:** DoRight's has covered an outdoor area, perhaps an acre or so, with a tight mesh (EX86), a sort of scrim weave. It is designed so that the whole roof can be pulled back or extended mechanically (Wadsworth). Dudley feels that it will probably carry them through as low as 25°F on things like petunias. It was done primarily to permit putting the hardier annuals outdoors earlier in the spring and also to improve the quality of them. The same thing for late fall primula. The goal is to be able to keep plants out up to 8° to 10°F below freezing.

Carl Blasig

Carl operates about 2½ acres of modern greenhouses in Hightstown, New Jersey. His grand plan is to expand his place as much as possible, and yet be able to do most of the work between him and his family—his wife and son. This means automating—and he reaches especially hard for automatic irrigation of all his crops. And from seeing his operation several times, it's clear that he is doing a top quality job—predominantly with automatic watering and with minimal outside help.

First, schedules/temperatures (it's nearly all grown from plugs). Again, growers must plan to sow one week earlier if the crop will be grown from bareroot seedlings.

			Weeks		
Sow Plugs	Transplant Plugs	Crop Salable	Sow to Transplant	Transplant to Sell	
Jan. 10	Feb. 25	Apr. 25	6	8*	Begonias (our slowest crop) Lot #1
Feb. 20	March 25	May 15	5	9*	Last lot
Feb. 15	March 20	Apr. 20	5	5	Impatiens—lot #1
March 15	Apr. 15	May 15	4	5	Last lot
Feb. 5	March 10	Apr. 25	5	7	Petunias—lot #1
March 15	Apr. 15	May 25	4 to 5	6	Last lot
Feb. 15	March 20	Apr. 15	5	4	Marigolds, African—lot #1
Apr. 1	Apr. 20	May 20	3	5	Last lot

*With good plugs

Here's what large-scale bedding plant/hanging basket production looks like across the United States—gutter-connected double poly roof, flats on the floor and baskets overhead.

Temperatures for growing on of flats of impatiens, begonias and vincas: 65°F night, 70°F day. For petunias and snapdragons: 55°F night and day.

On Growing Plugs

- **Temperature.** Carl maintains two temperature areas, one warmer and one cooler. Most annuals, including petunias, 68° to 70°F night and day. Begonias, vinca and impatiens, warmer. Also, tomatoes and marigolds are generally in a still cooler area.

- **Plug sheets.** Mainly 406 per tray, no 800s yet. Also says Carl, "We buy in a few of the larger 1″ plugs for fast turnover of crops."

- **Irrigation of plugs:** Carl uses two Grower System booms that do most of the job. "We do some touch-up by hand. But even begonias are mostly boom-irrigated."

- **Other points:** First, plugs are grown on a solid cement floor with buried hot water lines spaced 10″ apart and 4″ deep. This permits maintaining the desired soil temperature in the plug sheets.

Media: Carl uses a specialist-produced media, some Ball Plug Mix, some Pro Mix.

Seeders: One Blackmore and one Old Mill. By the way, he uses de-tailed marigolds and defuzzed tomatoes. Begonias are pelleted. He does use some of the high tech seeds, mechanically graded for higher germ.

No growth chamber here: "We're thinking about it, especially for things like begonias and summer pansies.

"We do use light reduction curtains in late spring, especially for things like begonias. We use one of the LS curtains.

"We do double-seed a few things—especially if germination on the package is listed below 85%. All our begonias are double-seeded. We get a better, fuller tray, 98% of plugs have plants. The same for most petunias—double seeded. Things like portulaca and alyssum we seed five to six seeds per cell, which we can do with either our Blackmore or Old Mill Seeder. We do B-Nine most plugs—improves quality."

How about pressing the mix in the plug sheet cells? Carl says, "We do, but take it easy."

"Eighty percent of our trays are new. We do dip a few into LS10 but it's a lot of work at a busy time. We wonder if it pays at $10 per hour."

Carl does often cool plugs down after they are well developed—60°F or even cooler.

Plugs sheets are set on an inverted plastic flat to keep them up off the ground. Otherwise they root through into the cement and results in uneven trays.

Growing on of Flat Annuals

Carl grows flat annuals primarily in eight packs of six plants—48 per 21″ flat. He does a considerable lot of pot annuals and various patio pots (details later).

Media for flat annuals is again, commercial mixes.

He does set up a belt-driven assembly line (I saw his wife with a team of high school people last spring doing the job very well). Flats in the production areas are grown on a layer of pea gravel—no soil heat. Oil-fired unit heaters are used throughout the range.

Production area flats are watered almost entirely with ITS boom irrigation. He finds this model, which can be moved manually from greenhouse to greenhouse, best. "We get very even coverage (18 nozzles on a 10′ boom)." Most of his 2½ acres of flat annuals are watered with ITS booms.

Peak week of sales of flats: April 25 to 30. "Flat sales are usually all through by May 20."

Pots and Patio Bedding Important Here

Carl reports roughly ¾ of his spring business is annuals in flats, but flat sales are steady or maybe dropping a bit, and both pot annuals and patio forms are coming up. Says Carl, "People don't seem to have time to make flower gardens with pack annuals anymore. They like the things they can set out on their patios. And if they are going to make a garden, they are more apt to buy 4″ and a lot of 6″ annuals to get color right now. We do some color bowls for Mother's Day, some 18″ window boxes, also an interesting 24″ long cylinder that hangs on its side—moss-lined and very colorful. Also 30,000 8″ hanging baskets. Baskets are big but the trend is only steady—they just can't be hung from a patio very well.

"We do a lot of 6″ bedding plants, lots of zinnias, some 4″. We do a nice 12″ sphagnum-lined hanging basket, 40″ across the top when in flower, for $45 wholesale."

Harold Ahrens—Cool/Dry Grower

The Ahrens family at Osseo (Minneapolis), Minnesota, are major bedding plant growers, all flats, and Harold is a classic cool/dry grower. First, temperatures. Example: for petunias, seed germination is at 75°F. After transplanting they start at 70°F for a week, then gradually cooler over the next three or four weeks, down to 45° or even 40°F until sale. These are night temperatures. Days are "cool as possible."

On watering says Harold, "always on the dry side. And no feeding beyond a little dry fertilizer plus Mag Amp in the original mix." The mix, by the way, is mainly local soil plus local peat.

The flat here is larger: 17″ x 21″, holds 18 packs. Impatiens and begonias are grown four per pack, also petunias. If this is scaled down to a 20″ flat it comes out to 48 plants per flat of impatiens, begonias, petunias and pansies.

B-Nine is used as needed. Result: A firm, short, stocky plant that will perform well in the lady's garden. And which, by the way, will stand up better at the garden center—better shelf life.

Here's the schedule for May 1 sales of petunias. By the way, it's all done bareroot (no plugs).

Sow	Transplant	Crop Salable	Weeks Sow to Sale Petunias
Jan. 7	Feb. 15	May 1	16 weeks

Ahrens', a family show by the way, grows only bedding plants. So that 16 weeks sow to sell costs only a little fuel, and less of even that in view of their cool temperatures.

The Kloosters of Kalamazoo

Mel and his wife, Elaine, (*Ball RedBook* cover lady, 13th edition) are classic Kalamazoo—Dutch-American growers. They operate M & L Greenhouse, located just off Sprinkle Road (one of horticulture's famous byways), and they're all bedding plants. Kalamazoo growers in total do about 4 million flats, 70 growers in Kalamazoo, $^2/_3$ of which are sold through their famous KVG co-op.

A widely-used way to move spring plants around a growing operation— various carts hooked together into a train and towed by either a garden tractor or golf cart.

Unique things at M & L (and at most KVG growers):
- **Temperature.** Most Kalamazoo growers carried a straight 70°F night and day on all bedding plants, as of the early 1990s. Now to control stretch they are almost

386

forced to cool day/warm night retarding, because of the ban on chemical retardants on vegetables (details later). It will still likely be an average of 70°F night and day. Example: maybe 67° day/72°F night.

Why the warm temperature here? Mainly because this area, being only bedding plants, strives for an early crop for the Southern market, and warm temperatures hurry that important early-sown crop into maturity sooner. And that in turn accommodates a major second crop—late April/early May maturity for the big Northern market. Since most of these growers do bedding only, this early Southern crop is the key to profit.

- **"We're slow on plugs."** Up to now Kalamazoo has done very little with plugs. After all there is no crop ahead of their first bedding crop so why strive to save several weeks' crop time? But several things are causing plugs to happen here. First, the much more rapid transplanting possible, especially with an assembly line belt system. Second, sandwiching in the two crops during the short spring weeks works a lot better when you can save three weeks of crop time (from plant to sell) on the second crop. Then there is the greater flexibility with plugs, you can hold a sheet of plugs longer without losing it versus a flat of seedlings.

But Mel is still doing bareroot seedlings: "I don't think it really pays to grow your own plugs until you get up to around 75,000 flats. Too much investment in equipment, and it's a whole new and difficult way of growing seedlings."

But clearly plugs are starting to happen in Kalamazoo.

- **Co-Op marketing.** Again, a unique thing here is that ⅔ of the area's 4 million flats are sold through their grower-owned marketing co-op. It's especially important in developing their all-important Southern market. By the way, these growers are very close—they tend to move more or less together on new things, they communicate freely among themselves (typical Dutch—and smart).

- **Specialization.** As the 15th *Ball RedBook* edition goes to press, the Kalamazoo growers are definitely moving toward specializing within the bedding plant crop. Example: One grower will do all impatiens, one will do marigolds and one will do maybe petunias, and with this the all-important advantages of specialization. Again, typically Dutch—and again, smart.

- **Schedule at M & L (all bareroot seedlings)**

Sow	Transplant	Crop Salable	
Nov. 28	Jan. 1	March 16	Begonias—lot #1
Dec. 23		March 15	Marigolds—lot #1
March 27		May 25	Marigolds—last lot
Dec. 5		Late April	Petunias—lot #1
Feb. 20		May 30	Petunias—last lot
Dec. 26		April 20	Geraniums—lot #1
Feb. 15		June 1	Geraniums—last lot

Note: Geraniums are shipped at first color. They use STS. Sales are up.

Other Cultural Notes

- **Root-zone heating:** Very little root-zone heating used for production of bedding plants here—Don Smith has one house of root zone. Nearly all growers do use root zone or some sort of effective soil heat for germinating seed and plugs.

- **Media.** For germinating seedlings, M & L uses commercial mix (Sunshine plus 25% vermiculite). For growing on flats they use HECO—mainly peat with nutrients plus 30% vermiculite plus 20% polystyrene beads. Says Mel, "This is normal for most of Kalamazoo. We don't sterilize these mixes."

- **Retardants on vegetables.** Strictly forbidden from here on out nationwide on *all* vegetable plants. The state of Michigan alone has 60 inspectors checking for retardants on vegetables. Says Mel, "We hope one grower doesn't violate this and make a big public furor." The other big result: Growers spring 1990 have gone over completely to cool day/warm night for height control on vegetable transplants and production crops.

  Mel and most growers here are very much aware of and using cool day/warm night technology to control height of bedding plants. They are also well aware of the importance of cooling the first two hours after sunrise to achieve an all-day cool day effect.

- **The crop is grown on the ground,** except that M & L and most growers use the plastic form that keeps the flats about 3″ off the ground. A big help, it keeps the occasional plant from growing through the flat and making a wild top growth and an uneven flat. And it keeps flats clean.

- **Growing containers.** There seems to be a mix of some 12 packs of four plants (48 per flat), some 18 packs of two to four plants (36 to 72 per flat) used in Kalamazoo. Most Co-Op bedding plants, though, are grown in 18 packs per flat.

  As usual, begonias and impatiens are often grown fewer plants per flat, and often they bring substantially more dollars per flat.

  Assembly line transplanting? Mel reports that about eight Kalamazoo growers are using this system now, and the trend is definitely up—especially with plug growers. "It's fast and easy to teach people to transplant with plugs."

- **Fertilizing:** Flat bedding plants at M & L are mainly watered with clear water, occasional fertilizer injected water "as needed." As with other good growers, these folks just don't feed bedding plants with every watering. Mel has two water lines through his range, one with constant-level fertilizer and one is clear water.

- **Four-inch pot annuals.** None at M & L's. Says Mel, "The Co-Op does a lot of 3½″ (A18 flat). We've tried hard on them. It's still small for us today and we're not gaining, except for seed geraniums. Somehow the East and the West and the Deep South are moving strongly into pot annuals, but not the Midwest."

  Interestingly, nearby Detroit-area growers do a lot of 4″ (May and June) and 6″(June and July). The trend is up in that area.

  Various forms for patio annuals, color bowls, window boxes, Dillen baskets, strawberry containers, etc. are also slow here. Among other things, Mel reports them difficult to ship—and Kalamazoo ships!

- **Several other points.** M & L uses HID supplemental light on seed flats. Says Mel, "We can sow weeks later on many crops, including impatiens, geraniums and petunias. It also speeds development of begonia seedlings—not earlier flowering but they grow better."

  Primed seed is used a good bit in this area.

  Light reduction is needed some from mid-April on. Mostly it's whitewash on the poly roof in this area. Says Mel, "It does cut down the amount of watering required."

  On watering: "It's handwatering all the way here on bedding plant flats.

  "We do not try to re-use trays here—most of our plants are shipped out of the area."

  How about cooling plants back for finishing? Not done here unless the weather is holding back demand.

  Should bedding plants be in color? Says Mel, "My market wants color. You really can't sell them without it unless the market is very tight."

  No guaranteed sale.

  Peak shipping weeks are April 15 to May 15 for the Northern market.

J & J Greenhouse—the Deep South

Jim and Judy Gordy operate J & J Greenhouses at Claxton, Georgia. It's a quality operation and, of course, located in the Deep South, actually the southern part of Georgia. They are heavily into flats and hanging baskets. Temperatures on things like begonias and impatiens will be 62° to 65°F at night, vents or fans on when it hits 75°F in the day. Petunias are often grown right outdoors right from the beginning, even though there may be a light frost, "We just wash it off." Plugs for these petunias for sale April 1 are planted February 25. Peak sales are about April 1.

Vinca are kept separate, and at 72° to 75°F nights and days if heat is needed. "Caution. Don't overwater. Let them dry out before watering. Avoid wet spots— you'll lose those plants." The key to vincas: warm and not too wet.

Almost everything is grown from plugs here—392 sheets all from specialist producers.

Scheduling for Most Deep South Growers—Main Lot of Petunias

Sow Plugs	Transplant Plugs	Crop Salable	Weeks Sow to Sale	
Jan. 21	Feb. 25	April 1	10	Peak week in southern Georgia

PROFESSIONAL PLANT GROWERS ASSOCIATION

PPGA, originally established as Bedding Plants Inc. (BPI), serves growers of all greenhouse crops, and members of related industries throughout the United States, Canada and the world. It offers a monthly newsletter, annual conference and trade show, membership directory and a catalog of reference materials, production and marketing aids.

PPGA's affiliated organizations include the Bedding Plants Foundation Inc., which funds scientific research selected by growers; Professional Plant Growers Scholarship Foundation, which helps support outstanding horticulture students; and the FloraStar trialing program which evaluates and promotes outstanding potted plants.

I urge growers everywhere to join PPGA and support its affiliated organizations. For membership information, contact PPGA, P.O. Box 27516, Lansing, Michigan 48909, (517) 694-7700.

Meet Claude Hope (if you haven't already). Claude is well known in the world of bedding plant growers and has been recognized by many national awards, including Society of American Florists Hall of Fame, the first ever Professional Plant Growers Association international award, the All-America Selections award of merit and the Alex Laurie Award for horticulture. He was also recognized as a fellow in the American Society of Horticultural Science "in recognition of his significant contributions to the development of improved open-pollinated and hybrid flowers through innovative plant genetics and breeding practices; for development of techniques and methodology for inbred maintenance and production of high-quality seed; for noteworthy leadership in the development of plant material for the bedding plant industry." I'd like to be sure that growers today are at least aware of a few things this remarkable plantsman/breeder/grower has done for floriculture.
Examples:

- *Claude fetched* impatiens wallerana, *then an obscure wildflower, out of the Costa Rican jungle, and bred it shorter and with flowers on top (lots of them). It's really the success story of the 50-year old-bedding plant industry. To this day, impatiens are a major part of U.S. bedding plants, often sold out by growers I talk with.*

- *New Guineas. Claude recognized the value of them, worked patiently for years, and introduced the first commercial impatiens with New Guinea blood. His Tangelow includes bloodlines from both New Guinea and other impatiens. Both Longwood Gardens and the U.S. Department of Agriculture were involved in the original acquisition and the early work on New Guineas.*

- *He has bred many other plants and is still working at it. Most important recently: Blue Lisa, the first satisfactory pot lisianthus. Also torenia Clown® (All-American Selections winner), and the original Elfin® impatiens and many improvements on them since then. He also bred the first red and the first yellow petunias. Claude did all the Rainbow coleus lines that are still widely used. He is currently active in both amaryllis and anthuriums that are designed for pot culture and has bred many of today's double petunias.*

- *Claude pioneered south-of-the-border production of F₁ seed. He was first to realize the problem of the costly and tedious work of hand-pollinating F₁ hybrid flowers and vegetables. He set up the first F₁ production in a low-labor cost area. The result: F₁ hybrid seed today, although still expensive, would be many times more so but for this great guy's foresight. He created his Linda Vista farm in Costa Rica which employs 900 Costa Ricans in F₁ seed production. Claude's commitment to the education and personal welfare of the native Costa Ricans he has employed over the years is a whole separate story.*

  A special Ball RedBook hats off to a great American plantsman!

BEGONIA

by Heidi Tietz
Petersen and Tietz Greenhouses
Waterloo, Iowa

TUBEROUS/NONSTOP BEGONIAS

There are many tuberous-type begonias on the market today. Traditionally, we think of the large (4" to 5") camellia-flowered begonias with fantastic color combinations, grown from tubers. These plants are indeed spectacular. There will always be a market for these plants but we must also be aware of new developments.

In addition to the traditional tuberous begonia from tubers, today's market has taken a giant leap toward the use of tuberous begonia types grown from seed. The most common of these types are Nonstops. They are easy to program for a uniform finish and can be grown in 4" or 6" pots as well as hanging baskets. Their numerous 2" to 3" blooms provide a lot of color; not as large as the traditional tuberous begonias, but much more show!

Other seed-propagated tuberous begonia types include the smaller flowering, more compact Clips (great for 4" pots) and the larger-flowering Memories (great for 6" pots and hanging baskets).

Although there are many types of tuberous begonias, they all require the same basic growing conditions.

Medium. Begonias prefer a well-balanced soil mixture with plenty of peat and perlite for good aeration.

Temperature. Ideal day temperatures are 68° to 75°F. Night temperatures below 62°F should be avoided as growth will be inhibited and tubers may form. Cooler temperatures are acceptable when flowering begins, but it will slow flower production. Likewise, temperatures of 85°F or above should be avoided. Lower the light intensity and temperature by using shade.

Fertilization. Begonias require less fertilizer than mums. They are considered moderate feeders. A very successful feeding program incorporates a weekly feeding with a peat-lite fertilizer like 15-16-17, alternated with calcium nitrate at the rate of 2 lbs./100 gals. Excessive amounts of fertilizer or ammonia can cause crinkled or curled leaves.

Lighting (daylength control). In fall-winter, tuberous/Nonstop begonias must have supplemental light at night to induce flowering and eliminate the growth of tubers. Mum lighting from 10 p.m. to 2 a.m., or by extending the daylength from dusk to 10 p.m., is sufficient. October through March is the crucial time period for this additional lighting, as the natural daylength occurring April through September is quite adequate for normal plant growth and flowering. Light intensity levels for good winter and spring growth are 3,500 to 5,000 fc. During the warm summer months, the maximum should be held to 2,500 to 3,000 fc.

391

Pinching. Tuberous/Nonstop begonias make beautiful 6″ pots or hanging baskets. To produce a full, well-branched plant, pinch the tips out two to three weeks after transplanting to the final pot.

Insects. The main enemies of begonias are spider mites, cyclamen mites and thrips. Pentac will control the mites. Avid, Mavrik and Orthene should control thrips.

Diseases. Use Banrot or Benlate and Subdue 2E at planting time for disease control. A second application four to six weeks after planting is also helpful.

Tuberous-type begonias come in a wide variety of flower colors and sizes as well as plant habits. A grower's own tastes and customers will determine which variety and pot size he chooses to grow. One thing is certain, with production times of just six to eight weeks for 4″ pots, and 10 to 12 weeks for hanging baskets when starting with 2″ liners, this crop has profit-producing tendencies.

RIEGER AND OTHER HIEMALIS TYPES OF BEGONIAS

Hiemalis begonia is a cross between the winter-flowering bulbous species *Begonia socotrana* and the summer-flowering *Begonia tuberhybrida*. The result of this cross is a winter-flowering begonia with characteristics similar to tuberous begonias. In 1955, Otto Rieger, of Germany, introduced new varieties that were more floriferous and more resistant to mildew; this was the beginning of the Rieger begonia.

Hiemalis begonias are very popular pot plants in Western Europe. Their many flower colors such as shades of red, pink, yellow, orange, white, and flower forms of single, semi-double and double combine with dark green or deep-bronze foliage to create a strikingly different pot plant or hanging basket. When hiemalis begonias are made available to U.S. consumers, the plants disappear from store shelves.

Starter plants are available as leaf (multistem) or stem tip cuttings. Multi-stem leaf cuttings contain three or more vegetative shoots that will produce a very full pot plant from one starter. Stem tip cuttings are excellent for 4″ pot production, but when producing 6″ pots, two or three starters are recommended.

Culture

The following cultural information is taken from a culture sheet from Mikkelsens, Inc.

Medium/pH. Hiemalis (Rieger) begonias perform best when grown in a fast draining, well-structured medium with sufficient peat moss for water retention. Supplemental superphosphate and micro-nutrients may be necessary to avoid any nutrient deficiencies. The pH should be 5 to 5.5 for a synthetic mix, and 5.5 to 6 for a mineral medium. When potting, the top of the young starter plant rootball should be ¼″ above the surface of the growing mix to prevent stem rot.

Temperature. Optimal temperature for Hiemalis (Rieger) begonias to develop lush vegetative growth is 70° to 72°F with a 14-hour or longer day. After desired size of the plant is reached the temperature should be lowered to 65°F with a 12-hour or shorter day. The lower temperature aids in flower initiation and provides deeper bloom color, better bloom production and an overall sturdier plant. Final development can be delayed by reducing the temperature to as low as 62°F. Air-cooled houses may be necessary in warm regions during summer production. Temperatures over 75°F will result in soft, undesirable growth and flower delay.

Carbon dioxide. Supplemental CO_2 benefits plants grown in low-light areas by better utilizing the limited daylight, providing faster growth, flowering and overall plant quality in greenhouses where CO_2 can be contained. CO_2 will increase photosynthesis when used at 1,000 to 1,500 ppm during daylight hours. When growing at higher CO_2 levels, greenhouse day temperature should be 5° to 10°F warmer.

Growth. Rieger begonias are not heavy feeders. For optimal vegetative growth, constant feed at 200 ppm N, 190 ppm P_2O_5, and 150 ppm K_2O. Continue to alternate one clear watering to one feed application. Overfed plants with crisp, lush green foliage do not produce as many flowers as plants slightly starved during flower development. Flowering is promoted when moisture and fertility is limited.

Lighting (Long-Day Treatment—LDT). During the vegetative growth period, interrupted or supplemental lighting of Hiemalis begonias may be necessary to maintain a 14-hour daylength. Lighting of begonias is basically to encourage growth, not for flower delay, as they are only slightly photoperiodic. Lights should be applied to extend the daylength. In the northern latitudes additional lighting is necessary from September 15 to March 15. Under these poor-light conditions Hiemalis begonias require additional lighting to prevent growth standstill until short-day treatment begins. Interrupted lighting of 50% on and 50% off will fill the plants' needs for added lighting. Light for three extra hours daily during months of September and March, four hours in October and February, five hours daily in November and January and six hours in the month of December. Twenty to 50 fc. of incandescent light will give more rapid growth than 10 fc., which is sufficient to control chrysanthemum flowering.

Be careful not to expose Rieger begonias to extremely high daylight intensities. During high-light periods apply shade to prevent sun scald (marginal desiccation and burning) and vegetative hardening, causing a reduction of growth. The amount of light intensity that can be tolerated is dependent on temperature. Begonias can be safely exposed to 3,000 fc. at 65°F or below, 2,000 fc. at 70°F and 1,500 fc. at 80°F.

Short-Day Treatment (SDT). Short-day treatment begins when the desired number of shoots have emerged and sufficient new growth has developed. Since Hiemalis begonias are only slightly photoperiodic, short-day treatment is basically provided to produce shorter, more compact plants and to develop uniform flowering. The older the plant the more readily it will produce flowers, even under long daylengths. The number of flowers and flower buds will be at their peak when the daylength is reduced to 10 hours and the temperature reduced to 64°F. Plants grown in longer daylengths appear to have more vegetative growth at the expense of flower development. Four weeks of short-day treatment (maximum 12-hour daylength) is necessary for good flower induction. During periods of high temperatures, black cloth material should be applied at 7 p.m. and removed at 9:30 a.m. to prevent heat buildup.

Growth regulators. Application of Cycocel or A-Rest is needed only when necessary to maintain compact growth. Apply the growth regulator early, 21 to 28 days after the start of short-day treatment for best results. Plants must not be under any physiological stress when applying growth regulars. Apply Cycocel as a spray at 1,500 ppm. Recommended application rate for A-Rest is 25 ppm. Reduction of water could also be used as a growth regulator during short-day treatment.

Pinching. Plants should be pinched when young plants show a dominance of one or two shoots overcrowding the other shoots. It is advisable to prune out the stronger growth to allow more uniform bottom growth. A pinch will be necessary on single stem plants to allow the plant to break along the main stem with new shoots emerging at the leaf axis. Pinching helps shape the plant and provides additional flowering shoots.

Diseases

Powdery mildew is the most frequent disease problem of Hiemalis begonias. Bayleton 25WP is effective not only as a preventive spray, but also has a growth regulator effect. Apply as a fine mist only, using a rate of 1 to 2 oz./100 gals. water after flower initiation. Karathane is also effective, but will cause burn if sprayed on open flowers. Good air circulation and humidity control are very helpful in preventing powdery mildew.

Xanthomonas begoniae (oil spot sickness or bacterial blight). Discolored spots appear which turn from yellow to brown. Small round greasy spots become evident on the underside of the leaf. The disease affects the stems as well as the leaves. Xanthomonas is intensified by high temperatures and high humidity. To control xanthomonas: 1) Secure plant material from propagators using cultured index stock; 2) eliminate watering over the foliage—use tube watering systems or capillary mats; 3) complete all watering by noon; 4) lower the relative humidity by using heat and ventilation; and 5) discard all infected plants!

Botrytis. Conditions of high humidity and poor air circulation are conducive to botrytis development. Fungicides such as Chipco, Daconil, Benlate and Termil can help prevent botrytis.

Foliar nematodes (eelworms) are wormlike parasites of plants, infesting stems and leaves with diseases. They cause small yellowish spots that turn the leaf a brownish black, or purple to red on some cultivars. The infected areas take on a water-soaked appearance on the underside of the leaf. Use of the chemical Vydate will control foliar nematodes. Good sanitary practices are also helpful in prevention.

Xanthomonas, botrytis, powdery mildew and foliar nematodes can all be controlled with good heating, ventilating and air movement practices. A Dexon-Benlate drench applied two to three days after potting will aid in suppression of root and stem pathogens. When potting, remove all damaged leaves to prevent soft rot from progressing to the new undergrowth. To increase air circulation within the plant, the so-called "mother" leaf can be trimmed out.

Hiemalis Begonia Growth Timing Chart*

Starter Plant Size	# Starters /Pot	Desired Finished Pot	Long-Day Treatment	Pinch	Short-Day Treatment	Total Crop Time
Stem tip cutting	1	4″ pot	Week 1 to 2	Week 1	Week 3 to 7	7 to 10 weeks
Multistem	1	4″ pot	Week 1 to 2	None	Week 3 to 7	9 to 12 weeks
Multistem	1	5″ pot	Week 1 to 3	Week 2	Week 4 to 8	9 to 14 weeks
Multistem	1	6″ pot	Week 1 to 6	Week 3	Week 7 to 11	12 to 16 weeks
Stem tip cutting	4	8″ to 10″ hanging basket	Week 1 to 3	Week 2	Week 4 to 8	10 to 16 weeks
Multistem	3	8″ to 10″ hanging basket	Week 1 to 3	Week 2	Week 4 to 8	10 to 16 weeks

*by Heidi Tietz

Feed schedule. Feed continuously at 200 ppm N, 190 ppm P_2O_5, 200 ppm K_2O through the third week of SDT. Apply clear water during the fourth week of SDT, then reduce the amount of feed to 100 ppm N, 190 ppm P_2O_5, 150 ppm K_2O on week 5 of SDT and continue to alternate one clear watering to one feed application.

Additional uses for Rieger begonias: Hanging baskets for year-round flowering sales (avoid Aphrodite cultivars in winter because of petal drop. Use double-flowering cultivars for better keeping quality and more color variety); use for interior landscaping because of the excellent keeping qualities. For outdoor plantings provide semi-shade; good as bedding plants, borders and container plants.

Fibrous Begonias

Very few spring bedding annuals have achieved such a rapid rise in popularity in recent years as the perpetually flowering, fibrous-rooted begonia. For many years they have been grown as pot plants or as specialty items for bedding. Today, with the availability of many excellent F_1 hybrid varieties, most growers offer them in packs just like petunias, marigolds, etc.

Begonias are free-flowering with excellent habit. They are adaptable to a wide range of planting areas. Most important of all, they are "low-care" items, which makes them so well adapted to the American homeowner's yard today.

In sowing, use very light, sandy material with some sifted peat to help maintain uniform moisture without the need of frequent watering. Sow the seed thinly and carefully in shallow rows, and on a well-watered, smooth surface. If gone over with a misty spray, the seed will be washed in enough to make further covering unnecessary, except for a piece of slightly tilted glass, which will maintain moisture without frequent waterings. At 70°F media temperature, germination should take place in 10 to 14 days. Because of begonia's extremely fine root system, dilute liquid feedings should be started as soon as the seedlings emerge to prevent post-germination stall.

This is the reason so many growers fail with germinating begonias! The tiny plant with so little nutrient in the seed, germinates, and the nutrients in the top quarter inch of the seed flat are quickly depleted—and the plant just starves. Do start feeding promptly!

When large enough to handle, the seedlings can be potted directly from the seed flat to a 2¼″ or 2½″ pot. Nice flowering 2½s can be produced in three to five months from sowing, which indicates sowing in early February for the main spring supply. While all begonias enjoy a fair amount of heat, some growers, with the coming of warm spring temperatures, run begonias out into frames. Full air and some cool temperatures bring out the rich, natural colorings of the foliage, many being rich red, others with red edges, and several with dark, metallic-bronze foliage that contrasts strikingly with the flowers. Botanically speaking, the gracilis type is a tuberous species, but the term has been applied to several varieties in the semperflorens group by German growers, and usually refers to those with finely fringed leaves.

While fibrous-rooted begonias, by the nature of their growth, divide themselves readily into three groups—tall, intermediate and dwarf—the dwarf class is by far the most popular and widely used. These three groups can be further divided into green-leafed and bronze-leafed varieties. In most areas, the green-leafed will retain a better foliage appearance when planted in full sun (F_1s).

The dwarf class averages 3″ to 5″ in height when grown in pots; 6″ to 8″ in outdoor beds.

See Chapter 12 for notes on growing begonia plugs.

Interesting note: A Franciscan monk named Begon first discovered the begonia in the Caribbean in the 1600s—and it has carried his name ever since.

BELLIS

by Jim Nau
Ball Seed Company

Perennial grown as an annual (Bellis perennis), 140,000 seeds/oz. Germinates in 7 to 14 days at 70°F. Variety should be left exposed to light during germination.

Due to extreme temperatures in the Midwest, bellis plants are often grown as annuals though are listed as tender perennials in many listings. They are best grown for spring color in borders, window boxes, or in pots. Flower colors include pink, rose, red, or white and flowers are commonly double in their form. In coastal areas plant in full sun; in other areas plant in afternoon shade.

Allow 14 to 16 weeks for flowering pot plants in the spring. For pack sales in mildest areas, grow along with pansies and treat the same. In the Midwest an October sowing will flower in mid-February when grown at 50 °F nights.

Super Enorma is still the most popular of the varieties available on the United States trade today. Flowers are double, frilled, and blossom out at 1″ to 2″ across. The mixture is the most commonly grown variety. Another variety of merit is the Pomponette series which has tightly held petals and a flower size of no more than 1″. Both varieties grow to no more than 4″ tall though the crop time of Pomponette is one to two weeks earlier than that of Super Enorma.

BOUGAINVILLEA

by Heidi Tietz
Petersen and Tietz
Waterloo, Iowa

Bougainvillea is commonly seen around hotels as borders and in planters in Florida and such tropical locations as Jamaica. These plants thrive on the heat, humidity and sun that those areas have to offer. But, there are other parts of the United States that also provide these conditions for a portion of the year. Can bougainvillea be adapted for these climates? The answer is yes.

Bougainvillea are very effective as ground covers, trellis plants and hanging baskets. How do you start? Growers located in warmer climates such as Alabama, Florida, Georgia, Louisiana, Southern California and Texas, have good success using rooted liners (2¼″ to 3″ pots) as the starting point.

For Northern growers, the greatest success stories come from growers that begin with bougainvillea in a prefinished form. Prefinished forms include a 4″ pot used as a jumbo liner, or a hanging basket that is ready to set flowers.

The flowering of the bougainvillea may seem complicated, but the following basic guidelines will help you understand this plant.

- Dry conditions and stress are required for flowering.
- Bougainvillea bloom heaviest when grown under short days.
- They are not a true short-day plant.
- Bougainvillea will flower on mature wood without short days.
- Summer conditions may enhance growth so rapidly that there is no mature wood available.
- Once plants drop flowers, plants will rebloom in six weeks.
- Iron is a very important nutrient to bougainvillea.
- Tests using Bonzi reveal that it aids the blooming process as well as greening up the plants. Different varieties respond to different rates of application.

Exploring the growth and blooming habits of bougainvillea, it is obvious that there is not one set of growing criteria. It is evident, however, that this is a new, different and money-making crop.

BRACHYCOME

by Jim Nau
Ball Seed Company

Annual (Brachycome iberidifolia), 155,000 seeds/oz. Germinates in four to eight days at 70°F. Seed should be left exposed to light during germination.

Brachycome is commonly called Swan River Daisy and is available as seed, plugs or liners. Predominantly sold as a mixture from seed, separate colors are also available in primarily blue or white, though off-types will be noted in each color. From cuttings, separate colors of yellow, pink, and lavender are also available. Flowers are single to semi-double and measure less than 1" across. Brachycome is basal branching and has a bushy habit in the garden. The stem itself is wiry, which allows the plant to be shifted easily by the wind; this often creates an uneven performance in flower beds when the plants are used in mass plantings or when used in large numbers in landscaping. Brachycome works best in sunny morning locations as a container plant or in borders. Plants grow to no more than 10" tall in the garden.

Sowings made in late March can be transplanted two to three weeks later into cells and grown on at 58°F nights. These plants will be ready for green pack sales in mid-May and in full bloom in late May. In general, allow 7 to 8 weeks for green pack sales, and 10 weeks for full bloom. Crop these as you would French marigolds, allowing a similar crop time and growing regimen.

BROMELIADS

by Russell Miller
GrowerTalks magazine

Bromeliads are members of the family *Bromeliaceae* and are native to tropical and subtropical areas of South, Central and North America. Texas and Florida have many native bromeliads that are protected by conservation laws. Spanish moss and ball moss are bromeliads found across the Southern states. The pineapple is the most familiar bromeliad. There are more than 2,000 recognized bromeliad species, as well as hundreds of hybrids. Each offers a uniqueness for the grower, retailer, and especially the interiorscaper.

Bromeliads have long been a favorite houseplant in Europe, having been grown in greenhouses there for the last 200 years. Since the early 1980s, bromeliads have become increasingly popular in North American homes and interiorscapes. This can be attributed to three very strong selling points bromeliads offer: Bromeliads are true eyecatchers, as they are available in a wide range of colors and often sport a combination of colors; they require very little maintenance and thrive on neglect; and with reasonable care, bromeliads will bloom on the store shelf or in the home for at least three to as many as four to six months or more.

Common bromeliad genera include Aechmea, Billbergia, Cryptanthos, Dyckia, Guzmania, Neoregelia, Nidularium, Tillandsia and Vriesea. Bromeliads can range in height from several inches up to 40', depending on the type. The most commonly sold varieties range in height from 20" to 30" high and are sold in 4" to 8" pots. Color development is commonly rated as low, medium and high, depending on the plant's maturity.

A colorful, well-developed bromeliad retails for $10 to as much as $40 or more, depending on size and characteristics. A large, rare bromeliad often retails for $75 or more. Due to the wide range of colors available with bromeliads, you can tailor specific ones to the holidays. Red bromeliads for Christmas, orange and yellow for Thanksgiving, pink, blue and peach for Easter and Mother's Day.

Bromeliads can be found growing naturally in diverse environments, from rain forests to cool mountains to hot, dry deserts. Most bromeliads available today are tropical, although there are a few desert types available.

Most bromeliads are naturally epiphytic, clinging to other plant material as they grow while producing their own nutrition through photosynthesis. Most bromeliads have a center rosette of leaves from which a blossom-bearing spike grows. On other varieties the colorful blush on the inner leaves is the flower. Many bromeliads have an inner central "cup" that holds water. The shape, size and color of the flower, as well as required culture and production methods, depends on the genus.

Growing bromeliads from seed is very difficult and, outside of some hard-core collectors of the plant and a few U.S. commercial wholesale growers, most commercial suppliers prefer to buy in bromeliads as bare-root cuttings or as potted plants that are in, or near, full color. Since growing techniques are genus-specific, and sometimes even variety-specific, you should obtain cultural guidelines from your bromeliad supplier. Additional information can also be obtained from the Bromeliad Society Inc., 2488 East 49th, Tulsa, OK 74105.

It takes two to three years to grow a bromeliad from seed before you have a saleable plant. Growing bromeliads from seed requires different types of media, media preparations and seed placement methods, as well as specific cultural methods after germination and strictly controlled climatic conditions. Much of this information is considered secrets of the trade. Interestingly, however, mass producing bromeliads from seed is considered easier than growing, for example, orchids from seed.

Epiphytic bromeliads are grown in pots, in hanging wood or wire baskets, or attached to boards, as is done with some orchids. The terrestrial bromeliads can be grown in well-drained, neutral to acid-medium soil. A peat-based media with sand, sawdust or crushed granite can be used, but a widely accepted mixture is one part peat to three parts bark.

Cryptanthus and Dyckias grow well in African violet soil. Dyckias also do well in cactus soil. Most gray-leaved Tillandsia do not grow well in pots. The most important consideration is that the mix must drain rapidly and that the pot used must have adequate drainage holes.

After germinating the lettuce-size seed, grasslike seedlings should be transplanted into flats after having grown to 4 cm. in size. From flats, plants can be moved to cell packs and eventually into individual containers as they grow larger. The more often a bromeliad is transplanted the better it grows. For each transplant provide more room on the bench, more light and, to a small extent, more nutrients. Don't crowd young bromeliads on the bench, as bromeliads thrive on aeration. Bottom heating has shown to increase the turnover in bench space required for commercially growing bromeliads from seed, as well as reduce heating costs.

The plant flowers once in its life cycle, and usually within one year after flowering the plant dies. After finishing its life cycle the plant produces side shoots, called "pups," that sprout next to the mother plant. As many as 12 of these clones may be left behind as the mother plant withers away. The common method of reproducing bromeliads is by snipping away and repotting these pups, then caring for them as you would their parent. The pups normally bloom in two to three years, and the cycle begins again.

Don't pot a bromeliad too deeply, just to the base of the leaves. Don't use a pot that is too large for the plant, as the danger of overwatering increases. Usually a 4" to 6" pot is sufficient. Use stable pots or containers, as any rocking or motion damages the tender, developing roots. Staking may be necessary until roots are well-developed.

To complete a typical bromeliad life cycle, a temperature range of 65° to 85°F and humidity between 60% and 80% is usually required. Tropical bromeliads prefer high humidity. Outside of a few bromeliad types that can withstand temperatures as low as 30°F with protection, for most you cannot allow night temperatures to drop below 50°F.

Bright, diffused light and genus-specific care improves growth and plant quality of most bromeliads grown for commercial production. Direct sun can burn the leaves of most bromeliads. A minimum of 200 fc. for indoor maintenance is best in preserving flower color.

Bromeliads thrive on neglect. Normally, a bromeliad requires water once every 10 days to as little as once every three weeks. Apply water to both the plant and the soil. Misting systems may be ideal for most bromeliads under proper growing conditions. Water requirements vary with the genus as well as the region and light intensities. A common rule of thumb is the less light the less fertilization and water required.

When watering, the water should run fast through the mix, then, after watering, drain off the water in the pot saucer. The roots of most bromeliads grow well in moist, but never soggy soil. Use room-temperature water, and, for most bromeliads, water should be applied onto the center of the plant, the cup, and allowed to run through the leaves into the soil. Mist the plants every few days if humidity is 50% to 60%, or daily under drier conditions. Softer-leaved plants require more water and humidity than stiff-leaved ones (most Vrieseas, Guzmanias and Nidulariums). Mounted plants need frequent misting and do well with a weekly dousing.

For bromeliads that have a center cup, apply water in the cup as well as the soil. Under low-light conditions, however, it may be best to water only the lower leaves and soil. Do not keep the central cup constantly full of water. Allow it to become nearly dry before adding additional water. Never allow the water in the cup to stagnate or remain in the cup for more than one month.

Use only water-soluble fertilizers. Under most conditions the "normal" fertilizer dosages are too high for some bromeliads, so it's best not to exceed 1/3 or 1/4 of the recommended rate.

Bromeliads can be artificially induced to flower by injecting ethylene gas into the cup of the plant at the right stage of the plant's maturity. The plant will begin blooming in a few days.

BROWALLIA

by Jim Nau
Ball Seed Company

Annual (Browallia speciosa), **125,000 seeds/oz. Germinates in 15 days at 75°F. Leave the seed exposed to light during germination.**

Browallia is a warm-season annual with star-shaped flowers on plants recommended for baskets or containers. If planted to the open ground, be sure to have fully developed plants and not seedlings or small transplants; these often perform poorly or not at all. Flowers are 1″ across, in colors of blue, lavender and white.

Allow 15 to 16 weeks for flowering 4″ pots, one plant per pot, or 20 to 22 weeks for flowering 10″ hanging baskets with no more than seven plants per pot. No pinching is necessary to encourage branching. As a hanging basket it does well in fairly heavy shade.

In the southern United States, browallias will overwinter in areas without frost. Plant from mid-September to November in the deep South for flowering until late April. In cooler areas have plants ready for sale once the danger of frost has passed.

The primary variety selection in the U.S. trade is the Bell series, which includes three shades of blue and a white. Blue Bells Improved is the most popular variety due to its true blue flower color. Marine Bells is a dark indigo color which makes it the darkest variety available in this series. Sky Bells has a powdery or mid-blue flower color and, finally, Silver Bells has a pure white flower color. The Bell series grows to 12″ in window boxes and containers.

BULB CROPS

SPRING BULB CROPS*

First, the case for spring bulbs—especially in pots.

1. Aesthetically and market-wise, they are colorful and delightful—the very essence of spring. People love them! A fresh breath toward the end of a long winter.

2. In the growers' year-round space plan, they offer a profitable, marketable crop to fill January/February benches—after poinsettias. A great Valentine's crop—both cut and pot.

3. To a retail grower, a special advantage over the chain: Bulbs have a short shelf-life. They are not well adapted to wholesale pot-plant channels, especially chains—but great for the well-planned retail grower.

4. They are not really difficult—just follow the rules.

Plan well. Before you order—plan! Write down how many tulips (or whatever), what varieties, pot size, bulbs per pot, flowering date, and prices. Also, a complete growing schedule. Again, bulbs are not long-lived. Use *The Holland Bulb Forcers Guide* by Gus DeHertogh. It is excellent! See your bulb supplier for a copy.

(Note: For their overall plan, Bachman's divides all bulb crops into an early lot (Group I) for January/February flowering and a late lot (Group II) for March/April flowering.)

Pot Tulips—The Heart Of It

Bachman's flowers pot tulips from early January through Easter. They are clearly #1 one in the spring bulb crops here.

Ordering/shipping. Todd Bachman does his annual ordering in February and March—mainly from Holland. "Watch currency exchange gyrations—I would rather order in dollars than in Dutch guilder. I know my costs." Shipping needs attention. Bachman's uses mainly ocean freight. Shipping dates must relate to planting dates—again in Group I and II. Beware of heat during transit, also delay—and high humidity. Bachman's prefers the plastic container—it is open and porous. "You can order a temperature recording instrument to be packed with the bulbs to be sure consistent temperatures have been maintained during transit."

Upon arrival, open and ventilate the bulbs. Ethylene builds up and can cause bud blast. "We always check our bulbs to be sure everything is there. Check for a sour smell as an indication of fusarium disease. We store our bulbs upon arrival at 60° to 65°F—with good air circulation. Cut flower bulbs are immediately put into a 55°F storage to start the vernalization process.

*Based partly on several Ohio Short Course talks by Todd Bachman, Bachman's, Minneapolis, Minnesota.

"Check bulbs for flower bud development. You slice a bulb open, look for complete flower parts, anthers, etc. If they are present, the bulb has reached 'G-Stage'—ready to go. Do not plant bulbs until 'G-Stage' is confirmed (DeHertogh's book)."

Pot sizes versus the market. Bachman's grows a variety of tulip pot sizes:
- four bulbs per 4½″ pot
- six bulbs per 5½″ bulb pan
- eight bulbs per 7″ bulb pan
- ten bulbs per 8″ or 15 bulbs per 10″ bulb pan

Be sure all pots drain well.

Potting. "We like soil a bit heavier than that for pot mums. Our mix includes sandy loam, Hypnum peat. With too light a mix, the bulbs' vigorous root systems tend to push them out of the soil. We do steam all bulb soils. We fill the pot half-way, set the tulips in (flat side to the outside of the pot), then fill up the pot. Do not push them in—it compacts the soil." There should be at least a quarter inch of soil over the bulb. Potting machines can work well for bulb crops. Set the equipment to fill the pot half full on the first pass. Plant the bulbs, then finish filling the pot on the second pass.

Pot tulips—the #1 pot bulb crop.

403

"Do label each lot carefully. Include plant date, date to remove for forcing, flowering date and supplier name. If you get two lots of the same variety, mark them Lot A and Lot B—they may not flower quite together.

"Temperature, when bulbs are first placed in the cooler, should be at 48°F. Within several weeks of potting, bulbs should show roots—also shoots. Keep the soil moist. On November 10, tulips should be dropped to 41°F for several weeks at this stage—a more ideal vernalization temperature."

Early January tulips. They can be flowered nicely right about January 5 to 15—a great after-poinsettia crop. To do this, bulbs must be artificially pre-cooled. Immediately upon arrival, they need six weeks at 48°F—starts vernalization. "We do it in our rooting room. Then to 41°F. Move to the forcing house four weeks before the flowering date."

Group I—the early ones. Group I should be potted and put in the storage room normally in mid-September. The better pot forcing varieties like Paul Richter will need 15 to 16 weeks in the cooler, plus three to four weeks to force. A total of 18 weeks plus from planting to flower. Group I goes into Room 1—Group II into Room 2, so that we can vary temperatures. By the way, the storage rooms have concrete floors, refrigeration, capability of drawing in cool outside air during winter to minimize costly refrigeration. Bulbs are stored on pallets—50 pots per pallet, 12 high—stacked pot on pot. They are moved by forklift. Be sure there is air circulation in the cooler room.

Group II—the later ones. Group II tulips should be ordered to arrive about October 1. Tulips are potted immediately and placed in the Group II cooler room. They are kept at 48°F until December 10, and then dropped to 41°F until they are ready for forcing.

"On all pot tulips, as soon as we see roots and shoots, we apply Benlate and Truban—8 oz. per 100 gal. of each—as a soil drench. Also, all hyacinth bulbs are sprayed once with Benlate—8 oz. per 100 gal. And, lastly, we burn Termil in the air as a botrytis preventative—before removing from the cooler."

Forcing. Tulips want a normally light house, reasonable humidity. It's really very simple—mainly 60°F—or 5°F more or less to time the crop. Later, spring crops flower faster, the earlier tulips will take three or four weeks to force. Moisture is again important at this stage. "Never let them dry. Also, we try to water in the morning so as to minimize botrytis." Again, reasonable humidity—avoid the extremes. Feeding, long felt to be unnecessary, is required to provide both calcium and nitrate, which tulips require in higher amounts than the base soil provides. One or two feedings of $CaNO_3$ at 140 ppm during forcing produces a better tulip.

Harvest date. (All harvest dates are for maximum longevity.) Pot tulips should go to the retail display when they are in the green bud stage. "We like slight color at the base of the flower. Again, they are short-lived, so they must be removed at the right time."

Varieties for pot forcing. Due to an increased demand in the marketplace for 4", 4½" and 5½" pot sizes for tulips, varieties fall into two groups: standard varieties and short varieties.

Short varieties for January and February flowering include: Christmas Marvel, Prominence, Kareol, Abra and Flair. Tall varieties for the same period include Paul Richter, Merry Christmas, Golden Melody, Christmas Marvel and Kees Nelis.

Post-Valentine's Day short varieties include: Arma, Sundance, Plaisir, Etude and Red Riding Hood. Tall varieties for the same period: Attila, Yellow Present, Red Present, Princess Irene and Couleur Cardinal.

Cut Tulips

These are rather important crops at Bachman's—all grown in wood flats 12" x 18" x 3½". They plant 10 rows of six plants per flat—60 bulbs. Again, steam the soil.

Cooler room and forcing procedures. In general, the same procedure used for pot tulips is used with cut tulips. By the way, the Valentine's Day cut tulip crop is big and important at Bachman's. Says Todd, "Good cut flowers tend to be scarce for Valentine's Day. We rely heavily on cut tulips."

Cut tulips are harvested as Todd says, "With slight color—a bit more color than pot tulips." Cut tulips can be stored two or three days at 33°F. Bachman's stores them horizontally. Some do pull tulips out bulb and all, but Todd feels they get about the same amount of life cutting them.

"Get them to the point-of-sale fast—they are beautiful, but short-lived. Give the customer the joy of watching them open."

Varieties for Valentine's Day at Bachman's are mainly Paul Richter and Trance, "It is a bit short, but a good red color for our use." For late flowering cut tulips, Bachman's uses Golden Melody, Attila, Oxford and Golden Oxford.

Here are cut tulips outdoors in coastal California. The growers are the Brothers brothers.

Crocus

Todd reports strong demand for January and February flowering crocus. The principal varieties they use are Remembrance and Purpurea. "Our crocus are grown mainly five bulbs per 4″ pot."

Cooler forcing regime for crocus. A rough schedule used at Bachman's: For early-flowering (January/February), bulbs are potted and put in a cooler on September 10. Forcing time "often under one week—can be done on carts in any light area."

For late spring (March/April), bulbs are potted and put in a cooler on October 10. Again, a week or less to force.

Harvest date for crocus. Bachman's moves them into the retail shop as soon as the buds' sheaths (not the individual buds) are visible. Again, "Let people enjoy watching them develop."

Pot Hyacinths

The normal pot size at Bachman's is one bulb per 3½″ geranium pot or three bulbs per 5½″ azalea pot for the mass market. For retail shops, five bulbs per 7″ pot.

For forcing hyacinths, Bachman's just takes them out of the cooler, puts them in a warm, sunny area (60°F) on carts—saves greenhouse space. Hyacinths, again, will normally be ready to sell within a week or less of removal from the cooler. Again, keep them watered and ventilated.

Hyacinth varieties. Anna Marie, Carnegie, Delft Blue and Ostara Blue are the main varieties of hyacinths used at Bachman's. "We sell hyacinths with just a little color showing—well before florets open."

Pot hyacinths are colorful, fragrant, delightful!

Daffodils

Two main pot sizes at Bachman's for daffodils: two bulbs per 4½" pot for the mass market—three bulbs per 6" pot for a retail shop.

Cooler procedure for daffodils. For early flowering, daffodil bulbs at Bachman's are potted and put in the cooler on September 10; for later flowering, bulbs are potted and put into the cooler on October 10.

Forcing. Daffodils need more time to force than tulips, normally three or four weeks. Temperature should be maintained at 60°F.

Daffodils go to the retail shop when buds are vertical—before they tip. There should be a slight tip of yellow showing.

Main daffodil varieties. Carlton is the main daffodil variety for 6" pots. Jack Snipe and Tete-a-Tete make excellent 4½" pots.

Retardants

Todd talked A-Rest mainly for height control of tulips. Also, it helps on stem topple with hyacinths—although "we like to solve this problem with better timing and culture." Bachman's uses ½ mg. with 4 oz. of water on a 6" pot tulip to shorten the plant—hyacinths, the same ½ mg. Be sure the pot is moist, and if the mix includes a large percentage of bark or peat, it may take more A-Rest. Try it on a small scale first. And, best of all, select dwarf varieties.

Problems

Too tall or too short tulips. Answer is more or fewer cold days—more days in the cooler mean taller tulips. Plant one week later if they are too tall. Also, of course, variety selection is important.

Bends or crinkles on tulips. This is often the result of overheating during the shipping of bulbs. Over 80° or 85°F often causes this problem.

Split on hyacinths. The flower stalk separates from the plant. Most often this is the result of freezing of bulbs. This can happen after they are potted if they are outdoors and not covered well enough.

Schedules

Paul Richter pot tulip schedule for Valentine's Day forcing
- October 4: Plant date
- November 10: Strong visible root—Benlate Truban
- Shoots developed—Chipco 26019 spray
- January 5: Drop temperature to 35°F
- January 18: Move to 60°F forcing area
- February 10: Bud stage—ready for sale!

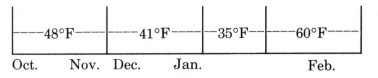

Paul Richter—Red   Optimum Cold—15 Weeks   Forcing Time at 60°F—23 Days

Paul Richter cut tulip schedule for Valentine's Day

- September 14: Plant date
- October 28: Strong visible root—Benlate Truban
- Shoots developed—26019 spray
- January 5: Drop temperature to 35°F
- January 18: Move to 60°F forcing area
- February 10: Bud stage—ready to cut!

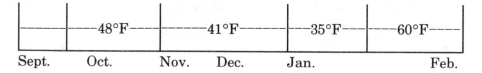

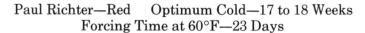

Paul Richter—Red   Optimum Cold—17 to 18 Weeks
Forcing Time at 60°F—23 Days

Table 1. Critical Dates at a Glance

Salable Dates	Dates Bulbs Should Arrive	Potting Dates[2] Temperature After Potting	Temperature, Phase II	Weeks Needed to Force at 60°F
POT TULIPS				
Jan. 5 to 15	Sept. 1	Pot on arrival (Sept. 1 provided you're at 'G-stage'). First 6 weeks at 48°F.	After 6 weeks move to 41°F.	4 weeks
Group I— Early—to flower Jan.-Feb.	Sept. 1	Pot Sept. 1 to Oct. 1. Then 48°F until root formation, approx. 4 to 6 weeks, then to 41°F.	For better vernalization, drop to 41°F on Nov. 10.	3 to 4 weeks for early crops
Group II— Later flowering— March-Easter	Oct. 1	Pot on arrival, put in 48°F cooler.	Drop to 41°F Dec. 10 until forced.	Faster than early crops
TULIPS FOR CUTS[1]				
Valentine's Day crop	Sept. 1	Sept. 15		3 to 4 weeks
Easter crop	Oct. 1	Approx. 20 to 22 weeks prior to Easter depending on variety.		3 to 4 weeks
POT CROCUS				
Jan.-Feb. flowering	Sept. 1	Pot Sept. 10, cooler temperature 48°F 4 weeks, then to 41°F.		1 to 2 weeks
March-April	Oct. 1	Pot Oct. 10, move to cooler temperature 48°F 4 weeks, then 41°F.		1 to 2 weeks

408

Table 1. Critical Dates at a Glance *(continued)*

POT HYACINTH

Valentine's Day crop	Sept. 1	Sept. 15	1 week
Easter crop	Oct. 1	18 to 20 weeks prior to Easter	1 week

[1]Store all cut tulips at 55°F at once upon arrival.

[2]The above dates assume no precooling. If bulbs have been precooled at 48°F for six weeks they must obviously be planted six weeks after the dates that appear here. Precooling is used by growers who do not have refrigerated bulb storage.

Table 2. Rooting Room Temperature Sequence for Pot Tulips

Room 1	Room 2
Early and mid-season varieties flowering through February 14.	Mid-season to late varieties flowering from February 14 to end of season.
48°F to November 10	48°F to December 5
41°F to January 5	41°F to January 5
35°F to finish	35°F to finish

DAFFODIL FORCING—POT AND CUT

by Teresa Aimone
Sluis & Groot
Fort Wayne, Indiana

Daffodils truly are the essence of spring! Their bright golden yellow color as cuts or pot plants is everywhere in February and March.

Pot Daffodils

See the following table for specific temperature schedules for pot bulb forcing.

Forcing temperatures in the greenhouse for potted daffodils are 60° to 62°F. Optimum stem length for pot daffodils ranges from 10″ to 14″. Be sure to check on the response of individual cultivars. A good rule of thumb: When scheduling, always plan your production for seven days prior to the date you want the bulbs to flower. For example: A grower would schedule his daffodils to flower on February 7 for Valentine's Day sales.

Here are height control suggestions from Gus DeHertogh of North Carolina State University:

Apply a 1,000 ppm (3.2 oz./gal.) to 2,000 ppm (6.4 oz./gal.) foliar spray of Florel (ethephon) when leaves or floral stalks are 4″ to 5″ long. Foliage should be dry. If required, use a second application two to three days later. Do not apply if flower bud is visible! The concentration and number of applications varies with cultivars and flowering periods. Bulbs should have received proper cold treatment for given flowering period prior to Florel application. Do not wet foliage for 12 hours after treatment. Florel should be applied in a well-ventilated, 60° to 65°F greenhouse.

Critical Data Summary For Pot and Cut Daffodils

Salable Dates	Dates Bulbs Should Arrive	Potting Dates and Temperatures	Phase II Temperatures	Greenhouse Forcing Time
Pot Daffodils				
Christmas	Late August	Oct. 1. After bulbs arrive in late August, store at 48°F until potting.	41°F until Nov. 1, then 32° to 35°F until Dec. 1.	Bring into green-house three to four weeks prior to sale. Force at 60° to 62°F.
Valentine's Day	Mid-October	Mid-October 48°F until Dec. 1.	48°F until Dec. 1, then 41°F until Jan. 1, then 32° to 35°F until bulbs are brought into the greenhouse for forcing.	Same as above.
March and April flowering	Mid-November	Mid-November 48°F until Dec. 1.	Same as for Valentine's Day. Hold at 32° to 35°F until time for green-house forcing (three to four weeks prior to sale).	Same as above.
Cut Daffodils				
Valentine's Day	Late September	Late September 48°F until Dec. 1.	48°F until Dec. 1, then 41°F until until Jan. 1, then 32° to 35°F until bulbs are brought into the greenhouse for forcing.	Bring into green-house three to four weeks prior to sale. Force at 55°F.
March and April flowering	Oct. 10 to 30 depending on desired flowering date.	Oct. 10 to 30. Hold at 48°F until Dec. 1	Same as above	Same as above.

CABBAGE AND KALE, ORNAMENTAL

by Jim Nau
Ball Seed Company

Annual (Brassica oleracea)*, 7,000 seeds/oz. Germinates in 10 days at 68°F. Cover seed upon sowing to keep light out.*

Gay Heibert with ornamental kale at Heibert's Greenhouses, Sioux Falls, South Dakota. Heibert's are finding a good demand for them. The nice thing about them: They can be set outdoors in the early fall and will be ornamental more or less until Christmas, even in the North.

Ornamental cabbage and kale are often listed under a variety of names in the seed catalogs, but are commonly listed under the "ornamental" heading or as "flowering" cabbage and kale. Regardless of the common name used, it defines a class of vegetables that are used primarily as bedding plants or as garnishes in restaurants. Plants have large leaves, up to 10″ across, in colors of white, red, rose, and pink. These colors intensify and become bolder as the temperatures become cooler. Plants grow to between 10″ and 14″ tall and are most common in the fall garden in the Midwest and South, rather than in the spring. The basic difference between ornamental cabbage and ornamental kale is the leaf shape; cabbage has rounded leaves and kale often has frilled or notched leaves. Both crops can handle repeated light frosts. Plants are edible, but are valued for their ornamental uses instead.

Plants are salable green in the pack with little or no foliage color in 5 to 6 weeks. The primary market is in 5″ and 6″ pots, which are salable in 12 to 14 weeks using one plant per pot. Once seedlings are large enough, transplant them up to their leaves. When ready to shift to 2¼″ pots, plant them deep, covering part of the stem. Grow on at 55 ° to 58 °F once the plants are established in the container, and grow along with other cool weather plants like pansies. Keep in mind that white foliage varieties will color up more quickly than their red-leaved counterparts, sometimes as much as two weeks earlier.

411

In varieties, there are plenty to choose from; the key question is whether or not seed is available. The U.S. ornamental cabbage and kale market has grown faster than the supply of the world's seed, making it difficult at times to get the varieties you want. In ornamental cabbage, the Dynasty and Pigeon series, along with Rose Bouquet, will give you some of the best varieties on the market. Dynasty is available in three separate colors plus a mixture, while the Pigeon series is available in red and white separate colors only; no rose or mixture. Rose Bouquet is a mounded plant that fills out a 6″ pot uniformly. Though only available in one color, this variety is an excellent choice.

In ornamental kale, the Peacock and Feather series have deeply cut leaves on plants that grow uniformly in the container. Both are available in both red and white variegated-leaved varieties. The Emperor series and the Chidori series are available in either red or white separate leaved colors, and have fringed or frilled leaf ends that are not notched like the previous two kale varieties. Regardless of which you choose, you will find excellent performance from these representative varieties.

CALADIUM *(Caladium bicolor)*

by Gary J. Wilfret
University of Florida
Bradenton, Florida

Caladiums, colorful members of the aroid family, are widely grown as pot plants and, during the warmer seasons, as outdoor bedding plants. Caladiums are grown outdoors in the southern states from April through November and in the central and northern sections of the United States from June through August. In climates where night temperatures are below 65°F, caladiums must be started in greenhouses until warm weather arrives. Caladiums originated in the Amazon River Basin of tropical America where environmental conditions exemplify the ideal growing parameters for this crop: high humidity, temperatures above 65°F, ample water and nutrition, and loose, well-drained soil.

Plants are grown from tubers produced on the muck soils of central Florida. Tubers are grouped into grades according to their diameter: Mammoth, 3½″ and larger; Jumbo, 2½″ to 3½″; No. 1, 1½″ to 2½″; and No. 2, 1″ to 1½″. New crop tubers are usually available in late December for Valentine sales. Some specialists, however, store tubers under controlled conditions of 70° to 80°F and 40% to 50% humidity, and can ship tubers through August, although plant vigor decreases with extended storage. Tubers are generally cured for six to eight weeks after digging and prior to shipping from Florida. Tubers which have not been stored for at least six weeks at 70°F will sprout slowly. If tubers cannot be planted as soon as received,

412

Overview of caladiums grown for tuber production in Lake Placid, Florida.

they should be unpacked and stored at 70°F with ample air circulation. Allowing exposure to temperatures below 60°F will cause tubers to have a rubbery texture, display slow sprouting and produce fewer leaves.

There are several ways of starting caladium tubers. They may be planted directly out-of-doors when night temperatures remain above 65°F. They may be started in flowering-sized pots, or they may be started in Jiffy (peat) pots for later transplanting. Some growers start tubers in peat moss beds and transplant into containers as soon as roots are visible. Many growers plant tubers in straight peat moss at 80° to 85°F with high humidity, although many of the commercial peat-vermiculite media produce similar growth and plant quality. Tubers should be planted as deep as possible in the pots (2″ to 3″ of medium covering the tuber), since new roots develop on the upper surface of the tuber. Medium should be moist but not saturated. Containers can be stacked in a pyramid formation and covered with a plastic tarpaulin until first leaf sheaths are visible in 10 to 20 days. If greenhouse space of 80° to 85°F is not available, electric heating cable may be used in a section of bench to provide the necessary soil temperature.

Caladium tubers are similar to a potato tuber in that new growth develops from eyes. Depending on the cultivars, there may be from one to five prominent eyes and numerous small eyes. These larger eyes will produce the first large leaves while the smaller eyes will form later peripheral leaves. With some cultivars it is necessary to carefully remove the large eyes, allowing the secondary eyes to sprout. Be very careful not to cut or damage the small buds surrounding the main bud or eye. This

413

"de-eying" procedure delays marketability up to 10 days, but produces a more compact plant with numerous leaves. A No. 2 tuber will fit easily into a 3″ pot, and one No. 1 tuber or two No. 2 tubers are adequate for a 4″ pot. A "de-eyed" Jumbo, three No. 1s, or five to six No. 2s are required for a 6″ container, and six No. 1s or three Jumbos are needed for a 10″ basket. Mammoth grade tubers produce large exhibition plants and should be used in large containers or in the landscape. Some growers cut tubers into pieces prior to planting to get more uniform growth, but this practice increases the chance of disease problems. Plants should be grown within a 70° to 90 °F temperature range and a light intensity of 2,500 to 5,000 fc. Lower light intensities will cause undesirable stretching of the petioles, oversized leaves and weak plants which become prostrate rather than upright. Higher light intensities can cause color fading and burning of the foliage. Plants should be kept well-watered and can be grown easily using a capillary mat irrigation system. If the primary roots are lost due to inadequate moisture, the plants never regain their optimum floral display. Fertilizer, in a slow release form, can be incorporated in the medium (e.g. 5 lbs./cu. yd. of 14-14-14) or can be applied with weekly solutions of 400 to 500 ppm N-P-K.

Caladiums destined for sale as bedding plants are best started in small containers (3″ to 4″) and sold in these pots as soon as three to four leaves are mature. Some retail growers plant small tubers (No. 2) in a multi-cell pack and sell them as multiple plant units. Temperatures should be maintained above 65 °F during shipping of the finished plants and in the selling areas.

Caladiums grow best with partial shade in outdoor plantings, although some cultivars (e.g. Aaron, Candidum Jr., Carolyn Whorton, Fire Chief, Gingerland, Pink Gem, Rosalie and White Wing) perform well in full sun. They always should be planted in a well-drained location and kept well-watered. Caladium troubles are usually caused by a too dry soil and/or too much light (foliage has a burned look), too low temperatures (tubers grow slowly and erratically), or disease (soft, mushy tubers with brown roots).

Cultivars

There are over 1,500 named cultivars, of which less than 100 are available commercially. Two distinct leaf types are available: fancy and lance. The fancy-leaved cultivars, with their tall, upright growth and large, fleshy heart-shaped leaves, account for 80% to 85% of the market. The lance-leaved cultivars generally have heavier textured, leathery narrow leaves. Plant growth of the lance type is generally more compact, with numerous leaves that do not burn or fade as easily in full sun. Lance cultivars produce smaller tubers and are priced one grade above their actual size, as compared to prices for fancy-leaved cultivars. Leaves of the lance cultivars have a good post-harvest life when cut and placed in water.

Probably 30% of all caladiums used are of the white cultivars Candidum, Candidum Jr. and White Christmas. The following list includes only a few of the many fine cultivars available, but is representative of the biggest selling cultivars for pots and the landscape.

A fine 6" pot caladium,
Florida Sunrise.

Fancy Leaf Cultivars*

White

- **Aaron** (6,D) Large white center with green margins.
- **Candidum** (4,6) White interveins with green veins.
- **Candidum Jr.** (4,6,HB) Similar to Candidums but shorter.
- **June Bride** (6,D) White overlay with finely netted green veins.
- **White Christmas** (4,6) Large white blotches with green veins.

Pink/Rose

- **Carolyn Whorton** (6,D) Rose blotches with red veins.
- **Fannie Munson** (4,6,D) Rose overlay with rose veins.
- **Kathleen** (6,D) Pink center with green margins.

*Code: 4 = 4″ pot; 6 = 6″ pot; HB = hanging basket; D = de-eying a must.

415

- **Pink Beauty** (4,6,D) Pink blotches with pink veins.
- **Rosebud** (4,6) Rose center with green margins.

Red

- **Blaze** (4,6,D) Bronze red with bright red veins.
- **Fire Chief** (4,6,D) Red/rose blotches with red veins.
- **Frieda Hemple** (4,6,HB) Crimson red center with green margins.
- **Postman Joyner** (4,6,D) Dark red with green margins.
- **Tom Tomlinson** (4,6,D) Red blotches with red veins.

Multi-Colored

- **Jubilee** (6,D) White with red spots.
- **White Queen** (4,6,D) White interveins with red veins.

Lance-Leaf Cultivars

- **Gingerland** (4,6,D) White with red spots.
- **Jackie Suthers** (4,6,HB) White with green margins.
- **Miss Muffett** (4,6,HB,D) Chartreuse with red spots.
- **Pink Gem** (4,6,HB) Pink with darker pink veins.
- **Red Frill** (4,6,HB,D) Ruffled red with green margins.
- **Rosalie** (4,6,HB,D) Deep red with dark green margins.
- **White Wing** (4,6,HB,D) White-green with pink overlay.

*Code: 4 = 4″ pot; 6 = 6″ pot; HB = hanging basket; D = de-eying a must.

CALCEOLARIA *(Calceolaria crenatiflora)*

by David W. Niklas
Clackamas Greenhouses, Inc.
Aurora, Oregon

This colorful low-temperature crop is traditionally grown for the spring holidays of Easter and Mother's Day. Calceolarias make excellent 4″ pot plants. Traditional cultivars are dependent on a combination of long days and cool night temperatures to initiate flowering. Some newer cultivars bloom independent of temperature and daylength, and these can be produced for Valentine's Day sales or indeed any holiday or desired bloom time. The best known of these independent varieties are Anytime and Melodie.

When growing the traditional varieties it is important to remember that the shorter the daylength during bud initiation, the cooler the temperatures must be to initiate buds. During the Easter crop bud initiation time (generally December and January), temperatures should be below 50°F for six weeks. Almost all calceolaria grown today are F_1 hybrids.

Calceolaria seed is very small and should be sown on top of a well-pressed germinating media, in the presence of light. The plants need shade as soon as germination occurs, and good air circulation is a must. Germinate the seeds between 60° and 70°F. Transplant the seedlings into 2″ or 2½″ pots or cells as soon as plants are transplantable. Because calceolaria are very fine rooted plants it is very difficult to bypass the intermediate container stage and transplant directly into the final container, as overwatering is hard to eliminate with this procedure.

Potted calceolarias are a popular late winter/ Valentine's Day cool crop.

To produce an Easter crop of 5″ or 6″ pots, sow the seed in early September. Four-inch crops can be sown later as less time is required to reach proper size for flower initiation. Temperatures after transplanting should be maintained at 60° to 63°F night temperature. When plants are well-established in the intermediate container, the plant can be potted into the final container. As crown rot can be a problem, the crown should be above the soil line rather than below. When plants have reached a proper size (approximately as wide as the final container), temperature should be lowered to 50°F for six weeks. After the cool period is completed, return temperature to 60° to 62°F until the crop is finished. Crop time from end of cool period is dependent on daylength. Late Easter and Mother's Day crops will develop in 9 to 10 weeks. Early Easter crops may take 10 to 12 weeks.

For Valentine's Day bloom, use Anytime and Melodie and assume a crop time of 18 to 20 weeks from sow to sell at 60°F constant.

417

Calceolarias are light feeders and subject to salt buildup and chlorosis if over-watered. The pH should be 5.5 to 6 and 100 ppm feed is adequate. Shade all plants at least 50% during bright light periods. In the North, shade is usually required from mid-February until mid- or late-October. Aphids and whitefly are the chief pests and should be monitored constantly.

Common varieties for 6″ plants are Brite and Early Mix, and Glorious Mix, although many special strains are available. For 4″ pots, Anytime and Dwarf Confetti dominate.

CALENDULA

by Jim Nau
Ball Seed Company

Annual (Calendula officinalis), 3,000 seeds/oz. Germinates in 10 days at 70°F. Seed should be covered during germination.

Calendulas are excellent cool weather plants that tolerate light frosts, though the flowers may burn. Most often available in orange or yellow flower colors, additional shades and tones include golden yellow, yellow with dark petal tips, a light yellow often called apricot, plus others. Flowers often grow to a size of 2½″ to 3½″ across on plants that range from 10″ to 28″ tall. Plants re-seed themselves in the garden.

Allow 8 to 10 weeks for green packs, and up to 14 weeks for flowering packs of 32 cells per flat. For 4″ pots give 13 to 15 weeks using one plant per pot. This culture is based on the dwarf varieties like the Bon Bon or Fiesta Gitana series.

In the southern United States allow seven weeks for selling dwarf varieties green in packs, 10 weeks for selling them in flower. Calendulas do well planted from September to April, though their performance isn't reliable in December and January. These plants rarely survive the heat of summer in the South.

The primary varieties used on the market today are the dwarf, double-flowering plants that make excellent 4″ pot plants or edging or border plants. Fiesta Gitana (Gypsy Festival) is available in orange or yellow, or as a mixture of these two plus several other colors. Plants grow to a height of 12″ to 14″ and are one of the more commonly grown varieties.

The Bon Bon series is similar to the Fiesta Gitana series in colors both available and overall plant performance, however, the plants grow to a height of only 8″ to 10″.

In the taller lines, the Pacific Beauty series was well-known for years as the leading variety chosen by cut flower growers and home gardeners for superior outdoor performance. Rarely seen in the U.S. trade today, this series was noted for its superior heat tolerance and large 3″ flowers in colors of yellow, orange, apricot, and cream. Pacific Beauty is still available, but is declining in popularity.

An historical note: George J. Ball Sr. established his seed business in the '30s with his outstanding strains of Ball calendula—then a rather important greenhouse cut flower world-wide.

418

CALLA LILY

by A.A. De Hertogh
North Carolina State University
Raleigh, North Carolina

Calla lilies *(Zantedeschia spp.)* originated in South Africa. The primary sources of calla lilies that are forced either as cut flowers or potted plants are grown in the United States, New Zealand, Israel and The Netherlands. Some are species types, but most are hybrids (see table.)

Species or Cultivar	Production Sources	Flower Color	Foliage Color(s)	Plant* Height(")	Average Minimum Ghse. Temp.	Approx. Days to 1st Flower
Z. aethiopica	Israel, U.S.	white	green	18-22	55°F	70-95
Z. albomaculata	The Netherlands, U.S.	white	spotted	14-18	55°F	60-85
Z. elliottiana	S. France, U.S.	golden yellow	spotted	14-18	60°F	55-80
Z. rehmannii	The Netherlands, U.S.	rosy pink	narrow and green	12-16	55°F	55-85
Z. solfatare	The Netherlands	golden yellow	spotted	14-18	55°F	55-80
Z. hybrid yellow	U.S.	golden yellow	spotted yellow	16-18	55°F	60-80
Z. Galaxy	New Zealand	lavender	spotted	14-16	60°F	55-65
Z. Golden Sun	New Zealand	dark yellow	green	14-16	60°F	55-65

Plant heights in inches without any plant growth regulator.

Unless one has previously forced callas, they should be tried only on a small scale to determine the adaptability of the species and/or cultivar under specific forcing and marketing conditions.

Depending on the locality and growing conditions, calla lilies can be in flower almost all year. However, the major flowering season for greenhouse-grown callas is early winter through late spring. They are also grown outdoors in very mild climates (climatic zones 8 to 11). The flowering rhizomes/tubers are usually sold in three sizes (diameters): 1½" to 1¾", 1¾" to 2" and 2" to 2½" and, from U.S. sources, 2½" and up. *Z. aethiopica* and New Zealand cultivars are available for planting in the fall, while the others are available after December. *Z. aethiopica* can be grown continuously and does not need to rest. The other callas generally have a rest period.

Very little specific information is available on post-harvest handling of calla lilies. After harvest, they are cleaned, inspected, graded and then given 68° to 86°F for seven days. Callas are subsequently stored at 35° to 48°F for the *Z. aethiopica* types and at 48° to 75°F for the colored types, with the lower temperatures generally

419

Golden State Bulb Growers, Watsonville, California, are major and the leading calla bulb producers in the United States. Tom Lukens of Golden State knows them well. He tends to divide callas into two groups: aethiopica *and* spring *(all others, including* albomaculata*). His experience indicated the* Z. aethiopica *likes more moisture and more organic content in its media. The spring group prefers a well-drained media, less than 40% peat and much less moisture. Also,* aethiopica *tends to need a larger pot size. Tom reports that the use of callas across the United States is rising steadily (Golden State has increased production from 1 million to 2.5 million in the past five years). Both pot and cut flower production are increasing and the same for home gardeners' use of them.*

being used if sprouting occurs. It appears that a minimum of six weeks of post-lifting storage is needed before the first planting can be made. Suppliers must inform forcers as to when the rhizomes/tubers were lifted.

On arrival, always check a few rhizomes/tubers to be certain they are free from serious diseases such as soft rots, physical damage, or physiological disorders like chalking. If a large amount of rhizomes/tubers has soft rot, do not try to save the crop. Report the problem to your supplier.

Provided the rhizomes/tubers have had at least six weeks of post-lifting storage, forcers should be prepared to plant rhizomes/tubers as soon as they arrive. If they must be stored, place them at 41° to 65°F.

Calla lilies require a well-drained, pH 6 to 6.5, sterilized planting medium that is fairly high in organic matter. Prior to planting, carefully inspect and discard any diseased rhizomes/tubers.

When callas are forced as cut flowers they are normally grown in pots or Dutch bulb trays so that they can easily be moved in the greenhouse. Generally, they are planted three to an 8½″ pot. It is usually best not to transfer the rhizomes/tubers from pot to pot but to continue growing them in the same pot for several years. For pot plants, use one rhizome or tuber per 5″ pot. It is anticipated that some shorter forcing types will be suitable for 4″ pots. When planting, cover the tubers with 1″ of medium.

When forced as potted plants, they can generally be grown pot to pot until the last two to three weeks, then they may need some spacing. When grown as cut flowers in pots, some spacing is generally needed as the plants come into flower. It will depend on the growth of the foliage and the layout of the greenhouse.

Callas should be forced in a medium to high light intensity (>2,500 fc.) greenhouse. Very low light intensities, especially as the flowers begin to color, can cause fading of some of the colored cultivars. They may need some shading in the summer months. There is no known pronounced photoperiod on flowering of calla lilies, however, short photoperiods can reduce plant heights, and long days (night interruption) can increase plant height.

After planting, water thoroughly. Then keep the planting medium only slightly moist. However, do not allow it to dry out, especially when forcing *Z. aethiopica*.

After planting, start plants at 60° to 65°F. Once the plants begin to sprout, grow white callas at a 55°F night temperature and 65° to 70°F day temperature, and colored callas at 60°F night temperature and 65° to 70°F day temperature. Use a well-ventilated greenhouse.

Calla lilies do not require a heavy fertilization program. Use 200 ppm N of 20-20-20, one to two times per month.

Use a preventive bacterial rot (Erwinia) control program. This is the major disease of callas. Always, inspect the bulbs prior to planting. Occasionally, there are leaf and flower blights and there can be some insect problems, but not many.

There are two disorders that can occur with calla lilies. Chalking has been reported, but the exact causes are not known—mechanical damage and sunburning have been implicated. Also, flower and leaf abnormalities can be caused by the use of excessive gibberellic acid preplant dips.

Zantedeschia aethiopica *pot grown outdoors in the Miami area.*

Although the testing is preliminary, three plant growth regulators have shown promise for calla lilies. Many of the colored callas have shown an increase in the number of flowers produced per rhizome/tuber by using preplant GA3 dips or sprays at 50 to 100 ppm for 10 minutes. Promalin is also being investigated to promote flowering. Extensive trials are needed in this area and none are EPA cleared at the present time. Calla lilies will normally begin flowering about 55 to 95 days after planting.

The flowers should be cut one day prior to pollen shed. If they are to be stored for up to three days, place them dry at 41 °F. Commercial floral preservatives containing sugar and a fungicide are generally advised to reduce stem splitting and rolling.

Market potted plants when the first flower begins to show color. Consumers should be advised to keep plants in coolest area of the home in order to obtain maximum life of the plant. They do, however, need direct sunlight.

CAMPANULA

by Nancy L. Drushal
GrowerTalks magazine

Campanula carpatica **Karl Foerster; family Campanulaceae; common name Karl Foerster Carpathian Harebell.**

The campanula genus consists of about 250 species, mostly long-lived perennials. They range from dwarfish rock garden forms to 5' giants that require support. Flower color is predominantly blue or lavender, but some species are white or pink. Flowers are bell-shaped, hence the Latin name campanula, meaning "little bell."

Campanula carpatica is a perennial that grows to 6", has a neat, moundy form and blue or white flowers. The Karl Foerster (sometimes listed as Karl Forster or Karl Foster) has large blue flowers that cover the entire plant. The cultivar White Clips has smaller white flowers, but is just as floriferous.

These plants are relatively easy to cultivate as flowering pot plants. Cuttings can be rooted in the spring and pots placed outside until brought in for forcing, usually December through February. These dormant roots require 10 to 12 weeks from start of forcing to finished product, both in 4" and 6" pots. Dormant liners can also be purchased and finished in the same time frame.

A well-drained, peat-lite soil mix should be used. When potting up, place plants at original soil level. The soil should be kept moist; do not allow it to dry out! Fertilize with 150 to 200 ppm NPK nutrient solution during the whole forcing period, using clear water every third watering.

Spacing should be pot tight the first three to four weeks, then place 6" pots on 6" centers and 4" pots on 4" centers. Night temperatures should be 63° to 65°F for the first two to three weeks or until foliage is full, then 55° to 58°F until finish.

Campanula carpatica is a long-day plant. Daytime light can be supplemented to 16 hour days of 3,000 fc., or broken night lighting can be implemented. Break nights from 10 p.m. to 2 a.m. with incandescent "mum lighting" at 10 to 20 fc. until buds are fully developed. Treatments should begin 10 days to two weeks after the start of forcing.

If plants are grown outdoors and brought in, they should be given a drench of appropriately labeled fungicides and insecticides immediately. Campanula are not bothered by many disease or insect problems, but if overhead watering is used during forcing botrytis in the crown may occur.

Growth regulators can be applied as follows:

B-Nine: 1 tsp. (85% active ingredient)/gal. of water
Cycocel: 1 oz./gal. of water
A-Rest: 1 oz./gal. of water applied as a spray or drench

These can be applied five to six weeks after planting, usually when the plant has reach ½ to ¾ of desired finished size. It is important to discontinue spraying when plants are blooming, as this will cause spotting on the open flowers.

When preparing plants for shipping, it is important to keep them moist to prevent blooms from inverting. A silver thiosulphate (STS) drench should be applied 10 to 12 days prior to shipping, at a rate of 1 oz./gal. (STS concentration: 40 grams of silver nitrate plus 160 grams sodium-biosulphate/gal.). STS splashed on open flowers will cause spotting.

Campanula does not take well to shipping at temperatures above 80°F, in fact, they will simply rot very quickly enclosed in a box during warm, humid weather. Shipping should be during the bud stage and limited to cool weather or nearby deliveries.

Any unsold pots in the spring can easily be cut back and will flower again in six to eight weeks for a second chance at the cash register.

CARNATION

CARNATIONS FOR CUTS

by Jeff McGrew
Ball Seed Company

Carnation production in the United States has been slowly declining every year since 1980. Although there are a few geographical areas (mostly in California and Colorado) where carnation production is holding on, the overall picture shows decline in virtually all mainland states. Even with this slowdown in U.S. production, the carnation is still a mainstay in the cut flower industry. The large demand for carnations is now being supplied by off-shore producers who can afford to deliver a much cheaper product than American growers. Colombia leads the way in this area, with Mexico, Costa Rica, Ecuador, and a few other South American countries supplying smaller amounts.

In the United States, standard carnations are produced basically in two areas: Colorado, and the Salinas Valley in central, coastal California. Standard carnations demand a more even growing environment than mini or spray types require. Large fluctuations between day and night temperatures will increase flower head splitting and bull heading, which adversely affect the flower quality and price. Therefore, standard types are economically grown in only a very small geographical area.

Miniature or spray carnation types are more tolerant to environmental conditions and, consequently, are extensively produced in areas including coastal California (San Diego to San Francisco), Colorado, Florida, Hawaii, and several other states to support local sales.

Structures

Virtually all carnation production in the United States is under cover, inside some type of greenhouse. Regardless of the structure used, the crop's requirement for cool temperatures and good air flow demands some type of efficient ventilation be present, regardless of the source. Depending on the growing location, production structures can vary from glass to poly to fiberglass to saran.

A typical house of Northern California cut carnations.

424

Planting and Spacing

A rooted cutting is planted into a bed spacing of 6″ to 8″ between plants or 3½ to 4½ plants per sq. ft., depending on where grown and type grown (spray type or standard). Commonly, production beds are 36″ to 42″ wide. Two to four layers of support wire are laid down at the time of planting. Plenty of support is necessary as the crop usually remains in production two to three years and becomes top heavy. The first wire grid is placed about 6″ to 10″ above soil; following grids are spaced 12″ to 18″ apart from the first.

Light and Temperature

Carnations grow best in environments of high light, but cool overall temperatures. Night temperatures of 50° to 55°F and day temperatures of 65° to 75°F, in conjunction with high light levels, are best to produce high quality product. High summer temperatures should be moderated by using any method possible, such as shading, fan and pads, exhaust fans, additional ventilators, etc.

Soil and Nutrition

Carnations are happiest when they are in a well-drained soil that is also high in organic matter (25% to 50%). A poorly aerated soil will quickly cause root problems that can increase susceptibility to other diseases by reducing overall vigor. A pH of 6 to 7 is best.

Carnations are fairly heavy feeders. They require adequate concentrations of calcium, nitrogen and potassium. Phosphorous and micronutrients are required in lesser amounts.

In modern carnation production, the use of drip irrigation is becoming more popular, especially in the water-conscious West. When a carnation is watered or fed, a thorough job should be done, but allow the soil to dry out somewhat between applications (no flagging).

Pinching

Generally, about four weeks after planting rooted cuttings, carnation growers start to pinch the crop. This helps build and develop a plant which will have a good production base or plane. The grower must read the crop and pinch only the plants that are ready; therefore, this procedure may take two to three weeks to fully accomplish. The grower should leave four to six sets of leaves on the plant after the pinch (this depends on variety response, growing environment, and culture practices).

Markets/Varieties

The mini or spray carnation types cost less (no disbudding or taping of splits) and are easier to produce (grow adequately in warmer climates). Minis are also heavily imported into the United States from Latin America, so the market is fairly volatile and occasionally oversupplied. The mixed bouquet industry is using mini types in the mixed bunches, so this has opened up certain marketing niches for some growers.

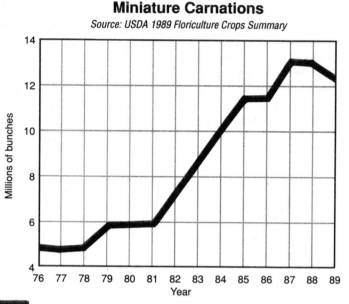

Miniature Carnations
Source: USDA 1989 Floriculture Crops Summary

(y-axis: Millions of bunches, x-axis: Year 76–89)

Here is the mini or spray carnation— widely grown in the United States. No disbudding labor!

Standards (large disbudded flowers) are generally more stable in the marketplace; however, off-shore production has dramatically increased in the last six to eight years and oversupply (low prices) is occurring more often than ever.

In the mid-1980s, several new standard varieties that were bred in southern Europe (the Mediterranean region) have made their way to the marketplace. These Mediterranean varieties (see variety list) have provided help to growers in certain areas: 1) Fusarium tolerance is improved; 2) high percentage of long stems;

426

3) head splitting is reduced considerably (no taping). Because of these positive characteristics, Mediterranean types have taken market share away from the "Sim" varieties, which have accounted for the majority of standard carnation production in the United States for the last 30+ years.

Color trends are changing, especially for spray types. Conventional holiday colors (red and white for Christmas, etc.) are still valid, but consumers are more and more frequently turning to new pastels, bicolors, and generally anything that is new.

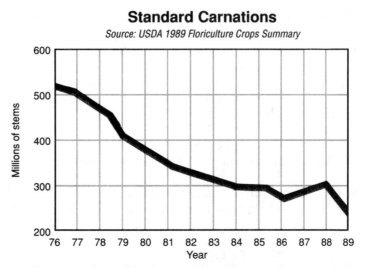

Standard Carnations
Source: USDA 1989 Floriculture Crops Summary

Carnation Varieties for the 1990s

Mini Spray Types	Color
Georgia Ann	White
White Elegance or Shiro	White
Etna	Red
Elsy Londonie	Red
Pink Ministar (several color sports)	Dark Pink
Light Pink Barbi	Light Pink
Improved Lilac	Lilac
Comanche	Purple
Moonlight	Light Yellow
Lemon Star	Yellow
Elegance Types	Variegated
Siri #1	Variegated
Maj Britt	Variegated
Lek's Paquita	Variegated

Standards	Color
Improved White Sim	White
White Candy (Mediterranean type)	Cream White
Flamingo (Sim)	Dark Pink
Nora Barlo II	Pink
Light Pink Candy (Mediterranean type)	Light Pink
Scania 3C (Sim)	Red
Tanga (Mediterranean type)	Red
Vanessa (Mediterranean type)	Purple
Pallas (Mediterranean type)	Yellow (Pink Edge)
Raggio di Sole (Mediterranean type)	Light Orange-Pink Margin
S. Arthur Sim (Sim)	White Background-Red Stripes

427

Disease/Insects

1) *Fusarium oxysporum*—a vascular wilt disease. The most serious carnation disease by far. No controls are available. Use greenhouse sanitation and harvest practices. Sterilize soil. Plant clean cuttings.
2) *Fusarium roseum*—generally a young plant disease. Fungicide drenching helps to control this fusarium type.
3) *Alternaria and stemphyllium*—both foliar leaf spot disease. Several fungicides are effective. Keep foliage dry.
4) *Rhizoctonia*—stem rot. Several fungicides are effective. Don't plant rooted cuttings too deep.
5) *Red spider mites, thrips, aphids*—all can distort and damage growing tips, foliage, and flowers. Conventional controls are possible.

CARNATIONS FOR POTS

by Vic Ball

Pot carnations are attractive, longlasting, flowering pot plants. Great shelflife. I see them regularly in commercial pot ranges—often a bench or two, occasionally a house of them.

There have been problems. First, to grow them from cuttings takes many months. It's slow and expensive. Second, disease problems have driven several propagators out of the crop.

As of the early 1990s, there are several possibilities available to the grower.

- **The Mini Pink carnation** propagated by Bay City Flower Co., Inc., Half Moon Bay, California, is available as roughly 2″ cell pack plants from Ball Seed and other brokers. Crop time is 14 to 16 weeks—not so bad. They can be pot-tight initially, then after eight weeks spaced at 2½ plants/sq. ft. Temperature: 60°F for three weeks, then 50° to 55°F until flowering. They like fairly high light, 4,000 to 8,000 fc.

  The propagator recommends not potting too deep—it may cause rotting. Lesan/Benlate drench as a preventative is recommended. Most commercial mixes with peat moss, fir bark, etc. are okay. At normal light levels no retardant is required. In a low-light situation, B-Nine at 2,500 ppm may be applied.

  A monthly spray with Captan as a general preventative is recommended.

  Pinching is recommended in the early stages of growth—remove developing flower stalks until the desired foliage density is attained. Again, they are showy, longlasting, and have been quite popular for four or five years.

- **Colorado Majestics.** This is the pot carnation from cuttings promoted actively by Ken Goldsberry of Colorado State University, Ft. Collins, Colorado. It is a showy plant. The main problem, again, is the long time required from cuttings to

John and Janet Kister, with their field-grown pot carnations in Fallbrook (coastal), California.

The Lillipot potted carnation.

finished plant. Cuttings are available from Denver Wholesale Florists Co., Denver, Colorado [phone (303) 399-0970]. The Majestics are often grown in 4″ or larger pot sizes.

- **Pot carnations from seed.** There are several interesting candidates here. At least most of them are varieties of dianthus caryophyllus. Seed is rather small, should be chilled for a week or two at 30°F, then kept at 70°F until established. Growing temperature: 50° to 55°F. Again, these pot carnations from seed tend to take four to six months from sowing to sale.

The Knight series is quite popular—lots of fine, large double blooms on a 10″ to 12″ plant. The Lillipot series is more compact, normally less than 10″. Listings and descriptions of these and others are found in current seed catalogs.

CELOSIA

by Jim Nau
Ball Seed Company

Annual (Celosia plumosus and C. cristata), 35,000 seeds/oz. Germinates in eight to 10 days at 80° to 85°F. Seed should be covered during germination.

Celosia are among the best annuals for warm weather color in the garden or as cut flowers. *Celosia plumosus* is characterized by having its flowers held in feather-like plumes that measure from 4″ to 12″ long and come in colors of red, scarlet, gold, cream, and rose. *Celosia cristata* is commonly called Cockscomb due to the tight, semi-rounded flower heads that measure from 4″ to 15″ across. *C. cristata* has the same flower colors as plumosus, and both varieties make excellent fresh and dried cut flowers. Both types have green and bronze leaf varieties, though bronze leaf plants are most often associated with red flowering ones.

In providing cultural suggestions, be advised that growing too cool or planting outdoors too early will cause premature flowering and spoil later performance. If this crop is allowed to flower using one plant per small cell pack (72 cells per flat and smaller), the resulting plants in the garden will be short, small flowering and will die prematurely. If selling in 72 cells per flat, sell the plants green or use 48 cells per flat to sell in colors. Allow seven to nine weeks for green packs and 10 to 12 weeks for flowering packs. Use only dwarf varieties when planning to flower in the pack. Allow 13 weeks for flowering 4″ pots using one plant per pot. If a growth regulator is needed to keep the plants dwarf, A-Rest is registered for use on this crop.

In the southern United States allow seven to nine weeks for green pack sales, and 12 to 13 weeks for 4″ flowering pots. Plant after all danger of frost has passed, until early April. If established before the weather gets hot, celosias will flower until August or September. Among the dwarf varieties, the feather or plume types show good color through mid-July, while crested types continue to display well until August. The taller varieties put on a good show until the first frost.

430

As for varieties, choose carefully for specific uses. The Century series and other upright spreading celosia, as tall as 20″, are ideal for mass plantings, filling in well on 12″ centers. The Centurys hold up longer and their colors shade less than other varieties, placing them among the top performers in the American garden. Smaller, dwarf varieties such as Geisha (10″) and Fairy Fountains Mixture (12″) make excellent border and 4″ pot plants, though the flower colors aren't as vibrant. However, the Castle series offers a medium, upright (but not tall) plant with bright, non-fading colors. Plants grow to no more than 14″ tall. Among the crested types, try the Jewel Box or Olympia series for 4″ pot and pack sales as border plants. Unlike dwarf plumosus types, crested varieties hold their color regardless of height.

For cut flowers or background plants, select taller varieties that hold their color well once cut. Among the feather types, the Century, Feather and Sparkler series are suggested for outstanding performance. Of the three, Century is the shortest, and the Feather series is the latest to flower in the garden. Crested types also make good cut flowers, such as Toreador, a dark red variety, and the Chiefs, an upright series reaching 3′ tall.

A colorful tray of pack celosia ready for the home gardener.

CENTAUREA *(Bachelor Buttons, Cornflower)*

by Jim Nau
Ball Seed Company

Annual** (Centaurea cyanus), **7,000 seeds/oz. Germinates in 10 days at 65°F. Cover seed lightly upon sowing.

Though *C. cyanus* is useful as a bedding plant, its primary market is as a fresh cut flower. Available in pink, white, crimson, and especially blue, cornflowers range in height from 12" to 30" tall, prefer cool weather, and do not tolerate hot, humid summers well at all.

Allow seven to eight weeks for green pack sales, and 9 to 10 weeks for flowering plants. Using two to three plants per 4" pot, allow 10 to 13 weeks to finish off in color. Once established in the packs, give 50° to 55°F night temperatures for several weeks to develop the root ball. If cooler temperatures are not given, the resulting plant and flower will be disappointing and unproductive.

As a cut flower in Florida, and the central coastal and southern regions of California, sow seed directly to the field in September for flowering plants from February to June. In the Eastern and Midwestern states, sow seed in the field from April to mid-May for flowering plants from July to September. Maintain a minimum night temperature of 55°F. In field production, seed sown during June and July will produce a few flowers on short plants, and then die. Plants started under short days and cool weather (i.e. fall and winter) will promote basal branching that elongates when given long days (i.e., mid-spring and summer). At the latitude of

The cornflower is a delightful flower for summer cut flowers and borders.

Cincinnati, Ohio, a September sowing will flower the following June, provided that winter protection is given unless adequate snow cover can be guaranteed.

The most popular variety on the market is Blue Boy, which grows to 3' tall and bears bright blue flowers. Blue Diadem is deeper in color than Blue Boy, but grows to approximately the same height. Snowman is a pure white variety to 2' tall, while Pinkie is a bright pink color on plants to 2' tall. There are some other varieties on the market as well, and the dwarfer ones make excellent 4" pots.

CHRISTMAS CACTUS

by Ed Harthun
Ball Seed Company

Schlumbergera truncata—**Thanksgiving cactus;** *Schlumbergera bridgesii*—**Christmas cactus.**

There is some confusion connected with the nomenclature of *Schlumbergera truncata* and *S. bridgesii,* species of commercial importance. They were formerly known as *zygocactus,* but are now in the genus *Schlumbergera.* The *truncata* blooms naturally in mid- to late-November, while the *bridgesii* blooms naturally in mid-December. The Thanksgiving cactus has sharp points on the margin of the leaves as compared to the smooth, rounded margins of the Christmas cactus.

Propagation is from cuttings rooted at a 70 °F temperature. Cuttings composed of one to three phylloclades should be removed from stock plants at the leaf joints. About three weeks rooting time is required. Plants propagated in December, January and February can be finished in 4" or 4½" pots. A March or April propagation should be finished in 3" or 3½" pots.

Rooted cuttings can be potted from March to May. Liners are usually made up from two rooted cuttings. These are usually potted up using one to a 3" pot and two or three to a 4" pot. Move one 4" pot up to make a 6" pot and three 4s to make a 10" basket. Many retail growers will buy liners in early summer or prefinished material shipped in October and November.

Plants do well in a good light soil mix amended with sand to add weight to the pot. Fertilization should be light, using 200 ppm every two weeks of a 20-10-20 or 15-16-17 analysis. Fertilization should be terminated six to eight weeks prior to bud initiation.

Holiday cactus should be grown under full sunlight through the fall, winter and spring. During vegetative periods of growth 60° to 70°F night temperatures are recommended. Flower bud initiation is brought about by short days or by low temperatures. Short day lengths of 12 hours or less, and temperatures of 59 ° to 68 °F are optimal for bud initiation. Twenty to 25 short days are enough for flower initiation. At a night temperature of 59 °F, flowering will occur 9 to 10 weeks after initiation. It should be pointed out that plants will flower when given night temperatures of 55° to 59 °F under any day length or when given short days under high night temperatures, up to 75 °F.

A growth regulator, benzyl-adenine (BA), has been found to increase bud count up to 40%. This cytokinin is applied at the rate of 100 ppm two weeks after the start of short days. Further research needs to be done on this chemical to better identify proper concentrations for best results.

Shattering has long been a problem with holiday cacti especially if shipped long distances. Causes range from various stresses to ethylene exposure. Silver thiosulfate (STS) has been shown to block the action of ethylene. Apply it two to three weeks before shipping. Spray to run-off with two ounces of STS stock solution per one gallon of water.

The main diseases attacking holiday cacti are Pythium and Phytophtora. These can be controlled with Subdue, Benlate and Banrot.

Caterpillars and fungus gnats are problem pests. Dipel, Resmethrin and Vectobac are effective controls.

Christmas Cheer, Koeniger and Norris are popular red Christmas varieties. Popular Thanksgiving varieties include White Christmas (white), Red Radiance (red), Lavender Doll (light purple), Peach Parfait (peach-red) and Christmas Charm (magenta).

A colorful (scarlet red) house of flowering cactus at the Hans de Vries range in Holland. Hans specializes in the Schlumbergera *Christmas and Thanksgiving cacti. This house is Easter cactus (*Rhipsalidopsis gaetner, *only botanically different from the* Schlumbergeras*).*

CHRYSANTHEMUM

by Vic Ball

BASICS OF CONTROLLED FLOWERING

Underlining the major success of mums the past 20 or 30 years is the fact of controlled flowering. Any mum crop can be forced to flower at any target date anywhere—if the rules are followed. The marketing implications of this are weighty and obvious. Mums today are big worldwide both as cut flowers and pot plants.

All this is based on the fact that mums are a "short day" crop. Simply stated, they will set bud and flower if exposed to a short day. Which of course reflects the way "natural season" or fall mums have been grown for hundreds of years. Here the formation of buds and flowers occurs precisely because the days do naturally shorten in fall. For the record, the researchers who discovered this most important phenomenon were two USDA scientists, Allard and Brown, in 1937. Since then many other crops have been found to be either short day responsive or, in some cases, will flower on long days.

So, in the late 1940s, growers began to force mum crops into flower early by early summer application of black cloth over the beds, typically from 5 p.m. to 8 a.m. Result: An artificial short day (9 hours long), and November varieties now flowered in September. And brought better prices! All of which gradually led to flowering mums, both pot and cut, 52 weeks a year. All by simply controlling length of day.

An interesting note: The short day principle was discovered in 1937. It took 13 years before the commercial trade realized the implications and the potential of the chrysanthemum in light of this new technology.

Need For a Long Day Period

If short days were applied immediately upon planting the new cutting, the crop would immediately go into bud and flower. Result: A pot mum perhaps 6" or 8" tall and a cut mum much the same. Obviously there was a need for, more or less, several weeks of long days immediately upon planting the cutting to allow the plant time to develop enough stem length and substance before flowering.

Response Periods

Again, early in the game, growers and researchers were able to sort out mum varieties according to "response period." Which means simply the number of weeks from the beginning of short day or black cloth application until the crop flowered. So now a typical crop would be planted, given two or three weeks of long days, then perhaps 10 weeks of response period. Result: A crop that took roughly 12 to 13 weeks from plant to flower.

Varieties varied in response period from as little as seven and eight weeks to as long as 14 to 15 weeks. In general, the very early responding varieties (seven and eight weeks) are the garden varieties that flower normally outdoors in September/early October. The great majority of commercial pot and cut mum varieties are nine-week and 10-week responders. These are varieties that naturally flower in early November. There is also a group of 13- to 14-week responders, which are varieties that naturally flower in December. Mainly they were a group of pompons, and formerly they were used importantly for winter flowering controlled crops in Northern greenhouses. Because of certain unreliabilities, they have been replaced largely by new and improved 10- and 11-week varieties for the Northern winter pompon crop.

Schedules for Northern Versus Southern Growers

I've talked mostly scheduling crops for the Northern greenhouse (latitude 40° to 45° north). Typically Northern *winter* pompon crops might need three or even four weeks of long days to develop enough stem and substance during the low light, slow growing, winter period. A grower in the same Northern greenhouse flowering a crop in summer or fall would reduce the number of long days to a week or two—since the crop grows so much faster in the higher light intensities and the longer days of summer and fall.

Another adaptation of this: Deep South growers (and south of the border crops) experience, in effect, high light and longer days year round. Therefore, schedules for these Southern crops year round tend to follow very closely the schedules and even selections of varieties used by Northern growers in summer and early fall.

Once all this basic knowhow was in place, propagators soon developed very complete schedules prescribing a precise number of weeks of long days and short days for crops to flower each week of the year. And schedules were developed for varying degrees of latitude from north to south. And typically these schedules also prescribed certain varieties for each of these crops in each latitude. Such schedules are available in fact to this day—from major propagators. Example: Yoder Brothers, Barberton, Ohio 44203. It's all a very striking example of technology descending upon our industry.

EXACTLY WHAT MAKES THE MUM FLOWER?

I've talked generalities up to now. Next question: Precisely what are the conditions of daylength and other environmental factors that will cause the chrysanthemum to set bud and flower, or to prevent flowering?

The answer unfortunately is not really precise since varieties differ substantially in their response. But some fairly safe ground rules can be laid down.

Let's start with the conditions to make the typical greenhouse pot or cut chrysanthemum variety set bud and flower.

- **Daylength.** Twelve hours or less daylength will cause most varieties to set bud and flower. A few short-day varieties will flower with 12½ hours of daylength. In fact, early researchers such as Kenneth Post pointed out that it's the long night, not the short day, that does it. But the answer comes out the same.

- **Temperature.** Another clear requirement to cause the mum to set bud and flower is temperature—normally stated as 60°F. Again, varieties differ; some will set bud and flower at 55°F, some require even a "warm" 60°F or perhaps 62°F. For most commercial crops of pot plants or cut flower growers maintain 60°F, at least until buds are set.

- **The very early seven- to eight-week sorts.** Some of the earliest of our garden varieties (naturally flowering in late August) and many of the English so called "early mums," which again flower outdoors naturally in late summer, seem to flower more in response to temperature than they do to daylength. If grown quite cool, 50° or 45°F nights, they will remain vegetative. If grown warm, 60° or 65°F, they tend to set bud and flower. In fact, some of the most "responsive" of these varieties will set bud no matter what you do! The Japanese also have a race of mums that are widely used for April and May flowering—without daylength control—which seem to flower more on temperature than on daylength.

How to Prevent Flowering

Now let's describe the conditions that will keep the mum plant vegetative—nonflowering. The heart of it is to maintain a long day which, of course, occurs naturally in Northern summers. To prevent flowering during the short-day fall and winter months it is necessary to supplement natural daylength with artificial light. The rule to remember: Buds will not form as long as the uninterrupted darkness periods are not over seven hours long. Example: In mid-winter assume natural light is from 8 a.m. to 4 p.m. Lights provided from 10 p.m. to 2 a.m. will produce two six-hour periods of darkness, 4 p.m. to 10 p.m. and 2 a.m. to 8 a.m. No buds will occur.

Note also that most varieties of chrysanthemums will simply rosette—make short, spreading growth and no stems or flowers—if temperatures are 50° or even 40°F—too cold.

Intermittent Light

Intermittent light can save a lot of electricity and will do the job. Use the same number of hours per night as with continuous light, but now, during the hours of light, turn lights on only six minutes out of each 30 minute period. In other words, six on, 24 off, then six on, then 24 off, etc. Some growers to be sure, use 12 minutes on, 18 minutes off.

How to Light

	Watt	Spacing	Height Above Soil
One 4' bed	60	every 4'	60"
Two 4' beds (One row of lights)	100	every 6'	60"
Three 4' beds (One row of lights)	150	every 6'	60"

Reflectors must be held up off the bulb. For a 20' wide house, a single row of 300 watt reflector bulbs facing down at a 45° angle, spaced every 10', will do it. Bulbs should be staggered on alternate sides of ventilators—not directly under because of rain damage to bulbs. Figure about 1½ watts/sq. ft. of ground covered. Use flood, not spot bulbs. It takes 10 fc. to prevent bud formation.

On large installations, half the area may be lighted before midnight, half after. This halves the demand cost. 230-volt lines reduce main sizes greatly.

Hours of Light Per Night

Latitude 35° to 40°		Latitude 25° to 30°	
North of Charlotte, North Carolina; Memphis, Tennessee; Bakersfield, California		Miami and Jacksonville, Florida	
June 15 to July 15	0	Dec. 1 to March 31	4
July 15 to July 30	2	April 1 to May 31	3
Aug. 1 to Aug. 31	3	June 1 to July 31	2
Sept. 1 to March 31	4	Aug. 1 to Sept. 30	3
April 1 to May 15	3	Oct. 1 to Nov. 30	4
May 15 to June 15	2		

Light Leakage

There have been cases where light "leaking" onto the crop by accident from some nearby source in effect delayed flowering of a crop. The effect is like heat delay. The tipoff nearly always is the area affected; plants nearest to a window of a nearby home (light shining out at night); or in some cases, lights used on main greenhouse walks by night men; or streetlights.

It is obviously important in year-round flowering to carefully "cage in" light being applied to a bench of young plants. If a bench is being lighted and the benches on either side are not being lighted, then the light must be confined to the one bench by means of sateen curtains, etc. Light that "leaks" to other benches will cause blindness—failure to flower.

438

Daylength Varies With Latitude

As you get near the equator, winter days are longer, and fewer hours of light are needed. In fact, growers in Bogota, Colombia, very close to the equator, find that no buds occur on some varieties even with no lights at all in mid-winter; same in Hawaii on certain varieties. Of course, the natural daylength at the equator is 12 hours year round; at the North Pole, it's zero hours in mid-winter and 24 hours in mid-summer.

Another Point

Speaking of preventing mum flowering, there is one other factor. A mum's proclivity to set bud and flower increases as the stem elongates. Propagators learn from experience that stock plants (beds to produce cuttings) allowed to grow older tend to set buds regardless of daylength. Conversely, the first flush of cuttings from a healthy, soft, succulent stock plant will nearly always be free of buds.

A mum stem physiologically tending toward buds and flowering will first display "strap" leaves (long leaves without notches) up near the growth tip. It is an early warning sign!

SCHEDULES

Here are samples of typical commercial pot plant growing schedules. Most are based on flowerings once a week year round.

				Flowering Dates		
Pot	Pinch	Lighting Periods	Shade	9-Week Variety	10-Week Variety	11-Week Variety
		Jan. 28-			Tall treatment*	
Jan. 28	Feb. 11	Feb. 3	Mar. 15	Apr. 8	Apr. 15	Apr. 22
		Jan. 28-			Medium treatment	
Jan. 28	Feb. 11	Feb. 10	Mar. 15	Apr. 15	Apr. 22	Apr. 29
		Jan. 28-			Short treatment	
Jan. 28	Feb. 11	Feb. 17	Mar. 15	Apr. 22	Apr. 29	May 6

Tall treatment is explained later in this chapter under the heading "Now a Production Plan."

Note that all varieties of the "tall treatment" group are potted January 28 and handled the same. The 9-week variety flowers April 8, the 10-week variety (one week longer response) flowers April 15 and the 11-week April 22. These flowering dates are from a short-day date of February 3. Shading in this case does not start until March 15 because days are naturally short enough until March 15.

Now let's go to the bottom "short treatment." This is a naturally short-growing variety. As mentioned above, these naturally short varieties need several weeks more time to develop strength and substance compared to a naturally tall variety. Therefore, from the same potted date (January 28), the short treatment varieties have a later short-day date (February 17 versus February 3). This is done to allow an extra two weeks from plant until short days—again, to allow the plant to develop more substance. Therefore, the short treatment 10-week variety will *flower* two weeks later than the 10-week tall treatment (April 15 versus April 29).

It's easy to see now why growers try very hard to plant a whole week's pot mums up with the same response group and the same "tall treatment—short treatment" group. It makes life a lot simpler.

For the record, all catalogs designate the pot varieties as tall, medium or short treatment.

Two essential conclusions here: Varieties that naturally grow short need several weeks more long-day time from plant to short days; and in the same way, crops grown during Northern, dark, mid-winter weather also need several more weeks of long days compared to summer or fall crops with high light.

Industry mum catalogs provide year-round schedules—52 flowering crops per year.

ALL ABOUT POT MUMS

Pot mums in the early 1990s are not booming but they are holding their own and are a big and steady part of the U.S. and Canadian pot plant business. Growers consistently complain about depressed prices and profits, but mums are the backbone crop on most pot ranges today.

Part of the success of pot mums is the dramatic rise in supermarket sales of pot plants generally. The pot mum with its long shelf life, bright colors and wide varieties of flower types is #1 among their flowering pot plants. Certainly the nonflorist outlets in total are selling ¾ or more of U.S. pot mums today.

Market the Crop First!

It makes so much sense to thoroughly study your market before you commit to any production. And a good starting point is to realize the wide variety of pot sizes and spacings available to the pot mum grower. All the way from 2" up to 7" and 8", including pinch crops and single stem. Another very important variable is simply your crop spacing. More and more I hear growers talking about growing a crop of pot mums or poinsettias to the "specifications of the buyer." If it's a quality retail shop, a 6" mum may get up to 15" x 15" of space. For a super or discount store wanting a lower price, the spacing will be crowded down and the pot will often go down from 6" to 5" or even 4". And fewer cuttings.

Suggestion 1: Go talk to several of your most promising prospective customers (or present ones); see what they are looking for and what sort of price they are

Norm White, Chesapeake, Virginia, is surely one of America's top quality pot mum growers. Here's Norm in his range of 4½". Close to half the crop is done in these small pots.

willing to pay. Offer them a variety of alternatives—with your pricing. Many or most will welcome this. Talk with experienced seasoned seed house sales people. They have a good grasp of the market, other producers, etc.

I am seeing more each year of a break from the standard 6" pot mum. Some major producers are moving importantly toward 5". Also, the 4" and 4½" mums are clearly coming up. Europe is almost entirely 12 cm. (4¾"). An interesting clue: One major West Coast grower recently has gone almost entirely to 4" poinsettias. In the early 1990s I see major interest in three cuttings per 4½" pot mum and also major production in Europe of 6 cm. (2") pot mums, and test production in the United States is occurring. Mini pot mums! What I'm saying is find your niche in the marketplace. By the way, for a niche story on pot poinsettias see *GrowerTalks*, "Viewpoint," October 1990.

Next suggestion: "Grow" the crop on paper first! A simplified cost forecasting is not that big a job. The objective, of course, is to be sure that for the crop you are planning, the spacing planned and your price, you will produce a fair profit including packing cost, selling cost, all overhead items and shrink. Computers are coming into this planning process. The goal: To be able, with computers, to try different spacings and different prices and quickly compute a net profit on each variable *before* you grow the crop.

441

Carl Blasig, a Hightstown, New Jersey grower with an Easter crop of 4" pot mums. Very even!

About expansion: Often, existing growers plan and build new greenhouse areas without really serious study of where the new product will be sold. The result is often a scramble, selling the product at distressed prices, at least at first, and so often, strained credit relations with suppliers.

An important point: The pot mum crop is potentially 52 crops a year—one each week. Poinsettias and lilies are one crop a year, and that's a big difference. The original, uniform production 52-weeks-a-year programs have given way in most cases to considerable peaking for major holidays. And, in some cases, pot mum production only in season when space availability or the market makes them profitable. A typical year-round grower will often "bump" his weekly average production by three to five times for Easter and Mother's Day.

Now a Production Plan

Having decided what you can produce, and at a profit, the next and very important step is to put your production plan in writing in detail—how many pots, what varieties, how many cuttings and what spacing for each phase of the crop. Most pot mums are grown in a starting climate (70°F and long days) for the first several weeks, then they are moved to final spacing. Some growers practice three spacings, not two. Of course, all this spacing must be carefully coordinated with available space. Again, this is starting to be done by computer.

Important! All this production planning really must be in writing a minimum of six months ahead of plant date. Several reasons:

- The plan is the basis for ordering cuttings from suppliers. Substantial discounts are offered for early orders, and late orders often don't get the desired varieties, especially for holidays.

- The quality profitable growers I talk to normally have a definite commitment from their major customers well in advance of even planting the cuttings.

442

• With six months planning you are in a much better position to plan other crops around space needed for the pot mums.

Such a plan must include varieties, complete schedules, pot size, spacing, date to pot, pinch date (some judgment here), short date and flowering date. Propagators' catalogs have tables providing suggested dates for all of this, also varieties. As you gain experience you'll of course adjust to your own circumstances.

Variety selection is a critical part of planning the crop. It's a point which requires constant communication with your customers. There is a constant stream of new varieties coming onto the market, most of which must be evaluated and some put in your program on a trial basis at least.

Sorting out varieties so that all pots in a planting are in the same response group is very helpful. Propagators classify pot mums as short, medium or tall varieties. The short ones are those which tend to grow short; the tall ones, of course, tend to grow tall. As you would expect, the short varieties are generally given a week or two more of long days, especially for winter flowering, to provide adequate stem length. The tall ones are given a minimum of long days. Commercial growers try very hard to include varieties of the same response group in a given week's flowering, and if at all possible, the same height group. Height of individual varieties can be controlled somewhat by more frequent retardant spray.

It's a lot less work, a lot less detail to watch, if a whole week's crop of pot mums can be grown on the same schedule all the way through! Simpler!

Well over half of the U.S. pot mum crop is sold in supers, discounts and other high-traffic outlets. Here's an example of a West Coast supermarket display. It's well done. I wish they were all so well presented.

443

A well-done Southern California pot mum operation. The grower is Jim May, May Floral Company, and his father Herman.

Finally, a crop well planned is a whole lot more apt to succeed than one thrown together the last minute. I hear growers saying, "Tell my supermarket buyer about that." Major crops of pot mums, especially for the big holidays, are sometimes a last-minute decision and often do succeed, but usually at a real penalty: Cuttings cost more; space is hard for the grower to find, so plants get crowded; you often take whatever varieties are available, and three or four different ones with different scheduling requirements, all of which cost more.

It seems that as the better growers develop a reputation for quality and reliable delivery they seem to find supers and good retailers willing to commit ahead. But you've really got to push for it.

Growing the Crop

Now some of the highlights of growing quality pot mums:

- **Soil mixes.** Most pot mums today are grown in commercial mixes. Some very large growers produce their own, but they are essentially the same ingredients of peat, pine bark, vermiculite, perlite, etc.

- **Irrigation and feeding.** Most pot mums today in the United States and Canada are fed and irrigated with a small tube leading to each pot. The grower can "water" a bench by just turning a valve for a couple of minutes—or even more frequently today, it's done by computerized controls. Dutch growers seem to often use mat irrigation with a thin sheet of perforated poly on top of the mats to prevent algae. It's often tied in with aluminum trays. Many use an "ebb and flow" system where the tray is actually flooded. This provides recirculation of the water and takes the

A good way to manage spaghetti tube irrigation of pot mums: Put one tube in a soda bottle at the far end of the bench. When the "right amount of water" has appeared, turn the water off.

pressure from contamination of ground waters. The irrigation water is used over and over again, normally treated for pH and nutrients between each use.

A word on feeding: Commercial pot mums are nearly always fed with tubes, and with each irrigation. The fertilizer is injected into the irrigation water line with a fertilizer injector. It's simple, nearly labor free. The normal injection level will be 200 ppm of nitrogen and potash, 300 ppm or more on the Northern winter crop. See John Peterson's notes on this point in Chapter 25, and see Chapter 9 on new irrigation concepts.

Last points on watering: water quality. Very hard high-salt water can and often does detract importantly from the quality, flower size, etc., of a mum or any crop. Typically the problem creeps up gradually; the grower isn't really aware of

Photo on the left shows Dutch trays with ebb and flow irrigation on a Danish pot range. Note the many supply lines going from benches down to the tanks. On the right is one of the houses of pot mums under the ebb and flow system. Typical of good ebb and flow culture, the crop was very even.

445

Highly-automated Dutch tray pot mum production at Green Circle Growers, Oberlin, Ohio. The pot mum operation covers about two acres.

it. One interesting way to put your finger on it is to grow a few plants with distilled water from a grocery on the same schedule, etc., as your tap water. The difference might surprise you. A solubridge will give you a definite reading on the salt content of your water supply. See Chapter 20 on fertilization.

Another point on water: temperature. Growers are beginning to realize the major impact of soil temperature on all pot crops, and that cold water will drop soil temperature 20° in a minute or less; so water heaters are appearing.

- **Temperatures.** Most year-round pot mum specialists carry a 63°F typical night temperature, 65°F cloudy days, maybe 70°F sunny days. Growers who have a separate area for starting their crops will typically maintain a warmer night temperature, often 70°F for the first several weeks.

  Where possible, a cooling down at the finish can do wonders for color and quality, maybe gradually dropping off to 55° or 50°F. Before year-round flowering, the mum was always considered a 50°F (night temperature) crop, but in warm, early fall weather, days were often 60°F, 70°F and more.

- **Toning.** Cloy Miller, Yoder Bros., a key figure in the early days of year-round flowering, was a great exponent of toning pot mum crops. Just as buds are starting to form, carry them on the dry side for a week or so. Just let them dry at the edges a bit, but not severely. You'll end up with a bit less flower size, but a lot more keeping quality and substance.

- **Plant a good cutting.** A quality crop must be done the quality way right from the beginning, including starting with a good cutting. Wherever it comes from, it should be a reasonably heavy stem, free of insects and diseases, uniform in caliper and length. Also very important, it must be succulent, not hard and woody. Rooted cuttings should have several ½" to 1" bristly white roots, not a mass of 2" to 3" roots. Roots should be solid, not hollow and tubular.

446

- **Heat delay.** Mums subjected to temperatures well into the 90s°F a week or two or three will typically flower late. In aggravated cases of a month or more of very high temperatures, this can result in a delay of seven to 10 days or even more in flowering, plus excess height. The clue is, of course, first simply a delay in flowering beyond the scheduled date. Also, you'll see "heat delay buds;" the little sepals coming up the side of the buds are curled inward in a very distinctive way. Look for it.

  The answer, in most cases, is evaporative pad cooling. In fact, most production of mums across the United States and Canada today is under pad and fan cooling. Some moderate summer areas such as the Northwest and New England may not need this. Mist cooling as an alternative is appearing especially in our dry Southwest areas.

  One point here: Some varieties are clearly more tolerant of high temperature than others. If you are in a high-temperature-prone area, be sure to lean on the heat tolerant sorts. Your propagator will know them.

- **Low winter light problems.** In areas such as the northern United States and the Northwest, winter quality of the pot mum depreciates seriously, and even worse in areas like Seattle or Cleveland. Depending on the number of cloudy days, I've seen a marked drop in quality as early as late November and December. The late December noon sun, when you can see it at all, rises only a bit above the southern horizon. By early February, as daylength increases, the sun rises higher each noon and cold clear days occur more often; quality starts up again. What to do about it?

  First, be sure the roof is clean and clear. In fact, a double poly roof, so often used today, allows perhaps 8% or 10% less light to get to the crop versus good, clean glass. Glass itself should be kept clean. I so often see summer shade still on the glass in November and December! Fiberglass ranges that have been allowed to deteriorate to a point of serious light loss are not great for winter mums in the North. Or anywhere for that matter. A light meter will often provide shocking news of light loss from even seven- or eight-year-old fiberglass.

  Part of the answer to the problem is to space the plants out a bit further (more light to each leaf), and allow an extra week or 10 days of long days to develop more substance. Another critical point is variety selection. Some varieties perform much better under marginal winter light than others. Again, talk to your salesman.

  Some growers have set up supplemental light programs—high intensity discharge (HID) lights. They deliver on the order of 500 fc. and are most often used during the first several weeks of the crop when many plants can be influenced at low cost. (A light meter is a valuable ally in appraising this sort of problem.) You'll see that 12,000 fc. (mid-day in July) shrink to 1,200 or even 300 fc. on a cloudy December day, and then it's light only six to seven hours versus 13 or 14 in July.

- **Height control:** On pot mums, B-Nine is very widely used and effective in controlling the height of pot mums, especially some varieties in some seasons. For taller varieties flowered in August and September (highest light and tallest plant), growers often make several applications. Dilutions:

2,500 ppm: 0.4 oz. of 85% wettable powder/gal. of water;
5,000 ppm: 0.8 oz. of 85% wettable powder/gal. of water.

The most important point about B-Nine is to be sure not to water the foliage immediately after application—you'll just wash it off. Application on wet foliage is okay. The first application is made normally 10 to 15 days after pinching—or with a minimum of 1″ to 1½″ new growth on new shoots. Applications are often repeated every three weeks and sometimes more often than that. One of the few penalties is the tendency for white varieties to turn cream. B-Nine is a great helper!

To get some idea of how much B-Nine can be applied without problems, I was surprised to find a grower producing single stem Bright Golden Anne in late summer, thanks to heavy B-Nine application. In fact, he applied B-Nine to the crop every Wednesday, from two weeks after pinch until near flowering date. The only casualty was that Cream Yellow Princess Anne would turn a heavy cream yellow. The flowers were huge, the stems short and sturdy. The plants were lovely.

Don't overlook the cool day/warm night approach to height control. It's very effective and inexpensive. See chapter 30 for details.

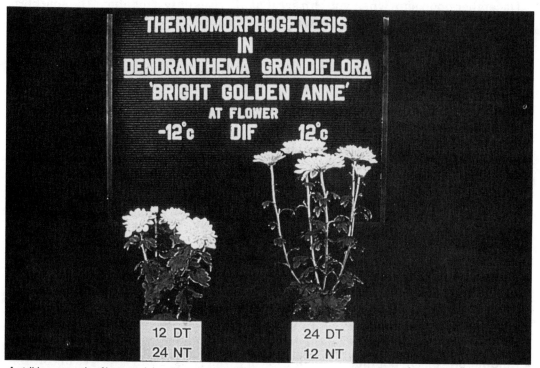

A striking example of how cool days/warm nights (DIF) can control the height of pot mums. The plant on the left was grown at 12°C (54°F) during the day and 24°C (75°F) at night and the plant on the right at reverse temperatures. Photo credit: Michigan State University.

448

These plants demonstrate the impact of B-Nine on pot mums, plus the importance of timing the application. The series was done at Ohio State. Cuttings potted October 8 and pinched October 22. Plant on the left was treated with B-Nine three weeks after pinch. Next right, two weeks after pinch. Next right was treated at time of pinch. And the plant on the extreme right was the untreated check. In the photo: Howard Jones, then an undergraduate of Ohio State, now production manager for Alexander Masson, Linwood, Kansas.

Pot mums too tall? A common problem. Things that can be done about it:

- Reduce the long day period—although most growers like to allow a minimum of one week.
- More applications of B-Nine—three or four times is not uncommon.
- Select shorter growing varieties.
- Less water/fertilizer.
- More light—is the roof glass clean?
- A little more space.

Now, what if plants are too short? Usually a much simpler problem. Mostly add some long days to the schedule; also select medium/tall varieties. Also, less B-Nine. Feed/water more. Are roots okay?

Question: What is the optimum height for pot mums? I've always used the rule of thumb of 12-12: The plant should be 12″ high from the pot rim, 12 open flowers on a plant. Recently though, supermarkets are wanting plants more like 11″ or 10″ from the pot rim.

As of the early 1990s, there are new grade and standard specifications agreed upon by a joint committee from Society of American Florists and Produce Marketing Association. Copies are available from SAF.

- **Crowd plants carefully—for profit:** The more space you give a plant the better the quality—and the lower the profit tends to be. Space costs a lot of money; therefore the pressure is on the grower to crowd plants down. The traditional 14″ x 14″ spacing for four or five cuttings per 6″ mum is giving way a lot these days to 12″ x 13″ or even 12″ x 12″. Or less!

The effect on profit in moving from 14″ x 14″ to 12″ x 12″ is monstrous. In fact, you get 27% more plants on a bench at 12″ x 12″. So pressure is on the grower to be able to crowd the plant down and still produce quality. Same thing, by the way, for poinsettias. So how do you do it?

To restrict height, more use of B-Nine is one obvious answer. Another more difficult response is less water and fertilizer. Another helpful answer is to select varieties that tend to grow more upright: Torch and, somewhat, the Annes. And don't forget the major potential of cool days/warm nights in restricting height of any crops.

Partly it's just a matter of being a good grower; it does take real skill to crowd plants down and still maintain quality—not a deluxe plant, but a somewhat more restricted plant, fewer flowers, but still quality. That's an important distinction.

- **Direct stick?** A few growers today are sticking unrooted cuttings directly into the flowering pot. They are rooted and flowered and sold in the same pot. The saving in time and labor is obvious. The problem: To maintain quality. For one thing, it's much more difficult to grade cuttings effectively at the unrooted stage. The result: Inevitably less uniformity with direct stick. Also, direct stick means the entire house of direct stuck pot mums must be handled as a rooting area. So in winter, 70°F or more soil temperature, and usually mist or an equivalent is needed to keep cuttings turgid until they start to root. Also, a lot more grower skill is needed in gradually withdrawing heat and mist at the right time to prevent softening of the plant.

For all these reasons the great majority of pot mum specialists today either buy rooted cuttings or buy unrooted and root them separately. Cuttings are again graded, but just before potting. If there is any trend here, it would seem really to be away from direct stick. The successful pot mum specialists really have to be quite

A well-done 6″ pot mum. The variety is Independence. In the photo: Sue Forbes, who has managed/typed several Ball RedBook editions.

As of the early 1990s, mini pot mums show much promise. European growers have been doing mini pot poinsettias and other crops for several years. They are just starting in the United States. Here's Yoder's new Fleurette—attractive in a 1¾" pot.

dedicated to quality, and direct stick makes it tougher to do a really top quality job.

Even with potting of rooted cuttings it's very helpful to create a starting area where plants will be grown for the first several weeks after potting. The temperature here is normally 70°F night and day, mist as needed at first, and HID supplemental light is very helpful. And of course, long days. A good starting area can do a lot to get a mum crop off to a quicker start, better quality, less days plant to flower.

- **About disbudding:** Traditionally, pot mums are disbudded. Each one of the eight or 10 or 12 stems is disbudded down, leaving only the top bud to flower. It's costly! I hear 25¢ and more a plant. With the immense pressure on labor cost, growers are looking hard for ways out of this cost. And there seems increasing evidence that the lady who buys the pot mums may not always really want the disbudded plant. For example, daisy pot mums sold today are virtually all not disbudded—and they seem to sell more each year. Removal of the center bud is practiced, but not lateral disbudding. Growers frequently put this job on a piecework basis, but that requires careful followup inspection of the work.

One helpful answer is variety selection. Some varieties will require twice as much or even more time per pot to disbud. The Annes are very fast to disbud, the white Puritan is very slow. The obvious answer is to select varieties that are faster to disbud.

You have to wonder, too, about the possibility of carefully selecting varieties that present themselves best with center bud removal only, and trying *them* on your customers. The Mandalays are a good starting point. I've seen them done

451

Pot Mums

Source: USDA 1989 Floriculture Crops Summary

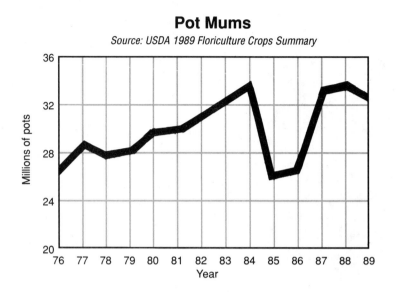

with only center bud removal and they're really a very colorful plant. The Annes are a good example of a variety that must be disbudded.

Watch Yoder's new Fleurette series with tiny, semi-single flowers, and dozens of them; a novel and showy plant, especially three to a 4½″ pot or even better, one cutting in a 2″ pot. Striking and unusual! And no disbudding needed.

- **Single stem pot mums:** Some growers consistently produce perhaps 5% or 10% or 15% of their crop single stem, typically 7″ pots with seven cuttings each. Each cutting is disbudded, grown up to a single flower; there is no pinch. The result, if well done, is of course a very showy plant for which there does seem to be demand, especially among the better retail shops. One of the problems involved is height control, and inevitably more B-Nine applications are used, and shorter varieties are often selected. The May Shoesmith group, white and yellow, are favorites for both their very large flowers and tendency to compact growth.

The question again is whether your market will pay the additional premium in space and cutting required to produce such a plant and still yield a fair level of profit.

An adaptation of this plan is the one cutting per 4″ pot. For years growers have done this, often using Nob Hill varieties. Again, the May Shoesmith family does well in this situation. Somehow it seems to be a favorite ploy of super and discount stores to contract for quantities of white flowers at such holidays as Christmas, then spray them with all sorts of colors and apply gimmick decorations: hearts for Valentine's Day, Santas for Christmas.

452

Two-inch pot mum (mini pots) production in Holland. The grower is Jake Strijbis who does 3 million a year, all Dutch trays, one cutting per pot with a pinch only, no disbud. It's all ebb and flow irrigation. The Dutch find a ready market on the Continent for these smaller pot mums, at rather low prices.

PRESSURES TO MECHANIZE

For several reasons, the U.S. pot mum is under ever-increasing pressure to automate. And there are good reasons:

- It is more or less a year-round crop, not a one-day holiday plant.

- It is a major U.S. crop, one of the two most widely grown.

- Good culture typically requires moving the crop from starting area to final spacing and then to headhouse. Lots of moving costs.

    Considering that moving crops from headhouse to greenhouse for growing, and back to headhouse for shipping, makes up the majority of the labor costs, it's easy to see why U.S. growers are moving toward automated moving of the crop. It's already widely done on Dutch trays for this reason.

    Several possible approaches:

- A full Dutch-tray system which eliminates 90%+ of the labor of moving crops in and out of greenhouses (see Chapter 7).

- Much less expensive, but again a major saving in this moving labor are powered belts. Note particularly in the chapter on belts, Jim Dickerson's operation at Gobles, Michigan, and also the Vander Lugts, Aldershot Greenhouses, Ontario, where the job is again done with belts.

- For the record, Dutch trays are not the province of only very large growers. John Van Bourgondien at Peconic, New York, a three-acre pot geranium grower, already has 25,000-sq.-ft. of Dutch trays and is considering more. He considers it a thoroughly practical way to cut labor costs and, by the way, recirculate his water, thus responding to acute environmental pressures on Long Island.

Growers discussing mechanization respond that the wide variety of crops necessary on most pot ranges preclude efficient mechanization. Several answers: First, many growers could halve the number of crops they grow, buy in a few from other specialists and simply not try to do everything themselves. Also a three or four acre pot range would probably have an acre or two of year-round mum production, which is ample to justify advanced automation.

Mini Pot Sizes Coming

Just coming onto the market in the early 1990s are the new mini pots—from three cuttings per 4½″ mum down to 2″ (6 cm.). They are already widely grown in Europe and are rapidly being developed by commercial pot growers in the United States. Yoder's new Fleurette series, a profusion of tiny, half-inch flowers in a 2″ pot are attractive, easy to grow and are at long last something really different in pot mums. Also, three cuttings per 4½″ is a major innovation in the 4″ pot mum field. They are bringing quite good prices, and growers report them more profitable than one cutting per 4″.

POMPONS

The U.S. production of pompon chrysanthemums is under major pressure especially from Colombia, but it's still a major U.S. crop, especially in California. I still see major production of cut pompons in Holland, even increases. They seem to compete with the very low labor and fuel costs in Colombia by doing a super job of mechanizing—and of quality and marketing. For details on automated Dutch pompons, ask for a video on this subject from *Grower Talks.*

The Colombian crop enters the United States through major "reshipping facilities" mainly in Miami. I hear of some production, by the way, starting in the Encinitas area, 100 miles or so south of San Diego on the Baja Peninsula in Mexico. This production enters the United States through San Diego. Also, there are some developments in pompon production in central Mexico. Then there is the classic Northern retail grower, who in many cases continues to grow pompons for his own retail shop, especially in the summer and fall months. The great point here: they are strictly fresh.

It's important to get a fair price! Which reminds me of a Minnesota grower who had been growing half an acre of year-round greenhouse pompons. He did his cost forecasting well and found that at the present going price he was just not making a profit. He called on a dozen of his key retail accounts, told them frankly that he was going to $3.50 a bunch for his pompons and if they wouldn't support that price he would give them up. To his surprise, they almost unanimously supported the higher price.

Pompon Chrysanthemums

Source: USDA 1989 Floriculture Crops Summary

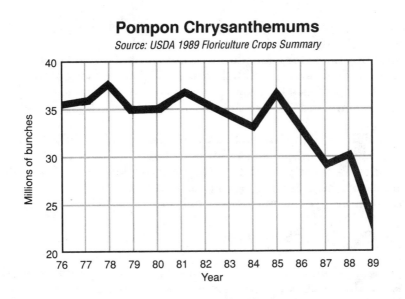

The bottom line of this: before production is committed, there must be a plan to market the crop, including certainly some commitment to handle most of the crop—and certainly with a close feel for likely prices.

And again from all this, there is the importance of projecting all costs and sales. And from this, ensuring a profit—before the commitment is made.

Plan Ahead

It's really critical to plan. I've always felt that a crop planned well in advance of planting time is a lot more apt to be profitable than one thrown together the last

Pompon production in Toronto.

455

minute. The plan (based on a marketing study) must include exactly what varieties and quantities will flower on what dates. And from that, specific planting, pinch (if any) and short day dates for each planting. Certainly it should include spacing the total cuttings needed. Again, published tables (from propagators and brokers) giving suggested schedules for crops in various latitudes are available. Typically they include recommended varieties for each season. Variety selection is so important!

Where specialist cuttings are to be used, propagators typically offer substantial discounts for cuttings ordered six months or more in advance of shipment. And most important of all, the grower gets the varieties he wants if he orders well in advance, otherwise, he gets what nobody else wants.

All of this planning of mum crops is gradually beginning to move to computers.

Year-Round Cut Flower Schedules

Schedules are designed to flower crops at predictable dates. And they are adjusted for dark winter weather versus bright summer or fall weather. Also, typically, cut flower schedules are done on a year-round basis—successive crops that flower one week apart.

Tables provide schedules for flowering each of the 52 weeks of the year, and often there are separate schedules for three or four zones across the United States— from Florida up to the northern United States and Canada, each with different natural daylengths.

Note the table below—similar tables are available for flowering 52 weeks a year in each of four or five daylength zones.

Plant Date[1]	Pinch Date	Modified Date[2]	Lighting Period	Start Shade	Stop Shade[3]	Response Group	Flowering Date
Jan. 7	Jan. 28	Feb. 4	Jan. 17-Mar. 3	Mar. 15	Note 1	10	May 13
Jan. 21	Feb. 11	Feb. 18	Jan. 21-Mar. 10	Mar. 15	Note 1	10	May 20
Jan. 28	Feb. 18	Feb. 25	Jan. 28-Mar. 17	Mar. 18	Note 1	10	May 27
Feb. 11	Mar. 4	Mar. 11	Feb. 11-Mar. 24	Mar. 25	Note 1	10	June 3
Feb. 18	Mar. 11	Mar. 18	Feb. 18-Mar. 31	Apr. 1	Note 1	10	June 10

[1]For single-stem crops, plant cuttings on pinch date.
[2]For crops produced in CO_2 environment or for retail production, use dates in this column.
[3]Stop shade on pompons when buds show color; stop shade on October through May standards when bud is size of a nickel; stop shade on June through September standards when bud is taken.

A Bit on Response Groups

Most commercial pomps are 9- and 10-week varieties, occasionally 8-week, and a few Northern winter crops use a few 11-week varieties. Several other points here:

- It simplifies the growing operation so much if a crop can be planned to include all the same response group: All 9-week varieties or all 10-week varieties. Again, that's 9 or 10 weeks from start of short days to flowering.

456

- Commercial growers are always pushing for faster responding varieties that will still make a quality pompon. A 9-week variety means substantially less total time on the bench than a 10-week. That means less overhead cost for the crop. And that can be the profit! Breeders are striving for these faster responding varieties, still being sure that it will be a quality crop.

- In grouping varieties, growers also strive to combine varieties that take roughly the same number of long-day weeks. A tall, rapid growing variety may well produce a quality crop with one week less of long days than a naturally shorter growing variety. The idea is not to mix the two and, whenever possible, use the naturally taller variety that will make a crop in a week's less time.

- Again, the summer and fall crops in the Northern greenhouse will be typically 8- and 9-week varieties; the winter crop will be 10- and 11-week varieties, often three to five weeks more plant to sell time. In Florida or Southern California, the 8-, 9- and 10-week varieties are used year round (it's really eternal spring in the South and West!).

Pinch Versus Single-Stem Crops

It's done both ways. Typically the quality greenhouse crop is single stem. All Dutch production is done this way, and much of California. The point is that overhead costs are so high under glass that the several weeks time saved on the crop more than offsets the added cost of cuttings for single-stem growing. On the other hand, most of Central and South American crops are pinched and most of Florida crops (cloth houses) are pinched, but not all. The grower striving for quality always tends toward single-stem crops. And the quality grower gets the price. In a soft market, quality pomps sell; the others don't.

Here's the case, again, for projecting cost. If you know your overhead cost per week, and you know the additional total crop time for a pinched crop, and you add the cost of the pinch, you can quickly make a decision based on cost. But there is also the heavy important element of quality involved. The single-stem crop is typically heavier and a better spray.

Where crops are to be pinched (tip pinched out several weeks after planting), the propagators' schedules normally include a pinch date. And the pinch, by the way, should be a soft one, always allowing several new leaf axils (in new soft growth) to provide breaks for the crop.

For the record, a typical "bunch" of pompons for most markets will include a minimum of five stems and weigh about 10 oz. Some retail outlets do like more than five stems. They want these because they can pull them off and use them individually in small arrangements. For tricks to produce longer peduncles see "culture." The opposite of long peduncles is a tight and "clubby" spray, with peduncles perhaps only an inch or two or three long. Not good. This can be partly a varietal problem, by the way.

Growing the Crop

Highlights of good culture:

- **Soil.** Pompons will grow in a variety of soil types! Excellent quality crops are grown in the rather hard clay found in northern California field soils. And equally good crops can be done in peat-lite (peat and vermiculite), which is very light and very porous. The essentials: the soil must drain reasonably well (mums just won't grow in a heavy, wet, poorly drained soil); soluble salt levels must be within reasonable limits, also pH, and the soil must be free of pathogens and soil-borne insects. Acres of pomps are grown in Florida—the typical mix of sand and some humus, and often peat. The typical Northern greenhouse crop will be in local soil with perhaps once-a-year additions of peat moss or other additives to provide better structure.

- **Irrigation/feeding.** These are nearly always mechanized today. You see it done with overhead nozzles, in Florida with "rainbird nozzles" that slowly rotate around a 360° radius. Many of the greenhouse crops are irrigated with plastic lines around the periphery of the bench—nozzles directing the spray toward the crop and not toward the walk. The big thing is to be sure that the job is automated. See Chapter 9 for Roy Larson's notes on mechanical irrigation of bench crops.

  Typically, fertilizer is injected with each irrigation. A normal rate of application would be 200 ppm of nitrogen and potash, which might be raised somewhat higher in winter, and also tends to be higher with very porous nonsoil mixes. See John Peterson's comments on fertilizers in Chapter 25.

- **Insects.** There is a tabulation of the main greenhouse insects and sprays for them in Chapter 14.

- **Temperature for the crop.** The standard rule for pompons is 60°F night temperature and 65°F on cloudy days, at least from planting cuttings until buds appear. The temperature may be and often is lowered gradually to 55° or 50°F as color appears—both to conserve fuel and to improve quality and color. Sunny temperature perhaps 70°F. Nearly all commercial varieties will set buds uniformly at 60°F minimum night temperature; a few prefer "warm side" (62° or 63°F). Some will set buds at 57° or even 55°F, but not many of the good ones. Grown too cool, the plant will "rosette" (make short clusters of leaves down near the ground). Crops grown much above 60°F (especially under low winter light conditions) will be drawn, thin, poor quality.

  In areas where mid-summer temperatures can go to 90° or 95°F, heat delay may be encountered. Buds will form but will fail to develop. Again, you'll see the little "heat bud"—a bud surrounded by stipules or little ridges that curl up around the bud; they will be concave-shaped. The only answer is pad/fan cooling, which is in fact widely used by mum growers in most areas where summer temperatures soar.

  Somewhat, the crop "remembers." Example: High day temperatures up to 75° to 80°F may offset night temperatures below 60°F. Even cuttings grown under

Leen Middelburg with his highly automated pompon production in Holland. There is very little hand labor in the crop. Harvesting, stripping and bunching is nearly all automated. The Dutch compete effectively with Bogota pompons done with very cheap labor.

An example of how well organized pompon production is in Holland. After the crop is finished, this tiller plows the bench up in minutes. It's a contract deal. This fellow plows beds for many growers.

high temperature tend to flower better at marginally cool temperatures. Ken Post, the great Cornell scientist, used to say, "The mum remembers."

Lastly, it's interesting to remember that the mum was originally a natural season crop, which meant planting and "long day" periods occurred during mid-summer (warm temperatures and long days). Then as fall approached, day length shortened and temperatures were typically maintained at 50°F until flowering. But normally, buds had been set during August/September during warm temperature and shortening days.

- **Winter crops—low light.** Substantial commercial crops of pomps are grown under Northern winter conditions, and that typically means low light. The best example is the Dutch crop, grown at 53° north latitude, equal to our Hudson Bay. There a winter day is short, with lots of cloudy weather. A truly low-light crop, which demands important changes in handling the crop.

First, certainly be sure that all possible available light gets to the crop. No place here for dirty glass or glass with summer shade still on the roof.

Next point, carefully select varieties—some will do better during dark mid-winter weather than others.

Third point: Extend the long day period, in effect giving the crop several weeks more total time from plant to flower. This allows time to develop a quality pompon even though light is sharply reduced.

And lastly, wider spacing is commonly practiced under such conditions. And by the way, crop irrigation must be carefully controlled. Don't overwater under

459

such conditions, especially on the ground. It may be weeks between waterings in mid-winter in Cleveland!

As mentioned before, these winter crops are typically done with 10- and 11-week varieties.

On selection of varieties: since varieties change so rapidly, specific varieties for each period of the year aren't recommended. Again, major propagators and broker catalog recommendations are updated annually and are the best source of information for the grower.

Other Cultural Points

- **Retardants on pompons.** The Dutch growers especially commonly use B-Nine on pompons. The application is made mostly on winter crops as it improves spray formation.

- **Clubby spray.** Again, the problem of short peduncles. Perhaps 1" or 2" long rather than the 8" or 10" that retailers love. It's partly a matter of variety, and is certainly always aggravated by cold, dark winter weather. However, there is also a daylength manipulation that can help. In effect, you inject a 10-day, long day period into the crop. Let's say the normal day to start short days would be February 1. You would start short days actually 10 days earlier (January 20), continue short days for 10 days, then inject a 10-day long day period into the crop schedule. After that (February 10) go back to short days to flower.

- **Crop too tall/too short?** If a pompon crop flowers out normally, good quality, but more than 3½' to 4' tall, it's a good sign that for the conditions of that crop the long day period was excessive. In other words, the same crop grown next year could be cut down to correct total height by reducing a week or perhaps two weeks of long days—with an important economy in cost. Of course, crops where bud development is delayed by excessive heat or excessive air pollution may stretch in height and perhaps never will flower. That's a different story.

  Pompon crops that flower too short and are still good quality indicate an insufficient long day period. For the same crop next year add another week of long days. If there are obvious quality problems in the crop, it may be an excessively wet heavy soil, nematode or other soil-borne insect problems, high salts, etc. And of course variety selection influences the height of the crop importantly!

- **Recommended spacing.** Spacing will vary with the season, especially in Northern areas. Winter pompons in the Midwest are typically grown (single stem) at 5" x 6". The same crop now flowered in August or September will be grown at 4" x 5". Pinched crops are adjusted accordingly. The pinched crops are often pruned to several stems per plant, typically one extra stem on the outside row. I often see growers completely omit the center row on a bench of Northern winter pompons or mums. The quality problems are worse in the center. By removing this row it gives the several center rows a lot more light.

  Spacing is one way growers can adapt their crop to a market that frankly

460

wants a little less quality, or conversely a quality retail shop that does want better pompons.

- **Plant a good cutting.** As with the bedding grower using good seed, starting with a good cutting is one of the basics to producing a good crop. And of course good cuttings aren't cheap. But planting a crop with cuttings that are hard, uneven, tending to bud prematurely, etc., is starting the job with a penalty, and worst of all, insect and disease problems.

   As always, there are few bargains here.

STANDARD MUMS

This is the football mum! Showy, large 5″ and 6″ blooms, great for large basket designs, wearing to football games, etc., they have been a major crop for years. However, demand has been steadily down in recent years. It's still a big crop, but apparently the very large flowers are just not what fits today's tastes.

Plan the Crop

Just as with pompons, so much can be gained by planning a crop well in advance of planting date—at least six months. You gain so much in so many ways, perhaps most of all in planning of your space requirements, fitting the mums into other crop rotations. And certainly, do a cost forecast before you commit the crop.

Growing the Crop

Many of the cultural details are identical to the preceding section on pompons. The Northern winter crop, however, is tough. Standard mums, perhaps even more than pompons, suffer in quality with the very short days and cloudy weather of the Northern winter. How do you maintain reasonable quality under these conditions?

Regional Crops

Just a bit on the way the crop is done in the principal producing areas:

- **Northern California.** Here it's almost entirely a greenhouse crop, often under poly, sometimes fiberglass or glass. There has been and still is a little of cloth house standards and pompons in summer and early fall in the West.

- **Florida.** Good looking standard mums are grown year round under saran mesh (outdoors) in Florida. You typically see heavy fungicide spray on the crop, but, with any sort of luck, growers seem to do quite well with them. The flower tends to be a bit soft and doesn't stand shipping to the Northern market. These are used mostly locally, whereas California is a "ship back East" crop.

Standard mums in the Northern greenhouse. It's a fine crop at Frank Clesen & Sons Greenhouse, South Elgin, Illinois.

- **Northern greenhouses.** Here it's under glass; sometimes wholesale specialists, sometimes retail growers or smaller—mid-size growers supplying a local group of retailers directly.

- **Bogota.** It's nearly all under poly here. Interestingly, some varieties really don't need black cloth shading, the natural daylength is so near the short day requirement that some varieties, even in summer, will make it without black cloth shade. The Bogota crop is of course shipped almost entirely to the U.S. market, with apparently mixed success. The standard mum doesn't ship as well as the pompon, and having to go through several "forwarding points" doesn't help the quality either. Result: locally grown standards often have an important advantage over the South American crop.

GARDEN MUMS *(Hardy Mums)*

by Bill Hamilton
Ball Seed Company

The term "garden mums" applies to mum varieties that will flower naturally in most parts of the United States early enough in the fall to be showy well before the first heavy frost. This contrasts with most commercial varieties, which bloom naturally late in October and early November and hence would be nipped long before flowering in most parts of the United States. The term "hardy" has been abandoned by most suppliers—not many pot flowering and cut flower varieties are indeed very "hardy"—the hardiness of garden mum varieties may vary significantly from one part of the country to another and from season to season.

Garden mums are selected for plant habit and flower characteristics second to earliness. The term "cushion" indicates plant habit forming a rounded 180° mound

462

Garden mums Cadillac style! The grower is Gordon Tyrrell, who, with his two able daughters, operates Springbank Greenhouses, Mississauga, Ontario, Canada. Cuttings for this fine plant were received June 1, potted one per 3½", then in late June potted one per 11" fiber pot. No short days. Two pinches. The photo taken in early October. They sold out (fall 1990) at $9.99 (U.S.) retail.

when the plant is grown in an uncrowded full-sun location. Read variety descriptions thoroughly; on occasion the word cushion is part of the name of a variety that has quite another habit.

The contrast to cushion habit is upright habit, describing a plant that displays a stiff vertical character. Semi-upright describes varieties that appear less formal in habit but have a marked vertical character. The growers' variety lists have completely eliminated varieties with tall heights in all habits. If grown in the open, garden mums are selected to be self-supporting.

Flower color, type and size are important aspects of garden mum variety selections. Mostly small, ¾" to 2" flowers are the rule; a few varieties bear flowers up to 5" in diameter. Generally these large flowers are not as durable in the outdoor environment. A full range of flower types is available, but the varieties with a hard texture—heavier, fleshier, stiff petals—are more durable and survive the breeders' selection process. Vivid colors dominate the scene, ranging from pure white through the full range of mum colors to the darkest, nearly black-red shades. Resistance to fading is seen in many of the more recent garden mum introductions.

For the grower, garden mums offer two main growing seasons—spring and fall. For spring sales, one cutting per 3″ to 4½″ pot is flowered for sale from early February in the South and West through May in the North. This crop may be grown under one of two production techniques.

No Lights/No Shade

For flowering up until Mother's Day, cuttings are planted, pinched seven to 10 days after planting and require no more than general growing care until maturity. A selection of 15 to 20 varieties will flower over a two to three week period, not all precisely on one date. This growing technique can be practiced from about September 15 planting through March 15 planting in the North. Not all varieties listed are suitable for this type of production; read variety descriptions carefully. The classic crop is potted March 1, no shade no light, and 60°F to flower early May.

Light and Shade

Garden mums can be and are often flowered any week of the year using this technique—just as are any other chrysanthemums. Four hours of light in the middle of the night are provided beginning when the plants are potted. The following schedule is suggested for mid-late winter growing:

- **Short treatment varieties:** Three weeks of light, pinch two weeks after potting.
- **Medium treatment varieties:** Two weeks of light, pinch two weeks after potting.
- **Tall treatment varieties:** One week of light, pinch two weeks after potting.

Almost all varieties accommodate this type of production; again, read variety descriptions. The ultimate retail customer takes home a flowering plant to use for decoration indoors or out. This plant, when past its prime, can be planted in the garden (cut back to just lower foliage) and it will produce a full-sized garden mum for natural fall flowering. The advantage to flowered sales is that the customer sees "in the flesh" the variety purchased.

Also for spring sales, vegetative plants sold with a color variety label are growing in popularity. This crop is timed to be marketed with the big push of the bedding plant season—with tomatoes, impatiens, begonias and the like. Cuttings are planted in single plastic pots, A-18s or A-24s; the larger size cell packs; AC4-8s or AC2-12s; or equivalent containers. For best results these plants should be placed where they will receive three hours of light in the middle of each night from planting until sale. They are ready for sale when breaks are ¾″ long or longer. If sales are slow, a second pinch can be made two to three weeks after the first. B-Nine will be helpful to control growth.

464

Fall Sales

These plants are in flower or at least showing color when sold. In some areas fall sales begin the first of August and run until frost. In the most favored climate areas, flowered garden mums are still selling in December for quick color effect.

August flowering plants are grown in containers, one plant per 4½″ on the small end to several plants double-pinched in an 8″ nursery container at the larger end. This crop can be precisely timed using the variety response information to develop a schedule and black cloth. For example, a crop of seven-week medium-treatment varieties to flower for August 10 should go under black cloth June 20. Production scheduling prior to black cloth can vary depending on the type of crop desired. See the following table for guidelines and comparisons.

Seven-Week Varieties for Flowering August 10

Type of Plant	Black Cloth Shade	Last Pinch	First Pinch	Plant Date
4½″—1 plant/pot	6/22	6/22	—	6/8
6 to 6½″—1 plant/pot	6/22	6/22	6/1 to 6/8	5/18 to 5/25
7 to 8″—1 plant/pot	6/22	6/22	6/1 to 6/8	5/18 to 5/25
7 to 8″—3 to 5 plants/pot	6/22	6/22	—	6/8
7 to 8″—3 plants/pot	6/22	6/22	6/1	5/18

This schedule can move easily forward and backward in the calendar. Shade one week later for six-week varieties, i.e. June 29, and one week earlier for eight-week varieties, i.e. June 15.

A second method of production for fall sales steps around the use of black cloth shade and employs natural season techniques. Field grown plants fall in this category and should be spaced at least 24″, preferably 30″, in the row, with rows 3′ apart. These plants are dug when color shows, and placed into containers or balled in burlap. This is probably the least used and least effective method for growing and marketing garden mums today. Vastly more popular, container-grown natural-season plants may not be as large as field grown, but without a doubt give the ultimate customer the greatest satisfaction and, at the retail sales point, much less grief. Container plants should be pinched the last time July 15 to July 20. This can be the only pinch if multiple plants per container are used, three to five plants per 7½″ to 8″ container. For two-pinch plants, allow two to three weeks from first pinch to last pinch, and in either case receive cuttings and start plants two weeks before first pinch.

	Last Pinch	First Pinch	Plant
1 plant/container—double pinch	7/15 to 7/20	6/22 to 6/29	6/8
3 plants/container—single pinch	7/15 to 7/20	6/29	6/15

465

Another natural season method for smaller pot plants in terms of height and spread is known as "fast crop." Cuttings are planted 7/20 to 7/25 and allowed to grow without pinch, shade cloth, lights or other manipulation. The result is a free-breaking plant flowering six to eight weeks from plant date, and ideal for quick sale, spot-of-color markets in late September and October. Not all varieties respond well; avoid taller ones and eight-week varieties.

About Culture

Here are some general garden mum cultural comments that apply to all techniques suggested above. Garden mums in the first three to four weeks of production should always enjoy a minimum 60°F night temperature. When the season allows for a cooler finish it will enhance flower color and shelf life. Avoid below 40°F to keep foliage color green. Garden mums respond to well-drained production media and a regular, balanced fertilizer program. They should be fertilized until they are sold, as long as some crop toning is practiced the last two weeks of the crop.

Generally, garden mums don't require any bud removal to improve habit. Neither are there important varieties in the trade that require disbudding.

The first two to three weeks after planting are very important to the crop. Warm growing temperatures, full sun, CO_2 if available, thorough irrigation practices, and regular liquid fertilization are all important. I suggest for crops that are to be grown single plants in 6" or larger containers that the cuttings be established in Jiffy-Pots or 32-cell packs, pinched there and grown until breaks are ¾" to 1" long, then placed in the finished container. This provides a much easier to maintain starting environment and may double the number of breaks on your crop. Depending on your work schedule, it may allow the more labor intensive part of the job at an easier scheduled time.

If a garden mum crop numbers more than a few plants, mechanical watering is important. Mechanical watering will do a consistently good job plant to plant, minimize labor and enhance crop management. Fertilizer should be a minimum of 200 ppm nitrogen and potassium each watering, with one leaching per week in media with mineral soils. Rates can range as high as 250 ppm nitrogen and potash in mixes of mostly peat, bark or peat and bark combinations.

B-Nine is an effective growth retardant for garden mums, and contributes to growing a well-tailored crop. The standard rate of 2,500 ppm is minimum strength. Experience may dictate that 3,750 ppm or even 5,000 ppm may be necessary in your growing environment. The first application may be three to five days after planting or after the first breaks are ¾" long. A second application two weeks later is suggested for all but field grown crops, and a third application may be appropriate (see elsewhere in this chapter for general B-Nine comments).

Sales aids are effective with garden mums, especially the green vegetative ones in spring. Major suppliers ship color variety labels for a small additional charge at the time the cuttings are shipped. Insert the labels as you plant and make one job of it.

A word about garden mum sources: The major mum propagators produce garden mums on a year-round basis for orders received 19 weeks before ship date. Their stock management techniques strive to produce soft vegetative cuttings for weekly harvesting. The variety list of these producers ranges from 50 to 60 varieties selected for their adaptability to this type of cutting production and to the two main garden mum production seasons addressed here. In addition, there are a number of garden mum propagators who address a narrower segment of the wholesale growing industry and often address retail customers. These producers may rely more heavily on seasonal climatic variations for stock management, may carry a much longer and broader list of varieties and deal in smaller quantities.

Garden mums are much used for early May flowering—no light, no shade. Colorful!

Best Varieties

by Ed Higgins
Yoder Brothers Inc.
Barberton, Ohio

Best Spring Flowering Garden Mum Varieties

White	Yellow	Pink	Bronze	Red
Ballerina	Allure	Debonair	Ginger	Bravo
Frolic	Donna	Grenadine	Grace	Minngopher
Illusion	Goldmine	Naomi	Remarkable	Red
Nicole	Jessica	Stardom	Sarah	Remarkable
Tolima	Target	Tinkerbell	Triumph	

467

Best Summer Flowering Garden Mum Varieties
For Black Cloth (Shaded) Programs

White	Yellow	Pink	Bronze	Red
Encore	Allure	Debonair	Bandit	Bravo
Frolic	Donna	Naomi	Minnautumn	Buckeye
Illusion	Goldmine	Stardom	Remarkable	Minngopher
Nicole	Jessica	Stargazer	Sandy	Red
Tolima	Target	Sundoro	Triumph	Remarkable

Best Garden Mums for Fall Container Programs

White	Yellow	Pink	Bronze	Red
Encore	Donna	Debonair	Ginger	Bravo
Frolic	Goldmine	Grenadine	Grace	Minngopher
Hekla	Jessica	Naomi	Minnautumn	Red
Nicole	Legend	Stardom	Sandy	Remarkable
Tolima	Target	Sundoro	Triumph	

Best Garden Mums for Fall Fast Crops Pot Plants

White	Yellow	Pink	Bronze	Red
Hekla	Donna	Debonair	Dark	Bravo
Illusion	Fortune	Grenadine	Grenadine	Red
Nicole	Jessica	Naomi	Ginger	Remarkable
Tolima	Legend	Stardom	Grace	
White Stardom	Target	Sundoro	Triumph	

CINERARIA

by David W. Niklas
Clackamas Greenhouses Inc.
Aurora, Oregon

Cineraria are colorful pot plants that when properly grown as compact, well-spaced plants can be a profitable addition to winter and early spring sales. Demand is high from January through April, especially for mass markets at Valentine's Day and Easter. Cineraria are traditionally produced in 5″ or 6″ pots, but new compact varieties make excellent 4″ pots that can be highly profitable. Cineraria come in a wide range of colors. Some strains have predominantly solid colors while others have a high percentage of white "eyes." Generally, a high percentage of bicolors are seen as desirable by retailers.

The following schedule is for January to February bloom in the mild winters of the Pacific Northwest. Desired blooming dates and local temperatures during the growing season will necessitate alterations in the schedule. After flower initiation

468

Cineraria is a colorful champion of the spring cool pot crops.

has occurred, a procedure described later, cineraria bloom dates can be controlled by manipulating forcing temperature. Cineraria can tolerate temperatures from 40° to 68°F although temperatures above 63°F should be avoided. At lower temperatures, growth is greatly retarded and care must be taken to avoid overwatering.

Sowing time for 6″ plants is in early August, while 4″ plants can be sown two weeks later. Temperatures should be moderate for germination, but prevailing outdoor temperatures often dictate what is obtainable. Seed is small (150,000 seeds /ounce) so select a well-prepared pasteurized media for sowing. Do not cover seed with media, but take steps to maintain high humidity.

As soon as plants are established, transplant to larger cells. This will avoid problems with damping off. Since cineraria are leafy plants, choose at least a 2″ cell. I prefer to use 50 cells or larger to avoid stretching problems. At this stage, temperatures of 60° to 62°F will promote good vegetative growth. Transplanting usually occurs in mid-September. Plants remain in the 50 cells for six to eight weeks, or until between October 15-30. An application of B-Nine at .25% applied as soon as plants are well established will reduce stretch and improve quality.

Between October 15-30, shift plants to the final containers. Keep temperature at 60° to 62°F at night for two weeks to promote rooting, then drop the temperature to between 45° to 55°F for a minimum of four weeks to initiate buds. During this cool period keep plants pot-tight. An additional spray or sprays of B-Nine at .25% should be used to control stretch if necessary. This will depend on pot size grown and variety selected.

In early December, space the plants and raise temperatures to between 60° and 65°F. Early flowering varieties will be 8 to 10 weeks from sale. Lower average temperatures delay flowering, but plants will exhibit less vegetative growth, resulting in more compact plants with less reliance on growth regulators.

469

During December, January, and early February, cineraria can take all the light available. In March and April, shade should be applied to reduce water stress. A sunny day in late January or early February can cause even well-watered cineraria to wilt. Cineraria are light feeders, and too much nitrogen will produce leafy plants that take up too much bench space to be profitable.

Cineraria are subject to the big three insect pests: aphids, whitefly, and thrips. Careful monitoring and a well-thought-out spray rotation are essential for control of all three. Tomato Spotted Wilt Virus spread by thrips has been reported on cineraria, so control of thrips is essential. Verticillium can be a problem in the early stages of the crop, so good sanitation must be maintained. Botrytis and powdery mildew can occur at flowering, but good air movement and cultural practices prevent these problems from occurring.

The following varieties are good for 5″ or 6″ production: Ball Florist Select, Cindy, Dwarf Erfurt, Tourette, Improved Festival, and Venus. For 4″ plants you can use the following: Amigo, Cindy*, Starlet, Dwarf Erfurt* and Cupid.

CLEOME *(Spider flower)*

by Jim Nau
Ball Seed Company

Annual (Cleome Hasslerana, formerly C. spinosa) **14,000 seeds/oz. Germinates in 10 to 12 days at alternating 80°/70°F day/night temperatures. Cover the seed lightly upon sowing.**

Cleome is one of the best old-fashioned annuals still available on the U.S. trade today. Robust plants, from 3′ to 5′ tall and up to 4′ wide, grow without branching for the first 10″ to 12″ and then branch off with three to five developing shoots that will all flower. The primary flower colors include white, rose, and purple, though other colors are known as well. The flower heads grow to 6″ across and often wilt in the afternoon sun, though they fully recover by nightfall. Cleomes have strongly scented foliage that may be overpowering in small, enclosed gardens. Plants also have short, sharp spurs along the stems, similar to thorns.

Cleomes should be sold green using one plant per 4″ pot since the plants may be rather tall by the time they flower. For green pack sales, allow seven to nine weeks and the plants will be 5″ to 8″ tall in the pack. Instruct home gardeners to plant out into the full sun and do not pinch the plants back. If pinched, cleomes often need staking before the season ends. In the southern United States plant from summer or

*Increased B-Nine applications required.

470

early fall until late December. Cleomes have not performed very successfully in the Deep South, including Florida and southern Texas.

In varieties, the Queen series is the only known variety on the market. Rose Queen is a soft rose-pink color, while White Queen (also called Helen Campbell) is a pure white. Both varieties grow to 4' tall, with large blossoms.

Cleome is an excellent background annual. It stands high temperatures and flowers all summer.

COLEUS

by Jim Nau
Ball Seed Company

Annual (Coleus x hybridus), 100,000 seeds/oz. Germinates in 10 days at 70° to 75°F. Seed should be covered with media upon sowing.

Coleus is an annual plant whose beauty lies in its foliage and not in its flowers. It has been one of the more popular bedding and indoor pot plants due to its versatility and ability to take low amounts of light and still put out true, sharp colors in its foliage. However, the market and varieties available have been decreasing for the past five years. Intensity of foliage color, especially important to landscape and garden design, is determined by the amount of light provided. In shaded plantings Wizard Sunset is bright bronze-scarlet, but in full-sun plantings its leaves turn deep, dark red.

For salable, colorful packs allow 9 to 10 weeks, or 12 to 13 weeks for 4" pots, using one plant per pot. In 10" hanging baskets, allow 14 to 16 weeks for five or six plants per pot to fill out and make a mounded habit. Though pinching of the newer varieties is not necessary to encourage branching, some of the older varieties and the vegetative material will branch more freely if pinched. This crop time is based

471

Coleus—Easy, Versatile Plants
Give a Burst of Color in Shade or Partial Sun

VARIETY	Rainbow	Saber	Carefree	Dragon	Fiji	Wizard
LEAF TYPE	Large, heart-shaped	Small, tapered	Small, deeply lobed	Large, moderately lobed	Large, fringed	Large, heart-shaped
HABIT	Vigorous growth	Base-branching. Slow to flower	Dwarf, self branching, very bushy	Vigorous, erect	Bushy and erect	Base-branching, compact
USES	Vigorous garden performance	Packs 4″ pots, baskets, tubs	Packs, 4″ pots, baskets, tubs	Tubs, good garden performance	Tubs, good garden performance	Packs, 4″ pots, baskets, tubs, good garden performance

on the Wizard series; crop times for other varieties, such as Saber or the Carefree or Fiji series, should be increased by one to two weeks since they are somewhat less robust than the Wizards.

In the southern United States allow 8 to 9 weeks for pack sales, and 11 to 13 weeks for 4″ pots. Plant in early spring after all danger of frost has passed. In the garden, coleus do best in the partial shade.

For varieties, selections are largely based on leaf shapes and sizes; see the Ball Seed catalog sketch of various types for more details. Among the large, robust varieties, the Ball Rainbows or Wizards are suggested. The heart-shaped leaves of these two series are some of the largest ones offered. They both grow to a height of 14″ in the garden and fill in quickly. The bushy, compact Carefree series features the smallest leaves, with attractive, deeply curled edges, on plants to 10″. For hanging baskets the Poncho series grows to a height of 12″ and branches freely to create a mounded effect.

COREOPSIS

by Jim Nau
Ball Seed Company

Perennial (Coreopsis Grandiflorum, sometimes *C. lanceolata), 10,000 seeds/oz. Germinates in 9 to 12 days at 65° to 75°F. Cover the seed lightly upon sowing.*

Coreopsis Early Sunrise is a champion perennial. It flowers all summer in hot weather and stays short.

Coreopsis offers single to double flowers of golden yellow on plants that grow from 18″ to 24″ tall. It is a dependable perennial with excellent color that remains stable throughout its flowering period. Flowers can have a slight scent, and are held on upright stems that work well in cut flower arrangements. Flowers are 1¾″ to 2½″ across. In Midwest gardens all coreopsis varieties tend to be short-lived, lasting only three to four seasons. Plants flower in June and July and are hardy to zones four to nine.

Seed is the most common method of propagation, though division can also be done in the spring or fall. If seed of Sunray or Sunburst is sown during winter, plants will not flower profusely the same season. In fact, if sown early February and planted up into cell packs, grown at 50°F nights, plants remain vegetative all the following spring and summer. However, in the case of the newest variety, Early Sunrise, sowings made in March, transplanted to cell packs and grown on at 50°F nights, flower profusely in mid-July until late August.

On most other varieties (with the exception of Early Sunrise) sow seed in July or August for overwintering in gallon containers, one plant per pot. These will flower in the spring of the following year. It is suggested to grow Early Sunrise from seed sown early in the year, as opposed to trying to overwinter this variety. Grow on at 50°F nights.

In varieties, Early Sunrise is the newest member of this family of plants. Early Sunrise grows to 2′ tall with semi-double blooms of golden yellow. Flowers are 2″ across and plants can bloom within 100 days of sowing. Early Sunrise is a 1989 AAS Gold Medal Winner. Sunburst is a vigorous performer to 3′ tall that has a somewhat open, rank habit in the garden. Its flowers are yellow, to 2″ across, with either a single or semi-double appearance. Sunray is an excellent double flowering variety to 2′ tall. It has a tidier habit than Sunburst, with flowers to 2½″ across. It also has some semi-double blossoms as well. Flower color is a rich golden yellow.

CROSSANDRA

by Ed Harthun
Ball Seed Company

Annual (C. infundibuliformis), 4,000 seeds/oz. Germinates in three to four weeks at 80° to 85°F.

Pot crossandra done very well by a Danish specialist, Jens Knebs. They are colorful, long-lasting and quite widely used in Europe.

Crossandra is an unusual and attractive pot plant that came originally from India. Introduced to the American trade by the Ball Company many years ago, it had declined in popularity until a few years ago when it started to make a rapid comeback. It is popular today as a 4″ to 5″ spring and summer flowering pot plant. The plants have glossy, gardenia-like foliage with flower spikes of overlapped, clear salmon-orange florets.

A minimum temperature of 75° to 80 °F is necessary for satisfactory germination, with a minimum of 65 °F nights for growing on. It needs rather rich, well-drained soil, and will flower seven to eight months after it is sown. Germination usually starts 10 to 14 days after sowing and will continue slowly and irregularly over a period of a month. Transplanting, therefore, must be done at intervals as the plants appear and when they are large enough to handle. Use care in transplanting so that the ungerminated seeds will not be disturbed. Light should be between 2,000 to 3,000 fc. for an average day length. Summer growing will require about a 30% shade. Crossandra is an average feeder, requiring about 200 ppm of N, P and K with each irrigation. It will send up flower spikes blooming over a period of time.

There are four other varieties available that are propagated from cuttings and are more cold tolerant than the above. These are Florida Flame, Florida Passion, Florida Summer and Florida Sunset. They should be pinched about two weeks after transplanting. The foliage is not glossy but will turn glossy and dark green when treated with B-Nine at 5,000 ppm when new breaks are 1½″ long following a pinch. A-Rest and Bonzi sprays are also effective. Other cultural factors would be similar to those listed above.

CYCLAMEN *(Cyclamen persicum)*

by Vic Ball

The traditional 15 to 16 month cyclamen crop is history. Sow September, flower January, a year later.

The fine work at the University of Minnesota by Richard Widmer developed a cookbook formula for an 8- to 10-month crop. Seed is now sown early April to flower a full 6″ plant for Christmas/early January. Through a combination of higher temperature, carefully selected varieties, and otherwise optimum culture, Dr. Widmer did cut the crop timing potentially almost in half! This was also demonstrated by crops grown at Cornell under John Seeley.

The big question: How is the crop grown by the real commercial world—as of the early 1990s? There are several answers.

Smaller Retail/Wholesale Growers

In most cases today, such growers will order in well-established specialist-

475

grown 3″ plants—normally received from June until September. They are carried at 55° to 62°F nights. Well grown, such plants will produce quality 6″ plants in flower for Christmas/January sales. Only six months later! The savings in bench time and labor are obvious. Another big plus—the grower avoids the germination and care of these plants through the busy spring months. These specialist-produced plants can come from the East, some from the Midwest, some from California. Typically 2¼″ plants grown in plastic trays, 15 to 18 weeks old, are potted and sold in bloom four to five months later.

Southern growers prefer to receive these 3″ plants after mid-September. Midsummer heat in the South is very tough on cyclamen! One St. Louis grower reports that a 108°F temperature "really destroyed our cyclamen crops." Even Northern growers should use evaporative pad cooling, as high temperatures can delay plants a month.

Why 3″? Several years ago there was much traffic in 4″ prefinished cyclamen. The shift to 3″ seems mainly a matter of major savings in freight cost.

Larger Growers—Sow Your Own

An interesting compromise has developed between Dick Widmer's 7-month crop and the traditional 15- to 16-month way. In fact, the commercial trade growing the crop from seed is typically growing a 10- to 12-month crop; about midway between the old and new. Several Iowa growers report sowings in December/ January to flower 12 months later.

Dick Widmer reports that many Minnesota growers are producing 6″ cyclamen in schedules varying from 10 to 12 months to sell. With good culture, 12 months tends to produce really too big a plant.

Applications of gibberellic acid are becoming fairly common practice among commercial growers. (See later in this section for details.) Conclusion: Cutting the crop time from 15 to 16 months to 11 to 12 months means a full four months less time on the bench. And that's a lot of economy.

Widmer's Basic Rules

What are the key cultural points in reducing all this crop time? Says Dick Widmer:

- Carry correct temperature: From seed sowing (March to early April) until the unfolded-leaf stage (130 days), an honest 68°F. Then, after the unfolded-leaf stage (now late summer), carry 62°F until flowering. Note that the 68°F temperature occurs mainly in spring, summer—little fuel expense.

- Use the right varieties: Some adapt well to faster crops, some don't. Important! The F_1s are more consistent in flowering, earlier, seed more costly. Tosca is fine.

- Media: Also critical. "I like peat. It's consistent."

- Feed: Follow the rules. Too much feed will produce cabbage leaves, few and late flowers. Too little produces a weak plant.

476

How about outdoor culture in summer? Dick Widmer is not in favor. "Too much exposure to disease. If you do go outdoors, plants should be up off the ground and protected from rain by a solid poly sheet to prevent disease. Also, reduce light to a maximum of 4,000 fc. and spray.

"An occasional very hot summer will tend to produce big plants, big leaves, late and fewer flowers."

How About Miniature Cyclamen?

"The Iowa growers use mostly standards. Lots of F_1s."

St. Louis area "mostly standards. The miniatures do make a nice $4\frac{1}{2}''$ to $5''$ plant. Trend seems to be up on them. Those $4''$ miniatures fit in nicely after poinsettias—with primula, calceolaria, etc."

Seven Month 4" Cyclamen—Widmer Plan

by R.E. Widmer, M.C. Stuart, and R.E. Lyons
University of Minnesota
Minneapolis, Minnesota
(adapted from a paper on cyclamen in the University of Minnesota State Bulletin, April, 1983)

First, the following schedule will produce $4''$ plants for Christmas flowering from a May 1 sowing.

May 1: Sow seed about May 1 if you have good bright greenhouses. If you are growing in double polyethylene-covered houses or for late winter bloom, plant production may require a few extra weeks. Germinate the seed in nutrient enriched moss peat (Table 1) or a peat-lite mix, at an air temperature of 68°F, in the dark.

Table 1. Recommended Chemical Additions to Sphagnum Moss Peat for Use in Cyclamen Production

Fertilizer	Grams*/bushel	/Cubic yd.
Ground limestone	200	9.7 lbs.
Magnesium sulfate	20	1.0 lb.
Potassium nitrate	7	5.5 oz.
Superphosphate	12	10.0 oz.
Osmocote (14-14-14)	16	12.5 oz.
Peters Fritted Trace Element Mix	1	.75 oz.

*28.35 grams/oz.

Cover the seeds with $\frac{1}{4}''$ to $\frac{1}{8}''$ of medium, and use a Benlate drench (1 oz./12 gals.) if any mold develops. Strive to obtain fresh seed (no more than one year old) for best germination. Germination of 80% to 90% is usually expected. No one cultivar is consistently highest; sometimes a higher or lower percentage is noted. Remember that seed quality and freshness is not the only factor influencing germination.

Keep the medium surface moist during germination. The containers of germinating seeds are moved from a dark to a humid (80% to 90% RH) shaded greenhouse when about half the seeds have germinated. This must be done promptly to avoid excessive stretching of the cotyledon hypocotyls. With good conditions the move

477

may be made about 28 to 30 days after seeding. Excessive light and/or low humidity levels at this time can result in shriveling and drying of the hypocotyl near the cotyledon; loss of or delay of plant growth by a month usually follows. A less humid (60% to 70% RH) atmosphere is satisfactory after several weeks. Continue at a 68°F night temperature with a maximum light level of 4,000 fc.

September 1: About 120 days after seeding, when the plants average five to six unfolded leaves, they are transferred to 4″ pots. Plant in nutrient-enriched moss peat as was used for seeding. We plant with the top of the "corm" flush with the surface. This practice provided more firmly "anchored" plants and sometimes results in wider spreading plants.

Following potting, the night temperature should be lowered to 62°F to encourage earlier flowering. Temperatures below 60° to 62°F will slow vegetative plant development. Recent Minnesota studies show that in the stage from 6 to 35 unfolded leaves per plant, the air temperature may be lowered to 50° to 52°F (especially nights, weather permitting) provided a 68°F root temperature is maintained, with no delay and sometimes earlier flowering. This regimen may also conserve fuel.

October 1: Flowering is advanced two to five weeks (varying by cultivar) if treated with gibberellic acid (GA3) at this stage. Plants should average 10 unfolded leaves at this time. An application of 8 ml. of a 10 ppm GA3 spray to the crown of the plant can now be recommended for most cultivars. Earlier application may be ineffective and later application may cause undesirable side effects on some cultivars. Growers who have not used the GA3 treatment before would be wise to use it on a limited scale for the first time or when growing a new cultivar. If GA3 is not applied, half or more of the crop may not flower in time for Christmas. When the additional production cost of one extra month in the greenhouse is considered, the benefit of using GA3 is most apparent. In addition to inducing earlier flowering, a much larger number of flowers open within the first two to four weeks of flowering.

Fertilization/Watering

Fertilization should begin within 60 days after sowing the seed, and 30 days after potting in the nutrient enriched moss peat. Quantity required increases with plant size. A constant flow of nutrients is necessary for optimum growth of good quality plants in the minimum time. Leaf size and plant habit can be controlled by the supply of nitrogen and potassium.

Monitor soil analysis readings and combine with plant appearance in order to determine appropriate fertilizer application rates that will encourage sturdy compact plant development. Insufficient nutrients will result in smaller plants and delayed maturity. An excess of nitrogen or potassium or both will result in rank plants with soft large leaves that lack substance. Insufficient light and crowding of plants are also common causes of stretched out, poor quality plants. Phosphorus should also be applied at regular intervals. Phosphorus is not retained as long in soilless media as it is in mineral soils. An application of microelements 60 days after transplanting into 4″ pots is also recommended. Mixing 90% moss peat and 10% loam or clay will slow leaching of nutrients from the growth medium.

We grow our plants on capillary mats covered with black polyethylene film with ¼″ holes at about 1″ intervals. Less leaching occurs, so fertilizer applications must be lowered accordingly, in contrast to top irrigated plants. Occasional watering from above may be desirable to prevent salt buildup in the medium. Mat watering saves time, lowers the frequency of watering required and lessens the likelihood of the development of botrytis crown rot.

Cyclamen sales are increasing on a national scale. Capitalize on this trend by producing quality plants on a fast schedule. Don't limit sales to the Christmas season. Depending on your geographic area, the plants should find a receptive market from early fall to late spring. In some areas summer sales are also practical.

The schedule provided herein can be modified for year-round production purposes. Providing proper culture makes good plant production relatively easy. Careless culture, neglect, or significant modifications of cultural practices will void the advantages of recommendations provided.

Cultivars

Fast crop production requires early-flowering cultivars. Cultivars with compact plant habit and small- to medium-sized leaves are also required. We have found that large-, medium- and small-flowered cyclamen are all suitable for culture in 4″ pots, if they meet the other prerequisites.

Recommended varieties (based on the appraisal of Jan Umstead, Ball Seed Company):

- **Opera series** (named after famous operas). (Pannevis). They are F_1 hybrids, quite large flowers, quite early, very free-flowering. The majority of U.S. cyclamen production is done with this group. Certainly they are adaptable to fast crop schedules. Examples: Boheme, Carmen, etc.

- **Sierra series.** Again, they are F_1s, similar to the Opera series above. Seed supply has been limited. Some variation in color within the straight color varieties.

- **Mirabelle series**—miniatures. The main advantage: more plants per square foot. They do take as long as standards from sow to sell, but closer spacing means less cost—and more plants per square meter. Not widely used in the United States, much more so in Europe.

- **Laser series**—very fragrant! Intermediate flower size and notably earlier flowering. Limited seed availability.

- **New Wave Mixture.** A new group, very large flowered and showy, nice plant, somewhat slower to germinate. Very popular in Germany, not much used in the United States.

Cyclamen Fast Crop Schedules*

Christmas Crop

Procedure or Stage	Pot Size		
	4"	5"	6"
Sow seed	May 1	April 1	March 1
Transfer to greenhouse	May 30	April 30	March 30
1 to 2 true open leaves	July 25	June 25	May 25
Potting	Aug. 30	July 30	June 30
About 6 open leaves	Aug. 30 to Sept. 10	July 30 to Aug. 10	July 10 to July 20
Apply GA (10 open leaves)	Sept. 20 to Oct. 1	Sept. 20	Sept. 20
Salable	Dec. 15	Dec. 15	Dec. 15

Valentine's Day Crop**

Procedure or Stage	Pot Size		
	4"	5"	6"
Sow seed	June 1	May 1	April 1
Transfer to greenhouse	June 30	May 30	April 30
1 to 2 true open leaves	Aug. 25	July 25	June 25
Potting	Sept. 30	Aug. 30	July 30
About 6 open leaves	Sept. 30 to Oct. 10	Aug. 30 to Sept. 10	July 30 to Aug. 10
Apply GA (10 open leaves)	Oct. 20 to 30	Oct. 10 to 20	Oct. 1 to 10
Salable	Feb. 1	Feb. 1	Feb. 1

*Schedules approximate for near optimum growing conditions and may vary somewhat by cultivar and geographic area.

**Slower than Christmas crop because of limited winter light in northern portions of United States.

Gibberellin Use to Accelerate Flowering

by Robert E. Lyons
Virginia Polytechnic and State University
Blacksburg, Virginia
and Richard E. Widmer
University of Minnesota
Minneapolis, Minnesota

The critical stage of cyclamen development for GA3 application occurs when the plants have 10 to 12 unfolded leaves, roughly 150 days after seeding. If the leaf petioles are spread apart and the crown carefully examined at this time, the first three flower buds should barely be visible as "pin heads" in the leaf axils. A full month or more can be shaved from the production schedule if GA3 is applied at this time (Figure 1). As small as they are, these flower buds are indeed receptive to GA, but, be warned, plants treated earlier will either not respond or will do so sporadically. Furthermore, given the wide range of cultivars available, some flowering response variability will likely occur. In general, the GA will enhance flowering by at least two weeks, with little fear of producing excessively long, weak stalks. One may wish to treat a small group of plants from the entire crop and examine cultivar differences the first year. There is also no need to prepare different GA treatment

480

Figure 1: *The effect of a single application of GA applied 150 days after seeding. Plant on right was treated, plant on left is control; both are in 5" pots and possessed similar leaf numbers at first flower. Cultivar is Swan Lake 238 days after seeding.*

concentrations for the F_1 hybrids, as has been done in the past; the treatment described below is universal.

Prepare a 10 ppm GA solution from any commercial source. Be sure to mix well and agitate frequently if the GA source is a wettable powder. Extra solution should not be stored and reused; GA loses its potency once it is diluted. To treat, aim the sprayer nozzle beneath the canopy and apply just enough (5 to 8 mls.) to wet the crown, assuring contact with the flower buds. Avoid the temptation to flood the crown with GA, and, by all means, do not make repeated applications. Research has shown that flower buds become increasingly sensitive to GA as they age, so excessive stretching is almost a certainty with late or repeated treatments. Should this happen the stalks are unable to support the weight of the flowers (Figure 2). Applied GA also enhances leaf development, so early-flowering plants should have a normal complement of foliage.

The GA method for cyclamen flower acceleration has contributed to a seven-month crop for many cultivars, while untreated plants often require four or more additional weeks to reach salable size. GA will not prevent heat delay, but will still enhance flowering relative to the delayed plants.

Figure 2: *The cultivar Swan Lake showing the effects of multiple applications of GA (plant on right) when first applied at 150 days after seeding and repeated at weekly intervals (five times). Both plants are in 5" pots and possessed similar numbers at first flower.*

481

DAHLIA

by Jim Nau
Ball Seed Company

Annual (Dahlia x hybrida), 2,800 seeds/oz. Germinates in five to 10 days at 80° to 85°F. Cover the seed upon sowing.

Though dahlias are available as tubers or seed, the dwarf bedding varieties are the most important in commercial bedding operations since they fit in well with pack and 4″ or 6″ pot growing practices. The tuber varieties, however, are larger flowered and available in more flower colors than their seed propagated cousins. As cut flowers, dahlias should be cut and seared to prevent loss of sap and wilting. The first part of this culture is how to grow from seed; tuber growing comments are provided at the end.

In general, for green packs allow 10 to 11 weeks, or up to 13 weeks for flowering packs. If growing in 4″ pots, use one plant per pot and allow up to 14 weeks to finish in color. B-Nine is registered for use on this crop and can help to tone the plant up

Dahlia Figaro is a colorful and much-used bedding plant that is fine in 4″ containers.

and keep it dwarf. Pinching is not necessary, though a better overall 4″ pot comes from a crop in which the first bud has been removed and secondary flower buds are allowed to show color; otherwise, you will have only one bloom on the plant at a time.

The majority of the varieties on the market from seed are available only in mixes. Some colors in a mixture may be weaker than others, so when most seedlings are ready, transplant them all. The weaker seedlings often develop into strong plants.

In the southern United States allow 9 to 10 weeks for flowering packs, and 12 weeks for flowering 4″ pots, one plant per pot. For best performance, plant after all danger of frost has passed. Dahlias continue to bloom up to September; however, flowers appear sporadically, at best, from July on.

The most popular varieties have double flowers, a dwarf habit and a full color blend in their mixture. Figaro Improved, Rigoletto and Fresco are all mixtures with an excellent color blend and a dwarf habit in packs or pots, and often look similar; especially if grown with B-Nine. The only difference is that Fresco flowers several days later than either of the other two. In the garden however, Rigoletto and Fresco grow to 20″ tall by frost, while Figaro Improved is about 15″ tall. All have double flowers to 3½″ across. In straight colors, the Sunny series is an F_1 hybrid available in red or yellow, with additional colors in development. While this is an outstanding variety with 3″ blossoms on plants that grow to 20″ in the garden, they have been having production problems for several years. Do not rely heavily on their availability until these problems are worked out.

In single-flowering seed dahlias, Dahl Face is a free flowering mixture in the same colors available on the double-flowering varieties. Flowers measure up to 3″ across.

Relative newcomers to the spring flowering pot plant line are the Dutch-grown tuberous rooted dahlias. Forced singly in a 6″ standard pot from tubers, crop time runs from 10 to 13 weeks when grown at 62° to 65°F night temperature. Key to quality production lies in the use of a growth regulator, which must be applied as a drench when shoots are only ¼″ long.

DAISY *(Shasta Daisy)*

by Jim Nau
Ball Seed Company

Perennial (Chrysanthemum x superbum [formerly *C. maximum*]*)*, **15 to 35,000 seeds/oz. Germinates in 9 to 12 days at 65° to 70°F. Cover seed lightly upon sowing.**

One of the backbones of the perennial garden, shasta daisies are some of the best perennials to use when white is a needed color in the garden. Large blooms, from 3″

483

to 4″, appear on plants that flower readily from seed. Plants vary in height from 10″ (Snowlady) to as tall as 48″ (Starburst and Alaska). The flowers have no scent and are most often single, though semi-double flowering varieties are also available. Double-flowering varieties grown from seed are not 100% reliable, nor are the blooms of high quality. Once a seed-grown plant produces a quality, double flower of any merit, it is advised to propagate it vegetatively instead of relying on seed to perpetuate it in the future.

For hardiness, shasta daisies are hardy to USDA zones 5 to 8. In the Midwest, these are most often treated as biennials due to their short life expectancy. Shasta daisies need well-drained soil to avoid winter kill; even then, Midwest winters are generally too severe for plants to last more than two to three seasons. Shasta daisies flower from June to August in the garden, and old blooms need to be removed as they fade to encourage re-bloom.

Growing shasta daisies from seed varies with the variety selected for production. For instance, both Alaska (single flowering white, 4″ blooms on plants to 24″ tall) and Snowlady (single flowering white, 3″ blooms on plants to 10″ tall) will flower from seed when sown before March. Alaska flowers sporadically with a higher profusion of blooms the second year, while Snowlady is an excellent pot plant. Sow Snowlady seed in January and February for flowering pot sales in May. For green packs, sow in early March and sell in May.

Other varieties like Silver Princess, Starburst, and any of the double-flowering varieties on the market will not flower the same year from seed if sown in January. For any of these, sow in the summer for overwintering in quart or gallon containers, and sell green next spring. Plants will flower in June. Growing temperatures should be 55° to 60°F.

From vegetative production, consider the double-flowering varieties of either G. Marconi or Diener's Double to offer to customers. Diener's Double is the dwarfer of the two, to 2′ tall, with frilled white flowers to 3″ across. G. Marconi is 3′ tall with pure white flowers to 4″ across. Both of these varieties are still in production though somewhat hard to find.

DELPHINIUM

Perennial (D. elatum), 10,000 seeds/oz. Germinates in 18 days at alt. 70° to 85°F.

Today's stately delphinium is an excellent garden perennial and has some commercial importance. While delphiniums are admittedly one of the most valuable hardy perennials for outdoor cutting, they also respond well to forcing. Outdoors, they seem to be profitable from Canada to Florida, though the finest flowers are produced where summer temperatures are moderate. In Florida they are largely grown as an annual. Some Southern growers find it best to use well-established seedlings that are started farther north.

Here's my wife Margaret Ball with an exciting show of hybrid delphiniums at Wisely Gardens of the Royal Horticulture Society in England. Unfortunately, delphiniums like these only occur in cool, moist climates.

Perhaps the best plan for producing strong plants to set out in spring is to sow about September 1 in finely prepared soil in a cold frame. Be sure the soil is perfectly level and well-watered, and don't spread the seed too thickly unless you plan to transplant (which is unnecessary). After the soil is frozen remove the sash and cover the soil with any coarse material to prevent too much thawing and freezing. Ordinary straw is inclined to pack and rot what it is supposed to protect. Cornstalks are ideal for protection. As it warms up in spring, remove this material and replace the sash, but don't soften the plants through lack of air; let them come slowly and be hardened off. Set out as soon as they are well in growth. Plant out in deeply prepared, fairly enriched, drained soil. Avoid using the same soil over, for delphiniums are susceptible to various rots that are carried over in the soil.

Another commonly used method of starting this crop is to sow indoors in January. With seed well-matured and temperatures cool at that time, germination should be at its best. Seedlings can be transplanted about 3″ apart in flats, grown cool, and set out early to harden before planting in the open. Some growers sow the seed direct into the open ground as early as it can be handled; and this, too, is a good plan, for it combines a minimum of labor with an unchecked start that promptly gets into rapid growth.

485

Belladonna-type delphiniums are field grown for cuts in Florida. The grower is Peter Nissen, near Stuart, Florida. It is an important cut flower crop here!

For forcing, the Giant Pacific strains are best. Sow the seed not later than August 1 in flats set in the coolest spot available, and later transplant the seedlings into frames. In late November, after they have had a short rest, they are taken up and planted in a cold house, spacing 6″ x 8″. About February 1, they are started into growth by a minimum temperature of 40° to 45°F; as spring advances this is increased to 50°F nights. This schedule gets them into full crop by Mother's Day and they continue producing nice stock well into July, after which they are discarded to be followed by other crops. If the Belladonna type is used (they are excellent) space them 6″ x 6″.

There are two distinct types of delphinium—the species *elatum*, to which most of the Giant Pacifics belong, and cheilanthum, which includes the belladonna types. The latter are not so strong in growth or as long-stemmed as the hybrids, but are more free-flowering. Belladonna Imp. is a very choice light blue. But little of the dark Bellamosum is wanted. Connecticut Yankees, an All-America Selection, produces bushy well-branched plants with very large florets in shades of lavender and blue. Decidedly the best strain of giants is known as the Giant Pacific Court series, which was developed from and offers the same quality as the original Giant Pacific strain (no longer available) originated by Frank Reinelt. It is available in a fine line of colors from light to the darkest blues, lavenders, mauve and white. The best varieties in the leading colors are Galahad, white; Guinevere, lavender; Summer Skies, light blue; King Arthur, royal violet; and Blue Bird, a mid-blue. Astolat contains lavender-rose shades, some of which are near pink. Most of them have a conspicuous center or "bee," as it is called. Nearly all come remarkably true to color. Also, they are quite mildew-resistant. There are two varieties of Dwarf Giant Pacifics available: Blue Fountains, which consists of blue shades blended with white, and Blue Springs, in shades of blue and lavender. In some areas these might be preferred for landscape and garden purposes because of their reduced height, 30″ to 36″.

486

Potted Delphinium—Delightful

(**Editor's note:** *Recent tests at Penn State show that delphinium makes an excellent spring and summer pot plant. The following from Jay Holcomb and David Beattie of Penn State reports on their experiences with delphiniums as pot plants.*)

Delphiniums are garden perennials whose flower spikes have graced perennial borders for many years. One of the advantages of perennials in pots is that they can be dual-use plants: They can be enjoyed as a flowering plant in the home, then planted to the garden and enjoyed for years to come.

There are a group of varieties that are naturally 2½′ to 3′, and these are the ones that we have been working with. The variety Blue Springs has worked well in our trials. Blue Fountain and Connecticut Yankee are two other cultivars that should work well.

Propagation

The most practical method of propagating delphinium is from seed. Timing seed sowing depends on when delphinium is to flower. For example, if you were to sow seeds in June, you would have plants large enough to force by fall. Delphinium seed germinates very well when fresh, but store the seed cold after collection.

Sow seed in plug trays in a well-drained medium, covering lightly. Most peatlite mixes have adequate drainage. It's best not to use a plug tray with more than 200 cells so that seedlings have some space to grow before transplanting.

Temperature is critical. Keep medium temperature 70°F with aerial day temperature between 70° and 80°F. Under these conditions germination should occur in 10 to 14 days. When germinating in summer, be careful temperatures don't get too high.

Growing On

Once seed has germinated, grow seedlings on at lower temperatures, as low as 55° to 60°F at night and up to 75°F during the day. For summer the best quality delphinium plugs will be produced in a fan-and-pad cooled greenhouse. You can also control high day temperatures with shading, but this also reduces light intensity. It takes seven to nine weeks for seedlings to grow to a transplant size of 1″ to 2″.

- **Forcing plants for flowering.** For forcing, grow plants in 5″ or 6″ pots. A 4″ pot is too small to hold the plant upright. Begin with plugs either from a commercial source or that you grew.

- **Light is critical for delphinium.** High irradiance appears to be more important than photoperiod. For example, in November, December and January, the naturally low light levels in Pennsylvania won't stimulate rapid flowering. If you want to flower delphinium in winter use supplementary light. In the brighter months of March and April, delphinium grow and flower rapidly under natural greenhouse conditions.

- **Temperature.** Plants tolerate night temperatures as low as 40° to 45°F, but growth rate is much slower. We grow our delphinium at a night temperature of 60°F and a day temperature of 70°F.

  In order to keep stem length as short as possible, keep day and night temperatures as close to the same as possible. If temperatures are 60°F night and day, crop time will be a little longer than if the night is 60°F and the day is 70°F.

- **Height control.** Use growing temperatures to control height. There are no growth retardants specifically labeled for delphinium. Our research has shown, however, that some of the retardants like A-Rest and Sumagic do reduce plant height.

- **Pests.** Delphinium will be affected by the same insects that affect other greenhouse crops. Scouting and yellow sticky cards are the first line of defense to controlling insects. Delphinium are also susceptible to some diseases, but starting with pathogen-free growing media should mean relatively few disease problems.

DIANTHUS

by Jim Nau
Ball Seed Company

Annual (Dianthus chinensis), 25,000 seeds/oz. Germinates in 7 days at 70° to 75°F. Cover the seed lightly upon sowing.

Biennial (Dianthus barbatus), [also called Sweet William] 25,000 seeds/oz. Germinates in 7 to 10 days at 65° to 70°F. Cover the seed lightly upon sowing.

Dianthus Chinensis

Dianthus is a diverse class of plants that is only briefly covered here. The market in the United States today centers around *D. chinensis* varieties and their uses in containers, as bedding plants and in the landscape. Predominantly cool-season crops, most *D. chinensis* varieties performed like pansies in the Midwest and South; showing good color for the spring and early summer and failing in the heat and humidity of August. Recent improvements in varieties have helped this class to become as popular as it once was in the gardens of yesteryear.

Green packs are salable 10 to 11 weeks after sowing, with flowering packs ready in 15 to 16 weeks. Using one plant per container, 4″ pots flower out in 15 to 16 weeks as well. If the plants become leggy and are in need of a growth regulator, both A-Rest and Bonzi are registered for use on this crop. Note that these plants are often robust once they come into flower, when grown in the pack. The shelf life of these plants is better if grown in pots and marketed as such.

In the southern United States sow seed in August for green pack sales in November. Plants will flower from February until May, or possibly June. Allow 9 to 10 weeks for green packs, and 11 to 12 weeks for flowering 4″ pots, one plant per pot.

In varieties, some of the best ones for all-around uses in the garden today include both the Princess and Telstar series. The Princess series is made up of five separate colors plus a mixture, while Telstar has four separate colors plus a mixture. In the Princess series the best varieties are the purple, salmon and the non-blushing white, while Telstar series has an excellent picotee and crimson. Both series have excellent scarlet flowering varieties. Both Telstar and Princess have excellent heat tolerance, flowering late into the summer, a time when other varieties have gone out of bloom.

Dianthus chinensis *is an increasingly popular summer bedding plant. Much good breeding here!*

In other varieties, consider both the Charms and Carpet series for 4″ pots and other containers. There are a number of separate colors in each series, and all have larger flowers than either the Princess or Telstar series. However, these varieties do not have the heat tolerance outside.

Though they have yet to be introduced at the time of this writing, two new series are headed to the market, combining the dwarf, pot performance of Charms and Carpet with the bicolor appearance and flower size of the old Baby Doll types. Both of these series, one called Rosemarie and the other Parfait, will be introduced into the marketplace in the early 1990s, and will be marketed for 4″ pots and as bedding plants. Flowers are over 1¼″ across and are characterized by having a prominent eye or spot of either purple or rose/red in the center of the flower.

Dianthus Barbatus

While annual forms of this old-fashioned garden favorite are available, most varieties are biennial. Sowings made in February or March usually grow to about 6″ to 12″ tall during the summer and flower sporadically at best. Once the plants go through the winter they will flower the following year, and can be used for garden accents or as cut flowers. In bloom the plants reach up to 18″ or 20″ tall for the cut flower types, while the carpet or prostrate varieties grow to only 12″ tall at best.

Green packs are salable 10 to 12 weeks after sowing, and the plants will flower the following May and June (a year later). Grow on at 50° to 55 °F nights and treat as you would pansies.

In selecting varieties, note that many of the U.S. brokers sell the dwarfer strains of *D. barbatus* in the perennial sections of their catalogs. These varieties are recommended for quart or gallon containers for summer or fall sowing and overwintering along with other perennials for sales the following spring. Varieties to look for include Double Mixture, which is a mixture of three colors with flowers that are "ringed" or spotted with red or rose. Indian Carpet Mix is a dwarf variety to 8″ with single blooms. Cut flower growers want to be sure to look for the long-stemmed varieties that are often not listed by most seed companies. However, these are available and are excellent plants even in Midwest summers.

DORONICUM *(Leopard's Bane)*

by Jim Nau
Ball Seed Company

Perennial *(Doronicum caucasicum)*, 26,000 seeds/oz. Germinates in 4 to 21 days at 70°F. Leave seed exposed to light during germination.

One of the earliest perennials to flower, doronicums are hardy plants in Midwest gardens, with golden-yellow flowers from 2″ to 2½″ across on plants to 2′ tall. Flowers are single, daisy-like, and have no scent. The foliage is kidney-shaped and deep green in color. Doronicum can be used within the perennial border as an accent planting. However, large mass plantings should be avoided due to the short duration of flowering and expected heat stall during the summer. Plants often go dormant in August under high temperatures and humidity in Midwest gardens. Plants flower in April and May and are hardy to USDA zones 4 to 7.

Doronicum is a spring flowering plant that will not flower from a winter sowing. If seed is sown in December and grown on in 4″ pots, plants will not flower until April/May a year and five months later. Sow seed in July, transplant to quart containers in late summer, using one or two plants per pot, and overwinter in a coldframe. Growing on temperatures should be 50° to 55 °F.

Most often the variety sold is labeled simply *D. caucasicum*. This variety is the species that was noted above in the description. It is 18″ to 20″ tall with golden-yellow flowers. Many times it is also listed as *Doronicum cordatum*. Magnificum is more uniform than the species, it looks similar in overall appearance and grows to 20″ tall. Spring Beauty doronicum has double-flowering yellow blossoms on plants 12″ to 15″ tall.

DUSTY MILLER

by Jim Nau
Ball Seed Company

Tender perennial (for genus and species, see below), germinates in 10 to 15 days at 75°F. Do not cover the seed upon sowing.

Dusty miller is actually a common name for a number of plants that have gray, woolly foliage. These plants are perennials in warm winter areas but are treated as annuals north of zone 8, especially if winter protection is not provided. The yellow flowers borne on these plants the second season after sowing are unimportant since it is the foliage that is sold on the U.S. bedding plant trade. However, dusty millers also make excellent dried foliage plants that work well in floral arrangements. The flowers are of merit, though, since they provide a unique contrast with the foliage and provide ample color in June and July in the southern United States.

In cropping, allow 11 to 12 weeks for all varieties to be sold without flowers in a cell pack. A 4″ pot will take up to 14 weeks to fill out the container using one plant per pot. If the plants get away from you, B-Nine is registered for use on this crop.

In the southern United States allow 8 to 10 weeks for foliage sales in packs, and 11 to 12 weeks for sales in 4″ pots, one plant per pot. Dusty millers are ideal for landscape and container plantings in the South, and overwinter best in the milder regions.

The genus, species and seed count per ounce will vary from variety to variety. Also note that all the heights listed below are based on the foliage in the garden without the flowers. Silver Dust *(Senecio cineraria,* 50,000 to 100,000 seeds/oz.), is one of the most popular varieties on the market today. Its deeply-notched leaves are covered with a woolly mat of gray on plants to 8″ tall. Cirrus is also listed under *S. cineraria* (50,000 to 100,000 seeds/oz.), but differs from Silver Dust by not having as much a gray cast to the foliage. Its leaves are the least notched of any of the dusty miller varieties in this listing. Cirrus grows to 10″ tall. Diamond *(Cineraria maritima,* also *Centaurea candidissima,* 50,000 seeds/oz.) is the most vigorous and largest leaf type of the dusty millers. It grows to 15″ tall and fills in well, making it a top choice for landscapers to use in mass plantings. Plants will appear very similar to Silver Dust except that they will be larger overall and with a slightly less-gray cast than Silver Dust. Silver Lace *(Chrysanthemum ptarmiciflorum,* 200,000 seeds/oz.) is one of the dwarfest varieties available on the bedding plant market today. It differs from the other varieties by having leaves that are twice notched—giving a lacy appearance to the plant. It grows to 10″ tall and has a lighter shade of gray in its foliage than the other varieties listed here.

ECHINOPS *(Globe Thistle)*

by Jim Nau
Ball Seed Company

Perennial *(Echinops ritro), 2,600 seeds/oz. Germinates in 14 to 21 days at 60° to 65°F. The seed should be left exposed to light during germination.*

Echinops is a blue flowering perennial from 24″ to 36″ tall. Flowers are globe shaped and range from 2″ to 2½″. Individual florets are small to ⅛″ across, and the globe opens from the top down. Leaves are distinctively thistle-like with spines at the ends; underneath, the foliage is gray-green in appearance. Plants can be used as either fresh or dried cut flowers, though they are primarily used in perennial border plantings at present. As a fresh cut flower, harvest when the topmost flowers emerge. As a dried cut, harvest when about one-third of the flower has opened and before the top blooms have faded or died. To dry, hang in a warm, dry place. Plants flower July and August and are hardy to USDA zones 4 to 9.

Any variety sold under the name of *E. ritro* is the species. This is available as seed, while the cultivars can be propagated by division or root cuttings. The species is more vigorous than the cultivars and can get 5′ tall after three years. Dividing the plants is done in the spring and is done every three to four years depending on the variety and how vigorous it grows.

Sowings made in the winter and spring seldom flower the same season from seed. Sowings are more often made in July and transplanted directly to a quart container. Seedlings do not like numerous transplantings and can often die for a number of reasons. For green plant sales in the spring, sow in January or February, transplant directly to 3″ or 4″ pots and sell 11 to 13 weeks later. Growing on temperatures are 55° to 58°F.

In varieties, our opinion is that the species type is a very good strain, though some variability is to be expected. However, it makes excellent cut flower plants. Tapglow Blue is the most popular cultivated variety today. Seed is not available on this plant with steel-blue flowers to 3″ across. Plants are 3′ to 4′ tall once established. Vetchii's Blue is a darker blue flower color than Tapglow, and it is earlier to flower in the garden. It is becoming more popular on the U.S. perennial trade. This variety is vegetatively propagated also.

EUPHORBIA

by Jim Nau
Ball Seed Company

The most popular euphorbia known on the market is the poinsettia. There are other types, however, that make excellent cut flowers or perennials. *Euphorbia polychroma* (also *E. epithymoides,* 6,500 seeds/oz.) is a perennial plant to 16″ that is admired more for its dense foliage than its inconspicuous yellow flowers borne in April and May. As the weather gets cooler, the foliage turns crimson in color. Euphorbias often exude a white latex or sap when the stem is cut or bruised. When taking cuttings or harvesting as a cut flower, be sure to sear the cut end with a flame before working with the plant. *E. polychroma* is hardy in USDA zones 4 to 8.

E. polychroma germinates in 15 to 20 days at 65° to 70°F, though without a pre-treatment, germination percentages often fall below 30%. If time permits, chill seed for 4 to 6 weeks at 35° to 40°F, then sow seed on moistened sand. Twenty-three to 35 days after sowing, seedlings can be transplanted into cell packs or 3″ to 4″ pots using 1 to 2 plants per container. Green packs are salable 8 to 11 weeks after sowing, but plants will not flower well the first summer after a mid-winter sowing.

E. variegata (also *E. marginata,* 2,500 seeds/oz.) is an annual plant commonly called Snow-on-the-Mountain. The foliage is green-and-white on plants to 2½′ tall. Like the preceding species, *E. variegata* is sold for its colorful foliage rather than its white flowers that color up during mid-summer in the garden. Plants are primarily used as fresh cut foliage, though they can be used as a bedding plant or as a pot plant.

E. variegata germinates in 14 to 20 days at 68° to 70°F, and the seed should be covered during germination. For cut flowers, sowings made directly to the field will be ready 9 to 12 weeks after sowing to the ground. In the Midwest the last sowing is in late June, which will produce large, robust plants suitable for cutting by Labor Day.

EXACUM

by Jack S. Sweet and Paul Cummiskey
Earl J. Small Growers, Inc.
Pinellas Park, Florida

Exacum is a beautiful blue-flowered plant that has exploded into popularity as a pot plant in just a few years. The myriads of dime-sized flowers, blue with bright yellow pollen masses in the center, tend to cover the whole plant when grown well. Plant and pot size vary with the grower and the market. Most seem to be grown as 6″ or

Exacum is an ever-popular, year-round pot plant—dozens of tiny, bright blue flowers!

6½" pots, but with the advent of some of the newer, faster growing, compact varieties, we should see a lot more grown in 4" or 5" pots. Some growers have a white exacum to add a little variety.

Most exacum are purchased from specialty growers as small plants ready for potting into 4", 5" or 6" pots. These plantlets may be from cuttings or from seed depending on method of propagation.

Seed is available, but it is quite tiny—even smaller than begonia seed—and must be handled very carefully. Exacum seed are slow to germinate—two to three weeks—and should be planted in a lightweight starting media with little or no covering. The seedlings will be ready to transplant in about six weeks into 2" pots. Then about seven weeks later can be put into the final pots for flowering.

The cultural procedures that follow are based on using plants, generally produced by specialty growers, ready for final transplant from 1½" to 2" pots.

Potting. Use a very light, well-drained potting soil, which is loose and has plenty of soil amendments such as perlite, calcine clay or Styrofoam, and peat to allow good root aeration. One plant per pot is sufficient and should be placed deep enough in the soil to stabilize the plant as it grows larger. Initial watering, and for the first 10 days, should be very light to encourage root action.

Temperature. Exacum grow best at 60° to 65°F nights and 75° to 80°F days.

Light. Plants should be grown under full sunlight in winter months. During the summer months, a light shade should be applied (4,500 to 6,000 fc.). During the spring and early fall, plants should be grown in full sun, and light shade applied when plants start to flower. Shading at this time will produce darker colored blooms. Excessive light and heat will cause flowers to be faded.

Media. Exacum grow best in a loose well-balanced soil mixture that has plenty of peat and perlite in it for good aeration.

Fertilization. Exacum are moderate feeders. We have found it grows best by alternate use of fertilizers such as 15-16-17 Peatlite Special and calcium nitrate at the rate of 2 lbs./100 gals. every third watering. If desired, Osmocote 14-14-14 may be incorporated in the growing media at the rate of ¼ to ½ tsp./6" pot of soil.

Some growers have experienced an excessive leaf curl or crinkle. This seems to be related to excessive light and possibly a low copper level in the leaf structure. A foliar spray using Tri-Basic Copper at 1 lb./100 gals. applied two weeks after potting has been very successful in reducing crinkle on exacum. Soil applications of copper on exacum have not been too useful.

Winter growing. Winter seems to produce more growing problems than summer. Apparently the lower light levels and shorter days make a softer plant that can be easily injured and attacked by disease. This must be compensated by lower fertilizer levels and reduced watering to make a "harder" plant. Starting around October, pots should thoroughly dry out between waterings. Water early in the morning so foliage is dry by late afternoon. Provide good air circulation around plants, and reduce fertilizer levels by half. Overwatering and high nutrient levels, besides promoting disease, cause delayed flowering.

Exacum requires much less fertilizer and soil moisture than pot mums, lilies or poinsettias, and responds poorly if fed with high levels of fertilizer on constant feed, with every watering, such as other crops may require. Remember, to accelerate winter flowering of exacum, one should lower fertilizer levels and make sure plants dry out between waterings. Light at normal mum intensity will force winter plants into bud and bloom.

Production time. Timing of the crop is seasonably variable, with a marketable 6″ flowering plant being produced in seven to eight weeks in the summer, and up to 12 to 14 weeks in mid-winter. Smaller plants grown in 4½″ or 5″ pots for mass market sales can be produced in less time and on less bench space, as exacum can be forced to flower at an early stage. No pinching is necessary as they are self-branching plants. In case of premature budding of small exacum, larger plants can be produced by removing the earliest flowers.

Disease. The major problem with exacum seems to be related to botrytis (gray mold). It can show up as a gray lesion at the soil line, or small gray lesions at the forks in branches, and cause all or part of the plant to wilt and die. This form of botrytis is actually caused by excess fertilizer, too much water, or water left on the leaves in evening or overnight. Specific botrytis control chemicals such as Chipco 26019 (Rovral) at 16 oz./100 gals. as a foliar spray only, or Benlate at 6 oz. plus Daconil 75 WP at 10 oz./100 gals. as a drench or spray will help control this problem, but less fertilizer strength and less water are also needed. Pythium and Phytophthora can be controlled by a tank mix of Benlate at 8 oz. and Subdue 2E at 1 to 1½ oz./100 gals. Banrot at 8 oz./100 gals. is also useful as a light drench right after planting. Regular use of the above chemicals can eliminate almost all diseases on exacum, but remember—they need it right after potting and repeated two to three times during production.

Insects. The most damaging insects to exacum are the broad mites. They are usually found on the upper parts of the plant, and cause the leaves and growing tips to become yellow and distorted, and the buds to fail to open. Broad mite can be controlled by various miticides such as Pentac, Kelthane, Vendex. All three can cause flower injury so caution is advised on mature flowering plants. Avid 0.15 EC has recently proven quite useful in control of mites and can be used on flowering crops without flower injury. Worms can be controlled with Thuricide or Resmethrin aerosol. Thrip injury to growing tips can be controlled by using Orthene, Lindane, Mavrik or Avid.

Height control. Height of exacum can be controlled by using B-Nine at regular mum strength (.25% solution) applied one week after potting, and, if needed, a second application can be given two to three weeks later for plants that are being grown under lower light conditions. Height can also be controlled by regulating the amount of water they receive. If small plants are desired they should be allowed to dry out more between waterings.

Supplemental lighting. Exacum react according to the total light energy on the leaves. Flower bud initiation is NOT affected by day length, but plant growth is increased by longer days. Therefore, the use of supplemental lighting in winter is very beneficial. Lighting such as HID lights or even mum-type lighting of 10 to 20 fc., used four to six hours a night starting at dusk, can speed up production time in winter months by two or more weeks.

Post-greenhouse care. Exacum should be placed next to a window or some artificial light source for long-lasting quality. Low-light conditions will cause flowers to fade. Exacum may also be placed outside in a semi-shaded area or on a patio. They are hardy to 32°F.

Varieties. There are several good exacum varieties used by commercial growers today: Blue Champion—an improvement on our original that we introduced many years back; White Champion, a white form of the original; Royal Blue, a new deeper color form that comes in about 7 to 10 days earlier and Little Champ, a smaller F_1 hybrid developed for the 4″ to 4½″ trade. It is smaller, grows smaller leaves, is sky blue in color and 15 to 20 days earlier than Blue Champion.

FOLIAGE PLANTS

by Charles Conover
University of Florida
Apopka, Florida

Production and Marketing

Although the foliage industry has been identifiable in the United States since the early 1900s, it is only within the last 30 years that it has become a major industry. The industry developed initially outdoors and under slat sheds in southern parts of Florida, Texas and California, but in recent years has moved into polypropylene shadehouses and plastic, fiberglass and glass greenhouses. In Northern areas, production has been centered in Ohio, Pennsylvania, New York and nearby states in glass and double-layer polyethylene greenhouses. More recently, Hawaii has developed a thriving foliage plant industry, mainly in production of stock plants for cane and cuttings. A number of companies have also developed stock production units in the Caribbean region for shipment of propagative units to the United States and Europe. In 1988, it was estimated that at least 30 million dollars of propagative material was shipped into Florida for finishing.

Major production areas within the United States are listed in Table 1. Concentration of the foliage industry in Florida, California, Texas and Hawaii is primarily because of reduced production costs associated with moderate winter temperatures and high light intensity year round. Production in Northern areas is facilitated by access to local markets and a product mix that stresses rapid turnover of easy-to-grow foliage crops in small pots and hanging baskets.

Table 1. Major United States Foliage Plant Production Areas and Estimated Sales (USDA 1989)

State	1988 Wholesale Value (millions of dollars)
Florida	254
California	79
Texas	15
Hawaii	12
Other States—24 total	42

Foliage crops were not of major economic significance in relation to other floriculture crops until the late 1960s. As late as 1970, foliage accounted for only $15 million at wholesale in Florida. The most recent USDA data (1989) indicates that the total U.S. foliage market at wholesale was nearly $402 million in 1988. Thus, foliage crops have become of major economic importance in a relatively short span of time.

498

Many definitions exist for foliage plants; however, they are so diverse in habit and use, it is difficult to develop one that is inclusive. One commonly-used definition that addresses itself to both form and use is: "Any plant grown primarily for its foliage and utilized for interior decoration or interior landscape purposes. While it may have flowers, these will be secondary compared to foliage features."

Detailed information on the national foliage plant product mix is unavailable, but it has been compiled for Florida (Table 2), which accounts for 63% of the U.S. production. The product mix data is not listed by genera throughout, since many diverse genera may be included in plants sold as combinations and, thus, individual genera may be responsible for very minor segments of the industry. On a national basis, this information is probably low for hanging basket and terrarium plants, which are often grown for local markets in northern areas of the United States. Also, larger foliage types would be listed at higher percentages than they actually are nationally, because Florida is responsible for well over 75% of plants grown in 10″ or larger containers.

Table 2. Foliage Plant Product Mix (%) in Florida

Product	1975	1988
Aglaonema spp.	2.0	4.0
Brassaia actinophylla	5.0	2.2
Dieffenbachia spp.	5.0	5.9
Dracaena spp.	11.0	9.4
Epipremnum spp.	3.0	9.1
Ferns	3.0	1.2
Ficus spp.	6.0	6.5
Ivy	*	3.1
Palms	7.0	5.8
Philodendron spp. (other)	6.0	1.7
Philodendron scandens oxycardium	14.0	3.0
Schefflera arboricola	*	1.3
Spathiphyllum spp.	3.0	3.3
Syngonium spp.	2.0	2.2
Combinations	2.0	1.0
Other	31.0	40.3

* Data not available.

Stock Plant Culture

● **Field.** Growth of foliage stock plants in the field (outdoors) is restricted to southern Florida, California, Hawaii and the tropics. For the most part, stock plants are grown in full sun or under polypropylene shadecloth that provides the required light levels.

Land selected for stock production should have good internal drainage as well as sufficient slope to allow surface water to drain off rapidly when excessive rainfall occurs. Temperature ranges should preferably be between 65°F minimum at night and 95°F maximum day for best quality and yield. Infrequent lows of 50°F and highs up to 105°F will not damage plants, but will reduce yields. Farm location should also be considered in relation to wind speed and frequency since winds may influence design of protective structures as well as types of crops grown. Wind-induced tipburn and foliar abrasion reduce crop quality and salability.

Structures can be constructed of treated lumber, concrete or steel with cable stringers to support the shadecloth. Height and size of the structure are important because they influence temperature at plant height. Because heat rises and air movement is slow through shadecloth, it is wise to provide a minimum 8', and preferably 10', clearance. Erection of 1- to 5-acre units with spaces between units will help prevent excessive temperature buildup in the center of the structure.

Foliage stock plants grown outdoors or under shadecloth are usually watered with impulse or spinning sprinklers, which are also used for fertilization. Therefore, it is very important to have a properly engineered system so that good coverage will be obtained. Use of low-angle trajectory sprinklers will be necessary to prevent contact of water with shadecloth. Normally, foliage plants grown under shadecloth require 1" to 2" of water a week. Native soils in tropical and subtropical areas are rarely satisfactory for foliage stock production; sandy soils usually require amendment with organic components, such as peat moss, to improve water- and nutrient-holding capacities, while heavy soils require peat moss, bark, coarse sawdust, or rice hulls to improve internal aeration.

- **Greenhouse.** Foliage stock plants can be grown in any type of greenhouse that provides sufficient light and required temperatures. Stock plants should be grown in raised benches or pots that provide sufficient medium volume for good root growth, drainage and adequate aeration. Benches with 6" sides and bottoms constructed to allow drainage serve this purpose best.

  Growing medium selection depends on local availability, cost, plant type and personal preference. Some excellent media for foliage stock plants include: 1) 50% peat moss/50% pine bark; 2) 75% peat moss/25% pine bark; 3) 75% peat moss/25% perlite; and 4) 50% peat moss/25% vermiculite/25% perlite.

  Selection of watering systems for stock plants grown in greenhouses is important since foliar disease is reduced when foliage is kept dry. Besides the economic advantage of reducing disease, and thus pesticide usage, is the reduction of unsightly foliar residues on propagation units. Irrigation systems directed at wetting the medium and not the foliage are desirable for these reasons.

  Temperatures needed for maximum yield from stock plants are 65°F minimum and 95°F maximum. Maintenance of the minimum temperature can be expensive during winter months and, if heat conservation is a problem, it is better to keep soil temperatures at 65°F minimum and allow air temperatures to drop slightly lower.

Here's a greenhouse of quality dieffenbachia in South Florida.

Growth of foliage stock plants in greenhouses is really limited only by economics. It is generally conceded that bench space in Northern greenhouses costs between $10 and $15 a year/sq. ft., while in warmer areas costs may range between $3 and $10. Size of plants in relation to yield of cuttings per square foot and need of specific crops to be grown under cover for pest protection govern the decision for stock plant production. Only a few fast-growing foliage plants yield sufficient cuttings to make them profitable where heating costs are high. Therefore, before establishment of a stock production area, it is wise to compare purchase costs per cutting versus those expected from a stock production area. Valuable and costly space devoted to stock plant production may be better used for potted plant production and propagation of purchased cuttings; in fact, many growers often utilize cuttings from plants being grown for sale since these plants are sometimes trimmed one or two times to increase quality and these cuttings can then be used as propagation units.

Propagation

- **Methods.** Propagation methods used for foliage plants include cuttings, seed, air layers, spores, division, and tissue culture. Using cuttings is one of the most popular propagation methods; cuttings can be tip, single- and double-eye leaf bud, leaf or cane. Selection of a specific method depends on plant form (upright, vining, etc.), availability of propagative material, and intended market date since some types of propagation take longer than others.

  Seed propagation is increasing in popularity because costs are lower than for vegetative propagation. However, seeds of many foliage plants are not available or plant type is not stable from seed. Some of the more popular foliage plants grown from seed include *Araucaria, Brassaia, Dizygotheca, Podocarpus* and nearly all of the palms. Seed of tropical foliage plants should be planted soon after harvest because germination percentage decreases rapidly with increased time between harvest and planting.

Air layering is decreasing in importance as a propagation method because of high labor costs and need for large stock plant areas. Plants most commonly air-layered include *Codiaeum, Ficus* and *Monstera*. One of the problems with air layers is that their large size makes the propagative units difficult to ship without mechanical damage.

Division is the only method of propagation for a crop like *Sansevieria*. This is a labor-intensive method and presents problems of carrying disease, insect or nematode pests to new plantings.

Spores are used to propagate a few fern genera, although most ferns are grown from tissue culture, divisions or offsets.

Tissue culture is becoming an important system of propagation for foliage producers. Rapid multiplication of new cultivars is an important advantage of tissue culture, but some old cultivars such as the Boston fern are also commonly propagated by this system. At the present time, about 20 cultivars of foliage plants are being propagated by tissue culture. Two major advantages of tissue culture are change in plant form and disease control. Genera such as *Dieffenbachia, Nephrolepis, Spathiphyllum* and *Syngonium* produce multiple crown breaks when grown from tissue culture and yield plants with more compact form and fuller appearance. Tissue culture has been successful in reducing disease problems with several genera since disease-free stocks can often be maintained free of disease when grown in enclosed greenhouses. Two major foliage crops (*Dieffenbachia* and *Spathiphyllum*) are grown from disease-free stocks and yield high quality potted plants.

- **Systems.** In the past the usual propagation system was a mist bed where cuttings were misted for 15 to 30 seconds each 30 to 60 minutes. Cuttings were stuck in the bed and then rooted, pulled, and potted. During the last 10 years, many producers have shifted to direct-stick propagation in which cuttings are placed directly in the growing pot, rooted and finished without being moved. This system is especially adapted to vining plants, and a dozen or more cuttings may be placed in each pot. The frequency of misting depends on light intensity and temperature, and should be set to keep some moisture on foliage at most times. In cooler climates, growers often use tents over the propagation bench to provide 100% humidity and eliminate misting. Mist application is very useful in lowering temperatures in summer months, but can prolong rooting during periods when medium temperature drops below 65°F. For this reason, the medium in propagation beds or benches should be maintained at 70° to 75°F at all times.

Numerous media have been used for foliage plant propagation, with sphagnum peat moss most commonly used, either alone or amended with perlite, polystyrene foam, pine bark or other organic components.

502

Production

Variability among foliage plants prevents development of a detailed crop production guide, but cultural factors influencing most foliage crops are discussed which will allow logical decisions to be made.

- **Physical factors.** Potting media used to grow foliage plants can range from 100% organic to approximately 50% organic and 50% inorganic. Key factors to consider in selection of potting media include aeration (measured as capillary and non-capillary pore space), moisture retention (water-holding capacity) and nutrient retention (cation exchange capacity). Several other factors that must be considered when selecting potting media include: consistency, availability, weight, and cost. Examples of components utilized in commercial foliage mixes, along with some of the commonly used mixtures, are shown in Table 3. Commercially prepared media sold premixed by suppliers are the most common source in the industry at this time.

Table 3. Physical and Chemical Characteristics of Potting Medium Components and Combinations Commonly Used to Grow Foliage Plants

Medium	Aeration	Water-holding Capacity	Cation Exchange Capacity	Weight
Composted pine bark	H*	M	M	M
Perlite	H	L	L	L
Polystyrene foam	H	L	L	L
Sand	M	L	L	H
Sphagnum peat moss	M(V)	H	H	L
Vermiculite	M	M	M	L
Peat:bark (1:1)	H	H	H	L
Peat:bark:polystyrene foam (2:1:1)	H	M	H	L
Peat:bark:vermiculite (2:1:1)	H	H	H	L
Peat:perlite (2:1)	H	M	M	L
Peat:sand (4:1)	M	H	H	H

* Abbreviations used: H, high; M, average; L, low; and V, variable.

Normally, pH is adjusted at the time potting mixtures are developed. The best range for most foliage plants is between 5.5 and 6.5, but several genera, including *Maranta* and most ferns, grow best with a range between 5 and 6. Dolomite is suggested for pH correction, but any calcium-containing material can be used. When fluoride-sensitive crops are being grown, the best pH range is 6 to 7. Superphosphate should not be incorporated into potting media unless intended for foliage plants not sensitive to fluoride. Micronutrients are normally included in the fertilizer program, although they may also be included in the potting medium.

- **Potting methods and systems** fall into two main categories: hand potting and automatic planters. Hand potting is still used by the majority of producers with small- or medium-sized operations. Systems vary, but potting media are usually delivered to a central site where potting occurs, and potted plants are then moved to growing areas. Most pot filling machines are stationary, and potting takes place in a central location; however, smaller, portable pot fillers are also utilized.

- **Spacing** of foliage plants directly controls final plant quality. Crowding of plants reduces light reaching lower foliage and may cause it to abscise, or may cause plants to grow tall without proportionate spread, which reduces value. Plants that will be finished within three months are usually placed at their final spacing when set on the bench; spacing distance varies from zero (pot-to-pot) to three times pot diameter. Plants grown in container sizes of 6″ or larger can take six months to two years to reach maturity. Such plants are often placed pot-to-pot until they become crowded and are then moved to their final spacing which, depending on plant form, varies from one to six times the container diameter.

- **Light intensity** is one of the most important factors to consider in culture because it influences internode length, foliage color, carbohydrate level, growth rate, and acclimatization. Production light levels have been included in Table 4 for many foliage crops. Light-green foliage or faded colors, such as in the case of *Codiaeum*, are indicative of excessive light and reduced chlorophyll levels. This can be corrected in most cases by increasing fertilization or reducing light intensity. Because increases in fertilizer often cause excessive soluble salts levels, the proper corrective method is to reduce light intensity.

- **Fertilization** directly influences growth rate, and thus profitability, but because fertilizer levels also influence longevity indoors, it is important that excessive amounts are not used. Maximum growth rate of acclimatized foliage plants can be obtained with moderate levels of soluble, organic or slow-release fertilizers applied constantly or periodically. Suggested levels of fertilizer (at recommended light intensities) in Table 4 are for production of acclimatized high-quality plants.

Fertilizer ratios for foliage plants need to be approximately 3:1:2 (N-P_2O_5-K_2O) when potting mixtures listed in Table 3 are utilized. A ratio of 1:1:1 is also acceptable, but because nitrogen is the key element in growth of foliage plants, this ratio will result in higher fertilizer costs to obtain the desired nitrogen level and is more likely to result in ground water contamination with the excess phosphorus and potassium. Rates listed can be calculated on a periodic basis and applied weekly or every other week. Periodic fertilization less frequent than every two weeks often results in reduced growth rate and/or quality. When a constant feed program is desired, the suggested level of nutrients at each application is 150 ppm nitrogen, 25 ppm phosphorus and 100 ppm potassium. Potting media used for foliage plant production are normally very low in micronutrients and, thus, most fertilizers used should contain at least the minimal micronutrient levels suggested in Table 5.

504

Table 4. Suggested Light and Nutritional Levels for Production of Some Potted Acclimatized Foliage Plants

Botanical Name	Light Intensity (fc.)	N	P$_2$O$_5$	K$_2$O
		Fertilizer Requirement lbs./1,000 sq. ft./year*		
Aeschynanthus pulcher	2,000 to 4,000	28	9	19
Aglaonema spp.	1,000 to 2,500	28	9	19
Anthurium spp.	1,000 to 2,000	34	11	23
Aphelandra squarrosa	1,000 to 1,500	34	11	23
Araucaria heterophylla	4,000 to 8,000	28	9	19
Asparagus spp.	2,500 to 4,500	20	7	13
Brassaia spp.	4,000 to 6,000	41	14	27
Calathea spp.	1,000 to 2,000	28	9	19
Chamaedorea elegans	1,500 to 3,000	28	9	19
Chamaedorea erumpens	3,000 to 6,000	34	11	23
Chlorophytum comosum	1,000 to 2,500	34	11	23
Chrysalidocarpus lutescens	4,000 to 6,000	34	11	23
Cissus rhombifolia	1,500 to 2,500	28	9	19
Codiaeum variegatum	3,000 to 8,000	41	14	27
Cordyline terminalis	2,500 to 4,500	28	9	19
Dizygotheca elegantissima	4,000 to 6,000	28	9	19
Dieffenbachia spp.	1,500 to 3,000	28	9	19
Dracaena deremensis (cultivars)	2,000 to 3,500	28	9	19
Dracaena fragrans (cultivars)	2,000 to 3,500	28	9	19
Dracaena marginata	4,000 to 6,000	41	14	27
Dracaena—other species	1,500 to 3,500	28	9	19
Epipremnum aureum	1,500 to 4,000	34	11	23
Ficus benjamina	3,000 to 6,000	41	14	27
Ficus elastica (cultivars)	4,000 to 8,000	41	14	27
Ficus lyrata	5,000 to 6,000	41	14	27
Fittonia verschaffeltii	1,000 to 2,500	20	7	13
Hedera helix	1,500 to 2,500	28	9	19
Hoya carnosa	2,000 to 3,000	28	9	19
Maranta spp.	1,000 to 2,500	20	7	13
Monstera deliciosa	2,500 to 4,500	34	11	23
Nephrolepis exaltata	1,500 to 3,500	28	9	19
Peperomia spp.	1,500 to 3,500	14	5	9
Philodendron selloum	3,000 to 6,000	41	14	27
Philodendron spp.	2,000 to 3,500	34	11	23
Pilea spp.	1,500 to 3,000	14	5	9
Polyscias spp.	1,500 to 4,500	41	14	27
Sansevieria spp.	3,500 to 6,000	14	5	9
Schefflera arboricola	1,500 to 3,000	28	9	19
Spathiphyllum spp.	1,500 to 2,500	28	9	19
Syngonium podophyllum	1,500 to 3,500	34	11	23
Yucca elephantipes	3,500 to 4,500	28	9	19

* Based on a 3:1:2 ratio fertilizer source—if growing medium is known to fix phosphorus and potassium, they should be added at the same rate as nitrogen—i.e., use a 1:1:1 ratio fertilizer source.

Table 5. Average Levels of Several Micronutrients Required for Foliage Crops

Element*	Spray Application lbs./100 gal.	Soil Drench oz./1,000 sq. ft.	Soil Incorporated oz./cu. yd.
B	0.01	0.03	0.010
Cu	0.10	0.30	0.100
Fe	1.00	3.00	1.000
Mn	0.50	1.50	0.500
Mo	0.01	0.01	0.001
Zn	0.30	1.00	0.300

One application is often sufficient for short-term crops, while reapplications are usually necessary for crops grown for six months or more.

- **Acclimatization** of foliage plants for interior use is necessary to ensure that they perform well indoors. Acclimatization is the adaptation of a plant to a new environment—in this instance, preparation for growth in a building with low light and humidity. One of the most important aspects of acclimatization is development of "shade" foliage, which is characterized by large, thin leaves with high chlorophyll levels. A second important factor is nutritional level, which should be as low as possible while still producing a quality plant. The major objective of acclimatization is to produce plants with low-light compensation points. Such plants are able to make the transition from production to interior environments without serious loss of quality. The most highly-acclimatized plants are those grown under recommended light and fertilizer programs for their entire production cycle (Table 4), for only with this system are leaves of all ages acclimatized. Also, plants grown under recommended light levels for full term will have a more open appearance, an adaptation to reduced light intensity.

    Foliage plants such as *Brassaia, Chrysalidocarpus* and *Ficus* are often grown in full sun and then acclimatized by placing them under suggested shade and lowering fertilizer levels for three to 12 months. Although chloroplasts and grana are capable of reorientation within sun-grown foliage, the leaf anatomy—small size and thick cross-section—prevents them from being so efficient after acclimatization as shade leaves. Therefore, such plants are less tolerant of low or medium light levels than plants acclimatized during the entire production period.

- **Temperature** control is very important, since most foliage plants are tropical and require minimal night temperatures in the range of 65°F. Soil temperatures are also important, and if they can be maintained at 65° to 70°F, the air temperature may drop as low as 60°F at night without significant crop response. Best temperature range for production of a wide variety of foliage genera is 65°F minimum night and 75°F minimum day. Night temperatures as high as 80°F and day temperatures as high as 95°F will not be damaging; however, it is often uneconomical to maintain these in temperate climates.

- **Irrigation** levels should be established that ensure that foliage plants receive sufficient water to remain turgid at all times. Watering requirements during

506

winter, when temperatures are low and growth rate is slowed, may be less than once a week; in spring or summer, daily irrigation may be necessary.

Use of water application systems that irrigate the potting medium without wetting foliage is desirable because this reduces foliar disease and residue problems. Some efficient watering systems include ebb-and-flow irrigation, capillary mats, troughs, and leader tubes.

- **Carbon dioxide** application to foliage plants is uncommon, although up to a 25% increase in growth has occurred with several foliage plants. However, it appears that temperature is the key to increased growth during periods when greenhouses are closed; therefore, unless a range of 65° to 75°F minimum is maintained, the injection of CO_2 will probably not be beneficial.

- **Humidity** requirements of foliage plants during production are not verified by research, but maintenance of 50% or higher relative humidity appears to be desirable. In areas where humidity falls below 25% it is desirable to install mist lines or raise humidity in some other way.

Biological Factors

- **Insects and mites.** Factors that affect pest populations include access to the structure, temperature, humidity, irrigation method and potting medium. When a particular pest, such as scale, becomes a problem, cultural procedures must be checked carefully to see if stock plants are infested and if crawlers or adults have been carried through propagation to potted plant production areas. It is imperative that stock be kept as free of pests as possible to decrease the need for spraying of potted materials for sale. Frequent and continued spraying is undesirable because it is expensive, increases potential for phytotoxicity, and causes hard-to-remove residues on foliage. Mites present the most problems in spring, summer and fall when temperatures are high, while caterpillars and thrips are heaviest in spring and fall. Temperatures above 80°F are conducive to rapid increases in mite populations, especially if humidity is low. Under such conditions, heavy dependence on chemical control is necessary to produce mite-free plants. Pest problems in unheated production areas are reduced by cooler temperatures, while in climate-controlled greenhouses they present year-round problems. Fungus gnats are more of a problem in greenhouses than outdoors, especially when organic potting media are kept too wet.

- **Control outdoors and under shade cloth,** where pest movement is unrestricted, requires spraying or drenching with pesticides as the primary method of control. Use of high pressure sprayers and careful application to both sides of foliage provides the best assurance of control. Air blast sprayers, while providing high pressure and wide dispersal, often do not properly coat both sides of foliage with pesticides.

- **Control in greenhouses** is somewhat easier, since producers can utilize many chemicals used outdoors or under shade structures, as well as smoke bombs or thermal fogs and biological control agents. However, smoke bombs or thermal fogs are only effective when greenhouses can be entirely closed for several hours or more.

Table 6 lists the major pests of foliage plants and some of the hosts upon which they most commonly feed. Chemicals registered for control of specific pests are subject to change; thus for up-to-date recommendations on chemical pest control procedures on foliage plants, check with your cooperative agricultural extension agent.

Table 6. Major Foliage Plant Insect and Mite Pests and Crops Commonly Serving as Hosts

Pest	Hosts
Aphids	*Aphelandra, Brassaia, Hoya, Dieffenbachia, Schefflera*
Broad Mites	*Hedera, Aphelandra, Pilea*
Caterpillars	*Philodendron, Dracaena, Brassaia, Maranta, Aglaonema,* Ferns
Fungus Gnats	*Schlumbergera,* Palms, *Peperomia*
Mealybugs	*Aphelandra, Ardisia, Dieffenbachia, Asparagus, Maranta, Dracaena, Dizygotheca, Hoya*
Scales	*Aphelandra,* Bromeliads, *Ficus,* Palms
Spider Mites	*Brassaia, Codiaeum,* Palms, *Cordyline, Calathea, Dieffenbachia, Maranta*
Thrips	*Brassaia, Ficus, Philodendron, Ctenanthe, Syngonium*

- **Diseases (fungi, bacteria and viruses).** Fungal and bacterial diseases are more troublesome when wet foliage is combined with high temperature and humidity. Therefore, these diseases are most prevalent in tropical and subtropical areas where rainfall is heavy. Even in these areas, however, growing plants under cover and irrigating without wetting foliage will nearly prevent their occurrence. Soil-borne fungal diseases become more severe when poor quality growing media (i.e. without good aeration and drainage) are used or when plants are constantly overwatered. Several bacterial diseases become more severe when plants are grown with excessive nitrogen fertilization or are stressed because of high soluble salts, excessive temperature, and/or high light intensity. Virus diseases are disseminated by insects, but since many foliage plants already contain at least one known virus, insect exclusion may not remedy the situation.

- **Control outdoors and under shade cloth,** common production areas in subtropical and tropical areas where heavy rainfall occurs, is difficult to achieve except with preventive spray programs. During periods of frequent rainfall, and depending on disease pressure, it may be necessary to spray weekly or more often; however, during dry seasons little, if any, pesticide application may be necessary. Irrigation applied to the soil, or overhead irrigation applied only during the middle of the day when rapid drying can occur, combined with proper plant spacing which will increase air flow, thus reducing humidity, will aid in reducing disease pres-

508

sure. Directed high pressure sprays, rather than air-blast sprayers, provide best control of disease pests and are usually worth the extra cost of application.

- **Control in greenhouses** of foliar fungal and bacterial diseases is easiest if foliage can be kept dry. When this is impossible, fairly good control can be obtained with chemical sprays to the foliage. Soil drenches for control of most of the soil-borne diseases are fairly successful in raised benches and in containers off the ground. No control procedures are presently recommended for plants with viruses except to rogue infected plants and use virus-free stocks. Table 7 provides a listing of some of the major disease pests and primary hosts. As with insecticides and miticides, the most up-to-date control information can be obtained from the local cooperative agricultural extension agent.

Table 7. Major Foliage Plant Disease Organisms and Crops Commonly Serving as Hosts

Organism	Area Affected	Common Hosts
Fungal pathogens		
Alternaria	Leaves, stems	*Brassaia, Schefflera, Polyscias, Fatsia, Calathea*
Fusarium	Leaves	*Dracaena*
Fusarium	Stems, leaves, roots	*Dieffenbachia*
Myrothecium	Leaves, stems	*Aglaonema, Dieffenbachia, Spathiphyllum, Begonia, Syngonium, Episcia, Aphelandra, Peperomia, Aeschynanthus*
Drechslera, Bipolaris	Leaves	Palms, *Maranta, Calathea*
Colletotrichum	Leaves	*Dieffenbachia, Hedera*
Rhizoctonia	Leaves, stems, roots	Many plants, especially ferns, *Hedera, Philodendron, Epipremnum*
Pythium	Stems, roots	Many plants, especially ferns, *Epipremnum, Philodendron, Peperomia*
Phytophthora	Leaves, stems, roots	Many plants, especially *Brassaia, Spathiphyllum, Dieffenbachia, Aphelandra, Philodendron, Saintpaulia*
Sclerotium	Stems, roots	Most plants grown on the ground are susceptible
Corynespora	Leaves	*Ficus, Aeschynanthus, Aphelandra*
Cylindrocladium	Stems, roots	*Spathiphyllum*
Bacterial pathogens		
Erwinia	Stems, leaves	*Dieffenbachia, Aglaonema, Philodendron, Syngonium, Dracaena, Saintpaulia*, and many others
Pseudomonas	Leaves, stems	*Caryota, Philodendron, Syngonium*, ferns, *Dracaena, Schefflera*
Xanthomonas	Leaves	*Philodendron, Dieffenbachia, Hedera, Aglaonema*

Packaging Systems

The two main packaging systems are boxing and shipping loose in specially constructed racks and trucks. When using the boxing system, cartons must meet interstate shipping regulations concerning weight of corrugated cardboard, and must either be waxed or moisture resistant to prevent deterioration of boxes in transit because of moisture in containers. Plants in containers up through 6″ are usually placed in a waxed tray, and the tray slid into a box of the proper height. Such boxes usually do not contain dividers or other restraints, although some producers have designed boxes with features for holding the pots in position and the potting medium in the container. Plants in 6″ or larger pots are usually sleeved and placed directly in cartons of the proper height or shipped loose in specially designed trucks.

In recent years, some producers and shippers are using adjustable racks that are wheeled directly into trucks. These racks have been designed to accommodate various-sized plants. Usually no dividers or restraints are necessary with this system, and physical damage is minimal.

Storage and Shipping

Storage of foliage plants is not a normal practice, but with increased sales in mass market outlets, which use central distribution points, there has been increased interest in how long plants can be held without significant decrease in quality. Research has shown that many foliage plants can be stored/shipped for two to four weeks in darkness provided they were acclimatized and that proper environmental conditions existed during the storage/shipping period. In actuality, storage and shipping are very similar in nature, and environmental conditions for

Foliage is very big in Europe. Here's a house of ficus canes just in from South Africa at Boekestijn's in Holland. Note the tray automation.

510

both are similar. However, plant preparation for storage and/or shipping does not start at the onset of the intended practice, but during the production period.

Preshipment Factors Affecting Plant Quality

- **Light.** Preshipment light levels have a strong effect on postshipment foliage plant quality. Plants grown under high light will not ship well because they are not properly acclimatized. High light production results in excessive leaf drop or other loss of quality either during shipment or after placement in an interior environment. Also, plants grown in higher light are not so likely to tolerate shipping temperatures without sustaining chilling injury.

- **Nutrition.** Preshipment fertilizer levels affect acclimatization and, in turn, subsequent interior quality. Foliage plants grown on higher than recommended nutritional regimens will not be well acclimatized and will ultimately lose more leaves and be of lower quality than those properly acclimatized. Serious reduction in plant quality during the shipping phase will be noticeable only if the fertilizer level is more than twice the recommended level.

- **Season.** Foliage plants grown during high-light and high-temperature periods are less tolerant of the shipping environment and are more likely to decline in quality during shipment. This may be due to lower levels of acclimatization or inability to tolerate lowered shipping temperatures. It appears that plants grown in summer and shipped then or in early fall require warmer shipping temperatures than plants grown and shipped in winter or spring.

Shipping Environment Factors

- **Light.** Although foliage plants would tolerate shipping for longer periods if light could be supplied, this is not possible with present equipment. Therefore, all research has been conducted on plants shipped or stored in darkness.

- **Temperature.** Controlling temperature at a level specified for the crop can be a major factor in maintenance of plant quality. Shipping at low temperatures, 45° to 60°F versus 65° to 70°F, can be beneficial in maintaining quality of some plants, provided there is no chilling damage. However, the best shipping temperature for specific plants changes with the season and is lower in winter and higher in summer. Duration of exposure to a specific temperature can also strongly affect plant quality; a temperature that might be optimum for two-week shipments might cause damage when plants are exposed for three to four weeks (see Table 8).

- **Soil moisture.** Plants should have adequate soil moisture at time of shipping; not too wet and not too dry. Plants shipped wet or with saturated media often have increased leaf drop, whereas low soil moisture during shipping periods increases desiccation of plant tissues and raises potential for leaf drop or injury.

511

Table 8. Suggested Shipping or Storage Temperatures (°F) for Acclimatized Foliage Plants

Plant Name	Duration[1] 1 to 14 days	15 to 28 days
Aglaonema Silver Queen	60 to 65	60 to 65
Aphelandra squarrosa	55 to 60	55 to 60[2]
Araucaria heterophylla	50 to 65	50 to 65
Aspidistra elatior	50 to 55	50 to 55
Asplenium nidus	50 to 65	50 to 65
Beaucarnea recurvata	55 to 60	55 to 60
Brassaia actinophylla	50 to 55	50 to 55
Cereus peruvianus	55 to 60	55 to 60
Chamaedorea seifrizii	55 to 60	55 to 60
Chrysalidocarpus lutescens	55 to 65	60 to 65[3]
Cordyline terminalis Baby Doll	55 to 60	50 to 55[3]
Crassula argentea	50 to 65	50 to 65
Dieffenbachia Tropic Snow	55 to 65	55 to 65[3]
Dizygotheca elegantissima	55 to 60	55 to 60
Dracaena deremensis Janet Craig	60 to 65	[4]
Dracaena fragrans Massangeana	60 to 65	60 to 65
Dracaena marginata	55 to 65	60 to 65[3]
Epipremnum aureum	55 to 60	55 to 60[2]
Ficus benjamina	55 to 60	55 to 60
Ficus elastica Burgundy	50 to 60	50 to 55
Ficus lyrata	55 to 60	55 to 60
Hedera helix Eva	50 to 60	50 to 55
Howea forsterana	50 to 65	50 to 65
Hoya carnosa Tricolor	55 to 65	55 to 65
Maranta leuconeura	50 to 55	50 to 55[2]
Nephrolepis exaltata Bostoniensis	55 to 60	55 to 60[2]
Philodendron scandens oxycardium	55 to 60	55 to 60[2]
Philodendron selloum	55 to 60	55 to 60
Phoenix roebelenii	55 to 60	55 to 60
Pilea Silver Tree	55 to 60	55 to 60[2]
Plectranthus australis	55 to 60	55 to 60[2]
Schefflera arboricola	50 to 55	50 to 55
Spathiphyllum Mauna Loa	50 to 55	55 to 60
Syngonium White Butterfly	55 to 60	55 to 60[2]
Yucca elephantipes	50 to 55	50 to 55

[1] *Plants shipped or stored for one to seven days should be held at the highest temperature listed for that plant.*
[2] *Plants observed to have severe loss in quality beyond two weeks.*
[3] *Plants observed to have a loss in quality of about 25% per week beyond two weeks.*
[4] *Data not available.*

- **Humidity.** Although all plants need to have adequate soil moisture during shipment, this will not prevent them from desiccating if humidity is too low. A relative humidity level around 85% to 90% is necessary for maintenance of foliage plants stored or shipped for long durations. This level can be obtained by putting plants in boxes or by setting the air exchange controls on the shipping container to the closed position with sleeved or unboxed plants.

- **Gases.** Research on foliage plants has shown that ethylene is probably the only contaminant that may occur in containers during shipping, unless there is pollution from an outside source. However, foliage plants require fairly high levels of ethylene (1 to 2 ppm) in relatively high temperatures (65°F or higher) for long durations before any damage will occur. Experience has shown that ethylene does not seem to be a major problem when foliage plants are shipped at cooler (65°F or lower) temperatures. In research on low-oxygen storage, no benefit was observed over foliage plants shipped in a normal atmosphere.

Selected References

1. Chase, A.R. 1987. *Compendium of Ornamental Foliage Plant Diseases.* American Phytopathological Society, St. Paul, MN. 92 pp.
2. Conover, C.A. and R.T. Poole. 1981. Basic Fertilization Guide for Acclimatized Foliage Plants. *Florists' Review* 168(4360):10-11, 29-32.
3. Conover, C.A. and R.T. Poole. 1984. Acclimatization of Indoor Foliage Plants. *Horticultural Reviews* 6:119-154.
4. Hamlen, R.A., D.E. Short, and R.W. Henley. 1978. Detection and Identification of Insects and Related Pests of the Commercial Foliage Industry. *FL Coop. Ext. Serv. Circular 432.*
5. Joiner, J.N. 1981. *Foliage Plant Production.* Prentice-Hall Inc., Englewood Cliffs, NJ.
6. Kucharek, T.A., G. Simone and R.S. Mullin. 1989. *Florida Plant Disease Control Guide.* Univ. of FL, IFAS, Gainesville, FL.
7. Short, D.E. 1989. Insect Control Guide. Vol. 1. Ornamentals and Turf. Univ. of FL, IFAS, Gainesville, FL

Market Dominance

An even dozen major foliage plant genera or groups comprise the majority (60%) of the foliage plants sold in the United States. Industry dominance by a single plant no longer exists, as was the case in the mid 1950s. Plants/groups that follow are listed not alphabetically, but by decreasing market share of the industry.

Dracaena
There are over 40 species native to tropical regions of Asia and Africa, and almost twice that number of selected cultivars. The most commonly sold species

Dracaena fragrans Massangeana *is often used as a single accent plant or with several plants of different heights per pot.*

Right, Ficus benjamina *and variegated cultivars, such as* F. b. Jacqueline *shown here, are used as small specimen trees in homes and as larger plantings in malls and hotels.*

Above, Epipremnum aureum *Golden Pothos. Varieties of this species are the most popular vining plant today and are especially attractive in hanging baskets.*

Dieffenbachia maculata *Camille branches well and is often seen as a single branched plant as an accent.*

514

include *D. deremensis, D. fragrans, D. marginata, D. reflexa, D. sanderana* and *D. surculosa.* The popularity of this genus is related to its tolerance of interior environments, its range of sizes from small plants in 4″ pots to trees in 200 gallon containers, and its diversity of form and coloration.

Most commonly-grown dracaenas are propagated by tip cuttings or cane. Best acclimatized plants are grown under light levels of 3,000 to 6,000 fc. with moderate nutrition. Disease pests of major importance include Erwinia, Fusarium, and Phyllosticta, while major insect pests include mites, mealybugs and thrips.

Epipremnum (Pothos)

About 10 species, all native to southeast Asia, exist within this genus. Popularity of this group has increased considerably within recent times. The most commonly sold cultivar is *E. aureum* Golden Pothos, although not all golden pothos look the same because of selection of "high color" strains by nurserymen. Other significant cultivars of *E. aureum* include Jade and Marble Queen.

Essentially all pothos are propagated from single-eye cuttings. Since bright coloration is very important with this crop, it is necessary to select cuttings from stock plants with the desired coloration. Best quality plants are grown under 2,000 to 4,000 fc. (use of lower light levels often reduces coloration) with moderate fertilizer levels. Disease pests of importance include Erwinia, Pythium and Rhizoctonia, while major insect pests include mealybugs, root mealybugs and thrips.

Ficus

Nearly 800 species of ficus exist, including trees, shrubs and even woody vines native to tropical areas. Although the potential for finding new species of ficus is good, mainly four species—*F. benjamina, F. elastica, F. lyrata* and *F. retusa* with their dozens of cultivars—are most often utilized in the industry. Most ficus are utilized as indoor trees in large plantings where their large size (10′ to 30′) can be observed, but they are also suitable for the home in sizes from 3′ to 8′ tall.

Most ficus are produced from cuttings or air layers, but *F. lyrata* is often grown from tissue culture, which yields an improved plant form. Ficus can be grown successfully under 4,000 to 6,000 fc. or in full sun and then acclimatized under the recommended acclimatization light levels for four to 12 months; the larger the tree, the longer the acclimatization period required. Nutritional regimen is moderate to high for this genus, but should be reduced prior to sale. Disease pests of importance include Glomerella, Botrytis, Cercospora and Corynespora, while major insect pests include scale, mealybugs and whitefly.

Dieffenbachia

About 30 species of this genus, native to Central and South America, have been identified, but most plants sold in the industry are *D. maculata, D. amoena,* or hybrids between species. Some of the most important cultivars include *D. maculata* Camille, *D. maculata* Exotica Compacta and *D. amoena* Tropic Snow. Some new introductions include *D.* Paradise, *D.* Triumph and *D.* Victory. Sales of this genus have increased with the introduction of cultivars with new colors and forms.

Chamaedorea elegans *is used as an accent plant in homes and as small specimens.*

Right, Philodendron selloum *(background)— a "self-heading" species often used as accent plants—and* Philodendron scandens oxycardium *(front), a vining species, sold in hanging baskets, small pots and dish gardens.*

Left, Spathiphyllum Gretchen, *as are many of the spathiphyllum cultivars, is sold with blooms.*

Hedera helix *cultivars. Variety of leaf shapes and colors and tolerance of low-light situations makes this species a popular plant for hanging baskets, small pots and planters.*

Dieffenbachia are propagated mainly by cuttings and tissue culture. Best color is obtained when grown under 1,500 to 3,000 fc. at moderate nutritional levels. Low light intensities or low nutrition will reduce basal breaks. There are many disease pests of significance, with Erwinia and Pythium among the most important, while major insect pests include mites and mealybugs.

Palms

The importance of palms has decreased slightly in recent years, even though the number of genera utilized in the industry has increased. Overall there are hundreds of palm species with nearly 25 common in the industry. Some of the best palms for interior use include *Caryota mitis, Chamaedorea* spp., *Chrysalidocarpus lutescens, Howea forsterana, Phoenix roebelenii* and *Rhapis excelsa*. Many other good palm species are available.

Palms are propagated from seed, which should be planted as soon after harvest as possible and germinated at 75°to 80°F. Different palm genera require varying light intensities for growth, but a range of 3,000 to 6,000 fc. is best for most species when grown on moderate nutrition. Numerous diseases affect palms, with Colletotrichum, Phytophthora and Helminthosporium among the more important, while major insect pests include scale, mites and mealybugs.

Aglaonema

Approximately 30 species of this hardy foliage plant are known from the wild, but only a few species and cultivars are commonly grown. *Aglaonema* Silver Queen is grown in greatest volume, while other good cultivars and species include *A. Maria, A. Romana, A. commutatum* Emerald Beauty and *A. crispum*. These are excellent plants for low-light interiors and have increased in popularity during the last 10 years.

Most aglaonemas are grown from cuttings or root clumps, although some are from tissue culture. These plants grow best in light levels of 1,500 to 2,500 fc. with moderate nutrition. Leaves oriented vertically, or bleached leaves indicate excessive light. Disease pests of importance include Xanthomonas, Erwinia, Pseudomonas and Pythium; the most serious insect pests are scale and mealybugs.

Spathiphyllum

This genus contains about 35 tropical species, but the industry sells mostly hybrids. Some of the most commonly available hybrids include *S.* Lynise, *S.* Mauna Loa, *S.* Petite, *S.* Starlight, *S.* Tasson and *S.* Viscount which include both small and large cultivars suitable for 6″ to 17″ containers. This low-light tolerant plant has had a considerable increase in popularity during the last 10 years.

Most spathiphyllum is now grown from tissue culture, although a few less important species are seed grown. These plants require low light levels (about 1,500 to 2,500 fc.) and moderate nutrition to achieve best quality. Generally spathiphyllum are easy to grow except for the disease Cylindrocladium, a severe root disease; other diseases of importance include Pseudomonas and Phytophthora. Major insect pests include mealybugs and scale.

517

Schefflera arboricola. *Compound leaves make this an unusual accent plant.*

Left, unusual leaf shape makes Syngonium podophyllum *White Butterfly a popular accent plant in smaller pots and hanging baskets.*

Right, Aglaonema *Silver Queen is an excellent plant for low-light interiors.*

Nephrolepis exaltata *Dallas is sold in large and small hanging baskets or pots and used as accent plants.*

Hedera (Ivy)

Although ivy has been used as a foliage plant for years, its popularity has increased in recent times. Hedera contains about 15 species native to southern Europe, Asia and North Africa, but there are several hundred named cultivars within the single species "helix." Some popular cultivars include *H. h.* California, *H. h.* Curly, *H. h.* Glacier, *H. h.* Gold Dust, *H. h.* Needlepoint and *H. h.* Sweetheart. The popularity of ivy is related to its tolerance of cool locations and the wide diversity of leaf colors and shapes.

Ivy is propagated by cuttings and grown in cool greenhouses. Although it will tolerate high light, it grows best at 3,000 to 5,000 fc. at low to moderate fertilizer levels. Ivy grows poorly at temperatures above 85°F, but will tolerate night temperatures of 55° to 60°F without reductions in growth. Major disease pests include Xanthomonas, Pythium and Rhizoctonia, while insect pests of importance include broad mites, spider mites and scale.

Philodendron

Philodendron scandens oxycardium was once the major plant of the foliage industry, but it now accounts for only 3% of the industry's sales, versus 34% in 1956. There are almost 200 species native to tropical America, but, except for the species listed above and *P. selloum*, mostly hybrids are sold in the industry. Most of these hybrids—*P.* Black Cardinal, *P.* Emerald Duke, *P.* Majesty, *P.* Red Princess, *P.* Royal Queen and others—were bred by Robert McColley who was responsible for all the major breeding work on *Philodendron*. Many of the hybrids are "self heading," meaning they stand up without support, but those with a vining habit require a pole or slab for support, or are sold as hanging baskets or in small pots or dish gardens.

Propagation is by cuttings and tissue culture, although a few species are air layered. Best light intensities for production are from 2,500 to 3,500 fc. depending on cultivar. Fertilization levels in the moderate range provide best growth without excessive softness. Numerous diseases attack Philodendron and the bacterial diseases—Erwinia, Pseudomonas and Xanthomonas—are the most troublesome. Insect pests include mealybugs, mites, scales and thrips.

Schefflera/Brassaia

These genera are often confused, since the names have been interchanged, but they are closely related. Brassaia (commonly called schefflera), a native to Asia, is usually sold in larger sizes for its dramatic leaf form, although plants in sizes as small as 6″ pots are also available. *Schefflera arboricola* (commonly called "arboricola") is somewhat like Brassaia, but it is smaller and leaflets making up the compound leaves are much shorter. *B. actinophylla* and the cultivar Amate are the only plants available in this genus, while there are many *S. arboricola* cultivars including *S. a.* Covette, *S. a.* Gold Capella, *S. a.* Trinette and others. The *S. arboricola* cultivars are especially tolerant of low-light interior locations. *Brassaia actinophylla* is propagated from seed, while *B. a.* Amate is produced from tissue culture. Propagation of *Schefflera arboricola* is by seed or cuttings, while the named cultivars are by cuttage or tissue culture. Brassaia can be grown in full sun, but a light level of 4,000 to 6,000 fc. is better, while best Schefflera are grown with 3,000 to 5,000 fc. Both genera grow best under reduced light at moderate nutritional levels. Major disease pests include Cercospora, Pythium and Rhizoctonia and insect pests of importance include mites, scales and thrips.

Syngonium

About 20 species of Syngonium are native to South America, but only one cultivar, *S. podophyllum* and its cultivars, are found in the industry. This vining plant is excellent in hanging baskets and is also sold in smaller pot sizes (4" to 6"). The most important Syngonium cultivar is White Butterfly, and it accounts for nearly 75% of sales. Some of the other cultivars include Jenny, Lemon Lime, May Red, Robusta and Pink Allusion.

Propagation of Syngonium is almost exclusively by tissue culture, because it produces the types of plant desired by consumers. Excellent plants can be produced under light levels of 2,000 to 3,500 fc. with low to moderate nutrition. Because of several disease pests, it is imperative that sanitary practices be maintained for this plant. The major disease pest is Xanthomonas, although Pseudomonas and Pythium may also present problems. Insect pests of importance include mealybugs and thrips.

Ferns

The majority of ferns grown in the foliage industry are cultivars of *Nephrolepis exaltata*. A small number of ferns from the genera of *Asplenium, Davallia, Pteris* and *Sphaeropteris* are also grown. Nephrolepis are considered sword ferns; Bostoniensis is the oldest commonly grown cultivar. Other important cultivars include Bostoniensis Compacta, Dallas, Florida Ruffle and Maasii. Ferns are sold mainly in hanging baskets, but 4" to 8" pots are also used.

Most Nephrolepis ferns are propagated from tissue culture, although runners/offsets are still utilized to some extent. Other ferns are still grown from spores, but are also produced from tissue culture. Best quality ferns are grown at 2,500 to 3,500 fc. at moderate nutritional levels. The primary disease problem is Rhizoctonia, although Cylindrocladium may also occur. The major insect pests are caterpillars (worms) and mealybugs.

GROWING FOLIAGE—UP NORTH

by Heidi Tietz
Petersen and Tietz Greenhouses
Waterloo, Iowa

Is it practical for growers outside the typical foliage growing areas of Florida, California and Texas to grow foliage? The answer is yes, if you are selective. Growers can successfully grow foliage if they choose to propagate softer items on their own, or if they use a liner of some sort to bump up.

Softer items that have offered a lot of success include baby tears and toes, strawberry begonia, Swedish ivy, spider plant, Tahitian bridal veil and wandering Jew. These plants require very little stock since they are so prolific. They are excellent plants for dish gardens or hanging baskets. In fact, the cuttings of the Tahitian bridal veil and wandering Jew root very nicely when placed directly into a hanging basket.

Some other selections you may choose to propagate yourself include Rex begonias, string-of-hearts and string-of-pearls. These plants are also very prolific and offer some more unique items to your customers.

Purchasing liners and moving them up for finishing also works well. Choose plants with quick finishing times, or plants that can be grown in hanging baskets to help you utilize your space most efficiently. For instance, although ferns can take some time to produce, you can grow them in hanging baskets. This allows you to use growing space that is not quite so obvious and may otherwise go unused.

There is also the possibility of purchasing overgrown small plants from typical foliage growers and moving them up one size. Consider purchasing an overgrown 3″ dieffenbachia that will easily make a nice 4″ pot, or an overgrown 4″ that in a very short time becomes a nice 6″ pot. Although this option is not always available, be ready when the opportunity presents itself. Overgrown plants can save you money since they are usually sold at a reduced price. They are also shipped at their usual density so this saves on freight costs.

You can be successful growing foliage. There are many plants you can grow, but many—like spathiphyllum with a crop time of 24 to 30 weeks for finished 6″ pots—that should be left to the typical foliage grower. Remember—be selective.

FINISHED—BUY IT IN

by Heidi Tietz
Petersen and Tietz Greenhouses
Waterloo, Iowa

The buying (from the South) and selling (in the North) of finished foliage is a huge market. Some of the reasons being that Northern growers cannot afford to tie up bench space for extended periods, the heat cost associated with growing large foliage, and the costs of producing quality finished plants in low-light conditions. The answer is "Buy it in." Leave the growing to the Southern nurseries.

Now that you are convinced that you belong in the foliage market, and buying finished product is the way to go, a couple of basic needs you must fill are reliable sources of supply and a good trucking company.

One thing you will learn quickly is that there are many, many growers of foliage. The majority are located in Florida, which divides itself roughly in two. The northern part of the state, around Orlando, specializes in production of small containers such as liners, 3″, 4″, and 6″ pots, as well as hanging baskets. These growers have invested in greenhouses due to the cool conditions that they experience in the winter. As we all know, greenhouse space is a little expensive, and these growers cannot afford the production time involved in large container plants.

The southern part of Florida, around Tampa, West Palm Beach and Miami, specializes in production of large container plants such as 6", 8", 10", 14" and specimen plants. The typical mild winter conditions allow these growers to use shade houses for production. This structure is considerably less expensive than a greenhouse, but still provides good growing conditions in the southern Florida climate.

How do you know which growers to contact? Your broker sales representative can help you, or you can obtain the Florida Foliage Locator from the Florida Foliage Association at 57 East Third St., Apopka, FL 32703, a non-profit organization.

There are also foliage brokers located in Florida. Some of these brokers do not even grow plants; they warehouse plants for a short period before shipping them on. Many of the growers also broker foliage from other growers. All of these systems work as long as you are working with a reputable company. It is okay to ask your source if they are buying plants in or growing their own. And do not be afraid to ask for a description or the specifications of the quality of the product that will be shipped to you.

In addition to some of the varieties listed in the European dish garden section, you will find the following plants and pot sizes to be good sellers for you: Aglaonema (Chinese evergreen), arboricola, croton, dieffenbachia, dracaenas, ficus benjamina (weeping fig), palms, rademachera (China doll), schefflera and spathiphyllum (peace lily) are all good movers in 6" and 8" pots. Spathiphyllum is available in bloom year round.

Pole plants like philodendron, pothos, and syngonium (arrowhead) are also in strong demand. Good hanging basket items include 6", 8" and 10" pots of chlorophytum (spider plant), cissus, philodendron, pothos and syngonium.

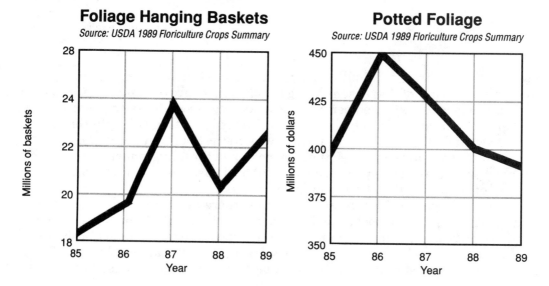

EUROPEAN DISH GARDENS

by Heidi Tietz
Petersen and Tietz Greenhouses
Waterloo, Iowa

European dish gardens incorporate a combination of many different small green plants and usually at least one small blooming plant into one common container. Consumers really appreciate this long-lasting gift item.

There are two ways for you to have European dish gardens available: buy them in or purchase the starter kit and build your own.

It is quite possible to purchase dish gardens already assembled from large foliage-producing areas such as Florida. The key here is to ship the dish gardens to the final destination in one piece. As a result you must look for an experienced source, as this is one of the main points they will have mastered. Gardens available include anything from a single braided fig tree with ceramic figurine to combination gardens that include shells or rocks to spice them up. How does the supplier keep the rocks and shells in place? A glue gun, of course.

If you are interested in becoming an artist yourself, find a good source of jumbo rooted liners or 3″ pots. And do not forget the blooming plant such as a kalanchoe or African violet to brighten things up.

When planting your own gardens, remember drainage is a must. Of course a drainage hole in the container is preferred by the plants, but will not make the homeowner happy. So you are going to use solid-bottom containers. Plants should be leached well prior to planting to help reduce the amount of salt build-up in the container at a later date. Create an area in the planter for excess water to move to rather than allowing it to engulf the roots. Use rocks or charcoal in the bottom of the container.

Some varieties of plants are more suited to dish gardens than others. For instance, pothos and Marble Queen (the white and green cousin) are closely related, yet Marble Queen can easily rot where pothos seems to survive. Other plants recommended for European dish gardens are: palms, dieffenbachia, aglaoenema; croton, and dracaena marginata and tricolor are good to use for their height. Some excellent filler plants include: pothos, philodendron, prayer plant, arrowhead (syngonium) and ivy. Good low-growing plants include baby toes, baby tears, strawberry begonias and airplane plants. Other blooming plants to consider beyond the already mentioned kalanchoe and African violet are mums, anthurium and small blooming peace lilies (spathiphyllum).

FREESIA

by A. A. De Hertogh
North Carolina State University
Raleigh, North Carolina

Freesias originated in South Africa. The commercial cultivars (Tables 1 and 2) are hybrids and products of extensive breeding efforts. They come in a wide range of colors, are fragrant, highly suitable for low-temperature forcing and have good keeping quality. They can be forced either as cut flowers or potted plants.

Normally, 5/7 cm. corms are used, and most corms used for forcing are produced in The Netherlands. Flowering is primarily regulated by temperature and light intensity. Because of the need to precisely control the growth and development of the corms, forcers must coordinate the cooling and planting schedule with their corm supplier. Corms for forcing must have been properly stored at 86°F until shipped to the forcer. Because the quantities used are generally small and transportation time needs to be short (less than seven days), air freight from The Netherlands is absolutely necessary.

The freesia is fragrant and colorful.

Cut Flowers

The information provided covers flower production in the greenhouse only from corms. It is also possible to produce flowers from seed (see Smith, D. 1985 (revised). *Freesias*. Grower Books, London).

Planting can begin in September in the northern areas, and be as late as December in the southern areas. Depending on the cultivars and forcing temperatures, flowering usually starts 110 to 120 days after planting and lasts for about four weeks. Forcers who want to have flowers for several months need to use staggered plantings. There are a wide range of freesia cultivars available (Table 1), and forcers should consult their suppliers for cultivars in addition to those listed. There are both double and single flowers. They are fragrant and available in a wide range of colors. Average plant heights are 20″ to 30″, but the actual cut flowers are usually 10″ to 14″ long.

When corms arrive, check a sample of the corms to be certain they are free from serious diseases or physical damage. Forcers should be prepared to plant the corms on arrival, but if they must be stored, place them at 55°F under non-ventilated conditions. They can be held for up to three weeks at this temperature.

The planting medium should be pH 6.5 to 7.2, free from fluoride-containing additives, and sterile. Plant in either well-drained ground or 8″ to 10″ deep raised beds. They can also be started in special propagating trays and then transplanted. The bed or bench needs to have a mesh support system.

Plant corms 2″ deep and use about 80 to 100 corms per sq. yd. Under most North American conditions, planting is usually from September to December. It is year-round in certain West Coast areas. Planting depends on prevailing soil temperatures, which should be 55° to 60°F. Keep planting medium moist, but not wet.

Cut freesias can be grown virtually outdoors in the central California (Watsonville) area. Paul and Suzanne Baldwin do them under plastic or sometimes saran only. Baldwin's is a major forcer for the Eastern cut flower market.

Freesias require a medium- to high-light intensity (2,500 fc.) greenhouse. Use 50° to 55°F night temperatures and avoid day temperatures over 63°F, especially during short days of winter. During warm temperature months it is advisable to use soil cooling systems to maintain a soil temperature less than 63°F.

Freesias can be forced in a greenhouse with 1,000 ppm CO_2 during the daylight hours. After plants begin to grow, use 200 ppm of 20-20-20 every other week.

Other than viruses, which come with the corms, Fusarium is the most common disease. The most common insect is the aphid. Freesias can exhibit flower abortion. As with Dutch iris, low-light intensities and/or high temperatures during the period of rapid flower development can cause abortion. Leaf scorch can also be induced by fluoride, so do not use superphosphate or other fluoride-containing amendments.

It is possible to harvest the corms and store them for forcing in the next season. This requires proper storage facilities and the use of specific temperatures, relative humidities and ventilation requirements (see Smith reference cited above).

Cut flowers when the first (lowermost) floret opens. For short term storage, hold flowers dry at 32° to 35°F and at 90% relative humidity. For long term storage, keep flowers in water at 32° to 35°F. Little or no storage is advised. Some flower preservatives will aid in the bud opening of cut freesias. Freesias are sensitive to ethylene in storage.

Table 1. Selected Freesia Cultivars for Cut Flower Forcing

Cultivar	Color
Athene	White
Aurora	Yellow
Ballerina	White
Blue Heaven	Blue
Blue Navy	Blue
Cote d'Azur	Blue
Elegance	White
Escapade	Orange-red
Fantasy	Creamy-white
Golden Wave	Yellow
Miranda	Creamy-white
Oberon	Red
Pink Glow	Pink
Polaris	White
Riande	Yellow
Rossini	Pink
White Wings	White

Potted Plants

This product is somewhat experimental. Forcers are advised to determine how the plants will force and market under their conditions. The objective is to produce a marketable plant in 60 to 80 days from planting, with an average total plant height of 10″ to 16″. At present, these goals are not always achieved with the cultivars and treatments evaluated, however, progress is being made.

When corms arrive check a sample to be certain they are free from serious diseases or physical damage. Then store in open trays at 55 °F at a high relative humidity with good air circulation, but no ventilation, for 45 to 49 days. Do not return corms to 86 °F! Forcers should not store corms in excess of 49 days since this can cause the corms to "pupate," i.e. to form a new corm instead of a shoot. It is possible that the 55°F treatment can be provided by the corm supplier, but if this is done, transportation time must be exceedingly short.

A preplant soak in paclobutrazol (Bonzi) can significantly reduce the flowering height of potted freesias. It appears that the concentration needed and perhaps the length of the dip will vary with each cultivar (Table 2). The dipping of the corms should take place after the 55°F storage treatment and immediately before planting. Normally, the corms should be dipped for only one hour. Also, it is important that the corms be planted immediately after dipping. Do not allow them to dry out. Additional trials are needed and will be conducted.

Pot freesias are being done in major quantities, especially in northern California—a delightful, fragrant, colorful pot plant.

The guidelines for preparing a series of concentrations of paclobutrazol as a dip are as follows:

50 ppm—12.5 ml./l. of water or 1.7 oz./gal. of water*
100 ppm—25.0 ml./l. of water or 3.4 oz./gal. of water
200 ppm—50 ml./l. of water or 6.8 oz./gal. of water
300 ppm—75 ml./l. of water or 10.2 oz./gal. of water

Plant corms 1" deep. Use four to six per 4" pot, six to 10 in a 6" pot, or 10 to 15 corms in an 8" pot. Use a well-drained, pH 6.5 to 7.2, fluoride-free, sterilized planting medium. After planting, keep the medium moist but not wet. For plants that require staking, special rings are available from suppliers.

Freesias require a medium- to high-light intensity (2,500 fc.) greenhouse.

Use 55° to 60°F night temperatures. Avoid temperatures above 63°F, especially during short days of winter. Forcing times range from 55 to 90 days depending on the cultivars (Table 2).

After plants begin to grow, use either 200 ppm N of 20-20-20 every other week or 14-14-14 Osmocote.

Market plants when first floret begins to open. If plants need to be stored, place at 32° to 35°F, but not for a long period. Homeowners should be advised to place plants in coolest, but well lighted areas of the home in order to obtain maximum life of the flowers.

Table 2. Selected Freesia Cultivars for Forcing as Potted Plants

Cultivar	Color	Average Greenhouse Days to Market Stage	Normal Plant Height (inches)	Paclobutrazol Preplant Dip (ppm)*
Amadeus	blue	65-75	16/40	100
Athene	white	70-80	20/50	200-300
Bloemfontein	pink	55-70	20/50	100-200
Blue Navy	dark blue	60-70	16/40	50
Fantasy	creamy-white	70-80	18/45	200
Florida	pink	55-65	20/50	100-200
Golden Crown	light yellow	70-80	22/55	200
Oberon	orange-red	70-80	22/55	200
Riande	light yellow	70-80	22/55	200
Rosalinde	deep pink	65-75	18/45	100-200
Rossini	deep pink	65-75	20/50	200
Vienna	white	65-75	16/40	300
Washington	red	60-70	18/45	100

*For a trial basis, 100 ppm is advised. All dips are for 1 hour. Concentration given is for about a 40% reduction in total plant height.

*1 ml. contains 4 mg. of active ingredient, 1 oz. contains 112 mg. of active ingredient.

FUCHSIA

Annual (F. hybrida), **20,000 seeds/oz. Germinates in four to six weeks at 65° to 75°F.**

Largely propagated from tip cuttings, fuchsias are only occasionally grown from seed. These cool-temperature plants enjoy a rather light soil with some organic material. The trailing varieties are fittingly used in hanging baskets or porch boxes, and the more upright varieties are used for pot plants and bedding; but when summers are hot, it's difficult to keep them in good flower unless they are protected from full sun. This gives them special value for use in boxes and baskets that are usually in at least partial shade.

Tip cuttings that are 2″ to 3″ in length will root in two or three weeks. Once they are rooted they can be planted direct in pots or hanging baskets. Usually one cutting per pot is used. For hanging baskets use one plant in January, three plants in February and five in March.

After six pairs of leaves have developed, pinch to leave four pairs of leaves. In order to produce stocky, well-branched plants, two or three pinches will be necessary. Allow seven to eight weeks from last pinch to sale.

The important fact to keep in mind when it comes to flowering fuchsias is that they are long-day plants and that they will flower when the daylength is more than 12 hours. A total of about 25 successive long days is required to assure flower development. Lighting with mum lights from 10 p.m. to 2 a.m. will do the job.

The more popular varieties include Dollar Princess and Winston Churchill. Varieties especially suited for hanging baskets include Marinka, Dark Eyes, Swingtime and Southgate. In a climate such as is enjoyed in California, they grow into fine, large specimens in the open and sometimes withstand some frost.

For specific handling information from several topnotch growers, see the chapter on hanging baskets in this book.

GAILLARDIA *(Blanket Flower)*

by Jim Nau
Ball Seed Company

Perennial (G. x grandiflora, formerly *G. aristata)*, **7,000 seeds/oz. Germinates in 5 to 15 days at 70° to 75°F. Seed should be left exposed to light during germination.**

An easily grown perennial from seed, gaillardia has mostly single flowers in either bright yellow or crimson, though bicolors between the two are common, too. Flowers range in size from 2″ to 4″ on plants from 12″ to 30″. Plants have excellent weatherability and flower consistently from June until frost. Flowers are borne heavily at

529

first and then provide better-than-average color the remainder of the season. Gaillardias are one of the few perennials to flower for the majority of the summer. Gaillardia is hardy to USDA zones 3 to 9.

Seed and division are the two noted methods of propagation. Division can be done in either the spring or the fall. From seed, sowings made in mid-winter or spring will flower sporadically the first year after sowing. Plants put on a better show the second season. Allow 10 to 12 weeks for green pack sales in May. However, for larger and fully blooming plants, sow seed in July, move up into quart or gallon containers and overwinter for sales next spring. Grow on at 55°F.

In varieties there are a number of seeded and vegetative forms to pick from. The key difference is habit and height; the seeded forms are bigger in both aspects. Baby Cole is propagated by division only; there is no seed available. Plants have red flowers with yellow margins on plants to 10″ tall. Dazzler has crimson red petal ends with yellow centers on plants to 16″ tall. The plants are commonly propagated vegetatively though seed is available. Goblin is also a vegetatively propagated variety to 12″. The seeded form of this variety isn't bad, though it can get to 15″ tall. The flowers can get up to 4″ across on established plantings, and the flower color has a red base with yellow tips. This is the most-preferred variety for its uniformity and overall performance in the garden. Monarch Strain is an upright and vigorous variety to 30″ tall. Flower colors are primarily a mixture of red and yellow combinations throughout. Excellent as a cut flower. May require staking in the garden.

GAZANIA

by Jim Nau
Ball Seed Company

Annual (G. splendens), 12,000 seeds/oz. Germinates in 10 days at 65° to 70°F. Seed should be covered during germination.

Gazanias are low growing annuals to 10″ tall, in bright colors of white, yellow, orange and crimson; though lavender, pink and red shades are also available as well. Gazania flowers, like portulaca, will close during cloudy weather and not re-open until the sun appears. Flowers measure up to 3″ across and are single in appearance. In warm-winter areas the plants are perennial, but they are treated as annuals where there are killing frosts.

Allow 11 to 12 weeks for green packs, and 12 to 13 weeks for flowering cell packs. Using one to two plants per pot, gazanias require 13 to 15 weeks to flower in a 4″ pot.

In the southern United States allow 10 to 11 weeks for flowering pack sales, and 13 to 14 weeks for flowering 4″ pots, one to two plants per pot. Gazanias can be planted out from late March to June for flowering during early summer. Plants are tolerant of salt and can be used in coastal regions very effectively.

530

In varieties, gazanias are divided between dwarf and vigorous types. Dwarfer varieties are best in pack and 4″ pot production, sold in full bloom. Among the dwarfer varieties, Chansonette Mixture provides the earliest flowering in packs. Another good performer, the Daybreak series, has separate colors with the same dark-ringed eyes as some of the colors in Chansonette Mixture, while the Ministar series has clear, unringed eyes. All of the above grow from 8″ to 10″ tall with a 10″ spread in the garden.

For more vigorous varieties, Sunshine Giants Mixture and Splendens Grandiflora Mixture both grow large and robust to 14″ tall. Plants fill in well on 12″ centers and look similar to the vegetative varieties often sold on the West Coast for roadside plantings. Both mixtures have a range of colors, though yellow and orange are the most prevalent.

GERANIUM

CUTTING GERANIUMS

by Richard C. Oglevee
Oglevee Ltd.
Connellsville, Pennsylvania

During the late 1950s and early 1960s, the commercial production of geraniums declined because slow crop turnovers and major losses due to systemic diseases made the crop unprofitable to grow. Today, however, the situation has changed dramatically. By 1989, sales of all geraniums totaled just over 100 million pots (60% cuttings, 40% seed). The change is due to an increase in consumer demand for better performing flowering crops and an increase in the supply of clean, disease-free plants for propagation.

As the popularity of bedding plants has increased, the consumer has been looking for plants that will grow and flower in all types of climate and soil conditions. The consumer also wants a plant that is relatively labor free, requiring little or no pinching, watering, fertilizing or spraying. The geranium seems to have these qualifications. According to a recent PPGA survey, cutting geraniums account for approximately 10% of the total bedding plant production, with the future potential looking good. At the same time the crop has become more profitable for the grower as turnovers and plant quality have been increased and crop losses minimized through the use of clean stock.

As the total market for geraniums grew, so did the variety of uses for geraniums. Previously, consumers usually purchased red geraniums to be planted on Memorial Day in the cemetery. Today, consumers want geraniums in a variety of colors, both flowers and foliage, that perform in either full sun or full shade. They

A fine house of zonal geraniums as grown by a fine grower family, the Kunans, in Holbrook, Massachusetts.

also want varieties that suit large open gardens, planter boxes, window sills and hanging baskets of various sizes. The increase in demand for geraniums along with the Culture-Virusing-Indexing (CVI) program, which includes breeding and selection, has resulted in a dramatic increase in the number of good, clean cultivars now available.

The ivy geraniums, for example, have greatly improved flowering ability, plant habit and cultural adaptability. The ivies are ideally suited for a sheltered area of a garden, used as a bedding plant or in a hanging basket. For areas receiving high light and warmer temperatures, a group of ivy geraniums called the Alpine Series is recommended. There are also dwarf ivy geraniums available, such as Sugar Baby, that are well suited to small hanging baskets.

The Brocade Series, known as "fancy leaf" or "variegated-leaf" zonal geraniums, flower more freely and have more plant vigor, thanks to the CVI program. The grower now has a choice of plants such as Wilhelm Langguth or Mrs. Parker that have green-and-white foliage and red or pink flowers. Velma Cox has multicolored leaves with a small salmon bloom.

Finally for the home there is the Regal geranium (*Pelargonium domesticum*). This flowering plant, which has attracted many customers, has not always been finished reliably. Recommendations for precision finishing have been vague at best and, more often than not, inaccurate. Moreover, Regal flowers were prone to heavy shattering. However, the Regals now available will bloom consistently on a timed schedule with less shattering. Varieties are being investigated and developed for use in the garden as well as indoors.

Colorful, wonderful Regal geraniums! They do require a precooling period to flower. They are generally not good performers in outdoor plantings in hot weather, but such a lovely plant. The "poor man's azalea." In the photo is Richard Craig, Penn State University, who has done so much for geraniums.

Culture Indexing—Control of Bacteria and Fungi

The major crop losses common 20 years ago were due to various bacterial and fungal diseases—especially bacterial blight (*Xanthomonas pelargonii*) and Verticillium wilt (*Verticillium albo-atrum*)—that plug the conductive tissues and make the translocation of water and nutrients nearly impossible. Because there are no chemical protectants or cures for these diseases, once the crop is infected the disease cannot be eradicated. Hence the losses became a part of growing. Growing plants infected with these bacteria and fungi meant managing the disease instead of the plant, through low temperature, fertility and water, which in turn slowed crop turnovers.

With the advent of culture-indexing, these bacterial and fungal diseases have been controlled. Briefly, culture-indexed geraniums are the product of a laboratory procedure that allows trained personnel to visually check for the presence of systemic diseases and select cuttings that do not have the diseases. To ensure that bacterial and fungal diseases do not escape detection, the indexing or testing procedure is repeated for three consecutive generations. The plant is then placed in a specialized greenhouses called the "nucleus house." As a further check, the nucleus stock is periodically culture-indexed, and no plants are held for longer than one year.

It should be noted that culture-indexing is a procedure that allows for the selection of those cuttings not infected and does not alter the genetic structure of the geranium. Therefore, culture-indexed plants have no change in their resistance or susceptibility to fungal or bacterial diseases. If any of these diseases are introduced during production, the plants will become infected. Indexed stock should never be mixed with nonindexed stock, and plants should not be held over from year to year. It is critical to realize that no matter how well a crop is managed there is always the possibility of reinfection. If this happens, all the advantages of using culture-indexed stock will be lost. For the best results, growers must follow the strict sanitation procedures discussed below.

Before planting stock plants, the greenhouse should be clean and free from weeds, pests and diseased plant material. If the house was used previously, the entire greenhouse should be sterilized. Steam sterilization should be used as a priority treatment. On items that cannot be steamed, chemicals such as a hospital disinfectant or commercial bleach should be used. Any debris such as dead plant material, especially under raised benches, should be removed.

All soil should be treated with either steam or chemicals. The chance of recontamination will be reduced if all the soil in a given greenhouse area is treated. The floors should be sterilized with a formaldehyde solution before dumping treated soil on them. Containers need to be new, steam-sterilized, or soaked in a disinfectant (one hour in a 10% hospital disinfectant solution or ½ hour in a 10% bleach solution).

Ground or raised pot benches need to be steam-sterilized or chemically treated. Wooden benches can be sprayed or painted with a brand of copper naphthenate such as "Cuprinol." Creosote should never be used in the greenhouse due to its toxicity to plants.

Any tool or material that comes directly or indirectly in contact with the geraniums should be sterilized. Automatic watering systems and growing implements (i.e., shovels) should be soaked in a disinfectant as described above. All watering hoses should be soaked in a disinfectant. These hoses should be hung up so the nozzles never touch the ground. The use of knives in taking cuttings should be avoided. When knives must be used, keep several soaking in a disinfectant. The cutting knife should be changed every 10 minutes for a "clean" knife that has been soaking in the disinfectant.

The "clean" geranium has given the grower the ability to manage the growth of the plant as opposed to managing the disease, which results in faster crop turnovers. No longer is it acceptable for a grower to lose 20% or more of a crop. A careful grower should not lose any geraniums. The use of culture-indexed plants in conjunction with advanced cultural practices has provided the industry with better performing plants that are more profitable to grow.

Virus Problems—And Answers

With the fungal and bacterial diseases under control, it was apparent that the next major limiting factor was viral diseases. Viral diseases are much different from bacterial and fungal diseases, due to the nature of viruses. Fungal and bacterial diseases are characterized by severe crop losses, but viral diseases usually affect the quality and the overall performance of the plant. Chlorotic spots and vein clearing may indicate the presence of virus, while other symptoms, not as obvious, are reduced plant vigor, fewer and smaller flower heads, stunting, poor plant habit and poor rooting. Unless a plant without virus is grown beside the plant with virus for comparison, these "symptoms" can go unnoticed. Plants may not show any of these symptoms and still carry a virus that may lead to further infection in the greenhouse.

As in the case of bacterial and fungal diseases, there are no chemical treatments to control or eliminate a virus. Virus can only be controlled using a systematic approach of heat treatment, meristem-tip culture and virus-indexing. Like culture-indexing, virus-indexing is a laboratory procedure to test for the presence of virus. Briefly, the process starts with a culture-indexed geranium that is heat-treated for three weeks at 100°F during a 16-hour day and 95°F during the night.

A well-done Balcon geranium mid-May. In the photo: Rich Scali, Ball Seed Company.

This helps to reduce virus levels in the plant. The meristem tip, a small 0.5 to 1.0 mm cutting, is removed and propagated in test tubes in the laboratory tissue culture under sterile conditions. The resulting plant must then be virus-indexed or tested for the presence of specific viruses. Heat treatment and meristem-tip culture do not guarantee virus removal, but only aid in removing virus.

The differences between virus-indexed material and non-indexed material is dramatic. Plants are more vigorous and break more freely. They have more blooms because there are more florets per bloom and the bloom lasts longer. These plants tend to bloom sooner and are more uniform in blooming time, size and overall quality. This increases the percentage of high quality plants that command a higher price, and leads to faster crop turnovers. It all adds up to higher profits for the grower.

It is important to note that virus-indexed plants are not immune to virus. Again strict sanitation is an important step in preventing reinfection. Moreover, many viral diseases are transmitted by insects, such as aphids. It is extremely important to follow a preventive maintenance program for these pests.

Insects and Diseases

There are several pest and disease problems that the grower must be aware of in order to manage the environment. Botrytis blight, a disease caused by an airborne fungus called botrytis cinerea, lives on aging tissue such as old leaves, blooms and debris. Under the right environmental conditions, botrytis can attack and damage young, soft, succulent tissue. The fungus produces spores that are carried through the air, on splashing water and on cuttings. Once on the tissue the spores will attack the plant if the conditions of high humidity and free water are found in the greenhouse. When the cutting stubs are infected, the disease can progress several inches down the previously healthy stem.

Botrytis is always present in the greenhouse environment. The best way to control botrytis is to make conditions less favorable for its growth and development. Flowers should be removed while in the bud stage. All dead and infected plants, parts, leaves and blooms must be cleaned up and removed from around the plants and under the benches. This reduces the sources of infection and therefore the load of spores present in the greenhouse. Because botrytis spores require moisture to germinate, holding the relative humidity below dew point will reduce the number of infections. The relative humidity can be lowered by venting on dry days or venting while heating on very humid days. Weekly applications of Exotherm Termil, Daconil 2787, Chipco 26019, Ornalin or Benlate are good preventative measures. However, Benlate should be used with caution; prolonged use of Benlate at recommended rates has been shown to inhibit the rooting of cuttings in certain cultivars such as Pink Camelia, Pink Fiat and Springtime Irene.

Geraniums are attacked by a number of greenhouse pests. Pests that are particularly bothersome to geraniums include aphids, whiteflies and spider mites. These pests are a problem because of the damage they cause and the potential to carry and reinfect plants with various bacterial, fungal and viral pathogens. The most effective method to control insect damage is to follow a carefully managed spray program. Weeds must be controlled throughout the greenhouse because they serve as an ideal reservoir for spider mites and aphids. During the warmer months of the year the grower should also screen the side vents of the greenhouse to prevent the entry of insects such as aphids and whiteflies.

Aphids injure plants by piercing and sucking the sap from the plant, which causes the leaves to curl. This affects the appearance and the performance of the plant. Aphids are commonly found in groups on the stems and leaves. The female aphid is capable of producing 50 daughters, each maturing within a week under average conditions! Aphids can also introduce certain viruses to geraniums.

Whiteflies can be a problem on geraniums, particularly regal geraniums. The adult whitefly is a tiny, white moth-like insect that can fly short distances in the greenhouses. The whitefly adults and nymphs feed by piercing and sucking on the underside of the plant's leaves. Damage due to whitefly can be in the form of a stunted and yellow plant. The whitefly completes one generation from egg to larvae to adult in about 30 days. Many recommended chemicals are aimed at only one phase of the insect's life cycle, and spraying schedules must be planned accordingly for effective control.

Two-spotted spider mites, nearly invisible to the naked eye, are persistent pests with geraniums. The adults and nymphs suck the sap from the plant, resulting in mottled, bleached-appearing foliage. If a plant is heavily infested, its photosynthetic rate is decreased, resulting in minimal new growth. Under average greenhouse conditions, the spider mite requires about 11 days to develop from egg to adult. As with whitefly, the recommended chemicals for spider mite attack only certain stages of the insect's life cycle. This must be taken into consideration when setting up spray schedules to control this pest. The varieties that are susceptible to spider mites include Red Perfection, Cardinal and most of the ivy geraniums, especially Sybil Holmes.

Because chemical registration varies between states and countries, it is impossible to recommend a general spray program suited for growers across the United States and Canada. This information can be easily obtained from the local extension agent.

Another disease problem in geraniums is oedema (or edema). Oedema is a physiological problem caused by environmental conditions. On a cloudy day when the soil is warm and moist but the air is cool and moist, the plant will absorb water rapidly, but it will lose very little water through its leaves. The cells of the plant, especially the undersides of the leaves, swell with the excess water and form blisters that eventually burst. These broken cells later harden and turn brown with a corky appearance. Generally, ivy geraniums and the Irene cultivars are particularly susceptible to oedema. Among the ivies, Yale, Cornell, Beauty of Eastbourne and Amethyst are very susceptible to oedema. Cultivars such as Double Lilac White, Sugar Baby and Galilee are the more resistant varieties. Although oedema is not caused by an insect, spider mite damage can resemble oedema. The grower must be careful in the identification of the problem.

In order to control oedema, there are several steps that must be followed. Soil pH should be 5.2 to 5.7 for zonals and 5 to 5.5 for ivies, and a peat-lite medium such as the one described previously must be used. High levels of nitrogen and iron must be maintained in this type of medium. The temperature during the day must be kept cool, and the light levels should be held at less than 3,500 fc. Proper irrigation is very important: Water plants only in the morning and remove all saucers from hanging baskets.

Several Points on Propagation

The ideal cutting for propagation is a 2″ to 3″ terminal with a good active growing tip and no physical damage. Terminal cuttings are preferred because they finish two weeks earlier than the eye or heel cuttings. For disease control, cuttings should be broken off whenever possible. When breaking, it is important to break cuttings evenly, leaving no jagged edges. When clean breaks are not possible and knives must be used, they should be soaked in a disinfectant and changed frequently. Before sticking the cuttings, the bottom inch of the cuttings should be cleaned. There should never be any petioles or stipules below the soil line, because this is a source of rot. Only those petioles and stipules which will be below the soil level need to be removed.

Some researchers recommend the use of rooting hormones, while others point out that rooting hormones provide little value to cutting propagation. Rooting hormones are probably unnecessary on fast rooting varieties without fertility imbalances. However, if there is a fertility imbalance or if a slow rooting cultivar is being propagated, the rooting hormone seems to be of value. The use of rooting hormones, such as Indolebutyric Acid (IBA), have been shown to improve the uniformity of root development and to speed up the root initiation, especially on slow rooting cultivars such as Pink Camelia, Wendy Ann and most of the ivy geraniums.

IBA can be applied by using commercial dust or solution. If the liquid form of IBA is used, care must be taken not to use more than a 0.10% solution or damage will result. A fungicide such as Benlate (10%) or Captan (7%) can be added to the rooting duster or solution to help control basal rots caused by various bacterial and fungi. There are unpublished reports that Captan has also been shown to increase rooting. Rooting mixtures should always be dusted or sprayed on to the basal end of the cuttings. For disease control purposes, never dip the cuttings into a powder or solution.

There are two stages in the propagation of geranium cuttings: 1) root initiation and development and 2) a growth stage. Both stages are important in development of high-quality cuttings, but root initiation and development is probably the most critical.

The objective of propagation is to quickly put roots on a cutting to relieve the dehydration of the cutting. When a cutting is taken, the natural water supply to the leaves from the roots is eliminated, but the leaves continue to lose water or transpire. The transpiration rate must be reduced to keep the cutting alive. This is usually accomplished by raising the relative humidity around the leaves, or through the use of mist. The use of mist allows the grower to use soft, succulent cuttings, which root faster but tend to lose water more rapidly than hard cuttings.

Mist is an effective propagation tool that lowers the transpiration rate of the cuttings by raising the relative humidity around the leaves. Mist also lowers the leaf and air temperatures. The cooling is so effective that leaf temperature is often 10° to 15°F lower than air temperature. The net effect is that geraniums can be propagated under relatively high levels of light to increase the growth rate of the cutting. This higher light intensity increases the photosynthetic rate, ensuring that the cutting has the necessary carbohydrates for root initiation and development. A cutting propagated under heavy shade without mist may lack the food necessary for rapid growth because the cutting's respiration rate is higher than the photosynthetic rate.

The optimum mist program will depend on light, humidity, temperature, cultivar and the cutting's age. Ideally, the grower should try to maintain a thin layer of moisture on the leaves during the day. During the night the cutting should be misted periodically to relieve the water stress caused by evaporation. Care must be taken not to overmist as this may leach the nutrients from the foliage, especially after the cutting is rooted.

Another key factor to initiating root development is proper temperature control. The grower should provide bottom or soil heating to maintain a soil temperature of 65° to 70°F. Air temperature should be 70°F during the day with night temperatures maintained at 62°F. Air temperatures above or below these recommended levels will have a negative effect on the cutting's development. Air temperature above 75°F promotes bud development in advance of root development, which increases the transpiration rate. Air temperature below the recommended levels lowers the cutting's growth rate.

Under ideal conditions and depending on the cultivar, a callus should form on the basal end of the cutting after five days. Roots should be developed within 10 to 14 days after sticking the cutting. At this stage those cuttings for finishing should be placed in 4" pots. Using lightly rooted cuttings will minimize transplant shock. More vegetative growth will be required if these cuttings are to be shipped.

The objective of the growth stage of propagation is to promote the development of vegetative growth. Cuttings at this stage are self-sufficient and should not require mist. Temperature is an important variable in the growth stage, and the temperature in the propagating area should remain above the temperature in the stock area. Day temperature should be at least 70°F and recommended night temperature is 65°F or higher. These rooted cuttings should be spaced at 20 to 25/sq. ft., and placed on a constant feed program of 200 to 300 ppm nitrogen. Carbon dioxide can be used to increase the vegetative growth of the cuttings. The growth stage should take approximately three weeks in order to prepare the cuttings for sale.

Fast Cropping 4" Geraniums

To profitably finish geraniums one must turn over as many geraniums as possible from a given area in the shortest time possible. The use of the culture-virus-indexed geranium with new fast cropping techniques has allowed the grower to finish a 4" product in less than six weeks—from a 2" plant. Furthermore, breeding and selection have produced varieties that finish pot-to-pot, maximizing the utilization of the bench area. These pot-to-pot varieties in the red category include Irene, Stadtbern, Improved Matador, Hildegaard, Glacier Crimson, Glacier Scarlet, Glacier Carmen, and possibly Yours Truly. The pink cultivars that can be grown this way are Pink Camelia, Didden's Improved Picardy, Cherry Blossom, Salmon Irene and Veronica. Of the fancy leaf cultivars (Brocade Series), Wilhelm Langguth, Mrs. Parker and Velma Cox do well pot-to-pot, and so do many of the ivy geraniums.

The fast cropping technique requires that the medium be tested and adjusted to proper pH, salts and fertility levels before the crop is planted, because there is no time to adjust afterwards and still grow a good crop. A slightly higher fertility regimen of 350 ppm nitrogen should be used at three out of every four irrigations. This higher fertility promotes more compact plant growth with short internodes and dark green foliage. High nitrogen and soft growth do not delay flowering of geraniums.

The plant should be pushed in order to maximize its potential. Plants should not be pinched because this delays flowering. Plant height can be regulated with Cycocel, A-Rest or B-Nine. Cycocel is recommended over A-Rest and B-Nine because it provides more uniform results over a broad range of cultivars. Florel should never be used to manage the height of a finished crop because it aborts flower buds for four to six weeks, thus delaying the crop. Water should not be withheld to control plant height because this slows plant growth and lengthens finishing time.

Before spraying with Cycocel, be sure the geraniums are moist and are well fertilized to prevent plant damage. The geraniums should be sprayed on a cloudy, cool day or early in the morning. When spraying with Cycocel, a 1,500 ppm solution should be used. This is equivalent to a 1:80 dilution. Do not use a spreader sticker with the Cycocel solution.

Cycocel should be applied 17 to 21 days after planting, when the axillary shoots are ¼" to ½" in length. At this time there should be approximately seven sets of leaves on the plant. The leaves should only be sprayed to glisten without any runoff. A 1,500 ppm Cycocel spray of ¼ to ⅓ of a gallon should cover 100 sq. ft. If at the time of the application you see Cycocel running to the center of the leaf, the foliage can be syringed. This will reduce but not completely eliminate damage to the plant. If sprayed properly, yellowing may appear on the leaves in seven days, but should disappear in three weeks, with the possible exception of one or two bottom leaves. If too much Cycocel was applied, or if the conditions were not right for spraying, yellowing of the leaves will appear in three or four days, with physical damage to the plant being the end result. The grower who is unfamiliar with using Cycocel, or wants to be cautious, can use a Cycocel spray of half strength (750 ppm) with two applications seven days apart.

Some varieties may require two 1,500 ppm applications of Cycocel to control plant height. The second application should be made 10 days after the first application. The following cultivars could be included: Sincerity, Yours Truly, Irene, Toreador, Cardinal, Wendy Ann, Penny Irene, Rockford, Springfield Violet, Pascal and the Sunbelt varieties.

Gibberellic acid has been reported to increase flower size and life on geraniums. Treated blooms have been reported to last seven to 10 days longer than blooms of nontreated plants. A grower wishing to try gibberellic acid should begin with a 1 to 2 ppm solution. Plants should be sprayed to glisten after two or three florets have opened. Because little work has been done with gibberellic acid, a small trial should be conducted before deciding to use the gibberellic acid on a large block of plants.

Ivy Geraniums

As previously mentioned, ivy geraniums require more attention than zonal geraniums with respect to oedema. This holds true for finishing as well, and the steps to prevent and control oedema must be followed in finishing. Zonal geraniums can receive up to 5,000 fc. of light before the foliage and flowers start to burn. However, ivy geraniums must be grown in a greenhouse with only 2,500 fc. of light. If the light is higher, the plants will be small with tiny, cupped leaves and small blooms and some burning. The grower may notice aborted buds and florets. This is due not so much to high light, but to high air and leaf temperatures. If the leaf and air temperatures could be kept below 80°F, the high light would not affect the ivy geraniums. Because leaf temperature is so important, ivy geraniums should never be hung close to the glass, as this only multiplies the problem of high leaf temperature.

Ivy cultivars can be separated into three categories depending upon their light tolerance capacity. Those cultivars which must be grown under very low light of 2,000 to 2,500 fc. are Sybil Holmes and Sugar Baby. Other cultivars such as Beauty of Eastbourne, Balcon Imperial, Double Lilac White and Balcon Royale can be grown with 2,500 to 3,000 fc. of light. The third category is the most light tolerant and can be grown with light levels of 3,000 to 3,500 fc. This category includes such cultivars as Pascal, Galilee, Yale, Princess Balcon, Cornell, Amethyst and King of Balcon.

SEED GERANIUMS

by Vic Ball

Geraniums of all kinds are seeing good times! Over 40 million seed geraniums alone were sold in 1989 per USDA figures (see seed and zonal geranium sales graphs in the bedding plant chapter).

The fascinating point about all this is that both seed and cutting geraniums seem to be holding their own in recent years; in fact, both are expanding steadily.

The quality 4″ geranium trade often prefers a cutting geranium. They often look nicer at the point of sale—but, again, 40 million pot seed geraniums are being sold each year. Also, a bedding grower selling 18 or 24 smaller potted plants in a 21″ flat will usually grow from seed. The same for those who produce three or four plants in a pack.

An interesting exception to this is the John Van Bourgondien family in Peconic, New York. They do 150,000 4″ geraniums a year, all from seed, and the quality is really topnotch. They are heavy plants and bring a price equal to good zonals. It can be done.

On this controversy, growers tell me three things: 1) Cuttings do often make more salable, showy plants in April and May; 2) Seed plants outdoors all summer, except in cool summer areas, will look a lot better than cuttings by September or early October, and 3) So often I hear, "I make more money growing seed geraniums versus cuttings."

If there is any trend at all it might be a bit in favor of seed. An interesting point here: The first true zonal or cutting geraniums *grown from seed* are just coming onto the market as the 15th edition goes to press. The two varieties are Freckles™ (bicolor) and Classic Scarlet. This says that probably in the next few years we will see a lot more seed propagated zonal geraniums.

Surely the excellent work done by Oglevee on virus and disease control has been a major factor in favor of cuttings. The ever troublesome *Xanthomonas pelargonni* would be a disaster without Oglevee. It doesn't seem to appear much on seed crops.

Hybrid Geraniums Offer Great Performance in Packs or Pots

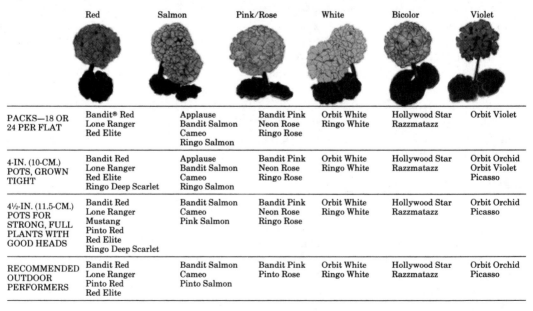

	Red	Salmon	Pink/Rose	White	Bicolor	Violet
PACKS—18 OR 24 PER FLAT	Bandit® Red Lone Ranger Red Elite	Applause Bandit Salmon Cameo Ringo Salmon	Bandit Pink Neon Rose Ringo Rose	Orbit White Ringo White	Hollywood Star Razzmatazz	Orbit Violet
4-IN. (10-CM.) POTS, GROWN TIGHT	Bandit Red Lone Ranger Red Elite Ringo Deep Scarlet	Applause Bandit Salmon Cameo Ringo Salmon	Bandit Pink Neon Rose Ringo Rose	Orbit White Ringo White	Hollywood Star Razzmatazz	Orbit Orchid Orbit Violet Picasso
4½-IN. (11.5-CM.) POTS FOR STRONG, FULL PLANTS WITH GOOD HEADS	Bandit Red Lone Ranger Mustang Pinto Red Red Elite Ringo Deep Scarlet	Bandit Salmon Cameo Pink Salmon	Bandit Pink Neon Rose Ringo Rose	Orbit White Ringo White	Hollywood Star Razzmatazz	Orbit Orchid Picasso
RECOMMENDED OUTDOOR PERFORMERS	Bandit Red Lone Ranger Pinto Red Red Elite	Bandit Salmon Cameo Pinto Salmon	Bandit Pink Pinto Rose	Orbit White Ringo White	Hollywood Star Razzmatazz	Orbit Orchid Picasso

Seed Germination

Geraniums germinate promptly and easily if the media itself (not air temperature) is kept at 75°F and uniformly moist. The germinating mix must be porous, screened, sterile and free of excess salts.

Some cultivars may produce one "flush" of seedlings seven to 10 days after sowing. Then a second flush may appear a week or so later. Simply remove and transplant seedlings as they are ready. Seedlings are fairly good size—better not aim for over 500 seedlings per 21" flat.

As of the early 1990s, probably the majority of seed geraniums are started in plugs. For details on plug cultures, schedules for seed geraniums in plugs, etc., see the bedding plant chapter elsewhere in this book.

Potting

Probably the majority of seed geraniums in the early 1990s are planted as plugs directly to 4" or 3" pots or to an A-18 (3½" plastic pot, 18 per flat). A few growers still transplant bareroot seedlings directly to 4" pots—but this uses more time. Nearly always one plug is used per 4" or 6" pot.

An interesting adaptation of seed geraniums to the mass outlets would be the crop at Henry Mast Greenhouses, Byron Center, Michigan. They do 1 million-plus 4" seed geraniums a year. A large Florida-grown plug (about 1") is planted direct to 4" pots the day after Easter pot mums go out. The crop will be "bud or bloom" and out the door in about five weeks. It's not a heavy 4" but it's clean and good, and if given good care by the home gardener will produce a fine bed of geraniums. Highly mechanized.

Growing Containers

1. It's mainly a 4" pot market—will vary from 3" to often 4½" or even 6" pots. All this depending on the grower's market. One Eastern grower reported 25% more dollars per sq. ft. using 3" plastic pots joined together. He spaces freely, gets top price. Mainly they are grown in plastic—but occasionally in clay.

2. Packs/smaller pots—a wide variety of containers are used here. Some are grown in A-18s (18 3" pots per 21" flat). Some in A-24s, some A-32s. Many are done in cell packs, eight packs of four plants each per flat. Some in open packs, six or 10 per flat, four or six plants per pack. Again, all depending on the market.

Soil Mix

Mostly a variety of commercial mixes are used—including Ball Choice. The majority of growers go this way today, mainly to save the labor of soil preparation. Also it gives them a predictable mix to make a predictable crop. In using mixes with heavy bark content be sure to start feeding as soon as plants are potted.

543

An example of the tight rotations used by growers to boost dollars per sq. ft. per year. Here's Hank Mast (right) and brother Jack, Byron (Grand Rapids), Michigan, with their May 4" seed geraniums. The Masts bring in well-established 1" plugs that take over space from Easter pot mums. In about 5 weeks most of the crop is gone!

Peat-lite mixes (peat/vermiculite), such as the Cornell mix, will grow good geraniums, much used by research workers working with geraniums. Actually any mix that's open, porous, free of excess salts and sterilized will do the job.

Temperature

Here's an interesting comment from Bob Bernacchi, a LaPorte, Indiana, grower: Bob suggests maintaining 70°F for seed germination and until the root shows through the side of the pot—typically three to four weeks after sowing. Then drop slowly to 60°F night and day for the rest of the crop.

Feeding

The best practice is to start liquid feeding with all irrigations the day plants are potted. A 20-20-20 mix at 100 ppm is recommended.

Retardants

Mainly Cycocel, will mean shorter, more compact plants and often a week earlier flowering. Cycocel is very widely used by commercial growers and is cer-

544

tainly recommended. Normal practice is one application at 1,500 ppm 40 days after sowing. That should be a plant well established in the cell-pack or Jiffy-7, etc. A rate of 1,500 ppm will mean 1¾ oz. Cycocel/1 gal. water. Spray until the leaves are wet. The second application may be made one to two weeks after the first; many growers do it—and depending on the crop it is recommended. Leaves will yellow for several weeks after the application of Cycocel—but it goes away quickly.

The cool day/warm night procedure will effectively retard seed geraniums. See the separate chapter on this subject elsewhere in this book.

Pinching

Pinching is almost never done with this crop. It will delay flowering. Seed geraniums are inherently very free branching and don't need a pinch.

Supplemental Light

HID light will hasten flowering on geraniums. Occasionally growers apply it to plugs, in some cases, on up to the 2¼″ stage. John Tomasovic, a St. Louis grower, applies HID lights to his plug flats of geraniums. He reports 10 days earlier flowering as a result. Jim Tsjuita, a Guelph, Ontario researcher, reports that 630 fc. from sowing to flowering will save four weeks time on a seed geranium crop.

When to Sow

Fortunately, there is ample data available to growers. Provided that correct temperatures, light levels, etc., are maintained, a crop of hybrid geraniums should be easily timed for the grower's market demand. You may occasionally lose three to five days in case of an abnormally dark February or March.

The table that follows is based on our own experience at West Chicago, plus reports from other growers and several university research projects, which also help bracket these critical dates. Of course, a grower's own experience under his own culture is the real key to accurate timing. If he keeps good records!

One more point on timing: What are the peak demand weeks for 4″ geraniums?

1. In the North, most growers' peak shipping is mid-April to mid-May. Mother's Day is big. Growers aim to be sold out by May 30.
2. In the South, the peak is April 15 to 25 or April 30. And the goal is to be sold out by Mother's Day.

Recommended Sowing Dates

The North—Chicago-New York Latitude

To Flower[1]	Sow Seed	Weeks to Sell
4″ Pots:		
April 15	Dec. 13	17½
May 5	Jan. 6	17
May 25	Jan. 26	17
Packs or Small Pots[2]:		
May 5[3]	Jan. 20	15
May 15	Feb. 2	14½
June 1	Feb. 22	14

The South—Atlanta-Oklahoma City Latitude

4″ Pots:		
April 1	Dec. 6	16½
April 15	Dec. 24	16
May 5	Jan. 13	16
Packs or Small Pots[2]:		
April 15[3]	Jan. 7	14
May 1	Jan. 26	13½
May 15	Feb. 13	13

[1] *"To flower" here means 75% of all plants showing a minimum of several open florets. Allow one to two weeks more to have a minimum of one fully open flower head per plant and second head well on the way—or showing color.*
[2] *For 2″ to 3″ pot size—or four plants per 5″ to 6″ open pack.*
[3] *"To flower" here means about 25% of plants showing at least some color. Two Cycocel applications were used one week apart.*

Many growers today are relying on Florida-grown, small 1″ or so started plugs of seed geraniums. It's a very fast turnover crop for the Northern grower—at a time when space is so valuable. Typically, it will be six to eight weeks from potting these Florida-started plants to flowering a salable 4″. Under especially favorable sunlight and growing conditions it takes as little as five to six weeks. The high sunlight in Florida gives them a great start. Seed geraniums are also available in small plugs—a ⅝″ "potted plant," a mature well-grown plug, will grow into a 4″ in remarkably short order.

Seed geraniums at Bryfogle's, Muncy, Pennsylvania. On the right is Ken Bryfogle with his grower. It's an A-24 crop (24 plants per flat).

Varieties—Which Are Best?

There are so many. But typical of these situations, it quickly boils down to two or three topnotch proven ones for each purpose.

A point: The major effort that had been made to improve hybrid geraniums by leaders the world over is a clue to what happens when breeders are given assurance of exclusive use of their winners. Which is the case in seed geraniums (being F_1 hybrids). In contrast, look at the restricted breeding effort and money being spent on such nonhybrid species as zonal or cutting geraniums, carnations, poinsettias and foliage plants (almost zero breeding to support our number one dollar crop)!

Back to "all the best" in seed geranium varieties:

Much intensive and very good breeding work is being done by seed firms the world over on seed geraniums. Here are five "families" all important in today's world. Growers tend to use one of these families of varieties since they tend to flower at the same time and the same height. Most of these families have a wide variety of colors.

Ringo. An older variety and still very popular. Good in packs, accommodates pot-tight growing.

Bandit. A new variety, very large flowers, lots of zonal coloring on the leaves. A fine 4″.

Elite. A wide range of colors, large flower heads, fine outdoor performance.

Orbit. Very free branching, a bit earlier than most.

Pinto. Widely used, attractive in spring pots, best outdoor performer.

There are several others worth mentioning:

Multibloom. New in the early 1990s, more but smaller flower heads. An interesting new approach.

Lone Ranger. A very intense, red color and very large flower heads—outstanding outdoors. Red only, for now.

The new tetraploids. These are the "zonal or cutting geraniums grown from seed." So far, only Freckles™, a bicolor (an AAS winner), and Classic Scarlet are available.

Petal Shatter on Seed Geraniums

A vexing problem. The grower works for months to produce quality plants, then just as they are set out on a garden center display rack, petals start falling. Messy! Several answers:

Silver thiosulfate. A spray that was developed in Holland, perfected at Michigan State University, which does control this shatter very well. Here are directions for preparing the STS solution—developed by Willie Faber, Extension Floriculturist at Ohio State University. This method first prepares a concentrate, then dilutes it:

1. Weigh 20 g. (¾ oz.) silver nitrate and dissolve in 1 pint distilled water.
2. Weigh 120 g. (4½ oz.) sodium thiosulfate (prismatic) and dissolve in a separate pint of distilled water.

547

Seed geraniums two different ways. The grower: Jack Tomasovic, St. Louis. The plant on the right was a 1" Florida plug, potted March 1. The plant on the left was Jack's own home-grown plug (with HID light), potted several weeks earlier. The Florida plant flowered earlier.

3. Pour the silver nitrate solution slowly into the sodium thiosulfate solution and stir rapidly to mix.
4. This will give you 1 qt. of stock solution.
5. For seed geraniums: Use 2 tsp. ($^1/_3$ oz.) of this stock solution to 1 gal. of water for a direct spray solution. Spray 10 ml. per plant, just as florets show color. This amount of stock solution will prepare 96 gals. of spray, which is enough to treat 36,000 plants.
6. For holiday cactus: Use 2 oz. of this stock solution to 1 gal. of water for a direct spray solution. Spray 10 ml. per plant at tight bud stage. This amount of stock solution will prepare 16 gals. of spray, which is enough to treat 6,000 plants.

Other ways to ease the shatter problem:

1. If at all possible, ship plants out just as they show color. Shatter won't be a problem.
2. Be sure plants are watered before shipping. Avoid tight boxes, tight truck bodies; ethylene builds up and aggravates petal drop.
3. During growing of the crop, provide ample ventilation. Somehow plants from low, humid, poorly ventilated, dark houses shatter worst.

DIRECT STICK GERANIUMS

by Robert Danielson
Ball Seed Company

One of the trends today along with material handling and mechanization has been the shift from liners (2" to 2½" plants) to the direct stick of unrooted cuttings. Many pot mums and kalanchoes are grown from unrooted, direct stick in the finished pot. Some geranium growers have practiced this direct stick with their later plantings of zonal geraniums with success. The most opportunities for the direct stick zonal geranium are for the late plantings of 3", 4" and 4½" for May and June flowering. The direct stick of geraniums is practiced most heavily by growers in the Sunbelt, Florida, Texas, and Southern California.

Unrooted geranium cuttings are available now from several off-shore sources and in large quantities. Transportation and delivery services have improved to almost every location in the country. The success of a direct stick unrooted program depends on receiving the cuttings promptly in prime condition and providing the necessary environment and sanitation to prevent any losses to disease problems. For this program to be successful, the product should finish in seven to 10 weeks depending on time of year and the growing environment. If the unrooted cuttings are purchased from a propagator, you should receive them within 48 hours from the shipping point. The unrooted cuttings should be stored below 55°F until stuck, and lower if possible. Unrooted geranium cuttings can safely be cooled to 40°F and below.

Sanitation and receiving clean cuttings are the two most important features of this program, providing you can provide a good growing environment. The geranium is very susceptible to a number of disease problems in propagation; Pythium, Rhizoctonia, Botrytis, and Bacterial Soft Rot. It is important to use sterile media, clean or new containers, and sterilized clean benches. The greenhouse environment should be able to maintain 65°F air temperature and have bottom heat for the

I see a lot of geranium baskets these days—colorful and they do flower well outdoors if given reasonable care. The mix of overhead baskets and flat annuals below is common in the industry! This photo taken at Young's Nursery Co., Gallatin, Tennessee.

propagation benches. In addition to or in place of bottom heat, it would be important to have internal horizontal air flow fans. They provide for a more uniform temperature within the house, and circulation of air around the clock maintains a disease-free environment. The area above the propagation benches should be free of hanging baskets or overhead shelves which can contribute to disease or light problems.

The growing media should be an open mix which retains moisture, has good aeration, and can be sterilized for ensured disease control. The filled growing container should be placed on the bench and be thoroughly watered prior to sticking the cutting. This practice makes it easier to firmly stick the cutting and reduces the need for applying a lot of water after sticking.

The average cutting is between 1½″ and 2½″ long and should be stuck deep enough to stand erect. This is between ½″ and ⅝″ deep. Remove any leaves or stipules that remain on the cutting below the soil line. This will prevent disease problems from entering the stem. The smaller cuttings with a good growing meristem do not need a pinch on the finished crop since the tip is not in a flowering mode, all the eyes that develop are ready to branch. Cuttings produced in high light areas have better meristems and branch freely given the right environment.

All preparation work, cleaning the benches, mixing the media, sterilizing media, filling and watering the pots thoroughly, should all be done prior to cuttings arrival. The cuttings should be removed from the box and stuck immediately upon arrival (maximum 24 hours). Geranium cuttings do not have a long shelf life at any temperature. The smaller cuttings with smaller leaves and good substance will not usually develop yellow leaves and disease problems as will cuttings with large leaves and soft stems.

The ideal rooting temperature is 72° to 75°F soil temperature and 65° to 70°F air temperature. It is important to maintain the turgidity of the cutting during propagation. To reduce stress during high light periods, cut the light on the benches to 3,000 fc. This will eliminate the need for excess mist and reduce disease problems. Direct stick geranium cuttings can be rooted without mist by reducing the light during the first three weeks, but return the bench to full sunlight as soon as cuttings are rooted.

The use of a rooting hormone can improve both density of roots and time of rooting if not overdone. Excess amounts cause over-callusing and prevent root formation. The best method is to use a #1 rooting hormone powder with 10% Captan which can be dusted lightly on the basal end of the cutting. After the cuttings are stuck, water lightly and drench with Subdue/Benlate combination at a safe rate. Drenches with either Banrot or Captan can also be effective as a prevention.

From this point on until rooted, use only enough mist or water to prevent stress or excessive wilting. The cuttings should have only light waterings until callus or root horns appear in 7 to 10 days. Flooding the pots and soaking the foliage creates a good environment for botrytis or other disease problems.

After 10 to 14 days, begin feeding with a complete fertilizer 20-10-20 or 15-15-15 at 200 ppm N and K. When the plants have developed a good root system and new foliage, a constant fertilizer program should be established. Also, a supplemental feeding of potassium nitrate and calcium nitrate can be used to develop a stronger plant with more substance and compact habit.

If the more vigorous varieties become too stretched for a close spacing, the use of Cycocel 21 days after sticking, at 1,000 ppm (1 oz./gal.), will control stretching and increase bottom breaks. When you have stuck the cutting pot to pot, not in carriers, it will benefit the quality and compactness of the plants to begin spacing four to five weeks after sticking.

The direct stick crop stuck on March 15 should be ready for sale May 15 to June 1 in a good growing environment. With an early Easter, a direct stick geranium can follow an Easter crop for early June sales. The direct stick method can be perfected for a quality product and be cost effective.

A TOP QUALITY GROWER'S APPROACH

by Vic Ball

Bernacchis, LaPorte, Indiana, pot plant and bedding plant producers know cutting geraniums, do a lot of them and do them well. Here briefly is their plan, mainly from Bob Bernacchi.

Stock Plant Handling

Most commercial growers today rely on either small 2", rooted cuttings or unrooted cuttings from specialists. Managing stock plants is another task during the busy winter/spring months. It's also very exacting disease-wise. Many growers are glad to turn the job over to specialists.

Bernacchis produce a major volume of cuttings for other growers, plus cuttings for their own 4" crop. So stock plants are important here—you'll see several houses of them. Here's how it's done.

Here's one of the 10" pots with three 4" geranium stock plants as it looked early October. In the photo, Bob Bernacchi.

They receive cuttings from Oglevee in mid-August, pot to a 4″ and, in mid-October, they put three of these 4s into a 2 gal. container—roughly 10″. Plants are pinched when ready. The first unrooted cuttings are available around January 1. They use a commercial mix. The temperature for stock plants in the fall is 68° to 70°F night and day. Bob Bernacchi says, "We seem to get better growth that way than we do with running a cooler night." A constant level feed is done at 250 ppm N. The tubs are spaced a bit as they develop. Says Bob, "We do apply Florel ¾ oz./gal. twice as plants develop. It does increase cutting production. The first application is done in the 4″ stage, four to five weeks after planting, then another one as needed."

Many growers pot one cutting to a larger tub or pot mid-summer. It works. There is substantial space saved by keeping the stock plants in 4″ pots for six or eight weeks.

The rooting procedure is covered in detail earlier in this chapter—including all-important sanitation! Bernacchis do carry 70°F night and day soil temperature during rooting, and do use some mist at first. They do not sterilize the commercial mix used in rooting.

Producing the Early Crop of 4″

The first flush of cuttings available around January 1 is direct-stuck and rooted in a 4½″ pot. Again, commercial mix (Sunshine) is used. In most cases they do not use rooting hormones—partly due to concern about spreading xanthomonas. The media temperature in the pots during rooting is 70°F night and day. After roots hit the edge of the pot, the temperature is dropped down slowly to 60°F night and day—until flowering.

Bernacchis do make one very soft pinch on this early crop, but no top cutting is taken. Says Bob, "Taking a cutting from this plant takes away from the final quality—and top quality is our goal."

"We space the plants about February 1, or after Valentine's Day. The temperature after roots are developed will be 60°F night and day. Feeding at this stage is constant injection at 250 ppm N."

Cycocel retardant is used especially on their seed geranium crop and also on some crops of zonal cuttings, as needed.

"The second flush of cuttings is taken about February 15, again, direct stuck one per 4½″ pot. They're rooted at 65°F night and day. They will be salable about May 15 (Mother's Day)."

Many good growers do root cuttings in a propagating bed. Direct stick does demand very careful watering—it's easy to overdo.

Xanthomonas—A Classic Encounter

Xanthomonas is a very tough problem. It destroyed the California geranium cutting industry 30 years ago. Even today we hear of growers losing their geranium crops—often very suddenly, the first warm days of spring—from this same problem.

Bernacchis had an encounter with xanthomonas quite a while ago (spring 1982), but it's such a classic story, tells so much about xanthomonas, I thought it worth including.

First, Bernacchis were and still are clean, top quality growers. Fresh stock plants from a top specialist are brought into a super clean greenhouse each season.

Back to spring 1982. All was well until early or mid-March. The first sign of problems: Several of their geranium cutting customers reported serious wilting of their plants on warm days.

To make a long story short, Bernacchis called in Allen Hammer, their able Indiana extension man, who quickly identified the problem as xanthomonas and developed a plan of action. They did these things:

- First, they temporarily discontinued harvesting and rooting of cuttings.

- They raised the temperature of the stock plant area sharply—up to minimum 75°F night and day and even 80° or 85°F on sunny days. The objective was to force out symptoms of xanthomonas on any plants that may have become infected.

  It worked beautifully. Bob Bernacchi still remembers, "Every day we'd find several dozen more stock plants with wilt developing. We immediately removed them from the house. This went on for several weeks. Each day we would detect and remove a few more infected plants. Then, rather suddenly, in spite of the high temperature, no more disease symptoms appeared." They assumed (correctly) that all infected plants had been identified by the warm temperature treatment. At this point they had discarded 1,200 of their 6,000 stock plants.

  Harvesting of unrooted cuttings was resumed—with strong emphasis on sanitation. Fortunately they had in fact removed all bad plants and they were able to complete production of cuttings for both themselves and for customers. Says Bob, "We replaced 38,000 cuttings—but the rest of them were good."

  Special credit to the Bernacchis for sharing this experience with other growers.

Dramatic evidence of what happens when you overwater a geranium. The plant on the left was watered daily, the smaller plant on the right, only as needed. Both were potted the same day. In the photo is Debbie Hamrick, a helpful contributor to this 15th edition.

RECOMMENDED VEGETATIVE VARIETIES

by Bill Kluth
Ball Seed Company

Variety	Flower Color	Foliage Color	Zone	Flower Response	Outdoor Performance	4" Performance	Overall Rating
Reds							
Crimson Fire	crimson red	medium	yes	medium	vigorous	vigorous	★★★
Kim*	scarlet red	medium	no	early	medium	medium	★★★★★
Mars*	scarlet red	medium	no	early	medium	medium	★★★★★
Sincerity	orange red	medium	yes	medium	vigorous	vigorous	★★★
Sunbelt Dark Red	dark red	medium	yes	late	vigorous	vigorous	★★★
Tango*	dark red	dark	no	early	medium	medium	★★★★★
Victoria*	crimson red	medium	no	early	medium	compact	★★★
Yours Truly	orange red	medium	yes	medium	vigorous	medium	★★★
Pinks & others							
Alba*	white	medium	no	early	medium	medium	★★★★
Aurora	purple	medium	yes	early	medium	medium	★★★
Blues*	pink w/dark eye	medium	no	early	medium	medium	★★★★
Charleston*	coral	dark	no	early	medium	medium	★★★★★
Cherry Blossom	light pink	medium	yes	early	vigorous	vigorous	★★★
Disco*	magenta/rose	medium	no	early	medium	compact	★★★★
Helena*	salmon	medium	no	early	medium	medium	★★★★★
Katie*	soft pink	medium	yes	early	medium	medium	★★★★
Pink Camellia	light pink	medium	yes	early	medium	medium	★★
Pink Expectations*	salmon pink	medium	yes	early	medium	medium	★★★★
Pink Satisfaction*	light pink	medium	yes	early	medium	medium	★★★★
Rio*	single pink w/eye	dark	no	early	medium	medium	★★★★
Risque*	pink w/dark eye	medium	no	early	medium	medium	★★★★
Snowhite*	white	light	no	early	medium	medium	★★★
Snowmass	white	light	no	early	vigorous	vigorous	★★
Sunbelt Coral*	melon	medium	yes	medium	medium	medium	★★★★
Twist*	bright coral/pink	dark	no	early	medium	compact	★★★★
Valerie*	coral	medium	yes	early	medium	compact	★★★★
Veronica*	magenta/rose	medium	no	early	medium	medium	★★★★★
Wendy Ann	salmon pink	medium	yes	medium	vigorous	vigorous	★★★

Patented variety

GERBERA *(Transvaal Daisy)*

Annual (G. jamesoni), **6,000 to 7,000 seeds/oz. Germinates in 10 days at 70°-75°F.**

by Michael Behnke
Highwoods Nursery, Inc.
Winter Haven, Florida

Gerbera daisies have now taken a place alongside geraniums in many greenhouses as an important pot and bedding crop. Significant improvements in uniformity, earliness, habit, color and flower form have been made in seed varieties since Happipot was first introduced. There are now cultivars that flower consistently double, others with dark eyes, separate colors, and bicolor petals. Among the dwarf pot types are Tempo, Parade, Nain, Cyclops and Festival, as well as Happipot.

Tissue-cultured gerbera have also been bred for production in larger 6″ pots. The most notable of these is the Sunburst series. Some shorter cut-flower varieties from Holland are adapted to pot production.

Breeding programs for cut gerbera in Holland and the United States are advancing at a rapid pace. The Dutch are emphasizing keeping quality and high productivity in their work, while American programs are selecting for stronger color and performance in higher light. There is also an interest in smaller flowers

Gerberas make a striking pot plant!

more suitable for bouquets. Top American cuts are Pensacola, Ohio, Oklahoma, Texas, Arizona and New Mexico. Among the many Dutch selections are Fleur, Tanja, Darling, Roulette, Maria, Tamara and Barcelona and the Terra series.

Propagation

Seed is the method most used for propagating potted gerbera. However, tissue culture is used more often for cuts. Division is now seldom practiced commercially.

A mix of 60% perlite and 40% peat is good for germinating gerbera. Approximately 1,000 seeds may be broadcast in a 14" x 18" flat and covered with a thin layer of vermiculite. About 70% usable seedlings at transplant is an average yield. Use bottom heat to maintain a soil temperature of 68 °F. Direct sunlight is to be avoided, and seeds must be kept moist at all times or germination is uneven. Emergence will be in 7 to 14 days. In about four weeks when two true leaves develop, transplant seedlings to cell-packs, 2¼" pots or Jiffy-Strips.

Tissue-cultured plantlets are usually sent to specialist propagators for adaptation to greenhouse conditions. At stage III of their growth they may come still in culture jars or in plastic bags. If the plants are shipped in jars, the agar medium must be thoroughly washed away with water. They should be immediately planted into cell-packs, 2¼" pots or Jiffy-Strips. Soil should be clean and well-drained. Several of the soilless plug mixes do a good job and are easy to handle. After transplanting, put plantlets under 50% shade with intermittent mist and drench with Banrot, Truban plus Benlate, or Subdue plus Benlate. Mist cycles will depend on the stage of growth and individual conditions at each operation. Mist can be gradually reduced, and most plantlets will be ready for planting in six weeks. Keep the temperature at 77 °F during the day and minimum 60 °F at night. Feeding may begin at the rate of 100 ppm N and K in two to three weeks or when plants become established. Since tender new growth is easily burned, soluble fertilizers should be rinsed from foliage.

Division is a method of propagation still used in the garden. June is a good time to divide one- or two-year-old clumps so that size is reached for flowering in the fall.

Pot Production

When five true leaves have developed, plant liners in a well-drained mix with a pH close to 6.5. Some research indicates that gerbera grow best in mixes with less than 20% bark. Crowns should not be buried. As gerbera are heavy feeders, 250 ppm N from a balanced fertilizer at each watering will provide adequate nutrition. In some programs Osmocote 14-14-14 at 8 lbs./cu. yd. is the only source of fertilizer. During warm weather in Florida, 14-14-14 releases too rapidly and, instead, slower 18-6-12 is used at the same rate. Magnesium and iron deficiencies are not uncommon when gerbera are grown in soilless mixes. Magnesium sulfate at 1½ lbs./100 gals. or chelated iron drenches will restore vigor quickly. Foliar application of minor elements is less effective.

Pot gerbera are done easily and well in the south Florida climate. Here is Jeff Lovell of Lovell Farms, Miami, Florida, in a house of 4″ plants.

Space requirements are dependent upon light quality and market demands. For the first month plants may be spaced pot-to-pot. Final spacing for 6″ pots is typically 12″. In northern areas more space may be needed in winter. Final spacing for 4″ pots can be as close as 7″ for dwarf types to 10″ for the larger varieties.

Growth regulators are helpful in situations where pots must be spaced tightly. B-Nine may be used as a 2,500 ppm spray two weeks after potting if leaf petioles appear to be stretching. Bonzi at 1 oz./gal. is effective and does not fade color or reduce flower size when applied late. A-Rest as a drench at 0.25 mg a.i. per 6″ pot is also used.

Gerbera grow best under maximum light intensity. Northern greenhouses should not be shaded at all during fall, winter and spring. Temperature is not as critical as with some other crops. Day temperatures of 70° to 80°F are optimum. For pot production most growers hold night temperature near 60°F, but some in Florida run regularly at 48°F.

Production time from 2¼″ liners to flower is approximately 10 weeks. Gerbera will not bloom at one time. The first few flowers appear about eight weeks after transplanting, and the last plants begin blooming about four weeks later.

Cut Flower Production

Ground beds are usually between 2½′ to 3½′ wide. Either two or three rows are common, with plants spaced on 10″ or 12″ centers. Growers generally mound beds or use sideboards. Beds are replanted annually and should be amended with peat or other organic matter to improve fertilizer retention and water-holding capacity. Soil testing is done, and if calcium, magnesium or phosphorus are needed, then dolomite or superphosphate is incorporated.

Raised benches are sometimes used, and several large Northern growers are planting in 2- or 3-gallon nursery containers instead of beds. The yield is slightly less, but containers help isolate soil-borne fungus that can be very damaging. Unthrifty plants may be immediately replaced, and at the end of the season the plants are sold for landscape use.

Trickle irrigation is the most common means of applying water and fertilizer. In Florida, beds receive two or three pounds of slow release 18-6-12/100 sq. ft., along with an additional 100 to 200 ppm N and K at each watering. If supplemental soluble fertilizer cannot be applied, four or five lbs. may be mixed into the first 6″ of soil before transplanting.

First bloom is 10 or 11 weeks after transplanting from 2¼″ liners, somewhat more for Northern locations.

Cut gerbera is a major crop in Holland. Growers do such a good job of packing them—each flower face up for both protection and display.

Most Florida gerbera for cut flowers are grown in open fields, sawtooth and saran houses. Structures in Florida are usually unheated, but in-bench or bottom heat appears to be a trend of the future. As long as the soil remains warm, air temperature at night may be set 10 degrees lower than normal. Northern growers, who seem to require higher night temperatures to keep plants active, set thermostats near 60°F.

For beds, average production of flower stems in a season is around 20/sq. ft., and 25 to 30 is considered very good. Blooms are harvested by pulling sideways when the first row of outer staminate flowers show pollen. Early harvesting may result in wilting or closing at night. Preservatives are useful, but flowers should be shipped as soon as possible. Do not store cold. Delivery upright in water prevents bending of flower stems, but most growers box and ship dry.

Pest Control

Pythium, fusarium, verticillium, phytophthora and rhizoctonia are soil-borne diseases that cause serious losses. Beds and benches should be steamed or treated with methyl bromide prior to planting. Soil must be allowed to dry somewhat between irrigations. Along with strict sanitation and clean stock, drainage is an absolute requirement. Some beds are mounded as much as a foot above walks. Field soils and ground beds are often ditched or tiled so that excess water can be moved away rapidly. Banrot, Truban, Benlate and Subdue are all useful.

Foliar diseases are pseudomonas, alternaria, botrytis and powdery mildew. Presence of these organisms suggests improper watering practices or inadequate ventilation.

Daconil and Manzate are effective chemical controls for fungi. As a bacteria, pseudomonas is difficult to manage. Conditions favorable to most other leaf spots also promote its spread. Pseudomonas seems to be more of a problem where leaf miner populations are high.

Spray programs effective against whitefly are usually adequate for thrip and leaf miner. Talstar, Plantfume 103, Thiodan, Premex and Safer Soap in rotation are presently widely used.

GEUM

by Jim Nau
Ball Seed Company

Perennial (G. quellyon, formerly G. chiloense)**, 10,000 seeds/oz. Germinates in 21 to 28 days at 65° to 70°F. Cover the seed upon sowing.**

Geum can be somewhat difficult to germinate; by alternating day and night temperatures by 8° to 10°F, germination can be increased. This is especially true if using seed saved from last year's sowing. Flowers are semi-double to double and measure up to 1½" to almost 2" across. Flower colors are predominantly red, yellow and shades between these two. Plants produce a mass of foliage in which long flowering stems to 20" develop. Overall, plants can get 18" to 24" tall. Geum is hardy in USDA zones 4 to 8, and flowers during May and June.

Sowings made in mid-winter to mid-spring will be of good size and salable 10 to 11 weeks after sowing. Plants will be sold green and will not flower the same season from seed. For blooming plants in June, sow in July of the previous year, transplant to quart or gallon containers as needed, and overwinter with other perennials.

Mrs. Bradshaw is the most common of the geum varieties on the market. It has 1½" flowers of bright red held on upright stems in May. Plants range in height from 18" to 24" tall. Lady Stratheden has deep golden-yellow flowers to 1¾" across that are semi-double or double. Plants bloom in May.

GLADIOLUS

by Vic Ball

Gladiolus could be called a major among the minor crops. It is an important crop in Florida—the largest grower does over a thousand acres of them. Florida is in crop from November until June. Other growers, spread all the way from Florida to Canada, flower crops from winter on as the spring season advances. The earliest Midwestern crop would be planted April 1 and would flower in mid-summer. It is also a delightful cut flower and border plant for the home gardener pretty much all over the United States.

Here's a brief outline of the crop as it is done by Manatee Farms, Bradenton, Florida's largest gladioli forcer. I talked with Whiting Preston.

The Florida gladioli are harvested from November through mid-June. A furrow is dug, bulbs are hand-set (upright), then covered mechanically. Rows are 6' apart, bulbs are spaced with an inch or more between the bulb. It's mostly sand in the southern Florida area so lots of feed is required—around 2,000 lbs./acre/crop.

Aphids are a particular problem both because of the aphids themselves and because they are a vector for cucumber mosaic which is another difficult problem. Also thrips are widespread in this area.

Watering is done by controlled subirrigation. In fact, the water table is brought up under the roots to provide water as needed. There is no roof—the crops are grown right outdoors in the area roughly from Bradenton to Naples.

Manatee ships cut glads all over the United States and Canada. They are all shipped upright in small buckets of water (gladioli are geotropic, so the tips would turn upright if the stems were laid flat). Stems are cut as the first color shows.

The trend on the gladiolus market as of the early 1990s is steady. There are lots

560

of problems in Florida: scarcity of good water, good land is being taken up by subdividers and freezes are difficult. Manatee does about 1,200 acres a year of cut glads plus a variety of other cut flower crops.

The gladiolus is, again, a delightful cut flower and border plant for the home gardener. Bulbs can be planted in the spring, around April 1, after the last freeze. They will normally flower in about 90 days. A succession of plantings can be made—the last must be timed to flower before killing frost.

GLOXINIA

by Jack Sweet and Paul Cummiskey
Earl J. Small Growers, Inc.
Pinellas Park, Florida

Gloxinias *(Sinningia speciosa)* have increased in popularity to the extent that many growers consider them to be a major crop. The wide variety of colors and types include double and single varieties, standard solid colors that run predominately red, pink, deep purple lavender, or white, as well as many shades of two-tones with white centers or white rims, and a few new spotted types are now appearing.

Gloxinias can be grown from tubers or seed; however, tubers are available only in mid-winter, so this limits their flowering period to the early spring months, whereas seedlings are available all year long. Gloxinias from seed are also much more economical because the tubers are imported mostly from Belgium and have increased in cost in recent years. Most growers purchase gloxinias as seedlings from specialty growers instead of planting seed.

For those who wish to start with seed they must use much care and have a warm moist house with 65° to 70°F nights. The seed is very fine, 800,000 seeds/oz., and should be planted in a light media with very little, if any, covering over the seed. The tiny seed takes two to three weeks to germinate and will be ready for first transplanting in about six weeks. Second transplanting goes directly into 6″ pots about four weeks later, making total crop time from seed to spring flowering about six months.

Gloxinia seedlings in small pots can be purchased any week of the year from specialty growers and have proven to be a very profitable crop. Many growers raise them as a year-round crop without any special requirements. They do require a reasonably warm night temperature of 65°F with at least 75°F days to grow properly, but no night lighting, black shade, pinching or disbudding is needed for normal growth.

There are two basic strains of gloxinia available as seedlings—the regular florist grade strains that are ideal for 6″ to 6½″ pots, and now the fast grower Super Compact strain developed for 4″ to 5″ pots that are so ideal for the mass market.

561

Gloxinias are an important "minor" greenhouse crop—especially for spring and summer. On the left is the late John Holden, the widely known American seedsman.

They are a much faster crop, flowering in six to nine weeks on the bench, and can be sleeved and boxed for shipping. These Super Compact strains will flower three to four weeks ahead of the standard types, can be grown on 9″ centers, and produce 2½ to 3 times as many plants in the same space during the course of one year.

Specialist-produced seedlings purchased in small pots should be unpacked as soon as received, placed in trays in a warm greenhouse, watered lightly to help acclimate them, and potted when convenient in a few days. Do not leave gloxinia seedlings too long in a small pot as they become stunted rapidly and will flower prematurely with a much smaller plant and only a few buds. In fact, any type of shock during the first few weeks after receiving gloxinia seedlings can produce stunted inferior plants that bloom early with only a few flowers. Too much fertilizer, high light, high temperature, or loss of root system causes premature flowering of gloxinias.

Starting with small gloxinia seedlings, the following procedures will produce good finished plants in 10 to 14 weeks depending on the season. They grow much faster in the long warm days of summer.

Potting

Plants should be potted deep, ¼" to ½" from crown of plant, in a loose potting soil containing plenty of peat and some soil amendments such as perlite, vermiculite, calcine clay or coarse sand for good aeration. Better grades of peat-lite mixes can also be used. Heavy soil mixes with poor aeration will result in poor root development and stunted foliage. Use a loose, well-balanced soil media that has plenty of peat and perlite for good aeration. Set the seedling well down into the soil to stabilize the plant, leaving only the four uppermost leaves above the level of soil. Gently tap the pot to level the soil, but do not pack around the plant as gloxinias like a very loose open soil mix. Next, the plant should be watered in lightly with a good dual-purpose fungicide such as Banrot, Benlate, or Benlate and Subdue. This will eliminate most disease problems that might show up much later in the crop.

Fertilizer

Gloxinias are moderate feeders and cannot use as much fertilizer as other flowering pots such as mums, poinsettias or lilies. Excellent results can be had using weekly feedings with 2 lbs./100 gals. of a 15-16-17 peatlite formula alternated with plain calcium nitrate at the same strength. If desired, slow-release fertilizers such as Osmocote 14-14-14 may be incorporated in the potting soil, but must be used at one-fourth recommended strength. Be careful not to use any fertilizer with excessive amounts of phosphate or urea (ammonia), as gloxinias react poorly to both. Remember 20-20-20 has a very high amount of both and is not recommended.

Temperature

Greenhouse temperatures should range from 65°F nights to 75°F days for best results. In northern climates, tempered water is recommended for gloxinias. Water below 50°F can cause injury to foliage and root systems.

Light

Optimum light intensity for gloxinias is between African violets and pot mums—about 2,000 to 2,500 fc. Excessive light above 3,000 fc. will cause yellow blotched foliage, hard growth, or small irregular light brown spots on leaves.

Height Control

To produce a choice gloxinia, B-Nine can be used 12 to 16 days after potting. This will shorten the main stem and leaf petioles, producing a sturdy well-shaped plant. The suggested B-Nine rate on gloxinias is only one-third that used on mums— approximately 0.10%. This can be made by dissolving B-Nine SP at the rate of 2 tsp./gal. of water. A second application may be used 7 to 10 days later for plants grown under low-light conditions (under 2,000 fc.). Bonzi has shown promise recently, particularly in reducing flower stem stretch during warm periods of the year. Use one application of Bonzi at 1 oz./gal. of water as a light foliar spray (ONLY) when buds start to grow above foliage (three to four weeks before flowering). This controls leaf expansion and stretch of primary flower stalks.

Disease

Immediately after potting, a good fungicide drench should be applied. Use either Banrot at 8 oz./100 gals. of water, or Benlate at 6 oz. plus Subdue 2E (Ridomil) at 1½ oz./100 gals. of water. A second application may be applied four weeks later for complete disease control to last the entire production time. A light foliar rinse should be applied after fungicide drench to eliminate possible injury to foliage from residue left on foliage.

Crop Production Time

Winter—December through March	13 to 14 weeks
Spring—April and May	12 weeks
Summer—June through September	10 weeks
Fall—October and November	11 to 12 weeks

Remember, the faster growing Super Compact strain of gloxinia will flower three to four weeks faster than the above schedules.

For growing temperatures below 65 °F, add two weeks to the above schedule. Do not allow temperatures to fall below 60 °F. Gloxinias are delayed by low day or night temperatures and dark overcast winter days. Auxiliary lights such as fluorescent or HID lights which produce 200 fc. or more at bench level, used in the daylight periods and extended into the night (8 a.m. to 10 p.m.), will speed up winter growth by several weeks.

Insects

Cyclamen mites are too small to be seen without a magnifier, but may be detected by stiffening and discolored reddish-brown center leaves. Pentac or Kelthane will kill cyclamen mites as well as other mites. Army worms or loopers can be controlled with Mavrik, Dipel or Resmethrin aerosol. Thrips attack the growing tips of small plants and can cause the leaves to grow out deformed with cuts, elongated holes or ragged edges. Because of increased thrip problems, including some strains of virus (tomato spotted wilt virus) that can be carried by thrips, it is suggested to control them with alternate sprayings of several different insecticides such as Lindane, Orthene, Mavrik or Avid 0.15 ED. During periods of heavy infestation, spraying twice a week may be necessary to control any influx of thrips that could come from outside, or freshly hatched adults from the soil pupae stage.

GODETIA

by Jeff McGrew
Ball Seed Company

Annual/biennial *(Godetia whitneyi)*, **37,000 seeds/oz., 1,300 seeds per gram. Germination in 10 days at 70 °F—dark.**

Godetia is being transformed from a garden plant into a dependable field-grown cut flower. Leading the way in this market transformation is a new F_1 class of godetia called the Grace series. This relatively new hybrid series (introduced in 1987 in the United States) is available in salmon, red, rose/pink, and shell pink, with lavender becoming available in 1990.

The new Grace series godetia is a promising cut flower for the central California (Watsonville) area. Here is Paul Baldwin with a several-acre field of them. They are at their best in late winter/early spring. This January crop was clearly delayed in flowering.

Godetia Grace series.

Godetia is a charming, colorful garden plant and now a promising cut flower.

Godetia prefers a cool growing environment; optimal temperatures of 60° to 75 °F days and 50 °F nights will produce the best quality. Night temperatures of 63 °F or above can delay flower bud initiation.

A plant height of 2' to 3' is possible, with 10 to 20 quality cut flower stems being produced per plant depending on cultural practices and growing conditions. Individual stem lengths of 12" to 18", which produce clusters of five to 10 flower buds on the top of each stem, will develop from a strong lateral branching growth habit.

Six- to eight-week-old seedlings (three to four true sets of leaves) are commonly planted out in February to April in temperate growing areas and after the fear of frost in colder areas. A crop time of four to five months is common if planted in spring or summer (from sow to harvest).

A crop spacing of 10" to 12" centers between plants is commonly used. For field production no pinching is usually practiced. In Japan, godetia is produced in the greenhouse in the winter months and a soft pinch, leaving seven to nine sets of leaves, is frequently done. Sometimes a thinning or removing of spindly growth and excess shoot development is done as a crop maintenance practice.

Godetia prefers a well-drained soil with a pH of 5.5 as optimal. Godetia has only average fertility requirements. Too high an availability of nitrogen can cause excess vegetative growth with stretched and weak shoots. Phosphorus is beneficial for proper flower development.

These plants are hardy and usually are not bothered by many insects and diseases. Watch out for fusarium or pythium (generally worse in heavy soils) and aphids and thrips.

566

GOMPHRENA

by Jim Nau
Ball Seed Company

*Annual (Gomphrena globosa), **seeds per ounce varies from 5,000 for uncleaned seed to 11,500 for cleaned seed. Gomphrena germinates in 10 to 14 days at 72°F and seed can be covered or left exposed to light during germination.***

Gomphrena is a heat- and drought-tolerant plant that can be sown directly to the field or transplanted to the field from cell packs. Flower colors are pastel and come in white, pink, lavender and bright purple. Plants will fill in quickly, and the flowers are a traditional dried cut flower.

As bedding plants, allow 7 to 8 weeks for green packs and 9 to 10 weeks for flowering packs of the dwarfer varieties (see comments below). For 4" pots allow 13 to 14 weeks and use one plant per pot.

For bedding, 4" pots and landscaping, the primary choice on the market is Buddy. Buddy is a deep purple-red flower color variety to 12" tall in the garden. In some catalogs you will find Buddy White or Cissy listed. For all practical purposes these two are the same variety. Both have off-white flowers on plants to 12" tall, like Buddy. While rose pink and lavender flowering plants have been available on the market in the past, there are none on the market at the time of this writing. However, there are several selections in the breeding stage of development which will be out by the mid-1990s, and some additional colors should be included in this group. In the taller strains, this group of gomphrena is most often just sold as the Globosa type instead of a variety name. These are available in separate colors of rose, white and purple on plants to 2' tall. These make excellent plants for cut flower growers or for landscapers who want a gomphrena with a little more vigor than the dwarfer strains.

GYPSOPHILA

by Jim Nau
Ball Seed Company

*Perennial (G. paniculata), **26,000 to 30,000 seeds/oz. Germinates in 5 to 10 days at 70° to 80°F. Leave the seed exposed to light during germination.***

Gypsophila is one of the more graceful of the garden perennials, with small white or pink flowers on plants that grow to 36" tall. An excellent cut flower (a major floral crop), gypsophila is used as a filler in either fresh or dried arrangements. Not

567

long-lived in Midwestern gardens, gypsophila is not tolerant of severe winters, and often winter-kills after two to three years. Plants are hardy to USDA zones 4 to 8, and flowers June and July.

From seed, allow 10 to 12 weeks for green pack sales. Plants will flower the same season from seed. In propagating the vegetative varieties, division and cuttings are the primary methods of replication. Cuttings are taken after flowering is complete, and division is done in early spring.

The primary varieties for use as cut flowers are either Bristol Fairy or, more important, Perfecta. Both of these varieties are vegetatively produced and not available from seed. Both have double white flowers on plants to 36″ tall. The primary difference is in flower size. Perfecta has the largest flower size available, from ¼″ to ½″ or larger, while Bristol Fairy has flowers slightly smaller. However, keep in mind that Bristol Fairy still has larger flowers than any of the seeded forms.

The annual gypsophila *(G. elegans)* is also valued for its cut flower performance in the field. The traditional variety Covent Garden Market is often seeded in successive sowings once every three to four weeks. The first seeding is around the last frost-free date until mid-June here in our latitude. The plants will flower approximately 2½ to 3 months later. While plants will perform well under full sun locations, growers in the Midwest or Northeast have had higher quality plants when the crop was covered with saran—especially for late summer crops.

HANGING BASKETS

by Vic Ball

Hanging Baskets—Important!

Baskets continue to be a major spring plant item on most U.S. and Canadian ranges. Twenty million of them were grown in the United States in 1989! Trend is strongly upward. (See the U.S. sales graph in the bedding plant chapter.)

Growers consider baskets in two groups: "hard" and "soft." The hard ones are generally vegetatively-propagated, including fuchsias, New Guinea impatiens and ivy geraniums. They are generally slower growing, and tend to bring more money.

Soft baskets are generally seed-propagated annuals such as petunias, Elfin-type impatiens and many others; colorful, widely used.

First, the Hard Baskets

Fuchsias are very widely used—and especially satisfying for the consumer in areas of cooler summers. Fuchsias are long-day plants and will flower when daylength is greater than 12 hours. They must be pinched (details below), and for late-May sales make the final pinch seven to eight weeks before the sale; if for Mother's Day, allow eight to nine weeks from last pinch to sale. Usually two or three pinches are needed. Most growers carry them at 68° to 70°F night temperature. Cool day/warm night temperatures are very effective for retarding fuchsias.

Here are several "real world" grower schedules and experiences:

Plant date	Sale date	Remarks
January	4/20 to Mother's Day	We plant three 2¼″ per 8″ basket. Two pinches are used. Two plants per 8″ doesn't make a quality basket.
1/15	4/15 to Mother's Day	Plant four 2¼″ per 10″ basket. Bernacchi's, LaPorte, Indiana. They also plant a top cutting 3/15.
1/25	color 4/25, flower Mother's Day	Plant three 2¼″ per 10″ basket. Jim Dickerson, Gobles, Michigan. "We pinch 2/1 and 3/1. Temperature 70°F night and day. Cool days/warm nights are very effective."
1/20	5/5 to Mother's Day	Plant one strong, well-branched 4″ per 10″ basket. Temperature 68°F nights. Pinch 2/15 and 3/15.

The typical way baskets are hung— up under the gutter. Note the ECHO automated hanging basket system that delivers baskets to the center walk as needed and permits watering from one position.

Ivy geraniums. Cuttings should be pinched two to three weeks after planting—as soon as well-established. Cycocel with 1,500 ppm when new growth starts after the pinch. Very dwarf varieties may not need Cycocel.

Again, several actual growers' schedules:

Plant date	Sale date	Remarks
1/25	Mother's Day	Plant three 2¼″ per 10″ basket. Temperature 68°F nights, 62°F days to restrict growth. First pinch is 3/1. Jim Dickerson.
1/15 (some late Nov.)	4/15	Plant four 2¼″ per 10″ basket. Bob Bernacchi.
Geraniums, zonal		
1/20	Easter	Plant three rooted cuttings per 8″ basket for a full, heavy basket. Carl Blasig, New Jersey.

New Guinea impatiens will make a spectacular basket. If they are fed lightly, watered regularly and given at least fair light they will perform all summer on patios in the Midwest and East. Better neither full sun nor heavy shade. Very colorful.

Growers report New Guineas "tough to grow," more than average of failures. I asked Jim Dickerson, Gobles, Michigan, grower, who does them very well, why? His comment (typical of many good growers), "Mostly you've got to follow the rules. They won't recover if they are neglected a bit. Example: Don't ever let them dry out—and at the same time don't let them get too wet. Also overfeeding can check them. They don't like too cold a temperature—they're a tropical plant; 60°F is too cold, 65°F is okay. If they're getting too tall, go to 65°F days and 75°F nights. We carry an average 70°F."

Jim does several 200′ houses of them each spring. They're lovely—and profitable. By the way, research at Michigan State University (Royal Heins) says, "Optimal temperature for the New Guinea impatiens is 68° to 70°F. Faster growth is at 75°F. Growth extremely slow at 65°F. These are average daily temperatures.

"We observed no photoperiod response. Response to cool day/warm night (DIF) is much smaller than that observed on lilies." Which checks with most reports we get from growers.

They are susceptible to tomato spotted wilt virus—carried, of course, by Western Flower Thrips. Jim has had no problem with this. We've seen almost no damage among other growers on New Guineas in recent years—thanks to clean stock from propagators, and better thrip control.

Again, several growers with schedules, temperatures, etc.:

Plant date	Sale date	Remarks
2/1	Mother's Day	Plant three 2¼″ per 10″. Jim Dickerson. He plants an unrooted cutting to a cell pack on January 10 for this purpose. Temperature 70°F night and day.
2/1	4/1	Plant three 1″ plugs per 10″. Mel Klooster, Kalamazoo, Michigan.

For more on New Guinea impatiens culture see the chapter on impatiens.

Nonstop begonias are an extremely colorful, mid-size flower version of the tuberous begonia. They are very free blooming, make a colorful basket. Must have some shade and good summer care to flower all summer in the Midwest.

Plant date	Sale date	Remarks
2/15	Mother's Day	Plant heavy 2¼". Jim Dickerson.
2/15	Mother's Day	Plant five 1½" per 10" basket. Post Gardens, Detroit—they use cell pack plants (72 per flat size).

Zonal geraniums also make very colorful and satisfactory hanging baskets! Gene Young, Nashville, Tennessee area, does them well.

Plant date	Sale date	Remarks
2/20	Mother's Day	Plant three rooted cuttings per 10" basket. Post Gardens, Detroit area. Temperature 68°F night and day.
Cuphea (Mexican heather)		
2/1	spring holidays	Plant five 1½" cell pack plants per 10" basket. Something different.

Probably the #1 hanging basket in today's world is Elfin® impatiens. The grower is Ben Miller, Stutzman's, Hutchinson, Kansas.

Each year I see more zonal geraniums as hanging baskets. Colorful!

Now the Soft Baskets

Again, these are the bedding annuals such as petunias, impatiens, vinca. They are very widely used as baskets. Very colorful, generally easier to grow—and faster. Typically six to eight weeks versus 12 to 15 weeks for the "hard" baskets, especially such champions as the Elfin-type impatiens, Madness™ petunias. They do make a great showing all summer long if watered and fed a bit (or better yet, some Osmocote put on by the grower).

In today's world most of these soft baskets are grown from plugs. Especially where the very large 1″ plugs (Expeditors) are used, a basket can be a very fast crop.

Plant date	Sale date	Remarks
3/20	Late May	Plant four plugs per 10″ basket. Bernacchi's, LaPorte, Indiana. Petunias (white and pink Madness).
3/1	April 10	Four plugs per 10″ basket. Mel Klooster, Kalamazoo, Michigan. For petunias and impatiens, their first lot.
4/1	Mother's Day	Plant four plugs per 10″—Klooster's last lot. Mix used here: Sunshine plus 25% vermiculite. Temperature 70°F day and night.
3/15	early May/ Mother's Day	Plant five plugs (200 sheet) per 10″ basket. Post Gardens near Detroit. Temperature 68°F nights. Grower reports, "Cool days/warm nights really work on Elfins." Petunias same schedule. Says grower Harold Schwall: "You get a much heavier basket if you use the larger 128 per sheet plug."
2/5	Mother's Day	Plant five plugs per 10″. Nonstop begonias grown by Post Gardens.

Browallia is one of the few annuals where good blue flowers can be obtained. Beautiful in baskets and satisfactory in shade areas. Sow seed mid-January for mid-May flowering.

Gazanias—they're very hardy, both heat and drought-tolerant, fine for patios where other things won't survive. Sow seed late January/early February for mid-May baskets. Temperature: 65°F night.

Portulaca—a very colorful hanging basket—great for full exposure in hot, dry situations. Grow best at 65°F night temperature. Figure 16 weeks from sowing to sale.

Thunbergia (Black-eyed Susan)—a very attractive hanging basket, it drapes artistically and does well in partial shade or full sun.

Vinca (periwinkle). Again, a very satisfying basket for the consumer. Sow seed in flats allowing for a warm 75°F soil temperature, and don't overwater or you'll lose them in the seed flat.

Tomatoes. There are several varieties adaptable to baskets. Sow late February for May sales.

Here's Tom Abramowski and his $3.75 baskets.

Tom Abramowski's Approach to Baskets

This is pure economics—and a very interesting, controversial point at that!

Tom (Rockwell Farm, Rockwell, North Carolina) is a very strong believer in producing a top quality but smaller hanging basket or poinsettia or whatever. He believes deeply that there is a major market (mass outlet) here in addition to the demand for larger plants at a higher price. His modern 9-acre range near Charlotte is proof that his approach can't be all that wrong.

Example: Tom does a good 10″ New Guinea hanging basket—which he wholesales at about $3.75. This against $6 and $7 for a 10″ New Guinea that I see at most other ranges (early 1990s). Both Tom's and the $7 basket are quality plants, but Tom's New Guinea is just not as large. Maybe half as big. His case for this: "First they are a lot easier to ship than a big basket, and of course a much lower cost to the customer means more volume. They take up a lot less space in the retail outlet. They take a lot less time on my benches and much less space—maybe 70 to 100 more baskets in each row versus most ranges. They are less apt to be abused in handling from greenhouse to retail outlet since they are not as big. Maybe most of all, the two weeks less crop time is big in the spring, to me, from a cost point of view."

Tom also does acres of 6″ poinsettias—at around $2 wholesale. Offhand this sounds like bankruptcy—but again, Tom hastens to add that these are grown at final spacing of 10″ x 10″. They are shipped bench run, but nearly always a minimum of three flower heads per plant. "And I get my money in two weeks." He firmly believes that he's making a profit on his $2 poinsettias.

Tom is very convincing.

573

Four genera of evergreen shrub are usually called heath or heather. *Calluna* is the Scotch heather or ling, *Daboecia sp.* includes the Irish heath and a related plant from the Azores, *Bruckenthalia* and the many species of *Erica* heath come from various other areas. Heaths and heathers resemble each other in that both have narrow, needle-like or scale-like leaves and bell-shaped, urn-shaped or tubular flowers.

Only a few heathers are fragrant, but one or more variety is in bloom every month of the year for continuous garden color. Foliage of some cultivars changes with the season to add extra interest.

Heathers grow best in neutral to slightly acid soil with good drainage. A sandy soil mixed with leaf mold, peat moss or compost and sharp fresh water sand is ideal. Fertilizers should be of the rhododendron type. Excessive fertilizing can cause heathers to lose their naturally compact form.

Pruning keeps heathers neat and encourages new growth. Cut back most of the Ericas for compactness, shearing off all the flowers as soon as blooms have faded. This includes all winter and early-spring flowering varieties. Callunas should also be cut back after flowering, except for late-flowering plants, which should not be pruned until the following spring. The sooner pruning is done, the sooner growth starts for the next season's bloom.

Plant heather right at ground level. Never cover the root ball with excessive soil, as this tends to smother the plant. A winter mulch of peat, bark or leaves can be used, but should not cover the crown of the plant.

Heathers do not need heavy watering after plants have been established. An occasional deep watering during the dry season is more beneficial than frequent sprinklings.

Heathers grow best in full sun or partial sun and shade. Plants will thrive in shady locations, but will not bloom as well and tend to get leggy. Avoid planting where they will get hot reflected sunlight. Ample room should be allowed between plants. Distances will vary depending on growth habit and desired landscape effect. A minimum of 12″ is usually best for dwarf compacts, with 18″ to 24″ needed for spreading types and even more room for specimen plants such as tree heaths. Heathers usually look best when planted in groups of three or more of each variety to create a solid, weed-smothering mat.

HELICONIA

by Jim Nau
Ball Seed Company

Tropical plant *(Heliconia psittacorum)*

A regal foliage plant, heliconias have banana-like leaves on plants that spread by means of a fleshy rhizome. Flowers are enclosed in boat-shaped bracts and last only a few days, though the bracts are present for some time—even if cut and used in a vase. Flowers are brightly colored and come in red, rose, pink, yellow and orange. Though heliconia can be used as a pot plant, its most common use is as a cut flower primarily in the southern United States.

As a cut flower, grow in full sun in ground beds for best performance and growth. When planted, you should use a cluster of rhizomes to fill out the bed faster and decrease your chances for disease and poor growth. Plant the roots about 1′ deep and on 1′ centers, and the bed should fill out in six to eight months. To keep the plants actively growing and flowering, be sure to keep the plants at 70°F and above. While plants will continue to grow at 58°F and above, all plant development ceases at 50°F. Plants can take cool temperatures for a period of time, however, temperatures in the mid-30s will kill the foliage, while temperatures at or below freezing can kill the rhizomes as well.

Plants will flower in eight to 10 weeks after the shoot emerges at the soil line, when grown at 70°F or above. The plant will develop four to five leaves first, and then the bud will be visible in the crown of the foliage.

Beds should be dug up after two years if plants begin to crowd. Though container production can be done, it is suggested that you use ground beds whenever possible to avoid root restriction. If restricted, the resulting flowers will be smaller and less productive than expected.

For harvesting, cut the bracts once two of them have opened. Note however, that no further opening is to be expected once the flowers are cut. Also, since the flowers are a terminal inflorescence, be sure to remove the whole stem down to the crown of the plant to avoid overcrowding. In general, while the bracts come in the range of colors noted above, the flowers themselves are most often yellow or orange in color.

In varieties, Andromeda is a light orange-and-red bract variety with orange flowers that has excellent performance; Lady Di, a rose variety with cream flowers; and Rubra, a red bract variety with orange flowers. While there are other varieties available, there are probably no more than 10 to 15 commercially available, although work on breeding and selection is being done all the time.

HEMEROCALLIS *(Daylilies)*

by Jim Nau
Ball Seed Company

Perennial (Hemerocallis species)

Very few of the species of the common daylily are grown within the American garden. Instead, it is the hybrids that have helped this class become one of the backbones of the perennial plant trade, and favored among plantsmen, enthusiasts and growers. Leaves are long and gracefully arching, providing a fountain-look to the planting. Leaves can be up to 1″ wide and up to 2′ long when fully extended. There are some evergreen and semi-evergreen varieties, too, the latter ones going dormant in Northern winters. Flowers are held upright on stems that range from 12″ to 3½′. Flowers are in a wide variety of colors, though ivory-white and blue are not available. Flowers range in size from 2½″ to 4″ long, are trumpet-shaped, fragrant and usually last only one day—hence the common name, daylily. Plants flower during the summer for up to two months, though there are some that will flower from June until frost. Hemerocallis is hardy in zones 4 to 9.

Division of the cultivars is the most common method of propagation, but tissue-cultured plants are also available. Division and digging are done either in the spring or fall, and most commercial sales are done on two-year-old plants. When separating the clumps, divide the roots so they have two to three shoots—many commercially propagated pieces will have only one to two, but the division will be larger overall.

If purchasing the plants in the spring, pot up into gallon containers for May and June sales. However, the plants seldom flower well the first summer. Sometimes the problem is that these are one-year-old divisions and are too small for flowering. Plants are still salable green in these containers about 8 to 10 weeks later, depending on the variety. A number of growers pot these up into two-gallon containers and grow during the summer and fall for next spring sales.

A second method of growing is to bring in clumps in late summer/early fall and pot up into gallon containers. Make sure that these are of blooming size (commonly called a #1 division) and not smaller. These can be brought in during late August and September and grown on with no lower than 45°F nights until these are established in the pot.

In regard to temperatures, if fall planted make sure plants have established themselves before temperatures drop consistently below 40°F. In general, a growing-on temperature of 45° to 48°F helps to develop root growth, and this temperature is often followed in fall and early spring growing schedules. As daylength increases in the spring, so can the temperature.

As for cultivars, the number of varieties in hemerocallis that are available are way too numerous to give all of the best. The following is only a short list of good varieties. One additional note: As you read through the various catalogs on varie-

576

ties to purchase, keep in mind that varieties will be listed as hybrids or possibly even as tetraploids. Tetraploid varieties have a larger plant and flower size than the standard hybrids, often with frilled or ruffled petals, and are usually more expensive than the standards as well.

Stella D'Oro flowers from June until frost. Flowers are 2½″ and golden yellow in color. Grows from 11″ to 15″ tall. Repeat bloomer.

Mary Todd has buff yellow flowers to 24″ tall. Flowers are lightly ruffled to 6″ across. Flowers in June. It is a tetraploid with foliage that is evergreen across the southern United States. It is dormant in the Chicago area. It has a later flowering time, and will re-bloom again after a flash of flowers 20″ tall.

Chicago Fire is a red flowering variety with a light band of yellow.

HERBS

by Marj Laskey
Molbak's Greenhouse, Inc.
Woodinville, Washington

Introduction

Molbak's, the leading Seattle garden center/grower, has been selling herbs for at least 15 years. As of three years ago, herbs were just a small part of our annual production. Since then, the herb production has increased over 300%, and herbs have become a major seller in the spring and summer.

Molbak's grows over 70 varieties of herbs. They are grown in 4″ round pots. They offer 10 of the major varieties in 6″ pots.

Scheduling

It is no easy task to schedule herb production, especially for the first-time grower. Obviously, one must know what customers want and when they want it. For example, at Molbak's we always have a fast turnover of sweet basil. This is mainly due to the fact that many of our customers who buy sweet basil, buy it for immediate use rather than for long-term growing in a garden. Therefore, we must always have a large quantity of sweet basil available. A second example is that the customers who tend to buy sweet woodruff or silvermound tend to be landscapers. They want to buy these herbs more in the early spring than any other time of the year. So, during March and April, we will have a large quantity of these herbs available and then lower the production numbers after those months. In conclusion, each variety has its own selling habits. It is up to the grower to discover these selling habits and to schedule accordingly.

The majority of Molbak's herb sales occur from March through July. The lowest sales occur during November and December. Because of this swing in sales, from September to March we only grow 25 herb varieties. Then from March through August we offer all 75 varieties of herbs that we grow.

Growing Herbs

When growing many varieties of herbs, you must take into consideration each variety's specific growing requirements. At Molbak's we give each variety of herb its proper growing requirements as closely as possible to produce a salable 4″ pot herb.

One major way we propagate herbs is through the use of seeds. There are many excellent sources of herb seeds. Most of the major seed companies now sell herb seeds, and there are also many other companies who specialize in selling herb seeds.

After receiving the seeds, they are stored in a refrigerator, cooled to 40°F, to help retain their freshness. Also, there are certain varieties whose germination percentages will increase when the seed has been prechilled.

We sow into 406 plug trays (all seed propagation is by plugs) filled with a basic seedling media that has been lightly watered in. We double seed most varieties, although there are some varieties that we will single seed, and a few varieties that we will sow four seeds per cell. All seeds are left uncovered unless a specific variety requires darkness for germination. All are germinated at 70° to 72°F under HID lighting and periodic misting. After the seed coats have been broken and the radicles have emerged, misting is stopped. The seedlings will then be irrigated with a fine watering head one to three times per day, weather dependent.

After the seedlings have slightly rooted in, the plug trays are moved to cooler temperatures, depending upon the need of each variety. The seedlings are watered at least once a day using fertilized water (200 ppm N). They are held in the plug trays until nice rootballs are formed.

The plugs are then transplanted into 4″ round pots. Usually we will put in two to three plugs per pot. The reason for this is to produce a finished plant in a shorter period of time (versus putting only one plug per pot).

There are a few varieties (coriander, dill, etc.) which are direct seeded into 1206 trays (12 six packs). They are covered lightly with vermiculite and watered in. They are germinated at 70°F under HID lighting and watered only when necessary. When the seedlings emerge, they are moved to a cooler temperature and are held until good rootballs are formed. They are then transplanted into 4″ round pots, one cell per pot. We find that the survival rate on these varieties is higher if begun this way.

All the seeded herbs will be finished at the most favorable temperature we are able to provide (variety dependent). They are all fed 200 ppm N each watering. They will be grown pot-to-pot until sold, unless spacing is necessary.

Another major way we propagate herbs is through the use of stem cuttings. We keep 8″ stock pots of 38 varieties of herbs. Half of the year the stock are grown indoors at 70°F, and half of the year they are grown outdoors in coldframes (55° to 85°F). The stock are fed 200 ppm N each watering. Each fall we repot new stock so that we get vigorous growth year-round.

Each month we take approximately 2″ cuttings off the stock. The cuttings are stuck into 1206 trays that are filled with a standard soilless media (we use Fisons Sunshine Mix #1). With the majority of the varieties, we will put three cuttings per cell. With a few varieties, lemon thyme for example, we will put four to five cuttings per cell.

All cuttings will be rooted at 70°F under HID lighting with periodic misting. As the cuttings callus and begin to root, misting is decreased. When the cuttings all have roots, misting is stopped. They are then fed 200 ppm N each watering.

At this time the flats are moved to a cooler temperature to be held until good rootballs are formed. Some varieties (most mints) will be pinched and held until breaks appear. They are then transplanted into 4″ round pots, one cell per pot. They will be finished at the most favorable temperature that we are able to provide. If necessary, we will pinch the plant again to get greater branching. As with the seeded herbs, they will be grown pot-to-pot until sold, unless spacing is necessary.

Pest Problems

Insects. Whitefly and aphids love herbs. Since the majority of our herbs are for culinary uses, we can only use organic solutions—insecticidal soaps, nicotine, etc. We find a weekly spraying of Safer Soap helps control the insect population.

Fungi. Seedlings can damp off if kept too wet. Pythium can also become a problem, especially with the young plants when first transplanted into the 4″ pots. Watering practices must be watched carefully. Water only when the soil media is dry. Powdery mildew can occur when the foliage is kept wet. Water early in the day so that the foliage can dry before night.

Selling Herbs

An informed customer is a happy customer. Therefore, all pots of herbs are labeled. In addition, behind each variety there is a sign telling about its growing requirements, uses, and folklore.

Favorite Herbs

Of the 75 varieties of herbs that Molbak's grows, 20 varieties make up over 60% of the herb production. The following chart lists each variety, how it is propagated, what type of tray is used, germination or rooting temperature, number of plants per pot, the holding temperature before transplanting, and the finishing temperature.

Molbak's Top 20 Selling Herbs

	Propagate	Plug Tray	# Plants Per Pot	Plug Holding Temp. (F)	Finish Temp. (F)
Sweet Basil *(Ocimum basilicum)*	seed	406	4	70°	70°
French Tarragon *(Artemisia dracunculus)*	cutting	1206	3	60°to 65°	60° to 65°
Munstead Lavender *(Lavendula angustifolia* 'Munstead')	seed	406	4	60° to 65°	60° to 65°
Extra Tripled Curled Parsley *(Petroselenium crispum)*	seed	406	4	60° to 65°	60° to 65°
Oregano *(Origanum vulgare)*	seed	406	6	70°	60° to 65°
Chives *(Allium schoenoprasum)*	seed	406	12 to 18	60° to 65°	55° to 60°
Rosemary *(Rosmarinus officinalis)*	seed	406	4	65° to 70°	65° to 70°
Sweet Woodruff *(Asperula odorata)*	cutting	1206	3	60° to 65°	50° to 65°
Spicy Globe Basil *(Ocimum basilicum* 'Minimum')	seed	406	4	70°	70°
Thyme *(Thymus vulgaris)*	seed	406	6 to 8	60° to 65°	50° to 60°
Coriander *(Coriandium sativum)*	seed	1206	4 to 5	60° to 65°	60° to 65°
Sweet Marjoram *(Origanum majorana)*	seed	406	6 to 8	70°	70°
True Mint *(Mentha spicata)*	cutting	1206	3	60° to 65°	50° to 65°
French Lavender *(Lavendula dentata)*	cutting	1206	3	60° to 65°	60° to 65°
Garlic Chives *(Allium tuberosum)*	seed	406	12 to 18	60° to 65°	50° to 65°
Silvermound *(Artemesia schmidtiana)*	cutting	1206	3	65° to 70°	65° to 70°
Santa Barbara Rosemary *(Rosmarinus officinalis* 'Lockwood de Forest')	cutting	1206	3	60° to 65°	60° to 65°
Greek Oregano *(Origanum heracleaticum)*	cutting	1206	3	60° to 65°	60° to 65°
Dill *(Anethum graveolens)*	seed	1206	4	60° to 65°	60° to 65°
Lemon Thyme *(Thymus x.* 'Citriodorus')	cutting	406	5	60° to 65°	60° to 65°

Germination temperature: 70° to 72°F for all the above.

Other Comments:

- **Sweet Basil** is a fast-growing, sun-loving herb. Quick turnover makes this our least expensive herb to produce.

- **French Tarragon** is an ugly-looking herb that sells well. During the spring and summer we root cuttings and sell them. During the fall we root cuttings and then overwinter them, still in the 1206 trays, out in coldframes. In early spring, while the stock is still dormant, we will bring the overwintered cuttings inside (in increments) so that an early crop will be available.

- **Munstead Lavender** is one of the fastest-growing lavenders from seed. Chill the seed for at least one week before seeding to get the best germination.

- **Extra Tripled Curled Parsley** is a must for year-round sales. Parsley is a biennial, but we treat it as an annual. When it goes to seed the second year, its leave lose their flavor.

- **Chives** is another good herb to overwinter for easy spring sales. It tends to fill out the pot more after being overwintered.

- **Rosemary** is a good seller during the winter months. It is very slow growing.

- **Sweet Woodruff,** when grown cool, tends to stay nice and compact. Landscapers tend to buy it more during the early spring. It is one of the few herbs we grow that likes shade.

- **Spicy Globe Basil** is not quite as fast-growing as sweet basil. Its unusual globe form makes it a good seller. It also has a strong odor.

- **Thyme** will damp off easily during the winter months. Watch your watering!

- **Coriander** is our second biggest seller during the spring. We have on the sign that coriander is also known as cilantro and Chinese parsley.

- **Sweet Marjoram** also tends to damp or rot off. You must let the pots dry out completely before watering.

- **True Mint** is fast in rooting. It is one of the favorite culinary mints.

- **French Lavender** has finely dentated foliage. Its unusual foliage and pretty flowers make it popular.

- **Garlic Chives'** germination percentage is lower than standard chives. Its flat leaves makes it unusual.

- **Silvermound,** a scented herb, is a big seller to landscapers in early spring.

- **Santa Barbara Rosemary** is a prostrate rosemary with very good flavor.

- **Greek Oregano** is truly the best tasting oregano. It is also a better winter-growing oregano (less tendency to rot).

- **Dill** is sold only during the spring and summer. It has the tendency to overgrow its 4″ pot, so you should sell it when it is young.

- **Lemon Thyme** is also a good seller during the winter.

HEUCHERA *(Coral Bells)*

by Jim Nau
Ball Seed Company

Perennial *(H. sanguinea* and *H. americana,* sometimes listed as *H. micrantha), 500,000 seeds/oz. Germinates in 21 to 30 days at 65°F. Leave the seed exposed to light during germination.

Heuchera is an excellent perennial with rounded rosetting leaves on plants to 3′ tall when flowering. *H. sanguinea* is the common Coral Bells with deep green leaves with red or scarlet flowers, while *H. americana* is the deep purple red-leaved type with yellow flowers. This latter variety is sold primarily for its leaf color rather than its flowers. Plants flower June and July and are hardy to USDA zones 3 to 8.

From seed, allow 10 weeks for green pack sales of *H. sanguinea,* and up to 13 for *H. americana.* Plants will not flower the same season when sown from seed. Sow seed during July of the previous year and move up into quart or gallon containers and overwinter. These plants will flower this season.

H. sanguinea has two varieties of importance, including Bressingham Hybrids, which is a mixture of scarlets and light crimson. Plants grow upright to 28″ tall. Splendens, the other variety, has deep red flowers on plants that are uniform. Seed is often sold under other names like Spitfire or Firefly.

In *H. americana,* Palace Purple is the most common variety available. Plants have dark red foliage that will bronze and turn deeper with a greater amount of sunlight. Flowers are off-yellow or cream colored in appearance on plants to 26″ tall. Plants do best in areas where they get afternoon shade.

HIBISCUS *(Hibiscus Rosa-Sinensis)*

by H.F. Wilkins
Nurserymen's Exchange Inc.
Half Moon Bay, California

For many years hibiscus has been popular in the homes of northern Europe, illustrating that it can be acclimatized to the home environment. In recent years growers in the United States and Canada are finding it a promising pot plant. This plant has become a specialty item in the North for home use, as well as in the South where it survives in the landscape under frost-free conditions. Regardless, this plant is tolerant to high temperatures and full sun in the South, as well as being an excellent patio plant in the North.

The genus *Hibiscus,* a member of the Malvaceae family, has been so commonly grown in gardens for so long that its site of origin is lost. However, it is believed to have originated in China and Cochin China (Vietnam), and is extremely common in the East Indies as well. In China, some varieties have indeed been cultivated since the dawn of history as recorded in ancient art and writings. Women have used the sap from the flowers to color their hair black, and the juice can also be used to stain shoes black.

There are about 250 species, which are widely diffused geographically but are particularly abundant in the tropics. The name hibiscus probably derives from ibis, a bird that was believed to live off certain hibiscus plants. In fact, many species of hibiscus are naturalized in marshy localities where such birds abound.

We do not know for sure how many varieties have been developed during the past centuries, or how many have been lost since *H. rosa-sinensis* was first introduced into Europe in 1731. This species is certainly the most beautiful of all the hibiscus, and there are numerous magnificent hybrids, each more attractive than the next.

The Commercial Pot Hibiscus

Hibiscus is a shrub whose leaves are a shiny dark green, can be variegated, and are usually simple and palmately veined. The flowers are mostly solitary in the leaf axils consisting of five petals with a bell-shaped calyx; the stamens are united into a tubular column that is frequently longer than the petals. The style usually has a five-branched stigma, which can be quite proliferated and ornamental. The ovary is a five-celled structure with three or more seeds per cell. Colors of the blossoms range from vivid red to white to various shades of yellow and orange. Flowers can be single or double. Contrary to the situation some years ago, single-flower types are common. Flowers last but a day; however, selections do exist whose flowers last somewhat longer. The senior author was amazed to observe in Hawaii that flowers can be harvested in the morning, placed on a table, and they will remain turgid and open for 20 or so hours without water.

Here's a colorful 4" hibiscus done by a Danish specialist.

Propagation of hibiscus can be achieved by seed, cuttings, grafting, or layering. However, hybrids of *H. rosa-sinensis* must be propagated from cuttings because they do not come true from seed. Four-inch to 5" cuttings with two or three leaves are taken from stock plants every two weeks. Researcher Karl Wikesjo states that in Sweden stock plants are grown in beds or in large containers for five to seven years. When stock plants are grown in containers for nine months to one year, they can be sold as specimen patio plants. Cuttings can also be obtained from plants in production when the pinch occurs. Thus, production can be self-perpetuating. In Florida, they are commonly placed in a medium of 50% Canadian peat/50% coarse perlite and placed under a mist. Wikesjo reports that rooting takes place in 35 to 40 days under milk-white plastic tents in the summer or under clean plastic in the winter without mist. Little air is allowed under the tent until rooting commences; then, the center is opened 1 cm. and afterwards gradually enlarged. Other literature shows maximum rooting was achieved in a sand/moss mixture (1:2 by volume).

No rooting hormone is required. However, rooting hormone hastens the process and may be desirable on some cultivars. Various concentrations have been recommended: 3,000 ppm IBA in talc, or Hormodin #1. Bottom heat of 72° to 75°F is beneficial and will speed rooting. Air temperatures for rooting and production are maintained at 55° to 61°F nights and 61° to 64°F days (minimum). A 68°F day is best, but do not go above 86°F days. Under these conditions, rooting takes four to six weeks and sometimes up to two months.

Cuttings can be stuck directly into small pots and later shifted into larger pots, or directly stuck into the final pot size. After rooting, cuttings can be transplanted, two or three cuttings per pot, into a well-drained and well-aerated medium consisting of loam, sand and peat, or similar media combinations. When cuttings are first stuck, a fungicidal drench combination can be used. Dead leaves should be continuously removed. Fungicidal sprays can be used on plants every second week under the tents during rooting.

Production of hibiscus may be a profitable summer fill-in crop. With the economics of energy as they are, winter production in the North could be questioned. However, with the rapidity of crop turnover when compared to other crops, this may not be true. Spring and summer sales are brisk. Cuttings taken in December can be predicted to be sold in late March; if taken in March, plants are ready to sell in July. The average production time from cutting to sales is 16 weeks. In winter it can be 18 weeks; in spring and summer 14 weeks.

Growth and flowering time of *H. rosa-sinensis* is greatest in the summer. It has been established that flowering of *H. rosa-sinensis* is not photoperiodic. High light and long photoperiods result in maximum flowering. Professors von Hentig and Heimann have illustrated that the plants respond to high light conditions (100 to 150 W/m^2).

Nutrition. *H. rosa-sinensis* is considered to be a moderate feeder. Recommendations for nutrition have varied. If regular or treble superphosphate is used, frequently only the N and K supply must be of concern. Osmocote (17-7-12) and micromix can be incorporated into the medium. A pH of 6 to 6.5 should be maintained. Criley, working in 1:1 volcanic ash:wood shavings, incorporated 4 oz.

Schematic Growing Program for Hibiscus Rosa-Sinensis
(Diploid Cultivars Type, Miesiana) (Wikesjo 1981)

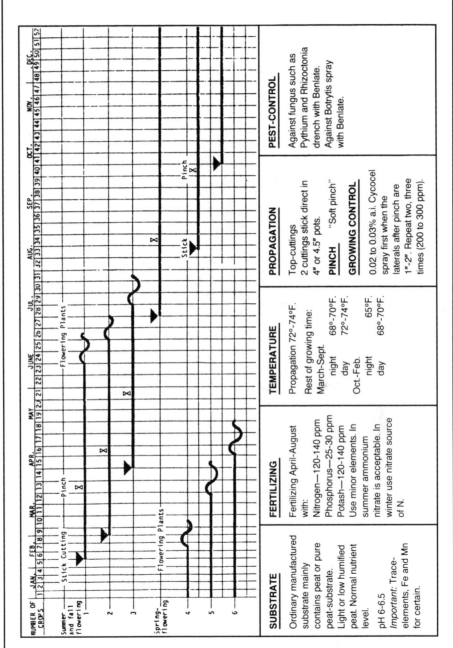

SUBSTRATE

Ordinary manufactured substrate mainly contains peat or pure peat-substrate. Light or low humified peat. Normal nutrient level.

pH 6-6.5

Important: Trace-elements, Fe and Mn for certain.

FERTILIZING

Fertilizing April-August with:

Nitrogen—120-140 ppm
Phosphorus—25-30 ppm
Potash—120-140 ppm
Use minor elements. In summer ammonium nitrate is acceptable. In winter use nitrate source of N.

TEMPERATURE

Propagation 72°-74°F.
Rest of growing time:
March-Sept.
  night   68°-70°F.
  day   72°-74°F.
Oct.-Feb.
  night   65°F.
  day   68°-70°F.

PROPAGATION

Top-cuttings
2 cuttings stick direct in 4" or 4.5" pots.

PINCH   "Soft pinch"

GROWING CONTROL

0.02 to 0.03% a.i. Cycocel spray first when the laterals after pinch are 1"-2". Repeat two, three times (200 to 300 ppm).

PEST-CONTROL

Against fungus such as Pythium and Rhizoctonia drench with Benlate. Against Botrytis spray with Benlate.

Osmocote (14-14-14), 2 oz. treble superphosphate, and 6 oz. dolomite per cubic yard of medium. Plants were also fed two times daily with 200 ppm N and K. Never allow plants to dry.

Height of outdoor plants in China can be up to 30'. In Florida and California it seldom reaches 15'. Pinching in the greenhouse can be used to control the growth and shape of the hibiscus plant. Von Hentig and Heimann report that when new shoots reach 3 to 5 cm. in length, they should be pinched. As many pinches as deemed necessary to achieve the desired shape and form can be used.

In commerce for houseplant and patio specimens, growth regulators are commonly used. Sprays of Cycocel or chlormequat not only induce shorter plant internodes and darker green leaves, but also more flowers, sooner, during the summer months. Initial sprays are applied two or so weeks after plants are pinched and active growth has commenced. Shanks used single aqueous sprays of Cycocel (1,000 to 4,000 ppm active ingredient), while Criley used 3,000 ppm to control growth of hedges in Hawaii. However, an application of two to three individual sprays spaced three to four weeks apart have evolved as commercial recommendations. Criley recommends 75 ppm (0.016% active ingredient), and Wikesjo recommends 95 to 140 ppm (0.02-0.03% active ingredient). The different levels could be relative between amount applied per plant, location (Hawaii versus Sweden) and cultivars. Criley used 0.05% Tween-20 as a wetting agent. A-Rest (ancymidol) has also been reported to retard growth on several cultivars.

Dwarfing of *Hibiscus rosa-sinensis* by the use of Cycocel has also been reported by Bhattacharjee et al., Bose et al., Hore and Bose. Bhattacharjee, et al., reported that a soil drench of Cycocel at 2,500 and 5,000 ppm suppressed growth on some 10 cultivars. With Cycocel drenches some cultivars produced fewer flowers, all produced larger flowers, and the effect persisted for over 360 days for most cultivars. Reduced flower numbers and persistent activity were also reported by Criley when drenches were used.

Common insects of hibiscus are red spider, aphid and whitefly. Temik, Pentac and Plictran are used as preventatives. Olson used Temik and Pentac year round, but during the summer he alternated Pentac with Plictran.

Applications of Captan, Benlate, Terrachlor, or Daconil can be used for any respective disease problems. A common disease is angular leaf spot. The best control for this is to keep a close watch over temperature, moisture, and humidity levels. Many times this disease cannot be controlled and infested plants should be discarded.

Hibiscus rosa-sinensis is very beautiful and useful as a garden, terrace, or balcony plant, or as a houseplant in the North or South. Cultivars reported to be used in greenhouse culture are: Apricot, Brilliantissima, Cooperi, Double Red, Flamingo, Freidsdorf, Holiday, Kona, Lagos, Laterita, Miami, Moonlight, Odense, Weekend and Yellow Koniger.

HOLLYHOCK

by Jim Nau
Ball Seed Company

Perennial (Althea rosea)**, 3,000 to 6,000 seeds/oz. Germinates in 2 to 3 weeks at 60°F.**

This old-fashioned garden favorite has been greatly improved and modernized with double flowers and an array of rich colors. They are usually sown in April, potted as soon as they can be handled, and either planted out or sold as pot plants. They can also be sown out in the open in May and, if kept thoroughly cultivated, will grow into strong plants by fall. An early-March sowing will usually flower some in the following late summer. Hollyhocks are annuals or short-lived perennials that are often termed "biennial." The plants can live as true perennials for several years if protected or covered with mulch once they are planted to the garden. In unprotected

Colorful hollyhocks!

587

garden locations, in areas of the country where frost can penetrate deep, the plants often fail to perform and can die out readily. Their best performance comes from plantings made close to foundations or up against barriers to the winter winds.

Hollyhock varieties are stately companions to the home perennial garden. Both single and double flowering forms are available, but it is the double flowering varieties which have the strongest acceptance. Chater's Double, Powderpuffs Mix and others will flower sporadically the first season when sown from seed in March or after. Mid-winter sowings, transplanted to quarter or gallon containers when ready, will flower more freely during the summer than their late-seeded counterparts. Powderpuffs Mix is a 4' to 5' variety with 3" to 3½" blooms in soft pastel shades, while Chater's Double grows to 7' to 8'. Chater's can be found on the market available in separate colors, but is the mixture which is the most popular. Both Chater's and Powderpuffs are short-lived perennials, but can live from year to year.

Many times the annual varieties will flower shorter than their perennial counterparts. Often growing 3' or so, these plants will flower profusely in July when planted to the garden from 4" pots from seed sown in February. The single flowering varieties are more popular in the annual form since they often reseed if not pulled too early from the garden in the fall.

HYDRANGEA

by James B. Shanks
University of Maryland
College Park, Maryland

Editor's note: Because production of cuttings, summer care, etc. has become the province of a few specialists, that portion of this excellent chapter on hydrangeas has been omitted. For anyone interested in a very complete presentation on the whole crop from beginning to end, I recommend the hydrangea chapter in the Ball RedBook *14th edition. Copies are available in most horticultural libraries.*

Native to Japan, the florist hydrangea, or pink-blue hydrangea as it is sometimes called, belongs to the Saxifrage family and is known botanically as *Hydrangea macrophylla* (Thunb.). Varieties designated as suitable for outdoor use may be bud hardy in USDA zone 6, but greenhouse forcing varieties are usually bud hardy only into the lower part of zone 7. Outdoor plants grow vigorously even though winter-killed to the ground, and early budding varieties may still develop flowers by late summer.

The inflorescence of the hortensia types used for greenhouse forcing is a globular cyme with perfect flowers capable of forming seed only in the inner regions, while the flowers making up the outer portions of the inflorescence are staminate. All flowers have a reduced corolla, but the staminate flowers have large petaloid

Minis are happening in hydrangeas, too!

sepals that make up the showy portion of the inflorescence. Thus, the hydrangea, like the poinsettia, has the capability of being a long-lasting flowering plant, as the showy parts are not petals which rapidly fade and fall. The outdoor types with flat cymes and staminate flowers only at the outer edge are known as lacecaps.

Hydrangeas growing outdoors make vegetative growth in July and August, with the initiation of terminal flowers in September and October, after which the flower buds are in a resting state and resume growth after normal winter chilling and leaf shedding. Overwintering flower buds are usually in flower by late June. The usual method of greenhouse forcing simply mimics the natural sequence, with propagation in May or June and the substitution of a controlled cold period of six to eight weeks for winter chilling, followed by 12 to 14 weeks forcing in the greenhouse. The period of availability as blooming pot plants extends from early March to early May.

The resting flower bud of hydrangea contains six to eight sets of leaves because, being a deciduous plant, the flowering shoot must develop a new set of leaves by flowering time. A relatively long forcing period is thus required for the development of leaves and flowers. The hydrangea, unlike the lily, also requires a great deal of bench space in forcing, so the hydrangea becomes an expensive plant to produce. Hydrangea production has declined in recent years because of the inability of the greenhouse operator to sell the product at a profit.

On the positive side of hydrangea production, the plant fulfills a need for a very showy and long-lasting plant that can be accurately timed for a holiday market. There is need for variety in flowering pot plants, and a well-grown hydrangea fulfills the demand for a distinctive, high-class flowering plant for all occasions.

In our present period of specialization, fewer hydrangea growers are performing all phases of growth, and specialists are performing the separate operations of cutting production and propagation, summer growing, cold storage and the greenhouse forcing of blooming plants.

Growth Characteristics and Cultural Requirements

Root media. Hydrangea growers have gradually changed to media containing little or no soil for many reasons including availability, uniformity and ease of handling. In addition, watering is easier, a more vigorous root system is possible, and, where plenty of peat moss is included, the all-important water supply to the hydrangea plant is provided. Soilless mixes contain little aluminum, and maintaining pink sepals becomes easier.

Fertilization and color control. Some understanding of the effects of fertilization on the color change in pink-blue hydrangeas is essential to good fertilization practice. The sepals of these hydrangeas contain a red anthocyanin pigment that becomes blue upon complexing with certain metals, including aluminum, which is abundant in most soils. The relative availability of aluminum is thus the principal factor in determining the color of the pink-blue florist hydrangea. Unless steps are taken to prevent aluminum uptake, the otherwise pink sepals gradually become blue; and unless enough aluminum is present to complex completely all the anthocyanin, an intermediate color will be produced instead of a clear blue color where the color change is desired. Intermediate colors are not attractive in most varieties.

Aluminum becomes more available to plant roots as soil acidity increases (pH values are lower), and liming to pH 6.5 is usually practiced in the production of pink hydrangeas, and acidification to pH 5.5 for the production of blue flowers.

Phosphorus will also render soil aluminum unavailable, and high phosphorus and high nitrogen during flower development promote clear pink sepals, whereas lower phosphorus and nitrogen, but an abundant supply of potassium, promote clear blue sepals where the soil contains plenty of aluminum.

Growth of hydrangeas in both plant production and forcing requires a relatively high nitrogen ratio; a 2:1:1 or 3:1:1 ratio is adequate. The object of summer growth is to provide a base for flower formation without excessive height, and a moderate program of fertilization with a 25-10-10 or similar analysis at 340 ppm of nitrogen each week or a biweekly application of 700 ppm nitrogen should suffice.

Plants are not fertilized in cold storage, but an application of 25-10-10 at 700 ppm should be made upon removal from storage. For the production of pink sepals this is continued at weekly intervals, except that ammonium phosphate (either mono- or di-ammonium) at 700 ppm nitrogen is used on alternate weeks after flower buds are visible. Fertilization is reduced when sepals are in full color and plants are hardening.

Standard hydrangea in 7" pot grown in equal parts sludge compost, pine bark and vermiculite.

In the production of blue flowering plants it is best to make an application of aluminum sulfate in September at the rate of 15 lbs./100 gals. of water. Fertilization for plants being forced for blue sepals is lighter than for pink sepals, and low phosphorus and high potassium levels should be used for the clearest blue color. Biweekly applications of 25-5-20 at 700 ppm should be adequate. Additional applications of aluminum sulfate made on several alternate weeks after flower buds are visible should assure complete bluing of the sepals. Additional applications may be required if the soil or water is alkaline.

Constant fertilization during the summer, and in forcing of plants for blue sepals, is done with 100 ppm nitrogen, while constant fertilization in the forcing of pink sepals is done with 200 ppm nitrogen. Levels must be higher if clear water leaching is practiced. White varieties are best fertilized on the pink sepal program for best plant appearance.

Growth Pattern and Effects of Environment

With the longer nights and cooler temperatures of late summer and early fall, the vigorous summer growth becomes slower, and internodal elongation gradually ceases with the formation of the large, terminal resting bud. The stem apex within the bud begins the formation of the branches of the cyme, upon which the first flowers formed are the inner perfect flowers followed by the formation of pistallate flowers. The buds may be in various stages of development as temperatures become too cold for further growth. While some development will take place during storage, such growth becomes very slow and without internodal elongation; we say that the flower buds are in a state of rest.

The resting stage gradually disappears as leaves are shed and the buds are subjected to a period of cold temperatures. This is followed by the ability of the buds to again make vigorous growth, indicating that the resting stage is terminated. Development is rapid, internodes long, leaves large and cymes and flowers become maximum size. The more completely rest is terminated, the faster the rate of development, the larger the growth and the cooler the temperature at which growth will take place. Efficient hydrangea forcing is thus possible only if rest has been

A fine hydrangea about ready to show color. The grower: Robert Miller, Dahlstrom & Watt Bulb Farm, Smith River, California.

completely terminated. An additional one or two weeks of storage may be more advantageous in making an early flowering date than the early removal from storage.

Minimal storage requirements vary with plant maturity and natural exposure. In the Midwest, plants stored in September need eight weeks of cold, while by late October a six-week storage may be adequate under constant temperature conditions. Under natural storage conditions of a shed, cold frame or greenhouse, where temperature fluctuates, the periods of time below the critical temperature are approximately additive, and a longer period is required for the accumulation of the 1,000 to 1,200 hours required.

The resting condition is alleviated by temperatures below 55°F and, for early forcing, a temperature of 52°F has been superior to colder temperatures. There will be bud development during the storage period and leaf abscission is more rapid at the warmer temperature. This is true only for a dark, controlled temperature storage. Any light reaching the plants stored in a greenhouse or cold frame situation will favor leaf retention and raise the bud temperature. In holding plants for late

The mistake of removing plants from cold storage too soon. The plant on the left was removed December 9; plant on the right removed December 23. Both forced at 62°F nights. At least 6 weeks of temperature below 50°F are necessary to force hydrangeas efficiently.

593

Hydrangeas force more rapidly at a warm temperature (plant on left), but stems and flowers will be small. The plant on the right, grown at a cool temperature, will be much taller and have larger leaves.

forcing, a colder temperature (to 35°F depending upon duration) is necessary to conserve plant strength and to prevent bud and stem elongation as rest is terminated.

Flower buds are visible and the size of a pea 8 weeks before full bloom, the size of a nickel 6 weeks and the size of a 50¢ piece 4 weeks before flowering at a temperature of 62°F.

594

A commercial crop growing in Vancouver, British Columbia. Excellent! The grower: John Vandermey, Fraser Nurseries.

Temperature, Photoperiod and Forcing

Photoperiod may affect rate of development and type of growth during forcing. Plants placed in cold storage early and forced under the long nights of November, December and January, or which have not had an adequate storage period, will be benefited by a night break with 10 fc. incandescent light. Additional light will have little effect on plants forced late in the season as these plants had a longer bud development and rest period.

There may be slightly greater promotion as the lighting period is increased to eight hours or all-night lighting, but a light break from 10 p.m. to 2 a.m. appears to have near maximum promotion in increasing the rate of development, height and flower size during forcing.

The temperature at forcing regulates not only the rate of development but the ultimate height, size of cyme, intensity of sepal color and quality of the finished plant. Basically, the hydrangea is a cool-temperature plant, making its best growth at night temperatures below 60°F, although the rate of development will be faster at a higher temperature. Night temperatures in the mid-50s will produce taller stems, larger leaves and larger flower heads than plants growing at 62° to 65°F.

595

Representative forcing periods at different night temperatures are 16 weeks at 54°F, 12 weeks at 60°F and 10 weeks at 66°F. At a temperature of 60° to 62°F buds are visible eight weeks before bloom, ¾″ at six weeks and ½″ in diameter at four weeks before flowering.

Single-bloom plants typically have larger flowers than plants of the same variety growth with two, three or more inflorescences. Usually only those varieties capable of producing large flower heads are used for single-bloom culture. Single-bloom plants are becoming more popular as they are easily produced, take less space at forcing and are more suitable for merchandising. They possibly could represent the most profitable hydrangea of the future. On the other hand, the two-or three-bloom standard plants, and the multiflowering plants, should be grown for the better trade with the emphasis on top quality and top price.

Early varieties are expected to force in 12 weeks, mid-season varieties in 13 weeks, and late varieties should force in 14 weeks under usual forcing conditions. Sepal colors are always more intense when forced at a cooler temperature.

Forcing

Dormant plants are placed in the greenhouse at forcing temperatures of 60° to 64°F immediately upon removal from storage. Spacing closely for the first two to four weeks will save on heat and space. Plants received with bareroot balls can be placed together on a solid bottom bed for up to two weeks. It is best to start forcing in the same size pot as for summer growth. The shift to final pot size is made after two to four weeks of forcing, depending upon the size of the original pot. Root growth will have resumed by this time, and it will not be necessary to break the old root ball as is done when repotting is done before growth has started. Final spacing can be made at this time and a lower forcing temperature selected if desired.

Every effort should be made during forcing to prevent plant growth from becoming soft and subject to excessive water loss or desiccation injury upon removal from the greenhouse. Maximum sunlight, adequate space and low humidity are important, and any wetting of leaves should be avoided. Tube watering is practical during the forcing period, but mat or capillary watering can be done. Growth will be more vigorous with a constant supply of moisture to the roots.

Growth regulators are frequently used to prevent excessive height in forcing as well as in summer plant production, and to reduce the space requirement. The use of such growth-retarding chemicals must be anticipated, and an application of a retardant in mid-September is an excellent means of reducing stem stretch at forcing without severely reducing the inflorescence size. Plants forced for Mother's Day particularly need an application of a retardant. Application of a retardant in the forcing season is made during the third week of forcing and usually at a lower rate than on summer growth. B-Nine at 2,500 ppm or A-Rest at 50 ppm is satisfactory as a foliar spray at forcing. Bonzi is also effective as a foliar spray at 50 ppm.

Should plants show signs of insufficient storage as evidenced by slow development, short internodes, small leaves or a general rosetted appearance, an

Application of B-Nine made during the summer can have a desirable shortening effect on the plant at forcing (plant on the right).

application of gibberellin should be considered. GA_3 at 2 to 5 ppm is used in the forcing period. A single foliar application may be adequate, but weekly applications may be made if plants do not respond. Careful observation is the only means of determining the number of applications necessary to restore growth.

As sepals enlarge and become pigmented it may be necessary to reduce the light intensity to prevent fading and injury to sepals from excessive transpiration. As the sepals approach maturity, plants should be hardened by giving cooler night temperatures and ample ventilation. If the plant growth has been restricted by environmental care and growth retardants, the staking and tying of flower heads should not be required. Multiflowering plants usually need no support. Mature hydrangea plants can be held under refrigeration at 35° to 40°F for several weeks if necessary.

Out-of-Season Forcing

Extending the period of availability would increase the market potential, add variety to available potted flowering plants, and reduce production costs by growing hydrangeas at times other than the coldest period of the year. Some of the principles involved in early flower initiation could be of value to Southern growers who lack the cool fall temperatures for flower initiation.

Forcing hydrangeas for sales later than Mother's Day has always been possible by holding plants in artificial cold storage. Much of the heat cost of winter forcing would be avoided, but a market potential would need to be developed as for any out-of-season production. A means of shortening the growing period, or simplifying production for the spring period, would of course have important advantages.

Summary of Hydrangea Production

The following suggestions are based on Maryland conditions. Adjustments may be necessary for other areas.

Easter to Mother's Day Flowering

Rest period. Controlled temperature of 52°F in dark for eight weeks minimum with careful watering and humidity control. For longer storage periods use 45°F. Defoliation with butynediol, ethylene or Vapam is possible.

Saran shade for starting young plants, getting better breaks and increasing summer growth. In the photo, the author of this chapter, Professor James B. Shanks, University of Maryland, now retired.

Forcing period. First three weeks at 65°F and close spacing, then 58°F or split-night temperature of 62°F until 2 a.m., then 48°F until 8 a.m. for the final nine to 10 weeks. Full sunlight until color, then light shade. Retard tall varieties and plants in small pots at final spacing with .25% B-Nine and shift to final pot size in peat or peat-lite mix. Fertilize heavily with high N and high P. Bloom 85 to 100 days.

Valentine's Day and Early Flowering
Rest period. Controlled temperature of 52°F in dark from September 10 to November 10 with natural defoliation.

Forcing period. Use 10 fc. incandescent light from 10 p.m. to 2 a.m. at 62°F immediately upon removal from storage. Bloom 100 to 110 days. Retard tall varieties at three weeks with .25% B-Nine.

Troubles

Cultural Problems
Failure to initiate flower buds or evidence of crippled buds during forcing may be due to poor culture during summer growth, frost injury, drying in storage or bud rot (gray mold) in storage. The initiation of flowers early in the summer may result in fewer than normal leaves at forcing, causing poor flower development because of lack of leaf area. Cymes containing leaves are also associated with early initiation. Removal of leaves in early forcing usually permits the cyme to develop normally.

Multiflowering plant in 8" pot.

Iron chlorosis (interveinal yellowing) is frequent in rapid forcing without adequate root development, or is due to alkaline soil, overfertilization or overwatering during summer growth. The young growth of hydrangea leaves and flowers at forcing is very susceptible to injury from insecticides, fungicides and growth regulators. Caution is advised in using any chemical spray, and dosages should be confined to the lower rates recommended for use.

Diseases

Hydrangeas are not often subject to root and stem rots provided usual sanitation and good cultural practices are followed. Propagation benches, all media, as well as pots, flats, etc., should be disinfected by steam or fumigation to eliminate pathogens and weeds. Good drainage is important, as is the avoidance of overwatering.

Botrytis-causing gray mold on leaves and stems in propagation, or bud rot in storage, occurs in high humidity and high moisture situations, frequently starting on injured or dead tissue. Injured leaves should not be permitted on cuttings, and fallen leaves should be removed from plants in storage. Ventilation, air circulation, and avoidance of overhead watering greatly reduce the incidence of gray mold. The

Plant production in air-conditioned greenhouse in Texas.

600

systemic fungicide Benlate is used on plants and cuttings to reduce susceptibility before placing them in a high humidity environment. Other fungicidal sprays may be used.

Powdery mildew is most prevalent on outdoor plants in the fall, and in the greenhouse under conditions of high humidity and crowding. Older leaves are most susceptible. A protective mildicide can be used in the fall, while humidity control is usually adequate to prevent serious infection in the greenhouse.

There is a wide range of variety susceptibility to both gray mold and powdery mildew, and susceptible varieties should not be grown where an environment conducive to disease cannot be avoided.

Viral Agents

The hydrangea ring-spot virus has been found in most present-day commercial varieties. Typical symptoms show only during winter growth, and the effect on susceptible varieties is generally weakened or smaller growth. Roguing is difficult, and virus-free plants of commercial varieties are not currently available.

Virescence, or the green sepal mycoplasma complex, has been responsible for a series of problems, and is divided into three distinctly different but related groups:

1. **Severe.** Extreme stunting, small leaves with vein yellowing and dwarf, green cymes followed by death of the plant.

2. **Intermediate.** Reduction in vegetative growth, but with normal leaf expansion and continued vein yellowing. Cymes contain both green or bronzed sepals, and normal-colored sepals.

3. **Mild.** Stock plants gradually decline in vigor. Forcing plants retain normal pattern of growth with green leaves, but cymes contain large, green sepals, and reproductive parts may revert to a vegetative type of growth.

The severe form of virescence can be readily eliminated by roguing as the symptoms appear at any stage of growth. Careful observation and continued roguing can eliminate the intermediate type. The mild form is the most dangerous, as symptoms appear only at forcing, so greenhouse-growth material or other flowering stock must be used to replace all plants used in cutting production. Hydrangea virescence has been virtually eliminated by most hydrangea specialists by careful roguing. Since Stafford and Rose Supreme currently appear to be most susceptible, the mild form of virescence would most likely appear in these varieties.

IBERIS *(Hardy Candytuft)*

by Jim Nau
Ball Seed Company

Perennial *(Iberis sempervirens)*, **10,000 seeds/oz. Germinates in 14 to 21 days at 60° to 65°F. Leave seed exposed to light during germination.**

A low growing, evergreen perennial that ranges from 9″ to 12″ tall, iberis flowers are pure white and held in clusters in early spring. Plants are dependably hardy and are one of the first returning perennials to show flower color in the spring. As they age, the base of the plants turns woody. Plants flower in April and May and are hardy to USDA zones 3 to 9.

Seed sown anytime after the first of the year will not flower the same season when grown at 50 °F. Green packs are salable 10 to 14 weeks after sowing, and plants will attain their full height the same season from seed. For flowering plants in April and May, sow seed in June and July of the previous year, transplant to cell packs by the end of August, and shift up to quart containers when ready. Overwinter and bring back into the greenhouse or coldframe. Plants dependably flower during the following months when grown at 50 °F night temperatures. California growers should sow seed in early November for flowering plants in mid- to late April using one plant per 4″ pot.

Snow White iberis is about the only variety sown from seed that is sold with a name on it. Snowflake is also sold, but is traditionally vegetatively propagated. Seed-grown plants produce smaller flower clusters than the vegetative material. Both varieties grow to 12″ tall with pure white flowers and deep green foliage. Keep in mind that the vegetatively propagated varieties are more uniform than seed sown material, and you will notice some variability in Snow White.

IMPATIENS

by Vic Ball

The 1980s were the decade of the impatiens! Growth in demand for the Elfin types has been strong and steady. Year after year they have been in short supply—and it's happening again in the early 1990s. Notes on culture and scheduling of the Wallerana types appear in the bedding plant chapter. Brief comments on varieties follow.

Elfin-Type Impatiens Varieties

Here's a brief rundown of the best of the Wallerana type impatiens as of the early 1990s. I'll talk classes, not individual colors—most classes have a full range of colors. Schedules, culture, etc. on Wallerana impatiens will be found in the bedding plant chapter.

- Dazzler® is a fine bedding plant and landscape impatiens. The Dazzlers seem especially adaptable to landscaper work, perhaps standing a bit more of full sun.

- Super Elfin® is the standard and very well-known bedding plant impatiens, very widely used. There's a unique color here: Red Velvet—a very deep red and dark foliage. Handsome.

- Accent is another major bedding plant class of seed impatiens. Noteworthy here is an especially wide range of colors.

Here's George Ball Jr. with a fine basket of Dazzler® impatiens. These Wallerana types are champion baskets and very widely grown. They do satisfy the consumer!

• Other groups: There are several as of the early 1990s including the Impacts, the Impulse group, and the Tempos—all new.

The other bright star in impatiens is the New Guineas. As both pots (4″) and hanging baskets (8″ and 10″) they have been coming up steadily through the late 1980s. In spring 1990 I saw acres and acres of especially fine 10″ hanging basket New Guineas. They have become a major spring basket and spring pot crop in the United States, Canada and Europe.

The following culture notes by Ed Mikkelsen of Mikkelsens Inc. give a good overview of culture. Also, I suggest referring to the grower experiences in the hanging basket chapter for more notes on growing New Guineas. Also, at the end of this chapter you'll find a summary of available varieties as of the early 1990s, including some very interesting seed-propagated material.

Culture of New Guinea Impatiens

by Ed Mikkelsen
Mikkelsens Inc.
Ashtabula, Ohio

New Guinea impatiens were not known to the gardening public prior to 1972. Since the time of their introduction, sales have climbed at an annual rate of over 15%. Many people thought that recent droughts would have caused sales to level off. Others predicted that the threat of the Western Flower Thrips/Tomato Spotted Wilt Virus would cause a slowdown of growth. They didn't. Sales increase about 15% each year. What is the explanation of this phenomenal growth? The answer, of course, is consumer satisfaction. The performance for the consumer is excellent.

Equally important for their popularity are the many advances that have been made by breeders. Plant habit and self-branching traits have been improved. Many vibrant tropical colors are available in combination with assorted leaf types/colors. Variegated leaves and dark-green to bronze colored leaves provide contrast to other gardening plants. New characteristics such as bicolored flowers continue to add variety to the cultivars available today. Other improvements will assure growth of sales of the New Guinea impatiens.

Growing New Guineas

It is important to start with good plant material. Obviously this means plants that are free of insect pests and diseases. The best cuttings do not have flower buds. If the cuttings are budded with no vegetative nodes below the tips, the plants will be slow growing and poorly branched. However, if the cuttings are budded but have vegetative nodes below, then the plants should still perform satisfactorily.

Matching the varieties to the size containers is also important. A short variety like Dawn should not be used in a hanging basket. A vigorous variety like Enterprise should not be grown in a 4″ pot. With the wide assortment of varieties available, a good color mix is possible for most pot sizes and growing temperatures.

Spectra™ is the first pot/hanging basket of New Guinea impatiens from seed, and many more are coming!

New Guinea impatiens have been successfully grown in a wide range of media. Growers have used media with soil, media of straight peat, or peat with various additives such as perlite, vermiculite, Styrofoam and/or bark. The media should have good aeration and be free of disease organisms. A common mistake that growers make is overwatering after transplanting. In order to prevent the overwatering of small plants in large containers, some growers prefer to transplant first into 4″ pots and then transplant the 4″ into 10″ baskets or other large containers. (See the hanging basket chapter in this book for schedules.)

After transplanting, night temperatures should be 65° to 68°F until the plants become well established. At this point night temperatures may be lowered to reduce stem elongation. However, most of the newer varieties don't require this, and temperatures below 62°F slow the crop down without any benefit to plant habit. Flower initiation occurs best at temperatures between 65° and 75°F.

New Guinea impatiens require moderate fertilization with 250 ppm or less NPK at every watering. However, they prefer low levels of minor elements. If the medium has minor nutrients, do not use them in your feed, or vice versa; minor nutrient toxicity has occurred when used in both the soil and in the feed. It may appear as brown or black spots on the leaves. Severe cases may show die-back starting at the plant tip and moving down the stem. Sometimes the stems may have dark areas that are firm, in contrast to being soft as with rot. Symptoms of minor element toxicities are sometimes mistakenly attributed to Tomato Spotted Wilt Virus (TSWV) infection. Plants exhibiting these symptoms should be tested for both high levels of minor elements and virus before concluding the cause.

Crop time for New Guinea impatiens can vary greatly depending on season and locality. Seven to 10 weeks are required to produce a 4″ pot crop, and 10 to 14 weeks for 10″ hanging baskets. With the newer self-branching cultivars a pinch is often not needed. Proper spacing of the pots is necessary in order to prevent internodal stretch.

Production of New Guinea hanging baskets at Bob's Market, Mason, West Virginia. Excellent.

Disease can be controlled with good environmental practices and, when necessary, appropriate fungicides. Two-spotted mites and thrips seem to be the most important insect pests. A vigorous thrips control program is a must if this insect is present, since New Guinea impatiens can become infected with TSWV.

There is every indication that the breeders have provided plant material free of TSWV. Plants have become infected by thrips infestation at some of the secondary propagators and/or at some of the growers. Thrips control programs initiated by propagators and growers have already reduced the incidence of TSWV. Annual renewal of propagators' stocks will add to the overall quality of the product. It is extremely important to remember that the best measures of control for TSWV are to start with clean material and continue with a sound thrips control program.

The outlook for New Guinea impatiens is bright. Consumer satisfaction is excellent. New varieties will continue to spark interest in them, and new characteristics and forms will keep them ever popular.

Comments on New Guineas From Other Growers

• Peter Konjoian is of the Konjoian's Greenhouse family, Andover, Massachusetts. He studies the response of his crops carefully to conditions. His comments: First, on temperature, "We try to maintain 62° to 65°F nights for the first week or two. After the first two weeks we maintain 60°F with excellent results."

A very well done New Guinea basket by Bob Barnitz, Bob's Market and Greenhouses Inc., Mason, West Virginia. They're doing a lot of them. It's a common sight in greenhouses almost everywhere. New Guineas make great baskets, can be grown overhead and need no bench space. Question: Are they taking trade away from geraniums?

On light: "We find the New Guineas more tolerant of hanging baskets overhead than either seed or cutting geraniums. We can afford to hang more baskets above our New Guineas than other crops.

"Humidity plays an important role, especially in the initial stages of the crop."

Watering: "New Guinea impatiens are thirsty plants requiring more water than geraniums. The exception is during the early stages of growth when you should keep them on the dry side. In fact, during the first several weeks after transplanting we try hard not to overfertilize or overirrigate—which may be a place where many growers get into trouble."

- Bob Barnitz, president of Bob's Market and Greenhouses in Mason, West Virginia. I visited Bob in late May; he had 12,000 10″ New Guinea baskets and they were great. Says Bob, "Temperature at first is 60°F nights/70°F days, and we water on the dry side at first. Later as the crop gets going we go up to 65°F and water more normally."

- Jim Dickerson, Gobles, Michigan. As noted in the hanging basket chapter, Jim considers them a 68° to 70°F night temperature crop all the way. He also does a fine job with them—and a lot of them.

- David Hartley, Paul Ecke Poinsettias: "Researchers make it very clear that the problem growers have starting New Guinea impatiens the first month or so is twofold: First, they must be watered sparingly for the first several weeks, until roots show at the edge of the soil ball; after that they like ample irrigation." (Editor's note: Oddly enough, I found on my own patio that even though they are allowed to wilt to total distress, they will come back very nicely.)

"Second, feeding should be avoided until roots have been well established, normally several weeks. Even after that they are light feeders. They will become established sooner, will grow faster, and flower sooner and more if grown at 65° to 68°F nights. At 60°F nights they will grow okay, but much slower. At 77°F nights they are unhappy. This is mainly from work done by John Erwin, then at Michigan State University. John noted that there was actually less growth on plants fed at 300 ppm nitrogen versus 150 ppm. Overfeeding makes crinkly leaves."

An interesting point: especially in the first three or four weeks after potting, New Guineas will do very badly if watered heavily. Elfins types, on the other hand, if watered heavily at this stage will simply grow faster and taller. When mature, both types tend to stretch if watered freely.

Dave also defines very clearly the sun and shade preference of New Guineas outdoors in the summer. Several examples he cites make this point clear: First, New Guinea baskets in full sun in Boston do well all summer if regularly watered. In other words, no problem with full sun in cool summer areas. The second example: New Guineas planted outdoors in the North Carolina State University trials—outdoors in the full sun, with no special mulch. Even though adequately watered they were very unhappy, some plants even gave up. A third example: New Guineas in Tulsa, Oklahoma (very hot summers) planted on the north side of a commercial building with little or no direct sun, but ample light, well mulched and watered, were successful in spite of the intense heat.

Apparently, New Guineas can stand full sun in cool summer areas, but in high-temperature parts of the United States they need shading from direct afternoon sun. Mulched and irrigated freely they will do well in partial shade, even in very high summer temperature areas. They are not at home in heavy shade —not nearly as happy in dense shade as is the Elfin type (I. wallerana). If grown in heavy shade they will flower sparingly or not at all. Pinching is not needed. They can be retarded with Bonzi (try 15 ppm), also Sumagic. B-Nine is not effective on them.

All this points up an obvious need for growers to provide care tags with their New Guineas, including some tolerance suggestions for your local climate.

Conclusion: It looks as though they can be grown from 60°F nights to 70°F nights, but as per the research at Michigan State, you get there quicker at 70°F and, since New Guineas are a tropical plant, there apparently is no penalty in quality.

Most Important Varieties as of the Early 1990s

by C. Anne Whealy
Ball Seed Company

Color	Mikkel Sunshine®	Kientzler Series	Celebration™ Series	Bull Series	Lasting Impressions™
Red	Mirach[2] Red Planet[2,4]	Aenea[2]	Celebration Bright Red[3]		Blazon[3]
Dark Orange		Epia[1,2] Marumba[2,3]	Celebration Dark Orange[1,2]		
Orange	Zenith[1,2] Nova[1]	Eurema[2]		Adelene[2] Tilly[1]	Ambrosia[2]
Salmon	Nebulous[2,4]	Melissa[1,2]	Celebration Salmon[2]	Olga[3]	Charade[1]
Coral	Dawn[1]	Sesia[1]			
White	Milky Way[2] Cirrus[3]	Jasius[2]	Celebration Blush White[1,2]		Innocence[2]
Light Pink	Equinox[2]	Caligo[2,3,4]			Illusion[2]
Medium Pink	Aurora[1,2]		Celebration Candy Pink[2]		
Dark Pink	Gemini[3,4]	Thecla[2,3,4] Delias[1]			Rosetta[2]
Hot Pink		Aglia[2]	Celebration Hot Pink[2,3,4]	Christine[2]	
Dark Hot Pink	Pulsar[2] Radiance[1,2]	Mimas[2,4] Isopa[2,3,4]		Lena[3]	
Lavender	Telstar[3]	Saturnia[2]	Celebration Light Lavender[2]		Heathermist[1]
Purple	Antares[1,2]			Veronica[2]	
Bicolor	Sunregal[1,2] Sundazzle[1,2] Twilight[2,4]	Vulcain[1,2] Flambe[2]	Celebration Red Star[2]	Dark Twilight[2,4]	

[1] *Compact cultivar*
[2] *Moderately vigorous cultivar*
[3] *Vigorous cultivar*
[4] *Upright habit*

Vigor ratings determined from greenhouse and field trials conducted at Ball Seed Company, West Chicago, Illinois, 1989 and 1990.

Mikkel Sunshine® and Lasting Impressions™ Series are products of Mikkelsens Inc., Ashtabula, Ohio.
Kientzler Series is a product of Kientzler Jungpflanzen, Gensingen, Germany.
Celebration™ Series is a product of Ball Seed Company, West Chicago, Illinois.
Bull Series is a product of N. Bull, Gartner-Siedlung, Gonnebek, Denmark.

Impatiens Brighten Shady Areas All Summer Long

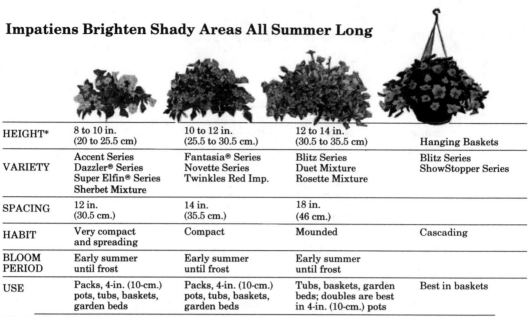

HEIGHT*	8 to 10 in. (20 to 25.5 cm)	10 to 12 in. (25.5 to 30.5 cm.)	12 to 14 in. (30.5 to 35.5 cm)	Hanging Baskets
VARIETY	Accent Series Dazzler® Series Super Elfin® Series Sherbet Mixture	Fantasia® Series Novette Series Twinkles Red Imp.	Blitz Series Duet Mixture Rosette Mixture	Blitz Series ShowStopper Series
SPACING	12 in. (30.5 cm.)	14 in. (35.5 cm.)	18 in. (46 cm.)	
HABIT	Very compact and spreading	Compact	Mounded	Cascading
BLOOM PERIOD	Early summer until frost	Early summer until frost	Early summer until frost	
USE	Packs, 4-in. (10-cm.) pots, tubs, baskets, garden beds	Packs, 4-in. (10-cm.) pots, tubs, baskets, garden beds	Tubs, baskets, garden beds; doubles are best in 4-in. (10-cm.) pots	Best in baskets

The height of impatiens is relative. Normal and large amounts of fertilizer and water cause excessive growth. Keep impatiens a little lean on feed and allow them to dry out somewhat between waterings for an improved, compact habit.

IRIS *(Iris Hollandica)*

by Henk Berbee
Leo Berbee Bulb Company
Marysville, Ohio

Forcing

Many growers, both retail and wholesale, find it profitable and not too difficult to force iris during the winter months. Here, we refer strictly to forcing varieties classed generally as Dutch iris. These bulbs are grown in Holland as well as in our Pacific Northwest. However, with the excellent quality produced in this section of our country, it is wise for a grower to limit his purchases to the American-grown bulbs.

Bulbs should be planted in deep flats (4″ to 5″) or into a bench. The top of the bulb should be level with the surface of the soil. Iris must be kept moist and should never be allowed to dry out. Since, in flats, iris form a thin matted layer of roots on the bottom, thorough watering is a must. Placing the flats too near the heating pipes will cause rapid drying out and subsequent bud blasting.

Spacing depends on the variety and size. Standard varieties: Ideal, Wedgewood, White Wedgewood—size 10/11 = 12/sq. ft., size 9/10 = 15/sq. ft. Special colors:

Apollo, Blue Ribbon, Golden Harvest, Purple Sensation, Blue Magic—size 10/11 = 8/sq. ft., size 9/10 = 10/sq. ft., size 8/9 = 12/sq. ft. Some growers mark the flat or bench at this spacing after thoroughly watering the soil, and then push the bulbs into the soil, covering them with an inch layer of peat which is again watered. If placing flats on a bench, it is a good idea to allow a 1″ air space between them.

Iris need plenty of light and ample ventilation with uniform temperatures. The bulbs should be planted in an ordinary loose, well-drained soil. After bulbs root and begin to grow, fertilize weekly with $Ca(NO_3)_2$ at 2 lbs./100 gals.

Due to the excellent work that has been done by the USDA and other experiment stations, fairly accurate schedules are available today that allow the grower to plan his crop by selecting the proper variety, size, temperature and treatment to force a crop from mid-December through May. East Coast growers can produce

Cut iris—the wonderful blue of the flower world.

611

from mid-December through May, but West Coast growers who are located in areas where the temperature does not exceed 70° to 75°F can produce year-around.

Bulbs are usually dug in July and immediately given a 10-day curing period at 90°F, which accelerates the formation of flower buds. Immediately upon arrival at warehouses, all iris that are to be shipped to customers for planting after mid-November are put into a heat-retarding chamber at 82° to 86°F with 80% to 85% humidity. They are left in this chamber until they go into precooling, which is approximately four to eight weeks before planting, depending on size, variety and time of year. Those bulbs that are to be planted before mid-November can be left in open storage for about 30 days until they go into precooling. By precooling, the bulbs force more quickly and uniformly. Bulbs are placed in a 45° to 48°F precooling storage at the proper time so that they can be removed at planting time. Precooled bulbs must be planted immediately, since a delay will nullify the precooling effect. Some growers have facilities to do their own precooling, and thus use regular or heat-treated bulbs, depending on the intended planting date. Generally, these are shipped six weeks prior to planting. However, the time of precooling varies from four to eight weeks, depending upon the time of the season, variety and size of bulbs. If a grower is in doubt about this, he should consult those firms where scheduling services are available. Note: recent trials have shown that a two-week temperature treatment of 65°F (either before or after the 45°F treatment) does reduce the amount of foliage and improves size of flower. Also, with this treatment there is an increased blooming percentage.

The most widely used varieties are Wedgewood, a light blue; Ideal, a lobelia blue sport of Wedgewood; Blue Ribbon, a dark blue; Golden Harvest, a deep yellow; and White Wedgewood, a creamy white.

Assortment of Dutch iris cultivars used for forcing as cut flowers are:

Cultivar	Color	Bulb Sizes (cm)		
		10/up	9/10	8/9
Apollo	yellow & white	X	X	X
Blue Magic	violet	X	X	X
Blue Ribbon (Prof. Blaauw)	dark blue	X	X	X
Golden Harvest	golden yellow			X
Hildegarde	light blue	X	X	X
Ideal	lobelia blue	X	X	X
Purple Sensation	violet-purple			X
Royal Yellow	buttercup yellow			X
Symphony	ivory with yellow veins		X	X
Telstar	light blue with violet	X	X	X
White Wedgewood	creamy white	X	X	X

X indicates commercially available bulb sizes.

Iris come in sizes measured in centimeters of diameter: 6/7, 7/8, 8/9, 9/10, 10/11, and 11+. Depending on the temperature, forcing time on iris will range from 9 to 12 weeks on standard varieties such as Ideal, Wedgewood, and White Wedgewood, while other varieties may take 11 to 14 weeks before they bloom.

Regular iris cannot be timed accurately, so only the grower with precooling facilities will be interested in the regular bulbs.

There are two principal troubles encountered in the forcing of iris: bud blast and flower abortion. Bud blasting is generally caused by too-high temperatures in forcing (about 60°F), overcrowding in the bench, or not enough water or light. An aphid infestation on the bulbs can also cause blasting. If bulbs are infested with aphids at time of planting, a methyl bromide treatment before planting will solve the problem unless the bulbs are already damaged.

In Dutch iris, flower abortion can occur at almost every stage of flower development, and many factors are involved. These include low light intensities, high temperatures, poor nutrition and improper watering. In general, when light intensity is low, it is best to reduce the forcing temperatures. Research has indicated that this is particularly critical about 14 days before flowering. This is about the time when the floral stalk is rapidly growing out of the leaves. Thus, forcers should observe the prevailing weather conditions and adjust greenhouse conditions accordingly.

In the past, there were reports of blindness (three leaves). This was caused by too early digging and too early precooling of the bulbs. Presently, the West Coast-produced bulbs are harvested at proper maturity stage. Holland-produced bulbs receive an ethylene gas treatment after digging. This initiates a flower into the bulb. Also, in Holland-grown iris there have been few reports regarding blindness. Blindness should not be excessive if bulbs are dug and cured by August 15, precooled September 1 to October 15, and planted on October 15. Although it is possible to harvest flowers from 95% to 100% of the bulbs planted, percentages of 80% to 90% should be considered satisfactory for the earliest crop.

When iris flowers are destined for long-distance shipping, they should be cut in the bud stage just as their true color begins to show. For local selling, flowers should be cut when they are nearly wide open. If iris need to be stored after cutting, hold flowers in water at 33° to 35°F.

The West Coast Iris Crop

by Jeff McGrew
Ball Seed Company

There are major field-iris producers in the Watsonville and Half Moon Bay areas; also other large growers from San Diego to Northern California, but all are located close to the coast.

Most production occurs in open field conditions in full sun. There is an increasing number of iris being grown under saran (40° to 50°F), usually in the summer months and more in Southern California than Northern. There are an estimated 28 to 30 million bulbs grown annually in California.

Bulb sizes are 8/9 and 9/10 cm. for spring/summer growing, and 9/10 and 10 cm. and up for fall/winter forcing. The most popular varieties are Blue Ribbon (Prof. Blaauw) and Ideal, along with Telstar, Apollo, White Wedgewood, Hildegarde and a few others.

Growers between Watsonville and Half Moon Bay often plant nine to 10 months a year. Only the months of high rainfall (December and January) keep growers from planting and harvesting. In Watsonville, an October/November planting will usually bring flowers in April. The same planting in Southern California will bring flowers about one month sooner. A January/February planting in Watsonville brings flower in May/June, with flowers in Southern California coming four to six weeks earlier.

This picture shows the Kubota Farms in Castroville (Salinas), California. Ted Kubota is the owner. He forces several million iris per year between Castroville and Arcata (Northern California). Credit Jeff McGrew.

KALANCHOE *(Kalanchoe Blossfeldiana)*

by Robert Danielson
Ball Seed Company

The kalanchoe is a member of the family *Crassulacae*, succulent herbs and pliable shrubs of the temperate and tropical regions. It is a short-day plant flowering in January or February in the temperate regions.

*Here's a fine 3"
kalanchoe grown by
Hollandia Flowers,
Carpinteria, California.
Holding the plant is
Peg Biagioni, who
managed the
production of this
XV edition—a big job
well done.*

The kalanchoe can be flowered year around on a scheduled program very similar to the pot mum program: long-day requirement, followed by short-day response, using a long-day period and growth regulators to control plant habit and flowering.

There are many new commercial varieties that have bright colors, pleasing foliage, long shelf life and customer satisfaction. Sales have been increasing for the smaller sizes flowered for mass market outlets. Plants are easy to care for in mass market displays.

The kalanchoe is gaining in popularity as a pot plant because of its versatility and the availability of cuttings and liners from specialty propagators. Crop time can be shortened and quality improved by following the cultural and environmental requirements of the crop.

Propagation. While kalanchoes have been propagated from seed in the past, it is no longer practical because of long crop time. The best method is to purchase either liners (2" potted plants) or unrooted cuttings from specialist propagators. The problems of maintaining disease-free vegetative stock plants is both costly and difficult. Most of the large growers purchase unrooted cuttings scheduled to arrive weekly or bi-weekly for a steady supply of flowering plants. For specific holiday or special events, larger numbers are available if ordered earlier. The cuttings or liners will be uniformly selected and graded to provide a more uniform finished product.

The best cutting is either a two- or three-node cutting, 1½" to 2½" long, from a clean stock plant growing under long days with a minimum of 13 hours of light.

615

These cuttings will root within 14 to 21 days, with soil temperature of 68°F, with about 40% shade and very little mist to prevent stress or wilting. No hormone is required.

Growing media. The root system is made of very fibrous roots and not a very heavy root system. The media should provide for aeration, but should hold about an 80% field capacity. The higher field capacity reduces the need for frequent waterings. A good soil mixture contains 50% peat, 25% soil and 25% perlite. In a bag mix look for a finer mix rather than a coarse mix—better water holding capacity for the fine fibrous root system.

The pH should be between 5.8 and 6.5, with a peat-lite mix being closer to 5.8. In any soil or peat-lite mix, calcium should be in good supply by the addition of dolomite; superphosphate and micro elements should be added if a complete water soluble fertilizer is not used.

Watering. The plants should not be watered overhead on a regular basis. Smaller sizes work very well on a mat or an ebb-and-flow system. The growing media and watering practices go hand in hand in plant culture. The plants do not have a high transpiration rate and dry out from air circulation rather than plant transpiration, which makes kalanchoes drought resistant.

The young plants in the early stages of growth through bud initiation should not be stressed by high temperature or lack of water. It is very important to maximize the growth of the young plants through the bud initiation to size up the plant in relation to the pot size.

After flower initiation, overwatering can soften and stretch the flower stems. It is a good practice to tone the plants at the finishing stages.

Fertilization. Kalanchoes require less water than chrysanthemums, which reduces the frequency of watering. Since you are watering less frequently, you need to increase the fertilizer concentration. Three hundred to 400 ppm of nitrogen and potassium is recommended through bud visibility, and after that stage clear water and fertilizer can be alternated or fertilizer reduced to 150 to 200 ppm N and K. As in all fertilizer programs, it is recommended that the pH of the media be regulated to between 5.8 and 6.3.

It is recommended that calcium nitrate and potassium nitrate be used rather than ammonium nitrate as a source of nitrate or a complete fertilizer such as 20-10-20. The kalanchoe requires a consistent fertilization and watering program and will not perform at its best if neglected as a crop.

Growing temperatures. There have been many complaints that kalanchoes are difficult to schedule: This is because temperature is critical. Low night temperatures slow down the growth and make schedules and plant size difficult. The minimum night temperature through bud visibility should be 65°F. A 65° to 68°F range is optimal. The bud initiation and development is slowed down by night temperatures over 75°F and heat delay can occur.

Should the crop be developing too fast, the night temperature can be reduced below 60°F after the buds are initiated. During the winter months, low light in the North, CO_2 can be beneficial at 1,200 and 1,500 ppm.

616

Knud Jepsen, a major Danish kalanchoe specialist. Knud does 4 million, mostly 3½″ kalanchoes per year.

Pinching requirements. Kalanchoes can either be grown pinched or unpinched depending on size of the pot and number of cuttings used. As a rule, with the smaller sized—2½″ to 4½″—single plants, no pinch is necessary if the minimum number of long days and growth regulators are used to develop a compact plant habit. In growing a single plant in a larger pot, apply more long days and a pinch to increase plant size. If growing three plants in a larger pot, crop time can be reduced by four weeks by not pinching.

When pinching kalanchoes it is best to take the tip with one set of leaves to get a plant with more basal breaks.

Plant spacing. Because of their compact growth habit, kalanchoes can be grown closer than most pot plants. They can be grown pot to pot until the foliage touches, usually at the beginning of the short day period. A final spacing can be established when short day begins.

Size	Spacing
4″ Pots	4 to 6 plants/sq. ft.
5″ Pots	7″ x 7″
6″ Pots	10″ x 10″
6½″ Pots	12″ x 12″—3 plants per pot

Long-day treatment. The number of long-day weeks is critical to the vegetative development—plant size and plant habit.

- Not enough long-day weeks reduces the height and size of the plant.
- Too many long-day weeks stretches the plant.
- The long-day weeks on pinched plants should be balanced. Example, three long-day weeks before a pinch, three long-day weeks after the pinch.

If too many long-day weeks are given, then the result is a top heavy plant, not a balanced compact plant. The schedules in the following table, under good culture programs, should produce a balanced plant for any size. There are varietal differences and experience will fine tune the results.

Long-day treatment consists of 10 fc. at plant level. Use two hours per night, March 1 through October 31, and four hours per night November 1 through February 28.

Using this schedule takes some of the details out of changing schedules every month. Mum lighting is compatible with kalanchoe lighting—time and light levels.

Short-day treatment (black cloth). Kalanchoes, being photoperiod short-day plants, require a longer night than chrysanthemums. At higher night temperatures the black cloth should be applied between 14 and 15 hours—6:30 p.m. until 9:30 a.m.

The consistency of applying black cloth to kalanchoes is more critical than chrysanthemums. Since most of the larger sizes require long crop time, do not miss any nights of black cloth application or the crop will be delayed. Short-day treatment should start March 1 and end October 1.

Growers should also prevent any lighting spillover from adjacent areas from October 1 until March 1. Heat delay can occur in summer production if there is high temperature build-up under the black cloth.

Growth regulators. B-Nine is used to control the internodal stretch of the stem and the size of the leaf on more vigorous varieties. B-Nine can be scheduled as often as every three weeks during the plant development period to produce a more compact plant. Usually no more than two applications of 5,000 ppm are necessary; 2,500 ppm is also effective for some growers, depending on how vigorous the plants are growing.

B-Nine can also be used to shorten the peduncle stretch on tall growing varieties. Use 2,500 ppm when the buds are clearly visible. Not all varieties need B-Nine to shorten peduncle stretch. Some markets like a very short kalanchoe with flower heads right down on top of foliage. Some growers have used Bonzi as a growth regulator on kalanchoes.

Light level for greenhouse and outdoor growing. It is better if the plants are not stressed during the early growing stages. Kalanchoes do not usually do as well under high temperatures and high light. Leaf temperature is everything in growing a good kalanchoe. Under high temperatures and high light, the leaves will bleach out and harden, even develop a red color. When temperatures exceed 75°F, reduce the sunlight to about 3,500 or 4,500 fc., a little less light than mums. Reduce the light to lower the leaf temperature.

Under low-light levels, the kalanchoe will stretch and not flower as heavily, and flowers will be thin and weak. In the winter or low-light periods, it can be advantageous to start the plants under supplemental light (HID).

Insect problems. The most common insect problem is aphids, at the later stages of maturity when buds and flowers develop. Plants should be inspected on a regular basis for any developing insect problems. Some of the other insect problems are worms, mealybugs, thrips and whitefly.

Kalanchoes are very sensitive to certain spray material. Emulsifiable oil spray often burns the leaves. This happens because many of the kalanchoe leaves cup up and hold the spray material, causing a burn.

The best materials for kalanchoes are wettable powders or water soluble. Oil-based sprays should always be tested before applications. If an oilbased spray is used, I suggest washing after a short period. Don't let spray material remain on the leaves. Also be cautioned against fog materials that have an oil base and can settle on the leaves.

All spraying material should be tested on plant material prior to general usage. Some material successfully used: Thiodan for aphids, whitefly; Orthene SP for aphids, worms; Oxamyl for aphids, mealybugs; Vydate for aphids, mealybugs; and Avid for aphids, whitefly.

Disease problems. The most difficult disease problem of kalanchoes is bacterial soft stem rot, which can develop at any stage of plant development. The crop should be started from disease-free plants, and sanitation is important in culture. The benches should be clean and treated for disease with bleach. If growing on the ground, the soil should be sterilized between crops.

A Benlate/Subdue drench after planting will control many soil problems. Spraying the plants with a fungicide for mildew or bacterial wilt is almost impossible. The best way to control foliage diseases on kalanchoes is through the environment. Keep the foliage dry at all times, have good air movement in the house, and water from the bottom, not overhead. In plastic houses, and where you do not have good air circulation, botrytis can often become a problem. The use of Daconil or Chipco can help in the control of botrytis.

Keeping quality. Kalanchoes should be about 40% to 50% open before shipping for the best shelf life under low light levels in the store or home. Shipping the plants before terminal flowers open will set the plant back and never develop the flowers fully. If the customer has well-lighted windows or a garden exposure, he can handle a budded kalanchoe. Be sure the plant has mature flowers before shipping. Plants shipped at this stage will have six to eight weeks of shelf life. Breeders continue to work for newer varieties that will perform better in the marketplace and be easier for growers to produce. This is an interesting old crop.

Kalanchoes from seed. Kalanchoes may also be propagated from seed. Vulcan is a bright-red variety to be sown carefully in a well drained soil. Keep the soil temperature at 70°F and do not cover the seed. Transplant into 2¼″ pots and grow at 62° to 65°F and move the plants into 4″ to 4½″ pots for finishing. Seed sown in June should provide finished plants for Thanksgiving. Plants should be given black

*A well done one cutting per 4″
kalanchoe. Colorful, longlasting,
a pot plant on the way up.*

cloth, short-day treatments from late August until October 1. For Christmas, shade from September 10 until October 1. To flower for Valentine's Day, light plants from September until November 1. Plants do not usually need a pinch or B-Nine.

Varieties. There are many new varieties available and this list represents the most popular ones:

Red Avanti, Garnet, Attraction, Stromboli, Inspiration
Deep Pink Fascination, Sensation, Singapore
Medium Pink Bingo, Satisfaction, Cherry Jubilee
Salmon Pink Eternity, Seraya, Citation
Orange Bali, Flamboyant, Tropicana
Yellow Goldstrike

Best for 4″ or smaller:

Red Avanti, Tijuana
Deep Pink Fascination, Sensation
Medium Pink Bingo
Salmon Pink Seraya
Orange Bali, Tropicana
Yellow Goldstrike

Kalanchoe Crop Schedule*
Long Schedule   Min. Temp. 65°F Night

Plant Size	Pot Size	Plants Per Pot	Long-Day Weeks	B-Nine[1] #1	Approx. Weeks Plant to Pinch	Short-Day Weeks	B-Nine[1] #2	B-Nine[2] #3	Weeks[3] Plant to Sell
URC[4]	2″ to 3″	1	0-2	Week 3	No	6	Week 6	Yes	9-15
URC	4″ to 4½″	1	3	Week 4	No	6	Week 7	Yes	12-16
URC	5″ to 5½″	1	5	Week 4	Week 5	6	Week 8	Varietal	14-18
URC	6″ to 6½″	1	8	Week 5	Week 6	6	Week 9	Varietal	16-20
URC	6″ to 6½″	3	4	Week 5	Optional	6	Week 9	Yes	13-17
Liners									
2″ to 2¼″	2″ to 3″	1	0	Week 2	No	6	Week 5	Yes	9-13
2″ to 2¼″	4″ to 4½″	1	2	Week 4	Optional	6	Week 7	Yes	11-15
2″ to 2¼″	5″ to 5½″	1	3	Week 4	Week 2	6	Week 7	Varietal	12-16
2″ to 2¼″	6″ to 6½″	1	6	Week 6	Week 3	6	Week 9	Varietal	15-19
2″ to 2¼″	6″ to 6½″	3	3	Week 4	Optional	6	Week 7	Yes	12-16

Schedule used from March through September in the North; Sunbelt year-round. Longer crop times may be required in winter. Lower light areas.

Note 1: B-Nine for height and foliage size control, 5,000 ppm, applied for example, third week after plants are potted.
Note 2: B-Nine for peduncle length control, 2,500 ppm, bud visible—apply only if needed. Some varieties will not need this third application.
Note 3: Two long-day weeks plus six short-day weeks totals eight weeks, not 11 to 15 weeks. Reason: You need not shade kalanchoe all the way to maturity. Also, why the range of weeks from 11 to 15? Reason: Varieties differ in their earliness.
Note 4: Direct-stuck unrooted cuttings.

Note: Short-day treatment is not needed in Northern areas from October 1 to March 1. Days are naturally short enough to induce flowering.

Minimum short-day weeks for flowering is six weeks (42 days). Why the long-day and short-day periods? Answer: The kalanchoe flowers when exposed to short days (normally under 12 hour daylengths). If short days are applied on cuttings that are just planted, the finished plant will be too small. Therefore some weeks of long days are included in the schedule—time for the plant to build strength before it is put into flower by application of short days.

LANTANA

by Jim Nau
Ball Seed Company

*Tender perennial (L. camara), **1,300 seeds/oz**. Germinates in 6 to 7 weeks at 65° to 75°F. Seed should be covered during germination.*

Though the information above would suggest that lantana would make an excellent crop grown from seed, it is available only as a mixture or in purple; propagation by cutting is strongly advised.

Lantana comes in a wide range of colors where the buds will exhibit one color and the resulting flower will show another, and then often shades even to a third color in some cases. Flowers come in pink, orange, yellow, purple, cream, and shades in between, and are held on plants that grow horizontally and flower as long as the temperatures stay warm. Lantana is treated as a perennial in selected areas of the Deep South and Far West, but are annuals in the Midwest. Plants grow to a height of 3' and should be grown in full sun. Space 18" to 24" apart to fill in.

The predominant culture of these plants was for growers to dig the plants in the fall, pot them up, and move to a 55°F house to take cuttings. Today, commercial propagators perform this task, and the resulting plants are shipped to growers to finish off. However, if you want to take your own cuttings, use only softwood cuttings and stick into sand or sand mixed with peatmoss. Provide a bottom heat of 65°F, and mist. Roots will develop in 3 to 4 weeks and finish off in another 7 to 9 weeks in a 4" pot when grown with a soft pinch.

If buying from a commercial propagator, allow 6 to 8 weeks to finish, unless otherwise noted by the supplier, and stick directly into 4" pots or 8" and 10" hanging baskets. Water and feed only when necessary, as plants will be shy to flower from an abundance of either.

LARKSPUR

Annual (Delphinium ajacis), *8,000 seeds/oz. Germinates in 20 days at 55°F. Dark.*

The half-hardy nature of the larkspur can be taken advantage of by outdoor growers in the near South. If a sowing is made in the open in this section six to seven weeks before the ground freezes, plants well enough established to winter over should be produced. An exceptionally severe winter will sometimes destroy them, but usually they come through very well. Most growers find that a covering of even coarse material tends to rot them. With perfect drainage and some coarse covering, a fall sowing outdoors does usually come through nicely if made late enough to avoid germination before the ground freezes. The advantage of such a sowing lies in the promptness with which larkspur germinates in early spring. Such a sowing will flower at least two to three weeks earlier than if sown out after the ground dries in the spring.

In figuring seed requirements for an extensive planting, do so on the basis of 25 oz. of seed covering an acre; this is figured on double 8" rows spaced 3' apart. Spacing plants in the rows is not so important. They will fill out the row if spaced 10" to 14", but will do so more promptly if allowed half that distance. Some growers

Larkspur—a widely grown cut flower.

plant out March 1-sown seedlings, usually getting good results, but we believe that if the fall sowing comes through it will be more profitable because of the cost of greenhouse plants and transplanting. If you are depending on spring sowings, two should be made two to three weeks apart. By all means, get the first one in as early as possible and use deep, fairly well-enriched soil, and it will pay to irrigate during dry weather if it can be done.

Larkspur is also an important "minor crop" among Florida cut flower growers. It flowers very well during the winter months in Florida. It is also, of course, a great favorite for the homeowner's cut flower garden. For this it can be sown direct. Plants should be supported.

LIATRIS *(Blazing Star, Kansas Gay Feather)*

by Vic Ball

Perennial (L. spicata and pycnostachya), 9,400 seeds/oz. Needs cool temperature for germination.

Liatris, especially *L. spicata,* has become an important perennial cut flower in recent years. The showy 12″ to 15″ spikes make great accents in cut flower arrangements.

Although they are a native United States plant, they have been shipped importantly from Holland—in fact the Dutch exports are what triggered the present interest in the crop.

They are often grown from tuberous roots, planted rather deeply (4″ or so) in well-drained soil. The tuberous roots can be divided at the end of the crop, one eye to remain with each root. They also can be successfully grown from seed, both *L. spicata* and *L. pycnostachya,* a taller species but of the same color.

Liatris has become an important item for Florida cut flower growers—it does well in sandy soils and in cooler winter temperatures of south central Florida.

Liatris *pycnostachya* is quite a bit taller and difficult to manage as a cut flower—it needs careful supporting.

Liatris is a colorful cut flower that fits well in today's smaller arrangements.

LILY

LILY, EASTER

by Robert O. Miller
Dahlstrom and Watt Bulb Farms Inc.
Smith River, California

Lilium longiflorum Thunb., the Easter lily, belongs to the sub-genus Eulerion, the true lilies. The Easter lily with a white trumpet is the most popular lily for greenhouse pot lily production. Asiatic and Oriental hybrid lilies are also gaining in popularity.

Easter lilies are a major holiday pot plant crop that have maintained their popularity over the years. It is a traditional plant and there appears to be a core of demand centered around the religious significance of the Easter lily. Although the lily of religious paintings and writings was the Madonna lily, "longiflorum" types replaced it for practical cultural purposes. Tradition has also played a role quite apart from religious considerations. Probably the most important factor contributing to the continued popularity of the lily has been, however, the profitable nature of the crop both for the producer and the seller, and the perceived value by the customer. The Easter lily was one of the first plants to be sold through mass market outlets, and it's adaptability for this method of merchandising has been important.

Economics of Production

Lilies are the most profitable major holiday pot plant crop produced. This is true even though the initial cost of a lily bulb is high. When combined with the cost of the pot, soil, and labor of potting, often growers have 30% to 35% of the selling price invested initially. The space occupied by the crop compensates for this, however, so that the return per square foot is high. Consider that a chrysanthemum, a poinsettia or a hydrangea may occupy 1 to 1½ sq. ft. of bench space at finishing spacing. If an average of 1¼ sq. ft. is used and if a price of $4 per plant is used, then the return per sq. ft. of finishing space is $3.20. Lilies are grown from 2 to 3½ per sq. ft. If 2½ lilies are grown per sq. ft. and sold at $3, then $7.50 per sq. ft. is realized. This is more than two times the per sq. ft. income to be realized from other holiday pot plant crops.

Varieties

It is interesting that the variety Ace first gained widespread popularity about 1953, and the variety Nellie White slowly was accepted from about 1964, replacing Ace in popularity probably in 1979. Recently with the more widespread use of low

Figure 1.

Figure 2.

day temperatures to control height, interest in Ace is increasing. These varieties are "old" by present horticultural standards. Persistent efforts to breed superior varieties continue, however Ace and Nellie White have many good characteristics and remain pre-eminent. Great hopes were held for the varieties Harbor and Chetco, but they have not met expectations.

A large number of varieties are being created and tested at the Easter Lily Research Foundation in Brookings, Oregon. There are numerous varieties from this project that have been released for testing at various universities and research stations. Most of these, while promising, are not necessary to mention at present, but two especially meritorious varieties will be discussed.

The variety 255-3 (Figure 1) is a third generation self-cross of the variety Ace. It can best be described as an Ace type with very long, dark green leaves which are retained at the base even under stress conditions. Further, leaves are upright, slightly cupped, stiff, and do not droop under most negative DIF conditions (see discussion of height control). Plants are strong; days to flower is nearly the same as Ace and Nellie White. Bud count is higher than Ace, being near one flower per inch of bulb circumference on pot cooled crops. Height varies but is near that of Nellie White. Stems show no purple coloration as does Ace. Field performance thus far appears good. 255-3 propagates well from scale and grows well. This is an important factor for both bulb and greenhouse growers to ensure stable supplies of bulbs. Possible problems for this variety in the field (which could impact greenhouse production) is basal plate breakage under some environmental conditions, and a tendency to "summer sprout." Neither of these problems is more noticeable with 255-3 than with Ace, and the summer sprout problem is apparently less severe than it is with Nellie White.

626

Easter Lilies

Source: USDA 1989 Floriculture Crops Summary

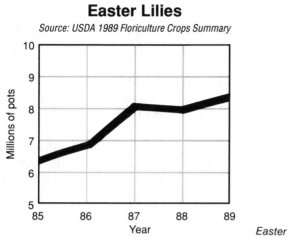

Easter lily sales 1985 through 1989.

Judged at present as second most promising in trials both by the Research Foundation and cooperators is 82-80 (Figure 2). This lily has excellent leaf retention, slightly higher bud count than Nellie White, flowers about five to seven days earlier than Nellie White, and is shorter than Nellie White. This is true even though 82-20 is an Ace type.

Since the major varieties continue to be Ace and Nellie White, a comparison of several traits follows:

Height. Nellie White is shorter than Ace.

A-Rest tolerance. Nellie White is more apt to suffer leaf yellowing from late or excessive growth retardant application than Ace.

Bud count. Nellie White will usually have one half to one fewer buds for a given size bulb compared to Ace. This is why most growers force larger size bulbs of Nellie White.

Flower size. Nellie White is generally credited with having larger flowers than Ace.

Forcing time. There is no difference. In most years Nellie White is slower to emerge than Ace, but from emergence to flowering it is faster.

Leaf number. Nellie White—for a given size bulb vernalized the same way—usually has fewer leaves than Ace. In some years 10 to 20 fewer leaves have been recorded. This is why Nellie White flowers in the same time as Ace even when it emerges later.

General toughness. Nellie White is not generally as "tough" as Ace. Ace is more tolerant of temperature extremes, A-Rest, root rot, fertilizer excess and deficiency, etc. Ace foliage does not curl down with the use of lower day than night temperatures (negative DIF) to the degree that Nellie White foliage does.

627

Precooling temperature. Nellie White is best vernalized (precooled) at near 45°F, while the optimum for Ace is 40°F.

Scorch. Nellie White is more resistant to true leaf scorch than Ace. Ace is much more resistant than the older variety Croft (no longer grown). Ace is not troubled by scorch if a few rules are followed (see fertilizer).

Space. Nellie White and Ace have the same space requirements.

Fertilizer requirements. Nellie White and Ace require essentially the same fertilizer. Nellie White may show higher leaf nitrogen content than Ace under similar regimes.

Timing from visible bud. Nellie White and Ace have the same time of development from visible flowers until flower opening. The same "bud stick" may be used.

General plant picture. Nellie White generally is given credit for having broader foliage and a more pleasing picture. It is difficult however to distinguish between well-grown Ace and Nellie White.

Georgia lilies, either from the southern United States or from Japan, once used in significant numbers are no longer important. Problems are height, virus content, and especially the overall plant appearance and lasting quality of individual flowers.

Attempts have been made by the Dutch to export Easter lilies into the United States. Varieties were obtained from Oregon State Lily Research or developed from them. While some varieties have been satisfactory in some situations, bulbs in Holland must be spring planted, and with their often wet springs they have not been able to deliver quality bulbs consistently. While cheaper, the greatest cost is in labor, heat, overhead, etc., and growers have not felt the risk worthwhile.

What Cultivar to Grow?

Grower preference is the single determining factor. Larger growers, especially, should be familiar with the forcing characteristics of both varieties and be prepared to utilize either. Nellie White is more prone to summer sprouting in the field than Ace. Since summer sprouting can on occasion affect 10% to 50% of the crop, summer sprouting could affect the supply of bulbs in a given year.

It is also true that weather conditions on the West Coast can affect bulb size of the cultivars differently. There are Ace "years" and Nellie White "years." The ability to handle either variety is an advantage.

Height is perhaps the single most important consideration, and the fact that Nellie White is the shorter of the two varieties is balanced in many instances by the fact that Ace is less likely to suffer leaf yellowing and can tolerate a higher negative DIF (see height control) or more A-Rest, and thus be held as short as Nellie White. The cost of A-Rest may be offset by the higher bud count obtained with Ace. Nellie White is more prone to leaf curling under excessive negative DIF conditions than Ace. Proper management of DIF will eliminate problems.

Field Culture

Most Easter lilies are produced on the West Coast on the Oregon-California border (many fields overlooking the ocean) between Harbor, Oregon, and Smith River, California. Production requires two to four years growth in the field, depending on size and whether scale production is utilized or plants are started from bulblets (small bulbs formed around the below ground stem above the bulb). Bulbs from scales (modified leaves broken from "mother bulbs"), called scalets, can be produced in one year. Scaling, combined with tissue culture, offers a means of more rapid build up of desirable stocks. Other factors being equal, scalets produce more uniform crops than bulblets.

Bulblets or scalets are graded and planted to produce 4" to 8" circumference bulbs called "yearlings" the first year. These produce "commercials" in the second year. Because of demand for larger-sized bulbs, some smaller commercials are replanted for still another year.

Packing and Size

Bulbs are harvested in late September and October, usually being completely packed by October 20. Rain is a determining factor in some years. The rainy season can begin on the Coast about September 15; thus rain can hold up the harvest. Forcers should be aware of this and be prepared to adjust their procedures should delayed harvest result.

Long standard lily packs are presented below. Changes are being considered to allow smaller cases for ease of handling and shipping.

Lily Bulb Size and Case Packs

Bulb Circumference	Number Per Case
6½" to 7"	300
7" to 8"	250
8" to 9"	200
9" to 10"	150
10" to 11"	125

Bulbs are packed in peat moss of a standardized moisture content. The ratio of bulbs, peat moss and moisture is of critical importance. Bulbs must not dry out during the vernalization period or afterward.

Vernalization (Precooling)

Easter lily bulbs of presently-grown cultivars have similar though not exact vernalization or precooling optima. Vernalization is the proper term to describe the cold treatment of several weeks duration that must precede initiation of flower buds. While vernalization is the proper word, the process is often referred to as precooling,

cooling, chilling, cold treatment, and others. It is important to remember that not only is the cold treatment critical, but it must be given under moist conditions. Cold received in late October, November and December is "remembered" by the stem to cause flowers to be initiated in January. If plants are not exposed to cold (or long days) the stem will eventually grow—perhaps indefinitely—and not initiate flowers. Stems with over 300 leaves have been recorded. Cold thus causes leaf making to cease and flowers to form.

Methods of Vernalization

Before specifics, the several methods of precooling should be broadly explained. "Case precooled" bulbs are precooled in the packing case, wherever it takes place. "Pot cooling" is a broad term also and means that plants are precooled after potting. Pot cooling has many variations such as "cold framing," which refers to early potting and placing in cold frame or other location which will prevent freezing but otherwise is not temperature controlled. "Outdoor cooling" refers to potting and placing outside with perhaps a straw cover to prevent drying, protect from heating during the day and frost at night. "CTF" or controlled temperature forcing is a popular and preferred system of pot cooling. The CTF system, or variations of it, allows more definite control of vernalization. When the investment in bulbs, soil, pots and labor is considered, we believe it prudent that all pot cooling be done under controlled conditions.

Case Cooling

Bulbs are shipped from the production area to either commercial cold storage facilities or to greenhouse growers who place them into refrigerators in the cases in which they have been shipped. It is important that temperature and time be carefully controlled. Table 1, though reflecting some variation in the data, illustrates the effect of too little or too much vernalization or precooling.

Table 1. Effects of Vernalization

Weeks of Storage	Days to Flower	Number of Flowers
00	196	10.0
01	176	9.7
02	160	9.1
03	135	7.1
04	123	6.4
05	114	6.5
06	109	5.6
07	112	5.6
08	110	5.2
09	103	5.0
10	100	4.9
11	98	4.4
14	103	4.5

From Lilies, edited by D.C. Kiplinger and Robert W. Langhans. February 1967.

Almost always a vernalization time of six weeks (1,000 hours) is recommended. With six weeks, expected forcing times of 110 to 115 days usually result. Longer vernalization results in faster forcing but lower bud count. This is a trade off. Nellie White has an optimum vernalization temperature of 44° to 46°F and Ace at 39° to 41°F. Times of longer than six weeks are not suggested.

Bulbs probably vary from year to year either in the amount of cold they have accumulated in the field or in the time requirement for vernalization, and perhaps temperature optima as a result of seasonal changes. It has not been necessary to vernalize longer than six weeks or less than four weeks. For practical purposes, never less than five weeks is recommended, and then only in some years if bulbs have received some cold in the field.

CTF Cooling

Bulbs are potted immediately after receipt in October. After potting, many schedules call for three weeks of 63°F for root growth, and six weeks at 40° or 45°F for vernalization. This is a total of 63 days. When bulbs are received early and Easter is relatively late this is no problem. When Easter is early and/or bulbs are received late, there is just not time to accommodate the entire CTF 9-week schedule. More on this later.

Many texts have placed the forcing time for Nellie White and Ace lilies at 120 days. Previous editions of the *Ball RedBook*, for example, say "timing of lilies for Easter centers around a basic rule that the bulb requires approximately 120 days from potting to flowering." Table 1 shows (after six weeks vernalization) 109 days. The point is, no less than 110 days should be allowed from bringing bulbs to the heated greenhouse until shipping, depending on when this is, and 120 days is good because of slower forcing. Usually 1/3 of the crop is shipped up to two weeks before Easter. Many growers in recent years have not allowed enough time for forcing.

Consider the following for a crop to be shipped seven days before Easter:

Easter Date	Description	Dec. 1	Dec. 8	Dec. 14
		(Days From Easter)		
March 26	Early	109	101	95
April 7	Early-Mid	121	113	107
April 14	Late-Mid	128	120	114
April 21	Late	135	127	121

For early or early-mid Easter dates, plants must be brought to the greenhouse by December 1 to 8 or earlier to allow time for forcing. On the latest dates enough time is available from a December 15 to 21 date.

Most practically, whatever the date of Easter, we strongly suggest that plants be in the greenhouse no later than December 15. On a very early date, December 1 is much preferred; this allows the plant time to develop. If December 15 is used as a date to begin forcing (no matter what the Easter date), then either the schedule before forcing or the forcing time must be adjusted or both. See the suggested schedule below.

Controlled Pot Cooling Schedule

Easter Date	Begin Forcing Date	Days to Easter	Days of Vernalization	Start Vernalization
March 26	Dec. 7	102	42	Oct. 26
April 7	Dec. 15	114	42	Nov. 3
April 14	Dec. 15	121	42	Nov. 3
April 21	Dec. 15	128	42	Nov. 3

Note that for the earliest Easter a vernalization date of October 26 is suggested, and earlier is better. If bulbs are shipped from the West Coast October 10, and require five days in transit and three days to get potted, it is obvious that it's October 18 or thereabouts and that at most there are only seven to eight days for 63°F rooting treatment. The movement to the greenhouse at the proper time, and a full vernalization treatment are more important than three weeks at 63°F, therefore the rooting period should be cut short. Note also that in many cases weather and other factors prevent early bulb shipments. Also as more and more forcers elect pot cooling more, and more shipments are made early as requested, it is obvious that all shipments can not be made at once. Further, bulbs are not always out of the ground to honor all these early shipments.

In summarizing pot cooling techniques, remember that Easter lilies need 110 to 120 days from the start of forcing to flowering. Many troubles in forcing result from bringing them to the greenhouses too late and "starting from behind." Pot cooling is to be recommended for those who can use it and understand it. The 63°F rooting period should be adjusted (eliminated if necessary) to allow for a full six weeks of vernalization and moving to the forcing greenhouse in time. In many cases a slower start in the greenhouse at relatively low temperatures helps early root growth. It is also critical that forcers understand that they must keep pots moist to ensure that the bulbs can perceive the proper cold temperatures. Many problems that have been caused by drying during pot cooling are blamed on bulbs.

With today's earlier poinsettia shipping schedules, lilies can be brought in at the proper time for the lilies. While this may require some special management, the extra trouble will be more than repaid by the crop quality that results. Raising the temperature of the storage after precooling and prior to moving the pots to the greenhouse, is a method to start forcing at the proper time if some problem prevents moving to the greenhouse on schedule and if sprouting has not started. Growth in storage is probably slower than in the greenhouse, however, because of no "sun heat," and this should be considered. There is also danger of sprouting in the dark in storage unless extreme care is used.

Modifications of Pot and Case Cooling

In the past, some growers have requested that bulbs be shipped to them early, prior to the finish of case cooling, so as to be potted in late November. They then run cool temperatures, near 50° to 55°F, until late December when they raise temperatures to 60° to 65°F to start forcing. This is a workable system. The cool temperatures during December allow for some rooting and also some vernalization. The four weeks at 50°F equate to near two weeks at 40°F. This is a system that was in wide spread use before the long-lasting poinsettia varieties became common.

In some warm areas such as inland valleys of California and in the South, a modified pot cooling program works, although controlled conditions are to be preferred. Some forcers allow bulbs to have two to four weeks of vernalization in the case, then pot, then allow the balance of the vernalization to proceed under natural conditions. This procedure, too, allows some rooting to occur.

Lighting

Long days can substitute for cold on a day-for-day basis. Long days also have the same effect as increased vernalization on reducing bud count. From a practical view, use of lights can be very beneficial if combined with sorting. Light of 10 fc. (mum lighting) four hours nightly is used. If a new installation is put in just for lilies, installation costs can be reduced by use of an intermittent lighting system. Lights should be applied immediately on emergence (have lights on one to two days prior to emergence) and left on for the number of days desired. There is one potential dilemma: early emerging plants could receive more long days then they need, and late emerging plants not enough. Observations indicate that slow emerging plants often have fewer leaves than early emerging ones, and thus flower in nearly the same time with slightly less lighting. Remember lighting for too long a period can cause reduced bud count.

Bud Count and Bulb Size

Bud count is controlled by bulb size, vernalization, and growing factors. Bulb size affects bud count. Table 2 is idealized but gives a rough idea of the number of flowers to be expected from a given size bulb treated properly. Note that "pot" cooling can increase bud count. Bud count is probably controlled by meristem area at the start of the flower initiation period near January 7 through February 7. Thus larger bulbs—which have larger meristems—have more flowers. Similarly, anything that promotes vigorous growth of the new stem can increase flower count; most recognized of these growth factors is temperature.

Forcers who use smaller bulbs such as 6½" to 7" Ace or 7"/8" Nellie White must bear in mind that should any difficulties arise during the forcing period, where they lose a bud or two, they may end up with an undesirable, nonsalable plant.

Robert O. Miller, shown here with his forced crop, is the author of this chapter and a major bulb producer.

Table 2. Bud Count

Bulb Circumference	Case Vernalized		Pot Vernalized	
	Ace	Nellie White	Ace	Nellie White
6½" to 7"	3 to 4	2 to 3	4 to 5	3 to 4
7" to 8"	4 to 5	3 to 4	5 to 6	4 to 5
8" to 9"	5 to 6	4 to 5	6 to 7	5 to 6
9" to 10"	6 to 7	5 to 6	7 to 8	6 to 7
10" to 11"	7 to 8	6 to 7	8 to 9	7 to 8

Note: Pot cooling in many of its variations will usually produce one or more buds than indicated above. Note, too, that the above figures are average, not maximum or minimum.

Temperature Dip

By reducing the night temperature during the flower initiation period, growth slows and the meristem apparently expands, allowing more flowers to form. Reducing temperature to 55° to 58°F for seven to 14 days can increase bud count appreciably. Perhaps more importantly it must be emphasized that raising the temperature during this period can cause a severe loss of flowers. It must be emphasized that in no case is it suggested that growers use a temperature dip unless the leaf count method of timing is being used to monitor crop development.

Other factors such as sunlight, good fertilizer, high carbon dioxide levels, good roots, proper watering, etc., all have a definite effect on bud count. The bad effects of over-vernalization have already been covered. The most beneficial effect of pot cooling is that roots are established when flower initiation occurs. This allows lots of water and nutrients to be absorbed to promote vigorous growth. Much as a pot mum cutting fattens after planting, a lily stem also expands. The better the growth, the more the bud count. A further effect of rooting prior to stem emergence is apparently a control of leaf elongation by the root system. Plants that emerge prior

634

Figure 3.

to rooting will have shorter lower leaves than those well rooted prior to emergence. In fact, one major cause of very short leaves, as seen in Figure 3, is lack of rooting caused by any number of factors prior to emergence.

Bulb Drying and Vernalization

Vernalization is a process that takes place under cool moist conditions. Drying during vernalization, either in the case or in the pot, can prevent the bulb from receiving the cold and result in uneven or partially vernalized bulbs. If vernalization is not complete, exposure to temperatures of near 70°F or higher can erase the cold treatment and can cause growth anomalies (see Figure 4). If vernalization has been completed (six weeks of temperatures near 40°F, under moist conditions), temperatures at or slightly above 70°F will not cause devernalization.

Figure 4. Here's an example of what can happen if precooled bulbs received in the fall are not placed in cold storage or potted immediately upon arrival. The bulb on the right was held at room temperature for two weeks before planting.

635

Potting

Bulbs should be potted upon receipt or upon completion of cooling. Delay in potting is a serious potential problem. See Figure 4.

Bulbs should be planted deep in standard (6" x 6" for example) pots to protect against early emergence in controlled storage, and to allow adequate room for the development of stem roots above the bulb. One inch of soil in the bottom of the pot is adequate, and two inches of soil over the bulb is preferred.

A few bulbs may sprout in the case. Sprouted bulbs are not hurt. The critical factor is to bury the entire etiolated (white) stem below soil level. Sometimes planting the bulb on its side can accomplish this. If the entire stem is covered, growth will be normal on emergence. If a portion of etiolated stem remains above ground, leaves will not elongate and small stem bulblets will form. If this is one inch or less, it will not be noticed at flowering.

Some forcers still prefer gravel in the bottom of pots, mostly for weight to prevent tipping. Gravel serves no drainage purpose; in fact it probably shortens soil, water columns and contributes to a wetter root area and is a practice which should be discarded.

With more height specifications by large buyers, more ¾ pots (6" x 5") are being seen. The 1" shorter pot could make a difference between three and four layers in a truck. Height is best controlled by A-Rest, negative DIF, spacing, etc., because deep potting is beneficial and should be a goal.

Soils

Good lily soils are soils with water holding capacity but good drainage and especially good fertilizer holding capacity. It is likely that the keeping quality of lilies grown in lightweight peat mixes is as good as that of lilies grown in heavier soil based mixes. Further, lily soils should have enough weight to prevent tipping should lilies get taller than desired.

Depending on physical characteristics, ¼ to ½ of the mix can be soil. Vermiculite is excellent to increase nutrient exchange capacity. Peat moss at ¼ or more, and bark (be sure to add nitrogen to correct for bark decomposition) is suitable. Because of absorption, bark can be a problem if A-Rest drenching is practiced. Remember that on a volume basis peat moss has very little fertilizer holding capacity. A useful mix has been:

> 1/3 soil
> 1/3 peat moss (or peat-bark, ½ each)
> 1/6 vermiculite
> 1/6 coarse sand.

636

The pH should be adjusted to 6.2 to 6.5 with calcium carbonate, using 2 lbs./yd. as a basis. Certain limestone deposits have apparently high fluoride content, and known sources of this material should be avoided. For this reason also, perlite should not be used in lily mixes. Calcine clay is an excellent aggregate where available. Styrofoam has been used but is not in favor because of the litter problem.

A complete fertilizer, 12-12-12 for example, can be added at the rate of 1 lb./yd. DO NOT use superphosphate (see leaf scorch). If bark is added to the mix we suggest an extra ½ lb. of urea formaldehyde fertilizer per yard be added to compensate for nitrogen tie up in bark decomposition. If soil is to be stored, organic nitrogen should not be used. Trace elements are probably best added in liquid form.

Easter lilies need fertilizing early in their development to produce vigorous stem expansion and a large leaf canopy. For this reason soils should contain adequate fertility. Good nutrition starts with a soil of high initial fertility but one not exceptionally high in total soluble salts. High soluble salts can cause erratic sprouting and in extreme cases can prevent sprouting completely.

Ace is more susceptible to leaf scorch then Nellie White, but Nellie White can show scorch symptoms. Leaf scorch is a serious disorder and many younger growers have not seen the extreme loss that can result. Fertilization of lilies should be based on elimination of leaf scorch as a problem, in addition to other considerations. Leaf scorch can be controlled—whatever its true cause—by high calcium levels and low phosphorus. This is the reason for lime for pH control, and no superphosphate in the initial mix. After potting, calcium nitrate coupled with soluble trace elements and potassium at 200 ppm is satisfactory depending on soil mixes and irrigation schedules. Calcium nitrate can be applied at 200 to 400 ppm regularly, and up to 750 ppm to boost fertility.

Use of phosphorus at 20 ppm in irrigation water is not likely to induce scorch and certainly provides adequate phosphorus.

One of the most important cultural considerations is to provide adequate nitrogen to prevent lower leaf yellowing and subsequent leaf loss. Experiments removing the lower 1/3 of leaves induced tall lilies. Lower-leaf loss caused by nitrogen deficiency is most likely to be a problem starting at bud initiation. A high nitrogen requirement at this time, plus a possible deficiency because of organic matter decay, can result in an incipient nitrogen deficiency. Often, also, it is difficult to make adequate liquid fertilizer applications at this time because of constantly wet soils due to dark weather and other liquid applications. Often the yellowing of a few lower leaves is attributed to root loss or drying and nothing is done. Nitrogen deficiency then becomes progressively more pronounced until it is too late to correct it. The best method to prevent this and to ensure a dark green, shiny, healthy leaf surface is to top dress with a dry long-lasting nitrogen source such as urea formaldehyde nitrogen (Nitroform for example), Osmocote or other slow release nitrogen form. One-half heaping tsp. of Nitroform per 6″ pot at mid-January and another February 15 is adequate. Application costs are more than repaid. Soluble salts should be kept below 2.0 micromhos/sq. cm. (2.0 EC).

For best keeping quality, plants should be well fertilized during the growing season so that the fertilizer level can be reduced in the greenhouse during the last two weeks. Clear water applications will leach out any excess salts. Lilies, like foliage plants, use much less fertilizer and are more susceptible to fertilizer injury when they are moved from the growing environment to a non-growing environment. This is especially true when lilies are boxed and cold stored prior to shipping.

Watering

Lilies, in most cases, should not be automatically watered by mat or drip tube from systems. Excess height almost always results unless special soil-based mixes make conditions prevail. Overhead sprinkling, however, is satisfactory. As with all crops, water management is tied up with soil management.

Heavier soils are harder to manage with respect to water relations than lighter extra soils, but the extra effort worthwhile.

Excessive watering can encourage root rot problems. It is probable that currently available fungicide drenches have allowed growers much more latitude in watering. With the loss of certain fungicides, watering may become as critical as in the past. Careful watch should be maintained on the root system should rot appear. Careful assessment of water level, soluble salt level and fungicide drench timing must be made.

Early in the life of the crop in the dark days of December and January, it is difficult to time fungicide drenches, liquid fertilizer applications and liquid growth regulator applications.

Crop Control

A great amount of work has been done in recent years that has made the lily crop more predictable. Timing and height control are two areas which were highly unpredictable as recently as 10 years ago. In spite of the progress made in recent years, however, lilies are a difficult crop to grow to perfection. There are several reasons for this:

1. Easter dates vary widely at a time of the year when the environment rapidly changes.

2. Bulbs are field grown and exposed to differing environmental conditions yearly.

3. Only one crop a year is grown.

4. Specifications by large buyers have been recently adopted. These criteria are perhaps overly restrictive given the nature of the crop.

5. Vernalization as well as season has a great effect on the number of leaves that are initiated prior to flower initiation, thus influencing the time to force.

Timing, height control with chemicals, height control with DIF, and crop monitoring will be discussed separately.

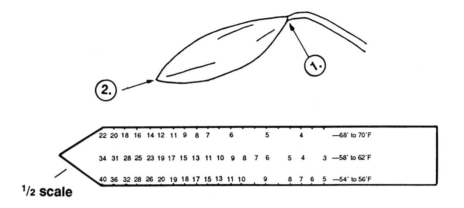

¹/₂ scale

Figure 5. Here's the famous lily "bud stick." For example, if you're growing Easter lilies at 68° to 70°F, place the bud stick tip where the flower joins the peduncle (1) and locate the corresponding number at 2 to find the number of days (at the 68° to 70°F growing temperature) until the bud will open. In this example, the answer is about 7 days. The only qualification: A lot of bright sun will hasten the process. Note: bud stick shown 1/2 scale.

Timing

Until A.N. Roberts of the Oregon State University devised the leaf counting method of timing lilies, most growers relied on height to time the crop until flower buds were visible. From visible flower buds timing was aided by "bud sticks" as pictured in Figure 5. The pattern can be traced onto a pot label to make a "bud stick." The pointed end is sharpened and then aligned with the base of the small developing bud (where the peduncle ends and the petals and sepals begin). The tip of the flower is then aligned with three numbers that show the number of days at three temperatures required to bring that bud into flower. Note that a bud nearly ½" long—about the visible stage—can be brought to flower in as little as 20 days by "hard forcing" at near 70°F night temperature (day temperature 10 to 20 degrees higher) or as many as 36 days at 54°F.

Time of emergence and height are still useful guides for early development. Such detailed schedules were published by many colleges in the past. Few are now. Here is a typical old schedule based on an April 2 Easter:

Date of Easter, April 2

Date	Weeks to Easter	Suggested Stage of Development
Dec. 3	17	Potted, 60°F
Dec. 10	16	Making roots
Dec. 17	15	Making roots
Dec. 24	14	Making roots
Dec. 31	13	Growth coming through

(Forcing timetable continues on next page.)

Date	Weeks to Easter	Suggested Stage of Development
Jan. 7	12	Growth 2″ to 3″
Jan. 14	11	Growth 4″ to 6″
Jan. 21	10	Growth 6″ to 8″
Jan. 28	9	Growth 10″
Feb. 4	8	Growth 15″
Feb. 11	7	You can feel the buds
Feb. 18	6	You can see the buds
Feb. 25	5	Buds ½″ to 1″ long
Mar. 4	4	Buds 2″ to 3″ long—few bending down
Mar. 11	3	Buds 3″ to 5″ long
Mar. 18	2	Buds fully developed
Mar. 25	1	Buds whitish-cooled
Mar. 28	½	Some opening-cooled
Apr. 2	0	Easter

Note that the essential fact of these height schedules is that they entirely fail to take into account growth factors which influence height. They are rigidly fixed in allowing six weeks for development from buds visible, and also relatively rigid upon emergence. The only flexibility is the "middle of the schedule." Since they allow absolutely no method of determining how fast development should be in the middle of the schedule they really are quite useless. If buds are not seen by a particular time, temperatures can be raised, but it would obviously be advantageous if an earlier measure was available. Such a system was devised by Oregon State University

A fine house of lilies just breaking color.

Research and has been widely publicized and refined by Harold Wilkins, formerly of the University of Minnesota. If the leaf counting procedure is followed, a grower can determine by mid to late January exactly how many leaves the crop has (remember the number of leaves varies with the amount of cooling). Since the rate of leaf unfolding is determined by temperatures, the temperatures to force can be determined as early as leaf count is determined. By monitoring the rate of leaf unfolding, development can be continuously monitored. The number of leaves the crop has must be determined after flower initiation has occurred. To count leaves use the following procedure:

1. January 15 to 20 select three to five representative plants of each major lot to be monitored.

2. With a felt tip pen or by notching a leaf, select the uppermost "unfolded" leaf.

3. Start at the bottom and count all leaves which have unfolded up to the notched or marked leaf (in 2 above). Write this number down.

4. Start with the notched or marked leaf and remove and count leaves toward the growing point. This is easy until the leaves get to be ¼″ to ½″ long. Then a mounted hand lens and needle will be necessary. Count the leaves right into the growing point—buds should be visible (see Figure 6). Write down the

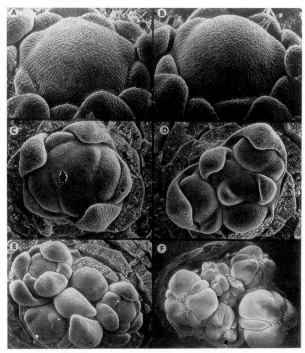

Figure 6. Six pictures of a lily growing point as seen under a binocular microscope or powerful hand lens. Development from A to D is a vegetative growing point to a stage of flower development just before buds would be visible.

A. Lily meristem in October. No floral development.

B. Early January. No floral development evident.

C. Mid-January. This is a reproductive meristem. This would be difficult to distinguish without a lot of experience.

D. Late January. A reproductive meristem with four or five buds formed. This is about the earliest stage that growers can verify bud set.

E. Further advancement of flower development. Four buds with either a flower bud or a secondary vegetative meristem in the lower center (covered by two leaf primordia).

F. Further advancement. Six flower buds evident.

number of leaves. The numbers written down would appear as follows, for example:

Leaves unfolded	50
Leaves not unfolded	45
Total leaves	95

5. Average, or look at the figures, for three to five plants. If, for example, this count was made January 15 and 45 leaves were left to unfold, compute as outlined below the number leaves per day to unfold:

A. Count back from Easter the number of days before Easter that buds should be visible. Usually six weeks is used (but less can suffice). So, for an Easter on April 19, less six weeks equals March 8. Now, from January 15 to March 8 there are 52 days.

B. Divide 45 leaves not unfolded by 52 days to unfold = .87 leaves per day. So .87 leaves per day need to be unfolded to see buds on March 8.

Now the question is, how many leaves per day can be unfolded?
After the leaves per day is determined, the following can be used as a starting place to pick a forcing temperature:

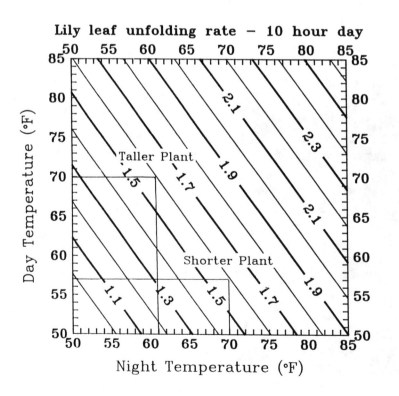

Figure 7.

It's nice to read in a book that for a "large bulb" 60°F will cause the unfolding of one leaf a day. It's even better to actually measure the average number of leaves unfolding per day after the indicated temperature change has been made. To accomplish this, follow the procedure below:

1. Select another three to five plants from each major lot. Put a pot label in each pot and use a tall flagged stake to mark it to make it easy to find.

2. Write the date on the label and notch or mark a leaf in the same relative position as the one in 2 above.

3. Wait four to five days and again mark a leaf in the same relative position as in 2 above.

4. Then count the number of leaves that have actually unfolded from the most recently marked leaf down to the earlier marked leaf. Write this down on the label with the new data.

5. Compute the leaves per day as follows:

> 5 = number of leaves unfolded
> 4 = number of days
> 1.25 = number of leaves per day

Computation in 5 above showed a need to unfold .87 leaves per day. This computation showed that 1.25 leaves per day are unfolding. Temperatures need to be slowly lowered to decrease the rate of unfolding to .9 to one leaf per day.

6. By counting leaves every four to five days, crop progress can be followed.

This is a workable system. All lily growers should use it. Remember leaf counting allows timing to start January 15 rather than when buds are visible. Growers have four to six weeks longer to manipulate temperature using this system.

Leaf counting also allows more reasoned decisions regarding temperatures, and this allows fuel savings. When coupled with "graphical tracking" (to be discussed later), keeping consistent records of the rate of leaf unfolding along with major cultural events—periods of high or low light intensity, irrigations and fertilizations, carbon dioxide additions, temperature changes, root loss, fungicide applications—makes it possible to determine the effect of these changes on growth rate. It thus builds a body of knowledge which can be used to judge the effect of future cultural changes.

Height Control

Chemical Growth Retardants

At this writing, A-Rest is the only practical chemical to reduce the height of pot lilies. While expensive, its use often times is necessary if height is to be controlled.

The material may either be applied as a drench, a spray or as a combination. If roots are present, soil application may be made early, before leaf surface is expanded to absorb a spray, and may have a more lasting effect (but only if a root

Sumagic, a chemical retardant, shows promise of being best for lilies—at one-tenth the cost of A-Rest. The photo above left shows the effect of Sumagic at .062 mg./6" pot versus the control plant. The photo above right shows .125 mg./6" pot, again versus the control plant. Both were applied as a soil drench, 3 oz. (100 ml.) per pot at the 4" to 5" height. Growers should certainly do a small field test for a year or two before a major application.

system is present). Shredded bark—especially pine bark—absorbs A-Rest, thus reducing its effectiveness. More material must be used to counter this loss. Greater expense is incurred and this may offset the advantage of soil application. Rates of about 0.5 mg per pot as a soil application, or 33 ppm as a spray (see A-Rest label) are effective under conditions of low light. In higher light areas, or if bark is not used (these rates presume use of bark media), it is probable that lower rates should be used. Spraying is gaining favor over soil applications because of flexibility, especially in view of negative DIF.

Some thought persists that A-Rest reduces flower count. However, it is unlikely that this is true unless it is applied excessively early at excessive rates.

A-Rest is to be avoided if possible. The known effect of rapid senescence (leaf yellowing from the bottom to the top) has been associated with A-Rest applications, particularly on Nellie White. Most yellowing, though, has occurred under conditions of "carbohydrate shortage." Prolonged high-temperature forcing, long shipping distances, long storage of boxed plants and late applications have been most detrimental. A-Rest is also expensive.

Growth retardant should be applied in relation to leaf number in order to have more predictable response from year to year. First spray applications can be readily made when 25 to 30 leaves have unfolded. Sprays much earlier have less dwarfing effect apparently because of lack of leaf surface. Usually two or more applications are necessary, the second seven to 15 days after the first. There may be some advantage to a first spray application, to have a rapid effect, followed by a drench, which seems to be slower to take effect but more long lasting.

Negative DIF

Work at Michigan State University by Royal Heins and his students has had a dramatic impact on height control of lilies. Studies have shown that reversing the normal pattern of day and night temperature has a profound effect on stem elongation. The normal pattern is a higher day temperature than night temperature. By changing this to a higher night temperature than day temperature, shorter plants result. Low day temperatures are most effective during the first hours of light each day. This is fortunate because it is sometimes impossible to maintain low day temperatures in high sunlight situations, or when outside temperatures are high.

When night temperatures are higher than day temperatures, it is referred to as a negative DIF situation. Conversely, with higher day temperatures than night temperatures, a positive DIF results.

The greater the DIF, positive or negative, the greater the height difference will be, taller or shorter. As a practical matter, growers have had good results with negative DIF's on the order of 5° to 15°F. Excessive negative DIF can cause growth changes, especially downward leaf curling on the variety Nellie White. Unless the negative DIF has been excessive, a few days of positive DIF will correct the problem.

While using DIF to control height, it is critical not to lose sight of the fact that the total amount of heat that a lily receives does control flowering. In the past, lilies

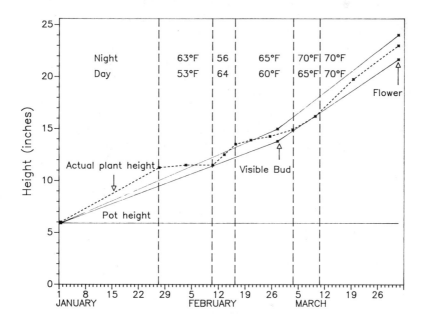

often were exposed to day temperatures considerably higher than today and thus were forced faster. For example if by reference to Figure 7 it is determined that an average 24-hour temperature of 65°F is needed to flower the crop on time, and it is determined that a 10°F negative DIF is needed, then the following computations can be made assuming (for example) a nine-hour light period and a 15 hour dark period:

> 24 hours x 65 degrees = 1,560 degree hours
> 15 hours x 69 degrees = 1,035 degree hours
> degree-hours remaining = 525

Dividing 525 degree hours by a 9-hour day gives a day temperature of 58°F, about a 10°F negative DIF and an average temperature of 65 °F.

Graphical Tracking

The tools to control height are largely available. The challenge is to apply them. Royal Heins has devised a method to track height changes on a graph on a regular basis so as to be able to use A-Rest or control of DIF to effect changes in the rate of stem elongation.

Figure 8 shows a graph illustrating tracking a crop for an April 7 Easter, with planned flowering one week earlier. The graphical tracking method is based on the assumption that the height of a lily will double (from the bottom of the pot) from buds visible to flowering. To follow the procedure, the date of emergence must be recorded on a graph and this is the starting point. The next step is to determine the desired final height—for example 20″ to 22″. Thirdly, specify the date buds should be visible. In the case illustrated, this would be February 28, 42 days before Easter. Assuming a height of one-half final height at buds visible, a buds visible range of height should be 10″ to 11″. Lines connecting the emergence date at the top of the pot to buds visible, then to final height, defines the envelope of height over time that is the goal. By measuring height at least two times per week, height can be monitored closely. The graphs should be filled in while in the greenhouse so that any modifying actions—temperature changes, A-Rest applications, etc.—can be entered at the same time, thus creating a record for future crops.

A potential problem is false information as a result of handling the plants to get the measurements. More than one uniform plant should be selected at the beginning of the tracking. This allows switching plants should stunting from handling occur. Graphical tracking is a practical method of following the progress of the crop. It is not, however, a substitute for watching other aspects of culture. It is interesting that while great progress has been made in methods to control and monitor growth, buyers specifications have become more demanding. Growing the crop has therefore remained difficult.

646

Diseases

Root Rots

Root rots are probably the most serious disease of lilies in greenhouses. Well-drained soils and attention to good irrigation practices are of importance. The wide array of soil drenches available have been of prime importance in control. This may change as chemicals become harder to obtain. Pythium, Rhizoctonia and to a lesser extent Fusarium appear to cause the most problems. The drench schedule below has proven effective:

Possible Fungicide Drenches

Pot Cooled Bulbs	4 oz. to 8 oz. Benlate per 100 gallons	½ oz. Subdue per 100 gallons	4 oz. to 8 oz. Truban per 100 gallons	4 oz. Terraclor per 100 gallons
At potting		X		X
January 15	X		X	
March 1	X	X		
Case Cooled Bulbs				
At potting		X		X
January 15	X		X	
March 1	X	X		

Roots should be monitored and the drench schedule adjusted as needed. One Terraclor application is important because of its effectiveness in Rhizoctonia control. Rhizoctonia infections may be associated with bulb mite infestations, and Terraclor is most effective in preventing this.

Viruses

Two major viruses affect lilies. When cucumber mosaic and lily symptomless virus are at high levels, "fleck" symptoms appear. This virus can be crippling. The "fleck" spots on the leaves and sometimes distorted plants can cause economic loss. All lilies in commercial production have lily "symptomless" virus. Clones made free of this virus grow much taller than infected clones; flower count and other characteristics are apparently not much affected.

Poor growing conditions can magnify virus symptoms. Low temperature starting, low humidity, and no doubt other conditions can cause more symptom expression. Due to rouging and aphid control in the field, viruses are usually not a problem.

Botrytis

Under low-light high-humidity conditions, botrytis can be a problem on unopened buds and flowers. Best control is by adding heat while venting to reduce relative humidity. Daconil sprays (1 lb. wettable powder/100 gals. with a recommended spreader) over the bulbs are also used. Botrytis is seldom a problem on

647

foliage in greenhouses, although it is the most important disease in field production. Under severe humidity and free-water situations, botrytis on leaves can occur.

Insects

Mites

There has been much publicity about bulb mites. Mites have long been associated with bulbs and are responsible for consuming the sloughed-off outer scales of the bulbs as they grow from inside out. Mites have been seen tunneling in stems, apparently entering between the bulb and the soil surface. It is debated whether the mites are primary, causing the lesion themselves, or secondary, entering a lesion caused, perhaps, by Rhizoctonia. It is to protect against the latter that Terraclor is specified as a drench at potting. Most severe bulb mite-type damage has been seen in pot cooled lilies. Plants are often bent because the lesions on one side of the stem stop growth while the opposite side elongates. Dwarfed, stunted growth with thickened leaves and crippled growing points has been attributed to mites, but this has not been established.

Bulb dips in Kelthane can be effective in elimination of mite populations. Rates are 1-1/3 lb. of Kelthane 35% wettable powder/100 gals. of water and immersing the bulbs for 30 minutes. Planting should be done immediately to prevent drying.

Aphids

Aphids transmit viruses in lilies and should be controlled in greenhouses rigorously. A few aphids early in the crop can cause considerable damage. Distorted foliage, honeydew secretions with subsequent black mold, as well as virus buildup can result from aphid infestations. Controls which have been effective are as follows:

> Vydate at 16 oz./100 gals.
> Orthene W.P., at 1 lb./100 gals.
> Diazinon AG 500, at 1 pint/100 gals.

Preventive sprays are not suggested, but beginning in early January careful monitoring of the crop is necessary. Spot treatment early can sometimes eliminate the need for general sprays. Aphids can build rapidly near the end of the crops due to warmer temperatures.

Fungus gnats can build up on lilies kept especially moist or when much algae is present. It is not known if direct damage can result, however, their presence is not a good sign. Granular Diazinon, as well as Vecto-Bac, have been used.

Other Troubles

Leaf Scorch was discussed under fertilization. Symptoms are very characteristic: half-moon shaped areas, often with concentric rings of varying colors of brown. These scorched areas are almost never located at the tip of the leaf, but are usually ¼" or more from the tip. Uniformly brown "dieback" of leaves is not true leaf scorch and, while occasionally seen, the cause of this problem is not known. Often such

648

symptoms are seen after a period of clear weather following a long period of dark weather.

"Greenhouse Twist"

The cause of "Greenhouse Twist" is debated. Some believe an organism—perhaps a bacterium—is the cause. Whatever its cause, twist can be serious in limited situations. Symptoms are circle shaped leaves appearing at the growing point, often with brown necrotic areas bordering the inside of the circle. The plant may produce only one or two such leaves or several, and the plant usually outgrows the problem with the plant being salable.

No Shows

Lily bulbs are a field crop and by the very nature of production all bulbs are not perfect. It is to be expected that yearly a percentage of the crop may not emerge. There are several causes of this phenomenon although some non-emergence cannot be explained. The most common causes are:

1. Broken Sprouts. If lily bulbs "summer sprout" in the field, that is if the stem that normally emerges in the greenhouse emerges in the field, the sprout may be broken off during the harvest operation. Bulbs are inspected prior to packing but the broken sprout may not be detected. A bulb with a broken sprout will make good roots and will eventually sprout, but the plant will be "off-cycle" and will not bloom for Easter.

2. "Die Back." Phytophthora and perhaps other soil-borne diseases can cause a dying back of the flowering stem in the bulb. This can occur on a prematurely sprouted bulb in the field or in a sprouting bulb after potting. Such bulbs are very difficult to detect at packing, or at times the dieback occurs after packing or potting. Such bulbs make good roots and eventually sprout, but they too, will be off cycle.

3. Broken Bulbs. During the harvesting process some bulbs are broken. This is evidenced by bulbs which do not emerge, and when dug up and scaled down, show excessive amounts of bulblet formation.

4. Unexplained Non Emergence. Some bulbs, while making roots, do not sprout. This is seldom a problem, but can be observed. Some bulbs do not sprout or make roots. The causes of non-emerging bulbs of this kind can arise either in the field, during vernalization, or in the greenhouse. Severe drying, anaerobic conditions from soils high in readily decomposable organic matter and/or water, and probably other factors, can cause dormance in the bulb. That is, even though the current environment is favorable, internal factors prevent sprouting and growth.

Bud Abortion and Bud Blasting

There are three phenomenon which pertain to loss of flower buds.

1. Blasting. Buds that have blasted are evident on the plant. The first sign of blasting is a stoppage of growth of the bud followed by shriveling starting at the

Lilies can be retarded with the cool day/warm night method down South. Here's Bill Clark, Memphis, Tennessee, with a cool-day retarded crop. Excellent!

base of the bud. This is followed by further browning of the bud. Causes are most often high-temperature forcing, especially if humidity has been allowed to be low. Lack of water is also critical. This situation is possibly made worse by root rot at this time.

2. Abortion. This bud loss occurs just after bud initiation. Signs of buds show that they were present but were lost. Again high temperatures just after the bud initiation set period are most often responsible. Drying or any other growth factor can affect this. Small scars, small "pimples," and bract like leaves (which always are present below a bud) are all signs that buds were there or were potentially there but lost.

3. Loss of Potential. In severe situations buds may be lost but leave no telltale signs. This phenomenon is best observed in comparing bulbs from the same case grown under different conditions; pot and case cooling for example. Again high temperature during the bud set period is most frequently responsible, but also poor growing conditions from potting though the bud initiation period is often at fault.

In most cases excessively low bud count is caused by greenhouse forcing problems. So many factors affect bud count that simple answers are often not possible. Most problems, however, relate to temperatures during the bud initiation period.

Leaf Yellowing

Leaf yellowing from the bottom up is of two types:

1. Catastrophic yellowing in a very short time usually associated with a carbohydrate shortage in combination with late A-Rest applications (and possibly negative DIF), which can cause nearly complete yellowing of the plant.

650

2. Gradual yellowing at the bottom of the plant, usually starting at bud initiation time and progressing to, often, an unsightly appearance at time of sale.

Avoiding late A-Rest applications, late high-temperature forcing, long box storage, and long delivery times are primary in controlling catastrophic yellowing. Some research shows higher phosphorus levels near shipping helps. There is also evidence to suggest gibberellin applications prior to shipping can help.

Gradual bottom leaf yellowing is a complex problem. Stress of any kind is likely of foremost importance. Research has shown that high density planting, above 2 ½ plants/sq. ft., is contributory. Excessive drying, root rot, lack of fertility, and high-temperature forcing are all also very important. Dry fertilizer applications to supplement liquid feeding is very important especially when it is difficult to sequence liquid feeding with fungicide or A-Rest drenching.

Shipping

Lilies are sold through retail florists or mass merchants. Most retail florists receive plants not boxed. Most mass markets are delivered in boxes. It is the practice in many instances to pack plants as they reach the "white puffy" stage, and place them in the cooler. This is the proper stage for packing, however, excessively early packing is being abused. Packing too early can result in reduced quality in stores and for the ultimate customers. Good quality means good future sales. Efforts should be made to reduce box time in all instances. Lack of keeping quality in stores and in the home is potentially the most severe problem in the industry. Long box time, high temperature forcing from late potting, soils with no soil base, high A-Rest rates and other factors must be considered.

LILY, HYBRID

by Ron Beck
Fred C. Gloeckner & Co. Inc.
New York, New York

Hybrid lilies have been classified into nine major groups based primarily upon a variety's parentage and physical characteristics (i.e., flower form). Aside from Easter lilies, the most important divisions for the commercial greenhouse grower for pot plant and cut flower production are the Asiatic hybrids (which include such varieties as Enchantment, Sunray, Montreaux, Dreamland, Corsica, Symphony, Orange Pixie, etc.); the Oriental hybrids (which include such varieties as Star Gazer, Sans Souci, Casa Blanca, Journeys End, etc.), and the Longiflorum hybrids (which include such varieties as Nellie White, Ace, White America, etc. Easter lilies).

651

Asiatic lilies are colorful!

The most significant improvement in recent years among the pot plant Asiatic varieties is the introduction of the Pixie series, true genetic dwarf varieties— varieties that stay short and compact (12″ to 18″ tall) without the use of growth regulators. The most significant recent improvements among the cut flower varieties is the addition of a complete selection of pastel colors, plus improved varieties that better tolerate adverse growing conditions such as warm temperatures and high light, or low-light intensities of fall and winter.

Basic Culture (Pot and Cut)

Hybrid lilies are not difficult to grow if a few basic cultural requirements are followed. In hybrid lilies, shoot emergence and forcing time are dependent upon several factors: bulb maturity, duration of cold storage, planting date, planting density, greenhouse temperatures and light intensities.

General Forcing Requirements

Bulb Preparation

Asiatic hybrids require a minimum of six weeks at 34° to 36°F. Oriental hybrids require 8 to 10 weeks at 34° to 36°F. Bulbs should be precooled (in the case) upon

Oriental lilies are large-flowered and very fragrant.

arrival (normally October to November). Additional cooling time at this temperature is not harmful. Once the bulbs are precooled (vernalized), do not leave them at temperatures above 36°F for an extended period of time or sprouting will occur.

Bulbs that will be used for late forcing (usually after January or February) should be kept at 28°F. Bulbs must be totally vernalized before freezing. The case must have adequate moisture, freezing temperatures are very drying and the bulbs can dehydrate easily. Allow for free flow of air between and around cases. Do not allow bulbs to thaw and then refreeze.

Defrost bulbs slowly at 45° to 55°F temperatures for one to three days or until they are thawed. As soon as the bulbs are thawed, they should be planted.

Planting

Upon arrival, precooled bulbs should be planted immediately in moist soil. If it is not possible to plant the bulbs upon arrival, they should be stored at 34° to 36°F. If they have not been precooled, it should be started at once.

Hybrid lilies must be planted deep. The top of the bulb must be covered with a minimum of 2″ of soil; 3″ to 5″ is not too deep, based on temperatures. The maximum depth is recommended for warm summer months. Minimum soil depth under the bulb should be 1″. Water the bulbs in well when planting to compact the soil around the bulb.

653

The bulb itself has enough stored energy to begin shoot growth. Once the shoot starts to grow it will develop a root system, referred to as the stem roots. It is these stem roots which provide the nutrients and moisture required by the growing plant. If adequate stem roots do not develop, the plant will be deprived of sufficient nutrients and moisture, and not develop a proper stem root system; thus, sufficient planting depth is of utmost importance, as are proper growing temperatures, to allow this underground root system to develop.

Bulb Size

The smaller-sized bulbs are recommended for forcing purposes. The majority of forcing varieties have a very high bud count on the smaller bulbs. Also, by using a smaller-sized bulb more bulbs per sq. ft. may be planted, yielding a higher profit per sq. ft. See Table 2. Use larger bulbs for pot forcing.

Media

A wide variety of soils and growing media are suitable for growing lilies. The growing medium should be sterilized or treated with aerated steam to control pests, disease organisms and weeds. The growing medium must be porous for good aeration and water drainage. A pH of 6.0 to 6.5 is recommended; too low a pH tends to produce leaf scorch susceptibility.

Lilies have been forced successfully in several types of growing media. Two successful media are:
1) 50% sandy loam, 25% sphagnum peat, 25% sharp sand
2) 25% sandy loam, 50% peat, 25% pumice
Caution: Bark should not be included in media for pot lilies if A-Rest is required for height control.

Fertilizer

The bulb is an excellent food reservoir up to flowering time, especially if fertilizer is added to soil mix before planting. Due to variations in soils, it is best for growers to use their own judgment as well as soil samples. A well-balanced liquid fertilizer containing 200 ppm N and P should be used once the plants' buds become visible, followed by an application 14 days later. This will deepen the foliage color and add to market appeal. Avoid over-fertilizing, especially with high nitrogen levels which can produce a lush appearance, but soft stems. Avoid fertilizers with superphosphate.

Forcing Temperatures and Times

High temperatures are not recommended for Asiatic lilies: 50° to 55°F night temperatures and 65° to 70°F day temperatures. A maximum day temperature should be 85°F for Asiatic hybrids. Oriental hybrids need a warmer night temperature, 60° to 65°F. Day temperatures for Oriental hybrids should not exceed 85°F. The forcer can increase or decrease the night temperature to control the flowering date. The night temperature can be dropped to 40°F if the plants are early, and increased to 60° to 65°F (but only after adequate stem roots have developed) if the plants are late and good light is available. Bright sunny conditions will promote rapid development; long overcast periods will retard development. Use of A-Rest will delay flowering three to five days.

Some Asiatic hybrids will force in 60 days for Mother's Day, while others will require 80 days. Some Oriental hybrids will force in 100 days for Mother's Day, while others will require 130 days. Forcing times vary depending upon variety and the season forced. Table 1 below is a generalization.

Table 1. Approximate Forcing Times*

Planting Date	Asiatic Hybrids Forcing Time/Days	Oriental Hybrids Forcing Time/Days
Dec. to Jan.	85 to 90	120 to 140
Feb. to March	70 to 77	110 to 120
Apr. to July	65 to 70	100 to 110
Aug. to Sept.	60 to 65	95 to 105
Oct. to Nov.	65 to 70	100 to 110

*The above forcing times are calculated using 55°F night temperatures and 70°F day temperatures for the Asiatic hybrids, and 60° to 65°F night temperatures and 70° to 75°F day temperatures for the Oriental hybrids.

Watering

Uniform moisture is important, especially during the first three weeks after planting. Watering must be carried out sparingly at that time, not letting the soil dry out, while at the same time not over-watering. The stem roots are usually well formed when the shoot is 3″ to 6″ tall, and water can then be safely increased.

Lighting

Lilies require low to medium light (2,500 fc.). In low-light intensity conditions (photoperiod less than 12 to 14 hours) an 8-hour night interruption is beneficial to help prevent bud abortion. Use mum lights from 8 p.m. to 4 a.m. An alternative method is to light the plants for 24 hours per day as soon as the buds are visible, using high pressure sodium vapor lamps.

Height Control

Cuts. The grower can raise the height of the plants substantially by crowding them in beds or flats and by extra shading during high-light conditions (summer). Crowding will help to extend height for cut flowers forced late in the season when days are longer. Shorter daylength produces taller plants.

Pots. A-Rest (ancymidol) has proved to be the most reliable growth regulator currently available for height control of hybrid lilies. With the growing media suggested earlier, satisfactory height control has been obtained with split applications applied as a soil drench using a maximum of .5 mg/pot. The first application, at the rate of .25 mg/pot, is applied upon shoot emergence (when shoot is ½″ to 1″ tall). If multiples are potted, apply A-Rest when the first two shoots to emerge are from ½″ to 1″ tall. It is not necessary to wait for all shoots to emerge before applying A-Rest. Follow 10 to 14 days later with a second application of .25 mg/pot.

Other rates of application that have also been successful are .175 mg/pot applied at shoot emergence, followed 10 to 14 days later by a second application of .325 mg/pot. Also a single application of .5 mg/pot applied at shoot emergence has been successful. Amounts of A-Rest will vary with climate, season forced, light intensity and soil moisture. Trials for your area and greenhouse environment will determine optimum amounts and application times.

Caution: A-Rest is not effective in growing media containing bark.

The newer pot plant varieties which are genetically dwarf, 12″ to 18″ tall, will not require the use of growth retardants.

Harvesting Hybrid Lilies

Cuts. Lilies are cut soon after the primary bud is colored and begins to swell. Stems should be cut before flowers open to ensure easy packing and better quality of the flowers upon arrival at the florist. Cut lilies can be treated with silver thiosulfate (STS) to increase flower life/vase life. The stems are placed in STS solution (0.2 mM silver nitrate and 1.0 mM sodium thiosulfate) for 24 hours at 68°F before being shipped. If flowers cannot be shipped after STS treatment, they can be held in cold storage at 38° to 40°F for three to five days. A floral preservative should be used during this storage period. It is not recommended that cut flowers be held in cold storage over five days, as prolonged storage will decrease the vase life as well as be detrimental to flower quality.

Pots. Potted lilies are ready for market at the same stage of development as cut lilies, that is, when the primary bud is colored and begins to swell. Pots can also be held in cold storage at 38° to 40°F. Pots held in cold rooms should not be sleeved.

Table 2. Planting Densities in Bulbs Per Square Foot—Cut Flowers

Planting Date	4/5″ 10/12cm	5/6″ 12/14cm	5/6″ 14/16cm	6/7″ 16/18cm	7/8″ 18/20cm
December	6½	5	4½	3½	3
January	7½	6	5	4½	4
February	8	6½	5½	5	4½
March	8½	7	6	5½	5
April	8½	7½	6½	6	5½
May	8½	7½	6½	6	5½
June to Aug.	8	7	6	5½	5
Sept. to Nov.	7	6	5	4½	4

Cut flower planting densities will vary between varieties due to foliage habit and height differences. The above table is a generalization. The smaller bulbs are planted denser than the large bulbs, and densities increase as the light intensities increase. A grower in Southern California will plant greater densities than a grower in the northeastern United States.

656

For pot plants, the following densities are recommended: 6 to 6½″ pots at 1½ pots/sq. ft. and 5 to 5½″ pots at 3 pots/sq. ft. This spacing refers to the finish spacing. As with the cut flower table this is a generalization. A grower in Southern California will be able to plant closer together than a grower in the Northeast. However, this spacing is a fair average. Densities will vary with the season forced and light conditions.

Grower Pitfalls

Growers could easily avoid many of the common pitfalls if they follow the suggested cultural recommendations and techniques. Frequent problems to avoid:

Small lots of hybrid lilies grown with other plants such as pot mums or Easter lilies. The temperature for these two plants is generally much too warm for hybrid lilies.

Crowding too many pots per sq. ft. The number of pots/sq. ft. varies with light intensities. Example: An Eastern grower would require more spacing than a Southern California grower.

Not allowing enough time to force, and having "too many pots" for the greenhouse space.

Not selecting the proper varieties. Select only the varieties recommended and select only the finest quality bulbs.

Not allowing sufficient precooling. Be sure bulbs are totally vernalized before planting.

Planting bulbs too shallow. Adequate stem roots cannot develop if bulbs are planted with less than 2″ of soil over the top of the bulb, thus preventing sufficient nutrients and moisture from getting to the plant. The bulb has enough stored energy to put forth the stem, but if supplemental nutrients are not received from the root system (stem roots) the plants will not be able to survive.

Overwatering. Bulbs should be watered in well when planted to compact the soil around the bulb. Water sparingly thereafter until the shoot is 4″ to 6″ tall. After this stage, the roots are generally well developed and overwatering is not as severe a problem.

Over-fertilization. The bulb itself is an excellent food reservoir and will support the initial plant growth through shoot emergence. Fertilizer is not necessary until the shoot is 4″ to 6″ tall. Poor fertilizing can produce pH problems.

LISIANTHUS

by Ed Harthun
Ball Seed Company

Annual (Eustoma grandiflorum), **624,000 seeds/oz. Germinates in 10 days at 70°to 75°F.**

The state flower of Texas, lisianthus is also known as the Texas Blue Bell. Available in colors of blue, lilac, rose, pink and white, it can be sold as a pot plant, bedding plant or cut flower.

As a pot plant, it is generally recommended not to mix colors. When the seedlings have reached the four- to five-leaf stage, they are ready to be transplanted to their finishing container, using one to a 4″ pot, two to a 5″, and three to a 6″ pot. When roots have reached the edge of the pot, it is time to pinch above the third node.

Since the plants are naturally upright growing, it is essential that a growth regulator be used. A B-Nine spray at the rate of 2,500 ppm is said to be effective in some areas, while in others a drench of A-Rest at .5 mg has produced desirable results. These growth regulators should be applied when new breaks have reached a

Pot lisianthus is almost a major crop in Europe. Here's a Danish grower, Jorgen Pedersen, and part of his 100,000 per year 3½″ crop.

length of 2″ to 3″. Under natural light conditions during the fall and winter the plants will rosette. To prevent this use night lighting from 10 p.m. to 2 a.m.

Optimal growing temperature is 65°F night. Proper light intensity is 4,000 fc., which means that in high-light areas during late spring and summer months they should be grown under a light shade (20%).

If sown around the first of the year, total crop time would run about 20 to 22 weeks when finishing in a 4″ or 6″ pot. If started from plugs the total crop time would be cut in half (10 to 12 weeks). It is very important to run the seedlings and transplants on the dry side. A light feed (150 ppm) of a complete fertilizer at each irrigation is adequate.

There is a very promising new pot variety, Blue Lisa™, which is very compact and early.

When grown as a cut flower from seed, crop time is about 22 to 24 weeks when sown about January 15. Lisianthus, when grown as a cut flower, will last about two weeks. They do not shatter and are easy to ship. Transplants with four to five leaves are generally spaced in the bench at 6″ x 6″ for a pinched crop. They require one or two tiers of support netting. Some growers find that the best time to grow lisianthus as cuts is the spring and summer, when crop time is much shorter. Flowers should be harvested when the first lateral buds open. Plants will reach a height of 24″ to 30″.

Lisianthus (Eustoma) Blue Lisa is a fine, dwarf, colorful pot plant.

Disease problems include root rot and damping off. Preventive drenches are recommended. It is also important to start with a well-drained, pasteurized media and to run the crop on the dry side.

Major insects infesting lisianthus are whitefly, mites, thrips and aphids.

LOBELIA

Annual (L. erinus), 1,000,000+ seeds/oz. Germinates in 20 days at 70°F (exception: Heavenly does best at 50°F).

Although more at home in a moderate climate such as England's, lobelias are used throughout the United States for their brilliant blue effects in combination boxes, pots and hanging baskets. With the development of many delicate-toned varieties, lobelias have gained in popularity and are highly valued plants in shady or semi-shady areas.

Culturally, they are not difficult. Being a bit slow-growing, lobelias should be started not later than February 1, if flowering pot plants are wanted for Memorial Day. The seed is very fine, don't cover. A moderate temperature, say 55° to 60°F, will keep them moving without undue softening. They stand transplanting satisfactorily, and do well in any ordinary garden soil. If you can give them some shade they will stand heat much better. They do not tolerate high temperatures.

Allow 8 to 9 weeks for green packs, 11 to 12 for flowering plants. For 4″ pots, lobelias require 12 to 13 weeks to fill the container and bush out. As for 10″ hanging baskets, allow 14 to 15 weeks and use 8 to 12 clumps of seedlings. "Clumps" of seedlings is a good way to transplant lobelia. Like alyssum, lobelia seedlings are very fine and hard to handle. When transplanting by hand, it is easier to grab hold of clumps of seedlings that have 6 to 12 individual plants per clump, and transplant these rather than using individual seedlings. The baskets will also fill out faster as well.

A popular lobelia variety is Crystal Palace—very dwarf, deep blue with dark, bronze-green foliage. White Lady lobelia is clear and showy, while Heavenly is a deep sky-blue with large flowers and compact habit. All of the above varieties will stay below 8″.

There is a trailing class of lobelia known as pendula that works out well for trailing over porch boxes and for hanging baskets. Outstanding is the variety Sapphire, deep blue with white eye and light green foliage. The Fountain series is available in three separate colors including blue, lilac and white. Plants make excellent baskets and fill out the containers quickly. Color Cascade lobelia is a mixture of rose, blue and white flowering plants that have some of the best trailing performances of any varieties.

LUPINE

by Jim Nau
Ball Seed Company

Perennial *(Lupinus polyphyllus)*, **1,000 seeds/oz. Germinates in 20 to 30 days at 65° to 75°F. Seed should be covered during germination.**

Sowings of lupine made in winter or early spring will not flower the same season from seed. If winter or spring sowings are needed, use a deep container (nothing smaller than 32 cells per 22" flat) or a 3" to 4" pot, with one plant per container. For green packs allow 10 to 12 weeks. Keep one point in mind: the roots on lupines are fragile, and once restricted will produce inferior plants and flowers. When the plants are ready to transplant, do not delay in getting the job done.

The Russell Strain is the most common variety sold on the market today that is available as both seed and as transplants. Plants grow to 3' tall with flowers to 1" wide. Separate colors are available and are sold under such names as My Castle, a brick-red flowering variety; Noble Maiden, with white flowers; and The Pages, which has carmine rose flowers. There are other colors in the series totaling six varieties.

In dwarf varieties consider using the Gallery series which has five separate flower colors plus a mixture. Plants grow to 20" tall and make excellent quart or gallon containers for spring sales.

Lupines are a colorful perennial—great especially in cooler summer areas.

MARIGOLD

by Jim Nau
Ball Seed Company

Annual, 9,000 seeds/oz. Germinates in seven days at 75° to 80°F. Cover the seed lightly upon sowing. African or American marigolds (Tagetes erecta); French marigolds (Tagetes patula); Triploid marigolds (Tagetes erecta x Patula).

One of the premiere of all the annual plants, marigolds perform well in dry as well as moist conditions and display color all season long. No annual garden is complete without the bright colors that marigolds add to any setting. Excellent in borders, as cut flowers, in the landscape, in 4″ pots and any other setting in which is needed long-term color. Marigolds are available as either single, semi-double, or fully-double flowers, in colors of yellow, orange and gold. Red and crimson are available in the triploids and French types, though these colors are absent in African varieties. However, there are white flowering plants as well in Africans, but at present these appear somewhat dull in their coloring. In double flowering varieties there are crested doubles where the blooms appear mounded and full, or an anemone form, which is a flat and wide flower where the center is recessed. Flowers range in

Four-inch marigolds, part of the 150-acre crop of outdoor 4″ annuals in Homestead, Florida. In the photo is Carol Troendle, Ball Seed Company.

size from 1″ on the French to as broad as 5″ on some of the Africans. Plants range in height from 6″ to 3′ tall on plants that fill in well when spaced out 12″ apart in the garden. Marigolds have a strong scent, which is one of their key faults. As cut flowers, strip the foliage away before shipping to decrease the scent.

French Marigolds

Crop times differ from variety to variety, but many will flower in eight weeks from sowing seed. For green packs allow six or seven weeks depending on variety. For blooming cell packs allow eight to 11 weeks, and up to 13 weeks for 4″ pot sales with one plant per pot. For those who like baskets, allow 11 to 14 weeks for five or six plants per 10″ basket.

In the southern United States allow seven to nine weeks for flowering packs, 10 to 11 weeks for flowering 4″ pots. Plant to the garden until May once all danger of frost has passed, and again in August for flowering until frost. Space 8″ apart in full sun to partial shade. Plants may heat stall during the hottest parts of summer.

In double-crested flowering varieties, plants range in height from 6″ to 8″ up to 12″ tall. The dwarfest variety on the market is the Little Devil series, which has 1″ blooms in five separate colors on plants to 8″ tall. Little Devil Fire is a top performer and is one of the landscape varieties used at Walt Disney World in Orlando, Florida. Fire has maroon petals with a gold border on a double-flowering crested type of flower. The Boy and Janie series are slightly taller to 10″ tall. Both series have 1¼″ blooms in five separate colors. Janie Tangerine is an excellent variety with deep orange flowers on mounded plants. Yellow Boy is still one of the top-selling yellow flowering varieties on the U.S. trade today. Unlike many yellow colored flower varieties on the market, Yellow Boy is a true yellow (bright yellow) as opposed to a golden yellow. The Bonanza series ranges from 10″ to 12″ tall with flowers that grow to 2″ across. Of the six varieties available, Bonanza Yellow, Bonanza Flame and Bonanza Orange are three of the series' best overall performers for the landscape and garden.

Finally, the Hero series is one of the top varieties, with a number of strong performers, and it has the largest flower size of any French marigold on the market today. Blooms range up to 2½″ across on plants to 12″ tall. Hero Red is a red-and-yellow bicolor with a red flecked yellow crest. Hero Flame is similar to Bonanza Flame except it has a larger flower overall, and Hero Orange is a deep orange that rivals Bonanza Orange as being the deepest orange available.

In fully-double varieties there is only one variety of any merit. Golden Gate is a large-flowered variety with fully-double blooms in mahogany with gold edges. The full doubleness of the variety comes out in 4″ pots and in the garden, but small cell packs tend to restrict the plant and decrease the overall performance of this variety. Once planted to the garden, Golden Gate will bloom fully double.

In double-flowering anemone or Queen types, the three best varieties are the Queen, Early Spice, and the Aurora series. The Queen (also called Sophia) series was the first variety in this group on the market. Queen Sophia is the grandmother of them all, with rust colored petals with golden bronze edges. The flowers lay flat and spread to 2″ wide, making this variety a prime choice for landscaping or 4″ pots. In the Aurora series, Aurora Yellow Fire is an unusual variety with golden yellow petals with a deep crimson blotch at the base of each petal.

In single-flowering marigolds the Disco and Fiesta series are the two key varieties on the U.S. trade. However, single-flowering marigolds are not as tolerant of heat and humidity as the double-flowering varieties are. Single-flowering marigolds perform best in English gardens and the areas of this country that have similar conditions.

African Marigolds

African varieties flower earlier under short days. For sowings after February 15, start short days upon germination and continue for 14 days, maintaining darkness from 5 p.m. to 8 a.m. Short days can actually be started from time of sowing on, using inverted standard flats to cover the germination trays. Although African marigolds require up to two additional weeks to flower than their French and triploid counterparts, a short-day treatment helps produce a smaller overall plant habit, plus earlier and more uniform blooming. Allow nine to 10 weeks for green packs and 11 to 12 for flowering cell packs. For flowering 4″ pots allow 12 to 13 weeks using one plant per pot.

In the southern United States, allow 10 to 11 weeks for flowering pack sales, 11 to 12 weeks for flowering 4″ pots.

In varieties, one of the best is Discovery Yellow. It makes an excellent 4″ pot plant or a bedding plant. Discovery Yellow has fully-double flowers to 3″ across on plants to 14″ tall.

Voyager Yellow has 3½″ to 4″ flowers on plants to 18″ tall. The flowers on Voyager Yellow have less tendency to break under their own weight like the Inca series can do. Voyager Yellow is an excellent landscape plant and works well in 6″ pots.

As for the Inca series, this is still one of the premier varieties for landscaping. The three separate colors of orange, yellow and gold have the largest flower size of any double-flowering African on the market today. Flowers grow to 5″ across on plants to 18″ tall in the garden. Sunshot is less daylength-sensitive than any of the other African varieties. It grows to 18″ tall with yellow flowers to 4″ across.

For taller African varieties, the Lady series is still one of the best choices for cut flower growers and for use as an annual hedge in the home garden. Primrose Lady flowers to 3″ across, and is the best primrose yellow flowering African on the market.

Triploid Marigolds

The triploid marigolds provide the longest overall color in landscape plantings of all types of marigolds. They tend to stay in color through the August hot weather. Though germination is considerably lower than for French and African types,

664

triploid marigolds offer the advantage of quick finishing—90% of the varieties bloom in just seven to eight weeks. However, since they are shy to set seed, it is difficult at times to get the varieties you want.

Green packs take seven to eight weeks, while flowering, salable cell packs take up to nine weeks. For 4″ pots and 10″ hanging baskets, allow 10 to 11 weeks.

In the southern United States allow seven to eight weeks for flowering packs, 10 to 11 weeks for flowering 4″ pots.

In varieties there are (or were) a large number from which to pick. However, the best ones are those that are available when you need them. To take nothing away from the varieties, though, the following are some of the best triploid marigolds for overall garden performance. The Nugget series has three separate colors on plants to 10″ tall with blooms to 2″ across. Orange Fireworks has 2½″ blooms of a deep orange color on plants to 14″ tall in the garden. Finally, Red Seven Star is a free-flowering variety with red blooms tinged with gold above 12″ to 16″ foliage.

Marigolds Offer a Variety of Flower Forms and Colors

GARDEN HEIGHT*	6 to 10 in. (15 to 25.5 cm.)	10 to 12 in. (25.5 to 30.5 cm.)	12 to 16 in. (30.5 to 41 cm.)	16 to 18 in. (41 to 46 cm.)	24 to 36 in. (61 to 91.5 cm.)
VARIETY	Boy Series Janie Series Little Devil Series	Bonanza Series Early Spice Series Hero Series Honeycomb Queen Series Red Cherry Royal Crested Mixture	Apollo Discovery Series Inca Series Sunshot	Galore Series Lady Series Perfection Series Voyager Series	Gold Coin Series Jubilee Series
FLOWER SIZE/TYPE	1 to 2 in. (2.5 to 5 cm.) double	1½ to 2 in. (4 to 5 cm.) double	2 to 3 in. (5 to 7.5 cm.) double	3 to 3½ in. (7.5 to 9 cm.) double	3 to 4 in. (7.5 to 10 cm.) double
SPACE	10 to 12 in. (25.5 to 30.5 cm.)	12 in. (30.5 cm.)	12 in. (30.5 cm.)	18 in. (46 cm.)	18 in. (46 cm.)
HABIT	Ball shaped, compact	Bushy, compact	Basal-branching	Hedge type	Tall, bushy
USE	Border	Foreground	Foreground	Background	Background

Based on Ball Seed Field Trials, West Chicago, Illinois.

665

MIMULUS

by Jim Nau
Ball Seed Company

*Annual (Mimulus x hybridus), **624,000 seeds/oz. Germinates in 5 to 7 days at 60° to 70°F. Leave the seed exposed to light during germination.***

Blooming in bold, bright colors, mimulus flowers hold up well, but require long days of 13 hours of light or more to appear. For sowings prior to February 15 in the northern United States, grow under a mum light long-day set-up. Transplant from sowing trays or plug flats direct to the final containers. We recommend this crop for areas with cool summers when it is to be grown in the garden. This is the climate that is found in the Pacific coastal regions and selected areas of the Atlantic seaboard states. In other areas, mimulus plants can be sold in 4" or 6" pots for spring and early summer color.

For green packs allow seven to eight weeks, and up to 10 weeks for full-blooming cell packs. Four-inch pots take 11 weeks, and 10" hanging baskets take up to 12 weeks to fill out. Add an additional two weeks to the baskets to get them to be more mounded and full in appearance. When transplanting seedlings, use one or two per 4" pot and up to eight for each 10" basket.

The Calypso and Velvet series are the two most predominant varieties in the trade. Both varieties have yellow and orange as separate colors, but it is most often the mixture of Calypso that is sold in the United States. Since there is little demand for this material due to our climate, only a limited number of varieties are available here. Both Calypso and the Velvet series grow to about 12" tall with flowers to 2" across. Flowers are often spotted with large crimson blotches.

NARCISSUS, PAPERWHITE

by A. A. De Hertogh
North Carolina State University
Raleigh, North Carolina

Paperwhite Narcissus that are used for cut-flower and pot plant forcings in the United States and Canada are primarily produced in Israel. The marketing season normally extends from mid-November to April. The bulb sizes available range from 13/14 cm to 16/up cm, with the most consistent results being obtained with 15/16 and 16/up cm bulbs. The cultivars available and the programming information are in the table.

666

Paperwhite Narcissus—first color showing, the correct stage to market the plant.

U.S. and Canadian flower-bulb wholesalers should have Israeli-grown paperwhite Narcissus shipped from Israel at 77° to 86°F. Upon arrival, they should be stored under well-ventilated conditions at 77° to 86°F until either shoots and/or roots begin to grow out of the bulb. Then the bulbs should be stored at 35°F. In general, it is advisable not to place paperwhite Narcissus at 68°F before November 1. Prior to shipping to the forcers, the bulbs should be placed at 63°F for two to three weeks. This would be true regardless if the bulbs were being held at the warm 77° to 86°F or low (35°F) temperatures.

Forcers should be prepared to immediately plant the bulbs when they arrive. Prior to planting, check them carefully. Discard any damaged bulbs. If bulbs must be stored, place them at 63°F under well-ventilated conditions, but only for a few days. Take care not to damage the shoot if it has emerged from the nose of the bulb.

Programming of *Galil, Shaleg,* and *Ziva* Paperwhite Narcissus

| *Galil* (all white) Forcing Program—Pot Plants | | Average |
Planting Date	Bud Date	Days to Bud
Oct. 15-20	Nov. 25-30	40
Nov. 15-20	Dec. 20-25	35
Dec. 15-20	Jan. 12-17	28
Jan. 15-20	Feb. 5-10	20
Feb. 15-20	Mar. 1-5	15

| *Shaleg* (all white) Forcing Program—Cut Flowers | | Average |
Planting Date	Bud Date	Days to Bud
Oct. 15-20	Nov. 25-30	40
Nov. 15-20	Dec. 18-23	33
Dec. 15-20	Jan. 15-20	30
Jan. 15-20	Feb. 15-20	30
Feb. 15-20	Mar. 15-20	28
Mar. 15-20	Apr. 10-15	25

| *Ziva* (all white) Forcing Program—Cut Flowers and Potted Plants | | Average |
Planting Date	Bud Date	Days to Bud
Oct. 10-20	Nov. 12-17	33
Nov. 10-20	Dec. 6-11	26
Dec. 10-20	Dec. 30-Jan. 4	20
Jan. 10-20	Jan. 25-30	15
Feb. 10-20	Feb. 20-Mar. 3	10

Cut Flowers

Use a well-drained, pH 6 to 7, sterilized planting medium. Plant in 4″ deep flats or trays. Use 35 to 50 bulbs per large flat. Paperwhite Narcissus can be planted bulb to bulb. The flats or trays do not need to be spaced out on the forcing benches.

Use a medium-light intensity (5,000 fc.) well-ventilated greenhouse. No fertilization is required for paperwhite Narcissus while in the greenhouse. Keep planting medium moist, and don't overwater.

Use 60° to 63°F night temperatures. Lower temperatures can be used, but the plants will take longer to reach the market stage. Normally, this is two to five weeks (see table).

Normally, diseases and insects are not a problem. However, forcers should always look for Botrytis and aphids.

The flowers should be cut when the first floret is fully colored. If the flowers must be stored, place them upright and dry at 32° to 35°F. Wholesalers and retailers should be advised to market paperwhite Narcissus when the first flower is fully colored. When this is done, the consumer will receive maximum satisfaction with the product.

668

Potted Plants

Use a well-drained, pH 6 to 7, sterilized planting medium. Plant three bulbs in a 5″ standard pot, four to five bulbs in a 6″ standard pot, or seven to nine bulbs in an 8″ pan. Grow plants pot to pot on the greenhouse bench. Keep planting medium moist, and don't overwater.

Use a medium-light intensity (5,000 fc.) well-ventilated greenhouse. No fertilization is required for paperwhite Narcissus while in the greenhouse. Use 60° to 63°F night temperatures. Lower temperatures can be used, but the plants will take longer to reach the market stage. Normally, this is two to five weeks (see table).

Normally, diseases and insects are not a problem. However, forcers should always look for Botrytis and aphids.

In order to reduce excessive elongation of the flower stalk and leaves of Ziva, the plants can be sprayed to runoff with 2,000 ppm ethephon (Florel) when the shoots are 4″ to 5″ long. A 2,000 ppm Florel solution is one pint in 2½ gallons and this treats about 500 6″ pots. It is important that the foliage be dry at the time of treatment. Also, do not wet the foliage for 12 hours after treatment. Thus, late afternoon is the best time to spray. This treatment can, however, delay flowering by two to four days.

The plants should be marketed when the shoots are 8″ to 10″ tall and the flowers are visible. Do not wait until they begin to show color. If the plants must be stored, place at 36° to 41°F. Wholesalers and retailers should be advised to market paperwhite Narcissus when they are in the "bud" stage of development. Homeowners should keep the plants in the coolest area of the home in order to obtain maximum satisfaction of the plants. In climatic zones 8 to 11, consumers should be advised that these bulbs can be planted outside after they have finished flowering. They will acclimatize outdoors in these areas.

NEMESIA

Annual (N. strumosa suttonii), **125,000 seeds/oz. Germinates in 10 days at alternating 55° to 60°F, dark.**

There are two distinct classes of this showy annual: Grandiflora and Nana Compacta. Grandiflora is the name of the taller strain that will draw up to a height of about 2′.

Of much greater value is the Nana Compacta type. Its dwarf habit, 10″ in the greenhouses, makes it popular to use in combinations. For this purpose, it should be sown in January and February for April and May flowering in 2¼″ or 3″ pots. While available in separate colors, it is chiefly used as a mixture. The Carnival Mixture is an excellent strain that is more heat resistant and will remain in flower several weeks longer than other strains.

Decorticated or cleaned seed is available of nemesia. This allows for many more seeds per ounce and much improved germination.

NICOTIANA *(Flowering Tobacco)*

by Jim Nau
Ball Seed Company

Annual (N. alta), 250,000 seeds/oz. Germinates in 10 to 15 days at 75°F. Leave the seed exposed during germination.

Keep germination temperatures uniform for nicotiana. Sell green in smaller packs such as 48s or 72s, or sell in bloom in large packs or pots. If plants are allowed to become restricted, they may remain too small to perform well in the garden. Among the most distinctive garden annuals available, nicotianas look sharp in 4″ pots and in tubs. Plants are self-cleaning and require no dead-heading in the garden, which makes them ideal for landscaping. For green packs allow six to eight weeks, and up to 10 weeks for flowering packs. For 4″ pots use one plant per pot and give 10 to 11 weeks to finish off in color.

If growing in spring and following the above recommendations for crop time, there should be no problem flowering either the Domino or Nicki series. Note that nicotianas are long-day plants and flower more evenly when given day lengths of 10 hours or more. If scheduling nicotiana for fall sales, it is suggested that they be grown under long-day incandescent lights (mum light set-up) for flowering dates of late September until February.

The Domino and Nicki series are ideal for pack production, and work well in garden plantings. The free-flowering blooms remain open all day. Domino White and Nicki Red offer especially good overall performances as pot, landscape, and bedding plants.

ORNAMENTAL PEPPER* AND CHRISTMAS CHERRY**
(Jerusalem Cherry)

by Ed Harthun
Ball Seed Company

Annual *(Capsicum species), 9,000 seeds/oz. Germinates in 12 days at 72°F. **(Solanum pseudo-capsicum), 12,000 seeds/oz. Germinates in 15 days at 70°F.

Ornamental Pepper

Ornamental peppers were formerly better known as Christmas Peppers. In some areas of the country they are still referred to as Christmas Peppers. However,

670

The ornamental pepper is a much-used plant for fall and Christmas sales.

currently there are many more of these colorful plants grown for sales during the months of September, October and November than for Christmas sales.

The majority of this item is sold in 4″ or 4½″ pots. A possible variation to this would be to pan three or four 2″ established plants to a 6″ pot sometime in late summer. Sowings are usually made from April until mid-July for sales from September until Christmas. Seedlings can be transplanted into cells (2″ to 2¼″ size) or directly into 4″ pots, using one plant per pot. Care should be taken to see that seedlings do not become crowded or stretched.

Most varieties benefit from a single or double pinch. Holiday Cheer and Fireworks are suitable for use in hanging baskets because of their growth habits.

A standard feeding program would require the application of 200 ppm nitrogen and potassium at each irrigation. This should be continued until fruit is set and then be reduced along with water.

Peppers require high light, good air movement and temperatures between 65° and 70°F for maximum fruit set. As they reach maturity, temperatures can be lowered to 60°F. Peppers are best produced in a greenhouse.

Most popular varieties include Holiday Flame F_1, which produces an abundance of slender, tapered fruit that turns from yellow to red; Red Missile F_1, whose red fruit is 2″ long and tapered, and Fireworks, which has a semi-spreading habit and produces early cone-shaped fruit.

Christmas Cherry

No longer commonly seen in the marketplace during the Christmas holiday season, there still are some grown for this time of year.

Finished mostly in 6″ pots, the seeds are sown in February, transplanted to cells or 2¼″ pots three weeks later, and then moved into the finished pot by late May.

During the summer the plants are grown outdoors to assure good fruit set. Brought inside before frost, they are finished at 50° to 55°F. Plants should be pinched after they develop four nodes. They can then be further pinched up until July 15. The two varieties still grown are the Ball Christmas Cherry and Red Giant.

PANSY

Pansies of all colors and sizes have "blossomed" in popularity in the past few years. Originally considered an early spring option that could withstand late spring frosts, pansies are now sought after by homeowners and landscapers almost year round—especially in the Mid- and Deep-South and West. The crop does hold value in the Northern regions for early spring gardens. In the warmer areas, such as in the moderate coastal and southern regions, pansies are planted in early spring, late fall, and even grown over winter. Because of the year-round demand for the crop, growers are facing new challenges producing plants of a "cool season" crop during warm seasons.

Culture

There is a variety of different sowings and cultural treatments used for pansies today. Midsummer has long been the traditional sowing time, generally late July or early August in the North. But any pansy plant that must grow from August 1 to April or May before being sold—about nine months in all—encounters many conditions that can reduce quality. The worst testing time is usually during winter, when exposure to weather can harden and damage outside leaves, even though the heart of the plant comes through in good shape. Good-looking pansies can be grown from summer sowings, though, by keeping the plants well-watered and fertilized during their growth and giving thorough winter protection. One other point: this system usually produces the heaviest plants.

The method being used by more growers each year calls for a December or early January sowing. Pansies can be grown steadily straight through to selling time with no dormant period. There is no hot-weather trouble during seed sowing and no damage from winter injury. Plants are either taken straight through in a 50°F greenhouse, or else shifted to frames when weather permits, usually early March. The greenhouse growing is often on shelves and racks or in little-used cold houses; heated frames also work well. This minimizes use of expensive greenhouse space.

Seed sown in November or early December and carried around 40° or 45°F make good, heavy plants, which often bring more than enough to justify the added time and expense. At the other end of the scale are late sowings made up to March 1. These produce young stock for sale with annual bedding plants, and can increase your overall pansy business.

Steve Barlow, Barlow Flower Farm, Sea Girt, New Jersey, a retail grower, does a lot of pansies and does them very well. In early March, Barlow's had an excellent

672

display with lots of color on a colorful wagon in front of the garden center. For this they sow September 20, and transplant October 20 (AC 8 packs of 6 plants each or 48 plants per flat). The pansies then go to a perennial greenhouse at 45°F until "the crown shows" and plants are in active growth, normally several months. About year end the temperature is dropped to 36°F until sale in March. The plants are sprayed with Benlate on alternate weeks to control botrytis. Steve does 1,500 flats at $2 per 6-pack or $15 per flat. Says Steve, "It's a good, early cash flow."

Special Problems

Problem: Thielaviopsis, Black Root Rot. Symptoms of Thielaviopsis include yellow bottom leaves, loss of root hairs, brown discoloration on roots, and slow plant growth or death. The root decline is similar to Pythium, but the affected roots have no odor and have a water-soaked appearance. Thielaviopsis is aggravated by high pH, high salts, and high temperature stress.

Solution: To avoid infestation use only new trays and sterile soil, maintain soil temperature of 62° to 78°F, and maintain the EC less than 1.0. The soil must dry slightly between waterings. Benlate and Cleary's 3336-F are registered for the control of Thielaviopsis. Sanitation is important. Remove infected plants from the greenhouse and avoid creating dust or water splash.

Problem: Pythium, Brown Root Rot. Pythium infects root tips and progresses upward along the roots, leaving them soft and dark. The rot is accompanied by a strong musty odor. Pythium commonly occurs under extremely wet and cold conditions.

Solution: Pythium can be controlled by similar cultural methods as described above. The disease can be controlled chemically with the use of registered chemicals such as Chipco 26019 or Truban.

Plugs—Big Help for Southern Growers

As of the early 1990s, most pansy crops grown for the ever-expanding Southern fall demand are plug-sown and grown in midsummer. Much of this is done, using refrigerated growth chambers, by Northern plug specialists so that growers are able to maintain the cool temperatures needed for good pansy germination. The plugs ship very well. It's the way that most of the major Southern pansy crop is done these days. For a detailed and excellent procedure for producing these plugs, see the pansy plug schedule in Chapter 12.

Year-Round Pansies in the North?

As the *Ball RedBook* 15th edition goes to press, several sources of successful pansy culture in the Northern states are emerging. Alex Gerace, Welby Gardens, Denver, is a pansy specialist and does 40,000+ pansy flats for the Southern trade.

Here's the way most Southern fall crop pansies are started. The grower is plug specialist Ron Wagner, St. Paul, Minnesota. These pansy plugs were germinated in a refrigerated growth chamber and averaged 91+% germination.

Here's Alex Gerace (right), Welby Gardens in Denver, and staff member Mark Sequin. In the background is part of the 40,000 flats of pansies produced here yearly for the Southern trade.

Alex has been testing pansy performance outdoors through the winter in the Denver area. He has planted three or four test beds, 5' or 10' each, in such places as the airport and city parks. Several of these beds were seen early October. Alex proudly pointed out that the beds had "survived -21°F the previous winter." He recommends fall, winter and spring pansies to Denver gardeners, and suggests planting pansies on top of fall bulbs. In this way they will be enjoyed through the fall and again with the earliest breaks in the weather in early spring. Normally, they are replaced during the summer.

Alex recommends that winter pansies not be covered (it tends to rot them). Also, place them in sunny locations so any snow cover will promptly melt.

Tests done by graduate students at Colorado State University, Ft. Collins, confirmed 80% to 85% survival of pansies outdoors in Colorado, and general success in color, etc. for the gardener. It's an interesting, promising new approach, certainly not proven across the whole eastern United States. It's perhaps worth trying in your area.

The pansy is rising rapidly—it's already a major crop among U.S. bedding plants!

674

Many pansies go out in packs, some quite small. There is also a major and expanding market for cool-grown, colorful 4" pansies.

Varieties

There are many! And lots of improvement coming from pansy breeders in recent years. Let's sort them into three flower size groups:

- **Small-flowering.** The principal contenders:

    Universals—quite widely used because of tolerance to both summer heat and moderately cold freezing weather. Also they are very free-flowering.

    Maxims—tolerant to heat and cold, and also very free-blooming. These smaller-flowered varieties do make a great show from a distance—but as you get closer, flower size becomes more important.

- **Medium-flowering.** Not as free-flowering as the small flowered, but some good classes here, too:

    Rocs—Some larger flower than the Universals, but inevitably not as free-flowering. They are somewhat earlier than the larger-flowered varieties—and are increasing in popularity.

675

Regals—Like all the above, they are F_1 hybrids. They are really a Swiss Giant type, offer the rich, strong colors of the old Swiss Giant strains. Also good weather tolerance.

Crystal Bowl—most pansies are "face" types—you see three or four prominent blotches at the center of the flower. The Crystal Bowls have no face blotches—the whole flower is the same color. Landscape architects and contractors especially like the Crystal Bowls because they make a better show (than the face types) as you go by the bed. The "Bowls" are extremely popular, excellent heat tolerance and very free-blooming.

- **Large-flowering.** Typically Americans do like large flowers on anything!

Majestic Giants—clearly the largest flowered commercial variety, fine strong colors and blotches, one of the leading and most used of all pansy strains today. They are a bit later-flowering.

Happy Face—similar—a bit shorter and a bit earlier.

Pansies—Favorites with Gardeners and Landscapers Alike!

FLOWER SIZE	1½ to 2½ in. (4 to 6 cm.)	2½ to 3½ in. (6 to 9 cm.)	3½ to 4½ in. (9 to 11.5 cm.)
VARIETY	Crystal Bowl Series Maxim Series Melody Series Universal Mixture	Crown Series Golden Champion Imperial Series Roc Series	Colossal Mixture Majestic Giant Series
SPACING	6 to 8 in. (15 to 20 cm.)	8 to 10 in. (20 to 25.5 cm.)	8 to 10 in. (20 to 25.5 cm.)

PEONY

by Jim Nau
Ball Seed Company

Perennial *(Paeonia officinalis)*

One of the old-fashioned perennial flowers for the home garden, peonies are long-lived plants that can survive from generation to generation of the families around

676

whose homes they are planted. Preferring cold winters so as to break the dormancy, peonies come in a limited range of colors: predominantly white, rose, pink and shades in between. Plants flower in May and are hardy from USDA zones 4 to 7. To be fair to the genus of Paeonia, it should be understood that there are a number of different species available to the trade in this class, and that this information in no way touches on the diversity of the line.

Peonies are propagated by tubers that are dug in the fall, divided and then replanted for sales next spring. Late-winter and early-spring dug tubers have flowered during the same year as dug, but not with the impact that fall-dug tubers have provided. Choose tubers with three to five "eyes" and plant them into gallon containers, leaving the tips of the "eyes" exposed out of the top of the container. If dug in September, there will be some root development below ground, though the foliage will stay dormant until next spring. Grow on at 45°F to get the plants established in the pot. Peonies require at least five weeks of 40°F or below weather to break dormancy and develop flower buds.

PERENNIALS

by Vic Ball

The demand curve for perennials climbs, consumer interest is strong. They sell! The new *Ball RedBook* talks perennials in two ways:

- Brief, individual chapters on several dozen of the leaders. They're included in the crop section alphabetically.

- The following tabulation of essential facts on 50 of the most grown species.

  But first, several comments on this rising star of the plant world:

- **Perennials from plugs.** They are being done by several of the specialist plug producers, and many growers themselves are starting perennials from plugs. The tendency to slow/irregular germination is less troublesome for the grower doing his own. It's very hard to turn out a 90% sheet of most perennials.

- **Several references:**

  Klaus Jellito, Jellito Seed, Postfach 560127, 2000 Hamburg 56, West Germany— a splendid catalog of seed-grown perennials.

  Matterhorn Nursery, 227 Summit Park Road, Spring Valley, NY 10977, offers a very informative catalog on perennials.

  White Flower Farm, Litchfield, CT 06759, offers a super catalog with lots of color. It's excellent.

  Wayside Gardens, One Garden Lane, Hodges, SC 29695, is an old firm, but still an interesting catalog.

  Walters Gardens, Zeeland, MI 49464, is another good source.

677

Herbaceous Perennial Plants by Allan M. Armitage is an excellent compilation of many, many perennials. Contact *GrowerTalks* BookShelf, P.O. Box 532, Geneva, IL 60134.

Hortus Third by the Staff of the L.H. Bailey Hortorium, Cornell University, published by Macmillan Publishing Company, is a very large and very complete compilation of virtually all cultivated ornamentals. It's expensive but useful.

Current issues of the Ball Seed catalog, P.O. Box 335, West Chicago, IL 60185, offer a variety of perennials with many helpful comments.

Pinewood Perennial Gardens, Main Road, Cutcheogue, NY 11935, offers a good catalog featuring 1-gal. plants.

- **Be aware of shade-tolerant perennials.** There are several dozen.

- **Color sells.** As with annuals, a little color on perennial plants will do wonders for sales. One Boston-area grower does several acres of them outdoors. He makes it a point to offer to his garden center customers each perennial species as it comes into color.

- **Use colorful annuals to fill in the blank spots.** I see more each year of various annuals planted among perennials in a border. Some perennials die out, others are thin and don't make a show. Both homeowners and landscapers are putting a few impatiens or other annuals in the blank spots.

- **Perennial gardeners are collectors.** Annual gardeners plant a few petunias, a few impatiens and often not much more. Any reasonably serious perennial gardener will have several dozen species of perennials in his border. And he's looking for more. In other words, to be in the perennial business you've got to have a fair collection of different species, which is a difficult challenge to keep on hand. But people will pay a fair price for them, and you've got to get that extra dollar per plant because of the nature of the perennial business.

- **Lastly, perennials are so showy!** When they're in season, doing their thing, perennials beat annuals hands down! An example: stately, bright blue delphinium; striking, rich scarlet Oriental poppies; masses of white Marguerite daisy flowers. And don't forget the very colorful early spring *Dianthus deltoides*, arabis and others of the "rock garden" perennials. These are what I see as the reason people are buying perennials. They are *not* easier to maintain, in fact you've got to encourage the weak ones, trim back the aggressive ones. In other words, a perennial border needs constant care, much more so than annuals. But it's this great show of especially the stars that bring people back more each year to perennials.

Pinewood Perennial Gardens—A Different Approach

This *Ball RedBook* perennial chapter and chart talk mostly 4″ plants—especially the chart. And it's true that the majority of perennials bought by the public are in 4″. The K marts of the world handle mostly 4″ perennials. But, there is also an important minority trade now done in 1-gal., 2-gal. and even 3-gal. containers. At the risk of oversimplifying, the garden center or landscape contractor serving the affluent trade and large industrial accounts tends to use the larger 1-gal./2-gal. plants.

Space does not permit details on these larger plants. In general, however, 1-gal. seed-propagated perennials offered in the spring are typically sown from April through July the summer before. Most seedlings are planted to a cell-pack, 48 or 72 per 20" flat, then planted as ready into 1-gal. nursery cans—the deep kind (many perennials are deep rooted). Divisions are also planted to 1-gal. cans in the summer or early fall. Both divisions and cell-pack seedlings are grown in cold frames or cold houses. Hoop houses are okay, but good ventilation is critical. No 90°F days! Some of these gallon-can perennials are carried at 40° to 45°F nights through the winter, and will make heavier plants for April and May sales in the spring. Other growers carry them at 28° to 32°F, semi-dormant. Less fuel cost, but a little less of a plant for spring sales. In general, these 1-gal. perennials, if they're good, strong plants and set out especially in April, will flower very nicely the first summer—of course, much more so than 4" plants. In fact, many of them will be in flower at the garden center display. Which, of course, helps sell them and command a better price.

I recently visited Pinewood Perennial Gardens at Cutchogue, Long Island, on the extreme east end of the island, and had a most interesting chat with Sandy Friemann, who, with his partner Hank Rienecker, runs the show. Pinewood is an all-out specialist in this 1-gal./2-gal. and larger perennial market. And they do them exceedingly well!

So here comes some of the procedures used by Pinewood to produce these 1-gal. plants that, by the way, go out of Pinewood at $4 to $4.50 (1-gal.), which is doubled or tripled by many garden centers. It's a real quality show.

First, propagating. Probably a good half of their production is done from divisions and a few cuttings. These divisions are often planted directly to 1-gal. containers in the early fall. Some are planted first to 4" pots and overwintered, then go to 1-gal. or 2-gal. containers in February. It all depends on the species involved.

The other important part of the business is done with seed-propagated things— and here this is done entirely with specialist plugs. I saw several hundred trays of them during my visit in early September. Says Sandy, "It's hard enough to get and keep a really good propagator, so we have just gone over to depending on plug specialists for plugs, and the same for major perennial propagators for many of our divisions." The plugs used are nearly all 72 or 128 per 20" flat.

- **About overwintering plants.** Pinewood covers a large area; typically you see long rows of low hoop houses (coldframes). The typical layout is a hoop house extending several hundred feet. Next to it will be a 10' wide bed of perennials set right out on the open ground, then space for truck access, then again a row of plants and another hoop house. In fact, the majority of their plants winter right outdoors in the spaces between the hoop houses. The hoop houses are used for some of the more tender plants. Good examples: delphinium and digitalis. Why do these need this protection? Sandy's answer: mostly it's crown rot. The single layer of poly, even with no heat, does give the plants considerable protection. Pinewood operates about nine acres of these overwintering hoop houses alone.

- **On irrigation:** Sandy says, "We irrigate only our 4″ plants here. Almost no supplemental water on 1- or 2-gal. plants. By the way, we welcome freezing. The only bad news is alternate freezing and thawing that occurs in late winter. We are able to open the end of the greenhouses and get some ventilation. Then, when the first warm weather of spring comes we just rip the plastic off." This eastern tip of Long Island, by the way, has a mild winter—it's surrounded by water, of course. It rarely goes below 10°F and Sandy's local area is reported to have the highest winter light level of any area on the East Coast (the reason why there are dozens of new vineyards within 20 miles).

- **Other comments.** I asked Sandy about the idea of delivering each species to the garden center about the time it begins to show color, since color sells. His response, "When we first started in business we wanted to do that, but when you get into the real world you find that if people want to plant a perennial garden they want to do it all at once. They want a variety of species available at a given time. That's just the way the business is done. We do sell mostly green plants.

  "Delivery is a tough problem for us. Out of desperation we operate our own fleet—four big trucks at $80,000 each, plus four smaller ones. We deliver 95% of our plants in our own trucks.

  "Our business is done mainly from April 1 to July 15. Our trading area is New England, Maryland, Pennsylvania and New Jersey."

  The phone rang during my visit. Obviously someone wanted to buy a lot of perennials. The response, "Sorry, we're 96% sold out today. We just don't have much left."

  Pinewood does publish an excellent catalog as listed above.

  A very interesting final comment from Sandy: "When the pressure is on, I'll be here until midnight." That only happens when there's family running the place and when it's a family who loves plants.

Echinacea
purpurea

Hemerocallis

Hibiscus

Aquilegia

Phlox

Perennials—a Tabulation*

Name	Use	Height	Colors	Sun/Shade[1] Preference	Flowering Season (Northern United States)
Achillea filipendulina Fernleaf Yarrow Coronation Gold	garden, rock garden, cut flower	3'	flower: yellow foliage: gray-green	FS	late spring to mid-summer
Aquilegia x hybrida Columbine	garden, pot	1' to 3'	red, pink, yellow, blue, white, purple	PS	spring to early summer
Arabis caucasica Rock Cress Syn: *A. albida*	rock garden or wall	8" to 12"	white, pink	FS	spring
Artemisia schmidtiana Silver Mound	garden, rock garden	1'	flower: yellow foliage: silvery white	FS	grown for foliage effect
Astilbe x arendsii False Spirea	garden, pot, cut flower	2' to 3'	pink, red, white	PS	early to mid-summer
Aubrieta deltoidea False Rock Cress	rock garden or wall	6"	red, rose, blue, purple	FS	early to mid-spring
Aurinia saxatilis Perennial Alyssum Basket of Gold	garden, rock garden or wall	9" to 12" prostrate	flower: canary yellow; foliage: gray-green	FS	early to mid-spring
Bellis perennis English Daisy	pot, garden, rock garden	3" to 6"	white, pink, red	PS	early to late spring
Campanula carpatica Carpathian Bellflower	pot, garden, rock garden	6" to 12"	blue, white	FS-PS	early to mid-summer
Campanula persicifolia Peach-leaved Bellflower	cut flower, garden	2' to 3'	blue, white	FS-PS	late spring to early summer
Chrysanthemum coccineum Syn: *Pyrethrum roseum* Painted Daisy	garden	1' to 3'	red, pink, lilac, white	FS	late spring to early summer
Chrysanthemum x superbum Shasta Daisy	cut flower, garden	1' to 3'	white with yellow center	FS	early summer to frost
Coreopsis grandiflora Tickseed	cut flower, garden	1' to 2'	yellow	FS	early to late summer

*Contributed by Nancy L. Drushal of GrowerTalks *magazine and Jim Nau, Ball Seed Company. Several helpful sources were* Hortus Third; Herbaceous Perennial Plants *by Allan M. Armitage; Steve Still of Ohio State University;*

[1]*FS = full sun; PS = partial shade; SH = full shade*

Will It Persist Beyond Two to Three Years	Hardiness Zone (USDA)	Special Cultural/ Soil Needs	Established 4″ Planted Out 5/1 in the North Will Flower?[2]	For This, Sow Seed or Plant Divisions on?
yes	3/4 to 9	well-drained, ordinary soil	July-August	divisions; early March
not usually	3/4 to 8	moist, rich soil with good drainage	NV; May	seed; September-October
yes (in Northern zones)	3/4 to 7	excellent drainage required; will melt out in South	NV; May	seed; September-October
yes (in Northern zones)	3/4 to 7	well-drained, ordinary soil; will melt out in South	(valued for foliage, not flowers)	divisions; early to mid-March
yes	4/5 to 9	moist, organic soil	6″ container better; June-July; NV	pre-cooled divisions early spring or late winter; allow 12 to 16 weeks for 6″ pot
yes (in Northern zones)	4/5 to 8	excellent drainage; cut back after flowering	May	seed; October
yes; melts out in South	3/4 to 8	well-drained; cut back 1/3 after flowering	—	—
yes	4 to 7	cool, moist, organic soil	May	allow 16 to 20 weeks from seed to flower
yes	3/4 to 7	well-drained	July	seed; allow 15 to 18 weeks for 1 plant/4″ pot
yes	3/4 to 6	well-drained	June	sow early summer and overwinter to flower following year
requires division every 2 to 3 years	3/4 to 7	well-drained; winter mulch required to prevent frost heave	July and August	December/January; allow 15 to 18 weeks from seed
yes	4/5 to 9	well-drained; many cultivars available	depends on variety; Alaska=August-September	depends on variety; from seed, sow February
yes in North no in South	4/5 to 9	well-drained; requires deadheading to prolong bloom period	depends on variety; Early Sunrise = July and August	depends on variety; seed early to mid-January

The National Arboretum Book of Outstanding Garden Plants *by Jacqueline Heriteau with H. Marc Cathey; and most of all, Jim Nau's extensive experience as manager of Ball Seed Company's perennial trials.*

[2]*Perennials are sold predominantly in 4″ pots but there is also an important trade in 1-gal. or larger plants. NV=Need vernalization.*

Perennials—a Tabulation* (continued from previous page)

Name	Use	Height	Colors	Sun/Shade[1] Preference	Flowering Season (Northern United States)
Coreopsis verticillata Threadleaf Coreopsis	cut flower, garden	1' to 2'	yellow	FS	early to late summer
Delphinium elatum Delphinium	cut flower, garden	3' to 6'	blue, red, pink, white, violet, yellow	FS	early to mid-summer
Dianthus barbatus Sweet William	cut flower, garden, rock garden, wall	8" to 12"	red, pink, purple, white, bicolor	FS	late spring to early summer
Dianthus deltoides Maiden Pinks	rock garden, wall, edging	6" to 12"	white, pink to deep red	FS-PS	late spring to early summer
Dianthus gratiano-politanus Cheddar Pinks	rock garden, wall, edging	9" to 12"	white, pink, rose, red	FS	mid-spring to early summer
Dicentra eximia Dwarf Bleeding Heart	garden	9" to 18"	flower: pink foliage: gray-green	PS-SH	early to late summer
Dicentra spectabilis Bleeding Heart	pot, garden	2' to 3'	pink, white	PS-SH	mid- to late spring
Digitalis purpurea Common Foxglove	garden	2' to 5'	purple, white	PS	mid-spring to early summer
Doronicum Leopard's Bane	cut flower, garden	1' to 2'	yellow	FS-PS	early to mid-spring
Echinacea purpurea Purple Coneflower	cut flower, garden	2' to 3'	purple, white	FS	summer
Echinops ritro Globe Thistle	cut flower, dried flower, garden	3' to 4'	blue	FS	mid- to late summer
Gaillardia x grandiflora Blanket Flower	pot, cut flower, garden	8" to 3"	red, yellow	FS	all summer
Geranium sanguineum Bloody Cranesbill	rock garden, garden	9" to 12"	magenta	PS	late spring to early summer

[1]*FS = full sun; PS = partial shade; SH = full shade*

Will It Persist Beyond Two to Three Years	Hardiness Zone (USDA)	Special Cultural/ Soil Needs	Established 4″ Planted Out 5/1 in the North Will Flower?[2]	For This, Sow Seed or Plant Divisions on?
yes; does well in South	3/4 to 9	well-drained; drought resistant	June to August	use one per 4″ pot to plant No. 1 transplants 6 to 8 weeks before sale date
no	3 to 7	well-drained, organic; basic pH; benefits from fertilizer	July and August	seed; January
divide every 2 years or let self-seed	3 to 9	well-drained, organic soil	NV; will be in flower until June	sow early summer and overwinter to flower following year
—	3 to 9	well-drained, slightly alkaline soil; shear after flowering	NV; will be in flower until June	sow early summer and overwinter to flower following year
—	3 to 9	well-drained, slightly alkaline soil; shear after flowering	—	—
yes	3/4 to 9	well-drained, moist organic soil	6″ will be in flower until early June	No. 1 transplants potted one/6″ pot mid-March; flowers early May
yes	3 to 9	well-drained, moist organic soil; usually goes dormant in summer	6″ will be in flower until early June	No. 1 transplants potted one/6″ pot mid-March flowers early May
biennial (self-seeds)	4 to 9	well-drained, moist, slightly acid, organic soil	—	—
no	4 to 7	well-drained, cool moist soil; usually goes dormant in summer	NV	sow early summer and overwinter to flower following year
yes	3 to 8	well-drained, ordinary soil; drought-tolerant	August	seed; January
yes	3/4 to 8	well-drained; very drought and heat tolerant	July and August	sow early summer and overwinter to flower following year
no	3 to 10	light, well-drained	June-July	seed; January
yes	3/4 to 8	well-drained, moist humus soil	—	—

[2]Perennials are sold predominantly in 4″ pots but there is also an important trade in 1-gal. or larger plants. NV = Need vernalization.

685

Name	Use	Height	Colors	Sun/Shade[1] Preference	Flowering Season (Northern United States)
Gypsophila paniculata Perennial Baby's Breath	cut flower, dried flower, garden	3'	white, pink	FS	early to mid-summer
Hemerocallis Daylily	garden	1' to 4'	wide range	FS-PS	varies with cultivar
Heuchera sanguinea Coral Bells	pot, garden	1' to 2'	red, pink, white	FS-PS	late spring to early summer
Hibiscus moscheutos Rose Mallow	garden	4' to 5'	red, pink, white	FS-PS	mid-summer to frost
Hosta (many varieties)	garden	6' to 3'	flower: lilac, purple, white foliage: green to yellow to blue	PS-SH	spring
Iberis sempervirens Candytuft	garden, rock garden or wall	6" to 12"	white	FS	spring
Iris hybrids Bearded or German Iris	garden, rock garden	8" to 4'	wide range	FS	late spring to early summer
Kniphofia uvaria Red Hot Poker	cut flower, garden	2' to 4'	red, orange, yellow	FS	summer
Lavandula angustifolia English Lavender	cut flower, garden, rock garden	1' to 3'	purple, lavender pink	FS	summer
Liatris spicata Spike Gayfeather	cut flower, garden	2' to 3'	purple, mauve, cream	FS	mid-summer to fall
Limonium latifolium Perennial Statice, Sea Lavender	cut flower, dried flower, garden	1' to 3'	blue, violet	FS	mid- to late summer
Myosotis sylvatica Garden Forget-Me-Not	garden	8" to 12"	blue, pink, white	PS	spring
Paeonia hybrids Peony	garden, cut flower	3'	red, pink, white, yellow	FS	late spring to early summer
Papaver orientale Oriental Poppy	garden	2' to 3'	red, orange, pink	FS-PS	late spring to early summer

[1]*FS = full sun; PS = partial shade; SH = full shade*

Will It Persist Beyond Two to Three Years	Hardiness Zone (USDA)	Special Cultural/ Soil Needs	Established 4″ Planted Out 5/1 in the North Will Flower?[2]	For This, Sow Seed or Plant Divisions on?
yes	3 to 8	well-drained, neutral to alkaline soil; may need staking	July and August	divisions; allow 6 to 9 weeks for one per 4″ pot to be salable
yes	3/4 to 9 (varies with cultivar)	well-drained	Divisions made in spring seldom flower profusely the same season. Some varieties like Stella D'Oro will flower in June and July from a divided plant in late winter and potted one "fan" to a 6″ pot.	
yes	3/4 to 8	well-drained, moist organic soil; mulch in winter to prevent frost heaving	NV; June and July	sow early summer and overwinter to flower following year
yes	5 to 9	moist organic soil	July and August	seed; mid-February
yes	3 to 8	well-drained, moist organic soil	depends on variety; July to September, many in August	depends on variety; for fast growing allow 6 to 8 weeks for one per 4″ pot
yes; shear back flowering; evergreen	3/4 to 8	well-drained	NV; will be sold in flower	sow early summer and overwinter to flower following year
yes	3 to 9	well-drained neutral soil	May and early June	divisions taken July-August and overwintered; 1 to 2 fans per 6″ pot
yes	5/6 to 9	well-drained, will not tolerate wet soils in winter	—	—
yes	5 to 9	well-drained	June to August	sow early summer and overwinter to flower following year
yes	3/4 to 9	well-drained	June and July	corms; when planted early March one per 6″ pot salable May
yes	3/4 to 9	well-drained	—	—
no, but will self-seed	4/5 to 8	well-drained moist soil	NV; in flower when sold	November and December
yes	3 to 8	well-drained, moist organic soil	—	—
yes	3 to 7	well-drained, will not tolerate wet winter soil; plant goes dormant in summer	May and June	sow early summer and overwinter to flower following year

[2]*Perennials are sold predominantly in 4″ pots but there is also an important trade in 1-gal. or larger plants.*
NV = Need vernalization.

Name	Use	Height	Colors	Sun/Shade[1] Preference	Flowering Season (Northern United States
Perovskia atriplicifolia Russian Sage	garden	3' to 4'	flower: blue foliage: gray	FS	mid- to late summer
Phlox paniculata Perennial Phlox	garden	2' to 4'	white, pink, red, blue, purple	FS	summer to early fall
Phlox subulata Moss Pink, Creeping Phlox	garden, rock garden	3" to 6"	blue, white, pink	FS	early to mid-spring
Physostegia virginiana Obedient Plant	cut flower, garden	2' to 4'	rose-purple, white	FS	late summer and fall
Primula x polyantha Polyanthus Primrose	pot plant, garden	6" to 12"	wide range	PS	spring
Rudbeckia fulgida var. sullivantii Goldsturm, Black-eyed Susan, Orange Coneflower	garden	2'	yellow	FS-PS	mid-summer to frost
Salvia x superba Perennial Salvia	cut flower, garden	2' to 3'	purple	FS	early to late summer
Scabiosa caucasica Pincushion flower	cut flower, garden	18" to 24"	light blue, white, lavender	FS	late summer to late fall
Sedum Autumn Joy Sedum	garden, rock garden	1' to 2'	flower: rosy-red foliage: gray-green	FS	late fall
Veronica spicata Spike Speedwell	cut flower, garden, rock garden	1' to 3'	blue, pink, white	FS	late spring to mid-summer

[1]*FS = full sun; PS = partial shade; SH = full shade*

Will It Persist Beyond Two to Three Years	Hardiness Zone (USDA)	Special Cultural/ Soil Needs	Established 4" Planted Out 5/1 in the North Will Flower?[2]	For This, Sow Seed or Plant Divisions on?
yes	5 to 9	well-drained, will not tolerate wet winter soil	—	—
yes	4/5 to 8	well-drained; susceptible to powdery mildew; many cultivars	late July-August	No. 1 divisions planted February or early March salable early May
yes	3/4 to 9	well-drained; shear back after flowering	—	—
yes	3 to 9	can be invasive	August	seed January
no	3/4 to 8	cool, moist, organic soil	sold in color	allow seed 24 to 28 weeks
yes	3 to 9	drought tolerant	July-September	sow early summer and overwinter to flower following year
yes	4 to 8	well-drained; drought tolerant	July	seed February
yes	4 to 8	well-drained organic neutral soil	July and August	seed mid-January
yes	3/4 to 10	well-drained	June	sow early summer and overwinter to flower following year
yes	3/4 to 8	well-drained; slightly acidic	July	seed; mid-January

[2]*Perennials are sold predominantly in 4" pots but there is also an important trade in 1-gal. or larger plants. NV = Need vernalization.*

PETUNIA

by Jim Nau
Ball Seed Company

Annual (Petunia x hybrida), **245,000 to 285,000 seeds/oz. Germinates in 10 to 12 days at 75° to 78°F. Do not cover the seed upon sowing.**

The following cultural notes and varieties are provided by class.

Grandiflora Doubles

Predominantly used as pot and bedding plants, the double grandiflora petunias are the showy stars of yesteryear. They have fallen behind the ever-popular grandiflora and floribunda singles in recent years, but provide a grandeur of individual blooms that is unequaled in bedding plants. Four-inch pots take 16 to 17 weeks to flower out, grown at 45°F.

Multiflora Doubles

Like the grandiflora doubles, multiflora doubles haven't fared well in popularity in recent years, either. Grown under the same conditions as the grandiflora doubles,

An interesting point here: The above bed of 4" pot petunias grown in England is all mixed colors, which seems to be a widely-followed practice in Europe. Bedding plants are very strong in England, and coming up. The grower: Eddie Fisher, Oaker Nursery, Great Yeldham.

690

An excellent pack of petunias. Note the vigorous side breaks coming up, compact habit and no flowers. This pack will perform for some lucky gardener, but I, too, know that color sells.

multiflora doubles will flower in approximately the same time. As for varieties, there are only two series of any popularity presently on the U.S. market: the Tart and Delight series.

California Giants

It will be interesting to see if this class continues to be written into any horticultural books that will be put out to the trade. As a class, the California giants are characterized by large, 4″ to 5″, single flowers in the most unusual color patterns available. At one time, this class was honored as the front cover variety for the Ball Seed catalog back in the 1940s.

Single Grandifloras

This is the most popular of the petunia classes on the market. Characterized by large flowers of 3½″ to 5″ across, the single grandifloras have dominated the market since White Cascade was introduced in the early 1950s. Today, nearly all the varieties offered are F_1 hybrids of either frilled or rounded petal edges, in a wide range of colors. The latest development is the advent of veined petals, where the flower color is predominantly salmon, pink, coral, or of orchid shade, with a characteristic veined petal surface that extends down into the throat. Sugar Daddy® was the first variety on the market to exhibit this characteristic in this form, but the latest trend has been to breed more-compact plants rather than the taller plants of yesteryear. However, these taller plants often gave superior hanging basket performance, and still have value in the market place.

For packs without color allow 10 to 11 weeks for well-formed foliage; 12 to 13 weeks for flowering packs when grown at 55°F. In 4″ pots allow 14 to 15 weeks and

691

Summer Madness™ is one of the important, new Madness (floribunda) group. They are somewhat larger than multifloras and very free-blooming.

up to 17 weeks for 10″ hanging baskets. Both B-Nine and Bonzi are registered for petunias and are helpful in darkening the foliage and keeping the plants in line. However, it is important that petunias be grown cool to keep them dwarf and basal branching.

In the southern United States, plants are hardy in areas with mild or no winters, doing well in full sun. A hard frost will kill petunias. Sow in January for pack sales in mid-March; plants will flower until August. Space 12″ to 15″ apart in the garden.

Single Multiflora, Single Floribunda

Hang on to your hats, it's going to be a bumpy ride. In no class of petunias has there been more work and development on the release of new varieties than in multifloras. In a class of petunias that was once considered unpopular due to small flower size, multifloras have come a long way. Since the advent of the floribunda variety Summer Madness in 1983, there have been no less than 60 varieties introduced into the trade; and more are on the way within the next two years. Floribundas offer the botrytis tolerance of multifloras, but with a 3″ flower size that is expected on medium-sized grandifloras. Soon, the small-flowered multifloras varieties, like Resisto and Joy, will become heirloom petunias as they fall prey to the large-flowered, heavily veined and compact varieties hitting the market annually.

Crop time on the newer varieties of multifloras is the same as was noted above for grandifloras. The older varieties need to be sown 10 to 14 days earlier to get them to flower at the same time. Though the older varieties have a solid show of color in the garden, they are late to perform.

692

In the 14th edition of the *Ball RedBook*, a number of varieties were listed as the best of their class. That edition came out in 1985, and now, in 1990, the listing has changed on all but one variety. Summer Madness, along with the other 10 varieties in the Madness series, is in the top 10 requested varieties nationwide.

Varieties like the Carpet and Celebrity series are of particular merit due to their compact performance in the garden. The Carpet series is getting more and more following in the southern United States as a variety that stands up well without lodging (falling apart) in the late season. The Celebrity series is noted for its larger than average flower size. Finally, if you prefer the smaller flower size of Resisto or Joy, you should give the Polo series a try. Flowers of 2″ to 2½″ on early blooming plants is the advantage behind this series.

Versatile F₁ Hybrid Petunias for Every Type of Garden or Container Arrangement

TYPE	Single Grandiflora		Double Grandiflora	Single Floribunda	Single Multiflora	Double Multiflora
FLOWER SIZE	3½ to 5 in. (9 to 13 cm.)	3 to 4 in. (7.5 to 10 cm.)	3 to 4 in. (7.5 to 10 cm.)	2 to 3 in. (5 to 7.5 cm.)	1½ to 2 in. (4 to 5 cm.)	2 in. (5 cm.)
VARIETY	Supercascade Series	Daddy Series Flash Series Falcon Series Happiness Supermagic Series Ultra Series	Ball All-Double Mixture Circus Fanfare Mixture Purple Pirouette Sonata	Madness™ Series	Carpet Series Celebrity Series Polo Series Sugar Plum Summer Sun	Tart Series Delight Mixture
SPACING	10 in. (25.5 cm.)	10 in. (25.5 cm.)	10 in. (25.5 cm.)	10 in. (25.5 cm.)	10 in. (25.5 cm.)	10 in. (25.5 cm.)
USES	Bedding, tubs, hanging baskets	Mass plantings, bedding	Porch boxes, tubs	Mass plantings, bedding	Mass plantings, bedding	Porch boxes
COMMENTS	The largest-selling type		Unique double types	Most disease and weather tolerant	Prolific bloomers	Popular novelties

PHLOX

Annual (P. drummondi), **14,000 seeds/oz. Germinates in 10 days at 60°F. Dark.**

Perennial (P. paniculata), **2,500 seeds/oz. Germinates in 3 to 4 weeks at 65° to 75°F.**

A very showy, colorful annual, phlox probably requires a little more attention than common annuals such as petunias when planted to outdoor beds. Phlox will easily make satisfactory-sized bedding plants for spring sales by sowing about the middle of March.

There are both tall and dwarf classes of phlox, known as Grandiflora (15" to 18") and Nana Compacta (6" to 8"), respectively. The former is not as widely used as the dwarf form, which is most popular and of greatest commercial value.

The most widely used dwarf forms are Globe Mixture, Petticoat Mixture and Twinkle Mixture. Globe Mixture has an almost perfectly round ball-like growth habit and an exceptionally free-flowering characteristic. It branches out beautifully from the base of the plant, in marked contrast to the other types of annual phlox, and has a good range of showy colors.

Twinkle Mixture, an early bloomer, produces an abundant amount of dainty starred flowers with pointed petals.

Petticoat Mixture is a variety of star-shaped flowers in a bright range of colors on plants to 8" tall.

Then there is the whole class of perennial phlox, about which a separate *Ball RedBook* might be written. Briefly, though, the most important group is the summer phlox *(P. decussata, P. paniculata, P. maculata, etc.)*. There are dozens of brilliant reds, purples, salmons and varicolored varieties in this group propagated by divisions and root cuttings. They like a fairly well-enriched soil and should be kept fairly moist. Let each clump have 4 or 5 sq. ft. to develop. Their normal flowering season is mid-July to September. Beltsville Beauty is a blend of *P. paniculata* types under one name. Seed should be exposed to freezing temperatures for several weeks for best germination.

For rock garden work, the dwarf perennial *Phlox subulata,* variety Nelsonii, makes a brilliant showing. It is division propagated, flowers in May and June and makes a mat of bright green foliage throughout the season. In addition to Nelsonii, there are a dozen or so other choice varieties varying from white through bright pink, red and crimson. All of this subulata group are procumbent, under 3", and are used for carpet plantings, rockeries, etc.

POINSETTIA

by Paul Ecke, Jr. and David Hartley
Paul Ecke Poinsettias
Encinitas, California

GENERAL REQUIREMENTS AND CHARACTERISTICS

Cultural programs have changed substantially in poinsettia production over the past decade due to the differences in growth habit of the new varieties. Fortunately, most of the changes in variety characteristics have made it easier to produce a quality plant.

As new varieties are developed, tested and introduced into the trade, there will undoubtedly be new approaches employed in their handling. However, certain basic characteristics of poinsettias will prevail, regardless of developments, and it is the purpose of this section to provide both background and practical-application information on handling this crop in particular. The information presented should be considered as guidelines only, since conditions differ in the United States from Northeast to South to Midwest to West. Therefore, schedules and programs must be adjusted to correspond to local conditions of daylength, temperature, light intensity, humidity, and markets.

The poinsettia is a short-day plant that is grown in greenhouses to produce colored leaves called "bracts." The flower itself is a relatively inconspicuous yellow organ. It has been demonstrated that in the northern hemisphere, flower bud initiation occurs in early October, and under favorable temperature conditions results in flowering during late November and December. Some of the varieties may flower earlier and others later than the average. One of the attractive features of poinsettias for Christmas production is that there is little or no need for daylength control. For other blooming periods, daylength must be artificially controlled. In general, it can be assumed that the bract development will be completed two to three months after initiation.

Although all aspects of the mechanism have not been clearly demonstrated, it appears that there is a certain minimum daylength requirement for the first stage of initiation. If this critical daylength remains constant, the plant may tend to split as if it had been pinched, and proceed to produce three vegetative branches. However, if the daylength is gradually reduced from time of initiation, the tendency then is to produce a single stem terminating in bract and flower. Thus, under normal conditions, initiation occurs when days are just short enough to stimulate this reaction, and as days gradually become shorter, they automatically satisfy the second requirement.

Poinsettias have been and currently are being grown in a wide variety of media. There is little question that the best root development and subsequent growth occur in growing media of high porosity. It has further been demonstrated that poinsettias thrive under conditions of high fertility and high moisture supply. The tendency has been to use very high fertility programs, but it is questionable whether they actually need to be any higher than for many other common pot plant crops, such as pot mums and Easter lilies.

The growing medium should be in the pH range of 5 to 6.5. Nutrients are thought to be most available if soil pH is in the range of 6 to 6.5. However, recent research indicates that for soilless or peat-lite mixes nutrients are most readily available if the pH range is 5 to 6. High pH results in reduced availability of metallic elements—iron, manganese and zinc—causing upper foliage chlorosis. Low pH results in reduced molybdenum solubility and increased solubility of metallic elements such as copper, zinc, manganese, iron, and aluminum, causing toxicity.

Susceptibility to unfavorable conditions of salinity, high boron, and high sodium are no greater than for other pot plant crops, and if anything, they're somewhat less susceptible. Domestic water containing chlorine and/or fluoride usually is not harmful to poinsettias.

Disease prevention deserves constant and persistent attention if successful production is to be attained. For most growers, the primary problems of disease are those which result in root deterioration during the development stages, and botrytis during the finishing stages. The latter becomes particularly important when temperatures are reduced. Normal botrytis precautions exercised for any other flowering pot plant crops are applicable to poinsettia production. Propagation is a particularly sensitive stage and is frequently the source of problems for the grower who does his own rooting.

Facilities required for pot plant production of poinsettias include an ability to supply heat with minimum temperatures of no lower than 60°F and preferably capability for higher minimum temperature. The facilities should also include means of controlling excessive temperatures, though this condition usually occurs only in the earlier forcing stages. Desired daytime temperatures are 70° to 85°F, though the plants will tolerate considerably higher temperatures. Extremely low temperatures will tend to retard growth and incite chlorosis, while extremely high temperatures with limited light encourages stretching and thin growth. It is desirable to keep different varieties in separate houses so they can be exposed to their own optimum temperatures.

Rising fuel prices have encouraged some poinsettia growers to conserve fuel and reduce costs by operating their greenhouses below recommended temperatures. There are guaranteed risks when cheating on temperatures. Low temperatures affect timing, quality, and disease control of poinsettias. Depending on local light conditions, schedules may have to be advanced under low temperatures to ensure maturity by time of Christmas sales. Low temperatures adversely affect root activity. Common symptoms of low temperature are poor uptake of nutrients and chlorotic plant leaves. Root rot diseases and botrytis are more prevalent and more difficult to control at lower temperatures.

Growth regulators are often used to restrict stem elongation, though this has become unnecessary, or nearly so, for some of the new varieties. The use of a growth

This was not a controlled experiment, but the plant on the left was grown in the low 60s and the plant on the right at a mid-50s temperature. Poinsettias are a tropical plant—they like it warm! Photo from Cornell University.

regulator is sometimes employed for "toning" the plant. Leaf color is darkened by this treatment. Another toning practice is that of reducing temperatures in final stages of development, particularly for purposes of creating deeper bract color.

The typical Christmas crop is grown either as a single-stem plant terminating in bract and flower, or as a multiflowered plant with each branch resulting from the pinch producing its own bract and flower head. New varieties make the multi-flowered plant highly attractive, both physically and economically. A properly grown modern variety will have a large bract and heavy stems, requiring no staking. Eckespoint®* C-1 will long be remembered as a first in demonstrating these desirable characteristics.

* Eckespoint is a registered trademark of Paul Ecke Poinsettias.

VARIETIES

Eckespoint Celebrate Red has a unique look with very erect bracts that do not droop, even after sleeving. The bracts actually bend slightly upward, giving finished plants a light buoyant appearance. Celebrate is best grown as fancy single-stem, non-branched plants. A medium-tall grower, Celebrate has oak-leaf shaped bracts and strong, stiff stems. It should be grown under high light conditions to enhance its strong features. If grown at Gutbier™ V-14 Glory temperatures during October and November, Celebrate will normally bloom around December 1.

Eckespoint Celebrate Pink is a pink sport of Celebrate with the same flowering response and cultural requirements.

Eckespoint Celebrate 2 is a strong, free-branching sport of Celebrate. With branching ability comparable to Gutbier V-14, Celebrate 2 makes an outstanding branched plant. It has the same bright red, erect bract presentation as Celebrate, which does not droop even after sleeving. Celebrate 2 is medium in height, and finishes shorter than Celebrate. Although its strong branching ability makes it ideal for branched plants, Celebrate 2 also makes excellent single-stem plants of the smaller sizes. If grown at Gutbier V-14 Glory temperatures during October and November, Celebrate 2 will normally bloom around November 25.

Eckespoint Jingle Bells 3 can be grown with the Gutbier V-14 cultivars. The bract color is dark red with an assortment of pink flecks.

Eckespoint Lemon Drop is a dark leafed, short growing, early flowering, yellow poinsettia. It can be grown as a branched plant or as a single-stem plant. Because of its slow growth habit, Lemon Drop should be propagated and pinched two weeks earlier than other varieties to attain the same height. Growth regulators are not required. Because of its compact growth habit, it can be grown at a closer spacing than most other poinsettia varieties.

Eckespoint Lilo features dark green foliage and bright ruby-red bracts. The plant is a short grower with an early flowering response. Leaf retention and keeping quality are outstanding. Certain cultural practices must be followed to increase branching and reduce the possibility of splitting.

Eckespoint Lilo Pink is a pink sport of Lilo with the same flowering response and cultural requirements.

Eckespoint Pink Peppermint is a novelty with pastel pink bracts, softly speckled with small red flecks. The bract presentation is flat and large with rather open centers. It can be grown either as a branched or single-stem plant, and requires the same cultural conditions as the Gutbier V-14 types.

Eckespoint Red Sails is an early flowering, short grower, with very dark green foliage and crimson bracts. The bracts have a concave appearance with very small, insignificant cyathia.

Gross™ SUPJIBI is a short growing, early flowering poinsettia with large red bracts. The center of the bract presentation is tight with large cyathia. The individual leaves and bracts of SUPJIBI are quite thick. These thick bracts may bruise more easily than those of other varieties, especially if the flowering plants must be shipped for some distance. SUPJIBI branches readily with thick, strong shoots that do not easily break off. This variety may need little or no growth regulator under normal conditions. It is quite tolerant of warm temperatures and seems to hold its bract color well, with little fading. SUPJIBI does quite well in Florida.

Gross SUPJIBI Pink is a pink sport of the Gross SUPJIBI, and as such has the same flowering response and cultural requirements.

Isn't this a spectacular poinsettia? It was grown by H.C. Williams, Williams Plant Farm, Sims, North Carolina; five cuttings per 10″ and planted 2¼″ September 6. The variety is V-14. I counted 23 blooms!

Gutbier V-10 Amy has light red bracts and an early flowering response. It is a short grower with excellent branching potential, but is sensitive to poor irrigation practices and low light conditions. It remains short in semitropical regions with high night temperatures.

Gutbier V-10 Marble is a pink-and-white color sport of Gutbier V-10 Amy. This novelty cultivar has excellent bicolored bracts, but the same flowering response and cultural requirements as Gutbier V-10 Amy.

Gutbier V-10 Pink is a pink sport of Gutbier V-10 Amy with the same flowering response and cultural requirements.

Gutbier V-10 White is a white sport of Gutbier V-10 Amy with the same flowering response and cultural requirements.

Gutbier V-14 Glory features large red bracts, a medium growing height, and excellent branching. It responds well to the high light intensity and warmer temperatures of Southern climates.

Gutbier V-14 Marble is a light pink-and-white bicolor sport of Gutbier V-14 Glory with the same flowering response and cultural requirement as Gutbier V-14 Glory.

Gutbier V-14 Pink is a dark pink sport of Gutbier V-14 Glory with large bracts and excellent branching potential. The flowering response and cultural requirements are the same as for Gutbier V-14 Glory.

Gutbier V-14 White is a white sport of Gutbier V-14 Glory with large bracts and excellent branching potential. The flowering response and cultural requirements are the same as for Gutbier V-14 Glory.

Gutbier V-17 Angelika is a variety with bright red bracts. It flowers earlier than Gutbier V-14 Glory, but the color intensity of the bracts is not as great. It grows to a medium height and branches very well. Leaf post-production lasting qualities are not as good as several other popular varieties.

Gutbier V-17 Angelika Marble is a pink-and-white bicolor sport of Gutbier V-17 Angelika. It has more pink color than most other marbled cultivars. Its growth habits and post-production qualities are similar to Gutbier Angelika.

Gutbier V-17 Angelika Pink is a dark pink sport of Gutbier V-17 Angelika. Its growth habits and post-production qualities are similar to Angelika.

Gutbier V-17 Angelika White is a white sport of Gutbier V-17 Angelika. The growth habit and post-production lasting qualities seem to be superior to Angelika.

Annette Hegg™ Brilliant Diamond features bright red bracts that retain their color when displayed under all types of fluorescent lights. The plant also has excellent branching potential and leaf retention. Flowering occurs at mid-season.

Annette Hegg Dark Red was an important cultivar in the northern United States. This poinsettia has dark red bracts, which do not fade when mature. It is a strong grower and has excellent branching potential and leaf retention. Flowering response is about the same as Annette Hegg Brilliant Diamond.

Annette Hegg Diva Starlight has large, brick red bracts on short bract petioles. The plant is a strong grower with excellent branching potential and excellent leaf retention. Flowering response is approximately one week earlier than Annette Hegg Brilliant Diamond.

Annette Hegg Lady is a cultivar with dark green foliage, dark blue-red bracts, and an early flowering response. This plant may flower one week to 10 days earlier than Annette Hegg Brilliant Diamond. It has excellent leaf retention, but may not branch as well as other Annette Hegg sports.

Annette Hegg Marble is a novelty cultivar with pink-and-white bracts. It retains the same excellent branching potential and leaf retention as the other Annette Hegg sports. Flowering response is similar to Annette Hegg Brilliant Diamond.

Annette Hegg Hot Pink is a cultivar with vibrant pink bracts and excellent branching potential. It has the same excellent leaf retention and keeping qualities of other Annette Hegg sports. Flowering response is similar to Annette Hegg Brilliant Diamond.

Annette Hegg Topwhite is a cultivar with genuinely white bracts. It is an especially strong grower with excellent branching potential and leaf retention. The flowering response is similar to Annette Hegg Brilliant Diamond.

Mikkel® Mini Minneken is a genetic pink dwarf and not a mutation. It is not as prolific or vigorous as Mikkel Mini Minstrel.

Mikkel Mini Minstrel is the brightest, most intensive red poinsettia developed by Mikkelsens. It breaks well from a pinch, is excellent for single pack (2″) production, and flowers early (November).

Mikkel Mini Mirabelle is a genetic white dwarf that rounds out the Mini trio.

Mikkel Yuletide bract color is similar to Merrimaker, and it does not require cooler growing conditions (below 60°F) to develop the deep red bract color. It does well in warm growing areas and the bract color holds well under warm temperatures and low light conditions.

Peace™ Cheers is a nine-week variety with bright red bracts and deep green foliage. It has an excellent branching potential. The branches develop evenly, resulting in a more uniform growth habit. To maximize bract size, pinch to leave a maximum of six to seven nodes.

Peace Frost is a creamy white variety with a 9½-week response time. The bracts are large and showy. It branches freely and is compact, but not as compact as Noel.

Peace Noel is a soft red variety with nine-week response time. It has a compact, freely branching habit and large bracts. Best results are obtained when finished under cool temperatures.

Peace Noel Blush is a bicolor sport of Noel. It has a soft blending of light pink centers with white margins.

Peace Noel Hot Pink is a hot pink sport of Noel with the same flowering response and cultural requirements.

Peace Regal Velvet is a nine-week variety with dark red bracts and dark green foliage. This variety makes an outstanding single-stem poinsettia. The blooms are long-lasting with tight cyathia that are slow to develop and slow to drop. Keep night temperatures at a minimum of 65° to 66°F during and after pinch. It is important to maintain this temperature until bracts show 50% color to promote proper shoot and bract development. Finish at 60° to 62°F at night.

STOCK PLANTS

To produce flowering plants true to variety, poinsettias are vegetatively propagated using stock plants of selected quality. The use of seedlings is confined to breeding, in the constant search for plants of better color, better structure, greater vigor and overall improved quality. Fortunately, the climatic conditions in Southern California are particularly favorable for year-round growing and breeding of poinsettias.

Not all growers produce their own cuttings. Many purchase rooted, callused, or unrooted cuttings directly from a specialist propagator. Specialists produce greenhouse grown cuttings where controlled environment ensures high production at periods of maximum requirement and also availability of vegetative plants the year round.

Where cutting production is to be carried out by the local grower, the procedure of developing stock plants starts with purchased liners from a specialist propagator in March, April, May or June. The specialist propagator by virtue of controlled environment, including artificial lighting for his own stockplants, can provide vegetative plants whenever the grower might want them.

701

Liners received for stock plant production should be planted as soon as possible into beds or containers in which they will be grown throughout their period of production. Placing a small liner in a large container will result in greater total growth than shifting it up from one size pot to another. However, this will require greater watering management in the initial growth stages due to the large soil volume. Growing medium and feeding programs should be the same as for Christmas crop production. Night temperatures of 65°F and day temperatures between 70° and 80°F will favor healthy development.

Spacing of plants placed in beds must be determined at the time of planting, as opposed to container planting where later spacing can be provided according to need. The earlier the stock is planted into beds, the wider the spacing should be. The earlier the stock is planted into containers, the larger the container should be. Since cultural practices as well as varietal characteristics will determine optimum handling in any given situation, only guideline approximations can be suggested (see Table 1).

Table 1. Stock Plant Bed Spacing/Container-Size Guidelines

Month Planted	Beds		Containers	
	Min. Spacing	Sq. ft./Plant	Min. Diameter	Final Spacing
March	18" x 18"	2.25	12"	24" x 24"
April	15" x 15"	1.55	10"	18" x 18"
May	12" x 12"	1.0	8"	15" x 15"
June	8" x 8"	0.44	6"	12" x 12"

There are many different and potentially successful approaches to the use of liners as a source of stock plants, but for purposes of illustration a typical program is outlined.

1. Upon receipt, liners should be immediately potted into sterile containers of pasteurized or otherwise disinfected soil of high porosity. Soilless media have been very successful. At this time it is important to maintain high humidity in order to encourage maximum growth and maximum number of breaks. If establishing plants from Oasis® rooting cubes, initial root establishment will be enhanced by thorough watering of the medium around the root cube during the first week of establishment.

2. Upon planting, drench with a fungicide using a combination of the following: Amount/100 gals. water, 2 to 4 oz. Truban 30% WP, or ½ to 1 oz. Subdue 2E with 4 oz. Terraclor 75% WP, or 4 oz. Benlate 50% DF, or 4 to 8 oz. Banrot 40% WP.

3. Maintain high fertility as for forcing of pot plants, using constant liquid feed or one of the other alternatives.

4. Provide medium shade (2,500 to 3,500 fc.) during establishment, with 65° to 70°F night temperatures, continuing to maintain high humidity during daylight hours. After plants are well established the shading may be reduced. It is suggested that light levels should not exceed 6,000 fc. for most established varieties. Day temperatures should not exceed 80° to 85°F, if possible to control.

5. As soon as liners are established, make a soft pinch (remove tip, including one fully expanded leaf). Depending on variety, five or more breaks should arise from nodes below the pinch. Research has shown that by removing any non-expanded foliage at the time of pinch, branching response may be enhanced.
6. When new growth has attained a mature state (leaves fully expanded as opposed to being paper thin and light colored) and when there is a minimum of four fully developed leaves on the shoot, it can again be pinched in the same manner as above. This will leave three mature leaves and respective nodes from which additional breaks can arise. Frequently only two breaks arise from the second and later pinches.
7. To avoid possible flower-bud initiation, use night lighting (10 p.m. to 2 a.m.) at 10 fc. until May 15.
8. Harvesting and propagation of cuttings can start in July and proceed through September. Many growers finish propagation by mid-September. Earliest propagations should be designated for branched plants or specimen plants and may require growth regulator treatment, depending on variety. The early propagations are more subject to "splitting" unless they, in turn, are pinched.
9. The grower who wishes to produce his own cuttings from stock plants will first want to estimate the number of stock plants required to produce the desired number of cuttings. There is no substitute for experience in this regard since so many factors enter into the calculation of production potential. Such items as time of planting, growing conditions, efficiency of pinching, efficiency of harvesting, success in propagation and, above all, the characteristics of the variety, must be considered. A table of procedure and production based on strictly theoretical considerations of a typical free-branching variety is provided (Table 2) for illustration.

Table 2. Theoretical Stock Plant Production

Plant liners	March 5	April 5	May 5	June 5
1st pinch (at 2 weeks) 6 breaks	March 20	April 20	May 20	June 20
2nd pinch (at 7 weeks) 15 breaks	April 25	May 25	June 25	
3rd pinch (at 12 weeks) 24 breaks	May 30			
Harvest 1st cuttings	July 10	July 5	Aug. 5	July 30
Number:	24	15	20	10
Harvest 2nd flush	Aug. 15 to Sept. 5	Aug. 10 to Sept. 5		
Number:	36	25		
Total cuttings/stock plant	60	40	20	10

In practice it is generally found that the first and the second pinches can be fairly accurately predicted. However, growth rates of some branches will be different from others. Also, it is not uncommon to obtain more than the theoretical number of breaks. For this reason, after the second pinch, it becomes necessary to examine the stock plants at about weekly intervals and pinch those stems that have matured sufficiently in the interim. The result is that stems ready for harvesting of cuttings will reach this stage at different times after any theoretical starting point.

From the time that cuttings are harvested for propagation it is usually desirable to repeat the cutting harvest at weekly intervals until the deadline date, which is frequently established as September 15.

PROPAGATION OF SOFTWOOD CUTTINGS

The term "softwood cuttings" applies to vegetative branch tips carrying one or more mature leaves. This is different from hardwood cuttings, which are taken from mature stems with or without leaves and usually stripped of leaves if they exist.

There are basic criteria which must be satisfied if success in propagation is to be assured. These include:

1. Absolute freedom from disease.
2. Elimination of moisture, heat and light stress once cuttings have been removed from the stock plant.
3. Adequate bottom heat (70° to 72°F) during rooting.

Conditions during propagation are highly favorable to spread of and infection by disease organisms. The program of sanitation must be directed toward eliminating disease rather than attempting to suppress it. This program must start before cuttings are taken from the stock plants.

In the outline to follow, one or more of the three criteria listed above are involved in each step. Normally, cuttings can be considered internally clean when removed from the plant. Surface carried, inactive fungal spores may be a source of contamination if not eliminated.

Procedures listed below have given excellent results in propagation. This does not mean that deviations and alterations of these procedures will not also be successful. Common sense and constant attention to sanitation are primary requisites for success.

1. Use a fungicide spray program on stock plants at one-week intervals occurring one or two days before the cuttings are to be taken. The objective is to provide protection against possible surface contamination being carried into the propagation bed. The following programs have been successfully employed: Amount/100 gals. water, 16 oz. Captan 50% WP with 8 to 16 oz. Chipco 26019 50% WP, or 8 to 16 oz. Ornalin 50% WP* with 1 oz. wetting agent,** or Exotherm Termil—1 can/1,000 sq. ft.
2. Rooting medium can be any clean and well-drained mix of sand, peat, perlite, vermiculite or other available materials of similar properties suitable for soil mix composition. Preformed foam media are also available and can be used. The medium should have a pH of 5 to 6.5 for best results, because excessive acidity slows rooting, and excessive alkalinity contributes to chlorosis. Fertilizers as

---

*Ornalin may be more phytotoxic to poinsettias when applied under warm, bright conditions. Like any chemical, test on small area for results prior to widespread application.
**Use of wetting agents seem to improve the ability of subsequent mist to wet leaf surfaces thoroughly. Results may vary due to varieties, water quality and wetting agent utilized. Some wetting agents may be phytotoxic to poinsettias and should be tested prior to widespread application.

704

used in regular potting media, incorporated into the rooting medium, do not seem to inhibit rooting. Cuttings can be rooted in the containers in which they will be finished, thus saving one or two steps in handling, and avoiding additional opportunity for contamination. This procedure is termed "direct rooting" and is rapidly attaining popularity for starting plants. The procedure saves approximately one week in the forcing schedule and will produce uniform pots if carefully managed. The procedure is fairly simple but does require special care in handling cuttings. Uniformity is most important. Cuttings should be of the same age (taken from the shoots of equal length). They should be similar in length, caliper and color, and should be stuck to the same depth. Finally, uniform mist coverage is required to produce plants of equal size and growth rate.

3. Cuttings 2″ to 3″ in length should be removed from stock plants by means of a clean, sharp knife, making the cut anywhere between the third and fourth fully expanded leaves on a mature shoot. Ideally the cut will leave at least two mature leaves on the stock plant stem as a source of new growth and subsequent cuttings. Leaves should be removed from the base of cuttings only when they interfere with sticking. Leaf removal reduces the stored food reserve and provides additional injury for possible infection.

4. Collect cuttings in sterile containers. Plastic containers prerinsed with diluted bleach are ideal (1 gal. 5% household bleach diluted to 10 gals. with water is satisfactory).

5. Avoid any moisture stress by undue exposure to dry air during period of collection. Ideally, though not always practical, cuttings should be taken in the evening, at night, or very early in the morning when moisture stress is minimal and cuttings are turgid.

6. For efficient and rapid handling, do not collect too many cuttings at any one time. Transport each batch under sanitary and moist conditions to the propagation area. Stick cuttings as soon as possible in steamed or otherwise decontaminated rooting media. Start mist as soon as possible to minimize moisture stress.

7. All personnel handling cuttings should thoroughly wash hands with soap and water, followed by a rinse with a hospital or dairy-type disinfectant. Other materials are equally satisfactory and nonirritating. Shallow tubs or basins of disinfectant should be kept handy for frequent rinsing of hands and/or tools, and changed as needed.

8. If cuttings are to be spread out on any surface for handling, be sure that such surfaces are sanitary. Film plastic covering is desirable and can be disinfected easily by washing with one of the hospital disinfectants or with bleach. Any cuttings which accidentally fall to the floor or contact nonsterile surfaces should be discarded.

9. Cuttings should be stuck by placing in preformed holes or by simply pushing into soft media. Do not flood them in after sticking, but do commence mist or other humidity supply immediately upon sticking. Flooding causes rooting medium to compact around the stem, increasing the moisture and reducing the air in this zone. This condition is highly conducive to bacterial soft-rot infection, which can occur within the first two or three days after sticking.

10. Mist frequency and duration should be such that leaves always have a light film of moisture covering them. A satisfactory program in California has been five seconds of mist at five-minute intervals on bright, sunny days. Should drying conditions occur at night, it may be necessary to use mist during this period. In very bright weather, moderate to heavy shading is required to protect against rapid drying and high-light intensity bleaching of the foliage.

11. At the end of one week to 10 days, there should be evidence of callus formation. At this time fertilizer plus fungicide can be employed as a protective drench and a means of setting the medium around the cutting. Callus formation seems to occur best when there is a large amount of air surrounding the cutting, but root initiation occurs most rapidly under slightly less open conditions. Choices of fungicide and/or fertilizer are numerous, with the following having been satisfactorily employed: Amount/100 gals. water, 4 oz. Terraclor 75% WP, or 8 oz. Benlate 50% DF with 2 to 4 oz. Truban 30% WP, or ½ oz. Subdue 2 E with 8 oz. ammonium nitrate.

12. At 14 to 21 days, root initiation should be at a stage that permits reduction or elimination of mist. If day temperatures can be controlled adequately, mist should be turned off, since surface applied water does have a bleaching and nutrient leaching effect on the foliage, as well as being an ideal environment for the growth of botrytis. All effort should be exercised to maintain good fertility in the rooting medium as soon as callus and root initials appear. If stretching and bleaching are problems, spray with Cycocel at 1,000 ppm to reduce stretch and hold color.

13. Transplanting should occur as soon as practical after roots are established in order to minimize shock due to root disturbance. Use of fertilizer in mist is practiced by many growers and has been advocated by numerous researchers. Experience to date indicates considerable variation in results due to materials and methods employed. Unless previous experience has provided the necessary background, the grower is advised to approach this program on a trial basis. Elements most rapidly leached from the foliage by mist are nitrogen and potassium. Phosphorus, when applied through mist feed, seems to encourage stretching and may cause damage to the growing tip. As a guide for initial trials, the following mist-watering composition is suggested: Amount/1,000 gals. water applied, 4 lbs. ammonium nitrate, 2 lbs. potassium nitrate, 1½ fl. oz. sodium molybdenum stock solution (use 1 lb./5 gals. to prepare stock solution).

Rooting can take place in a variety of media and containers. Preformed rooting media are being successfully used. Any new approach should be given adequate trial before being used on a large scale.

Where rooting media are shallow, there is frequently an interface effect that results in waterlogging in the zone, occupied by the base of the cuttings. Such a condition will cause darkening and deterioration of the stem and give the appearance of disease, even though disease organisms may not be present. The reaction is actually due to lack of oxygen. Where direct rooting in shallow containers is practiced, the containers should preferably be placed on sterilized sand, perlite or vermiculite to increase effectively the soil column height. Good contact with a wood surface can also provide a certain amount of "blotter" effect, causing free water to move out of the bottom of the pot.

Excessive crowding of cuttings in the propagation bed should be avoided in order to reduce soft growth, stretch, and slower rooting. In bed rooting, allow at least 12" (2" x 6") per cutting. For rooting in 2¼" pots, Jiffy 7s and 9s or Oasis Rootcubes, allow 15 sq. in. (3" x 5") per cutting. Units should be spaced so that the leaves barely touch, to allow air movement around the cuttings. Tips should not be covered by other cutting leaves.

Although rooting hormones are not used by all propagators and are not essential to root initiation of poinsettia cuttings, experience has indicated that they do speed up the rate of rooting and improve uniformity. Normal acceleration is several days.

One of the most convenient methods of hormone treatment is to provide a quick dip of cutting base in liquid solution. Indolebutyric acid has been successfully employed at 2,500 ppm strength. A calculated risk in employing this treatment is the possibility of spreading disease from one infected cutting to all other cuttings dipped in the same solution. An insurance practice, which has been shown to be beneficial, is to add 10 drops of household bleach per pint of hormone solution. The use of hormone powders reduces the chance of cross contamination. Dusting the powder on the base of the cutting is less apt to spread disease than dipping the cutting in powder. However, the use of powder provides less uniform treatment than the liquid quick dip.

Some growers use fan and pad cooling in their propagation areas. This is hardly necessary where frequent mist cycles are in use, but may be helpful under some circumstances. Ideally, the foliage of the cuttings should be kept cool and humid while the stem in the rooting medium should be kept warm, but not water-logged. The ideal mist system would maintain air humidity at near 100%, but would supply little or no free water to the rooting medium. Some compromise is commonly necessary in practical procedure.

PRODUCING A CHRISTMAS SEASON CROP

Although detailed discussion of specific phases of plant handling is provided in sections to follow, it may be helpful to have a generalized program in mind and at hand when reviewing subsequent sections, if only for use as a point of departure. There can be many successful alterations to any outlined program, including that to follow.

The first step in planning the Christmas crop is to determine the desired final product in terms of:

1. Pot size
2. Varieties
3. Blooms per pot
   a. Single-stem
   b. Branched
4. Date ready for sale

A production plan can then be drawn up and compared with space available in order to make final decisions on the intended inventory. It is quite important to be certain that there will be sufficient space at each stage of production, since crowding will definitely reduce quality. Table 3 provides a typical worksheet for this purpose.

Table 3. Poinsettia Production Plan for (Variety)

Container Size	4"	5"	6"	7"	—
Single stem					
Total pots					
Plants/pot					
Cuttings required					
Final space (sq. ft.)*					
Sales price/pot					
Theoretical gross					
Branched					
Total pots					
Plants/pot					
Cuttings required					
Final space (sq. ft.)*					
Sales price/pot					
Theoretical gross					
Total cuttings required					
Total bench space required				sq. ft.	
Total theoretical gross $					

* See Table 7. Select two or three flowers/sq. ft. spacing. For branched plants, program pinch to produce three or more flowers/plant.

Following the preparation of the plan, a "deadline" log should be prepared to indicate exact dates for completion of action for each phase of production. Since growing conditions are variable as to both location and facilities, this portion of the planning should be carefully reviewed by experienced personnel and adjusted to suit the particular conditions anticipated.

Table 4. Cutting Propagation and Pinching Date Guidelines*

Pot Size and Form	Direct Rooting in Finishing Pot	Propagate in Rooting Media	Pinch
7" SS 5-7 plants	Aug. 25	Aug. 20	
7" Br 1-3 plants	Aug. 1	July 25	Sept. 1
6" SS 3-5 plants	Sept. 1	Aug. 25	
6" Br 1-2 plants	Aug. 10	Aug. 5	Sept. 10
5" Same as 6"			
4" SS 1 plant	Sept. 15	Sept. 10	
4" Br 1 plant	Aug. 25	Aug. 20	Sept. 20
Smaller pot sizes—same as 4"			

*For Midwest; SS = Single stem, typical Eckespoint Celebrate; Br = Branched, typical Gutbier V-14 Glory.

708

All plants for the Christmas crop should be established in their final containers by September 25. A possible exception would be the 4″ pot or smaller size where direct rooting can be started as late as September 25, in some parts of the country, in order to assure short plants. Earlier propagations are required for large-size containers to attain desired height at time of maturity.

Where single-stem, multiple-plant pots are to be produced by direct rooting, it is essential that all cuttings be uniform, if a uniform finished plant is to be produced. Cuttings should be selected from stems of equal length to ensure equal stage of maturity and should be equal in length, stem size, leaf number and color. Finally, they should be stuck in the rooting medium to the same depth.

Varieties like Eckespoint Celebrate and Peace Regal Velvet are especially well suited for single-stem culture. Celebrate normally blooms about December 1, and Regal Velvet blooms later, nearer December 10. Although Eckespoint Celebrate 2 and Gutbier V-14 Glory are usually grown as branched plants, they, too, are excellent choices for fancy single-stem plants. These branching types are naturally shorter and make excellent three-, four- or five-bloom, single-stem pots.

Table 5. A Typical Three-Bloom, Single-Stem Production Guideline for a Variety Like Eckespoint Celebrate 2

Date	Temperature (°F) Night	Day	Cultural Procedure
Sept. 1	72	80	Direct-stick uniform unrooted cuttings close to pot edge. Rooting is slower below 70°F soil temperature. Use automatic mist during daylight hours. Use medium shade. Do not water in.
Sept. 7	72	80	Water in with 8 oz. ammonium nitrate/100 gals. of water. Continue mist.
Sept. 15	68	80	Reduce mist. Start constant liquid feed (CLF). Drench with ½ oz. Subdue/100 gals. plus 4 oz. Benlate/100 gals.
Oct. 1	65	80	Space 14″ x 14″. Avoid waterlogging. CLF. Beginning of bud initiation. Spray with Cycocel at 1,500 ppm.
Oct. 15	65	80	Drench with ½ oz. Subdue/100 gals. plus 4 oz. Benlate/100 gals. CLF.
Nov. 7	65	75	Color showing in upper leaves. Use Termil once each week until sale to protect from botrytis. If possible, ventilate and heat at night to reduce humidity. Use internal circulation of air. CLF.
Nov. 15	65	75	Drench with ½ oz. Subdue/100 gals. plus 4 oz. Benlate/100 gals. Terminate fertilization.
Nov. 25	60	70	Bracts approaching maximum size. Lower night temperatures will enhance color. Reduce light intensity if weather is bright.
Dec. 1	60	70	Ready for sale. Can be held in good condition for at least two weeks.

Note: If direct rooting of unrooted cuttings is not used, then plant 2¼″ liners or rooted cuttings in 6″ pans on Sept. 15; drench with Subdue, Benlate and ammonium nitrate. Then follow the schedule.

Branched plants can be programmed to produce a desired number of flowering stems, particularly in the case of the free-branching varieties. This is accomplished by removing the top of the plant at a point which leaves the desired number of nodes above the soil line. Each node will generally produce a flowering stem. Where this procedure is used, earlier propagation or transplanting can be employed since height will be controlled by removal of more of the top of the plant should it be excessively tall.

Table 6. A Typical One-Plant Branched Production Guideline for a Variety Like Gross SUPJIBI*

Date	Temperature (°F) Night	Day	Cultural Procedure
Aug. 10	72	80	Direct-stick uniform unrooted cutting in center of pot. Rooting is slower below 70°F soil temperature. Use automatic mist during daylight hours. Use medium shade. Do not water in.
Aug. 20	72	80	Water in with 8 oz. ammonium nitrate/100 gals. water.
Sept. 1	68	80	Commence constant liquid feed (CLF). Drench with ½ oz. Subdue/100 gals. plus 4 oz. Benlate/100 gals.
Sept. 5	68	80	Program pinch to leave four or five nodes above the soil, depending on how many flowers are desired. Maintain high humidity. Avoid waterlogging. CLF.
Sept. 23	66	80	Beginning of bud initiation. Breaks should be about 1" long.
Oct. 1	66	80	Space to 14" x 14". Drench with ½ oz. Subdue/100 gals. plus 4 oz. Benlate/100 gals. CLF. Spray or drench with Cycocel.
Nov. 1	64	75	Color development well underway. Use Termil once each week until sale to protect from botrytis. If possible, ventilate and heat at night to reduce humidity. Use internal air circulation. CLF. Drench with ½ oz. Subdue/100 gals. plus 4 oz. Benlate/100 gals.
Nov. 25	62	75	Ready for sale.

Note: If direct rooting of unrooted cuttings is not used, then plant 2¼" liners or rooted cuttings into 5" or 6" pans on August 20; drench with Subdue, Benlate and ammonium nitrate. Then follow the schedule.
*Based on Midwest conditions. Northern areas may require earlier programming, with later programming for Southern areas.

Where cuttings are rooted in 2¼" pots or preformed rooting media, panning should be scheduled for 21 to 28 days from time of sticking. By this time, roots should be well established and yet not root-bound.

In order to avoid stretch, all finished containers should be placed at final spacing as early as possible and no later than October 1.

Fertilizing should be carried out, preferably as constant liquid feed, from the earliest date possible after roots appear. At transplanting, the new pots should be drenched with fungicide solution as a matter of precaution against accidental contamination. Subsequent drenches should occur at 30-day intervals.

In producing branched plants, the shoot tip should be removed at an early enough date to provide sufficient growing time to produce the length of stem required for the pot size. Immediately following the pinch, it is very important to maintain high humidity by frequent misting until branches have started to develop (approximately one week). Temperatures should be about 80°F in the daytime and no lower than 65°F at night. Moderate shade will help in maintaining humidity. Care should be taken to avoid excessive water application to the roots, since plants will use less moisture due to fewer transpiring leaves. Waterlogged media will cause new leaves to be yellow.

Cool days/warm nights (DIF) at work on poinsettias. Plant at right, because it was near an outside door that was open much of the day, received cool day temperatures. The plant on the left received warm day temperatures. Notice the difference in height! That's Gus Corso, Sandusky, Ohio, on the left and Mark Evans, Ball Seed Company, on the right.

The period of flower initiation normally will be between September 23 and October 10. High temperatures seem to counteract the stimulus to initiate flowers. Night temperatures of 65° to 70°F are considered satisfactory for normal development, with day temperatures not exceeding 80°F. Lowering temperatures below recommended levels causes longer production schedules.

Since some varieties flower earlier than others, consideration must be given to providing proper temperatures and/or special treatment, depending on variety and desired date of maturity. Typical examples are Gross SUPJIBI as an early-flowering type and Gutbier V-14 Glory as a mid-season flowering type.

If the early-flowering type is being grown, a night temperature of 64° to 66°F after initiation will usually bring it in for Thanksgiving (November 23 to November 27). A mid-season type, being grown at 64° to 66°F after initiation, will usually flower December 1 to 10.

Where a mid-season flowering type is being grown, it will be necessary to use black-cloth shading from September 15 to October 10 to obtain earlier initiation for a Thanksgiving crop. After initiation, night temperature should be approximately 65°F, with day temperature about 80°F. Obviously, it will be necessary to advance the propagation and planting schedules where normal season varieties are being shaded for early flowering.

Some temperature manipulation may be required as plants reach maturity, to ensure their being in prime condition when sold. Lower temperatures during the final one to two weeks of forcing will enhance bract color. The one adverse feature of lower temperatures is the risk of botrytis infection. Protection can be afforded by providing good air circulation at night along with some heat and ventilation to dry

711

out the air. Also, certain thermal dust fungicides can be used at regular intervals (usually once per week) to present a barrier against botrytis infection.

Fan and pad cooling can be used during periods of extremely high temperatures and will, under these conditions, have a very beneficial effect. However, it is important that day temperatures be in the range of 80°F for best plant performance. If the crop should appear to be ahead of schedule, air conditioning can be used to drop the temperature to 70° or 75°F and hold the crop back. Usually, this is not practiced until fairly late in the production cycle. If temperatures are too low during the bract-maturation period, size may be adversely affected.

SPACING FOR FLOWERING PLANTS

For best quality, plants should be spaced early in their growing period to final location on the bench. This avoids temporary periods of crowding, reduces labor, and permits use of automatic irrigation for maximum periods of time.

As a rule of thumb, maximum density for a high quality product of the large type should be figured as two flowers/sq. ft., with square patterns most commonly employed. Depending on variety, method of handling, and market acceptance, up to three flowers/sq. ft. can be produced.

A guide for spacing distance (Table 7) is provided as a convenient means of determining the number of plants that can be grown in a given area. This approach assumes that pinched plants have three or more flowers per plant, and that planting into the final container size will have occurred by September 30. Where quality is less important than quantity, later planting and closer spacing can possibly be employed. Growth regulator sprays and drenches can be used to minimize stretch, which does occur under close spacing conditions. Usually the flower head is smaller and plants are less vigorous with weaker stems when spacing has been reduced.

Table 7. Spacing Guide for Poinsettias

Pot Size (inches)	Plants/ Pot	Pinching Treatment	Two Flowers/sq. ft.		Three Flowers/sq. ft.	
			Spacing (inches)*	Sq. ft./ Pot	Spacing (inches)*	Sq. ft./ Pot
4	1	none	9 x 9	0.56	7 x 7	0.34
4	1	pinched	9 x 9	0.56	7 x 7	0.34
5	2	none	12 x 12	1.00	10 x 10	0.67
5	3	none	15 x 15	1.56	12 x 12	1.00
5	1	pinched	15 x 15	1.56	12 x 12	1.00
6	3	none	15 x 15	1.56	12 x 12	1.00
6	4	none	17 x 17	2.00	14 x 14	1.35
6	1	pinched	15 x 15	1.56	12 x 12	1.00
6	2	pinched	21 x 21	3.05	17 x 17	2.00
7	4	none	17 x 17	2.00	14 x 14	1.35
7	5	none	19 x 19	2.51	15 x 16	1.67
7	7	none	22 x 23	3.50	18 x 18	2.25
7	2	pinched	21 x 21	3.05	17 x 17	2.00
7	3	pinched	25 x 25	4.33	21 x 21	2.90

*Approximate—rounded off to nearest inch.

ACCIDENTAL BUD SET DELAY

Each year, some growers have trouble getting poinsettias to set bud properly in the autumn because of unnoticed extraneous lights shining into the greenhouses at night. The proximity of well-traveled highways, new and improved street lighting, and large, well-lighted shopping centers near poinsettia-producing greenhouses impose new threats. If it is impossible to eliminate the unwanted light source, it is necessary that black cloth be pulled starting October 1 to ensure a 14-hour dark period until plants are ready for sale. Black cloth will ensure bud set if the temperature is not above 70°F at night.

FERTILITY MAINTENANCE

Poinsettias in particular seem to require a substantial rate of nitrogen application with modest phosphorus and modest potassium rates. It has been observed that very low soil potassium is still sufficient to supply the requirement of poinsettias. Apparently, this plant is capable of extracting potassium with greater efficiency than many other crops.

Table 8. Poinsettia Liquid Feed Programs

	Constant liquid fertilizer Amt./1,000 gals. water applied	ppm in water N P K
Make your own:	3 lbs. ammonium nitrate 5 lbs. calcium nitrate 3 lbs. potassium nitrate 10 fl. oz. 75% food-grade phosphoric acid 1½ fl. oz. molybdenum stock solution*	264-46-135 +0.1 ppm Mo
Prepared mixes:	14 lbs. 15-5-25 or 10½ lbs. 20-10-20	252-84-420 252-126-252
	Intermittent liquid fertilizer (Every 2nd or 3rd irrigation) Amt./1,000 gals. water applied	ppm in water N P K
Make your own:	6 lbs. ammonium nitrate 10 lbs. calcium nitrate 6 lbs. potassium nitrate 20 fl. oz. 75% food-grade phosphoric acid 3 fl. oz. molybdenum stock solution*	528-93-270 +0.2 ppm Mo
Prepared mixes:	28 lbs. 15-5-25 or 21 lbs. 20-10-20	504-168-840 504-252-504

*Molybdenum stock solution: Dissolve 1 lb. sodium or ammonium molybdate in 5 gals. water.

TEMPERATURE MANAGEMENT

Traditionally, higher day temperatures than night temperatures have been recommended for optimum poinsettia growth. For example, 80°F day and 64°F night temperatures have been suggested during October. This seems to be a logical temperature regime since outdoor temperatures are normally higher during the day. Researchers at Michigan State University have suggested manipulating the difference (DIF) between day and night temperatures to control plant height. Their work shows that as the difference between day and night temperatures increases, stem elongation and plant height increases. For example, plants grown at 75°F day and 65°F night will be taller than plants grown at 70°F day and night, even though the average daily temperatures would be the same.

On the other hand, poinsettia flower development is mostly controlled by the average daily temperature. Other things being equal, flowers develop faster at an average daily temperature of 70°F than at an average temperature of 65°F. To increase plant height without changing the rate of flower development, one could increase day temperature and lower night temperature and maintain the same average temperature. Therefore, by proper temperature manipulation it is possible to control plant height and the rate of flower development at the same time.

In parts of the world where day and night temperatures can be controlled, management of average daily temperatures and daily temperature differences can be used to help produce high quality flowering poinsettias.

CHEMICAL HEIGHT CONTROL

With the advent of new, naturally short growing varieties, the importance of growth regulators and their effect on height control have been somewhat reduced. However, in the period following flower initiation, it may be desirable to apply growth regulators as a spray or drench. This practice seems to improve plant quality by darkening foliage and strengthening stems, even though varieties being grown may be naturally short. Varieties that tend to grow tall may need several applications.

Factors affecting the action of growth regulators include concentration of active ingredient, quantity applied, time of application in relation to flowering date, stage of root development at time of application, temperature and humidity prior to and after treatment, plant moisture content, interaction of other spray materials, and method of treatment, whether by spray or drench. In general, growth regulators are less effective when temperatures are high, humidity is high, light is reduced as from crowding, and when nitrogen supply is largely ammonium or urea. Media containing pine bark will generally reduce the effectiveness of growth regulator drenches.

There are possible undesirable side effects from treatment. These include reduced bract size, crinkling of bracts, blotchy yellowing of leaves, marginal leaf burn, and delayed flowering. By early application under favorable environmental conditions, the yellow blotching which sometimes occurs will gradually disappear. Soil application seldom produces these undesirable reactions. However, foliar application permits the best opportunity to even up the height of the plants.

Cycocel is applied either as a soil drench or foliar spray. The soil drench application will usually provide greater height control than spray application per treatment. Cost of material and labor of application are higher with the soil drench procedure.

Solutions of desired strength (Table 9) should be made by measuring the appropriate quantity of growth regulator into an empty container and then adding enough water to make the desired final volume.

Table 9. Cycocel Growth Regulator Solution Preparation (based on 11.8% concentrate)

Desired Concentration		Fluid Ounces to Make:		
%	ppm	1 gal.	10 gals.	Dilution ratio
0.1	1,000	1	11	1:116
0.15	1,500	1½	16	1:80
0.2	2,000	2	22	1:58
0.25	2,500	3	28	1:46
0.3	3,000	3½	32	1:40

Note: Fluid ounces rounded off to nearest ½ ounce.
8 fl. oz./cup   32 fl. oz./qt.
16 fl. oz./pint   128 fl. oz./gal.

Soil drench application should be made as early as practical after plants are well rooted in the container. Late applications affect bract size and form. In Northern areas it is not recommended that application be made later than October 15. In Southern areas applications have been successful as late as November 1. Treatment of branched plants should occur approximately two weeks after pinching when new shoots are 1½" long.

Treatment by foliar spray normally should be completed by October 15 or earlier. Spray should be applied to the top side of all foliage of the plants for maximum benefit. Some growers make a practice of treating individual plants in multiplant containers in order to equalize the height. Applications late in the day when temperatures are lower will decrease chances of leaf yellowing. Spray treatment should be given only when soil is well supplied with moisture. Further moistening of foliage should be avoided for at least 24 hours. This permits maximum absorption.

Rates (Table 10) are usually higher in strength for early applications than for late. Numerous variations on treatment have been tried by researchers and growers with results equal to those advocated here. When a program is providing desired results, no changes should be made except by comparative trial. Since the spray approach is most apt to cause leaf yellowing or burn, it is desirable to test spray a few plants one week ahead of the intended general treatment as a check on possible damage. Even this precaution is not foolproof.

Don Layser does several acres of poinsettias in Myerstown, Pennsylvania. One important block (an acre or more) is finished at 10" x 10" spacing, and here's the plant. Not a blue ribbon at a flower show, but yes a winner when it comes to profitability.

Table 10. Typical Rates for Growth Regulator Application

	August	September	October
Cycocel soil drench*	3,000 ppm	3,000 ppm	3,000 ppm
Cycocel foliar spray	2,000 ppm	2,000 ppm	1,500 ppm

2 fl. oz./3" pot; 3 fl. oz./4" pot; 4 fl. oz./5" pot; 6 fl. oz./6" pot; 8 fl. oz./8" pot.

Another effective growth regulator is A-Rest. Used as a drench, one pint of A-Rest should be mixed in 16 gals. of water, then apply 4 oz. of this solution per 6" pot, two times, one week apart. A-Rest is less effective as a drench in pine-bark-based growing media. Although not labeled for use as a spray, some growers have experimented using A-Rest successfully this way. Their recommendation is to mix one pint A-Rest to three pints of water and apply this solution to 100 sq. ft. two times, one week apart.

Tank mixes of Cycocel and B-Nine can be used as foliar sprays and seem to be more effective in reducing plant height than either chemical used separately. Rates commonly range from 1,000 to 2,000 ppm Cycocel plus 1,000 to 2,500 ppm B-Nine. Use of the Cycocel/B-Nine combination is suggested only before flower initiation.

716

Flower initiation occurs about October 1 under natural daylength. It is generally conceded that the Cycocel/B-Nine combination applied after flower initiation will delay flowering and reduce bract size. Late growth retardant applications, if needed, should not be the Cycocel/B-Nine combination.

Paclobutrazol (Bonzi) is very effective in reducing the height of poinsettias at relatively low rates as either a foliar spray or as a soil drench. Spray application rates are labeled from 16 to 63 ppm, depending on minimum night temperatures. Growers in cooler climates should use lower rates. Drench applications are labeled for Florida only.

Results of using Bonzi seem to be variable. Bonzi is usually quite effective in warm, humid areas where height control is difficult to achieve. Some Northern growers also have good results, especially on early propagated material. However, when Bonzi is applied above recommended rates or at late dates, plants may be too short and flowering may be delayed.

NEW FORMS OF POINSETTIAS

- **Mini poinsettias** are generally grown upright in very small, individual 2½" to 3" pots. This miniature form is especially popular throughout Europe. Eckespoint Lilo and Lemon Drop are generally used for mini poinsettias.

Table 11. Guidelines for Producing Mini Poinsettias

Variety and cutting size: Eckespoint Lilo cut to a length of 1½".
Media and container: A basic planting media with good water-holding capacity; use a 2½" plastic pot.

	Direct Stick	Lights On	Lights Off	Flower
Schedule:	8/28	—	—	11/24
	9/4	—	—	11/30
	9/4	9/15	10/1	12/5

Temperature: 62° to 64°F night temperature after propagation.
Watering: Subirrigation is best. Daily watering is generally necessary, or as the soil dries.
Fertilization: Feed with a complete fertilizer including all of the micronutrients with each irrigation.
Light intensity: Shade to 2,500 to 3,000 fc. to lessen stress on the small plant.
Growth regulators: Cycocel sprays as needed.
Spacing: Final spacing 7" x 8" or .38 sq. ft./pot.

- **The Arrangement Pack** consists of a four-cell pack containing four compact, flowering, branched plants. These miniature poinsettia plugs provide the raw material for a floral designer's ingenuity. They can be popped out of their containers and used in an unlimited number of ways—from holiday dish gardens and wreaths to festive boutonnieres and bridal bouquets. Eckespoint Lilo, Lemon Drop, Gutbier V-10 and Annette Hegg varieties are all recommended for arrangement packs.

- **The Pixie** is usually grown in a 4" pot. The objective is to produce a very short, branched plant that is under 12" tall, including the pot. Eckespoint Lilo, Lemon Drop, Gross SUPJIBI and the Annette Hegg varieties are all suitable for pixies.

Poinsettias can be done in many forms. Here's a Pixie in a 4" pot, one plant branch in the 6" pot, a standard tree in an 8" pot, a 12" tub display plant and a 10" hanging basket.

Table 12. A Guideline for Producing Eckespoint Lilo 4" Pixie Type Poinsettia and Arrangement Pack Poinsettias

Bloom Date	Direct Stick into 4" Pot or Arrangement Packs	Temperature at Plant Level	Day	Night	Lights On	Pinch	Lights Off Start Black Cloth	Stop Black Cloth	CCC Spray at 2,000 ppm 1:60 2 oz./gal.	Bloom Date
Nov. 25	Aug. 15	Aug. 15 to Sept. 15	75	70	Sept. 7	Sept. 7	Sept. 23	Oct. 21	Sept. 1	Nov. 25
		Sept. 15 to Nov. 7	70	64					Sept. 23	
		Nov. 7 to Nov. 25	65	60					Oct. 5	
									(if needed)	
Dec. 8	Aug. 25	Aug. 25 to Sept. 25	75	70	Sept. 7	Sept. 17	Oct. 1	Oct. 21	Sept. 7	Dec. 8
		Sept. 25 to Nov. 17	70	64					Oct. 1	
		Nov. 17 to Dec. 8	65	60					Oct. 10	
									(if needed)	

Note: If lower temperatures are used in October and November, naturally the schedules for sticking and pinching will have to be advanced accordingly. Remember that light intensity and light duration in the fall will also have a great influence on any schedule.

Note: This schedule, prepared for the Midwest, does allow enough time to produce a good plant with three perfect blooms—of course local conditions will require certain adjustments to the schedule. Be sure the plants are not exposed to any unwanted lights from such sources as other crops being lighted, streetlights, floodlights or freeways—if in any doubt, shade.

● **Centerpiece Basket**—This mini hanging basket is grown in a 5" container. The finished product is generally not more than 16" in diameter. The hanger can be

718

removed and the basket can be used as a living centerpiece arrangement for the holidays. Eckespoint Lilo, Lemon Drop, Gross SUPJIBI and Annette Hegg varieties are excellent choices for centerpiece baskets.

- **Hanging Basket**—The hanging basket is a popular poinsettia form which does not occupy valuable bench space during production. These cascading baskets are usually grown in an 8″ or 10″ container, which the consumer may hang or place on a fern stand. Eckespoint Lilo, Lemon Drop, Gutbier V-14 Glory, Gross SUP-JIBI and Annette Hegg varieties have all been used successfully for hanging baskets.

- **Poinsettia Trees**—Poinsettia trees may be grown in a range of sizes, depending primarily on the date the tree is started. Large trees started from rooted cuttings on May 1 generally reach an overall height of 40″ to 48″ by December. Mini trees started on June 1 reach a height of 26″ to 30″, and bonsai trees started on July 1 will be 18″ to 20″ tall. The Gutbier V-14 varieties produce excellent shaped poinsettia trees.

Table 13. Guideline for Producing a Mini-Poinsettia Tree Using Gutbier V-14 Glory (2-pinch program)

Pan up established rooted cuttings	June 10 approx.
1st Pinch	Aug. 10
2nd Pinch	Sept. 10
Full bloom	Dec. 10 approx.

Notes: Pot size: 7″ azalea pot has good soil volume and good appearance.
At the beginning it is very important to grow the plant under warm, humid conditions to get height on the stem. Staking from time of potting until October 10 will ensure a much straighter stem.
Starting about July 10, remove the volunteer side shoots that will normally develop near the lower part of the plant. Leave eight shoots at the top of the plant.
Pinching: First pinch, remove ½″ of the growing tip (soft pinch). Remove lower leaves on stem three weeks after first pinch. Use a sharp knife to cut the leaves off, so the stem will not be injured. Second pinch should be done so there will be two or three nodes left after pinching. This will allow two to three blooms per shoot.
Temperature: use V-14 schedule.
Feeding should be on a constant basis.
CCC drench at 1:40 October 5 to 10.
This mini-tree should be about 25″ to 30″ in height, including pot.

PHYSIOLOGICAL DISORDERS

Leaf Crippling, Distortion, Puckering

For many years leaf deformity has been seen in some stock plants and often on pot plants in greenhouses. The symptoms are extremely variable. In some cases damage has occurred only at the tip of the immature leaf and it will give the appearance of having been chopped off at a later stage of development. Where the entire margin of the leaf has been affected in earlier stages, later growth of all except the margin causes a "puckered" appearance as if a drawstring around the leaf margin had been pulled up tight.

On Christmas-season plants leaf distortion frequently occurs in late September and early October after the plants have been moved from propagation to the finishing area. Branches that develop after pinching may have two to three mis-shapen and distorted leaves. In most instances these leaves remain distorted, but green, throughout the forcing period. Leaves that expand later are usually normal and hide the damaged leaves by market time.

The causes of leaf distortion are not well understood. It seems that when cells in very young leaf tissues are ruptured or killed, the leaf becomes misshapen as it expands. Drying of tissue, burn from fertilizer, nutrient deficiency and chemical burn have all been suspected of damaging young leaf cells. Plants under stress from bright light, extremely warm temperatures or moving air often have more leaf distortion. It is helpful to provide shade and syringe the foliage until roots are well established and the side branches begin to develop.

Many plants, including poinsettias, have leaf structures that include hyda-thodes or vein endings opening along the edges, tips, and sometimes leaf surfaces. Under cool, humid conditions, with ample growing medium moisture supply and elevated growing medium temperature, pressure of fluids in the conducting system may occur. If a rapid rise in temperature and drop in humidity occur simultane-ously, as frequently does happen in the morning of bright days, dissolved contents will become more concentrated. Sudden use of air-conditioning fans or natural movement of air from wind can cause the same effect. This concentrated solution may be strong enough to cause cell damage, and when sudden stress on the plant occurs simultaneously the concentrated fluid may be drawn back into the vein endings and cause damage to cells in and around the area. Since the phenomenon occurs only on immature leaves still undergoing expansion, subsequent growth in areas of cell injury will be inhibited and developing leaves will be distorted. Control of this leaf-edge damage can best be achieved by maintaining low humidity at night and avoiding conditions of rapid drying in the morning. Syringing of foliage in the early morning may also help by slowing transpiration. A complicating factor is frequently that of infection of injured tissue by botrytis.

Bract Edge Burn

Although botrytis causes an injury that is typically observed as a burn, all such injury is not necessarily due to the fungal disease. Severe bract burn has been encountered where extreme rates of fertilizer have been used. Under these condi-tions the leaves may show no damage. One theory is that during growth there is a diluting effect of plant-absorbed fertilizer, but at flowering new tissue development has virtually ceased and the fertilizer salts accumulate in the youngest mature and most sensitive tissue—the bract. This accumulation causes cell damage usually starting on the bract edges.

Where slow-release fertilizers are used, the rate should be modest and applica-tion should be early enough to ensure almost complete depletion at time of flower-ing. It may also help to increase intensity of irrigation in the finishing stages to ensure adequate leaching and removal of accumulated salts.

720

Bract burn may also be triggered by environmental factors. Research has demonstrated the effects of water stress, temperature, light intensity and humidity on bract burn, which typically occurs on transitional bracts (those structures that are usually colored, but are between the green leaves and true bracts). Changes in the environment, such as large temperature fluctuations, may be conducive to this malady.

Variety differences are usually noted. Those varieties with large bracts, like Gutbier V-14 Glory, are more susceptible to bract edge burn than the Annette Hegg varieties, for example.

Investigations at the University of Florida have led to a better understanding of bract edge burn, also named "bract necrosis." In essence, cultural and environmental factors which keep poinsettias in a soft, actively growing condition, late into the production period, promote bract necrosis. Some of these factors are: high fertilizer rates and heavy watering during the final four weeks of production; fertilizers containing nitrogen mostly in the ammonium form; and high relative humidity within the greenhouse environment.

To reduce the incidence of bract necrosis, the following practices should be observed.

- Avoid high fertility rates and heavy watering practices during the final four weeks of the production period. It may be advisable to discontinue fertilization and use water only, beginning two weeks before the flowering plants are to be sold.

- Avoid the use of fertilizers that contain 50% or more of their nitrogen in the ammoniacal form. Fertilizers which contain mostly nitrate nitrogen are readily available or are easily formulated.

- Avoid using high rates of slow-release fertilizers that maintain high fertility levels late into the production period. Second applications of slow-release fertilizers late in the production period should be especially avoided.

- Modify the greenhouse environment to reduce humidity and increase air circulation during the final three weeks of production. Chemical disease control methods may be used to minimize the spread of botrytis on the bracts.

Premature Cyathia Drop

During some Christmas-flowering seasons the true flowers, or cyathia, may drop from the center of the bract presentation before the flowers reach maturity. This may occur before the plants are ready for market, particularly in northern climates with low light conditions. Because this detracts from the appearance of the poinsettias, and makes them appear to be overly mature, it also reduces their economic value.

In 1982, a study began at Michigan State University to determine the cause of premature cyathia drop. Briefly, it was determined that premature cyathia drop is caused by low light levels and/or high forcing temperatures. Water stress aggravates the problem. These conditions allow the food reserves of the plant to become depleted. As the food reserves become low the plant reacts by dropping the cyathia.

It is not uncommon for skies to become overcast during late October and November in northern states. With the cloudy weather comes lower light levels and cooler temperatures. These are not ideal conditions for high quality poinsettias. With lower light levels plants do not make as much food. Also, as poinsettia bracts develop they shade the green leaves below and further restrict the amount of light available for photosynthesis. If poinsettias are grown at lower than optimum temperatures during the early part of the production period, flower development may be delayed when the cloudy weather begins. To speed up the rate of flower development it then becomes necessary to raise greenhouse temperatures. As temperatures increase the plants food reserves are used at a faster rate.

To produce high quality poinsettias and reduce the possibility of premature cyathia drop it is important to follow the old adage, "Make hay while the sun shines." Especially in Northern areas, it is important to maintain optimum greenhouse temperatures for rapid poinsettia development during the early part of the production period. When cloudy weather begins it may then be possible to start lowering greenhouse temperatures and slowing the depletions of food reserves.

The Michigan State University research also demonstrated that if the growing medium is allowed to dry to the point that the poinsettias begin to wilt, after the time the flower buds become visible, the chances of premature cyathia drop become greater.

To lessen the possibility of premature cyathia drop, the following cultural guidelines are suggested.

- Schedule your poinsettia program early enough so that the plants can do most of their "growing" early in the fall while good light intensities are available.

- Do not attempt to grow a poinsettia crop at lower-than-optimum temperatures during the early part of the production period in an attempt to save energy and reduce fuel costs.

- Grow your crop under a clear greenhouse cover to admit as much light as possible during October and November.

- If the crop develops properly it should be possible to reduce temperatures late in the production period when light levels are low, thus preserving part of the plants food supply.

- Do not allow the growing medium to become excessively dry. This only hastens the start of premature cyathia drop.

Latex Eruption

Plants belonging to the Euphorbia family contain latex, which is exuded upon cell injury. This became a problem in poinsettia production when the variety Paul Mikkelsen and its sports first became popular. The malady is sometimes termed

722

Here's a fine poinsettia held by Dana Groot of El Modeno Gardens, Irvine, California. By December 5, 95% of their crop was out the door. All of it was pulse-irrigated.

"crud." The mechanism is one of bursting cells resulting from high turgor pressure, with latex spilling over the tissue and, upon drying, the creation of a growth-restricting layer. When this occurs at developing stem tips, distortion or stunting of growth results. The exuding of latex has also been observed on fully expanded leaves, sometimes giving the appearance of mealybug infestation due to the white splotches scattered over the leaf surface.

All contributing factors have not been clearly defined, but several obvious ones include high moisture availability and high humidity, both of which result in high fluid pressure within the cells. Low temperature is an important contributing factor. Mechanical injury from rough handling or from excessively vigorous air movement may also increase injury to cells. High rates of photosynthesis may contribute by building up a high osmotic pressure in cells from carbohydrate accumulation.

Control is best attained by using growing media which dry out in a reasonable length of time, and avoiding extremes of high humidity, particularly during the night. Moderate shading in extremely bright weather might also be helpful. Sudden lowering of temperature can trigger the reaction. Fortunately, most varieties are not highly sensitive to this problem.

Stem Splitting

Under certain conditions poinsettias, which do not normally branch unless pinched, will suddenly produce stem branches at the growing tip. Careful examination will reveal that the true stem tip has stopped growth or aborted. This first became a prominent factor in 1964 when the Paul Mikkelsen variety was being heavily propagated. Many growers encountered splits and splayed flower heads. The phenomenon is not peculiar to the cultivar Paul Mikkelsen, but was brought about by a major change in cultural practice at that time. Propagators soon learned the reason for splitting and have taken steps to reduce it.

Splitting is actually a first step in flower initiation. The stimulus to flower increases with age of stem and with lengthening of night. Even with short nights and normal 60° to 70°F temperatures splitting can be expected if the stem is permitted to grow until 20 to 30 leaves are present. Stem tips that are continuously propagated carry an increasing tendency to flower. To ensure against this, lights should be supplied to stock plants until May 15. Propagations prior to July 15 should be grown as multiflowered or branched plants with tips discarded. Probably no hard and fast rules can be laid down, since new varieties may exhibit different tendencies. It is always good insurance to discard early pinches instead of trying to propagate them. Also, stems which are heavily shaded by a canopy of higher foliage may be subjected to enough reduced light to cause them to split, even in periods when daylength would be considered adequately long to keep apexes vegetative.

Bilateral Bract Spots

Often called "rabbit tracks," this condition is characterized by breakdown of the tissues between the veins located on either side of the midrib. It occurs in late November and early December during the flowering process. Although the plant is not killed, the condition can effectively lower the quality of the plant, rendering it unsalable.

Bilateral bract spots seem to occur under a wide temperature range, in various types of houses, under both gas and oil heat, and on about eight different varieties. The condition might be confined to a few plants or be found throughout the greenhouse.

A study was conducted in West Germany to consider certain factors that may predispose poinsettias to bilateral bract spots. Most obvious were varieties of the Annette Hegg family, which are more susceptible than most other commercial varieties. Also, cultural and environmental factors had their greatest influence during the bract development stage.

In this study incidences of bilateral bract spots were associated with high relative humidity or changing humidity levels. High temperatures, above 70°F, especially high night temperatures during the bract development phase caused a greater incidence of bilateral bract spots. And high levels of nitrogen fertilization near the end of the crop, or high nitrogen content in the plants caused a higher frequency of bilateral bract spots.

Leaf Drop

The older varieties were much more prone to sudden loss of leaves than are modern varieties. There are several indirect causes of leaf drop. Under conditions of moderate to severe stress, it is not uncommon for older leaves to form an abscission layer at the juncture of the petiole and the supporting stem. It is believed this is due to loss of auxin from the leaf blade under stress conditions. Once started, the reaction is irreversible and the leaf petiole is virtually severed from the stem. Also, when plants are kept under very low light intensity for a period of several days, lower leaves will turn yellow and drop.

Many of the older varieties were very susceptible to leaf drop. Before better sanitation procedures reduced or eliminated disease problems, leaves would frequently drop in the greenhouse as root disease reduced the ability to supply water to the top of the plant. A parallel contributing factor was also the deliberate attempt by growers to keep the growing medium dry in an effort to restrict disease organism activity. Even with healthy roots, many of the cultivars would drop leaves within a day or two after being moved from the humid glass house to a warm, dry home or office. The change in environment caused more water stress than the leaves could tolerate. The moisture loss exceeded the ability of the roots to supply water.

Modern varieties are far more resistant to leaf abscission, though not completely immune. Modern methods of sanitation should make it unnecessary to impose dry growing medium conditions in the greenhouse or the home. Healthy poinsettias thrive under high moisture availability and moderate to high light intensities. Waterlogging should be avoided, however.

Insects

Poinsettias are subject to attack by various insect pests under greenhouse conditions. Whiteflies, fungus gnats, mealybugs and spider mites are the most prevalent pests of poinsettias, although other pests may occasionally cause problems.

One of the first "lines of defense" against insect pests is prevention of their entrance into the greenhouse. With increasing regulations and restrictions of chemical pesticide use, screening of all vents and doors may become an effective and economical means of excluding insects from greenhouses. Sanitation and cleanliness are also of utmost importance in an effective control program. Weeds and ground covers in and around greenhouses provide favorable locations for pests, which may easily move onto cultivated plants. Growers with the fewest insect problems are usually those with the cleanest operations.

Another essential element of pest management is an effective scouting and monitoring program. Frequent and thorough inspections of plants for the location and identification of insect pests may help prevent an infestation from becoming an unmanageable epidemic. Yellow, sticky insect traps are an effective tool for monitoring insect populations.

Biological control is becoming an important pest management option, as an alternative to chemical pesticides. The use of parasites, predators, and diseases of insect pests is receiving more attention and appears more promising. Effective biological control of whiteflies, fungus gnats and spider mites on poinsettias may soon become a reality.

The use of pesticides, although an effective and necessary part of pest management, continues to become more restricted and expensive. This situation increases the importance of sanitation, prevention, scouting, monitoring, and bio-control in any insect management program. Pesticide registrations may vary from state to state. It is the grower's responsibility to read and follow the label rates approved in his or her state.

Greenhouse Poinsettia Diseases

Pathogens of primary importance include fungi and bacteria. For disease to occur, the organism and the host plant must be in close proximity. Fungi infect plants through wounds, natural openings such as stomates, and intact epidermal surfaces. Bacteria infect primarily through wounds or natural openings including stomates, lenticels, nectaries, hydathodes, and glandular hairs. Under favorable conditions, wounded tissue is quickly covered by a suberin film, which protects against bacterial infection.

Disease control can be attained only by using clean plants, clean growing media, and complete sanitation, and providing appropriate environment. All other procedures must be considered as suppression—not control! The use of chemicals anticipates that the control measures will not be, or have not been, properly executed.

The diseases described include pertinent information on the ecology of the pathogen. This background often provides the most important basis for planning control measures and preventing infection.

Where chemicals are to be used, limited trials should be employed before treating an entire crop, unless there has been adequate prior experience.

Rhizoctonia solani (stem and root rot). Plant symptoms: Brown rot of stem at soil line; roots may have brown lesions and leaves can become infected under mist propagation where they touch soil. Infected plants are stunted, with leaves yellowing from the bottom and sometimes dropping. Complete plant collapse under severe conditions.

Organism characteristics: A fungus which carries over in the growing medium or on infected plants. Easily spread by water. No airborne spores. Favored by moderately high available moisture, high temperature and factors which weaken the host, such as salinity.

Suppression: Rogue infected plants and avoid scattering debris from infected plants. Drench with fungicides such as Terraclor 75 WP (PCNB) at 4 oz./100 gals., Benlate 50 DF at 4 oz./100 gals., Chipco 26019 50% WP at 6½ oz./100 gals., or Banrot 40 WP at 8 oz./100 gals. Keep growing medium on dry side.

***Pythium spp.* (water mold root rot).** Plant symptoms: Root tips and cortex rotted. May advance up stem. Plants stunted. Lower leaves yellow and drop. Entire plant may collapse. Growing medium tends to stay wet, since roots are incapable of removing moisture, leading to the erroneous diagnosis—"too much water."

Organism characteristics: Carries over in growing medium or infected plants and is spread in water. No airborne spores. Requires high moisture availability. Active at cool temperatures. Inactive spores may live in dry growing medium for several months.

Suppression: Rogue obviously infected plants, taking care not to spread debris to healthy plant areas. Maintain low moisture in growing medium. Drench with fungicides such as Truban 30 WP at 4 oz./100 gals., Subdue 2E at ½ to 1½ oz./100 gals., or Banrot 40 WP at 8 oz./100 gals.

***Thielaviopsis basicola* (black root rot).** Plant symptoms: Roots develop black rotted areas. Stem may accumulate black sclerotia, which form in the pith area. Plants show lack of vigor, leaf yellowing, leaf drop, and sometimes sudden collapse, particularly after temperatures have been lowered below 60°F.

Organism characteristics: A fungus having long life in growing media as sclerotia resting stage. Favored by cool, moist environment. Slow growth at elevated temperatures and in acid growing media (pH below 5.5). No airborne spores.

Suppression: Rogue infected plants, avoid low temperatures, use acid growing media and acidifying fertilizers. Drench with Benlate 50 DF at 8 to 12 oz./100 gals. or Banrot 40 WP at 8 oz./100 gals.

***Rhizopus sp.* (rhizopus rot).** Plant symptoms: Poinsettia plants growing under high humidity, high temperatures (80° to 90°F), and poor aeration are subject to a soft, wet rot of foliage and stems caused by rhizopus. Cuttings in propagation during hot weather are attacked especially when they are placed too close together. The stems, leaves, and/or leaf petioles become very soft, brown, and mushy. When rhizopus attacks the stem of poinsettia cuttings the resulting rot can resemble bacterial soft rot.

Organism characteristics: The spores can be carried by air currents, and the organism can live over in plant debris. It requires high temperatures (80° to 90°F), high humidity, and wounded or weakened host tissue for activity. It grows rapidly, forming abundant and visible surface mycelium. The mode of attack is similar to bacterial soft rot, with an enzyme being released to cause cell deterioration.

Suppression: Improving environmental conditions for the plants or cuttings, such as lowering the temperature and humidity, should help control this relatively uncommon but potentially destructive disease. Suppression is best attained by sanitation, careful handling of the cuttings to avoid injury, and possibly applying a fungicide such as Captan 50 W at 2 lbs./100 gals. of water, or Zyban 75 WP at 1½ lbs./100 gals. water.

***Phytophthora parasitica* (phytophthora crown and stem rot).** Plant symptoms: This fungus is closely related to pythium, but the pattern of symptoms that develops on the plant is quite different. Poinsettias infected by phytophthora may have no root rot at all. A characteristic sign is a brown canker just above the soil line about ¾" long. The canker often shows a black rim around it. Under more humid conditions, gray, wet lesions develop at the soil line. As the disease progresses the affected stem or the entire plant may wilt and die.

Organism characteristics: Phytophthora is an organism that historically has not been as prevalent or damaging as pythium root rot or rhizoctonia stem rot. Phytophthora crown and stem rot is caused by a water mold, as is pythium root and stem rot. The organism is able to invade tissue very rapidly through wounds. This fungus often attacks plants at the soil line where optimum levels of humidity exist. A lesion or brown canker is formed just above the soil line. Additionally, a black streak may run up the stem from the canker. The shoots above the stem discoloration eventually become brown; stems may become extensively brown and shrivel. Any or all of these symptoms may be on a given plant. The disease affects the vascular system, so wilting may precede the externally visible black discoloration.

Suppression: This problem can be overcome with strict sanitation. All plants with symptoms must be discarded, and healthy plants must not be handled after touching diseased plants. Splashing during watering is very likely to spread the contamination. This organism can be carried over in soil, and contaminated soil or pots should be disinfected before re-using. Chemicals that suppress other water molds such as pythium root rot are also usually effective against phytophthora. Drench plants with fungicides such as Truban 30 WP at 4 oz./100 gals. or Subdue 2E at ½ to 1 oz./100 gals. of water.

Botrytis cinerea (gray mold). Plant symptoms: Rotting of tissue, frequently starting on young leaf edges or other immature tissue. Sometimes causes damping-off symptoms at or near the soil line. Red varieties develop purplish color on infected bracts. Difficult to distinguish from edge burn due to chemicals or salts when bracts are affected.

Organism characteristics: A fungus whose spores are airborne and can be assumed to be present everywhere at all times. Not an aggressive parasite unless favored by injured, aging, or succulent tissue, moderately low temperature, and 100% humidity at site of infection. Thrives on plant debris on the floor of greenhouse.

Control: First line of defense is control of the environment. Avoid physical injury to plants, maintain air circulation at night, use night heat plus ventilation to lower humidity, keep temperatures above 60°F if at all possible. Remove all dead plant material. The dense habit of multi-flowered types presents a special problem of leaf and bract overlap.

Suppression: Numerous fungicides are effective as inhibitors to germination of spores and growth of mycelium. New developing plant tissue must be repeatedly covered to provide continuous protection. Materials that leave no residue are preferred to maintain salability. Fungicides employed include Exotherm Termil thermal dust, Ornalin 50 WP at 1 lb./100 gals., Chipco 26019 50 WP at 1 lb./100 gals., Zyban 75 WP at 1½ lbs./100 gals., and Benlate 50 DF spray at 8 oz./100 gals. Exotherm Termil programs have been widely used with little or no damage on blooming plants.

Erwinia carotovora (bacterial soft rot). Plant symptoms: Bacterial soft rot occurs primarily in propagation. Cuttings develop a soft, mushy rot beginning at the basal end within three to five days of "sticking."

Organism characteristics: The bacterium is prevalent on dead plant material and can be carried on windblown dust, non-sterilized tools, and the hands of workers. It spreads readily in water and may be found in pond water. Wounded tissue, waterlogging of rooting medium, high temperatures, and other factors that stress the cuttings favor this organism.

Suppression: Grow stock plants under cover or other controlled environment. Use good sanitation practices throughout the harvest and propagation of cuttings. Avoid waterlogging of the rooting medium. Keep temperatures below 90°F in propagation. Avoid stressing the cuttings as much as possible.

Corynebacterium poinsettia (bacterial canker). Plant symptoms: Black, elongated, and watersoaked streaks occur on green stems. Stem tips abort or bend over. Spots or blotches occur on leaves. In a favorable (warm, humid) environment, disease progresses rapidly, resulting in death of stem above infection and/or entire plant. Not a common disease except during hot humid weather, such as found in the summer climate of the midwestern, eastern, and southern United States. It has shown up in other areas where inoculum was present and the environment favorable.

Organism characteristics: A bacterium transported in water, soil, on contaminated tools and on the hands of workers. Enters plant through stomates or wounds. Spreads in plant through thin-walled parenchyma cells.

Suppression: Severe roguing should be practiced and all overhead irrigation or syringing avoided. Humidity should be kept as low as practical and excessive temperatures should be avoided. Plants should be protected from wind and/or rain. If stock plant infection is suspected, sterile knives should be used in removing each cutting to avoid spread.

Practice Sanitation

Good sanitation practices are essential for avoiding or minimizing disease problems. The following is a list of sanitation practices which should be used as a first defense against poinsettia diseases:
1. Keep hose ends off the floor.
2. Disinfect hands, knives, and other equipment before handling plants.
3. Use copper naphthenate on all wood, metal, or composition surfaces.
4. Pre-steam all soil or sand benches.
5. Steam or fumigate all growing media or use a clean, ready-to-use, soilless mix.
6. Avoid inoculation from dust.
7. Keep plants high enough off the ground or the soil mulch so that splashing water will not come in contact with pots.
8. Keep feet off benches.
9. Never use cuttings which have fallen on the floor. Disinfect tools which have fallen on the ground before re-using them.
10. Remove soil and plant debris from tools, pots, and benches before disinfecting them.

Three generations of Eckes! From the left is Paul 3, Paul Sr. (nearing 96) and Paul Jr. And of course, poinsettias.

11. Rogue diseased leaves and plants and remove them from the greenhouse.
12. Eliminate weeds and debris inside and outside the greenhouse, as they can harbor disease and insects.
13. Think "clean."

OTHER POINTS

Sales and Marketing

Poinsettias are not only the most popular Christmas plant, but the number one flowering potted plant in the United States. Even with its traditional selling period of just six weeks, the poinsettia has far outdistanced the second place chrysanthemum and third place zonal geranium in terms of wholesale dollars.

According to the U.S. Department of Agriculture's 1988 Floriculture Crop Summary, the wholesale value of the crop has increased from $37.6 million in 1976 to $157.7 million in 1987, a jump of 400% in just over a decade.

Historically, poinsettias have been marketed through flower shops, garden centers, and nurseries. With the introduction of the long-lasting varieties, poinsettias are now being sold in mass market outlets such as supermarkets and chain stores. Many of the new, longer-lasting varieties bloom earlier than the older varieties, and sales are starting in mid-November. It is possible to ensure flowering in time for early sales by using black cloth treatment beginning September 15 for three weeks. Naturally early-flowering varieties will generally not require this treatment.

Production Costs

The pricing of poinsettias varies greatly, depending on many cost factors. Some of the major factors that influence cost are geographic location and investment in production facilities.

It is obvious that poinsettia producers in New England, where the investment in glass greenhouses and fuel is high, must get more for their plants than those in Florida growing in the field under saran covering. Where plants were grown primarily as single-stem types, many growers sold their crop by the bloom. Now that there are good varieties producing excellent branched plants, more growers are marketing the plants by the pot. In either case, the producer should determine the cost of production and then attempt to sell the plants based on costs and a reasonable return.

A number of methods have been utilized to determine production costs of growing poinsettias. One method that is relatively easy to understand and adaptable to various situations involves calculating direct or variable costs, indirect or fixed costs, production space utilization in square feet weeks, and losses.

Direct costs include the costs of cuttings, pots, growing media, chemicals, and packaging (sleeves, boxes, care tags). The actual figures will vary among individual growers depending on cutting source, cultural practices and materials used.

Indirect or fixed costs relate to the general operating expenses of the business and include items such as advertising, depreciation, electricity, fuel, insurance, interest, taxes, telephone, and wages. Once the total indirect costs have been calculated for a year, the cost per square foot of bench space (actual production area) may be determined by dividing the total of each item by the total square feet of production area. This will provide cost per square foot per year. To determine the cost per square foot per week, divide the cost per square foot per year by 52.

Only after the production cost has been calculated should pricing be considered. Before the price is set, however, a grower must look at anticipated losses. Shrinkage, or loss of product, will affect total sales revenue, and needs to be taken into account when addressing anticipated profits. Losses in poinsettia production may be caused by crowding, cultural errors, diseases, insects, overproduction, poor nutrition, and sub-standard growing medium. Losses may be significantly reduced by focusing greater attention on quality control and eliminating mistakes. Additional shrinkage may occur if plants are left unsold at the end of the season and must be dumped.

Finally, the desired return on investment must be considered in determining pricing.

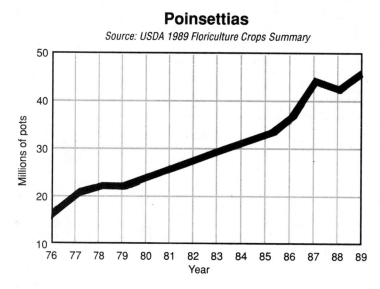

Poinsettias

Source: USDA 1989 Floriculture Crops Summary

This graph shows 14 years of poinsettia production in the United States, all in units. Production has gone up steadily and is still climbing. The poinsettia is the #1 pot plant in the United States.

Spacing Considerations

The most important factor influencing production costs is the productivity of greenhouse bench space. Many growers have reduced poinsettia production costs through space efficiency gains. In many cases, however, productivity advantages gained with closer spacing will be offset by reduced quality and reduced market price. Therefore, growers must carefully evaluate these tradeoffs.

Propagation Decisions

Poinsettia growers have the option of purchasing cuttings in the spring to establish stock plants for producing and propagating their own cuttings. Or, they may choose to purchase cuttings in the summer for direct Christmas crop planting. In deciding whether to buy or propagate a cutting, a grower needs to compare the cost of propagating with the cost of purchasing a cutting. In addition, the grower needs to consider the opportunity cost for alternative use of the facilities during the spring and summer months.

Postproduction Care and Handling

Today's poinsettia varieties are genetically improved to last longer and give greater satisfaction to the customer. But, even with the superior keeping qualities of the varieties currently available, poinsettias cannot withstand mishandling or exposure to adverse environmental conditions without suffering a decrease in quality. Special attention to care and handling at the retail level is necessary to ensure that the ultimate customers will receive the best quality plants possible. The following guidelines are recommended for poinsettia retailers:

- Poinsettias are sensitive plants that must be protected by boxes and individual sleeves during transit. The boxes must be unloaded immediately upon arrival at the store. Plants are very susceptible to chill damage, so never leave the boxes out on a cold dock, and never refrigerate them.

- Upon receipt of the poinsettias, unbox and unsleeve immediately. Prolonged storage of poinsettias in any type of sleeve may result in epinasty, a condition characterized by leaf and bract droop. While a moderate degree of epinasty may be reversed by allowing the plants one to two days to recover in the proper environment, it is clear that if retailers desire immediately salable plants, they must unsleeve them immediately. Of course, if the plants have been in transit for four to five days, unsleeving them immediately upon arrival isn't going to help much. Ideally, poinsettias should not be left in their sleeves for more than 24 hours from the greenhouse to the store.

- If the retailer's poinsettia orders are too large or the distribution system too complex to permit immediate unsleeving of plants, the store should arrange for smaller and more frequent shipments, or direct store deliveries from its suppliers. Some stores actually order on a daily basis and have their grower deliver door-to-door on a daily basis.

- The best way to remove the sleeve is to gently tear it along the seam, carefully avoiding any rubbing or abrasion to the bracts and leaves. Poinsettia bracts are fragile and if the plants are handled roughly, bruises in the form of black or white marks will develop on the bracts.

- After unsleeving, space plants apart in a 65° to 75°F room with enough light to read fine print.

- Now is the time for a thorough inspection by the quality assurance personnel. Most major retailers and growers agree on plant specifications far in advance. Any substandard conditions or shipping damage should be reported to the supplier immediately.

- Make sure that the plants are watered thoroughly before setting them out on display. The soil should feel moist to the touch at all times. When watering the plants the excess water should be allowed to drain through the holes in the bottom of the pot. It is important to discard the excess water. Remember, poinsettias don't like wet feet!

- Be sure to pass along good care information to the customer. A proper care tag with detailed instructions for the customer should accompany every plant. Obviously this tag should do much more than simply identify the name of the plant. It should give the customer useful information on how to care for the poinsettia in the home.

Poinsettias Are Not Poisonous

For years there has been adverse publicity during holiday time concerning the alleged poisonous nature of poinsettia plants. Past research at The Ohio State University has disclosed that laboratory rats are not subject to any ill effects from eating leaves and bracts. This research indicates that the poinsettias are not harmful to humans and animals, though, of course, it is not recommended that they should be taken internally.

A Note to Southern Growers

The unique climatic and environmental conditions that exist in the far southern regions of the United States need to be considered when applying the information presented in this chapter. Because of the high temperatures and humidity, poinsettia schedules need to be adjusted, fertilization practices altered, and more liberal use of growth retarding chemicals may be required. Also, there are several major poinsettia diseases in these semitropical regions which are not known elsewhere.

Specific recommendations for Southern growers are available in the Florida Poinsettia Manual, available from:

University of Florida
Department of Environmental Horticulture
1505 Fifield Hall
Gainesville, FL 32611

The Poinsettia Manual

For a more complete poinsettia publication, the new 3rd edition of *The Poinsettia Manual* has been completely revised and updated for the 1990s. Written and published by Paul Ecke Poinsettias, the new hardcover book has over 260 pages of cultural information with 136 full-color photographs.

The *Poinsettia Manual* details all aspects of poinsettia production, including stock plant management, propagation, and flowering programs. It is an invaluable reference tool and can be obtained by writing to:

Poinsettia Manual
Paul Ecke Poinsettias
P.O. Box 488
Encinitas, CA 92024

Price: $48.95 postage paid (pre-payment required)

POPPY

by Jim Nau
Ball Seed Company

Perennial (Papaver orientale and Papaver nudicaule), **100,000 seeds/oz. Germinates in 7 to 12 days at 65° to 75°F. Leave the seed exposed to light during germination.**

Papaver nudicaule is the Icelandic or Arctic poppy, which is treated as an annual throughout North America since it will flower in 15 to 17 weeks when grown using one to two plants/pot at 50° to 55°F for May sales. Flowers are single and measure from 3″ to 5″ across. They do not tolerate the hot summers of the central and southern United States, and perform their best as container plants with morning sun and afternoon shade. Flower colors include white, cream, scarlet, bronze, orange, pink and yellow, and most often the varieties are sold in mixes rather than separate colors.

The most popular variety to the trade in recent years is Champagne Bubbles, an F_1 mixture of colors on strong bushy plants. Sparkling Bubbles is very similar except that it is open pollinated and takes several days longer to flower than Champagne Bubbles.

The Wonderland series is about the only variety with separate colors available to the trade at this time. This includes Wonderland Orange, a true orange flower with no eye color; Pink Shades, which has flowers in both rose and pink; and, finally, Yellow Shades, which has flowers in both primrose as well as golden yellow. The Wonderlands have the largest flower size of any Icelandic poppy, as well as the earliest flowering plants available.

The Oriental poppies *(Papaver orientale)* are characterized by having large orange or scarlet color blossoms with a prominent black mark in the center of the flower. Flowers are single, measure to 5″ or 6″ across, and are displayed in either May or June. The flowering time is relatively short and the plants will go dormant during the summer. Be sure to mark the spot where they grew in the spring, because by late August little is left to let you know where to plant your fall bulbs and other autumn-planted perennials.

As cut flowers, harvest as the bud opens but before it fully expands. Next, sear the end of the stem to prevent "bleeding" of the white latex, and place the stem into water.

Seed propagated varieties are fine, though shades can vary between plants. Of particular value is Allegro, a scarlet-red variety to 3′ tall in bloom. Plants require two years from seed to flower, but are salable green in packs 10 to 12 weeks after sowing.

PORTULACA *(Moss Rose)*

by Jim Nau
Ball Seed Company

Annual (P. grandiflora), 280,000 seeds/oz. Germinates in 10 days at 80°F to 85°F. Leave seed exposed to light during germination.

Portulaca is an excellent flowering plant for areas with poor soil and full sun. Plants work well in rock walls as well, but will not tolerate poorly drained soil. Flower colors range from yellow, white, cream, fuchsia, scarlet, all the way to violet. Flowers are double in appearance and can develop to 2½″ across. The greatest area for advancement in this class are those selections whose blooms stay open even under cloudy conditions. At present only a limited number of varieties do so, and even these don't remain fully open.

For green packs allow 10 to 11 weeks, and 13 weeks for flowering cell packs of three to five seedlings per cell. Most often portulaca is sown directly to the final cell pack, like alyssum, where at least 8 to 10 seeds have been used per cell. Thinning is not necessary unless filling cells void of any seedlings. For something a little different, offer portulaca in 10″ hanging baskets, allowing 13 to 14 weeks to flower and become salable.

Portulaca is a champion for hot, dry spots.

In the southern United States allow eight to nine weeks for blooming flats. In late winter, plant out after all danger of frost or cool weather has passed, for blooming plants until October.

The large, double blooms of Sundance Mixture and similar varieties are usually the quickest to flower and stay open. The Sundial series also blooms early and offers a good range of separate colors, plus a mix. Double Mixture and Calypso Mixture display a wide range of colors, but their flowers close up if light is limited.

In a different species closer to the true purslane type, Wildfire Mixture is the earliest variety to flower in baskets and the most vigorous garden performer. The single flowers bloom in rose, yellow, and white. However, flowers open and close more erratically than other types, plus Wildfire Mixture can re-seed itself and become a nuisance.

PRIMULA

by Debbie Hewlett
Skagit Gardens
Mt. Vernon, Washington

Hardy Primula

To many, hardy primula herald the coming of spring; their brilliant flower colors are a promise that winter will soon be over. They are often called English Primroses, although many of these short-lived perennials are native to China. Primula is a broad genus with over 400 species but only a small percentage of its varieties are of importance to commercial growers.

P. acaulis

P. acaulis is probably the most widely grown of the primulas. Their leaves form compact rosettes, and flowers grow one per stalk with many blooms radiating from the center of the plant. These make excellent 4″ or 6″ pot crops as well as wonderful bedding plants in areas where springs are mild.

Primula can be difficult to germinate unless environmental conditions can be closely controlled. For best results, keep humidity high, temperatures at a very constant 59° to 65°F, and never allow the seed to dry out. Seed also requires light to germinate, so do not cover. Since sowings should be done during summer months to produce a crop for sales the following spring, it is often difficult for growers in warm summer climates to maintain ideal growing conditions. Plugs can be brought in from a specialist propagator to avoid risks.

Plants should be ready for potting about eight weeks after sowing. Pot into a well-drained, light soil with a pH of 5.5 to 6.5. Fertilize with a low nitrogen (calcium

Primula acaulis *provides a great bit of color and fragrance for early spring.*

nitrate is the best form) high-potash mix every third irrigation to avoid excessive leaf growth. Allowing plants to approach a slight wilt between irrigations will help control size as well as prevent botrytis. After transplanting, grow at 55° to 60°F. Once plants have six to 10 leaves and an established root system, lower the temperatures. Grow cool! For the ideal crop, grow at 35° to 45°F day and night temperatures. Do not exceed 55°F nights or 70°F days if possible, as temperatures higher than this result in tall, weak flower stalks and cabbage-like foliage. Shade primula in areas of high light to avoid sunburn.

Recent breeding has brought us many wonderful F_1 hybrid varieties that can be classified by bloom time. The early group blooms December through January and includes Pageant, a dependable variety with a very wide range of colors; Ducat has large uniform blooms in a bright color range; Peso also has large flowers and uniform, compact plants; and Saga was also bred for earliness and uniformity. In addition, the early group also has some miniature types. Julian is a true miniature and should be grown for 3″ pot production. The variety Lovely is a semi-miniature; the plants are truly compact but can be grown in 4″ pots. These early varieties need minimal cold for flower induction, so they are a good choice for warmer climates.

The mid-season varieties include the very large flowered variety Dania/Festive; also Crown, which is an improvement on the well-known Aalsmeer Giants; and Paloma, a floriferous variety with several pastel shades in the mix. Mid-season varieties bloom late January through early February.

Finesse is a unique late-season variety. This spectacular mix has uniform, compact plants with striking silver-and-gold-edged flowers. Sterling has many brilliant

738

colored flowers on strong plants. Late varieties are more frost tolerant than early season ones and, in fact, need more cold for flower induction; because of this, they are not wise choices in warmer climates.

In recent years, primula breeders have introduced some spectacular bicolored and flame-type flowers. Elara, a rich pink with a yellow center; Dione, a regal purple with a yellow center; and Leda, a yellow with a flamed, red margin are early varieties that make excellent pot crops. In addition to these single colors, many of the *P. acaulis* varieties can be purchased by color. Straight colors are an advantage over mixes for several reasons: growers wishing to put several plants in a 6″ pot can match colors, landscapers in mild climates are discovering the joy of mass plantings of primula in their designs and may have specific color needs, and straight colors are easier to germinate.

P. polyanthus

Although very similar to *P. acaulis* in cultural needs, *P. polyanthus* are more vigorous growers. Their flowers consist of one large stalk with full clusters of blooms at about 12″ high. This is more impressive than the acaulis type when tucked in the garden, since the flowers reach out to greet you. Ideally grown in 6″ pots, they can be produced quite nicely in 4″ pots if water management is used to control size.

Pacific Giants is an old favorite with clear, large flowers on long stems. Jewel Mix is a dwarf strain with the mix heavy on yellows and reds. Hercules has strong, even growth, thick flower stems and a brilliant color mix. All varieties are late and therefore tend to be somewhat hardy.

P. malacoides

P. malacoides is fondly known as the fairy primrose. Soft, green rosettes of foliage boast lacy, loose whorls of pastel flowers. These primula make excellent pot crops and are used as bedding plants in mild winter areas (plants will only take a light frost). Crop time is approximately three to four months from seed, and because of their cool growing conditions and natural bloom time they make marvelous Valentine's Day or Easter pot crops.

Germinate under conditions similar to *P. acaulis*. They should be ready to transplant after seven weeks. Plant into a well-drained, light soil mix with a pH of 5.5 to 6.5. Grow on at 58° to 65°F until established, then drop night temperatures to 45° to 50°F. Plants can be grown cooler but will require longer to finish. Fertilize with a low-nitrogen, high-potash mix. *P. malacoides* are very sensitive to high soluble salts and water stress, so leach plants every third watering and do not allow to wilt. They are responsive to B-Nine, but if grown with adequate space a growth regulator is not necessary.

Two of the early varieties offer a nice delicate fragrance; Pink Ice, a rose pink shade, and Snowcone, a pure white, are suitable for 4″ pot production. The Polar series offers a pink, a rose, a white and a mix; it is also an early flowering variety. For late season flowering, try the King series. Colors available in this series are carmine, lavender, red, salmon, true rose, white and a mixture.

Primula Saga Mix is a great, early spring, budget pot plant.

P. obconica

With the introduction of the Juno series there has been a resurgence of this old-fashioned pot plant. *P. obconica* is also known as the German primrose, and is a very free-blooming, easy to grow crop. The Juno series offers a full complement of seven pastel colors along with a mix, and is known for its early flowering and uniform plant habit. Cold temperatures are not needed for flower induction, so crops can be grown year round. Allow five to seven months finish time from seed. These attractive plants have round, soft, hairy leaves and full upright trusses of flowers that can provide show in a pot or in a garden in mild climates. Use caution when handling the plants since some individuals are sensitive to the foliage and may develop a rash.

P. obconica germinates at slightly warmer temperatures than other varieties of primula—try 68°F for best results. After about eight weeks, transplant one plant per 4″ pot, or one to three per 6″ pot; use a well-drained, light soil mix. The growing on temperature is also warm; grow at 60° to 65°F and then, when plants have filled the pot, drop temperatures down to 50° to 55°F for highest quality. Plants should not dry to a wilt between waterings as edge burn may result. This symptom may also be caused by high soluble salts. Follow the same fertilizer program as recommended for *P. malacoides* to avoid salts build up.

P. sinensis

Chinese primroses or *P. sinensis* have been grown as a favorite pot crop in Europe for many years, and are now being discovered here. The soft, tender foliage with its scalloped edges pleasantly shows off the brilliant flower clusters. Fanfare is a new line that is available in white, light rose, dark rose, blue, scarlet, orange and a mix. Sow July through September for January through March sales in 4″ or 6″ pots.

Treat *P. sinensis* like *P. acaulis* during germination stages. After potting, finish at 50° to 59°F. Allow adequate space and treat like *P. malacoides* in respect to water and fertilizer, since this variety is also sensitive to salts.

P. denticulata

Although not grown much in commercial production, this primula merits more attention as a landscape plant in cool winter areas. Grown as a perennial, foliage will die back in fall and re-emerge in very early spring accompanied by dense ball-shaped flower clusters in shades of lavender to rose. Plant hardiness is listed at -30°F. Forcing this crop for Valentine's Day sales has some possibilities, but timing and crop information is scarce.

PROTEA

by Nancy L. Drushal
GrowerTalks magazine

Family Proteaceae; common name protea.

Protea is a relatively new crop of cut flower and landscape plants in the United States and is characterized by large, unusual, showy flowers on woody evergreen shrubs. They are mainly grown in Hawaii and California, basically because of their particular cultural requirements.

Proteas require low humidity, cool night temperatures, good air circulation (as in strong wind), six to eight hours of sunlight a day, acidic soil and excellent drainage. There are many varieties, but most do well where temperatures stay above freezing. The preferred temperature range is from mid-30° to mid-80°F.

Plants are propagated either from fresh seed (from Australia) or semi-hard cuttings. One-year-old starts planted in the ground will begin flowering the fourth year on short stems. Florist quality flowers should be produced by the sixth year.

Seed or cuttings should be planted in a well-drained, slightly acidic (pH 6.5) peat-lite mix and starter under 50% shade until well established. A light fertilizer of 25 ppm should be applied monthly only to potted plants, never to field-grown stock. Protea are sensitive to phosphate toxicity, and therefore no phosphorus should be used in fertilizer.

Proteas like to be kept on the dry side and have few pest or disease problems other than some foliar fungi.

PYRETHRUM

*Perennial (Chrysanthemum coccineum, **though it may also be listed as** C. roseum, Pyrethrum coccineum **or** P. roseum), **18,000 seeds/oz. Germinates in two to three weeks at 60° to 70°F.***

Among the most valuable and best known of the easily grown perennials is *P. roseum* or "painted daisy." It includes a number of useful, long-stemmed, cut flower varieties that bloom heavily in June with a few scattered flowers during the rest of the summer. In England, named varieties that are propagated by divisions are very popular, the climate there enabling them to be marketed on heavy 2' to 3' stems. We have tried some of this division-propagated stock, but found they die out shortly, while seed-grown plants will do well for three to four years. Double strains of pyrethrum have been developed and they improve upon the single form, but the strength of at least 2-year-old plants is necessary to produce double flowers; the first year nearly all will be singles. While there are separate-color varieties available, the Double Mix strain is most popular. Another English strain known as Robinson's Mixture produces large, single, attractive flowers.

For green packs for spring sales allow 10 to 12 weeks when grown at 55° to 60°F.

ROSE

THE CUT CROP

by Bob Danielson
Ball Seed Company

Rose growing has long been assigned to the specialist, for it does adapt itself to a large operation with many thousands of plants. Producers of cut roses need a constant supply of blooms during all seasons of the year. In order to do this you need a large number of plants to produce enough roses to grade out fancy, long, medium and short lengths for the various needs of the retail outlets. As a producer you need a selection of varieties that will give you types (hybrid teas and sweethearts) as well as the color classes (red, yellow, pink, white and bicolors). It is obvious, then, that 1,000 or 2,000 or even 5,000 plants will hardly carry all the needs of one flower shop. However, with 20,000 or 30,000 plants—one acre of roses—one grower and five employees can profitably supply the roses required within a limited market area.

With the application of new technology in heat shields, high energy lighting, drip irrigation and fertilizer application, high pressure fog for cooling and humidity control, and CO_2 enrichment, high quality roses can be produced in many areas from which they had disappeared in recent years. The market for these locally

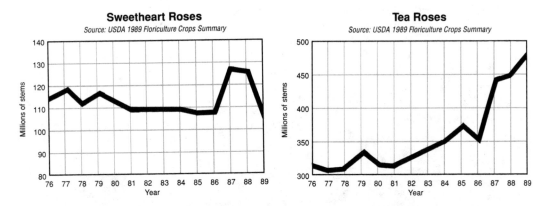

These graphs show USDA totals of sweetheart and tea rose stems sold in the United States for 14 years. There is a third class, the intermediates, that confuses these figures since some intermediate production is probably included in the tea rose graph, inflating the totals. (Intermediates are long-stemmed, similar to the tea rose but smaller-flowered, and the bud size is perhaps twice the size of a sweetheart bud. They are becoming rather popular in the United States.) By the same token, sweetheart roses seem to be dropping precipitously, but in fact the intermediates are probably, to some extent, taking the place of sweethearts. My guess is tea rose production in the United States is holding steady or better, but unfortunately, imports, mainly from Colombia, are already a strong 1/3 of the tea roses used in the United States, and this percentage is slowly rising. Roses are still big business in the United States, but can we keep our share?

grown roses in the Midwestern and Eastern areas of the United States and Canada has been good. Growers using this new technology are very satisfied with the results, both in the quality and profitability.

Rose plants are very specific in their requirements and therefore should be more or less isolated in one house or area where this can be achieved. They are more exacting in their light, temperature and humidity requirements than most other crops. It is very difficult to control disease and insect problems if they are not restricted to a given area.

Structures for Growing Roses

The most practical type of structure is one that will give full sunlight to all plants in the house. There should be no shading from other greenhouses, buildings or trees. Preferably the greenhouse should have adequate ventilation so it can be ventilated during all seasons of the year without cold drafts. The house should have at least 7' gutters so that the roses will not touch the glass when they are at their highest level of production.

Whether roses are grown in ground beds or raised benches makes little difference as long as good drainage is supplied. Those grown in ground beds are generally easier to manage and generally give more long-stemmed flowers.

Roses are generally planted four plants across a 42" bench, with 12" spacing down the bench. This planting gives you approximately 1 sq. ft. of area for each plant.

Len Busch, with his family, is a major U.S. rose grower near Minneapolis. Len pioneered use of acrylics for roses and does well with them.

The heating of a rose house should be adequate to supply 60°F in the coldest weather. The source of heat should be from the floor of the house; this creates rising air currents that will give the maximum circulation. You should also have pipes around the perimeter of the house, which can be left on at all times to keep plants dry at night. Roses grown in ground beds may have the pipes around the perimeter of the beds, thereby giving even heat to the house. Controlling the temperature is a very important part of rose culture, especially for timing and quality. The structure should supply a warm, humid atmosphere with high light intensity during the daytime, and at night a lower humidity with an even, warm 60°F. Good quality roses can be grown with a cooler night temperature, but production will be reduced.

Double-poly structures used to grow roses must be equipped properly to provide even distribution of heating, ventilation and air circulation, and other necessary environmental conditions. Humidity will remain higher in a poly house, and air can become stagnant if proper circulation is not provided. To grow real quality and get satisfactory yields in most Northern areas, supplemental light (high intensity discharge) is needed.

Gas-fired unit heaters can be used with poly convection tubes for distribution as an alternate source of heating, but some provision should be made to increase the soil temperature to 65°F for winter production. Also, all gas-fired unit heaters should be provided with outside outlets, both for intake and exhaust requirements.

Environmental Controls

- **Cooling and humidity.** The rose plant requires a specific environment in order to control quality and productivity. The past 10 years have seen the use of new technology in environmental controls for greenhouse production. Computer control of greenhouse environments based on outside environment and crop requirements has enabled the grower to fine-tune the growing environment.

  Fan and pad cooling has been used for many years to reduce stress on plants during high temperature periods; as an alternative, roses require a high humidity environment, and this can be accomplished by installing a high-pressure fog system in the structures to provide summer cooling and year-round humidity control.

- **Supplemental light.** During the shorter-day period of the year, supplemental light for photosynthesis can be supplied with high intensity lighting (HID), high pressure sodium vapor.

  Research today has determined that supplemental light at a minimum of 350 fc. and up to 500 fc. for 16 hours per day between September 15 and March 1 will increase production of quality roses by 25%. Producers should cut seven to nine more roses during the peak demand season.

  The optimum installation of high pressure sodium fixtures would use 1,000 watt bulbs, with a density of 250 units per acre (167 sq. ft./fixture), and up to 300 units per acre (125 sq. ft./fixture).

  In some areas off-peak demand electrical rates can be attained, reducing the cost of lighting. Spacing for even distribution of light is important depending on the width of the structure.

It is necessary to increase the use of CO_2 and fertilizer with HID lighting. The CO_2 level should be established between 600 and 800 ppm during sunlight hours.

The fertilizer level should be raised to compensate for the increased growth rate with HID lighting. You may need to double the rate of application in the feeding program and monitor the minor elements by soil testing. Deficiencies of minors can show up under lights.

Planting Stock

The time to plant roses is usually between January 1 and June 15. It is generally believed to be a better practice to plant in January or February and bring the plants into production in the early summer. This gives you time to build a large plant to go through the following winter.

The bud graft on a plant is very noticeable, and the plants should be set in the soil with this union about 1″ or 2″ out of the soil. This will allow the root system good aeration near the soil surface. It will also allow room for a mulch as the plants come into production.

Starting the New Crop

Roses are very heavy feeders, and as they grow and produce the soil should have a good supply of the necessary elements. When soil is placed in the bench, room at the top should be left for a mulch that can be applied later as the plants begin to grow. The bench should be filled to a depth of at least 6″. Leaving room for 1″ or 2″ or more of mulch on the bench is always necessary. At this time, 5 lbs. of 20% superphosphate/100 sq. ft. should be applied to the soil. The pH should be adjusted to 6.5. This may be done by adding flowers of sulfur to the soil. As the plants begin to grow and become fertilized, the pH can be controlled by the addition of fertilizers that will control the soil reaction.

The first six weeks of the new rose planting is very important to success. The plants should be watered thoroughly several times and then not be watered until the soil has dried out thoroughly, or until there is sufficient top growth. Instead of watering plants, the top should be syringed four or five times a day during this period. This practice will induce top growth. Rose plants at this time are not losing water to transpiration, and any water tends to reduce the amount of air in the soil. The grower should strive to get maximum root growth to drive new vegetative growth out of the new eyes breaking above on the plant. A rose plant that develops top growth without root growth will soon die.

To build up a plant for production of cut flowers, all new growth must be pinched when buds appear. This soft pinching is usually practiced at this time. Pinch all new growth back to the second 5-leaflet leaf. The new growth resulting from this pinch will be pinched, and so a partial crop may be had for Mother's Day by selecting a few of the stronger canes to flower at this time. At no time should a heavy crop be taken from young plants. Rose plants should be at their maximum growth during September and October in order to produce during the winter months. The recommended practice is to build plants up during the summer and fall and cut down on the wood during January through May.

Supporting the Plants

The usual method of supporting rose plants is to string layers of wire down the bench and cross them with bamboo canes tied to the wire. This makes a maze to support new breaks on the plants.

Watering

Watering of a rose crop is very important, and a number of factors enter into the amount of water they need at any one time. If the plants have a lot of top growth and are coming into a crop, water requirements are high. The bench dries out quickly, and watering should be adequate to prevent checking of the growth. In general, a rose crop should be watered thoroughly and then allowed to dry. If roses are cut back or if a crop is taken off, the water requirements will be less than for a full production crop. Rose plants should require considerably less water in winter than in the summer months. Mulching will tend to reduce the amount of water necessary during the summer months. It will also tend to keep the soil open and aerated. A soil that is not mulched soon becomes compacted from the great amount of water applied. Mulches of corn cobs, hulls, peat or other similar material can be applied at almost any time. Cattle-manure mulches must be applied at a time when the houses can be ventilated adequately, from early March through September. Care should be taken not to put too much manure in the house at one time, or an ammonia buildup will occur that will burn the foliage and leaves and give plants a real setback. When mulch is applied, or even manure, an application of nitrogen is needed to offset the reaction caused by the decomposition of the mulch. A good practice is to apply 1 lb. ammonium sulfate/100 sq. ft. Then go ahead with your regular feeding program.

Occasionally a heavy hand watering with a full flow breaker will be required to even out the moisture within the bench, or for leaching purposes.

Feeding

Feeding roses is, again, based largely on the time of the year and amount of top growth. You may follow an injector feeding program based on soil tests and supplement this with special applications of lime, sulfur or gypsum to adjust the pH and calcium levels of the soil.

Feeding is usually discontinued during the darker months of winter and again during the warmer months if roses stop growing. A very good practice is to discontinue feeding during December and January, and test your rose soils regularly.

Disease and Insect Control

The health of rose plants depends largely on success in controlling diseases and insect pests in the plantings. In contrast, we should say that all factors work hand in hand. Red spider must be controlled since roses simply will not produce on starved and spider-infested plants. You must have a regularly scheduled program of prevention to control insects and diseases. Spraying is generally preferred to eliminate spiders.

The second most important pest is powdery mildew, and the spores occur when environmental conditions are optimum for the spread of the disease when moisture condenses on the leaf surface. Mildew can ruin a rose crop unless checked. Watch for cold drafts from ventilation or broken glass during the heating season. Avoid sudden drops in temperature.

Black spot on roses has been a problem in the past, but it largely disappeared when the practice of syringing roses was discontinued.

Rose plants will often lose mature leaves if sprayed or fogged when the soil moisture is low. Leaves will ripen and fall when the soil is allowed to dry out too much between waterings.

Rose Cutting

Rose cutting is a very important part of rose production. Where you remove the rose from the plant largely determines the ability of the plant to produce subsequent crops. Many systems of cutting have been used, the most common being to cut to the second 5-leaflet leaf on the new wood. This will assure you of another rose within seven weeks (42 to 45 days) from this cut. This type of cutting in the summer and fall will tend to build up your plants. The hooks produced by this type of cutting can be removed by cutting below the hooks in the late winter and spring months. Another method is to soft pinch all breaks as they appear and cut the rose back below the pinch. With this method of cutting, you will have a long stem and better quality, but production will be reduced.

During the spring and summer, knuckle cuts may be practiced on older wood, where cuts are made just above the branch and adventitious buds appear and develop; later these knuckles can be removed with the next cut.

Roses must be cut twice a day to assure that none will open on the plant and be allowed to develop. It is also important that benches be cut at the same time every day, since one or two hours will result in a lot of blasting. These roses cannot be held, but must be used immediately. A new method recently practiced is cropping roses by pinching specific benches in rotation.

Roses cut at the right stage of development will last five to seven days under refrigeration at a 32° to 35°F temperature with 80% humidity. Sweetheart roses and some hybrid teas will last well over a week.

As the roses are cut they should be placed in water as soon as possible. The water should be room temperature and deep enough to immerse all the stems in 8" to

10″ of water. They can then be placed in a cooler at 32° to 35°F for a few hours to take up water. The roses should be graded by length and quality. Water for cut roses should be "relatively salt free and soft. Deionized water is recommended. Soft water is not recommended—too much sodium." All this per Harry Tayama of Ohio State.

The number of roses per pack varies by market, but usually 25 roses of equal length and quality are rolled into a pack with parchment, wax-coated paper or similar waterproof paper.

About preservatives: Immediately after cutting, put roses into pails of water adjusted to pH 4 to 5 with aluminum sulfate. After grading, roses should be placed in a preservative of room temperature water with 2% sucrose and 200 ppm 8-hydroxyquinoline (8-HQC), then refrigerate at 35°F. RoGard is a widely used commercial preservative.

There is a book about postharvest care available: *Post Harvest Care and Handling of Cut Flowers*. Contact the University of California, Dept. of Environmental Horticulture, Davis, California.

Resting Roses

It can be very desirable at times to rest roses. This will give you an opportunity to clean out the old wood and bring a more vigorous plant into production. The first practice is to dry the soil back until it cracks and the plants seem to be almost dormant. Then cut back all the plants to between 18″ to 24″ above the soil; also, be sure to remove all the dead wood from the plants. It usually takes about one month to dry rose plants back for pruning. Immediately after pruning give plants several very good waterings, soaking the soil thoroughly. Once the soil is absolutely soaked, return to normal watering. Rose plants will break out in new growth at once, and again, these shoots have to be pinched to bring the wood up to a new productive level. You will be back in production in September if you dry plants back in June.

Once planted in the bench, plants can very well last for four years or longer with good growing practices. They should be gone over regularly to pinch out blind shoots, remove the dead wood and die back, and return long, irregular growth to a good production level. If this is done, rose plants may never have to be rested, but can be kept in steady production.

A common practice is to cut up on roses in fall and early winter, and reverse the process and cut down in spring and early summer, thereby maintaining an optimum level of production.

Timing of the Rose Crop

There is always an increased demand for roses for Christmas, Valentine's Day, Easter and Mother's Day. To meet this demand you must pinch off enough of your crop prior to the holiday. Count the number of pinches to control the crop. This is done by determining when you wish to start cutting, probably seven to 10 days before the holiday. Soft pinches are generally several days later than hard pinches.

It is a good practice to soft pinch earlier and hard pinch later when timing a crop.

The Christmas pinch date is based on 49 days for most varieties. You would then pinch your roses on the last two days of October and the first two days of November for the Christmas cut.

Valentine's Day would depend largely on the return crop from what you cut at Christmas, since only seven weeks separate the two holidays. Both the Easter and Mother's Day crops would result from a pinch 45 days before the cut date.

The use of HID lighting has made it possible to cut a bearing crop for both Christmas and Valentine's Day peaks.

THE SPRING POT CROP

by Ian MacKay

Roses suited for pot forcing have been sold to the greenhouse trade for many years. Originally, sales of the plants were limited to Easter and Mother's Day, but new and improved varieties, together with the aid of HID lighting, are extending this selling season to include Christmas. Indeed, there is no reason why certain varieties cannot be sold year round. Being hardy, roses can also be planted in the home garden, provided they are not allowed to freeze; if planted in active growth, or if sold in the summer, they have sufficient time to acclimatize to the outdoors before fall frosts occur. No other pot plant offers such versatility and value.

Culture

Regardless of class, all pot-forcing roses require almost the same handling and culture. Budded plants will perform best in 6″ or 7″ pots, while the intermediate and miniature classes will be satisfactory in 4″ pots or larger. All plants should be pruned to promote strong vigorous shoots. The bare-root sweethearts should be reduced to within 6″ to 8″ of the scion union with the understock, and any weak or broken canes removed. Also, these plants should have any excessively long roots cut back, but only so they can be placed in pots without breaking. The smaller classes, received in pots, should be cut back to within 3″ of the soil level, and any very weak or spindly canes removed.

Roses should be potted in a good, well-drained soil mixture. The soil around the roots should be firm to ensure that no air pockets are left around the roots. Plants should never be allowed to dry out in the air during the potting operation. Keep them moist at all times. As soon as the pots are placed on the bench they should be heavily watered at least twice.

Roses initiate growth best in an atmosphere of high humidity. This can be achieved by covering the plants with white opaque polyethylene, damp burlap, or by repeated misting. These measures should be discontinued as soon as the first leaves open fully. Ideally, roses should be kept in a temperature of 45° to 50°F for the first week or 10 days, which reduces stress to the plant and encourages further breaks. Once the plants are growing, the heat can be raised to 58°F.

The question of whether or not to pinch pot roses varies with growers. Some growers do not pinch at all. Others use pinching not only to develop more flowers, but also to help time their crop. For instance, if an April 1 Easter crop is planted January 1 and given a soft pinch February 1, the plants should be in flower by April 1 — 8 weeks after pinching. A Mother's Day crop should be pinched 7 weeks before flowering. Control of flowering time is also possible by adjusting temperatures. The basic forcing temperature should be 58°F, but the crop can be advanced with a higher temperature (62°F) or retarded with a lower temperature (55°F). Bear in mind, however, that temperatures above 58°F are apt to result in loss of quality in the finished plant. For instance, flowers grown on plants forced at too-high temperatures are much more apt to shatter than those grown at lower temperatures.

A crop of pot roses for Mother's Day should be potted the first week in February. Otherwise, the same cultural practices apply as for the Easter crop. Plants unsold for Easter may be pinched back for a later crop. A pinched-back plant should flower in about 6 weeks from an Easter pinch.

GARDEN ROSES

by Ian MacKay

Garden roses remain the most popular, hardy, flowering ornamental plants. Their wide adaptability to climate, ease of culture and wide range of types and

Garden roses are a lovely addition to American gardens—really nationwide, but always best in cool climates.

751

colors make their reputation well deserved. There is no other hardy flowering plant that has so long a season or can provide so many bouquets of cut flowers for the home.

While rose plants were formerly sold exclusively by mail order nurseries and garden centers, they later became available in grocery and other chain outlets, being sold dormant with the roots enclosed in foil or polyethylene bags. Unfortunately, many of the latter sources allowed the plants to languish in locations unsuited to perishable products, resulting in high mortality and disappointed customers. Today's buyer is more discriminating in how he spends money, and wants some assurance that he will receive satisfaction for his purchase.

This is where the retail florist and garden center with growing facilities enter the picture. By potting and growing on a good selection of garden roses, they will find that they can attract a much larger clientele than is possible with bedding plants and run-of-the-mill nursery stock alone. Potted roses growing and well maintained are a drawing card that inevitably leads to increased sales of all other materials. Garden rose growers are an enthusiastic group who provide much word-of-mouth advertising when they find a good source of plants. A further advantage of handling potted roses is that they can be sold throughout the summer to provide quick and colorful additions to the home garden.

Culture

There is no problem in starting potted roses, provided a few rules are followed exactly. In our business of selling dormant, bareroot garden rose plants to florists, we have found a considerable lack of basic information concerning rose requirements. From our own experience, the following rules are applicable for starting potted roses.

1. Order your bareroot dormant plants for delivery at least two months before you want to sell them as started growing plants. For your own convenience, you can order your plants delivered in more than one shipment to spread out your workload and to give you a succession of plants to sell throughout the spring and summer. Rose plants do not have to be sold as soon as they are started. A plant properly started will remain in salable shape for several months.

2. When your rose plants arrive, you will find them packed in containers and in material that protects them from frost and drying out. If the shipment arrives damaged, be sure to file a claim with the trucking company immediately. If your plants arrive frozen, it is wise to file a claim, even though there is a good chance of thawing them out with no loss. If, when you open the shipment (and it should be opened immediately upon arrival), you find the plants frozen, pack them up again and store the shipment in a cool (temperatures between 34° and 40°F are ideal), dark place for two or three days, especially if frozen hard. This will give the plants a chance to thaw out gradually, which is the secret in salvaging frozen rose plants. Dormant rose plants can stand considerable frost, *if* they are thawed out gradually.

752

The most important, basic point in handling rose plants is to be sure the plant is *never* allowed to dry out—neither its roots or canes. As soon as roses are dug in the growing field, they are pruned, graded, and immediately packed in moist packing material and put into cold-temperature, high-humidity storage. If, when you receive them, they are allowed to stand out in the open sun and wind for a few hours, all this careful handling will have been for nothing and the plants may die. Even if the plants do not die, they will be sufficiently injured to cause slow starting and poor subsequent growth. It is a good idea to soak the plants in water for an hour or two as they are unpacked. In case the plants have dried out a little in transit, this dip will replenish their supply of moisture.

3. Rose plants should be pruned and potted immediately upon receipt. If you can't get to them immediately, leave the plants in their shipping containers until you are ready to pot them. However, don't leave them packed any longer than necessary—a day or two at most.

Pruning rose plants is a second important fundamental. At the time of potting, the plants should be cut down to within 6" or 8" of the crown of the plants. This should leave two to four "eyes" from which growth will start. Don't be afraid to cut most of the cane off. Long canes produce weak new growth and small blooms. Also, the plant will be more subject to injury from desiccation. Remember that until new root hairs are produced, the plants have no way of compensating for moisture lost from the canes, and the longer the canes, the greater the loss. Grading by the American Nurserymen's Association requires,

Schroeder's Flowers, Green Bay, Wisconsin, is a classic example of a retail grower doing a good job of pre-starting and displaying garden roses. Here's a view of their display. In the photo is Lee Hansen.

among other things, canes of a certain length, which is the reason canes are left long when shipped to you. Also, trim off any damaged roots or any roots that are excessively long. The finer roots are the important ones—heavy, thick ones do not produce the all-important white roots that the plants need to start growing.

This pruning procedure applies to all varieties and types of roses, including the climbing varieties.

4. Immediately after potting, the pots should be thoroughly soaked with water. This can be done by repeated hose waterings until the soil in the pot is completely saturated. The pots should be placed on a surface that allows drainage out of the bottoms of the pots. Gravel, for instance, is a good material to place pots on. Newly potted rose plants must be protected from wind and sun until root action starts. The best method of getting strong initial growth is by using white opaque polyethylene. Cover the plants completely and tuck the plastic under the outer pots. When growth starts and the first leaves have appeared, the sides of the poly can be folded back to allow the plants to become adjusted to a lower humidity gradually, and then removed completely after a couple of days. Caution: Where air temperatures are likely to exceed 80°F, do not use clear polyethylene unless you spray it with shading compound. Should high temperatures follow within 48 hours of potting, heat buildup under clear poly will sometimes result in the plants being killed outright. Once the roots are active, they can tolerate any temperature to be experienced in a greenhouse. Roses started outdoors under plastic should present no problems.

5. Once the rose plants are growing, the only care they need are an occasional spraying and feeding. Blackspot and mildew are the principal diseases of roses, both of which can be easily controlled with modern fungicides. Blackspot is a defoliating disease that does not often occur in a sales lot, but it is well to be on the safe side and practice prevention. Mildew, on the other hand, under certain weather conditions, can appear and be disfiguring to the foliage. Both mildew and blackspot can be controlled by spraying at 14-day intervals with Benlate, or a combination of Folpet and Actidione.

DIRECT STICK MINI POT ROSES

(The following information about Ed Melon's roses is adapted from a story by Russell Miller that appeared in GrowerTalks *September 1987. Ed is founder and vice president of Green Acres Wholesale Florist Inc., Newfield, New Jersey.)*

First, we find rising demand for the mini pot roses. Consumers love the colorful, tiny rosebuds on a houseplant, and it can be planted out later on as a hardy garden plant.

"Depending on varieties and types of material selected, you can use anywhere from one to four plants in a 4″ to 6″ pot. We have found, in our own production, the use of three to four plants to be best," Ed says. "There are many varieties to choose from and, if you have the time and the serious interest, it is well worth your while to experiment around a little for your needs."

Growing Mini Roses

Roses can be vegetatively propagated by direct sticking cuttings in pots, Oasis or soil cubes.

Another choice a grower has is to purchase dormant material, usually available during winter and spring, from a propagator. These roses have been grown-on for one season, and this is known as the "long cycle," says Ed. "These plants, depending on temperature and overall environment, will take an average of eight to 10 weeks to finish, giving usually a larger, fuller plant than the shorter cycle material."

Your third and fourth choices, together, are to start with prerooted cuttings or prepotted, prefinished material. The rooted cuttings must be grown-on for approximately four to six weeks, pinched back approximately 2″ above the soil level, and then allowed to grow on and set buds for another six weeks. Here, most of the varietal selections and difficult propagation have been done for you.

The prefinished material should arrive prepinched and leafed out, according to Ed. Approximately five to seven weeks are then needed for blooming. These could be finished in existing 4″ pots or shifted into 6″ pots for a larger product.

Soilless mix compositions should consist of 80% chunky peat moss, with the remainder being perlite or Styrofoam. You'll want to incorporate trace elements as well, he says; "Peter's FTE at 3 oz./cu. yd. could be recommended.

"Do not pack the soil when transplanting. We've seen crops set back many

Knud Jepsen, a major Danish pot producer, does an acre or more of direct-stick pot roses. They are top quality and highly automated. Plants move from headhouse to growing area in Dutch trays on a computer-controlled "robot." Knud also does several million excellent kalanchoes a year.

weeks due to soil packing. Good aeration in the soil is very important," says Ed, adding, "Sand is definitely not recommended."

Optimum temperatures for growing on miniature roses are 60° to 65°F nights and 68° to 75°F days; however, Ed says a miniature rose crop can "put up with extremes in temperature, but this will adjust overall quality and crop timing."

Dormant material should be started at cooler temperatures, about 55° to 58°F, with a gradual increase to the proper temperatures. Humidity should be kept high, at least 80%, until the shoots are 2″ long. For growing on, Ed recommends 60% to 70% humidity; "It prevents disease and allows for more constant feeding."

Good ventilation is important for miniature roses, but avoid drafts. High light, at a minimum 4,000 fc., will result in fuller bushes with a greater number of blooms, Ed says. Outdoors, roses can take full sun in the summer. "We apply light shading, 10% to 15% in our area (New Jersey), from June until August to reduce overall leaf temperature. They can take the light; high temperatures are not good."

Watering, Feeding and Spacing

Ed warns against letting your roses dry out. "Always, always moist but never soggy," is his advice. Watering should be done during the morning, allowing full leaves to dry by midafternoon, if you use overhead watering. Bottom irrigation is highly recommended after the plants are well rooted, and throughout the growing on and finishing stages.

This house of direct-stick mini roses is at Knud Jepsen's in Denmark. Note that all plants are in Dutch trays and ebb and flow irrigated.

756

Here's Ed Melon with one of his direct-stick pot roses.

The finishing spacing for 4″ pots should be approximately 4 to 4½/sq. ft., and for 6″ pots, 10″ or 12″ on center.

Holding and Shipping

"When holding the finished product, definitely allow for good air circulation. Keep the plants at their finished spacing and, if you're going to cool them down to a climate such as 38°F, gradually decrease the temperature so that the plants acclimate," Ed says. "A very versatile plant, the rose gives you great ability to store material for holidays."

Ed did an "extreme" test where he held material for four weeks at 38°F in the greenhouse during the bud stage. The plants did not "visually advance." He's also done numerous experiments in cooler facilities where he held plants for as long as four weeks without any detrimental effects. "If you're trying something for the first time, advance your crop a little bit and let it come in early. At the finishing stage, you can always hold it back."

Ed also recommends shipping the plants cold so that the finished product arrives at the store in good shape. "It's very important to keep one point in mind: the longevity at store level. Cut down on fertilizer levels just prior to shipping. Water retention in the pot is most important."

To conserve moisture during shipment, Ed says there are different approaches to consider. "A wetting agent applied to the soil mix or as a top dressing afterwards could be used, but that's something we're not currently familiar with. What we use is a wet sponge placed in the bottom of the pot saucer. We have found this literally doubles the shelf life, and we have seen other growers starting to apply this method with other crops that need a lot of water at store level.

"I don't have to imply to growers—how many stores have you been in after you've grown a quality crop and seen the way the plants get neglected? There are ways to overcome that problem, and the pot saucer with our wet sponge method, we've found, is one."

Roses can be shipped very long distances in closed or open carts, Ed says. "The main point to keep in mind is to have ventilation slots in your cartons to reduce ethylene buildup during long periods. Whenever possible—not entirely necessary but beneficial—ship your plants at a cool 40° to 45°F if you're going a major distance." He also points out that light encourages growth, therefore you want storage conditions to be cool and dark.

RUDBECKIA *(Gloriosa Daisy)*

by Jim Nau
Ball Seed Company

Perennial *(R. hirta)*, 27,000 to 80,000 seeds/oz. Germinates in 14 days at 70°F. The seed can be lightly covered during germination.

Rudbeckia is widely used to decorate our nation's capital in late summer. Pictured here is Goldilocks.

758

Rudbeckia is an excellent class of plants for well-drained areas in full-sun locations. Gloriosa daisies are often treated as annuals in the Midwest or in any areas where the autumn can be cold and wet. They do not appreciate overly moist conditions, and the shorter varieties can often die from foliar diseases brought on by excessive moisture in combination with high humidity. Plants flower readily from seed the first season, and varieties like Marmalade and Goldilocks will even flower well in pots or packs.

For flowering 4″ pots in May, sow Marmalade and Goldilocks in January and use one plant per pot. For the taller varieties, allow 11 to 15 weeks for green packs.

In varieties, both Marmalade and Goldilocks are dwarf selections to only 15″ tall in the garden. Marmalade does have problems with foliar-borne diseases, as noted above, but provides color from planting until August. Flowers are single to 3″ across in a golden yellow to light orange flower color.

Goldilocks is a semi-double to double flowering variety to 12″ tall in the garden. Flowers range from 3″ to 4″ across and the variety is excellent in packs or pots.

In the taller varieties, Double Gold is of particular value for cutting or as a background plant in the garden. Double Gold has double flowers up to 6″ across, in a stable flower color of golden orange.

We hear reports of large, spectacular, beds of rudbeckia across our nation's capital. It's widely used and very colorful! A great perennial.

SAINTPAULIA IONANTHA *(African Violet)*

by Arnold W. Fischer
Arnold Fischer Greenhouses
Fallbrook, California

African violets are pot plants that never go out of style. The long-lasting house plants can be cropped year-round. The African violet crop is timeable and, grown efficiently, it brings a good return.

Varieties differ in colors, shapes and sizes. Most common for mass production are compact and miniature varieties that have a fast and uniform growing habit and show a good flowering performance.

To grow the plants successfully it is necessary to maintain a proper environment: the pH and salt levels have to be right; the plantlets have to be healthy and must come from a good propagator's stock; best bench space and greenhouse should be available.

Starter Environment

After potting, keep the soil moist. The plants should be kept in a warm, humid micro-climate with soil temperature of 75°F for 25 to 30 days, depending on growth performance. Lower temperatures will prolong crop time. An under-bench heating system is recommended to keep a uniform soil temperature. Watering should be done overhead, with the water temperature equaling room temperature.

Blooming Environment

The plants can now be spaced out on the benches. The air temperature should be about 69° to 70°F day and night. To prevent botrytis, the humidity has to be controlled. Plants can be grown on capmats, ebb and flow, or trough watering systems. A liquid fertilization should be maintained with every watering. Early morning watering is recommended. Water temperature must be about room temperature (70°F) to prevent the occurrence of white ring spots on the foliage.

Crop Time

From a potted liner to a blooming African violet takes, in general, 10 to 12 weeks. Miniatures flower in 8 to 10 weeks. The crop time depends largely on the growing environment.

Lighting/Shading

African violets do not like direct sunlight. Their growing environment should preferably supply them with about 1,500 fc. of diffused light. In summertime this

It's a special joy to see African violets as they are done in northern Germany—such wonderful heads of flowers. Above photo is of Arnold Fischer's German range. It is trough irrigated to provide better aeration from below.

light level can be obtained by shading. The greenhouse ought to have at least one movable shading system on the inside, combined with a permanent summer shade outside. Artificial lighting in wintertime is not required, but can be helpful. Supplementary light from HID or Gro-Lux lamps (900 fc.) can benefit the starter period during December and January. Artificial lighting is a must for double-deck benching.

Media/Fertilizer

The media must have a high air capacity in addition to being able to hold a good reservoir of water, combined with a buffer for holding nutrients. Violets perform best in a light, well-drained peat-light mix or soil based media. The soil should contain a minimum amount of nutrients, but must be low in total soluble salts. A pH of 6 to 7 and salts below 1,200 mg/cu. yd. ensure a good growing environment. To predict the availability of a fertilizer, it must be measurable. A high percentage fertilizer has less ballast or filler salts and therefore smaller amounts are needed. Never use organic fertilizer! The total salts in the soil determine the plant growth and the requirements of liquid feeding. Recommendable is a light liquid feed program. One must use caution not to over-fertilize. It is always possible to adjust unless the plant's leaves are thick and brittle from over-fertilization. Leaves should always be flexible and soft. Violets are very sensitive to high salts. A testing of soil and water for nutrients, pH and salts must be done regularly. CO_2 can be helpful in the wintertime to supplement sunlight between November and February; 400 to 600 ppm being enough.

Again, here is excellence in violets—
this time a German grower in Sydney, Australia,
Bill Siererding. The variety is Meta.

Disease Prevention

The basics for disease prevention are: clean greenhouses and surroundings; best source for plantlets; healthy plants; on-time potting; right environment; good facilities, and preventive spraying. Chemicals and formulas change and are often regulated by the government. Prevention rather than cure is easier to manage and not as costly. Preventive application of sprays should of course be used only as needed. Some pesticides can act as growth regulators, and vigorous growth can be jeopardized by some specific chemicals. The most common pests and diseases are phytophthora, powdery mildew, botrytis, thrips and leaf nematodes.

Conclusion

To successfully produce African violets year round, one cannot underestimate the requirements of proper environment, culture, and timing. Culture instructions for the finished plant production of African violets can only be used as guidelines that need to be tailored and defined to the production methods and to the capability of the people of each individual greenhouse operation.

SALVIA

by Jim Nau
Ball Seed Company

Annual (Salvia splendens), 7,500 seeds/oz. Germinates in 12 to 15 days at 75° to 78°F. Seed should be left exposed to light during germination.

Tender Perennial (Salvia farinacea), 24,000 seeds/oz. Germinates in 12 to 15 days at 75° to 78°F. Seed should be left exposed to light during germination.

Both types of salvia are excellent in 4" and 6" containers and cell packs, and are of special importance in the landscape and home garden. *S. splendens* includes such varieties as Red Hot Sally and the Carabiniere series, and is characterized as a group by having flowers in bold colors of red, white, lilac, salmon, wine (burgundy) and blue. Flowers are held on upright spikes, and plants fill in readily on 12" centers in the garden.

S. farinacea is available in either pastel blue or off white, and works best in settings with other pastel colors or contrasting bold colors. Plants have a finer leaf on plants that grow taller than the splendens varieties. *S. farinacea* types make excellent dried cut flowers and background plants for the flower garden. Treated as an annual in the northern United States and as a tender perennial in the South, this class is an overlooked variety that does well in warm, dry locations.

762

For flowering packs of *S. splendens*, allow 9 to 11 weeks for the dwarfer varieties, and sell taller strains, like America and Bonfire, green in the pack seven to eight weeks after sowing. Four-inch pots require 11 to 13 weeks for the dwarfer strains to flower. *S. farinacea* requires eight to nine weeks for salable green packs, and up to 16 weeks for flowering 4″ pots. *S. farinacea* does not flower well in the cell pack, though it can be grown for this market. It does better going to the garden from a 4″ to 6″ pot.

In the southern United States allow eight to nine weeks for flowering packs of dwarf splendens varieties; sell taller types green. Space splendens 10″ to 12″ apart in full sun to partial shade in the garden. Planted from March to May, they will flower until November, though blooming sporadically in July and August. Not a hardy crop, splendens cannot tolerate frost.

For *S. farinacea* allow eight to nine weeks for green pack sales. Plant to the flower bed from September on; once established, farinacea varieties will flower until the next fall.

In varieties, for free flowering performance look to Red Hot Sally and Fuego; both among the earliest and most compact salvias. Red Hot Sally is a slightly darker shade of red. Another excellent choice is the Empire series which is made up of six separate colors. Of particular value is the Empire Lilac, a light purple flowering variety. For taller, background accents, try Bonfire or America. These are among the latest of the splendens varieties to flower, and these two varieties provide a long season of color, right up until frost. In the farinacea types, the Victoria series is excellent all around, providing free-flowering performance from planting until weather extremes take away from it. For something a little dwarfer try Rhea, which grows about 4″ shorter than the Victorias do.

Salvias Blaze with Continuous Color From June 'Til Frost

GARDEN HEIGHT*	8 to 10 in. (20 to 25.5 cm.)	10 to 12 in. (25.5 to 30.5 cm.)	14 to 16 in. (35.5 to 41 cm.)	18 in. (46 cm.)	26 to 30 in. (66 to 76 cm.)
VARIETY	Fuego Red Hot Sally	Carabiniere Series Empire Series St. John's Fire	Red Pillar Rhea	Victoria Series	Bonfire
TYPE	Splendens	Splendens	Splendens/ Farinacea	Farinacea	Splendens
BEST FOR LANDSCAPING	Red Hot Sally	Carabiniere Series Empire Series	Red Pillar	Victoria Series	Bonfire
BLOOMS**	June 20	July 1	July 10	July 15	August 1
USES	Garden borders	Garden borders	Foreground	Background, herb gardens or cuts	Background or foundation

Based on Ball Seed Trials, West Chicago, Illinois.
**Blooming date from green plants set out in late May—West Chicago, Illinois.*

SCABIOSA

Annual *(S. atropurpurea)*, **4,500 seeds/oz. Germinates in 12 days at 70°F.**
Perennial *(S. caucasica)*, **2,400 seeds/oz. Germinates in 18 days at 60°F.**

Often called "pincushion-flower," the annual form of scabiosa is another outdoor summer-cutting item that provides reasonably long stems under trying outdoor conditions. Scabiosa should be placed out as early as soil will permit. Fall sowing under favorable conditions is even better. Annual scabiosa also does well forced for spring flowering in a cool house (50°F), but in a warm house or during warm weather the naturally slender stems draw up rather weak. For May flowering, the seed should be sown in March and benched in April. For cutting purposes on a small scale, the Giant Imperial Mix is a good strain.

The perennial form, like the annual, is a cool-temperature plant. While both suffer in excessive summer heat, the perennials are inclined to die out if it gets too trying. Probably for this reason they are not widely used in the Midwest, but are very choice where summers are more moderate. In the annual form, try House Mixture, which will flower in September from a June sowing. Better performance can be had by sowing in May for mid-summer flower. In the perennial form the best variety is Fama, a mid-blue-flowered variety on plants to 3' tall.

SEDUM

by Jim Nau
Ball Seed Company

Perennial *(S. acre* and *S. spurium)*, **400,000 seeds/oz. Germinates in 14 days at 70°F. Seed should be left exposed to light during germination.**

S. acre is a small-flowered sedum variety with flowers to ½" across. Flowers are single and yellow in color. Plants are 2" to 4" tall and are smaller overall in habit than *S. spurium.*

S. spurium is more invasive than the previous variety, with bronze red foliage that appears more intense as the evenings cool in autumn. Flowers are bright rose in appearance, and up to ½" across. Flowers are single and held on foliage 6" tall. *S. spurium* has broad leaves rather than the needle-like foliage of *S. acre.*

Both varieties are hardy to USDA zones 3 through 9. *S. acre* flowers in June while *S. spurium* flowers in July and August.

Division, cuttings, and seed are the common forms of propagation. Sowings made in winter or spring of either variety can be sold green in the packs 11 to 14 weeks later. *S. acre* will not flower the same season from seed, and needs to be overwintered in a quart or gallon container to be most effective. *S. spurium* will flower the same season from seed, usually in late July or August. However, the best bloom comes the second season from seed.

In varieties, *S. acre* is sold under the name Golden Carpet, though the most uniform of the selections are those vegetatively propagated. In *S. spurium,* the species is often sold under this name or *S. spurium coccineum*, and both work well in the perennial garden. This latter species has scarlet flowers instead of rose.

SNAPDRAGON

by Ed Harthun
Ball Seed Company

Annual (Antirrhinum majus), 180,000 seeds/oz. Germinates in one to two weeks at 70° to 80°F.

Greenhouse snaps are grown more each year in Northern greenhouses, and in Florida and California. They provide a delightful, colorful, "spiky" vertical effect to arrangements. Wholesale market price as of the early 1990s is $4.50 to $7.00 for 10 spikes, depending on time of the year and marketplace.

Along with the rise in demand for cut flowers in the last few years has come an increased demand for good quality snapdragons both in the central part of the

Snaps are done importantly in both Florida and the West Coast. Here's a crop a few miles south of San Francisco. Excellent!

country as well as in the coastal areas. Positive factors in favor of this continued demand in the marketplace are snapdragons' low energy requirements and freedom from overseas sources. Snapdragons can be produced on a year-round basis, and returns are much better now than they were in the mid-1980s.

Propagation

While there are snapdragon growers still starting their crops from seed, the increasing trend is to start with plugs produced in trays holding 375 to 400 plugs. The big advantages to using plugs are reduced crop or bench time, resulting in a crop or two more from the same area in a year, and also reduced labor costs (faster planting time). Most plugs are three to five weeks old when shipped. It should be pointed out that seedling trays are also available.

When starting from seed, a light sterile medium should be used such as a mix of one-half peat and one-half vermiculite. Sow in rows and use ITP (2,000 seeds) for two standard size flats. Cover the seed lightly with vermiculite and keep the temperature at 70° to 80°F. Seedlings should be ready to transplant about three to four weeks after sowing. The use of supplemental lights during this period will aid in producing a stronger seedling at the darker times of the year.

Soils

Snapdragons can be grown in a variety of soils, but they don't like wet feet. The soil mix should be coarse, light and open. Adding peat, unless it's very coarse, can increase the water holding capacity to the point where slow drying can affect plant growth and invite disease problems. The pH range for optimal growth should be maintained at about 6.3.

Transplanting

It is extremely important to bench a seedling or plug at the proper time. Delayed planting will produce a stretched or hardened seedling that will never attain its maximum potential. The young plants should be transplanted at the same soil level at which they were grown. Good spacing is 3" x 5" during the higher light periods of the year. Increasing that spacing to 4" x 5" during the darker months will produce a better quality flower stem. Some growers produce year-round on a 4" x 4" spacing. Figure on using seven to nine plugs or seedlings/sq. ft.

Watering and Fertilizing

It is very easy to overwater snaps during the short-day periods of the year. On the first watering only the immediate area around the small plants should be watered. Once those small plants are established, they should be watered thoroughly and allowed to wilt slightly between waterings. When spikes begin to color, plants should no longer be allowed to wilt. Feeding with every watering is a common practice. Using 100 to 200 ppm of nitrogen and potassium, depending on the time of the year, is acceptable. Stay away from high ammoniacal forms of nitrogen. Feeding should be discontinued when buds start elongating.

Temperature

At the time of planting and for a two-week period following, running a night temperature of 60°F will help plants get off to a fast start. Then temperatures should be dropped to around 50°F, which is the temperature that most schedules are based on. A crop can take cooler temperatures than this, but it will lengthen crop time.

CO_2

The use of supplemental carbon dioxide can shorten crop time by as much as four weeks when used from October through March in the northern part of the country. The rate to use is 800 to 1,200 ppm.

Scheduling and Varietal Classification

Greenhouse snapdragons are classified into four groups based on their growth response to temperature and daylength. Group I varieties flower best in the winter

Snaps are also an important bedding plant in Florida. Here's George Caple with a 4" crop— part of the 100+ acres of 4" annuals at Caples Farm, Homestead, Florida.

under low light and cold temperature conditions. On the other end are the Group IVs which require higher temperatures and longer days. Group II and III varieties are the most versatile. (See Table 1).

With technical advances in the field of lighting and growing, the lines separating the four groups are no longer so definite or specific. For example, a few growers in the very northern part of the country are working on flowering Group III varieties year-round, using HID lighting (600 fc.) for 12 hours out of 24 and running night temperatures of 60 °F. Reported crop time reduction is 40% less. Growers in highlight areas such as Colorado and parts of California use only Group IIs and Group IIIs and flower out a crop in 12 to 14 weeks from sowing.

Table 1. Snapdragon Growing Schedule

	NORTH		SOUTH	
Group	Sow	Flower	Sow	Flower
I	Aug. 15 to Aug. 31	Dec. 10 to Feb. 15		
II	Sept. 11 to Dec. 10	Feb. 15 to May 10	Aug. 22 to Dec. 20	Dec. 1 to May 1
	July 24 to Aug. 9	Oct. 25 to Dec. 10		
III	Dec. 10 to Mar. 21	May 10 to June 30	July 6 to Aug. 16	Oct. 1 to Dec. 1
	June 18 to July 16	Sept. 10 to Oct. 25	Jan. 7 to March 8	May 1 to June 15
IV	Mar. 28 to June 10	July 1 to Sept. 10	Mar. 15 to July 2	June 15 to Oct. 1

Table 2. Top U.S. Varieties

Group	Variety	Color
I	Oakland	White
	Bismarck	Lt. Pink
	Cheyenne	Yellow
II	Oakland	White
	Maryland Pink Imp.	Lt. Pink
	Bismarck	Lt. Pink
III	Potomac White	White
	Potomac Ivory	Off White
	Potomac Yellow	Yellow
	Pan American Summer Pink	Lt. Pink
IV	Potomac Ivory	Off White
	Potomac Yellow	Yellow
	Winchester	Lt. Pink

Insects and Diseases

Aphids, mites, thrips and whitefly are the major insects attacking snapdragons. There are adequate chemical controls available.

Common snapdragons diseases include Pythium and Rhizoctonia, Powdery Mildew, Wilt, Botrytis and Rust. The best preventives for controlling soil-borne diseases lie in thorough sterilization and good sanitation practices. Useful in controlling airborne diseases are materials such as Chipco 26019, Benlate, Karathane and Manzate 200.

768

Harvest and Care

Snapdragons require light for continued flower development, but are harvested when the florets on the lower third of the spike are open. Snapdragons respond favorably to floral preservatives. Typical vase life in distilled water is one week, but may be extended to as long as three weeks. Storing upright in clean, well-ventilated coolers at 40°F will maximize keeping quality and prevent crooked flower tips. If snapdragons are to be delivered the same day as harvested, they may be shipped dry in boxes.

Shatter and tip breakage are sometimes problems. Although promising work has been done with silver thiosulfate sprays to prevent shattering, selection of varieties which are more shatterproof and less prone to tip breakage is the best solution.

Snapdragons for Bedding

The majority of bedding plant growers and retailers list two or three types of garden snaps on their sales sheets. The well-known F_1 Floral Carpet is the dwarf strain so widely used for edging and mass plantings. Growing 6" to 8" tall, it will flower well in packs and 4" pots after 10 weeks from sowing in the South and about 14 weeks in the North.

Here's a good example of snaps as bedding or border plants at the Marriott in Palm Desert, California. Very colorful!

On the tall end of the scale are the F_1 Rockets, usually grown for cut-flower purposes, and reaching a height of 30″ to 36″. In some areas the Rockets are grown for commercial cut-flower purposes.

The third type most commonly grown is the intermediate class (14″ to 18″) as represented by Sprite Mixture.

All snapdragons perform best at cool temperatures (45° to 50°F).

F_1 Hybrid Snapdragons Stand Tall and Colorful Through Summer's Heat

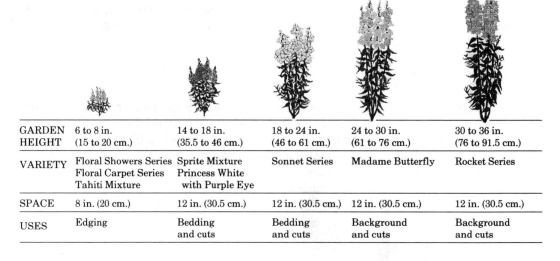

GARDEN HEIGHT	6 to 8 in. (15 to 20 cm.)	14 to 18 in. (35.5 to 46 cm.)	18 to 24 in. (46 to 61 cm.)	24 to 30 in. (61 to 76 cm.)	30 to 36 in. (76 to 91.5 cm.)
VARIETY	Floral Showers Series Floral Carpet Series Tahiti Mixture	Sprite Mixture Princess White with Purple Eye	Sonnet Series	Madame Butterfly	Rocket Series
SPACE	8 in. (20 cm.)	12 in. (30.5 cm.)	12 in. (30.5 cm.)	12 in. (30.5 cm.)	12 in. (30.5 cm.)
USES	Edging	Bedding and cuts	Bedding and cuts	Background and cuts	Background and cuts

STATICE *(Sea Lavender)*

Annual or Perennial** (Limonium species), **13,000 seeds/oz. Germinates in 15 to 20 days at 70°F.

Botanically, the genus Statice is no longer recognized; the various species now belonging to the genus Limonium. However, the term "statice" has been used so long that we shall continue to refer to them under this name. Principal use of statice is to furnish dried material for winter bouquets, wreaths, etc. The annual type, *S. sinuata,* is grown by the acre in Florida, while the perennial types are found all over this country and Europe, and are handled as hardy perennials.

Sinuata is sown in Florida during the midsummer, usually in late July or early August. This crop will flower during midwinter—January and February—right outdoors. The flowers are used both for the tourist trade and for shipping to Northern markets. Later sowings keep a succession of bloom until spring. Incidentally, it requires about 3 lbs. of annual statice seed to plant an acre.

Sinuata can also be grown as a spring greenhouse crop in the North; sow in January and plant into a deep ground bed for a fine crop of flowers in the summer. Under good culture, it should reach a height of 2½′.

The Russian, or rat-tail statice, known as Suworowii, produces lavender spike-type flowers that can be sown in October, spaced 8″ x 8″ in a light soil mix, grown at 45°F, and will flower from late February through May.

In the perennial species, *L. tatarica* (also listed as *Goniolimon tataricum* and *L. dumosa*) is the most popular with cut flower growers around the country. Fifteen to 18 weeks are required for green packs that will not flower the same season from seed and need to be given a cold treatment first. Plants require up to three years to put out their best flowering performance. This is similar to *L. latifolia,* which also requires three years to become established and put out a high yield of cut flowers. However, it requires only 11 weeks in which to fill out a cell pack and be sold green or moved to the field. Finally, we treat *L. perezii* as an annual in the Midwest, though it is a tender perennial rather than a hardy one. Green packs are salable 10 weeks after sowing, and plants will flower the same season from seed in the Midwest, but are not overly free-flowering.

STOCK

by Vic Ball

Annual (Mathiola incana), 16,000 to 20,000 seeds/oz. Germinates in two weeks at 65° to 75°F.

Columnar, or nonbranching, stocks at one time were a major greenhouse cut flower crop in the midwestern, eastern and southern United States. They were introduced to this country in the 1930s by George J. Ball. Today the cut flower crop is largely produced outdoors in California and Arizona. There are, however, several other new forms that are interesting as pot and bedding plants.

- **Midget series.** They're very early, dwarf (8″ to 10″) and fine for outdoor bedding and 4″ pot crops. They are available in red, rose, violet and white. Violet finishes 10 days later than others in the series. It's possible to eliminate the singles by keeping only the plants with serrated leaves. The selection is done at an early stage. The plain leaf types will be single and may be discarded if you wish.

All stocks are uncomfortable at high temperatures, and generally fail to flower past May or June in Northern summers (except trysomics). Optimum temperature for blooming is about 50°F nights, although the plant can survive at temperatures as low as freezing. Sowings can be made from August through February to bloom from October through March. In mild winter areas the Midgets will bloom continuously from November to April.

771

I saw a planting of them at Norm White's in Chesapeake, Virginia, planned to follow poinsettias. Plugs were planted to 2¼s November 30. On December 21, they were planted three plants to a 5½″ pot and they flowered in February, compact and very attractive. Probably plugs could be potted directly three to a pot. Again, singles can be removed at the three- or four-leaf stage by saving only the plants with notched leaves.

- **Trysomic dwarf double.** This 7-week strain is rather widely used for bedding plants in some sections of the country, especially California. Growing to a height of 12″ it is the only strain that will flower under high temperatures. Plants will usually throw a central spike in May and then produce numerous side shoots that will flower later. This variety can be flowered in the pack. Seed should be sown in February. As soon as seedlings become established they should be moved to a cold house. Chiefly grown as a color mixture, the strain is also available in separate colors.

STRELITZIA

by Nancy L. Drushal
GrowerTalks magazine

Strelitzia nicolai; **family Strelitziaceae; common name White Bird of Paradise**

The common orange-and-blue Bird of Paradise flower *(Strelitzia reginae)* has been used in the floral industry as an unusual tropical cut for years. *S. nicolai* produces similar flowers in white and does well as an interiorscape foliage plant. It has large, shiny leaves and grows in a planar fashion similar to compass tree. This usually occurs when the plant is roughly 10′ tall and approximately five years old. They will bloom in an interiorscape that has 400+ fc. of daylight.

Strelitzia *(S. nicolai* or *S. reginae)* can be grown from seed, but takes seven years to flower. In Hawaii division of the rhizomes is common. Stage 4 liners from tissue culture are often used to begin plants in 6″ or 8″ pots, two seedlings per pot. Crop time to a finished 10″ pot will be 14 to 18 months.

Spacing should be pot tight until plants reach 12″ to 14″. They can then be potted up to a 10″ pot, two plants per pot, and finished spacing should be 18″ to 24″.

Any well-drained common potting mix with high organic matter can be used. The pH should be between 5.5 and 6.5. In good light these plants have a high water consumption, but should not be kept wet. No more than 30% shadecloth should be used, and temperatures are best kept between 65° and 90°F.

Strelitzia do not like high soluble salts. A slow-release granular (12:6:8) can be used as a top dress, or a light nutrient solution under drip irrigation.

Scale and mealybugs can sometimes be a problem, and some fungal diseases occur. There are several well-known pesticides and broad-spectrum fungicides labeled for strelitzia.

It is important to acclimatize these plants for shipping. Increase shade, cut back water and leach well two to three weeks before shipping. Temperatures during shipment should range from 55° to 80°F.

Due to the slow growth rate and structure of the plant, careful handling is critical during shipping to prevent broken or damaged leaves. The plant simply will not "fill in" a missing leaf, therefore the void will remain permanently and can cause serious disfigurement.

Generally, finished plants in 10″ pots are 3′ tall, in 14″ pots 5′ to 6′ tall, and 17″ pots 7′ to 8′ tall. Strelitzia can be field grown as specimen plants in sizes 10′ and up. They should be root pruned six months before digging. After digging place plants in 28″ to 60″ containers of potting mix, irrigate well and place in sun again until rooted to the sides. To acclimatize, place plants in shadehouse 45 to 60 days before shipping, cut back on water and leach well.

STREPTOCARPUS

by Russell Miller
GrowerTalks magazine

Newer hybrids of streptocarpus, or cape primrose, are making commercial production both easier and faster. This flowering houseplant, which is also sometimes used in interiorscapes simply for its foliage effect, can add a unique dimension to a grower's or retailer's product line. Since the introduction of Concorde, the first F_1 streptocarpus, newer hybrids have been introduced that offer a fuller and longer color range, and are more tolerant to a wide range of greenhouse conditions.

Flowering plants can be produced from seed in about four to five months during summer or five to six months during winter.

Leaf Propagation

Streptocarpus can be produced by three techniques involving leaf sections. One technique is to use leaf tip sections that are about 3″ long and 1½″ wide. Stick the bottom ½″ of the leaf section into the propagation media. Another technique involves cutting the leaf just above the midvein (the leaf should be about 8″ long and 4″ wide) and sticking the leaf lengthwise into the propagation media. In another technique, the bottom portion of the leaf is removed just below the midvein (both the bottom and top halves can be used). Turn the leaf over and make ¼″ incisions 1″ apart on the midvein.

773

Media for leaf section propagation can be straight vermiculite, or one part peat, one part perlite and one part vermiculite. Media should be kept moist and media temperature should be 70° to 75°F.

In all three types of leaf propagation, a rooting hormone and fungicide dip should be used. Mist isn't required, nor should it be used for most varieties. Plantlets emerge from the base of the leaf section edge in about two months. Expect 20 to 30 plantlets per leaf. Carefully separate the plantlets from one another. Transplant these one month later into final containers. Streptocarpus does not react well to periodic container shifts and repotting, so only one transplanting should be done. Since streptocarpus is capable of producing plants from a single cell, you can expect some variation to occur from leaf propagation.

Seed Propagation

Streptocarpus seed is very fine (990,000/oz.). Sow in a light, porous media, such as one part peat, one part vermiculite. Maintain 70°F media temperature, keep under 40% shade, and use intermittent mist. Do not cover seed, as light improves germination. Delicate seedlings appear in two weeks. Keep them in the flat until crowding occurs (about two months after sowing). When seedlings are 30 days old, apply a weekly feeding of 100 ppm 20-20-20 until transplanting.

Culture

Cultural techniques are the same once plantlets or seedlings are transplanted. Streptocarpus requires light, well-drained media since their root systems are fine and shallow. A good media is one part peat, one part perlite and one part vermiculite; or peat, sand, and perlite in the same ratio.

Maintain 65°F night and 80°F day temperature, and 50% humidity. Streptocarpus will grow well with 1,000 to 1,500 fc. Ventilation helps keep heat stress down under high-light conditions. With sufficient light, streptocarpus will bloom throughout the year.

Feed weekly with 100 ppm 20-20-20. Do not constant feed. When plants are flowering, feed once every two weeks with 50 ppm 20-20-20. Allow streptocarpus to dry slightly between waterings. Due to its shallow, fine root systems, be careful not to overwater or overfertilize.

You can grow streptocarpus in 2¼" to 8" pots and baskets. Four-inch pots are commonly used. Plant one plant per 4" or smaller pot and use multiple plants for larger containers. Spacing on the bench can be close, as long as leaves from one pot don't touch another plant's leaves.

Diseases and Pests

Crown rot and botrytis can occur, but are uncommon. To prevent crown rot, improve soil drainage, avoid overwatering and use sterile soil. For control, use

774

Benlate or Banrot. Botrytis can be prevented with proper sanitation, spacing and repotting on schedule. For control, use Benlate or Ornaline.

The main insect pest is fungus gnat larvae on seedlings, and mealybugs, aphids, and thrips on older plants. Vectobac or Diazinon drenches control fungus gnats, and Knox Out PT265 or Orthene sprays keep mealybugs, aphids, and thrips under control. Malathion can damage streptocarpus foliage.

Varieties

Varieties include the well-known Weismoor hybrids (pink, white, blue, lilac, and red shades of fringed, orchid-like 4" to 5" flowers); the Concorde series (White, Deep Blue, Light Blue, Mid-Blue, Pink, Tri-Color, and Mixture); and the Nymph series, Constant Nymph (blue), Mini Nymph (blue), Blue Nymph (light blue), Cobalt Nymph (deep blue), Netta Nymph (deep blue with dark blue veination) and Purple Nymph (deep purple).

Other varieties include Delta (mid-blue); the Royal series (very strong, intense colors: Electric Blue, White, Deep Purple, Red, Pink, and Mixture); Baby Blue (a dwarf mid-blue); Mirage (blue), and Saxorum (blue).

Earlier streptocarpus hybrids are sensitive to heat, but Holiday Hybrids, a recent introduction from Park Seed, tolerates a wide temperature range. Four to six months after sowing, Holiday Hybrids bear year-round, large, 2" to 3½" flowers. It blooms without stretching under light conditions ranging from 1,000 to 6,000 fc.

Blue Angel, another introduction from Park Seed, also tolerates a wide temperature range. It also branches freely, so it's ideal for hanging baskets as well as pots. It becomes covered with 1½" to 2", deep blue, white-eyed flowers, six months after sowing. Grow at 1,000 to 8,000 fc.

Blue Angel and Holiday Hybrids are best propagated from stem cuttings. Provide bottom heat at 70° to 75°F. Keep leaves moist and transplant into 2½" pots when roots are about 1" long. Detach and move each plantlet to 2½" pots. Grow in diffuse or filtered light, and transplant to 4" pots after 6 to 8 weeks for Holiday Hybrids, and 10 to 12 weeks for Blue Angel. Plants in 4" pots are ready for sale in 6 to 8 weeks, or in 10 to 12 weeks for baskets.

Holiday Hybrids and Blue Angel should not be top-watered, and once seedlings are established a constant liquid feed (15-30-15 at 75 to 100 ppm) is recommended. After transplanting into final pots, use 15-30-15 at 150 to 200 ppm N.

SWEET PEA

by Jim Nau
Ball Seed Company

Annual (Lathyrus odoratus)**, 350 seeds/oz. Germinates in 15 days at 55°F. Seed should be covered for germination.**

Often in horticulture, certain crops or classes of plants go through a period of breeding and improvement, are offered to the trade and enjoy a place of prominence for years to come. Sometimes, as in the case of cut flowers, the market changes dramatically and the crops fall out of favor and go by the wayside—such is the case of the sweet pea.

Sweet peas offer softly-scented flowers in pastel colors atop foliage that grows and trails well. There are two classes of sweet peas; those that are summer flowering and those that are winter flowering. Summer flowering varieties branch close to the ground and produce a number of active shoots. The winter flowering varieties produce one vegetative shoot which first flowers and eventually will branch along the stem. Of the two classes, the summer flowering varieties are long-day plants and will not flower under the short days of winter. Therefore, since most of the cut flower material is sown in the summer months for winter flowering, use only winter flowering varieties in Northern greenhouses for best performance.

In cropping, sow seed in June, July, August and September to flower from October to March or April. However, growers have to ascertain whether they have the market to sell such a crop that is familiar only to older Americans.

THUNBERGIA *(Black-eyed Susan Vine)*

Annual *(T. species)*, 1,100 seeds/oz. Germinates in 12 days at 70° to 75°F.

Where a splash of real color is wanted in annual climbers, porch boxes, or hanging baskets, you'll find Alata hard to beat. It's easy and cheap to propagate, fast-growing, and has lots of black-eyed orange, buff and yellow flowers. It is also very useful as a screening material when planted to open ground and allowed to cover a trellis or fence. Allow eight to nine weeks for flowering 4″ pots that are sown direct without transplanting, since the roots are tender and resent frequent repotting. For 10″ hanging baskets allow 10 to 11 weeks with six to seven seedlings per container. Plants trail tremendously and flower profusely. The Susie Series, a fairly recent introduction, consists of three distinct colors: orange, white and yellow with eyes, as well as a mixture that contains both eyed and solid colors. These are especially suited for hanging baskets.

TOMATO—FOR BEDDING

By all recent tabulations, tomatoes are number one of all U.S. bedding plants—in flats or plants sold. They're the champion of home gardeners coast to coast, United States and Canada—because they produce the most fruit for the least amount of work. And really they are the easiest to grow.

776

As a bedding plant, tomato culture is quite simple. Tomatoes will grow fastest at 60°F with ample moisture and fertilizer. But generally in a bedding plant situation, growers don't want this rapid thin growth. Retardants are illegal on all vegetable plants. To restrict growth grow tomatoes cool, dry, and hungry or use cool days/warm nights. Wide extremes of temperature won't hurt the plants—they just grow faster if they are warm and wet and well fed.

For some reason, a great many growers, especially retail growers, produce tomatoes in 3″ Jiffy-Pots—and they are widely sold in this form. Many also go in cell packs. Also, many growers produce them in 4″, 6″, and even larger pots or small tubs. Often, the larger plants are staked—and sold in flower or even with green fruit.

Many wholesale growers organize this crop so as to produce as many as three or even four crops of cell-pack plants on a bench during one season.

Tomatoes are a strictly full-sunlight crop. Grown as bedding plants they should always have full light. Probably the biggest limitation of successful tomatoes in the home garden is that maybe half of all U.S. gardeners put them in some shade—and here they will make a lot of leaves and not many tomatoes. Also, they are less successful in cool summer areas like Seattle. Or England! Such areas use earlier varieties such as Early Girl Improved.

Tomatoes Love Heat!

Many home gardeners successfully grow tomatoes in urns or tubs—up to 15″ and 17″ in diameter. Good, heavy plants, bearing a lot of fruit, can be grown this way.

Hybrid Tomatoes—The Most Popular Garden Vegetable, Bred Especially For Disease Resistance, Higher Yields and Bigger Size

VARIETY	Sweet 100	Early Girl Imp.	Heartland	Celebrity	Floramerica	Lemon Boy	Pink Girl	LaRoma (Roma Hybrid)	Champion™	Super Fantastic	Better Boy	Beefmaster
SIZE	1 in. (2.5 cm.)	4 to 6 oz. (113.5 to 170 g.)	6 to 8 oz. (170 to 227 g.)	7 oz. (200 g.)	8 to 12 oz. (227 to 340 g.)	7 oz. (200 g.)	8 to 10 oz. (227 to 283.5 g.)	4 oz. (113.5 g.)	10 oz. (283.5 g.)	9 to 12 oz. (255 to 340 g.)	10 to 14 oz. (283.5 to 397 g.)	Over 12 oz. (340 g.)
GROWTH	Indeterminate (Pole)	Indeterminate (Pole)	Indeterminate (Dwarf Pole)	Determinate (Bush)	Determinate (Bush)	Indeterminate (Pole)	Indeterminate (Pole)	Determinate (Bush)	Indeterminate (Pole)	Indeterminate (Pole)	Indeterminate (Pole)	Indeterminate (Pole)
MATURITY (DAYS)	65	52	68	72	75	72	76	62	62	70	70	80
DISEASE TOLERANCE	—	VF1&2	VFN	VF1&2NT	VF1&2	VFN	VF	VF1&2	VFNT	VFN	VFN	VFN
NOTES	Extremely sweet.	Earliest yet. Smooth. Good flavor. A Ball Seed Exclusive.	Dwarf variety for small space gardening. Dark foliage. A Ball Seed Exclusive	Large, glossy fruit with light green shoulders. Medium-sized vine.	Widely adapted. Grow in cages or on short stakes.	Lemon yellow fruit. Very mild flavor. Very productive.	Pink Fruit. Crack-resistant. smooth.	Heavy yielding Italian-type tomato.	Large fruit. Medium-early tomato with good disease resistance. A Ball Seed Exclusive.	High yields. Good flavor. Continuous cropping. A Ball Seed Exclusive.	Most popular. Excellent flavor. Smooth. Grow on stakes or sprawled.	Beefsteak-type. Rough. good flavor. Tolerant of cracking or splitting.

As with many other bedding plants, breeders have made great advances in recent years—especially through use of F_1 hybrids. One result of this is the inevitable problem of winning the home gardener away from his lifetime favorite old standbys like Marglobe and Rutgers. But if such varieties are put alongside new hybrids in impartial trials (Ball Seed Company does this every summer) the difference is almost shocking. The old inbred or open-pollinated varieties are uneven, often diseased, and produce a small fraction of the amount of fruit of the new F_1 hybrids. The hybrids, by the way, now are almost normally bred to resist such diseases as verticillium, fusarium, and other diseases spread by nematodes. The acronym is "VFN resistant." It is important—it means a lot more success for a lot of gardeners.

Back to F_1 hybrids, here is a list of some of the old, open-pollinated varieties—and F_1 hybrids that are recommended to replace them.

Old Standard	Suggested Hybrid Replacement
Beefsteak	Beefmaster VFN
Bonny Best (John Baer)	Super Fantastic VFN or Champion VFNT
Earliana	Early Girl Improved VF1&2
Glamour	Champion VFNT or Better Boy VFN
Heinz 1350	Sunripe VF1&2N
Homestead 24	Sunripe VF1&2N
Jubilee	Golden Boy
Marglobe	Floramerica VF1&2
Roma	La Roma (Roma Hybrid)
Rutgers Imp. VF	Floramerica VF1&2
Super Sioux	Champion VFNT or Better Boy VFN

Probably the #1 all-around tomato as of today is Better Boy. It is VFN resistant and is an F_1.

TORENIA

by Jim Nau
Ball Seed Company

Annual (Torenia fournieri), 375,000 seeds/oz. Germinates in seven to 15 days at 70°F. Seed should be left exposed to light during germination.

Once used as a summer pot plant, torenias are chiefly used today as a summer bedding annual, where they make a surprisingly bright showing, flowering from June until frost. They can also be used as a midwinter pot plant, at which time their bright blue blooms are most welcome. Pinching will help develop a bushy plant.

Flowering cell packs are ready 12 to 13 weeks after sowing, and 4″ pots will flower 13 to 15 weeks after sowing using 55° to 60°F. They have no particular soil preference; grown outdoors, they do best in cool, moist, partly-shaded places, but make a surprising showing in full hot sun.

In varieties, an old favorite, Fournieri compacta is an excellent plant in landscape plantings spaced 10″ to 12″ apart. Clown Mixture offers less vigor, but blooms in a bright range of colors: space 10″ apart. Clown Mixture requires an additional one to two weeks for pack and pot sales, and also makes excellent 4″ pots.

VEGETABLES AS BEDDING PLANTS

by Jim Nau
Ball Seed Company

Cole crops include broccoli, Brussels sprouts, cabbage, cauliflower, collards, kale and kohlrabi.

The interesting thing about this group of plants is that all have a lot of similarities between each other. For instance, while each has a different botanical name, all those listed above have predominantly 7,000 seeds/oz., germinate in 10 days at 70°F, and their seed should be covered upon sowing. They prefer cool temperatures.

In cropping, allow 6 to 8 weeks for green packs and 8 to 9 weeks for green 4″ pots with one plant per pot. This is true for all the crops noted above. As for crop time, the number of days from planting to the ground until the crop can be harvested are: broccoli, 50 to 58; Brussels sprouts, 80 to 90; cabbage, 40 to 90; cauliflower, 45 to 68; collards, 70; kale, 45 to 55; and kohlrabi, 45 to 55.

Peppers. Annual *(Capsicum fruitescens)*, 4,000 seeds/oz. Germinates in 10 days at 72°F. Leave the seed exposed to light during germination.

Peppers are a warm weather crop that perform best once the night and soil temperatures reach 58°F or above. In the northern United States plants should be ready for sale in mid-April for homeowners who plant into the garden with night protection. Allow 6 to 8 weeks for green packs and 8 to 10 weeks for 4″ pots with one plant per pot. Plants will fruit 60 to 80 days after planting.

Pepper varieties are extensive and diverse, with over 50 varieties that vary in size and color, and range from the mildest of blocky-shaped bells to the red-hot taste of Fire! Among the best include: Better Belle (65 days), a blocky green bell with a sweet mild taste ideal for cooking, stuffing, and snacking; and California Wonder (75 days), a non-hybrid blocky green bell variety with thick walls and a flavor perfect for salads and snacking. For a superb yellow bell, try Sun Bell (70 days), a bright, golden yellow pepper highlighted by a delicious, sweet taste.

Vine crops. This class includes cucumbers, muskmelon, squash, pumpkins and watermelon. While this class differs in its botanical names and other particulars, you will find that, as a group, there are a number of practices that are similar among them. First, none of this group appreciates being transplanted where the roots are going to be disturbed. Instead, they all prefer to be sown where they are to flower and fruit. They do remarkably well when three seeds are planted to a Jiffy Pot and allowed to germinate and develop this way. Many trial gardens use this method to get an early start on the season. Thin to two plants per pot and bury pot and all into the ground when the vines are 3″ to 4″ long. On all the crops noted above, allow 4 to 6 weeks between sowing and selling the Jiffy Pots. The only exceptions are cucumbers, which are ready in 3 to 5 weeks, and can quickly become overgrown; and watermelon, which requires up to 8 weeks before it is ready to be sold.

Keep in mind that all the above plants need only to be started before they are ready to be sold. It is best to have them out of your greenhouse before the tendrils start to develop. Otherwise, it will be difficult to separate your plants.

As for days to maturity, the following crops and their number of days from planting to the garden to fruiting are: cucumber, 48 to 70; muskmelon, 72 to 90; pumpkin, 90 to 120; squash, 49 to 85; and watermelon, 70 to 85.

VERBENA

Annual (V. hortensis), **10,000 seeds/oz. Germinates in 20 days at 65°F. Dark.**

One of our old standby bedding plants, verbena owes its popularity to its bright and varied colors, delightful fragrance, low-cost propagation, and a free, all-season flowering habit, even under full sun.

Propagation is usually from seed sown in mid-February, if 3″ blooming pot plants are wanted by Memorial Day. They may be sown as late as the end of March, transplanted into packs or flats, and will still make a good showing outdoors, but not as early as when started in pots. Germination is not rapid; give them around 65°F soil temperature for several weeks and keep them on the dry side. There is some indication that overwatering at time of sowing will reduce germination. Some growers have had better success by preparing the seed flat in the late afternoon, watering it, and then sowing the seed the following morning without any further watering. Once established, verbena should be carried along at about 50°F nights, and should be pinched back early. A February sowing kept moving and pinched should make nice bushy plants with several flower heads—not hard to sell!

There are two basic types of verbenas: the spreading type is procumbent or carpet-like, covering a fairly wide area; the upright type is free-branching but distinctively bushy in habit.

Verbenas are a colorful, much-used bedding plant. The only problem is a bit irregular germination.

In the spreading class, the best varieties include the Showtime and Romance series. Both of these varieties have basal branching plants with numerous clusters of ¼″ blooms in a wide range of colors. Showtime is more vigorous (grows to 12″) and works well on embankments and over walls, as well as an edging plant along the annual border. Romance is slightly shorter (10″ tall) and works well in containers and in the annual border.

As for the upright verbena, the best are the Novalis series and Trinidad, which is a salmon rose flower color on plants to 14″ tall. Novalis grows to 12″ tall in the garden and is characterized by having basal branching plants that are free-flowering.

VERONICA

by Jim Nau
Ball Seed Company

Perennial *(Veronica spicata)***, 221,000 seeds/oz. Germinates in 16 to 25 days at 65° to 75°F. Leave the seed exposed to light during germination.**

Veronicas are excellent summer flowering perennials that bloom freely the first season from a winter sowing. The blue, white, or rose red flowering spikes are borne in June and July and the plants will flower until August. Veronica as a group is hardy to USDA zones 4 to 8.

Of easy culture, *V. spicata* is salable green in a pack in 10 to 13 weeks after sowing, and will flower during the summer. Plants flower more dependably the second season after sowing.

In varieties, *V. spicata* is available in both seed and vegetatively propagated material. Those that are seed-propagated will be of several different habits and heights as well as differing shades of blue. Though strong garden performers without being too vigorous, more uniform selections are available from cuttings or division.

Related material includes *V. repens,* which is a dwarf flowering plant to 1″ tall that flowers in April and May. Plants are best used in rock gardens where the soil is allowed to dry out. Plants are salable in 10 to 12 weeks after sowing and are available in single flowering forms only. Finally, *V. incana* is the most unique of the three types, but also the most difficult to germinate and grow. If the variety does not germinate well, place the seed into moist peat and refrigerate for 10 days to two weeks and then sow as you would as noted above. Plants have a gray green foliage like dusty miller, and require 12 to 14 weeks to be salable green in the cell packs. Neither *V. repens* or *V. incana* will flower the same season from seed.

VINCA

by Jim Nau
Ball Seed Company

Annual (*Catharanthus roseus,* formerly *V. rosea),* **21,000 seeds/oz. Germinates in 7 to 15 days at 78° to 80°F. After three days drop to 75° to 78°F for the remainder of germination. Seed should be lightly covered upon sowing. Upon sowing, place the flats into total darkness and move to the light once the seedlings have emerged but before they have stretched.**

Vinca is one of the up and coming classes in horticulture where a lot of time is being spent to perfect these species. They are considered to be difficult to grow. However, they are still one of the leading plants for warm, dry locations in full sun. They do not appreciate cool conditions, and prefer well-drained locations. Vinca is drought-tolerant if it is allowed to become established before water is limited. Much of the information available on this class has only recently come onto the trade and it is presented below.

Vincas are very sensitive to overwatering and cool temperatures. Grow plants warm at 65°F for the first three weeks after transplanting, then drop the night

Vincas are coming up rapidly in the bedding plant world. They withstand heat and dryness! An important cultural point: Keep them on the warm and dry side as seedlings, 70°F for the first two weeks after transplanting. Benlate on plugs after transplanting helps.

temperatures to 60°F once the roots have established in the container. In regard to seed, it has been found that vinca germinates better when seed is older as opposed to fresh. If seed is left over from sowings in the winter, hang onto the seed. It should germinate better 4 to 6 months later. For this reason, many of the seed companies are bringing in seed months earlier than needed so as to hold onto it and allow the seed to break dormancy to improve germination by sow date.

In the southern United States allow 11 to 12 weeks for flowering packs sales, and 15 to 16 weeks for flowering 4″ pots, one plant per pot. In the northern United States allow 14 to 15 weeks for flowering pack sales, and 16 to 17 weeks for 4″ pot sales using one plant per pot. For something unique, try a 10″ hanging basket using five plants per pot. Plants are salable 18 to 20 weeks after sowing.

There have been a number of varieties introduced into the trade over the years, but nothing like what is planned for the 1990s. At present the top selling variety is the Little series, which consists of five separate colors including Little Bright Eye, a white with rose-red eye. Slightly shorter but with more rounded petal edges is the Cooler™ series, made up of Peppermint Cooler, a white with rose eye, and Grape Cooler, a rose flowering variety with a dark rose eye.

The next class is the Sahara Madness™ series, which is a dwarfer variety than the Coolers, and excellent as an edging plant, in containers, or in mass. Sahara Madness Bright Eye is white with rose eye on plants to no more than 12″ tall, but with an upright and basal branching habit. Sahara Madness Pink is to be introduced in 1991 and it is a rose pink flower with a dark rose eye. The dwarfest series available is the Carpet series which is only 8″ to 10″ tall and is the only super dwarf variety available. Excellent where a trailing plant is needed for warm, dry locations such as embankments and over rock walls. Four separate colors plus a mixture make up this series.

Here's vinca, Pretty in Pink—fine warm pink. Vincas are fast becoming a major bedding plant—heat resistance!

Very popular, too, among the vinca clan, are the forms of *V. major,* a foliage vine usually seen in its variegated form. It is the traditional edging for window box and urn plantings, and, like its close relative *V. rosea,* it stands heat and drought exceptionally well. Propagation here is by cuttings, either tip or 3″ sections of old stems. Finished 4″ stock takes two years to grow, which adds to its cost, but its exceptional and lasting popularity stands it well. The cuttings are stuck in October or November. As soon as they are rooted they can be potted to small pots in which they will hold through the spring. From here they usually go outdoors, over the summer until fall. Clumps are then dug, divided, tops cut back to 4″ or 5″, and heeled in closely in a cool house. About January 1, they are potted into 3″s and 4″s, set up along the southern edge of a bench, vines hanging downward, where they make their final growth. Frequent feedings of nitrogen-bearing fertilizer help fill them out. It is very important to break the taproot that frequently forms through the drain hole during this stage, or the plant will suffer greatly when moved out.

The most popular type grown is *V. major Variegata,* a green-and-white variegated sort. Next in popularity is Reticulata, green-and-yellow variegated. The pure green species is sometimes seen but not highly prized.

A third, and again highly useful, vinca is *V. minor.* Unlike both major and rosea, it is completely hardy and makes a fine ground cover, especially in deeply shaded places. It flowers profusely, having a heavy crop of 1½″ single purple blooms during spring and early summer. Propagation is usually by stem cuttings rooted in June. Old clumps may be divided as a further means of propagation. The plant is also a favorite for rock gardens; often, it is commonly referred to as "myrtle" or "common periwinkle."

VIOLA

by Jim Nau
Ball Seed Company

Perennial (V. cornuta), 24,000 to 43,000 seeds/oz. Germinates in 10 days at 65°F.

Invaluable as edging plants, violas are also very effective when used in mass plantings to front a shrub border. Although not as large as pansies, they are more free-flowering and may be obtained in a wide range of colors—yellow, red, purple, lavender, apricot and white. Their culture is much the same as for pansies; late summer or fall sowings are, if anything, even more successful because of violas' unusual hardiness. Violas will do very well in light shade, although they prefer full sun. They will do well in any good garden soil, but in order to do their best they should be planted in a fertile soil with a good supply of organic matter.

In general, allow 12 to 13 weeks for flowering cell packs for either spring or fall sales when grown at 50° to 55°F nights.

In the class of small-flowered violas referred to as Johnny Jump-Ups, keep in mind that these have a lot in common with the standard violas but are far more popular. The specific difference is that this class will flower earlier and can become vigorous in the cell packs if not sold soon after they flower. For flowering cell packs allow 11 to 12 weeks when grown at 50° to 55°F nights for varieties like Blue Elf, a purple flowering variety (also called King Henry or Prince Henry), and Helen Mount, a violet, lavender and canary yellow flowering variety.

ZINNIA

Annual (Z. elegans), 3,000 to 6,000 seeds/oz. Germinates in 7 days at 75°F.

Zinnias' big claim to fame—they're really showy and they do stand summer heat! And heat is one thing you'll find plenty of during most summers in the majority of our states. If given reasonably good soil and water, zinnias will yield quantities of the brightest colored of all summer cut flowers. They are easy to grow.

Florists' main interest in them is the sale of pack-grown or 2¼″ plants in May for outdoor planting, and second, their use as a summer cut flower. Properly grown, they can be moneymakers on both scores.

For Spring Plant Sales

Sow four to five weeks before desired selling time in order to have good, hardy plants for green sales in packs or 2¼″ pots. Exceptions to this are Thumbelina,

Pulcino zinnias make a fine 4″. Here's Tom Abramowski, Rockwell Farms, Rockwell, North Carolina, with a flat of them.

Dasher, Peter Pan and the Pulcino Series, which should be sown about a month earlier to have plants in flower for pack sales. The big trick—seed flats must be kept at 70°F, at least, until seed is through the ground. Most complaints on zinnia germination are the result of trying to germinate the seed at 50°F or lower; they just won't come through—and, in fact, will soon rot in the ground. After seedlings are through, the flat may be carried along at 60°F, and the trayed or potted plants will be "huskier" if grown at this temperature.

Plant breeders have done excellent work with zinnias in recent years and have developed new and improved varieties to such an extent that today there is nearly a type, size or color available for any conceivable garden use.

As Cut Flowers

Most-popular zinnia handling for the retail florist is a late March sowing of pot or pack-grown plants carried in a 55°F house and planted out in late May. These plants, if given water outdoors, will give a good crop from early July on through the summer. They should be spaced 12″ x 12″ outdoors. The "dahlia" and "cactus-flowered" classes are preferred, although the tiny Lilliputs are often included to provide variety.

A direct sowing made outdoors June 1 will be in flower by late July—they grow very rapidly if given good soil and water as needed. Sow in rows 2′ apart, thin to about 6″ in the row, making it easier to cultivate than if a 12″ x 12″ spacing were used. Later sowings may be made on through June. Disbudding will greatly improve the quality of the flowers.

Types and Varieties

The "giant cactus-flowered" class has rapidly developed into one of the most popular types of zinnias. It produces huge flowers up to 6″ in diameter with long, curved petals, irregularly arranged in a pleasing manner. Largely responsible for their great popularity has been the development of F_1 hybrid varieties. Prominent in this class are two series, Big Top and Fruit Bowl. Available as a mixture, they are truly outstanding and are rapidly gaining popularity over the inbred varieties.

State Fair Mix, a giant tetraploid (30″ to 36″), produces 5″ to 6″ flowers with broad petals in a full range of bright colors, and has been very popular for many years. It has high resistance to alternaria and mildew, and probably outsells all other varieties in the large-flowered class.

Ruffles Series F_1, consisting of five separate colors plus a mix, is a tall growing variety (30″) that produces 2½″ ruffled double flowers on long stiff stems.

In the medium height class (18″ to 24″) are three separate color varieties worth noting: Gold Sun F_1, with 4″ bright gold dahlia flowered blooms; Red Sun F_1, a 4″ bright scarlet double-dahlia type, and Sombrero, a bright colored red-and-gold single.

One of the most popular members of the zinnia family is the F_1 hybrid Peter Pan, currently available in eight colors—Peter Pan Pink, a coral pink; Peter Pan Plum, a rose; Peter Pan Scarlet, a brilliant scarlet; Peter Pan Orange; Peter Pan Cream; Peter Pan Flame, a brilliant red; Peter Pan Gold, a yellow gold; and Peter Pan Princess, a luminous pink. These free-flowering All-America winners produce extra large, fully double, 3″ flowers on very bushy plants only 10″ to 12″ high. The only non-All America winner is Princess.

More dwarf than the Peter Pans but with similar flower size is the F_1 Dasher Series available in five separate, bright colors and a mix.

The Pumilas (2′ to 2½′) are between the "giants" and Lilliputs in flower size, the latter being more widely used. It produces small pompon-type flowers (2″) on bushy plants 1½′ to 2′ tall. Both of these are largely grown as color mixes.

The Pulcino Series (12″ to 15″) contains six very vivid colors plus a mixture. Excellent for 4″ pot production.

Thumbelina (6″ to 8″) is an extra-dwarf formulated mixture of bright colors that is particularly well adapted to edging. The compact, uniform plants flower early in packs and pots.

HOLIDAY DATES

	1991	1992	1993	1994	1995	1996
New Year's Day	Jan. 1	Jan. 1	Jan. 1	Jan. 1	Jan. 1	Jan. 1
Lincoln's Birthday	Feb. 12	Feb. 12	Feb. 12	Feb. 12	Feb. 12	Feb. 12
Valentine's Day	Feb. 14	Feb. 14	Feb. 14	Feb. 14	Feb. 14	Feb. 14
Ash Wednesday	Feb. 13	Mar. 4	Feb. 24	Feb. 16	Mar. 1	Feb. 21
Washington's Birthday	Feb. 22	Feb. 22	Feb. 22	Feb. 22	Feb. 22	Feb. 22
St. Patrick's Day	Mar. 17	Mar. 17	Mar. 17	Mar. 17	Mar. 17	Mar. 17
Palm Sunday	Mar. 24	Apr. 12	Apr. 4	Mar. 27	Apr. 9	Mar. 31
Passover	Mar. 30	Apr. 18	Apr. 6	Mar. 27	Apr. 15	Apr. 4
Easter Sunday	Mar. 31	Apr. 19	Apr. 11	Apr. 3	Apr. 16	Apr. 7
Secretaries' Day	Apr. 24	Apr. 22	Apr. 21	Apr. 27	Arp. 26	Apr. 24
Mother's Day	May 12	May 10	May 9	May 8	May 14	May 12
Memorial Day	May 27	May 25	May 31	May 30	May 29	May 27
Father's Day	June 16	June 21	June 20	June 19	June 18	June 16
Labor Day	Sept. 2	Sept. 7	Sept. 6	Sept. 5	Sept. 4	Sept. 2
Grandparents' Day	Sept. 8	Sept. 13	Sept. 12	Sept. 11	Sept. 10	Sept. 8
Rosh Hashanah	Sept. 9	Sept. 28	Sept. 16	Sept. 6	Sept. 25	Sept. 14
Yom Kippur	Sept. 18	Oct. 7	Sept. 25	Sept. 15	Oct. 4	Sept. 23
Bosses' Day	Oct. 16	Oct. 16	Oct. 16	Oct. 16	Oct. 16	Oct. 16
Sweetest Day	Oct. 19	Oct. 17	Oct. 16	Oct. 15	Oct. 21	Oct. 19
Election Day	Nov. 5	Nov. 3	Nov. 2	Nov. 8	Nov. 7	Nov. 5
Thanksgiving Day	Nov. 28	Nov. 26	Nov. 25	Nov. 24	Nov. 23	Nov. 28
Hanukah	Dec. 2	Dec. 20	Dec. 9	Nov. 28	Dec. 18	Dec. 6
Christmas Day	Dec. 25	Dec. 25	Dec. 25	Dec. 25	Dec. 25	Dec. 25

SPRAY DILUTION TABLE*

	1 to 50	1 to 100	1 to 200	1 to 300	1 to 400	1 to 500	1 to 600	1 to 800	1 to 1000	1 to 1600
1 gal.	72.5 ml. or 5 T. plus ¼ t. or 2.56 oz.	36.2 ml. or 2 T. plus 1¾ t. or 1.28 oz.	18.1 ml. or 3¾ t. or .64 oz.	12.2 ml. or 2½ t.	9.1 ml. or 2 t.	7.3 ml. or 1½ t.	6 ml. or 1¼ t.	4.5 ml. or 1 t.	3.6 ml. or ¾ t.	2.3 ml. or ½ t.
10 gals.	724.5 ml. or 25.6 oz.	362.2 ml. or 12.8 oz.	181.1 ml. or 12 T. plus 2½ t. or 6.4 oz.	120.8 ml. or 8 T. plus 1½ t. or 4.27 oz.	90.6 ml. or 6 T. plus 1¼ t. or 3.2 oz.	72.5 ml. or 5 T. plus ¼ t. or 2.56 oz.	60.3 ml. or 4 T. plus ¾ t. or 2.13 oz.	45.3 ml. or 3 T. plus ½ t. or 1.6 oz.	36.2 ml. or 2 T. plus 1¾ t. or 1.28 oz.	22.6 ml. or 1 T. plus 1¾ t. or .8 oz.
25 gals.	1811.2 ml. or 64 oz.	905.6 ml. or 32 oz.	452.8 ml. or 16 oz.	302.8 ml. or 10.7 oz.	226.4 ml. or 16 T. or 8 oz.	181.1 ml. or 12 T. plus 2½ t. or 6.4 oz.	150.8 ml. or 10 T. plus 2½ t. or 5.33 oz.	113.0 ml. or 8 T. or 4 oz.	90.6 ml. or 6 T. plus 1¼ t. or 3.2 oz.	56.6 ml. or 4 T. or 2 oz.
50 gals.	3622.4 ml. or 1 gal.	1811.2 ml. or 64 oz.	905.6 ml. or 32 oz.	602.8 ml. or 21.33 oz.	452.8 ml. or 16 oz.	362.2 ml. or 12.8 oz.	302.8 ml. or 10.66 oz.	226.4 ml. or 8 oz.	181.1 ml. or 12 T. plus 2½ t. or 6.4 oz.	113.2 ml. or 8 T. or 4 oz.

*This table, from the Ohio Florists' Association Monthly Bulletin No. 198, is a real timesaver in figuring spray dilutions. Note that dilutions are figured in tablespoons (T.), teaspoons (t.) and milliliters (ml.). Milliliters are simpler and more accurate. One source for cylinders graduated in milliliters is Central Scientific, 11222 Melrose Avenue, Franklin Park, IL 60131.

INDEX

Frost protection curtains, 55
Fuchsia hybrida, 529
Fuchsia, hanging baskets, 568
Fuel
  coal, 47, 48, 49
  costs, 25, 46, 49
  natural gas, 46, 49
  oil, 47, 49
  propane gas, 48, 49
  wood, 49
Fungi-beneficial pathogens, 166
Fungus gnats, 173-174
Fusarium, 280, 647

Gaillardia aristata, see *Gaillardia* x
  grandiflora
Gaillardia x *grandiflora*, 529-530, 684
Garden mums, see Chrysanthemum
Garden roses, see Rose
Gazania splendens, 530-531
  hanging baskets, 572
Geranium, 552-554
  Balcon, 535, 541
  Botrytis, 536
  Culture Indexing, 533-535
  direct stick, 549-551
  diseases, 534-535, 549
  fertilizer, 544
  four inch, 540-541, 549-551
  germination, 543
  growth regulators, 540, 544-545, 551, 552
  hanging baskets, 549
  insects, 536-537
  Ivy types, 532, 537, 541, 570
  media, 534, 543
  oedema, 537
  propagation—cuttings, 538
  Regal, 533
  seed, 145, 152, 541-548
  sowing dates, 546
  stock plants, 551-552
  STS, 547
  Xanthomonas, 533, 552
  zonal, 532-541, 549-553
Gerbera jamesonii, 228, 555
  cut flower cropping, 558-559
  four inch pots, 557
  packing cut stems, 559
  pest control, 559
  pot culture, 556-558
  propagation, 556
Germination chambers, 142
Geum Quellyon, 559-560
Gladiolus spp., 560-561
Globe thistle, see *Echinops ritro*
Gloriosa daisy, see *Rudbeckia hirta*
Gloxinia, 561-564

  disease control, 564
  fertilizer, 563
  height control, 563
  insects, 564
  media, 563
  propagation, 561
  temperature, 563
  tomato spotted wilt virus, 294
Godetia whitneyi, 565-566
Gomphrena globosa, 567
Grandiflora petunias, see *Petunia* x *hybrida*
Graphical tracking, 285, 646
  also see DIF
Greenhouse cooling, 57-66
  fan jet, 64
  fan/pad, 57
  fog/mist, 62
Greenhouse coverings
  acrylic, 13
  fiberglass, 13
  glass, 13
  polycarbonate, 13
  polyethylene, 13
Greenhouse temperature—cool days/warm
  nights, see DIF
Greenhouses, 3-18
  benches, 50
  cold frames, 14
  cooling, 57
  cooling/venting, 57-66
  CO_2, 229
  curtains, 6, 9, 52
  design loads, 8
  environmental control, 37-44
  headhouses, 50, 51
  heating, 19-36
  irrigation, 97-122
  mechanization, 15, 50, 69-95
  physical plant, 45-55
  snow loads, 8, 17
  space use, 50
  structure costs, 12
  supplemental light, 259
Ground water pollution, 289
Growth chambers, 142
Growth regulators, 428, 540
  aster, 335
  bedding plants, 369
  begonia, 394
  chrysanthemum, 447
  daffodil, 409
  delphinium, 488
  DIF, 284
  Easter lily, 643
  impatiens, 608
  poinsettia, 697, 706, 714
  plugs, 143
Guzmania spp., see Bromeliads

millipedes, 175
mites, cyclamen, 175
mites, 2-spotted, 175-176
pathogens, 165
scale insects, 176
scouting, 161
sowbugs, 177
springtails, 177
thrips, 177
whiteflies, 177-178
Insecticides, 170-178
Integrated Pest Management, see IPM
IPM, 160, 161
record keeping, 161
scouting, 161
Iris hollandica, 610-614
bulb size, 612, 613
California production, 613
cultural problems, 613
forcing, 610-613
harvest, 613
planting, 610
spacing, 610-611
temperature treatment, 612
varieties, 612
Iris hybrids, 686
Irrigation, 97-122
booms, 107, 108, 109, 113
cut flowers, 120
ebb and flow, 99
ebb and flow floors, 103
low-volume, 196
NFT, 122
plugs, 114, 140
pulsing, 119
recirculation, 290
runoff, 119, 289
spaghetti tube, 105, 106, 107, 445
sprinklers, 112
Irrigation mats, 111
Irrigation mist, 114, 115
Irrigation troughs, 103, 104
Ivy, see *Hedera helix*

Johnny Jump-Ups, 785

Kalanchoe Blossfeldiana, 614-621
crop scheduling, 621
diseases, 619
fertilization, 616
insects, 619
long-day treatment, 618
media, 616
pinching, 617
propagation, 615
seed propagation, 619-620

short-day treatment, 618
temperatures, 616
Kalanchoe, see *Kalanchoe Blossfeldiana*
Kale, see Ornamental kale
Kansas Gay Feather, see *Liatris spicata*
Kniphofia Uvaria, 686
Kurume azalea, see Azalea Kurume

Labor
career opportunities, 265
compensation, 266
costs, 69
Lantana camara, 621-622
Larkspur, 622-623
Lathyrus odoratus, 775-776
Lavender, French, see *Lavandula dentata*
Lavandula angustifolia, 580, 686
Lavandula dentata, 580, 581
Leaching, 117, 248
Leafminers, 174
Leopard's Bane, see *Doronicum*
Liatris pycnostachya, 624
Liatris spicata, 624, 686
Light intensity, 305-306
Lily, Easter, 625-651
bud development, 641, 642
bulb size, 629, 633-634
case cooling, 630-631
CTF cooling, 631-632
DIF, 284, 286, 645-646, 650
diseases, 647-648
growth regulators, 643-645
insects, 648
leaf counting, 639-643
leaf scorch, 637, 648-649
long days, 633
nutrition, 637-638
pre-cooling, 629-633
soils, 636-638
temperature, 634-635, 645-646
timing, 639-643
varieties, 625-627, 628
vernalization, 300, 629-630, 635
Lily, hybrid, see Hybrid lilies
Lilium longiflorum, see Lily, Easter
Lime, 247
Limonium latifolia, 770-771
Limonium latifolium, 686
Limonium Perezii, 771
Limonium spp., 770-771
Limonium tactarica, 771
Lisanthus, see *Eustoma grandiflorum*
Lobelia Erinus, 660
Lobularia maritima, 318-319
Low-volume sprayers, 127
Lupinus polyphyllus, 661

Thielaviopsis, 205, 673, 727
Thrips, 177, 392, 606
  also see Tomato spotted wilt virus
Thunbergia spp., 776
  hanging baskets, 572
Thyme, see *Thymus vulgaris*
Thyme, lemon, see *Thymus x citriodorus*
Thymus vulgaris, 580, 581
Thymus x citriodorus, 580, 581
Tillandsia spp., see Bromeliads
Tissue Culture, 225-228
Tomato spotted wilt virus (TSWV), 280, 282,
  293-297
  control, 296
  plant testing, 296
  symptoms, 294, 295, 296
  thrips vector, 295
Tomatoes, 139, 152, 776-778
  ethylene injury, 239
  gas toxicity, 239
  hanging baskets, 572
  varieties, 777
Torenia Fournieri, 778-779
Transplanting line, 123-126
Transplanting, costs, 138
Transvaal daisy, see *Gerbera jamesonii*
Tray mechanization, 50, 75-86
  cost, 78, 79
  ebb and flow irrigation, 77
  order assembly, 77
  roll-out, 84, 86
Triploid marigolds, 664
Tropical hibiscus, see *Hibiscus rosa-sinensis*
Trough irrigation, 103, 104
TSWV, see tomato spotted wilt virus
Tuberous begonias, see Begonia
Tulipa spp.,
  culture, 402
  rooting room temperatures, 409
  schedule for cuts, 408
  schedule for pot forcing, 407

U Factors, 35
U.S. Department of Agriculture, The, 308
U.S. Bureau of Census, Census of
  Agriculture, 308
Unit heaters, 47, 237
Unvented heaters, 237-242
USDA Floriculture Crops Report, 307
USDA Hardiness Map, 306

Van Wingerden, Aart, 76, 83, 104
Vegetables—bedding plants, 779
Ventilation 57-66
Verbena hortensis, 152, 780-781

Vernalization, 299, 405, 407
  Easter lilies, 629
  hydrangea, 592
Veronica incana, 782
Veronica repens, 782
Veronica spicata, 688, 781-782
Verticillium Wilt, 205, 277, 280, 533
Victoria salvia, see *Salvia farinacea*
Vinca
  hanging baskets, 572
  see *Catharanthus roseus*
Vinca major, 784
Vinca major Variegata, 784
Vinca minor, 784
Vine crops, 780
Viola cornuta, 785
  also see Pansy
Virus indexing, 279, 535
Viruses, 533, 647
  beneficial pathogens, 166
  tomato spotted wilt virus, 293
  wilt virus, 293
Vriesea spp., see Bromeliads

Wall Cress, see *Arabis caucasica*
Water
  acidity, 247
  alkalinity, 254, 256
  pH, 247, 255
  soluble salts, 248
  testing, 243-258
Watering, see Irrigation
Watermelon, 780
Western flower thrips, see Thrips
White Butterfly, see *Syngonium
  podophyllum*
Whiteflies, 163, 177-178, 537

Xanthomonas, 277, 281, 533, 552
Xanthomonas begoniae, 394
Xanthomonas pelargoni, 542
Xeriscaping, 195-196

Yarrow, see Achillea
Yucca elephantipes, 505, 512

Zantedeschia spp., 419
Zinc, 254
Zinnia elegans, 139, 785-787
Zonal geraniums, see Geranium
Zygocactus, see *Schlumbergera*